D1095029

WITHDRAWN

THE
FIFTY-YEAR
MISSION

ALSO BY **MARK A. ALTMAN** AND **EDWARD GROSS**

The Fifty-Year Mission:
The Complete, Uncensored, Unauthorized Oral History of Star Trek.
The First Twenty-Five Years

THE FIFTY-YEAR MISSION

THE COMPLETE, UNCENSORED, UNAUTHORIZED
ORAL HISTORY OF *STAR TREK*

The Next 25 Years
From *The Next Generation* to J. J. Abrams

MARK A. ALTMAN
AND EDWARD GROSS

THOMAS DUNNE BOOKS
ST. MARTIN'S PRESS ✦ NEW YORK

THOMAS DUNNE BOOKS.
An imprint of St. Martin's Press.

THE FIFTY-YEAR MISSION: THE NEXT 25 YEARS. Copyright © 2016 by Mark A. Altman and Edward Gross. All rights reserved. Printed in the United States of America. For information, address St. Martin's Press, 175 Fifth Avenue, New York, N.Y. 10010.

www.thomasdunnebooks.com
www.stmartins.com

The Library of Congress Cataloging-in-Publication Data is available upon request.

ISBN 978-1-250-08946-5 (hardcover)
ISBN 978-1-250-08947-2 (e-book)

Our books may be purchased in bulk for promotional, educational, or business use. Please contact your local bookseller or the Macmillan Corporate and Premium Sales Department at 1-800-221-7945, extension 5442, or by e-mail at MacmillanSpecialMarkets@macmillan.com.

First Edition: August 2016

10   9   8   7   6   5   4   3   2   1

FROM MARK A. ALTMAN

To my wonderful wife, Naomi, whom I married despite the fact she likes Captain Picard way more than Captain Kirk. Thanks for "tolerating" me....

To my incredible kids, Ella and Isaac, who may one day like *Star Trek* as much as *Star Wars,* but I kinda doubt it.

To my amazing mom, Gail, who took me to see *North by Northwest* at the Thalia when I was a kid, beginning an obsession with movies and television that would last a lifetime.

To my fabulous brother, Ira, for being *way* cooler than me.

To my incredible dad, Michael, for occasionally turning off the hockey, baseball, tennis, golf, and football games so I could watch *Star Trek*.

To our charming cats, Ripley, Giles, and Willow, for staying off my Mac keyboard while I wrote these books . . . most of the time.

To *Cinefantastique*'s Frederick S. Clarke, for proving there was a place for intelligent entertainment journalism about the genre and giving me the incredible opportunity that led to the creation of this book.

Ditto to my own Professor Kingsfield, the brilliant and inspirational Thomas Doherty.

Also a final nod of gratitude to the late Larry Goldman, one of the founders of the PR firm Bender, Goldman & Helper, who, for reasons I continue to find unfathomable, received a query letter from a young college student and invited him and his college roommate to Los Angeles to tour the sets of *Star Trek: The Next Generation* in 1987—which began a thirty-year journey that led to the writing of this book—and bought lunch at the commissary to boot.

And to three other people without whom this book would not be possible: Edward Gross, my incredible partner in crime, who truly is the hardest-working man in showbiz; the jocular bard of book publishing, Brendan Deneen, our editor and enthusiast-in-chief; and, last and certainly not least, the late, great Gene Roddenberry, without whom there would be no starship *Enterprise A, B, C* or bloody *D*.

FROM EDWARD GROSS

To Eileen, my best friend who also happens to be my wife: I can't remember a time when I was on this voyage without you, and I would never want to.

To my sons, Teddy, Dennis, and Kevin (all of whom have inherited the geek gene): I don't know how I could be as blessed as I am to have three children who have turned into such fine men. I'm grateful for all of you.

To my daughter-in-law, Lindsay: Welcome to the family. We couldn't be happier. And thanks for being a geek, too.

A life is like a garden.
Perfect moments can be had, but not preserved, except in memory.
—Actor/Director/Poet Leonard Nimoy, his final Tweet

The destiny of Google's search engine
is to become that *Star Trek* computer, and that's what we are building.
—Amit Singhal,
the head of Google's search rankings team, at South by Southwest

There are three sides to every story: your side, my side, and the truth.
And no one is lying. Memories shared serve each differently.
—Robert Evans, *The Kid Stays in the Picture*

DATABASE

PREFIX

I n 1987, as a young college student writing about the fledgling *Next Generation* series for the student newspaper, I first set foot on the bridge of the starship *Enterprise* during production on the first season episode, "Too Short a Season."

It would lead to many published articles about the making of *Star Trek* over the years (as well as myriad subsequent visits to the bridge of multiple starships, numerous away missions to *Deep Space Nine*, and the set of several of the feature films). My love affair with *Trek*, of course, predated my arrival in the twenty-fourth century by almost two decades, but this was the beginning of a professional association that continues to this day.

Revisiting the world of *Star Trek* with Edward Gross after these many years for this book reminded us both of one thing: the world needs *Star Trek*. In a cynical twenty-first century consumed by dystopian visions of the future, *Star Trek* is unique. It postulates a future in which we are better than we are today and where technology has allowed a united Earth to colonize the stars while leaving behind a planet that is a paradise; no longer ravaged by war, disease, hunger, climate change, or the Tea Party.

Over the years *Star Trek* has been great, its been awful, and, at its worst, it's been plain mediocre. But when it's good, *Star Trek*'s unique lens for observing the human condition is unparalleled in examining our society in a way that no other series in popular culture has even come close to.

The drama behind the making of the series is far less utopian, but someone had to make the sausage, and this is their story; honest, uncensored and unabridged. At the end of the day, whether you love each of these individual series—or only some of them—there is not one person interviewed in this book that didn't care deeply about the work and didn't make every effort to make their corner of the *Star Trek* universe great. For that, we thank you.

Knowing the late Michael Piller would appreciate this baseball analogy most of all, I would be remiss not to acknowledge his thoughtful and prescient decision to recruit rookie writers over the course of *Trek*'s many years in space, which led to him assembling a deep bench of talented wordsmiths akin to the 1927 Yankees of the Writers' Guild of America. Among those he discovered, or who were subsequently hired as a result of the open submissions policy he championed, are such now legendary showrunners as Ronald D. Moore (*Battlestar Galactica, Outlander*), Bryan Fuller (*Pushing Daisies, Hannibal, American Gods*), Brannon Braga (*Cosmos: A Space-Time Odyssey, Salem*), René Echevarria (*Dark Angel, Castle*), Naren Shankar (*The Expanse, CSI: Crime Scene Investigation*), Rob Doherty (*Elementary*), Mike Taylor (*Defiance, Turn: Washington's Spies*), Ken Biller (*Legends, Perception)* and Mike Sussman (*Perception*), to name only a few of the exceptional talents that toiled in the *Star Trek* universe under Piller's sage tutelage and mentorship.

So now it seems only appropriate that as we celebrate five decades of *Star Trek* and prepare to once again boldly go on future *Trek*s yet to come, we look back and see the many things these immensely talented craftspeople did right—and admittedly wrong—over the years, and hope that as *Star Trek* lives again on television in 2017, their aspirations to do it even better the next time will be realized as this unstoppable franchise continues to boldly go where no one has gone before.

Keep watching the stars.

Mark A. Altman
February 2016

DRAMATIS PERSONAE

STAR TREK ABBREVIATIONS

Star Trek: The Original Series: TOS
Star Trek: The Animated Series: TAS
Star Trek: Phase II: Phase II
Star Trek: The Next Generation: TNG
Star Trek: Deep Space Nine: DS9
Star Trek: Voyager: VOY
Star Trek: Enterprise: ENT
Star Trek: The Motion Picture: TMP
Star Trek II: The Wrath of Khan: STII
Star Trek III: The Search for Spock: STIII
Star Trek IV: The Voyage Home: STIV
Star Trek V: The Final Frontier: STV
Star Trek VI: The Undiscovered Country: STVI
Star Trek: Generations: Generations
Star Trek: First Contact: First Contact
Star Trek: Insurrection: Insurrection
Star Trek: Nemesis: Nemesis
Star Trek (2009): Star Trek
Star Trek Into Darkness: Star Trek Into Darkness
Star Trek Beyond: Star Trek Beyond

J. J. ABRAMS is a director, producer, and writer best known for his work directing *Star Trek, Star Trek Into Darkness, Mission Impossible 3, Super 8*, and America's highest-grossing motion picture of all-time, *Star Wars: The Force Awakens*. He is also the cocreator of three hit TV series: *Lost, Alias,* and *Felicity*.

MARC ALAIMO is a television actor who is best known for his role as Gul Dukat in *Star Trek: Deep Space Nine* as well as multiple roles in *Star Trek: The Next Generation*.

LARRY ALEXANDER is a television writer who has written episodes for such series as *The Streets of San Francisco, MacGyver,* and *The Six Million Dollar Man*.

JOHN ALONZO was the legendary cinematographer who shot such films as *Chinatown* and *Scarface,* as well as *Star Trek: Generations.*

DEBORAH ARAKELIAN is an Emmy-nominated television writer who wrote episodes of *Cagney & Lacey* and *Quantum Leap.* She also worked as a production assistant to Harve Bennett on *Star Trek II: The Wrath of Khan* and *Star Trek III: The Search for Spock.*

BURTON ARMUS was a former police officer and producer, whose credits include *Airwolf, NYPD Blue,* and *Star Trek: The Next Generation.*

RICHARD ARNOLD was a research consultant on *Star Trek: The Next Generation* holding the position of official "*Star Trek* Archivist."

RENÉ AUBERJONOIS is a screen and stage actor. He is known for his role as Father Mulcahy in Robert Altman's *M*A*S*H,* Clayton Endicott III on *Benson,* and Odo on *Star Trek: Deep Space Nine.*

JEFF AYRES is the author of *Voyages of Imagination: The Star Trek Fiction Companion.*

DENNIS RUSSELL BAILEY is a television writer who has written episodes for *Star Trek: The Next Generation* and the *Star Trek* fan film, *Starship Farragut.*

STUART BAIRD is an editor, producer, and director whose films include *Executive Decision, U.S. Marshals,* and *Star Trek: Nemesis.*

SCOTT BAKULA is an actor known for his role as Sam Beckett on *Quantum Leap* and Captain Jonathan Archer on *Star Trek: Enterprise.* He currently stars in *NCIS: New Orleans.*

MAJEL BARRETT starred as Christine Chapel on *Star Trek: The Original Series* and Lwaxana Troi on *Star Trek: The Next Generation.* She was also the wife of *Star Trek* creator Gene Roddenberry.

STEPHEN BECK is a former doctor and currently writer/producer who wrote episodes of *Chicago Hope, Seven Days,* and *Star Trek: Enterprise.*

IRA STEVEN BEHR is a television writer and producer best known as an executive producer and showrunner on *Star Trek: Deep Space Nine.* He is currently a writer and executive producer on *Outlander* and has previously worked on such series as *Fame, Alphas,* the TV version of *Crash,* and *Star Trek: The Next Generation.*

HANS BEIMLER is a television writer known for his work on *Star Trek: The Next Generation* and *Star Trek: Deep Space Nine.*

ROBERT BELTRAN starred in the cult classics *Eating Raoul* and *Night of the Comet* and may be best known for his role as Commander Chakotay on *Star Trek: Voyager.*

CHRISTOPHER L. BENNETT is an author of numerous short stories and novels, many of them set in the *Star Trek* universe.

HARVE BENNETT was a film and Emmy Award–winning producer as well as screenwriter. He produced several *Star Trek* films, including *Star Trek II: The Wrath of Khan* through *Star Trek V: The Final Frontier.*

RICK BERMAN is a former documentarian and producer of *The Big Blue Marble* for PBS, and studio executive who went on to executive produce *Star Trek: The Next Generation* and later cocreate and produce *Star Trek: Deep Space Nine, Star Trek: Voyager,* and *Star Trek: Enterprise.* He was also the producer on all *The Next Generation* feature films.

CASEY BIGGS is an actor known for his role as the Cardassian Glinn Damar on *Star Trek: Deep Space Nine.*

KEN BILLER is a television writer. He has written for such series as *The X-Files, Smallville, Perception,* and *Star Trek: Voyager,* on which he served as showrunner for the seventh season.

CHRIS BLACK is a television writer and producer. He has worked on a number of series, including *Desperate Housewives, Ugly Betty, Reaper, Sliders, Mad Men,* and *Star Trek: Enterprise.* He is currently the showrunner on *Outcast* for Cinemax.

JOHN D. F. BLACK is a television writer, producer, and director who is known for his work on such series as *The Mary Tyler Moore Show* and as story editor for *Star Trek: The Original Series.*

MARY BLACK is the former assistant to John D.F. Black on *Star Trek: The Original Series,* whom she later married.

ROBERT BLACKMAN is a television and film costume designer. He is known for his work on *Star Trek: The Next Generation, Star Trek: Deep Space Nine, Star Trek: Voyager,* and *Star Trek: Enterprise.*

JOLENE BLALOCK is a film and television actress and former model. She is best known for her role as T'Pol on *Star Trek: Enterprise.*

ANDRÉ BORMANIS is the former science consultant to several *Star Trek* series and has written for *Star Trek: Voyager* and *Star Trek: Enterprise.* He was also technical consultant on *Star Trek: Insurrection.*

ROB BOWMAN is a film and television director and producer. He is known for his work directing episodes of *The X-Files, Castle,* and *Star Trek: The Next Generation.*

BRANNON BRAGA is a television writer, producer, and director. He is known for his work on such shows as *Threshold, Terra Nova, Flashforward, 24, Salem, Cosmos: A Spacetime Odyssey, Star Trek: The Next Generation,* and *Star Trek: Voyager.* He was executive producer and cocreator of *Star Trek: Enterprise.* He also cowrote the screenplays for *Star Trek: Generations* and *Star Trek: First Contact,* as well as *Mission Impossible II.*

LARRY BRODY is a television writer who has worked on shows that include *The Six Million Dollar Man, Manimal, The Fall Guy, The New Mike Hammer* (which he cocreated), and *Star Trek: The Animated Series.*

FRED BRONSON is a journalist, author, television writer, and former network publicity executive at NBC. He is known for his *Chart Beat* column in *Billboard* magazine and wrote episodes for *Star Trek: The Animated Series* and *Star Trek: The Next Generation.*

AVERY BROOKS is an actor and director who is best known as Hawk from ABC's *Spenser: For Hire,* based on the books by Robert B. Parker, as well as for his role as Captain Benjamin Sisko. He also directed several episodes of *Star Trek: Deep Space Nine.*

BRYAN BURK is a prolific film and television producer. He has worked as a producer on such films as *Cloverfield,* the *Mission Impossible* series, *Star Trek* (2009), and *Star Trek Into Darkness.* He is also a producer on such series as *Alias, Lost, Person of Interest,* and *Westworld.*

LEVAR BURTON is an actor and director who is best known for his role as Kunte Kinte in ABC's groundbreaking miniseries *Roots*. He is also the host of PBS' *Reading Rainbow* and portrayed blind engineer Geordi LaForge on *Star Trek: The Next Generation* and its subsequent motion picture series.

DAVID CARREN is a television and film writer and producer. He has worked on a variety of shows, including *Stargate SG-1*, *G.I. Joe*, and *Star Trek: The Next Generation*.

J. LARRY CARROLL is a television writer. He has worked mainly in television on shows including *Dennis the Menace*; *Murder, She Wrote*; and *Star Trek: The Next Generation*.

DAVID CARSON is a television and film director. He is known for directing episodes of *Star Trek: The Next Generation* and *Star Trek: Deep Space Nine*. He also directed the first *Next Generation* feature film, *Star Trek: Generations*.

SCOTT CHAMBLISS is a production designer for film and television. His credits include *Star Trek* and *Star Trek Into Darkness*.

JOHN CHO is a film and television actor. He is known for his role as Harold Lee in the *Harold & Kumar* films as well as Hikaru Sulu in the J.J. Abrams' *Star Trek* films.

RICHARD COLLA was a television and film director. He directed the three-hour premiere episode of *Battlestar Galactica*, the Gene Roddenberry TV movie *The Questor Tapes*, as well as episodes of *Miami Vice* and *Star Trek: The Next Generation*.

JEFFREY COMBS is a television and film actor. He has portrayed various roles on *Star Trek: Deep Space Nine*, *Star Trek: Voyager*, and *Star Trek: Enterprise*, and memorably starred as Dr. Herbert West in *Re-Animator*.

JAMES L. CONWAY is a film and television director whose work includes *Supernatural*, *Charmed*, *Burke's Law*, the Sunn Classic Pictures films *Hangar 18* and *In Search of Noah's Ark*, as well as episodes of *The Next Generation*, *Deep Space Nine*, *Voyager*, and the two-hour premiere of *Star Trek: Enterprise*.

MANNY COTO is a writer, director, and producer for film and television. He was the executive producer and showrunner for such shows as *24*, *Dexter*, and *Star Trek: Enterprise*, as well as cocreator of *Odyssey 5* for Showtime.

GREG COX is an author of original and licensed fiction, particularly those works based on the *Star Trek* franchise.

JAMES CROMWELL is an actor who starred in such films as *The Green Mile; I, Robot; L.A. Confidential;* and *The Artist.* He starred as Zefram Cochrane in *Star Trek: First Contact*, a role he reprised on *Star Trek: Enterprise.*

DENISE CROSBY is a television and film actress. She is known for her role as Tasha Yar on *Star Trek: The Next Generation.*

BENEDICT CUMBERBATCH is an English actor and producer who has starred in such films as *Atonement, The Fifth Estate,* and *The Imitation Game.* He stars as the titular *Sherlock* on the popular BBC series and played John Harrison aka Khan Noonien Singh in *Star Trek Into Darkness.*

MARC CUSHMAN is a television writer, journalist, and author of the three-volume book series *These Are the Voyages*, devoted to the original *Star Trek.*

DANIEL DAVIS is a stage, television, and film actor. He is best known for his roles as Niles, the butler on *The Nanny,* and Professor Moriarty on *Star Trek: The Next Generation.*

ROXANN DAWSON is a television director and actress who portrayed the role of the half-Klingon/half-human B'Elanna Torres on *Star Trek: Voyager.*

NICOLE de BOER is an actress who played Ezri Dax in the seventh season of *Star Trek: Deep Space Nine.*

FRED DEKKER is a television director and writer. His films include *Night of the Creeps, The Monster Squad,* and *RoboCop III,* and he worked as a consulting producer on *Star Trek: Enterprise.* He is currently writing a remake of *Predator* for 20th Century–Fox.

JOHN de LANCIE is an actor, producer, musician, and writer. He is best known for his roles in *Breaking Bad* and as Q on *Star Trek: The Next Generation, Star Trek: Deep Space Nine,* and *Star Trek: Voyager.*

ELIZABETH DENNEHY is a television and film actress who is best known for her role as Commander Shelby on *Star Trek: The Next Generation* as well as being the daughter of actor Brian Dennehy.

DAREN DOCHTERMAN is a film illustrator and set designer. He has worked on such films as *Get Smart, Monster House,* and *Batman vs. Superman,* and was the visual effects supervisor on the director's edition of *Star Trek: The Motion Picture.*

THOMAS DOHERTY is a professor of American Studies at Brandeis University and author of such books as *Pre-Code Hollywood: Sex, Immorality, and Insurrection in American Cinema; Hollywood and Hitler; Teenagers and Teenpics: Juvenilization of American Movies in the 1950s;* and *Cold War, Cool Medium: Television, McCarthyism, and American Culture.*

JAMES DOOHAN was a television and film actor and veteran of the invasion of Normandy as part of the Royal Canadian Artillery. He is best known for his role of Chief Engineer Montgomery Scott in *Star Trek* as well as such series as *Jason of Star Command* and *Homeboys from Outer Space.* His son, Chris Doohan, plays Scotty in the fan series, *Star Trek Continues.*

MICHAEL DORN is an actor and voice artist who is best known for his role as Worf in the *Star Trek* series.

DOUG DREXLER is a visual effects artist, designer, sculptor, illustrator, and a makeup artist. He worked as a makeup artist on *Dick Tracy,* for which he won an Oscar, and *Star Trek: The Next Generation.* He went on to work as a designer, digital artist, and effects artist on *Star Trek: Deep Space Nine* and *Star Trek: Voyager.*

RENÉ ECHEVARRIA is a television writer and producer. He was worked on a variety of shows, including *The 4400, Terra Nova, Castle, Star Trek: The Next Generation,* and as supervising producer on *Star Trek: Deep Space Nine.*

DAVID ELLISON is a producer and financier whose credits include *Star Trek Into Darkness, World War Z, Terminator: Genisys, Mission Impossible: Rogue Nation,* and *Star Trek Beyond.*

HARLAN ELLISON is a legendary author and screenwriter. He has written for *The Outer Limits, Babylon 5,* and *Star Trek: The Original Series.*

JOEL ENGEL is a journalist and author of the book *Gene Roddenberry: The Myth and the Man Behind Star Trek.*

ALICE EVE is an actress who portrayed Carol Marcus in *Star Trek Into Darkness.*

TERRY FARRELL is an actress and model. She is best known for her roles as Regina Kostas in *Becker* and as Jadzia Dax on *Star Trek: Deep Space Nine*.

BOBAK FERDOWSI is a systems engineer at NASA's Jet Propulsion Laboratory. He served on the Cassini–Huygens and Mars Science Laboratory *Curiosity* missions. He is best known to the millions who watched *Curiosity* land on the Martian surface as "Mohawk Guy."

PETER ALLAN FIELDS is a television writer best known for his work on *The Man From U.N.C.L.E.*, *It Takes a Thief*, *McCloud*, *The Six Million Dollar Man*, *Star Trek: The Next Generation*, and *Star Trek: Deep Space Nine*.

LOUISE FLETCHER is an Oscar-winning actress (for her work in *One Flew Over the Cuckoo's Nest*) who memorably starred as Kai Winn on *Star Trek: Deep Space Nine*.

DENNY MARTIN FLINN was an author and screenwriter. He is known for co-writing *Star Trek VI: The Undiscovered Country* with Nicholas Meyer.

DOROTHY "D.C." FONTANA is a television writer who is best known for writing for *Star Trek: The Original Series*, *Star Trek: The Animated Series*, and *Star Trek: The Next Generation*. She also worked on such series as *The Streets of San Francisco*, *Fantastic Journey*, *Logan's Run*, and *Buck Rogers in the 25th Century*.

MICHELLE FORBES is an actress best known to *Star Trek* fans as Ensign Ro Laren. Her additional credits include *24*, *Battlestar Galactica*, *The Killing*, *True Blood*, *Powers*, and *The Returned*.

ALAN DEAN FOSTER is an author known for his works of science fiction and fantasy. He has written novelizations of myriad motion pictures and adapted *Star Trek: The Animated Series* into the *Star Trek Log* collection of books. He also has a story credit on *Star Trek: The Motion Picture*.

JONATHAN FRAKES is an actor and director. He is best known for the role of Commander William T. Riker in the *Star Trek: The Next Generation* series. He also directed the films *Star Trek: First Contact* and *Star Trek: Insurrection* as well as episodes of *Castle*, *Leverage*, and *The Librarians*.

MICHAEL JAN FRIEDMAN is a television, radio, and comic book writer as well as an author of many *Star Trek* novels and has written for *Star Trek: Voyager*.

BRYAN FULLER is a critically acclaimed television writer and producer. In addition to creating and executive producing the popular series *Pushing Daisies, Dead Like Me, Wonderfalls,* and *Hannibal,* he was a writer and coproducer on *Star Trek: Voyager.* He is currently the executive producer of the new *Star Trek* television series debuting in 2017.

MORGAN GENDEL is a writer and producer for television who has written for such series as *V.I.P., Law & Order, Wiseguy,* and *The Dresden Files.* He is best known as the writer of several *Star Trek: The Next Generation* and *Star Trek: Deep Space Nine* episodes. He won the prestigious Hugo Award for his *TNG* episode "The Inner Light."

DAVID GERROLD is a television and film writer as well as author. He has written for *Land of the Lost, Star Trek: The Original Series,* and wrote numerous popular sci-fi novels including the novelette *The Martian Child,* which was adapted into a feature film starring John Cusack.

MICHAEL GIACCHINO is a composer who has written scores for a wide variety of films, television shows, and video games. He has composed the soundtracks for *Alias, Cloverfield, Lost, John Carter, Star Trek,* and *Star Trek Into Darkness,* among others.

VINCE GILLIGAN is an Emmy Award–winning film and television writer, producer, and director. He is best known for creating the TV series *Breaking Bad* and *Better Call Saul,* and working as a co-executive producer on *The X-Files.*

WHOOPI GOLDBERG is an Oscar– and Emmy Award–winning actress, comedian, and talk show host. She starred in such films as *Ghost* and *Sister Act* and is a regular on ABC's *The View.* She had a recurring role as the alien bartender Guinan on *Star Trek: The Next Generation.*

JERRY GOLDSMITH was a legendary composer and conductor who was best known for scoring television and film. He won an Academy Award for his score to *The Omen.* Among his hundreds of classic movie scores are *Patton, Planet of the Apes, Total Recall, Star Trek: The Motion Picture, Star Trek V: The Final Frontier,* and *Star Trek: First Contact.*

DAVID A. GOODMAN is a television writer and producer. He has worked on such shows as *Family Guy, Futurama,* and *Star Trek: Enterprise.* He is also the author of *Star Trek: Federation—The First 150 Years* and *The Autobiography of James T. Kirk.*

CHRIS GORE is a comedian and writer who was a regular on G4TV's *Attack of the Show*. He is the founder of *Film Threat* magazine.

PETER GOULD is a television writer and producer. He is known for his work on *Breaking Bad* and as cocreator of its spin-off, *Better Call Saul*.

BRUCE GREENWOOD is an actor and musician. He has worked on such films as *Double Jeopardy; I, Robot;* and portrayed Captain Christopher Pike in *Star Trek* and *Star Trek Into Darkness*.

JAVIER GRILLO-MARXUACH is a former NBC network executive and writer/ producer best known for his work on such series as *Lost, Helix,* and *Medium,* and as creator of *The Middleman* for ABC Family. He is also the cohost of the screenwriting podcast *Children of Tendu*.

MAX GRODÉNCHIK is an actor who is best known for portraying the role of Rom, Quark's Ferengi brother, in *Star Trek: Deep Space Nine*.

ROGER GUYETT is a three-time Oscar-nominated visual effects supervisor, whose credits include the *Harry Potter, Star Trek*, and *Star Wars* franchises.

DANI HAIDER is a Web developer and longtime *Star Trek* fan.

TOM HARDY is a producer, writer, and actor who is best known for his starring roles in such feature films as *The Dark Knight Rises, Mad Max: Fury Road*, and *The Revenant*. He also starred as Shinzon, Picard's evil clone, in *Star Trek: Nemesis*.

JEFFREY M. HAYES is a writer/producer whose credits include the 1988 TV version of *Mission: Impossible, Time Trax, Chemistry,* and *Crusoe*.

CHRIS HEMSWORTH is an actor who is known for portraying Thor in the *Thor* and *Avengers* series of films. He also played the role of George Kirk in the film *Star Trek* (2009).

SONITA HENRY is an actress who has appeared in a variety of films and television shows, including *Doctor Who, Chuck,* and *Star Trek*.

J.G. HERTZLER is a television actor who portrayed the Klingon General Martok on *Star Trek: Deep Space Nine*.

MAURICE HURLEY was a television and film writer. He worked on such shows as *Miami Vice, Baywatch Nights, Kung-Fu: The Legend Continues,* and *Star Trek: The Next Generation.*

GENNIFER HUTCHISON is a former assistant to John Shiban on *The X-Files* and *Star Trek: Enterprise,* producer for *Breaking Bad* and *The Strain,* and coexecutive producer on *Better Call Saul.*

GERALD ISENBERG is a longtime film and television producer and former partner of Jerry Abrams, J.J. Abrams' father. He was hired to produce *Star Trek: Planet of the Titans* by Paramount in the mid-70s.

ANDRÉ JACQUEMETTON is a television writer and producer. He has written for such shows as *Baywatch Hawaii, Mad Men,* and *Star Trek: Enterprise.*

MARIE JACQUEMETTON is a television writer and producer. She has written for a variety of shows including *Baywatch Hawaii, Mad Men,* and *Star Trek: Enterprise.*

RICHARD JAMES is a set and production designer who worked on *Star Trek: The Next Generation* and *Star Trek: Voyager.*

ERIK JENDRESEN is a writer/producer whose credits include *Band of Brothers* and *Killing Lincoln.* He is also the writer of the unfilmed script, *Star Trek: The Beginning.*

BARRY JENNER is a television and film actor. He has appeared on such shows as *Saved by the Bell* and *Walker, Texas Ranger,* and he had a recurring role as Admiral William Ross on *Star Trek: Deep Space Nine.*

MIKE JOHNSON is a television writer/producer as well as a writer of comic books, including the IDW series set in the J.J. Abrams version of the *Star Trek* universe.

RON JONES is a composer who has written scores for a variety of television shows including *Family Guy, DuckTales,* and *Star Trek: The Next Generation.*

ROBERT H. JUSTMAN was a producer and assistant director on such series as *The Outer Limits.* He was one of the original producers on *Star Trek: The Original Series* and also worked as a supervising producer on *Star Trek: The Next Generation.*

MICHAEL KAPLAN is a costume designer who designed the costumes for both *Star Trek* and *Star Trek Into Darkness* as well as *Star Wars: The Force Awakens*.

DOMINIC KEATING is a television, film, and theater actor. He is best known for his role as Lieutenant Malcolm Reed on *Star Trek: Enterprise*.

DEFOREST KELLEY was an actor best known for his roles in films such as *Gunfight at the O.K. Corral* and as Dr. Leonard McCoy in the *Star Trek* series.

LUKAS KENDALL is a prolific producer of soundtrack albums as well as the editor of *Film Score Monthly*. He also cowrote and produced the film *Lucky Bastard*.

CHRISTOPHER KNOPF is a longtime television writer and friend of Gene Roddenberry.

WALTER KOENIG is an actor and writer. He is best well known for his roles as Alfred Bester in *Babylon 5* and Pavel Chekov in *Star Trek: The Original Series*.

WINRICH KOLBE was a television director and producer. He directed forty-eight episodes of *Star Trek* spanning four series, including *Star Trek: The Next Generation*, *Star Trek: Deep Space Nine*, *Star Trek: Voyager*, and *Star Trek: Enterprise*.

JOE KRAEMER is a composer who worked on such films and television series as *Jack Reacher*, *Femme Fatales*, *The Way of the Gun*, and *Mission Impossible: Rogue Nation*.

ALICE KRIGE is an actress who has worked in such movies as *Ghost Story* and *Sleepwalkers* and starred as the Borg Queen in *Star Trek: First Contact*, a role she reprised on *Star Trek: Voyager*.

ALEX KURTZMAN is a film and television writer, producer, and director. He was cocreator of the television show *Fringe* and cowrote the screenplays for the films *Star Trek* and *Star Trek Into Darkness*. He is currently an executive producer of the new *Star Trek* TV series for CBS.

LES LANDAU is a director and former assistant director. He has worked on *Star Trek: The Next Generation*, *Star Trek: Deep Space Nine*, *Star Trek: Voyager*, and *Star Trek: Enterprise*.

JONATHAN LARSEN is a former producer for such news outlets as ABC News, CNN, and MSNBC, where he was executive producer of *Up with Chris Hayes* and *Up Late with Alec Baldwin*.

ROBERT LEGATO is a visual effects supervisor and second unit director who won Oscars for his work on *Titanic* and *Hugo*. He was visual effects supervisor for *Star Trek: The Next Generation* and *Deep Space Nine*.

DON LEVY is a producer and publicist who has worked on such films as *The Lost World: Jurassic Park, Desperado,* and *Star Trek: Generations*.

JIM LEWIN is the son of *Star Trek: The Next Generation* producer Robert Lewin.

ROBERT LEWIN was a television writer and producer who worked on such shows as *The Streets of San Francisco, Hawaii Five-O, Man from Atlantis, The Paper Chase,* and *Star Trek: The Next Generation*.

DAVID LIVINGSTON is a unit production manager, producer, and director who has worked on *Star Trek: The Next Generation, Star Trek: Deep Space Nine,* and *Star Trek: Voyager*.

HAROLD LIVINGSTON is a longtime writer/producer and novelist and the sole credited screenwriter of *Star Trek: The Motion Picture*.

CIRROC LOFTON is an actor best known for his role as Jake Sisko in *Star Trek: Deep Space Nine*.

JOHN LOGAN is a playwright, screenwriter and producer. He is a three-time Oscar nominee whose credits include *Skyfall, Gladiator, Hugo,* and *The Aviator*. He currently produces *Penny Dreadful* for Showtime and was the screenwriter of *Star Trek: Nemesis*.

DAVID LOUGHERY is a screenwriter and producer. He has written a variety of films including *Lakeview Terrace, Dreamscape,* and *Star Trek V: The Final Frontier*.

PAUL LYNCH is a director who has worked on such shows as *The Twilight Zone, Star Trek: The Next Generation,* and *Star Trek: Deep Space Nine*.

STEPHEN MACHT is a television and film actor. He has appeared in a variety of film and television programs, including *Galaxina, Castle, Femme Fatales, Suits,* and *Star Trek: Deep Space Nine*.

DAVID ALAN MACK is an author who has written many novels set in the *Star Trek* universe and coauthored two episodes of *Star Trek: Deep Space Nine*.

ADAM MALIN is the cofounder of Creation Entertainment, which specializes in producing conventions for fans of comic books, television series, and films.

SCOTT MANTZ is a film critic and producer who has appeared on such programs as *Access Hollywood* and *The Today Show*.

CHASE MASTERSON is an actress and producer who has starred in such series as *The Flash, E.R.,* and *General Hospital* as well as in Mel Brooks' *Robin Hood: Men in Tights,* but is best known for playing the role of Leeta, the dabo girl, on *Star Trek: Deep Space Nine.*

TOM MAZZA is a television producer and executive. As executive vice president of creative affairs at Paramount, he oversaw a variety of programs including *Mac-Gyver, Nash Bridges, Star Trek: Deep Space Nine, Star Trek: The Next Generation,* and *Star Trek: Voyager.*

ERIC MCCORMACK is best known as the star of the NBC hit series *Will & Grace,* TNT's *Perception,* and the star of the cult classic *Free Enterprise.*

DAVID MCDONNELL is a veteran journalist and served many years as the editor in chief of *Starlog* magazine.

MALCOLM MCDOWELL is a television and film actor with an expansive list of credits including *A Clockwork Orange, O Lucky Man!, Time After Time,* and *Star Trek: Generations.*

GATES MCFADDEN is an actress and choreographer best known for her role as Dr. Beverly Crusher in *Star Trek: The Next Generation.*

ROBERT DUNCAN MCNEILL is a television actor and director who played the role of Tom Paris on *Star Trek: Voyager.*

COLM MEANEY is an actor known for his role as Miles O'Brien in *Star Trek: The Next Generation* and *Star Trek: Deep Space Nine,* as well as a noted character actor who has appeared in such films as *Layer Cake, Con Air,* and *Law Abiding Citizen,* and most recently starred in the TV series *Hell on Wheels.*

JOE MENOSKY is a television writer who has worked on such shows as *Star Trek: The Next Generation, Star Trek: Deep Space Nine,* and *Star Trek: Voyager.* He is currently a writer on the new *Star Trek* series.

NICHOLAS MEYER is a screenwriter, producer, director, and author. He is the writer of the bestselling novel *The Seven-Per-Cent Solution*, which was adapted by Herbert Ross into a feature film. In addition to writing and directing *Star Trek II: The Wrath of Khan* and *Star Trek VI: The Undiscovered Country*, he cowrote *Star Trek IV: The Voyage Home* with Harve Bennett. He is also a consulting producer on the new *Star Trek series*.

DANIEL MINDEL is a cinematographer whose credits include *Enemy of the State, Star Wars: The Force Awakens, Star Trek*, and *Star Trek Into Darkness*.

JOSE MOLINA is a television writer and producer who has worked on such shows as *Castle, Haven, Firefly, The Vampire Diaries*, and *Agent Carter*.

ANTHONY MONTGOMERY is an actor and graphic novelist. His credits include *Single Ladies, House M.D.*, and *Star Trek: Enterprise*, on which he played Travis Mayweather.

RONALD D. MOORE is a television and film writer and producer. After dropping out of Cornell University and having his spec script lead to a staff position on *Star Trek: The Next Generation*, Moore became a co-executive producer on *Star Trek: Deep Space Nine*. He would later go on to produce such series as *Carnivàle* and *Roswell* and develop and executive produce the critically acclaimed remake of *Battlestar Galactica*. Subsequently, he developed and executive produced the series *Outlander* for Starz. He is also the screenwriter for *Star Trek: Generations* and *Star Trek: First Contact*.

DIANA MULDAUR is a film and television actress whose credits include *L.A. Law, Born Free, Star Trek: The Original Series*, and *Star Trek: The Next Generation*, in which she played Dr. Katherine Pulaski.

KATE MULGREW is a film and television actress. She is best known for *Mrs. Columbo* and her Emmy–nominated role as Red on *Orange Is the New Black*. She starred as Captain Kathryn Janeway on *Star Trek: Voyager*.

DONNA MURPHY is a two-time Tony Award winner for her work in musical theater. She was the voice of Mother Gothel in Disney's *Tangled* and starred as Anij in *Star Trek: Insurrection*.

ED NAHA is an author, journalist, screenwriter, and producer. He has written for the magazine *Starlog* and produced the spoken-word album *Inside Star Trek* as well as wrote the popular film *Honey, I Shrunk the Kids*.

NICHELLE NICHOLS is an actress, singer, and performer. She is best known for her role as Lieutenant Uhura on *Star Trek: The Original Series.*

LEONARD NIMOY was a prominent actor, director, poet, and producer. While he is best known for his legendary portrayal of Mr. Spock in the *Star Trek* series, he also directed numerous films including *Three Men and a Baby, The Good Mother,* and *Star Trek III* and *Star Trek IV.* In addition to starring as Paris in the *Mission Impossible* TV series, Nimoy starred in the TV movies *A Woman Called Golda* and *Never Forget,* as well as in *Fiddler on the Roof* and *Equus* on Broadway.

GLEN C. OLIVER is a film and TV critic who writes under the pseudonym "Merrick" for the popular pop culture Web site, *Ain't It Cool News.*

ROBERTO ORCI is a prolific film and television writer and producer. He is the cocreator of *Fringe* as well as the cowriter on *Star Trek* and *Star Trek Into Darkness.*

LINDA PARK is an actress known for her roles as Maggie Cheon on *Crash* and Hoshi Sato on *Star Trek: Enterprise.*

SIMON PEGG is an actor, comedian, screenwriter, and producer. He is known for his roles in the films *Shaun of the Dead, Hot Fuzz,* and as Scotty in *Star Trek* and *Star Trek Into Darkness.* He is also the cowriter of *Star Trek Beyond.*

RON PERLMAN is an actor and producer who starred in such films as *Hellboy, Pacific Rim,* and *Fantastic Beasts and Where to Find Them* as well as in the TV series *Beauty and the Beast, Sons of Anarchy,* and *Hand of God.* He also costarred as the Viceroy in *Star Trek: Nemesis.*

ETHAN PHILLIPS is an actor whose credits include *Inside Llewyn Davis, Benson,* and *Star Trek: Voyager,* on which he played Neelix.

ROBERT PICARDO is an actor and singer who starred in such cult films as *The Howling, Legend, Gremlins II: The New Batch,* the TV series *Femme Fatales,* and portrayed the role of The Doctor in *Star Trek: Voyager* and in the film *Star Trek: First Contact.*

MICHAEL PILLER was a television writer and producer who is best known for his work on *Star Trek: The Next Generation* and for cocreating *Star Trek: Deep Space Nine* and *Star Trek: Voyager.* He also developed and executive produced *The Dead Zone* TV series as well as *Legend,* starring John de Lancie. In addition, Piller wrote the screenplay for *Star Trek: Insurrection.*

SANDRA PILLER is the wife of Michael Piller and a country music singer.

CHRIS PINE has starred in a variety of films including *Into the Woods, Jack Ryan, Horrible Bosses 2,* and, most memorably, as Captain James T. Kirk in the new *Star Trek* feature film series.

ANDREW PROBERT is a conceptual artist who helped design the U.S.S. *Enterprise* for *Star Trek: The Motion Picture* and the *Enterprise-D* for *Star Trek: The Next Generation.*

ZACHARY QUINTO is an actor and film producer. He is best known for his role as Sylar in *Heroes* as well as for his role as Spock in the new series of *Star Trek* films.

GARFIELD REEVES-STEVENS has written numerous nonfiction books about the *Star Trek* franchise. With his wife, Judy, he was a coproducer on the final season of *Star Trek: Enterprise.*

JUDY REEVES-STEVENS, in addition to writing for such shows as *Flash Gordon, Phantom 2040,* and *Beyond Reality* with her husband, Gar, was a coproducer on the final season of *Star Trek: Enterprise.* Together, they also cocreated *Primeval: New World.*

GENE RODDENBERRY was a television and film writer and producer, and futurist. He is famous for being the creator and executive producer of the original *Star Trek* series that inspired the *Star Trek* franchise as well as the creator of *Star Trek: The Next Generation.* He also executive produced *Star Trek: The Motion Picture* as well as numerous TV pilots, including *The Questor Tapes, Planet Earth,* and *Genesis II.*

ROD RODDENBERRY is CEO of Roddenberry Entertainment and a respected philanthropist. He is the son of Gene and Majel Roddenberry.

GRANT ROSENBERG is a television writer and producer whose credits include *Baywatch, MacGyver, Time Trax,* and *Star Trek: The Next Generation.*

DAVE ROSSI is a producer and former assistant to Rick Berman. He has worked on *Star Trek: The Next Generation, Star Trek: Deep Space Nine, Star Trek: Voyager,* and *Star Trek: Enterprise* as well as the restoration of *Star Trek: The Original Series.*

MARVIN RUSH is a director of photography and worked on *Star Trek: The Next Generation*, *Star Trek: Deep Space Nine*, *Star Trek: Voyager*, and *Star Trek: Enterprise*, as well as *Moonlight* and *Hell on Wheels*.

TIM RUSS is an actor, writer, and musician. He is best known for his role as Lieutenant Commander Tuvok on *Star Trek: Voyager* as well as the director of several *Star Trek* fan films.

JERI RYAN is an actress best known for her role as Seven of Nine on *Star Trek: Voyager* and appearances on *Boston Legal*, *Bosch*, *Body of Proof*, and *Leverage*.

SUSAN SACKETT is a former executive assistant to Gene Roddenberry for more than seventeen years. She also cowrote two episodes of *Star Trek: The Next Generation* and several behind-the-scenes books about *Star Trek*, including *Letters to Star Trek* and *The Making of Star Trek: The Motion Picture*.

NICK SAGAN is an author and screenwriter. He wrote episodes of *Star Trek: The Next Generation* and was a story editor on *Star Trek: Voyager*. He is also the son of famous astronomer Carl Sagan.

ZOE SALDANA is an actress and dancer who is known for her roles in *Avatar* and *Guardians of the Galaxy* as well as Nyota Uhura in *Star Trek*, *Star Trek Into Darkness*, and *Star Trek Beyond*.

BARRY SCHULMAN is the former vice president of programming at the Sci-Fi (now Syfy) Channel. He was involved in the channel's airing of remastered episodes of *Star Trek: The Original Series* as well as the creation of bonus material for their debut on the channel.

ALLAN SCOTT is a screenwriter for such films as *Don't Look Now* who was attached to cowrite the aborted *Star Trek* film *Star Trek: Planet of the Titans*.

NAREN SHANKAR is a television writer, producer, and director. In addition to being a science consultant for *Star Trek: The Next Generation*, Shankar went on to executive produce *CSI: Crime Scene Investigation*. He also wrote for *Farscape*, *The Outer Limits*, *Grimm*, *Star Trek: Voyager*, and *Star Trek: Deep Space Nine*. He recently developed and executive produced *The Expanse* for Syfy.

WILLIAM SHATNER is the legendary actor, writer, singer, and director who portrays the iconic Captain James T. Kirk in *Star Trek*. In addition, he won an Emmy for his work as Denny Crane in *Boston Legal* and also starred as the titular *T.J. Hooker* in the hit ABC series as well as the host of *Rescue 911*. In addition to directing *Star Trek V: The Final Frontier*, Shatner has also starred in such films as *Judgment at Nuremberg, The Intruder, Kingdom of the Spiders, Airplane II: The Sequel,* and played an unhinged version of himself in the romantic comedy *Free Enterprise*.

HANNAH LOUISE SHEARER is a writer and producer whose credits include *Knight Rider, Star Trek: The Next Generation,* and *Star Trek: Deep Space Nine*.

ARMIN SHIMERMAN is an actor, voice actor, and author. He is best known for playing Principal Snyder in *Buffy the Vampire Slayer* and Quark in *Star Trek: Deep Space Nine*.

ALEXANDER SIDDIG is an actor who is best known for his role as Dr. Julian Bashir in *Star Trek: Deep Space Nine*. He has also starred in such films as *Syriana, Kingdom of Heaven,* and *Reign of Fire,* as well as *24, Game of Thrones,* and *Da Vinci's Demons*.

ALEXANDER SINGER is a director whose credits include numerous episodes of *Star Trek: The Next Generation, Star Trek: Deep Space Nine,* and *Star Trek: Voyager*.

MARINA SIRTIS is an actress best known for her role as Counselor Deanna Troi on *Star Trek: The Next Generation* and subsequent *Star Trek* films.

MELINDA SNODGRASS is a television writer and author. Her credits include *The Outer Limits, Reasonable Doubts,* and *Star Trek: The Next Generation*.

BRENT SPINER is an actor and performer best known for his portrayal as Lieutenant Commander Data in *Star Trek: The Next Generation* and the four subsequent *Star Trek* films, as well as *Independence Day, Out to Sea, Independence Day: Resurgence,* and *Introducing Dorothy Dandridge*.

JOSEPH STEFANO was a screenwriter and producer known for writing the screenplay to the film *Psycho* as well as creating the original *The Outer Limits* for ABC. He wrote "Skin of Evil" for the first season of *Star Trek: The Next Generation*.

ANTOINETTE STELLA is a television writer and producer whose credits include *Necessary Roughness, Rizzoli & Isles,* and *Star Trek: Enterprise*.

DAVID STERN was editor for Pocket Books' *Star Trek* book line as well as a writer for DC Comics.

PATRICK STEWART is a television, film, and stage actor. He is best known for his roles as Professor Charles Xavier in the *X-Men* film series and as Captain Jean-Luc Picard in *Star Trek: The Next Generation* and its subsequent films. He currently stars in the TV series *Blunt Talk* for Starz.

ERIC STILLWELL is a former assistant to Michael Piller. He has worked on such series as *The Dead Zone*, *Star Trek: The Next Generation* (for which he contributed the story to the third season episode "Yesterday's Enterprise"), and *Star Trek: Voyager*.

GREG STRANGIS is a writer and producer whose credits include *Falcon Crest*, *War of the Worlds*, and *Star Trek: The Next Generation*.

MIKE SUSSMAN is a former journalist and television writer and producer who has worked on such series *Star Trek: Voyager* and as a producer on *Star Trek: Enterprise*. He is cocreator of the TV series *Perception*, which starred Eric McCormack, for TNT.

FARAN TAHIR is a television and film actor whose credits include *Iron Man*, *Elysium*, and *Star Trek*.

GEORGE TAKEI is an actor, author, and activist. He is best known for his role as Hikaru Sulu in *Star Trek: The Original Series*.

JERI TAYLOR is a television writer and producer. She is known for her work on such shows as *Quincy M.E.*, *Jake & the Fatman*, *In the Heat of the Night*, *Star Trek: The Next Generation*, and *Star Trek: Voyager*, which she cocreated with Rick Berman and Michael Piller. She has also written three *Star Trek* novels.

MICHAEL TAYLOR is a television writer and musician who has worked on *Star Trek: Deep Space Nine* and *Star Trek: Voyager* as well as such series as *The Dead Zone*, *Battlestar Galactica*, *Defiance*, and *Turn: Washington's Spies*.

BRADLEY THOMPSON is a television writer and producer whose credits include *The Twilight Zone*, *Battlestar Galactica*, *The Strain*, and *Star Trek: Deep Space Nine*.

GEOFFREY THORNE is a novelist and comic book writer.

TONY TODD is an actor and producer who has appeared in *Star Trek: Voyager, Star Trek: Deep Space Nine,* and *Star Trek: The Next Generation.*

TRACY TORMÉ is a screenwriter and television producer. He is best known for creating the popular sci-fi series *Sliders* and as a writer for *Star Trek: The Next Generation,* for which he won a Peabody Award for "The Big Goodbye." He also wrote the film *Fire in the Sky.*

JESÚS TREVIÑO is a television director whose credits include *Babylon 5, Star Trek: Deep Space Nine,* and *Star Trek: Voyager.*

CONNOR TRINNEER is a film, stage, and television actor. He is best known for his roles as Michael on *Stargate: Atlantis* and Charles "Trip" Tucker III on *Star Trek: Enterprise.*

KARL URBAN is an actor who has appeared in such films as *The Lord of the Rings* trilogy, *Riddick,* and *Dredd,* and as Dr. Leonard McCoy in *Star Trek, Star Trek Into Darkness,* and *Star Trek Beyond.*

NANA VISITOR is an actress best known for her roles as Jean Ritter in *Wildfire,* Nancy Loomis in the remake of *Friday the 13th,* and the Bajoran Kira Nerys in *Star Trek: Deep Space Nine.*

GARRETT WANG is an actor who is best known for his role as Ensign Harry Kim on *Star Trek: Voyager.*

APRIL WEBSTER is a casting director who has worked on such projects as *Lost, Mission: Impossible III,* and *Star Trek* (2009).

DAVID WEDDLE is a television writer and producer who has worked on such shows as *Battlestar Galactica, Falling Skies, The Strain,* and *Star Trek: Deep Space Nine.* He is also author of the biography of *Wild Bunch* director, Sam Peckinpah, *If They Move . . . Kill 'Em: The Life and Times of Sam Peckinpah.*

MING-NA WEN is an actress who has starred in *Stargate: Universe* and *The Joy Luck Club,* and currently stars in Marvel's *Agents of S.H.I.E.L.D.*

MICHAEL WESTMORE is a makeup artist from the legendary Westmore family, whose credits include *Star Trek: The Next Generation, Star Trek: Deep Space Nine, Star Trek: Voyager,* and *Star Trek: Enterprise,* as well as the four *Next Generation* features.

WIL WHEATON is an actor, blogger, and writer. He is best known for his roles in *Stand by Me* and *Toy Soldiers* as well as playing Wesley Crusher in *Star Trek: The Next Generation*.

JOHN WHELPLEY is a writer and producer known for his work on *MacGyver, Star Trek: The Next Generation*, and *Star Trek: Deep Space Nine*.

LISA WILKE is a writer who worked uncredited on the "Tin Man" episode of *Star Trek: The Next Generation*.

BERNIE WILLIAMS was a line producer whose credits include *Daredevil, A Clockwork Orange*, and *Star Trek: Generations*, as well as the original Patrick McGoohan classic, *The Prisoner*.

RALPH WINTER is a producer whose credits include *X-Men, Star Trek III: The Search for Spock, Star Trek IV: The Voyage Home*, and *Star Trek V: The Final Frontier*.

ROBERT HEWITT WOLFE is a television writer and producer. His credits include *Andromeda, Elementary, Star Trek: The Next Generation*, and *Star Trek: Deep Space Nine*.

ALFRE WOODARD is a film, television, and stage actress who is best known for her roles in *Primal Fear, K-Pax, Desperate Housewives, True Blood*, and on Marvel's *Luke Cage*. She starred as Lily Sloane in *Star Trek: First Contact*.

HERB WRIGHT was a television writer, producer, and director. His credits include *Shadow of the Hawk, Stingray, War of the Worlds*, and *Star Trek: The Next Generation*.

ANTON YELCHIN is a film and television actor. His credits include *Alpha Dog*, the remake of *Fright Night*, and starring as Pavel Chekov in *Star Trek, Star Trek Into Darkness*, and *Star Trek Beyond*.

BRYCE ZABEL is a journalist turned writer/producer whose credits include *Lois & Clark: The New Adventures of Superman, Dark Skies*, and *Animal Armageddon*.

THOMAS ZELLER is a longtime *Star Trek* fan and disabled veteran of the war in Afghanistan.

MARC SCOTT ZICREE is a television writer and producer whose credits include *Sliders, Star Trek: The Next Generation,* and *Star Trek: Deep Space* Nine, as well as the fan film *Space Command.* He is also author of *The Twilight Zone Companion.*

HERMAN ZIMMERMAN is an art director and production designer. He worked on all the *Star Trek* series from *Star Trek: The Next Generation* through *Star Trek: Enterprise* as well as the *Next Generation* feature films and *Star Trek V: The Final Frontier.*

REBIRTH OF A [TREK] NATION

"THESE ARE THE VOYAGES OF THE STARSHIP *ENTERPRISE* . . .
HER CONTINUING MISSION . . . TO BOLDLY GO WHERE
NO ONE HAS GONE BEFORE."

In a press conference in 1986, Paramount Television president Mel Harris proclaimed, "The speculation is over. The answer is 'yes.' *Star Trek* lives. Starting next fall, beginning with a two-hour telefilm followed by twenty-four one-hour episodes, *Star Trek* will return to television in the form of a new series, *Star Trek: The Next Generation*." In an era before sequels, spin-offs, and reinventions were de rigueur, the return of *Star Trek* to television was nothing short of miraculous.

It had been twenty years since the September 8, 1966, debut of the original *Star Trek* series on NBC, and in the subsequent two decades, the franchise had only grown in popularity. Buoyed by fans who embraced the series in television syndication in the early seventies, it became a vibrant movement that spawned well-attended conventions, extensive merchandise, and ultimately, a blockbuster feature film franchise. *Star Trek* confounded the naysayers by continuing to boldly go even as its seventy-nine original episodes played on local TV stations again . . . and again . . . and again before eventually being released on home video via VHS and, later, LaserDisc, DVD, Blu-ray, and streaming. The days of fans recording episodes on their audio cassette recorders at home from the tinny mono speakers of their Zenith and RCA TVs were long over.

The questions facing the studio, of course, were how long would even the most ardent fan continue to watch these same episodes repeatedly, and, just as important, could lightning indeed strike twice? The answer to the latter was a resounding yes, and with the success of *Star Trek: The Next Generation,* which debuted in first-run syndication in 1987, dubious fans eventually embraced the new series, many even preferring it to the original. But one thing was clear: *The Next Generation*, unlike the classic series, was a hit (in the ratings, at least) from the outset, and its success immediately inspired further sequels.

Star Trek: Deep Space Nine premiered in 1993, depicting a space station on the fringes of Federation space filled with myriad alien species that was a powder keg ready to explode. With *The Next Generation*'s seven-year run transitioning into a motion picture series, *Star Trek: Voyager* took its place in 1995 as the flagship of UPN, the United Paramount Network. Breaking new ground, this was the first in the series to boast a female captain at the helm, Kate Mulgrew's Kathryn Janeway, commanding a starship that had been flung to the outer reaches of the Milky Way and who now leads her crew in a desperate quest to get home. Finally, in 2001, *Enterprise* (sans *Star Trek*, initially) premiered, which was a prequel to the original series, taking place decades before the adventures of Captain Kirk and toplined by versatile *Quantum Leap* star Scott Bakula.

With the sputtering starship seemingly exhausting its supply of dilithium crystals, as evidenced by the ratings freefall of *Enterprise* and the failure of the last of the *Next Generation* movies, *Nemesis*, to engage audiences, it appeared that *Star Trek*'s *long* journey into night might truly be over.

But like the proverbial phoenix from the ashes, a new and shinier starship emerged from the brain trust at Bad Robot under the assured aegis of director J.J. Abrams and producer Bryan Burk, who, in 2009, reintroduced *Star Trek* for a new generation by taking it back to where it began with the all-new adventures of Captain Kirk, Mr. Spock, and the crew of the original *Enterprise* as portrayed by a new cast.

Whether *Star Trek* will continue to live long and prosper for another five decades remains to be seen, although the greenlighting of a new CBS TV series spearheaded by Alex Kurtzman and Bryan Fuller premiering in 2017 bodes well for the future. After all, if its fans have anything to say about it, you might just be seeing new *Star Trek* adventures for another fifty years. While every iteration of *Star Trek* has had its ardent defenders and detractors, one thing everyone can agree with Mel Harris about is that *Star Trek* does indeed live.

Of course, the birth (and rebirth) of *Star Trek* begins with one man. The late Great Bird of the Galaxy, Gene Roddenberry, whom Paramount reluctantly—due to numerous skirmishes over the years—tasked with the relaunch of their prized franchise, a role he himself initially approached with much trepidation.

GENE RODDENBERRY (creator/executive producer, *Star Trek*)

The first *Star Trek* took years out of my life, separated me from my family, and kept me away from my children, and I really didn't want to go through that again when Paramount asked me if I would like to bring *Star Trek* back. And there was a career consideration. Why rock the boat? You're ahead, you've got a show that's a success, and suppose you go in and everything goes boom, nosedive? No television series had ever succeeded in coming back again. None. It never happened. There were physical considerations, too. At sixty-seven years old, I was not the same man I was when I was forty-five when I started *Star Trek*.

ROBERT LEWIN (producer, *Star Trek: The Next Generation*)

Starting from ground level was the only way to go. I thought the idea was wonderful. The old show was not a big hit, and became a big hit during the seventies because the ideas at the time were advanced. While the show does look very primitive, it has a lot of content. The idea for *The Next Generation* was to provide that same content but in a 1987 capsule, within 1987 parameters.

FRED BRONSON (writer, *Star Trek: The Next Generation*)

I used to have dreams that *Star Trek* was back after the original was canceled. It usually involved reading *TV Guide* and there was a description of the new episode. So, to me, it was literally a dream come true that *Star Trek* was back on the air. After all the fighting and petitions and being totally devastated when it went off the air, to have it back was kind of unbelievable. When I say it was literally a dream come true, it's probably the only dream I ever had that came true.

MING-NA WEN (actress, Marvel's *Agents of S.H.I.E.L.D.*)

I would hear that theme music and I would get *so* excited. That to me was the ultimate, because I've always wanted to travel in space and to boldly go where no man has gone before. *Star Trek* made me feel, like, "C'mon, let's go!" And I got to meet William Shatner, which was *amazing*!

RICK BERMAN (executive producer, *Star Trek: The Next Generation*)

We tried to bring back the magic of a television show that had been off the air for twenty years, yet had continued to grow in popularity. The fans we had been in touch with felt you can't go home again. There's no way you can give us a new *Enterprise* with a new crew. Their attitude was one of great skepticism. It was a great challenge in that sense. If we had tried to re-create younger or older versions of Kirk or Spock, or had we tried to make characters who were extremely similar to characters on the old show, we would probably have failed. What we got was the *essence* of *Star Trek* as opposed to the specifics of what the show was about.

CHRIS BLACK (co-executive producer, *Star Trek: Enterprise*)

Star Trek had to evolve. I am a fan of the original series. It's still my favorite. To me *Star Trek is* William Shatner's Captain Kirk and Nimoy's Spock. There's a line from David Goodman's episode of *Futurama*—when he talks about *Star Trek*, he says, "TV show. 1966–69. Seventy-nine episodes. Thirty good ones." It's kind of true. But even the cheesy ones are entertaining, and I have great affection for them.

DAVID MCDONNELL (editor, *Starlog* magazine)

Like so many other people, *Star Trek* changed my life. I wouldn't have all the friends I have today, all the nifty experiences I've had—cruising the Caribbean with Sarek, Q, Koloth, and Kor; meeting Chuck Yeager and Chuck Jones, visiting Skywalker Ranch, ILM, Disney Studios, Paramount, and Pixar—without my time at *Starlog*. That magazine began as a *Star Trek*–oriented one-shot in 1976 and then was driven primarily for its thirty-three years and 375 issues of publication by its coverage of *Star Wars* and *Star Trek*. I'm happy to have been a part of it during those years, essentially serving as the maître d' of the science fiction universe.

GLEN C. OLIVER (film & TV critic, *Ain't It Cool News*)

Classic *Star Trek* was that slightly rough girl who is a touch unrefined, a tad bratty and disheveled, but dripping with sex appeal to the point where you can't help but want to bang her. And when you do, the sex feels noticeably naughty and maybe a little messy, but so, *so* hot. And you end up wanting more.

TNG was that more subdued, shy, refined girl whom you end up taking to bed—hoping for the best. But no matter how hard she tries, innate passion and chemistry just isn't there. And the entire experience feels a tad unrewarding, and is frustratingly laborious.

Not that I'd know.

CHRIS BLACK

The problem I had with the first two seasons of *Next Generation* was that they tried to make the same show with different actors and didn't acknowledge that it was almost two decades later. When Michael Piller came in, he said, "I love those shows, they were great, but you have to do a show for the mid-1900s, not the late 1960s."

MICHAEL PILLER (executive producer, *Star Trek: The Next Generation*)

As Gene had a chance to look at the change in our country and the change in the world, he felt that what really the message of *Star Trek* should be was that we should be out there exploring to learn more about ourselves instead of trying to teach everybody else what our values were. We were very sure of our values in the early sixties, but we've begun to question those values. We have a lot to learn as a civilization and the fundamental message of *The Next Generation* was where can we learn? Where can we go? And what can *we* learn from *you*?

DAVID A. GOODMAN (coexecutive producer, *Futurama*)

Tonally, the Rick Berman/Michael Piller years are very different from the original series, which was an action show. You had to have a fight scene every episode, and *Next Generation* had to be more cerebral without the requirements of action/drama.

JONATHAN FRAKES (actor/director, *Star Trek: The Next Generation*)

I was one of the people who didn't know the original show very well. I was aware of its existence, but not of its place in the popular culture. I had no concept that by being part of this family, that we would become iconic. My wife, Genie [Francis], did. She used to have a poster of Shatner on her wall when she was a kid.

NAREN SHANKAR (science consultant, *Star Trek: The Next Generation*)

Next Generation was truly a different version of the same concept. The only connection point to me between the original series and *Next Generation* was to boldly go where no man has gone before. The Prime Directive, which was ignored all the time on the original series, basically became gospel on *Next Generation*. It's a totally different attitude, different characters, different intellectualization of what their mission was. It's a very different thing.

JOHN LOGAN (writer, *Star Trek: Nemesis*)

To me, I've always found *Next Generation* a worthy successor to *TOS* because the reason classic *Trek* worked so well is because of the triumvirate of Kirk, Spock, and McCoy. You have emotion. You have logic. You have compassion. And Kirk always had to balance the scales between those characters, which is what made those morality tales of the original series so exciting.

I think *Next Generation* has something of the same thing in that Captain Picard has to be the fulcrum while you can have Worf expressing sort of the vainglorious, heroic aspect or Data expressing sort of the logical, cool, dispassionate response or Deanna Troi representing the empathic or sympathetic response to the situation. Instead of a triangle, it's sort of like a wheel with Picard in the center of all the spokes. I found that really dynamic dramatically.

DOUG DREXLER (special makeup effects artist,
Star Trek: The Next Generation)

The original series is the masterpiece. It's the original. It will always be the top one. But I was always very proud of *TNG*. I felt like it was *Star Trek* grown up. I understood that on television you had to have your fistfights, the captain always had to kiss the girl. There were certain things you had to have in 1960's television, but when they did *TNG* you had this very thoughtful captain who rarely ever struck anybody, never made a pass at the girl, and was an amazing diplomat.

GENNIFER HUTCHISON (coexecutive producer, *Better Call Saul*)

I've been a genre fan since I was very little. My mother grew up watching *Star Trek,* and it was her favorite show. She was always a huge Spock fan. She was one of the many girls in love with him. When I was about seven, she was going to college, getting her degree, and she took a sci-fi class as an elective. It was a night class and my dad was working, so she would take me to class. We would watch *Forbidden Planet* and old *Twilight Zone* episodes and old *Star Trek* episodes, so that's really when it cemented for me as something that I really loved. We watched *Next Generation* together and we watched all the movies. For years after watching *The Voyage Home* I wanted to be a cetacean biologist.

RENÉ ECHEVARRIA (producer, *Star Trek: Deep Space Nine*)

When *Next Generation* premiered, I checked it out. Patrick Stewart sort of saved it for me. I was in because of him. He was so interesting to watch, and also, it was such a different choice. But it was a rocky start for me. A lot of those early episodes felt like they were about going to the planet where the people do things some way and we teach them the error of their ways or something like that.

PATRICK STEWART (actor, "Jean-Luc Picard,"
Star Trek: The Next Generation)

It's a medium that has to be taken very seriously. Television is probably the most potent, whereas how many people does the theater touch? [The show] could play to over two million people in the Los Angeles area alone every week. That's more people than I've played to in a lifetime while acting on stage.

ANDRÉ BORMANIS (science consultant, *Star Trek: The Next Generation*)

Star Trek has shaped our perception as a culture of what the future ought to be. It makes people ask "Could we actually do that?" I'm still blown away when I think about the original series when you would see Spock or McCoy putting one of those little square discs in the computer. Twenty years later we had three-and-a-half-inch floppy disks. It's exactly the same thing. The flip phone, same thing. Some engineer at Motorola thought, "Hey it'd be cool to make this look like the communicator, but we need to make it smaller. Or fold it. You can flip it open like Kirk and Spock did, because that was so cool." It's been such a touchstone and such a cultural presence.

BOBAK FERDOWSI ("Mohawk Guy," Jet Propulsion Laboratories)

I've always loved trying to figure out how things work, but *Star Trek* and a general love of science fiction is what pushed me toward space exploration.

BRYAN FULLER (executive producer, *Hannibal*)

You look at the legacy of the writers that were coming in at that time with Brannon Braga and Ron Moore and René Echevarria and Joe Menosky. The quality of storytelling was so thoughtful and also trippy in a way that it was able to knock down the barriers of reality to tell really broad, fascinating stories. Stories that then came back to a science fiction explanation that was totally satisfying, yet had all of the tropes of a fantasy show just grounded in a bigger-than-life, high-concept, science-fictionalization that you weren't seeing anywhere else on television.

JAVIER GRILLO-MARXUACH (supervising producer, *Lost*)

Star Trek: The Next Generation was a writing school that turned out some of the best talent working in the medium today. It is to Michael Piller's great credit that his application of the show's "open submission policy"—and the way in which the show's upper management thought about story and ran the writers room—

yielded so many great writer/producers who continue to define the face of modern television.

It is a truly enviable accomplishment that Piller and company's "coaching tree" includes such talent as Ron Moore, René Echevarria, Naren Shankar, Brannon Braga, Bryan Fuller, and so on. Because I was taught how to break story by a *Next Generation* veteran, I have been the beneficiary of that tradition as well. And as someone who loves television, it's hard for me to not love *Star Trek*, both for its impact on the popular culture as well as for its effect on the creative and business culture of an art form I love.

ARMIN SHIMERMAN (actor, "Quark," *Star Trek: Deep Space Nine*)

On *Deep Space Nine* we had phenomenal writers, and the writers told incredible stories about hope, the future, and mankind. We weren't busy trying to correct other worlds' problems, we were busy trying to correct our own problems. The other most important factor in the show's success was the enormous power and talent of our cast. I may be slightly prejudiced, but I would venture to say our cast was far and beyond the most talented *Star Trek* cast.

ALEXANDER SIDDIG (actor, "Julian Bashir,"
Star Trek: Deep Space Nine)

Deep Space Nine was a trailblazer for the genre in the sense that *now* so many shows have got these long, sweeping arcs, but outside of David Lynch's *Twin Peaks,* I'm scratching my head to think of other shows at that time where you had to watch the whole of it to *really* get it. Every show does that now. Even *Game of Thrones*—you've got to watch fifty of them before you know what the hell is going on, and then you *still* don't know what's going on. People needed educating to be able to cope with that complexity, and that education started around that time with a bunch of shows, one of which was *DS9*. Ira Behr can be immensely proud of that.

IRA STEVEN BEHR (executive producer, *Star Trek: Deep Space Nine*)

I was there during the third season of *The Next Generation*, and I remember what it was like before *TNG* was put on the mountaintop. I remember when people were still bitching and moaning about what a lousy, stinking, rotten show *TNG* was compared to Kirk and Spock and "Charlie X" and the good old days. Well, then *TNG* became the godhead and *Deep Space Nine* was the one struggling to make a name for itself. I always felt if people would just allow it to happen, they would have said, "Hey, this is different *Star Trek*." We did something just like *TNG* did: we developed a new wrinkle in the franchise, which is what we set out to do. How often do you accomplish what you set out to do?

BRYAN FULLER

Deep Space Nine was for geeks *by* geeks. Everybody in that room was a *Star Trek* fan. Everybody loved the genre. Everybody enjoyed playing with the tools of the genre. And with *Voyager* there was a small element that was "we've got to be better than *Star Trek*." And it's, like, no, *Star Trek* is pretty great. Don't worry about being better and just worry about delivering. *DS9* was definitely like the hardcore *Star Trek* fans. Compared to *Voyager,* where there was a little bit of that, *DS9* knew *Star Trek* was cool, *Voyager* wasn't so sure.

GLEN C. OLIVER

Of the three series which followed *TNG*, *Deep Space Nine* took the most chances dramatically and conceptually, and in doing so felt most closely akin to its *TOS* progenitor. I believe that this is why *DS9* continues to resonate so strongly for so many *Trek* fans. Despite its awkward and clunky opening season or two, the show grew into itself nicely, developed its characters fully and took a few chances along the way, and in many regards felt more "true" to itself than either *Voyager* or *Enterprise*. It didn't feel timid, and didn't feel ashamed to present human beings as, well, acting like human beings.

MICHAEL PILLER (cocreator/executive producer, *Star Trek: Voyager*)

Voyager was a very contemporary kind of message to be dealing with. We said to ourselves, this is what Roddenberry had to deal with back in the original days when he was trying to figure out what *Star Trek* was going to be. The original *Enterprise* really was about being alone out there. It was about being in a ship in space, facing unknown aliens. If you look at the years since, it's gotten very crowded in our part of the galaxy. We know all the political scenarios there are in *Star Trek*; we know the Bajorans and we know the Klingons, we know the Vulcans and we know the Cardassians. When we sent this ship to the Delta Quadrant alone, the canvas was clear, and the same things Roddenberry had to do are the things we would have to do. It was really back to basics, and that was a huge creative challenge.

KATE MULGREW (actress, "Kathryn Janeway," *Star Trek: Voyager*)

I'm not even remotely surprised at how much attention the fact that the show had a female captain attracted. This is the human condition. It's a novelty. I think that it piques a mass kind of curiosity, and it's very typical of our nature as human beings. I do suppose that one has to always refer to the gender in this regard. I am a woman, and that lends itself to maternity, to compassion, to warmth—to a lot of qualities which our culture has encouraged in women.

DANI HAIDER (web developer, age 31)

Growing up as a young girl, you think that you can do anything or be anything that you want to be, but as I grew older and became an adult, it became clear to me that things *weren't* as great as I thought they would be. There's still an inequality between men and women and with racial discrimination.

Having Captain Janeway as a role model for me growing up as a young girl was *so* important in making me feel that I could try to be something that I otherwise might not have been able to be. Be a leader, be a scientist, or whatever. Janeway is such an important person in my life because she portrayed a strong woman who wasn't sexualized, who no one really pointed out, "You're a female and you're a captain. That's different." She was just the captain, and it didn't matter whether or not she was a woman.

JONATHAN LARSEN (executive producer, MSNBC)

The extent of gender equality that *Star Trek* did muster, giving women, albeit short in years and hem lines, "real" jobs and occasionally real authority, paved the way for public acceptance not just of future female Federation captains . . . but actual, real-life female astronauts, too. As in so many other regards, even when it came to elements of our politics and our culture, in imagining our future, *Star Trek* made it possible.

KATE MULGREW

It's extremely gratifying that it carries on. That speaks to the strength of the whole vision. Gene Roddenberry understood this, didn't he? A perfect genius, I think. It gratifies me. It's a testament to the mythology and the fact that science fiction is actually rooted in science. The fires are literature inside these young girls' imaginations, which actually takes them into the field of science, in very, very deliberate ways. The fact that I've been even a small part of that is an extraordinary thing.

SCOTT BAKULA (actor, "Jonathan Archer," *Star Trek: Enterprise*)

It all starts with the fact that I'm a fan of the original series. I never thought, "I'd like to be a captain on that," but I *did* think that I'd like to be with a group of guys like that. That's what was so appealing to me about the original. I wanted to have buddies like that. I was in college when it was in reruns and it was kind of a religion to watch it every night. I had really good friends and I was really struck by those three guys [Kirk, Spock, and McCoy] and how much they cared for each other and loved each other, and their life-or-death situations. It was a sexy show to me. It was fun and it had those relationships. That was the initial hook of *Enterprise* for me, and that part of it didn't let me down.

BRANNON BRAGA (coproducer, *Star Trek: The Next Generation*)

Enterprise had its virtues. It also had things that you felt you'd seen before. There was some groundbreaking stuff, and *Enterprise* is being reevaluated and viewed more favorably. In England, they loved *Enterprise*. I've done a couple of conventions there and people are like, "Why did you cancel it?" They were baffled, because it was successful and popular there.

DAVID A. GOODMAN

Every new *Star Trek* generation has people that say the last one was better, why are they doing this, why are they doing *Next Generation*? Why are you doing *Deep Space Nine*? So there's no pleasing us, and that's part of the fun.

RENÉ AUBERJONOIS (actor, "Odo," *Star Trek: Deep Space Nine*)

There is a sort of a generic concept of what a *Star Trek* fan is, which is the way *Saturday Night Live* portrayed them. But the thing that really interests me about the fans of *Star Trek* is the demographic of it. It goes from seven-year-old boys to M.I.T. physics professors to matronly painters, motorcycle jocks—you can't really pigeonhole it.

SCOTT MANTZ (film critic, *Access Hollywood*)

The most misunderstood thing about *Star Trek* are the fans themselves. People make fun of them. They still do. They were called Trekkies, now they are called Trekkers. There is a condescending and derogatory inflection that comes from calling a fan a Trekkie or a Trekker. But you know what? Whether you are influenced by the story, the characters, the messages, the optimism, the point is that *Star Trek* fans are really good people.

Sure, there's a certain percentage that go a little overboard, but it's no different when you're watching the Rose Bowl or some football game in Wisconsin in January and it's thirteen degrees outside and people are painted in football colors. I was made fun of when I was a kid for being a Trekker. It hurt, but I felt empowered by it because I was proud. It made me happy. I've got news for you, I wouldn't be here if it wasn't for *Star Trek*. Everything I am I owe to *Star Trek*. It changed my life. It wasn't just a show I liked and enjoyed. It was a show that inspired me in ways I didn't realize.

MANNY COTO (executive producer, *Star Trek: Enterprise*)

I personally miss the exploration; I actually like a lot of the early episodes of season one and two of *Enterprise* finding new planets and new worlds. They weren't always successful, but I liked what they were attempting to do.

BRANNON BRAGA

Going to these conventions, it's very enlightening. People aren't talking about the movies at all. I'll get a couple of "Oh, I liked *First Contact*," but all the questions are about the television series. That's how it started. That's what it is. Some of the movies are great. Some are not. It's not the same. *Star Wars* is all movies. *Star Trek* is TV.

MANNY COTO

The problem with *Star Trek* is that the universe has been so explored. The new movies were very smart in going back and starting over again and redefining the universe.

BRYAN BURK (producer, *Star Trek Into Darkness*)

What pulls people to *Star Trek* is the sense of wonder of what our future might hold when we boldly leave Earth to learn from different species and worlds. We're all drawn to that promise of a future where there's no more war on Earth and whatever problems we have, we work them out together. *That's* the *Star Trek* vision.

DAVID A. GOODMAN

J.J. [Abrams] explored Kirk and Spock in a way that had never been explored before. They talked about love and what love means on Vulcan, which are questions that never were answered before.

BRANNON BRAGA

It's definitely a reinvention that is still faithful to the mythology of *Star Trek*.

DAVID A. GOODMAN

It was a reinvention that did a trick to make it palatable to old *Star Trek* fans.

GLEN C. OLIVER

Many people seem to feel the Bad Robot films are highly off base. I'm not sure I agree with this assessment. They are hugely entertaining, energized, and exhilarating—qualities *Star Trek* had been missing and craving for a long while. They are undeniably spectacular—perhaps more so than any other *Star Trek,* ever. For the first time ever, *Star Trek* is the best that it could be in terms of production values and presentation—both of which are vital in how modern audiences perceive and embrace a franchise.

SCOTT MANTZ

The impact of J.J.'s movie became clear to me when I went to my high school reunion over Thanksgiving 2011. I was picked on a little bit when I was a kid because

I was a big *Star Trek* fan. This guy, Todd Capriani, comes up to me and puts his arm around me and says, "Mantz, I used to pick on you all the time for being a Trekkie, but that new movie was pretty good." And I said, "Todd, welcome to the bandwagon." That was it. That was the moment I realized that it was not just a great *Star Trek* movie, that it was a great movie, period. And my mom liked it.

ANDRÉ BORMANIS

When it comes back to TV, I hope they do something more in the spirit of the original. Everybody in Hollywood who has ever had even the smallest association with *Star Trek* I'm sure has a "How would you do the next *Star Trek*?" answer. I would probably do something a little more like Captain Pike's adventures. Go back to that era where it was a little more rugged, a little more fifties' sci-fi sensibility.

MANNY COTO

Darker is much easier—darker is always easier, and I'm guilty of that, too. *24* is very dark, but it's always easier to be dark; it's harder to be lighter and inspirational, uplifting here and there. It's easier just to be dark, kill everyone, make everyone rotten. And by the way, it's in vogue now to the point that it's cliché. Every cable series does it—*The Sopranos, Breaking Bad*. All shows I love, but enough already. Not everyone is rotten and not everything has to be. Hollywood thinks darker is grittier. I don't like the new *Batman* movies. I prefer *The Avengers*.

BRANNON BRAGA

I miss the freedom of storytelling. With *Star Trek* you could do anything, and I really miss it. I know that most of the people I used to work with miss it, too.

MIKE SUSSMAN (creator/executive producer, *Perception*)

I don't think *Star Trek* gets the credit for being as diverse as it is in terms of the stories it chooses to tell. Look at the difference between *Star Trek: The Motion Picture* and *The Wrath of Khan*. The same actors were in it and some of the same sets, but it's like they took place in different universes. It's this weird thing, because you have all these disparate people working on it with different ideas and theories about what the show could be. I think it was Nicholas Meyer who said it was like the Catholic Mass. This week we're doing it in Latin, next week we're doing it in English.

GENNIFER HUTCHISON

One of the things that I love about genre is I feel like it's such a great way to tell a story about basic human experience, just because you get to have this fantastic environment and a world where they're exploring. They're exploring other planets, they don't know what's out there, and it's such a great setting to tell stories about people. I feel like with *Breaking Bad* it was about drugs and crime, but it really was just a setting that provided high stakes to tell a story about people.

Part of that is having that humor and being able to set your own tone and not just have to stick with "We're only doing drama" or "We're only doing space battles." Or "We're only doing a sitcom." *Star Trek* really did set a standard of, you can tell a different kind of story with interesting characters in an amazing world that a lot of people will identify with.

DOMINIC KEATING (actor, "Malcolm Reed," *Star Trek: Enterprise*)

I went to see *Into Darkness* on a date and the girl I took was a *Star Trek* fan. Right at the end, where Spock is beating up on Benedict Cumberbatch, this little kid's voice came screaming out from a couple of rows behind me: "Way to go, Spock!" I turn around and it's this kid who must have been about eight years old, and I thought to myself, "Would you look at that. Fifty years on and they're bringing it still. Isn't that amazing?"

BRANNON BRAGA

Star Trek is obviously evolving. The fact is, once something becomes a phenomenon, it becomes owned by everybody. *Star Wars* is bigger than George Lucas. It's the same way that *Star Trek* went from Gene Roddenberry to Nicholas Meyer to the group that was there during my time to J.J. Abrams, and eventually beyond J.J.—this thing will still be around when we're all dead.

THE NEXT GENERATION

(1987–1994)

BACK TO THE FUTURE

"IF WE'RE GOING TO BE DAMNED, LET'S BE DAMNED
FOR WHAT WE REALLY ARE."

To commemorate the twentieth anniversary of the original *Star Trek*, Paramount Pictures produced *The Voyage Home*. Released on November 26, 1986, it was the fourth entry in the ongoing film series featuring the original cast and is commonly referred to as "the one with the whales." With a U.S. box-office gross of over $109,000,000, it was, by far, the most successful of any of the *Star Trek* films to that date.

Although the film's blockbuster success reinforced the potency of the cast led by William Shatner, Leonard Nimoy, and DeForest Kelley, Paramount was nonetheless anxious to jump-start a television franchise that promised lucrative weekly returns on their investment. Knowing it would be too expensive to corral the films' cast for a new television series, the studio's long-range plans for the franchise involved creating an all-new show with an original, and younger, dramatis personae. Translation: a new series for syndication, featuring an all-new cast and set seventy-five years beyond the adventures of Captain Kirk, Mr. Spock, and the rest of the *Enterprise* crew.

After exploring the opportunity to relaunch the series on NBC, as well as the then-fledgling Fox network (neither of which were willing to commit to enough episodes to justify the massive start-up costs involved), Paramount instead chose to produce a season's worth of episodes for first-run syndication to local stations hungry for original content. The studio would be able to charge premium advertising rates, and the stations would not be solely dependent on old television shows and shopworn feature films, as was common in the pre-Internet era. (Technically, on an average budget of $1.3 million first season, Paramount was selling $980,000 in national commercial time, deficiting about $320,000 an episode at the time.)

And thus *Star Trek: A New Beginning* (or *The New Adventure*, as it was initially called) was born, eventually becoming *The Next Generation*.

TOM MAZZA (executive vice president of current programming & strategic planning, Paramount Television)

It was a very exciting time. I was involved in putting the presentations together to help sell it when it first went into syndication. I thought it was a really bold move.

The first-run syndication market was at its heyday. For the longest time, *Star Trek* was in the top three. Only *Wheel of Fortune* and *Jeopardy* were constantly beating it. It was the highest rated one-hour scripted drama. It was a great economic opportunity. You could produce twenty-six episodes and sell the back end of the show ahead of time, so you're ensuring profitability . . . or, at minimum, breaking even.

LEONARD NIMOY (actor, "Mr. Spock")

I was among the first people Paramount approached to produce the show, but I didn't want to do it. But not because I didn't think it was a good idea or anything like that. I just didn't want to be doing that for the next two or three years of my life. I did have mixed feelings about the series. Of course, anything was possible. It was a tough challenge. There were going to be constant comparisons.

GENE RODDENBERRY (creator/executive producer, *Star Trek: The Next Generation*)

When Paramount originally approached me to do a new series, I turned them down. I did not want to devote the tremendous amount of time necessary to producing another show. There is only one way I know to write and produce, and that is to throw my energy at the project all the time. So when they began to think about a second series, I said I would not do it.

When I turned them down, Paramount had someone else work on a new *Star Trek* [the father-and-son producing team of Sam and Greg Strangis, who subsequently developed a *War of the Worlds* TV series for the studio]. It had a Vulcan captain and a lot of space cadets who seemed to mainly say, "Gee whiz, Captain."

GREG STRANGIS (executive producer, *War of the Worlds: The TV Series*)

It's not like I was a *Star Trek* atheist, but I was agnostic. My premise was relatively simple: It was a time when, in the future in the existing *Star Trek*, the Klingons weren't enemies anymore and were allies. I wanted to create Starfleet Academy on a ship. You'd have a lot of younger players and older, senior leaders, and it was going to be the naval academy on a starship.

I did some preliminary work and shared it with [Paramount Television executive] Lucie Salhany and whoever else was running syndication then, and it was going along swimmingly . . . until I got a phone call that said, "You're out, Gene's gonna do it." I eventually saw Gene's work, which mostly consisted of drawings, hardly any written words, that didn't really mean much. And that was it. I was done.

GENE RODDENBERRY

I really feared doing it until I got angry enough to try.

RICHARD ARNOLD (*Star Trek* archivist)

The original series' twentieth anniversary was coming up, and the studio seemed to be showing more respect to Gene than they had in a long time. But then he found out that they were going ahead with a new *Star Trek* series without him, which infuriated him. He called for a meeting with the heads of the studio, where he basically threatened to sue them if they proceeded without his approval.

Someone said that he was probably right, that you couldn't get lightning to strike twice in the same place, to which Gene responded, "Damnit, I could!" He walked out of that meeting having agreed to produce a new *Star Trek* series . . . hardly what he had planned going in. He was approaching his sixty-fifth birthday, and he had intended to retire and spend more time with his son, Rod, who was still very young at the time.

DAVID GERROLD (creative consultant, *Star Trek: The Next Generation*)

The studio's reluctance to come to Gene first was understandable. Roddenberry would go out to various speaking engagements and say, "It's difficult. How do you convince the studio executives that what you're talking about is changing the world?" and he'd do it very slyly. Studio executives are maligned by everyone who works for them. If a studio makes fifteen hit pictures a year, who gets the credit? The directors, the actors, the executive producers of the picture, but the studio executive who said, "I'll buy this picture, I'll finance it"—he's just lucky enough to be sitting there when they brought the project to him. They can tell the difference between a good story and a bad story. They get excited when they work with exciting people. You don't get to be the head of a studio by accident.

GREG STRANGIS

I wanted to create a universe where there was a parallel to the world we were living in at the time. It was jihad in space. You wouldn't call them jihadist by name, but that was what they were. Even before people knew what a jihadist was. That was going to be the ongoing adventure. That was the great story arc. Good guys and bad guys in an eternal battle. I knew Gene had seen it. I suspect other people internally had seen it as well.

There was a parallel story that only comes together at the final moment when Gene ended up closing a deal with Paramount, and I could have been the leverage they used to get Gene to cooperate. You have to understand those executives at Paramount; they're devious and like ex-CIA when it comes to working false flags, fake left, go right. They were really, really smart. For Gene to accept the idea that someone else was going to take his baby forward—without him being involved—would've been impossible for him, and I'm sure [his attorney] Leonard [Maizlish] was all over them like a cheap suit.

RICK BERMAN (executive producer, *Star Trek: The Next Generation*)

There were many ideas that were discussed, including making it a prequel to the original *Star Trek* and thoughts of it being set on a starship that was run by cadets in Starfleet Academy. Some suggestions were made by the studio, some by others. Gene's idea was to create an entirely new cast of characters and set it eighty years further into the future, to continue the premise and philosophy of *Star Trek,* but to do it with a new *Enterprise* and a new generation of characters.

RICHARD ARNOLD

On the one hand, Gene was very empowered by what had just come down, but on the other hand, he was, I think, a little scared. He was finally going to get the chance to prove that he wasn't a one-trick pony, but he knew it was going to be an incredible amount of work, as had been the original series, which had caused near-mental breakdowns for many of the people working on it. Gene immediately began bringing in the people he knew he could count on, and we all got to work putting together the new series.

GENE RODDENBERRY

Put yourself in my place. You think you did it all, that you're really basically responsible for the first *Star Trek*, but so many years have gone by and success has many fathers. For twenty-two years there had been a collection of people who have said, "He didn't really do it. It was me or my brother or my friend or this or that person." I found myself thinking, "They could be right." The first sign of insanity is that everybody is out of step except you. The net result of all of this made me mad, very angry.

Star Trek, I said to myself, may be an ego-bent dream, and the rumormongers may be right, but at least I'm going to have the courage to say "Fuck you" as I go back to it. The more I considered it, the angrier I got. If someone could create Star Trek more easily, why didn't more people do something like it in the twenty-two years since we did the original series?

RALPH WINTER (producer, Star Trek VI: The Undiscovered Country)

When they first started, they came to me and asked if I wanted to run the TV show.

I sat down with Rick [Berman] and [Paramount TV V.P.] John [Pike] and had lunch in the commissary. They said, "Yes, come do this and it will be a lot of fun," and I turned them down because I wanted to do something else. I didn't want to be just a Star Trek person for the rest of my career. So, Rick Berman said, "If you don't do it, I will." So, he left the studio and became the executive producer.

RICK BERMAN

I had a lot of people who told me I was nuts. But I had a feeling it was going to work, and I decided it was worth the risk of leaving a well-paying job at a movie studio to work on a science-fiction sequel syndicated television series.

GREG STRANGIS

I knew Rick Berman because I was trying to sell him stuff. We played golf together. I still have a putter he gave me. He was in charge of Paramount's movies-for-television, but they were closing down that department. It was going nowhere. The industry was changing, there weren't that many special projects being done anymore.

RICK BERMAN

I was "in charge" of overseeing all of the current programming, which included Cheers and Family Ties and Webster and MacGyver and a show called Call to Glory, and it was kind of overwhelming. But you're really not in charge of anything. The job of a current executive is just to try to put out fires and calm people down when they get a little bit crazy. I continued doing that, and then I got promoted to vice president in charge of movies and miniseries, which was an interesting job because Paramount wasn't really that interested in doing movies *or* miniseries.

Word had come down that Gene Roddenberry had finally agreed to do another *Star Trek* series. They had been trying for years to get Roddenberry to do another series, and the general opinion was that Roddenberry was a cranky old bastard and nobody wanted to have anything to do with him. But, finally, he agreed to do one. And most of the brass at Paramount Television were not super-fond of Gene. He was kind of ornery. He was resistant. He was not as pliable as the producers that they liked to work with. Since I was the lowest-ranked vice president in the group it was, like, "Let him do it."

GREG STRANGIS

They basically parked Rick [at *Next Generation*] and said, "This is your going-away gift. We'll give you this. It's never going to be a hit, never going to last. You handle Gene Roddenberry." And damned if he didn't. It was his retirement package. I think Roddenberry probably was more respectful of him, because he *wasn't* a writer. Roddenberry is very threatened by writers. Gene was an insecure, troubled individual.

RICK BERMAN

I went to the first meeting and there was some contention, because the studio wanted a two-hour pilot and Roddenberry only wanted to do a one-hour pilot. During the course of this meeting both Gene and his trusted lawyer and companion, Leonard Maizlish, spent a lot of time sort of glancing around the room. The first meeting had nothing really to do with me. It was everybody: Mel Harris, who was the president of television; and John Pike, and this guy Jeff Hayes.

JEFFREY M. HAYES (senior vice president of creative affairs, Paramount Television)

The *Next Gen* launch had the cachet of a title-intensive series and a great deal of success in syndication based on the old series. Paramount threw a lot of money at it. The general idea of starting up an hour show is they all have their problems in common. On *The Next Generation*, you were dealing with a bigger cast, and Gene

Roddenberry was involved, and it was the first foray into the first-run market with a new hour show, so it had its own unique set of problems.

RICK BERMAN

It's really hard to describe, but at one point in the meeting, somebody said something really stupid. I don't remember who it was. Leonard Maizlish, whom I had never met before in my life, looked over to me, and I sort of raised my eyebrow with a "What an asshole" kind of a look. He just thought that was the coolest thing he'd ever seen. So when the meeting was over, I got a call from Leonard Maizlish saying, "Do you want to have lunch?"

I went and had lunch with him the next day, and we had a very pleasant discussion. He was a very strange little man. So, Leonard and I talked at length about lots of different things, and about an hour after I got back to my office from lunch I got a call from Leonard saying, "Would you have lunch with Gene tomorrow?" I was a little nervous, but I went and had lunch with Gene. We talked about a lot of things, and I explained to him that I was not a *Star Trek* fan. I probably saw one or two of the movies. I did not know that much about *Star Trek*. Gene found that kind of refreshing, because he was surrounded by a group of people, most of whom were all not only incredibly knowledgeable about *Star Trek,* but had worked on the original series twenty years earlier.

I explained to Gene that I had spent most of the late 60s and 70s making documentary films and traveling. We talked a great deal about faraway places. Parts of Africa and the South Pacific and Egypt that he and I had both been to. When I told him that I'd been to Upper Volta, he said, "What's the capital of Upper Volta?" And I happened to know it. I said, "Ouagadougou," and he was very impressed because he'd been there, too. Upper Volta is now called Burkina Faso, by the way.

We had a nice lunch and it ended with me thinking I had a nice relationship with this guy whom I'm going to be dealing with. And then the next day, I get another call from Leonard saying, "Can I come over to your office?" And he came over and he said, "Would you consider leaving your job at Paramount and coming to produce this show along with Gene and some of the others?"

I was totally thrown for a loop. This show already had three strikes against it. One strike was that it was a sequel, which had never really worked on television. Another strike was it was going to be a syndicated dramatic series. The third strike was that it was science fiction and you'd be hard pressed to find any science fiction on television in the mid-80s.

But, I was so tired of being a studio executive and wanting to get back into producing, I went home, talked to my wife, and called Leonard back the next day and said yes. I went to John Pike and asked if I could get out of my contract as a

Paramount executive to come work for them, and Pike said yes instantly. I think one of his reasons was that he felt I was loyal to him, which I was, and he thought it'd be great to have an insider in the organization. It was risky and strange, but I was delighted and I had a great deal to learn.

ROBERT H. JUSTMAN (supervising producer, *Star Trek: The Next Generation*)

When I left *Star Trek* in 1968, it was a disaster. It was a failure as far as the network and the industry were concerned. The only thing that saved *Star Trek* two years in a row were the people who cared about it. By the time the third season rolled around, the handwriting was on the wall and Gene and I both knew that it was. I had a need to return to prove that the show did have value and was successful and could be successful again, and that you can go home again. *And* prove to the people who doubted you that there was value there all along, that this was a worthwhile, if you'll pardon the expression, enterprise.

There were mixed emotions about being involved with the show. I couldn't keep out of the back of my mind the fact that when the first feature, *Star Trek: The Motion Picture,* was made, I was disappointed in Gene because he contacted me about working on it and then played hard to get and I could never reach him. That really hurt a lot, so it was not easy for me. I wanted to come back and do it and I wanted to work with Gene again, because, overall, I was still his friend. But it was still stuck in the back of my mind. I told [producer] Ed Milkis of my disappointment with Gene. Eddie told Gene, because I'd said, "Gene broke my heart." But Gene always found it difficult to take responsibility or to tell people things they didn't want to hear. I don't think that he didn't want me to work on the movie, I think that he found out that Paramount was severely restrictive on what he could do.

RICK BERMAN

I joined the staff of what was going to become *Star Trek: The Next Generation*. There were two fellows who were producers under Gene: Bob Justman, who stayed for the first year, and Eddie Milkis, who had some kind of a disagreement with Roddenberry and had left just about the time that I came aboard.

DAVID GERROLD

There were some memos written the day the show was announced, and there was one floating around the studio that listed fifty story areas . . . one-liners. We suggest you consider stories dealing with these issues: poverty, hunger, terrorism, child abuse—and it was like somebody had gone through the newspaper. So very early on, Rick Berman handed me a copy of the memo and said, "I wrote this memo, what do you think about it?" I read it carefully and I said, "I think this is exactly what *Star Trek* has to be for it to be the kind of show that this studio can be proud of." He said, "I'm glad to hear you say that." I said, "This memo makes me feel good about this show, because it says the studio will support us in doing some dangerous stories."

RICK BERMAN

The person who I was sort of married to from the moment I started on the show was Bob Justman, who taught me a great deal. I watched all three of the *Star Trek* movies released at that time, and I watched as many episodes of the original series as I could take in one shot. Maybe twenty of them. And then the process began. Did I know it was going to turn into a nineteen-year gig and that I was going to do 624 hours of television? Definitely not.

GREG STRANGIS

The consolation prize for me was *War of the Worlds*. Paramount owned the underlying rights. That was something I was really excited about. I read the book, saw the movie, heard the radio broadcast, and knew quite a bit about it. It was intriguing, and it was an opportunity with no expectation to come up with some ideas. I guess they thought of it as a companion piece to *Star Trek*.

The studio, of course, was more than happy to fill the vacuum of network notes. It's like anything else, anytime there is a power removed, that giant sucking sound is someone filling in the space. You have no idea about the fights on *War of the Worlds*. It was always, "Make this series for people that drink beer." That was it. No wine. I didn't last the full first season. There was a script that we were about to go into production on that the people that drink beer won't understand, and this conversation turned into a screaming match. Only one person was screaming. It was a studio executive. I told her as I was walking out of the office that if they want to scream at someone, they can scream at my attorney.

Mel Harris, the president of Paramount Domestic Television, announced at the time, "Twenty years ago, the genius of one man brought to television a show that has transcended the medium. We are enormously pleased that that man, Gene Roddenberry, is going to do it again. Just as public demand kept the original series on the air, this new series is also a result of a grass-roots support for Gene and his vision."

RICK BERMAN

Gene was cranky if he felt anybody was pressuring him. He had become a bit of an icon. He was already close to seventy years old, and he didn't want to take crap from anybody. I had an absolutely delightful relationship with him, but I know people who didn't. He had very, very strong ideas on what he wanted the show to be, and he wasn't going to let anybody mess with that.

GENE RODDENBERRY

I had an interesting reaction at first from fandom. People were writing me and saying, "If you get rid of Kirk and Spock, you've gotten rid of me, too." We got literally tens of thousands of letters like that.

ROBERT H. JUSTMAN

Some people were afraid of the new *Star Trek*, because the old people wouldn't be in it. It was a threat to them. But I don't think that lasted very long. You form new relationships all through life, sometimes the old relationships are the best, sometimes not. But there's room in the world for diversity. People resist change for various reasons, it's just a natural reaction to put a show, or an enterprise, down out of hand, but it's not very science-fictiony. The great thing about people interested in science fiction is that they have open minds. They're eager for new ideas. Otherwise, why do anything different? Let's do *Space Patrol*. It was on and people liked it.

Among those who most vociferously objected was *Star Trek*'s original cast. In 1986, DeForest Kelley offered, "It's a mystery to me why they're doing it. I assume Paramount thinks they can hold on to the *Star Trek* phenomena. There's no doubt we can't go on forever, so they're trying a way to keep it going. But there's only one *Star Trek* and that's ours." James Doohan, never one to mince words, said, "I just regret that they are calling it *Star Trek*, when we know what it is, which is the characters. They are trying to fool the public, and that's bad business."

Not surprisingly, William Shatner also criticized the sequel. "I don't feel good about the new series. I think without the cast as we know it and not in the time we know it, it's hard to understand why they are calling it *Star Trek*. In addition, there's a risk of overexposure."

TRACY TORMÉ (writer, *Star Trek: The Next Generation*)

To some people, The Beatles are just Paul McCartney's band before Wings.

GLEN C. OLIVER (film & TV critic, *Ain't It Cool News*)

I vividly recall both the anticipation and discord leading up to the premiere of *The Next Generation*. Many folks were shouting loudly that such an undertaking should never be attempted. That it would fail. That the same heart and energy generated by *The Original Series* could never be replicated. They seemed to feel *TNG* was a dead end, and had determined as much before the show even hit the air.

I never agreed with this concern. Such criticism felt like reckless and unfair prejudgment. This type of consternation suggested to me that the people making so much noise about *TNG* had never really watched *Star Trek*. Or, if they had, they'd never really understood it. By my measure, *Star Trek* had already proven time and time again that its format supported any number of approaches and tones; action, drama, high adventure, shoot-em-up, comedy. The gamut. To write off a show categorically before understanding what stories it was trying to tell, before understanding how it wanted to tell them, seemed, well, somewhat "Herbert."

With producers Robert Justman and Eddie Milkis already on board, Roddenberry was quick to recruit other original series stalwarts, including "The Trouble with Tribbles" scribe and novelist David Gerrold, and former *Star Trek* story editor and animated series producer D.C. Fontana, who in the intervening decade had been a successful writer for numerous series, ranging from *The Six Million Dollar Man* to *The Streets of San Francisco* to *Buck Rogers in the 25th Century*. Fontana was also active in the Writers Guild of America.

DAVID GERROLD

It was a Friday, October 10, 1986. I heard the announcement about the show and confirmed it with Gene's assistant, Susan Sackett. Then I dropped a note in the mail that said, "Congratulations, this is great news. . . ." The kind of thing that said you worked hard and deserve the best. Gene and I had been friends for twenty years despite the fact that we had never really specifically worked together on anything.

I also called Dorothy Fontana right away and said, "It's just been announced," and she and I joked, "Okay, when Gene calls me, I'll tell him he has to hire you, and when he calls you, you tell him he has to hire me." As it happened, that's exactly what took place.

DOROTHY FONTANA (associate producer, *Star Trek: The Next Generation*)

I was very excited about the news. I thought it was a wonderful opportunity to do something new. Leonard Nimoy said that it was difficult to catch lightning in a bottle twice, which is true, but the potential of moving it ahead in time with totally new characters gave it a new venue. A new playground. I thought all of those *possibilities* were exciting at the time.

Early in October of 1986 I was informed in a telephone call from Gene Roddenberry that Paramount was prepared to go ahead with a new *Star Trek* television series. Roddenberry invited me to dinner with him and his wife, Majel Barrett. During the dinner, we spoke generally about possibilities for the new show—primarily things Roddenberry wanted to avoid and a few things he definitely wanted to accomplish the second time around.

DAVID GERROLD

Gene and I went out to lunch. We sat, talked, and he said, "What would you do with *Star Trek*?" He did *not* say, "I want to hire you." I nonetheless outlined my ideas for *Star Trek*, which were to shift the show to a first officer and let the captain stay on the ship. This allows you to simultaneously run shipboard stories and planetside stories. Before, the focus of the stories always stayed where Kirk was.

If you break it up and have a captain who's always on the ship, then you can stay with him if there are reasons to cut back to the ship, and yet you don't have him putting himself in danger on the planet. If your first officer is strong, then you have a focus there. So you have two heroes instead of one hero and a sidekick. I pitched it pretty hard; it's an idea I've had since way back in the early seventies. He thought that was a good idea.

ROBERT H. JUSTMAN

There is one element which I always felt was lacking in our original series. Although our ship was engaged in a "five-year mission," there were only crew members aboard. For the new series, we postulated travel through space could last for an even longer period of time. To expect people to leave everyone and everything they hold most dear for such a long journey is, I think, unconscionable. Why should our *Enterprise* crew be denied the opportunity to live a full and rewarding life? Therefore, I proposed that we have men, women, *and* children on board throughout the whole new series.

GENE RODDENBERRY

We always figured there would be some families aboard [the *Enterprise*]. And the reason is, these Galaxy Class ships go out for a longer time. And if you want people to join Starfleet, you want to take families, to have a healthy family life. It's a better show because we deal with that.

ROBERT H. JUSTMAN

There would be births, death, marriages, divorces, etc. Crew members would go "home" to the various living quarters aboard at the end of their duty with their homework or, if unattached, pursue the opposite sex. What we would have then is, indeed, "*Wagon Train* to the Stars." The pioneers didn't leave their families or their desires behind when they migrated westward, so why should we deny our people the same human rights? Most of the time we would not make a big deal out of the presence of children on board—we'd just see them in various areas of the ship, in passing.

DAVID GERROLD

During our first meeting, Gene said, "Here's what I want you to do. Next week we're going to start screening science fiction pictures to get a sense of what's been done in the genre over the past ten years. You, Ed Milkis, Bob Justman, and I and Dorothy Fontana, if she's available, will sit down and watch films and get a sense of living in the future rather than living in the twentieth century." Just really to charge our batteries.

I have to say that these were some of the most fun times, because we'd come in at ten A.M., and we saw *Blade Runner, Aliens, Brazil* . . . one day we even looked at *Ice Pirates,* because we wanted to see what could be done on a low budget. If you forget the story, it's an impressive picture. If you look at the story, it's a good argument for the death penalty. In fact, it was Gene's joke. He said, "This is the picture that is singularly responsible for bringing back the death penalty to California."

In the second week, we saw all four *Star Trek* films over four consecutive days, which I have to tell you is an exhausting process. Sitting through *Star Trek: The Motion Picture* . . . I don't think Bob Justman ever saw the film, and I don't know if Eddie had ever seen it. These guys kind of looked at each other and said, "God, that was awful."

SUSAN SACKETT (assistant to Gene Roddenberry)

I remember before it went on the air, we were having a great time. We were sitting around in a private room in the commissary and they would bring in food. Gene was somewhat sexist in those days. Everybody kind of was. If I had something I wanted to contribute, I would have to take him aside, since I was the lowly assistant and I wasn't an executive or head writer. He brought in all the writers that he liked: David Gerrold and Dorothy Fontana and Rick Berman, who was a studio man at the time. It was just a lot of fun.

DAVID GERROLD

Eddie Milkis called up the head of the motion picture division to say, "Okay, we want a screening of *Star Trek IV* for Gene Roddenberry," and they said, "I'm sorry, but you're the television division and you're not entitled to a screening." Eddie Milkis said, "Look, this is for Gene Roddenberry, the man who created the whole *Star Trek* series. We want to see what the new picture is," because this was a couple of weeks before it was released. They said, "We're sorry, but you're television and we're movies, and movies don't do nothin' for television." Eddie Milkis has been on the Paramount lot for twenty years, so he got on the phone to somebody topside and said, "We'd like a screening of *Star Trek IV*," and they scheduled it for exactly the time we wanted it.

TRACY TORMÉ

Gene and I had many golf cart rides across the Paramount lot. We would go from one end of the studio to the other, taking these long meandering drives. He would wave at people he knew, saying hi to the security guards, and he used these times to talk to me about a number of things: personal things, professional things, great stories about the old *Trek*, stories about Shatner, stories about Majel, stories about his ex-wife, his divorce, his relationships with women.

He told me he thought I would be running my own show one day and things I needed to know about how to work with the network executives; how sometimes they will give you the stupidest notes in the world and you would have to choose when to nod your head and say, "That's kind of interesting"—and then hope that it never comes up again.

DAVID GERROLD

At the time, we were the fair-haired boys at the studio. Every day after we'd seen a screening, we'd all troop over to the executive dining room, which is a big boardroom where you get personal service of the highest caliber, and you have to call to reserve it. Well, Gene had it every day for three weeks straight, and we'd come marching in and you'd hear the conversation stop. As we walked through into the executive dining room, you could hear people say, "There goes thirty million dollars on hooch."

We'd sit down and talk about the movie we'd just seen and spark ideas. Like after *Aliens*, Gene would say about Jenette Goldstein, "That woman created a whole new style of feminine beauty. We should have something like that in *Star Trek*." So we started off with a character named Macha Hernandez, who eventually became Tasha Yar. That sparked an idea for Gene.

ROBERT H. JUSTMAN

I, too, was taken with the girl who played the Latina in the landing party in *Aliens*. If we could get her, she could be a member of the *Enterprise*'s onboard Marine or MP contingent. This would enable her to serve in a military capacity within our landing parties. Her feistiness, coupled with her earthy physicality, could create interesting opportunities for drama.

DOROTHY FONTANA

David Gerrold had been brought aboard the show and was serving as a consultant. Early talks about the direction of the new series were taking place. I was told at the same time there was no place for me as yet, but I began to receive copies of memos sent to Gene Roddenberry from Robert Justman and from David Gerrold. I was invited to comment on all memo suggestions—which I did as of early November [1986].

DAVID GERROLD

In a period of about eight weeks, Bob Justman and I wrote about five hundred memos. Bob's memos were mostly "how to's" and mine were "what to's." We did memos on the look of the ship, technology of the ship, warp speed, star dates, casting, show format, stories we should buy, actors we should cast . . . everything about what the show should be.

ROBERT H. JUSTMAN

I thought we could establish a new series "regular"—an android programmed by Starfleet Command with all of the familiar abilities and characteristics of Spock fused with the leadership and humanistic qualities of Captain Kirk. A new character like this would give us any number of dramatic or humorous avenues. There are several ways to go when casting an actor to play such a part. I was impressed with the actor who portrayed the android in *Aliens* [Lance Henriksen].

SUSAN SACKETT

Gene was always fascinated by artificial intelligence. Data was sort of like the Spock character who could be logical and see things in a different way. The difference is this one wants to be human, unlike Spock, who did not want to be human. I don't think he was consciously thinking of *The Questor Tapes*.

ROBERT H. JUSTMAN

[I also thought] there should be a "special" area on board the *Enterprise* where a crew member can go to be psychically connected with his, her, or its home planet in an emotionally evocative connotation. People have a deep need to "go home again" and it would be marvelous if our future technology could afford them this opportunity. Although in the original *Soylent Green* movie, Edward G. Robinson experienced Earth as beautiful as it used to be while he lay dying, we would not confine ourselves to such a situation but would, instead, explore all the dramatic possibilities inherent therein.

DAVID GERROLD

At the time, Gene kept telling me how thrilled he was with all the work I was doing. The studio execs were receiving copies of the memos and they would stop me on the lot and tell me how thrilled *they* were with the work I was doing. They were *so* enthusiastic and so delighted, and *I* was thrilled, because at that point I was in an interesting mental state. I made up my mind that this was the most incredible opportunity in the history of television, and my job was not about making David Gerrold look wonderful or about being right; my job was totally to see that *Star Trek* turned out to be the best that we could make it. And it was not about me having a good office or a great parking space, or a lot of money, or any of that stuff. Everything I did, I would ask myself the question, "Is this good for *Star Trek*?"

We started looking for offices on the lot. For the first few weeks, I moved into Gene's office. I brought a computer from home, put it in [*Star Trek* archivist] Richard Arnold's office. It was a three-office complex, and I would work in there. So I was on the lot every day, writing and typing like crazy, then I'd go home and write and type like crazy, then I'd print the stuff out, and I'd bring in another pound of memos every day. Finally, Gene said to me, "I'm putting you on staff."

Actually, for the first week, I didn't know if I was going to get a job or not. The first week was all research. I was just saying, "I'm here as a friend to advise you, and when you want to put me on staff, I'm available." Gene finally said on the Thursday or Friday of the first week of screenings, "David, I want to put you on staff and your title will be creative consultant." I said, "Great." I figured that was worth about three grand a week. The following Tuesday, Gene said to me, "I want you to keep doing everything that you've been doing."

DEBORAH ARAKELIAN (writer; assistant to Harve Bennett)

Gene certainly created it. He did something that everybody wanted to do and didn't do. He created something in the time that was uniquely unlike anything else. I think that creates a natural animosity. The people that end up working on it, who in fact sometimes did make it better, probably felt they weren't getting their due credit. And Gene's probably thinking you wouldn't have anything to work on if I hadn't made it in the first place. It's writers being territorial.

After *Star Trek III*, I sold my first script within six weeks of having left the lot. And then it was nominated for an Emmy and a Writers Guild Award. That *Cagney & Lacey* was the second script I'd ever written in my life. So, when I came back to the lot as a guest of Susan Sackett, who had invited me back to see the set of *Next Generation*, she was giving me a tour when we saw Gene giving an interview to *Newsweek*. He stops the interview and motions for me to come in and says, "I want to introduce somebody to you. This is a writer that you're going to hear from again. She's going to do great things."

And I was like, Gene, first of all, no pressure. But, second, this is a side of Gene that every other person that I've ever known that has dealt with Gene has never seen. He was kind and generous to me from the first day he met me to the last time I saw him. I don't know of anybody else that can say the same thing, and I'm proud to say it, because I do consider him a friend.

DAVID GERROLD

My idea was that if I saw a problem that I could fix, I would fix it before it was a problem so that I was continually bringing solutions to the show. At the same time, I was being very careful not to step on anyone's toes. I would always communicate with Bob Justman, Eddie Milkis, and Gene: "What do you think about this? Should I do that?" I never did anything I wasn't supposed to. Anyway, Gene calls me into his office and says, "Leonard Maizlish [his lawyer] advises me that I shouldn't give you the title creative consultant, because it gets into all kinds of Writers Guild stuff. David, I'm not backing off on anything, but at this point we don't have the budget and we don't . . ." I said, "Gene, my main concern is *Star Trek*, the quality of the show. It's not a big thing to me whether I'm creative consultant or whatever, as long as I'm not washroom consultant." He said, "Fine. We're old friends."

This started to become a theme: "We're old friends, and I knew I could count on you." I thought, "Well, we'll see." They finally offered me the deal another week later. I did not get a paycheck or anything or a deal negotiated for three weeks. They finally called my agent and offered $750 a week for eight weeks. Which is a *terrible* deal. I went to him and said, "Gene, this is like hiring a writer for below Guild wages, and you and I both know that this is inappropriate." He said, "Let me talk to the studio . . . That's what the studio offered." And the studio said to my agent that that was what *Gene* had authorized.

At that time, I did not know that Leonard Maizlish was running the negotiations angle for Gene. That was coming from Leonard, and that's all he was willing to authorize. They upped the offer to $1,000 a week for ten weeks. Gene said, "Come January first, when this deal expires, we'll get you a proper contract on staff and you'll be working here a long time. It's going to work out fine, David." And I thought, "Well, I honestly don't know what's going on. Maybe the studio is not going to release big amounts of development money until they see what he is developing." So I took the deal against my better judgment, because I thought I could contribute to *Star Trek,* we could still have the very best *Star Trek,* and I'll just use this as an opportunity to prove that I'm worth more.

ROD RODDENBERRY (son of Gene Roddenberry)

Leonard Maizlish was sort of an uncle to me. He did come over to the house often, and he would always bring me gifts. He brought me very nice, expensive gifts, a refrigerator, TV, a leather trench coat once when I was older. I mean, pretty high-end stuff that twelve- or thirteen-year-olds don't really get. But, he was always nice to me. I was just not in that world. I didn't know what happened. It was actually a shock to me years later when I heard so many bad things about him—and I don't buy into those things necessarily. Everyone just points at him, and they always praise my father. I do, too. I'm just saying that he wasn't a perfect guy, but I'm not a perfect guy. I think he really loved my father. They had a very, very close relationship.

DAVID GERROLD

We blocked out three or four of the characters, and Gene said, "Okay, go home and do a character profile on each of those. Give me two pages on each." Then the next day we sat down and talked about two more characters, and he said, "Give me profiles of those," and I did that. I would bring the pages in to him, he would sit down and type up new character profiles. I did a rough-draft bible for him, then he sat down and did the bible that came out. I think it's dated November sixteenth. That came out of Gene's computer, but a lot of it was rough-drafted in my computer and Gene sat down and rewrote it. You can see that the relationship between what I did and what he did was very, very close.

DOROTHY FONTANA

When I read the early draft of the bible, I felt a lack in the characters as proposed, primarily because I didn't see any references to friendships, relationships. Each character proposed seemed to have limited communication with others, and each seemed to have a lot that will go on inside his/her head or in private. The captain keeps his emotions private, goes to his cabin and communes with books. Con talks to the captain, but only to differ with him. She deals with *her* emotions in private. Ops talks to the ship. Number One has disagreements with the other senior officers and heads the contact teams. Who does he talk to, besides the "few women who know him well enough to call him by his real name"?

The references to Data's [the android who wants to become human] relationship seem sexual only. Macha [later Tasha] deals with her feelings privately and expresses temper or displeasure aloud in dealing with stupidity or intolerance. Who does *she* talk to? Geordi is the only one who seems to have the capability of forming relationships.

The backbone of *Star Trek* has always been relationships and human stories. Gene didn't want the buddy system that evolved before, but people do form friendships and trusts, loves and hates, in their working and personal lives. Both are contained side by side on this ship, and they must be seen in the characters. A base is there for the Captain and Con. If they don't have a relationship—one in which all elements know, trust, and depend on one another—that "team" is not a team. It is in trouble.

DAVID GERROLD

In November we had developed a bible, so we were able to talk about the show in a little more depth. We hadn't quite developed all of our characters. That was the first week in November, so we were still talking about who our characters were and what the approach would be.

GENE RODDENBERRY

[I wanted] armaments and militarism to be deemphasized over previous *Star Trek* series and very much deemphasized over the *Star Trek* movies. We go back to the flavor of the previous series' first year when emphasis was on "strange new worlds" rather than on space villains and space battles.

DAVID GERROLD

I was using a program called Think Tank and had been making notes in it for a couple of weeks about the bible. I titled it the "Not Yet Official *Star Trek* Bible," and he [Roddenberry] had said, "I want to see all your notes on what we should do." So I did a real quick printout and gave it to him. He read it and lavished praise on me about how thrilled he was with its development, how I had organized this and clarified who our characters could be, what our technology would be, what stories we could tell, what stories we would avoid. He was very pleased and said, "This pushes us very far forward."

It was my goal that we should have a bible in place and scripts in development by December so that we could be very ahead of the game with scripts by the next year. By now, what had happened was, we were getting calls from agents and writers who wanted to pitch. Gene said we would handpick the first six writers, which is what I told the agents and writers.

DOROTHY FONTANA

There were a lot of egos involved, and they weren't our egos. We just wanted to do a good job, and we were not allowed to do a good job due to other people's egos. That's what *really* came into play on that show. I feel that was to its detriment. The first time around, everyone was simply trying to do a good job—just "Let's tell the best stories that we possibly can"—and there wasn't a lot of ego involved that I could perceive. People were just pitching in as a team. There wasn't a team feeling on *The Next Generation* at the time.

DAVID GERROLD

I finished the bible and asked [illustrator] Andy Probert to give us a sense of the size of the new *Enterprise*. He overlaid a map of the studio with the size of the *Enterprise*. And the new *Enterprise* is bigger than Paramount's lot. It's a great gag and we loved it. So we decide we're going to use it as [the bible's] cover, which is a great bible for a TV show. I show it to Bob Justman, he takes it out of my hands and walks into Gene's office, comes back and says, "You can't have that cover. I'll have Andy Probert design you a new cover." Apparently Bob thought the cover would offend the studio executives instead of saying, "Good job, David, you busted your ass."

Then Andy Probert designed a back cover which, on one side, shows the Paramount mountain, and the other side is the Starfleet logo, with a series of in-betweens as the insignia mutates. It's wonderful. That got pulled because somebody was afraid that it would offend the studio.

ANDREW PROBERT (production illustrator, *Star Trek: The Next Generation*)

Robert Justman said, "Let's put the Paramount logo on the back page of the bible." And I said, "I'm working on a bit of a surprise that I think you'll get a real kick out of." Justman, despite his deficiencies, does have a pretty decent sense of humor. So I thought he would appreciate it, but as soon as he saw it, he said, "You could lose your job for this." Hey, guys, what's the big deal?

SUSAN SACKETT

Everyone started out quite optimistic. David Gerrold kept saying "I can't believe I'm getting paid to do this, it's so much fun." Gene had him work on the bible and Gene took credit for it. He was not adverse to taking credit for other people's work on occasion, because he felt he gave them the ideas. On the bible, David did all the work and Gene got all the credit.

DAVID GERROLD

Two days after I finished the bible, while I'm still waiting for someone to say thank you, I get a copy of the new Lincoln Enterprises [Gene and Majel Roddenberry's *Star Trek* merchandise mail-order house] catalog, and they are taking orders for the bible. They're selling it. *Two days!* I'm working on the bible for six weeks, not because we needed a bible for the show, but because Majel had been bugging him for something to sell through Lincoln Enterprises. Gene realized this little twenty-page one we had was not a good enough collector's item, so we need a fifty-page one. Why not just say, "David, I want you to write something for Lincoln Enterprises, and I'll pay you." Instead, he plays this head game.

DOUG DREXLER (special makeup effects artist, *Star Trek: The Next Generation*)

When I first went out, there were no sets and they were still writing the first episode. Bob Justman kept me with him all day long. I remember meeting Eddie Milkis, and they were talking about doing some alien, and Milkis is saying, "You know, Bob, remember that thing we did on *The Outer Limits* with Cliff Robertson." And I was, like, "Wait, wait, let me explain it!" They were so amazed that I knew exactly what they did. And then while I was talking to Eddie and Bob, Roddenberry bursts into the room and says, "I've got it! The captain stops the ship, turns around, and surrenders." And Gene turns and looks at me and he sees a blank look on my face, and Bob says, "Gene, you don't realize what you just did to this guy."

He then took me in his office and opened it up and there was a small model of the *Enterprise-D*. It was pretty rough, the windows were drawn on with pencil and stuff. It was something that was made to show him basically what it would look like. He took it out of the box and goes, "I'm only showing this to you because you're a professional. You *are* a professional, right?" I'll never forget how proud he was of it. The first thing he said, "There's not a straight line on it." Which in producer-speak means it's really expensive.

ANDREW PROBERT

The *Enterprise* is a character, and you can't change a character drastically. Knowing there was a horrendous amount of apprehension about the new show, I wanted to maintain as many of the characteristics about the old ship as possible, and yet update it. The one thing that I was really adamant about doing, that the producers accepted, was to lower the engines so they're closer to the center. It always bothered me that the engines were above. So I lowered the engines, and enlarged the saucer considerably, because, in my opinion, being a primary hull, it should be the primary shape supported by engineering, which is considerably smaller. Then I flattened it out, giving everything basically an oval cross-section, and when it came time to do the down view, I gave the saucer an oval as well, so the ship was now basically a series of ovals. Which is my way of attempting to unify, make more cohesive the design.

David Gerrold was a big help in sort of pushing the design of the *Enterprise* that I was aiming toward. I felt it was too early; we were still heavily into designing the bridge and I didn't want to bring up a new subject and have them, out of haste, or not wanting to devote energy to the *Enterprise* design at that moment, just shoot it down without having the time or ability to devote the thought to it. But David got a Xerox of one of my drawings and, apparently, the producers liked it right away, so that was a nice bit of timing on his part.

DAVID GERROLD

At the end of November, the beginning of December, 1986, something weird started happening. Leonard Maizlish started coming into the office . . . a lot. I don't mind seeing him in there once a week or so, because I figured he needed to advise Gene, but all of a sudden he's in there *every* day, and he has one- or two-hour discussions with Gene behind closed doors.

Up to this point, Gene's door was always open. I could knock on the door, stick my head in, and say, "I have a question for you . . ." I did not create anything on the show without going to Gene and talking it over with him. I always made a big point of establishing that Gene is the great bird of the galaxy, because I was terrified that someone would accuse me of being ambitious at Gene Roddenberry's expense. I bent over backward to show that all I wanted to do at that point was work in Gene's field.

DOROTHY FONTANA

On January eighth, I turned in the first-draft outline for the pilot, "Encounter at Farpoint." On January nineteenth, I turned in the revised outline for the script. On January twenty-first, I was given the go-ahead by the studio to go into first-draft script. Also, during this time, the length of the premiere episode began to come into question. It had been decided between Roddenberry and Justman that the outline I had was enough for ninety minutes and that I should develop that material.

As I began writing the script, and throughout the writing of the first draft, the length of the script kept bobbing up and down from two hours to an hour and a half to one hour and back up again. I was told that this was due to the fact that the decision had not been made as to whether the premiere would have a "history of *Star Trek*" section, a behind-the-scenes section, or an extended preview section in addition to the dramatic story. Or whether it would be all story.

Every few days I was approached by Leonard Maizlish, who had begun to come to the studio daily, as to whether I thought the script could be an hour and a half, an hour, or back up to two hours. I was finally told by both Roddenberry and Maizlish to simply concentrate on my ninety minutes.

DAVID GERROLD

While they're changing their mind, Dorothy is trying to develop the outline. How do you develop an outline when you don't know if you're writing one hour, two hours, or ninety minutes? So Gene gave her instructions to write a ninety-minute outline. Now her contract specified that she would get a bonus if she did a two-hour pilot. So what happens is that she does the ninety minutes, which does *not* entitle her to the bonus, and they finally decided to do a two-hour episode. Gene said, "Don't worry about expanding your story. I'll put a frame on it, Dorothy."

DOROTHY FONTANA

Although I was ready and willing to expand my story to encompass the additional half hour, I was told that Roddenberry would write what came to be called "the prequel."

DAVID GERROLD

Dorothy writes this story of "Encounter at Farpoint," and Gene writes this framework of Q around it. We're all looking at each other, saying, "It's Trelane [from the original series] all over again." We all hated it, and very gently suggested to Gene that it wasn't very good. Of course, this fell on deaf ears. He said, "Trust me, the way I'll do it, the fans will love it."

DOROTHY FONTANA

During this time Roddenberry told me I would be on staff, but that he was having a very difficult time selling anyone on the idea of having me as associate producer. My agent was not contacted at all on the subject of my joining the staff.

DAVID GERROLD

When Gene said he would put the frame on it, Dorothy said, "There goes my bonus." Gene said, "Don't worry, we'll take care of you." As we're walking out of the meeting, Dorothy says, "I forgot. Working for Gene Roddenberry always costs me money. I remember something that I had been blocking out of my mind . . ." Way back on the animated *Star Trek*, Dorothy had been paid "X" amount of money for the show. Gene came to her and said, "Will you take a cut in salary and the title Associate Producer?" In other words, "We'll give you a higher title, but will you take a cut in salary, because we have to keep the show on budget?" She said yes, and later on she found out that her cut in salary coincided with Gene's raise in pay.

She was pissed as hell about that back in '73 or '74. It suddenly hit me what she was talking about, that working for Gene cost her money. So I'm thinking, "Well, producers are always looking out for number one. I'm going to keep my mouth shut. Maybe Dorothy's being a malcontent here." I even thought that way back when Harlan Ellison and Gene Roddenberry were going at it. "What does Harlan Ellison know about TV?" In 1968, that's the way I felt, because Gene had been right because he was the boss. It did not occur to me that we were going to get a replay in history.

I truly believed Gene's publicity at that time. In fact, I had been guilty for having spread some of that publicity, because I wanted it to be really true. It was like I believed if I said it enough, it would come true. I hate to admit stupidity on my part, but I am this personal optimist that things are going to get better. I could be standing there at ground zero in a nuclear war saying, "What an opportunity for slum redevelopment."

DOROTHY FONTANA

When I was on the animated series, I had the salary cut request. Gene had to have his salary, so I had to take a cut in salary. On *Star Trek: The Next Generation*, when salary "offers" for my staff services were tendered to my agent by Paramount, the first one was for $1,700 a week, which both shocked and astonished us. It was, in fact, below the WGA minimum for fourteen weeks employment for a staff writer.

When I refused it, the second offer came in—approximately $2500 per week—under the fourteen-week minimum figure WGA requires for a writer with additional capacities. I also refused this offer through my agent. Leonard Maizlish came to my office and wanted to know why I didn't accept these excellent offers. I informed him that I *could not* accept any offer that was below Writers Guild minimum, nor could Paramount legally offer one; and if such an offer was put forth again, I would have to inform the Guild. The next offer was for $3,000 a week, and Paramount informed my agent they refused to pay anything higher. We decided to accept the offer on a fourteen-week contract. It was insane. Gene had to have his salary, so I had to take a cut in mine.

DAVID GERROLD

Suddenly we're into negotiations for the renewal of my contract. My agent calls me and says, "Here's what they're offering: staff writer, minimum wage, twenty weeks." I said, "What happened to executive story editor? You go back and tell them that I was promised the position of executive story editor." He goes back and tells me that this came from Roddenberry. Actually, I found out later that it came from Maizlish, who said that was all they were going to offer. But I figured I would put my best face on, because I made a promise to myself that the most important thing we were doing in this office was *Star Trek*. So my agent tries to negotiate and there's no negotiating room. Take it or leave it. The only thing that they'll guarantee is that if I do a script, I get paid extra for the script.

SUSAN SACKETT

Dorothy Fontana was in some kind of position with the Writer's Guild, but her stuff was being rewritten and she didn't like that, and Gene was very concerned that it start out right. You hire people, but he wanted it to be his way, and they didn't care for that. There was animosity because of that and there was animosity because Gene's attorney, who had no Guild membership and no writing credentials, was doing it. Gene was happy to have input from Leonard Maizlish, and all the other writers resented Maizlish. And you can't blame them, because he was not a particularly warm and fuzzy person. He was a very strange man.

DAVID GERROLD

We start talking to writers and the first writer we talk to is Nelson Gidding, and he comes in with a presentation. He had worked with Robert Wise on *The Hindenburg*. What we get is this slightly befuddled old man who starts talking to us about pricklys and gooeys, that some people in the world are prickly and some are gooey, and he wants to do a water planet where the people make love by getting in a hot tub together. The man has been living in California too long.

Then he goes on to pitch for an hour and it's making no sense at all. I looked at Eddie Milkis to see his reaction, and he is absolutely blank-faced. I look at Bob [Justman] and *he's* absolutely blank-faced. I go back to making notes dizzily. Later on, Eddie said to me, "Don't ever do that again. You gave me such a look that I nearly burst out laughing." I thought we should get on the horn with his agent, thank him profusely, and pass, but we didn't have the authority *not* to buy it. Gene had to hear the pitch.

I said, "You cannot call the writer back to pitch this story a second time just so Gene can have the pleasure of rejecting the story. It's not fair to the writer." They said, "No, Gene should have been at this meeting and he has to reject it." So they brought him back in and he pitched it again, and he's real enthusiastic. A second meeting is a clear signal in Hollywood that "we're interested in buying your story." Instead they thank him, call his agent, and say, "We're not going to buy it," and we never hear from him again. But we've wasted a lot of our time already.

DOUG DREXLER

Bob [Justman] took me with him to a meeting with ILM where they showed that first shot from the title sequence, where the *Enterprise* comes under the camera and you see somebody walking through the observation lounge and then it snaps to warp. I love the rubber-band snap. I never liked what they did in the movies with the flashy red, white, and blue. I hated that. I thought the rubber-band thing was very clever. But when we came out, I said, "Bob, was it my imagination or was somebody walking through [in the windows]?" And he just, like, lit up into a big grin, because that was his idea. He wanted that and he pushed for it. It really makes such a visceral connection to how big the ship is, that there are people inside of it.

DAVID GERROLD

I'm suddenly hearing that Eddie Milkis is going to be leaving the show and someone was going to take over for him. Now Rick Berman was a studio vice president at the time, and I thought that was not a bad idea, because having a studio man around is okay because you know he's going to be reporting to his supervisors at the studio. If the guy's a Trekkie and he loves *Star Trek,* then we'll have a lot of studio support. That's just my feeling. Later I learned that Eddie was leaving, because he knew something weird was going on. Apparently the writing was on the wall very early.

DAVID LIVINGSTON (supervising producer,
Star Trek: The Next Generation)

I was the production manager for the pilot in February of 1987. I was in a trailer by myself. The rest of the guys were in the writers' building, but they didn't have any space for the production. I was the only one in it for a couple of weeks while they were gearing up. They already started building the sets and they were doing some preproduction planning. They needed someone to come in and finalize the pilot as well as hire the crew.

Shooting the pilot wasn't difficult. The only thing that stands out in my mind was the issue over the color of the walls. I had to go in on a weekend to discuss the color of sets for painting. All the creative people and producers were standing around on a weekend discussing the color of a wall. It was crazy. It wasn't necessary. To me, it was silly. If that's the most profound thing I remember about a problem, then you can gather the pilot went over smoothly.

DAVID GERROLD

I'm meeting with writers, taking pitches, I'm told pitches are good to go to outlines; later Gene calls me into his office and says, "We're not buying those stories."

"Why?" "Their credits are junk." "Gene, what are you talking about? Their credits are *not* junk. These are proven writers." Gene bawls me out, saying, "I'm going to tell you this straight out, David. There's talk around here that you're acting like a loose cannon on this show." Where did *this* come from? I would check in with everybody on a weekly basis: "How am I doing so far?" "You're doing great, just keep it up." So who the hell's got Gene's ear? I was crushed.

HERB WRIGHT (producer, *Star Trek: The Next Generation*)

I'm a student of the *I Ching* as well as being involved in martial arts for years, and the wisdom of every one of those people that I really respect and think a lot of, all say the same thing: any group endeavor starts at the center, and Gene and Leonard [Maizlish] are the center. The chaos, the confusion, the lies, the manipulation, the second, third, and fourth thinking of everything we do, and the general hubbub of every day starts there. We'd been constantly played off each other.

DAVID GERROLD

They bring in Bob Lewin. Bob's done *McMillan & Wife* and *The Paper Chase* and a whole bunch of other shows. I said, "Hey, he did *The Paper Chase*. Can't argue with that. Maybe this guy is what *Star Trek* needs." I'm meeting with him two or three times a day to bring him up to speed, and Gene says, "Use Dorothy as a story editor and use David as a story editor." And so I'm screening stuff for Bob and I'm happy. I figure I'm doing the work I should be doing on the show, we have a producer, and despite all the bumps that hit us in December, things are shaping up.

ROBERT LEWIN (producer, *Star Trek: The Next Generation*)

I began back on *The Rifleman* and *Rawhide*. I've written for Westerns, doctor shows, lawyer shows. The first year on a series is backbreaking, even if it's a half hour. It's agony. After about ten or fifteen shows you really know a lot of these people, but it takes that long. Spock was not the hero that he became during the early part of the first series.

HERB WRIGHT

First year of a series is a very exciting time. It's the riskiest, but also the most exciting. That's when you're making the rules; there are none and you're making them. There's no one saying "I've got the secret," because you're all trying to figure it out together. There's a sense of it becoming.

ROBERT LEWIN

It was impossible for people to conceive a perfect idea from the outside. One of the reasons it was so difficult is because we didn't always know what we wanted.

HERB WRIGHT

On *Star Trek* you really had excitement, a new ship, a new cast, and an opportunity to do shows that you couldn't have done twenty years before. You had a much healthier effects budget and no more rubber monsters and cardboard walls. You walk on those sets and you think you can fly, but there was so much strife and turmoil the first year I couldn't deal with it anymore. First season, no one got protected. Everyone had a target drawn on their chest when they came in.

TRACY TORMÉ

During one of the first meetings I went in on, Walter Koenig [Chekov] was there, so they decided to give me and him a tour of what was going on at the show. I had recently read the bible and now, literally, they were building the bridge and I was being led through the sets. Koenig and I were led around and shown everything. It made a big impression on me.

I had absolutely no desire to get back into TV at that point, I was deeply into trying to make movies and I have to admit after having read the bible and then actually being there to see how the show was piece by piece being put together, that was interesting to me. I thought it would be fascinating to create something and then watch it come to life as opposed to doing a movie. It opened up my mind to getting back into TV and doing this again.

DAVID GERROLD

I was still getting calls from agents. I told them, "I think we've got an edict from the studios that we're not to talk to new writers right now." I got called into Gene's office again. "Don't you dare tell agents that! There's been no edict. It's *my* decision." The first time he tells me that the studio says we can't buy those scripts because the writers have junk credits. In that first meeting I said to him, "What should I tell the agents?" He said, "Lay it off on the studio." So I lay it off on the studio, he calls me back into his office and says, "How dare you lay it off on the studio? It makes me look like I'm not in control of my own show." "Gene, that's what you told me." "I said no such thing." "All right, Gene, you're the boss. Do you want my resignation?" "No, I don't want your resignation, you're doing fine work," and he started backing down.

TRACY TORMÉ

At that point, even though I knew there was a tremendous amount of turmoil, and I had witnessed some of it—I'd seen some screaming matches between David Gerrold and Maizlish in the hallway—I was immune to it all. Maizlish was extremely nice to me from the beginning. I kind of remember that Maizlish was a fan of my father [Mel Tormé] and for that reason he went out of his way to be nice to me. I could see him doing things I knew were going to drive people crazy, taking on the role of the head writer, and it was really bothering people a lot.

HERB WRIGHT

At one point Leonard [Maizlish] was in my office telling me that he was going to give me Bob Lewin's office down on the first floor and his secretary. After the fourth time he told me, I went down and told Bob, "I don't want to take your office or your secretary, and I don't think that's right." He went in and confronted Gene about it, and, of course, Gene said, "I don't know what you're talking about. We've never considered moving you. We do need to get in a big exec to help us with the production, but we think the world of you," and so forth. Not a half an hour later Gene was in my office apologizing that he wasn't going to be able to move me downstairs and that he wanted to.

This is when I realized that everybody's been king of the heap for twenty minutes. And when I've been king of the heap or low man on the totem pole, I haven't done anything different. I've come in, done my work, turned things in on time, given my comments on other things. But what changed was their attitude toward you based on what they feel your loyalty is that week, and that's completely subjective to *them*. It has nothing to do with what you've done or what you haven't done. It just has to do with a certain kind of attitude about who you are that week. It's very schizophrenic.

DAVID GERROLD

What had happened was that Leonard Maizlish was running the negotiations and when the studio guys told him they were thrilled with my work, he saw me as a threat to Gene's power on the show. He was spending more and more time closeted with Gene, advising him how to run the show. *He* was the one who told Gene I was trouble. Then I realized what Leonard had done: He put me into an embarrassing position two weeks before my deal is to be negotiated, so I have no negotiation strength on the show for the story editor deal. They give me the stupid "take it or leave it" deal instead.

HERB WRIGHT

Leonard Maizlish was allowed to rewrite scripts, and he's not a Guild member. He told directors what to do on the set, and was in the cutting room telling people what to cut out. This is a man who's an attorney. He knows *nothing* about filmmaking, and has taken it upon himself on Gene's behalf to act as Gene's surrogate, and took that mission as seriously as Cardinal Richelieu took his.

DOROTHY FONTANA

Herb Wright turned in his final draft of a script titled "The Last Outpost." The script disc was turned over to the show's typist to format and print out a copy, which would then go to the print shop for formal copying. On our way out of the building, at about six P.M., Herb, his assistant, and I stopped in the script typist's office to say good night. We all saw that there were handwritten changes being made to Herb's script before anyone else had seen it. And *before* it went to the print shop. From long experience of working with Gene, I knew it was not his writing. Herb's assistant recognized it as Leonard Maizlish's. The typist confirmed Maizlish was sitting in Susan Sackett's office, making these line changes. Herb immediately went in and confronted Maizlish. Bob Lewin was leaving via that office and was witness to Herb's questioning of why Maizlish, a lawyer, not a writer, was making changes.

Maizlish said he was just putting in some word changes that Justman and Berman wanted and Roddenberry had also had some last-minute thoughts. Herb's counter to that was: how could anyone want word changes or have last-minute thoughts when no one *except him* had seen the script yet? And, in any event, such changes could have been conveyed to him and *he* would have made them. Herb immediately took his complaint to Rick Berman and thought he had effectively stopped this kind of script tampering by someone not a writer.

ROBERT H. JUSTMAN

I don't like to have anyone interfere in what I'm doing creatively as a producer. But suppose I don't call it interference, but I think, "Hey, here's another set of eyes looking at something." As long as I'm in a situation where I can use what I want and discard what I don't want, all's well and good. If it gets in my way when I don't have the time to deal with it, I would get annoyed.

I don't think an attorney should do that sort of thing, but at the same time that attorney as business manager and confidant and protector of Gene Roddenberry, having the benefit of what Gene has said to him, may know some things Gene wants done that perhaps other people don't know. Into each life some rain must fall. If everything went well, we'd have nothing to complain about.

History repeated itself on Fontana's script for "Too Short a Season," about an aged ambassador, Admiral Jameson, sent to negotiate a hostage release from terrorists, who is mysteriously turning younger. The script suddenly included handwritten changes as well as a pair of new scenes, including one with the teenager Wesley Crusher, that Maizlish claimed had been written by Roddenberry.

DOROTHY FONTANA

Berman knew Roddenberry had been out of town and could not have written the scenes and asked if Maizlish had written them. Maizlish was strongly pushing the inclusion of the Wesley character in all scripts. He admitted to Berman that he had. Berman said he told Maizlish he could in no way present these scenes to me for inclusion in the script. The next morning, Berman and Bob Justman had come in early to make sure [that day's scenes] were ready to go to the stage, and they had found a Maizlish-written scene inserted in the revised pages. In addition, there were Maizlish-originated line and word changes incorporated into the revised pages. Berman and Justman were outraged.

Berman called Roddenberry at home and informed him of the incident and also told him that I had every right to go straight to the WGA and begin a suit against Maizlish, Roddenberry, and Paramount, and that Berman would back me one hundred percent if I did so. [And] Justman called Maizlish personally and ripped him up one side and down the other for having the gall to insert his own material in a script.

DAVID GERROLD

Leonard [Maizlish] told people what they wanted to hear. Gene was afraid he would have his show taken away from him again. They took it away from him twenty years earlier, they took the movies away from him. They keep taking it away from him, and he was terrified of it. Anytime Leonard said that he had to protect himself, Gene freaked. They did it to Dorothy. The studio was thrilled with her work on "Encounter at Farpoint," and what happens to Dorothy? She starts getting walked over and bullied. The studio says to Leonard Maizlish, "We think Herb Wright is doing so well that he should be put in charge of story development." That's when Leonard bawls him out for being totally useless. Herb goes to Gene and Gene says, "I agree with that. Leonard's absolutely right. You're useless to the show." It's a horrifying story.

DOROTHY FONTANA

I do not feel Paramount is at fault in any of this. The show, as I understand by contract, [was] under the control of Roddenberry. And as has been painfully demonstrated time after time, Roddenberry seemed to be under the control of his lawyer, Leonard Maizlish.

DAVID GERROLD

All of that bullshit about how we really encourage new talent is just that from Gene Roddenberry. It's bullshit, because the way he treats new talent is they're no better than typists who need to be trained and he is the guy who's going to do it. There's no recognition of the fact that the new talent is enthusiastic, full of energy, full of bright ideas, and needs channeling, not training. Discipline. Gene wants to be the feudal lord of the kingdom. The way he treated people is bizarre.

HERB WRIGHT

During the first couple of months when it was the honeymoon period, I was the wonder boy on the block. Gene was taking me out for drinks after work, and

I could do no wrong at that moment. Everybody else had written a script for *Star Trek* and everybody had mixed reaction to each of the scripts. So I handed in mine, and I was the last one to do so, because I was the last guy to come on staff before Maurice Hurley. And I waited. Within forty-eight hours everybody, including the studio, loved my script, and I knew I was in deep shit, because it meant I would be the next target out there.

DOROTHY FONTANA

During the period of April and May [1987], I delivered the outline, revised outline, first and second draft scripts for "The Naked Now." While the script was given a good reaction by almost everyone, the Roddenberry pattern of dealing with scripts befell it. After a staffer turned in the official second draft of the script, they were not allowed to touch it again. No matter how good a script appeared to be, it would be rewritten by Gene Roddenberry. If possible, scenes of sexual content would be inserted into the script. When two such scenes were put into "The Naked Now," in addition to other scenes which I felt debased the female characters of the series, I put my sentiments into a frankly worded memo of comment on the script. My comments were ignored.

DAVID GERROLD

Maurice Hurley got hired about the same time as Herb Wright. Herb was supposed to get the downstairs office. Maurice insisted on a "run of the show" deal and he insisted on an office at least as big as Gene's. So he got the office that Herb was supposed to get. Herb got shoved into Dorothy's office, and she got pushed into another office. It's office roulette. Nobody knows what Maurice is. We hadn't met him. Herb just jumped right in saying, "Give me all the memos and scripts." He's there a couple of weeks before I finish the bible, and I finish it and see a memo from Herb Wright saying, "Gene, what a great bible that you've written."

What happens is that Herb, Dorothy, and I become a partnership to do our best in the face of massive disagreement in the face of whatever is coming down. Maurice Hurley has been advising Gene, "Why are we hiring outside writers? Let's have this show all staff written."

DOROTHY FONTANA

For freelance writers, there was a different complication. Scripts and stories were being pulled away from them—either at story or at first-draft script—and assigned to staff by Roddenberry. The freelance writers were not given an opportunity to work further with the producer to whom they had been assigned, nor were they allowed to do further work, even though, in the case of the scripts, they would have to be paid second-draft money. While this is not illegal, according to the Guild, it is not especially fair, either. Roddenberry's feelings about freelance writers was summed up in a staff story meeting at which Bob Lewin, Herb Wright, Maurice Hurley, and I were present. Roddenberry stated he had "forgotten how bad freelance writers were." From that point on, almost every freelance writer's script was taken away from them and given to staff.

DAVID GERROLD

I was always trying to put the best face on it, because I know how much of an emotional investment every single *Star Trek* fan on the entire planet had that this show be a success, and I will be goddamned if I'm going to be the guy who blew the whistle, badmouths the show, and spoilsports things. I'm thinking, "Maybe it's me. I don't understand what they're doing. Maybe I'm still a beginner, but I'm not going to be a bad sport. I'm not going to be Harlan Ellison."

HERB WRIGHT

Paramount had apparently suggested to Gene three or four times during my golden boy heyday there that I take over the writing staff, because they were having serious problems with what Gene was doing with scripts and how long it took for him to get them out and so forth. *Nothing* could have been more detrimental to my relationship with Gene. I was then seen as a threat, and on that day, the day which Gene saw me as that, my relationship with them changed.

Now, I never got into an argument with Gene. I *did* with his lawyer, but not with Gene. My attitude about work was, it's his show, it says "Gene Roddenberry's *Star Trek*," and I wanted to try and give him what he wanted and try to be true to what Paramount wanted. Well, what he wanted and what Paramount wanted and what the rest of the staff wanted are as different as if you'd been given the Tower of Babel to put together, and everyone is trying to pull you in opposite directions.

DOROTHY FONTANA

About the middle of June, Bob Lewin, Herb Wright, and Maurice Hurley were all approached by Leonard Maizlish with the proposal that all writing staff should take a cut on the pay they would receive on scripts, from network to syndication rates, because "the show was over budget and we have to cut down." I was not approached; I was told about this by Herb and Bob. Bob, Herb, Maurice, and I all agreed, and our agents agreed, that this was not the arrangement for which we had contracted, and we banded together to form a front that refused to accept such a cut in script rates. Our various agents had elected to have Marty Shapiro of Shapiro-Lichtman be spokesman for all of them, and Marty was scheduled to go in to the Paramount executives and have it out on this subject on a Wednesday morning. On the evening before, Leonard Maizlish came to Herb Wright and said we would be paid network rates on all script work we did, but that Roddenberry was very unhappy about it. The following morning in our weekly staff meeting, the subject was brought up again, and Roddenberry expressed his disappointment with "some members of the staff," but that network rates would continue to be paid "for now." The subject never came up again, possibly because the thoroughly united stand against it was one Roddenberry couldn't overcome.

HERB WRIGHT

There was no strongman in the center. Gene is not a strong guy. He will not tell you to your face that he does not like your ideas in the scripts. He'll tell you that they're all terrific, he'll pat you on your back, and you say "Gee, that's great." And you'll walk out of the office thinking that everything is great, and then you find out the next morning that he hated it all.

DAVID GERROLD

You can actually compare Captain Picard's relationship with his crew and Roddenberry's dealings with the writing staff. That's how Gene saw himself. He was in command of a floating executive hotel, and he's the boss. He's in charge of women, the wives, the children, the husbands, everything. In the script you'll see someone comes to the captain and says, "Some of the families are concerned," and the captain says, "This is not a democracy. You don't get to vote on it." At least we acknowledged that people on the ship were concerned about the danger. Gene crossed that off and said, "Nobody argues with the captain's decisions."

In other words, "Our people all know that the captain is going to make the right decision." That's the way he perceives his relationship with his staff. Nobody else's opinion has any validity. If you look at the relationship of Picard with all of his top officers, whenever they make a recommendation, they're wrong. Picard always knows better. He's got the best and brightest there, and his way of managing them is to show them that they're incompetent. You can see in the scripts Gene rewrote how he treats his staff.

TRACY TORMÉ

It seemed early in the show that everyone was surrendering all the time. That was a big running joke, like we surrender as soon as anything happened. I guess I'm a bit more hawkish in nature, so that's why I tried to do some things that made it a little more controversial, harder edged. I thought it was too soft in the early going.

DAVID GERROLD

[Conceptual designers] Rick Sternbach and Andy Probert were doing a technical manual about how things work, and most of the stuff is too complex to hand to writers. It's way too complex to hand to Gene Roddenberry. I explained to Gene how we could really make stardates work, develop a good system for making the warp drive number system work. He listened politely and made up something else. He said, "No, no. It's like the Richter scale, and each one is an order of magnitude." I said, "Okay, Gene." I'm not arguing anymore. When he hired me, he said, "David, your job is to keep me honest and disagree with me." But ten weeks later I know if I disagree with him I'm going to get bullied, so I just say, "It's your show, Gene. You can have it just the way you want it."

Arthur Sellers shows us a first draft script, and it's too heavy on the techno-jargon, but structurally correct. Arthur was so eager to please Gene that he went to talk to Rick and Andy about the science. He wanted the science to be accurate. Rick and Andy got enthusiastic and invented some great stuff for him. Gene reads the script and hits the ceiling. "This is bullshit science. Not on my show." The funny thing is that these things were really science.

Gene said, "If I call my good friend Isaac Asimov and ask him, would he understand?" Arthur said, "Probably, since we got this out of scientific articles." He calls it bullshit and then throws it out. Then he calls in Andy and Rick and bawls them out, telling them not to talk to the writers on the show. "I'm in charge of science on this show," he said. They played it down, but they were hurt. So Arthur Sellers' script got cut off.

MAURICE HURLEY (coexecutive producer, *Star Trek: The Next Generation*)

In the beginning, there was a lot of clutter. Too many ideas being thrown into one script. The show suffers if it gets too complex and there are too many things trying to be stated. The overlay becomes a diversion, a distraction. It takes away from the real point of the show. There was a tendency to sometimes do a very quick wrap-up. Too much in the bag, trying to fill the bag too full.

ROBERT H. JUSTMAN

You can't turn out a Picasso every week.

HERB WRIGHT

What happened is that the initial thrust of the series, where there was a lot of innovation . . . and, frankly, a lot of that innovation came from within the staff and outside the staff and not from Gene . . . was beaten down, honed down, and kind of blended out so that more and more we were doing the same kinds of stories that were done before back in the sixties. And we were not allowed to do dramatic resolves. So many times Gene took the guts out of the villain.

I'm not talking about melodrama. I'm talking about the actual conflict. Instead, they just have a serious argument. I wrote a thing where we were fired upon by the Ferengi, and I had us firing back a warning shot to slow them down, because we were in chase. Gene ripped that out, saying that we weren't allowed to fire back. He said we wouldn't do that. I said, "Gene, it's an act of war. They've fired at us and they've stolen something of ours." "We wouldn't do that. That's stupid."

We came across that time and time again, yet when he did a rewrite of the episode "Code of Honor" [in which a planet of primitive tribesman abduct security chief Tasha Yar], he had the *Enterprise* firing on a planet . . . with all of its power! *As a warning*! So the rules that he made he forgot, or only applied to other people. It was really impossible to write that way, because there's no consistency in the direction of what you were doing.

TRACY TORMÉ

That episode ["Code of Honor"] was offensive. It was like *Amos 'n' Andy* in the way African Americans were depicted.

BRENT SPINER (actor, "Data")

Worst episode we ever did was "Code of Honor," which was an inadvertently racist episode.

DAVID A. GOODMAN (consulting producer, *Star Trek: Enterprise*)

As weirdly offensive as people think "Code of Honor" is, I, at least, liked it because it felt new and different. There was some action, and it had a great score—it probably has the best score of any *Next Generation* episode. Fred Steiner from the original series did the score. But I stuck through it, and that's why I consider myself an unapologetic *Star Trek* fan. I not only watched it, I videotaped every episode on slow VHS speed. I didn't have cable, so I had to get my antenna exactly right. Then toward the end of the season it started to pick up a bit and I was, like, "OK, not bad." "Conspiracy" and "The Neutral Zone" were watchable.

ROD RODDENBERRY

"Code of Honor" is the one that people say is the most racist, but I just didn't see it. Is it the best episode ever? No. But did I enjoy the episode? Sure. I just saw them as people on a planet that happened to be of dark skin that evolved in this certain way.

DAVID GERROLD

And *then* things get *really* weird. Dorothy and Herb were telling me things that were going on in meetings that Gene is starting to say. Sexist and racist remarks about black people being spearchuckers. I'm hearing things like he's in a meeting with a woman writer who has been brought in, and he's explaining how our captain is an older man who is irresistible to women. Then he looked at her and said, "Executive producers often have the same problem." Everyone else in the room kind of looks up at the ceiling. It's things like that.

DOROTHY FONTANA

We had a black writer who was very badly treated. I said as much to him, and I said, "It isn't you. It comes from up top." I had seen him basically insulted as a black man in story meetings. Just off-the-cuff remarks from Roddenberry. You just want to leap out of your chair and say "Stop!" but nobody did. I know it must have gotten under his skin and hurt. *I* was offended by some of the things that were said.

HERB WRIGHT

Gene knew all of the right words to say, but he didn't believe them. I sat in on a story meeting with Patrick Barry, who was an outside writer. The story was called "Angel One," which was made. It was all about a reverse-world society in which women ruled and men are subservient. It's been done a thousand times already.

So one of the major issues that we didn't want to do was an Amazon Women kind of thing where the women are six feet tall with steel D cups. I said, "The hit I want to take on this is apartheid, so that the men are treated as though they are blacks of South Africa. Make it political. Sexual overtones, yes, but political." Well, that didn't last very long.

Everything that Gene got involved with had to have sex in it. It's so perverse that it's hard to believe. The places it was dragged into is absurd. We were talking about how women would react, and Gene was voicing all the right words again, saying, "Oh, yes, we've got to make sure that women are represented fairly, because, after all, women are probably the superior sex anyway, and it's real important we don't get letters from feminists, because we want to be fair and we don't want to infer that women have to rule by force if they do rule, because men don't have to rule by force." Very sensible stuff.

All of a sudden something kicks in and he changes: "However, we also don't want to infer that it would be a better society if women ruled, because as we all know," and he's getting louder and louder, "women are goddamned cunts! You can't trust them! They're vicious creatures who will cut your throat when you're not looking!" Then he looks out the window, looks at the outline, and says, "Okay, on page eight . . ." and continues like that didn't even happen.

TRACY TORMÉ

An exact quote from him that I still remember to this day was, you've always got to be careful of women because "women will suck the marrow out of your bones."

DOROTHY FONTANA

Back on the original show, Gene was a true liberal in the sense of women, race, and that kind of thing. He gave every opportunity to black actors and to black crew. He hired me as his story editor. No question, those days were good days. I have absolutely nothing bad to say for those times. But since then it seemed that things had gone sour for Roddenberry. I don't know what the elements were, but he was clearly carrying a grudge for younger writers, for women writers, for . . . I'm venturing to say, this is my perception, members of different ethnic cultures.

TRACY TORMÉ

I was on another one of my quests to create a new character for the show, so I had an idea: who would be a really interesting alien on *Star Trek*? And I got the idea of John Cleese. So I created an episode called "Genius Is Pain" and it was about a race of aliens who are mathematical geniuses—they spend the first twenty or thirty years of their lives devoted to mathematics, and they're off-the-chart geniuses, they can do things that engineers can't do, the whole race. But once they turn thirty, they have a philosophy of life that all life should be devoted to bohemian pursuits, so if you invite them to your house and they feel like spray-painting a four-letter word on the wall of your nursery, they're going to do it, because to suppress it would be against their nature.

I submitted the outline for "Genius Is Pain," which was about five pages long, and one day I'm sitting in my office and Roddenberry calls me, and he sounded lit, like he was not all there. And it started with "Hello, friend," and he went into this long, long rambling speech. "I love the title of your outline 'Genius Is Pain,' because, let me tell you something, genius *is* pain, you're absolutely right. But in fact, all of life is basically divided into two things, pleasure and pain."

And then he started to list things that he found painful: the pain of dealing with network executives, the pain of going through divorce, the pain of seeing your children's faces when you have to tell them you don't love their mother anymore, the pain of spending eighteen straight hours writing a perfect scene and someone saying it has to be changed for some fucking stupid reason—so he's going on and on. It was really one for the ages, and I was wondering when this was going to come to an end. So he finally comes up for air, and then says, "As for pleasure, my idea of pleasure is waves and waves and waves of cum exploding out of me."

I absolutely was shocked—and he had said it in this sort of Irish voice—that quickly I covered the phone as hard as I could and stuck my head as far out of my office window as I could and uncontrollably started laughing. Like I couldn't believe what I'd heard—and it was said to me by a leprechaun. So now I'm terrified to come back to the phone, that he's going to have heard my reaction and my relationship with him is going to be destroyed for all time. I very warily sneak my-self back onto the phone and he's in the middle of talking about more things that bring him pleasure that I had completely missed. That was one of the funnier and stranger moments of my life.

HERB WRIGHT

He was unquestionably ill, and had probably been that way for some time. Whether it was the first stage of Alzheimer's or whatever, he couldn't remember my name, the project we were talking about, the name of the story we had discussed ten min-utes earlier. He sent memos on projects I was not supervising, saying, "Sorry I'm late on this." He took notes for projects of mine and gave them to other people who came in and gave them to me.

TRACY TORMÉ

He had extreme self-confidence in his own thinking process, one of those guys who really believed that when he thought of an idea, and was going to add it to someone else's script, it was worth its weight in gold. He never lacked for that kind of confidence, always felt that anything that had sort of gone wrong with the orig-inal *Trek* were all the responsibility of the idiots above him.

I think that his politics were not fully understood by people, because they were very all over the map. He was very conservative on some things, but his overall view of the future was pretty liberal. That was confusing to some people. When you would have personal conversations with him, especially if he'd been drinking at all, there would be an almost draconian conservative side to him, like you could see how he would be very hawkish on some things. It was hard to get a handle on him. Powerful temper, his whole face would get red when he got angry.

ROBERT H. JUSTMAN

The original *Star Trek* was a failure. It was a good show with great ideas and it taught some serious lessons in human morality. It showed people that it's really good to be a moral person. I was glad for the show and glad for Gene. And I wasn't glad for Gene because I didn't have a piece of the show, but I know it kept some of the actors alive for a while. And I particularly wanted to prove that *Star Trek* could be successful right out of the chute, and that's the main reason I came back to work on *The Next Generation*.

DAVID LIVINGSTON

I'm very fond of Bob [Justman]. He was always good to me. Basically, he gave me free rein. He didn't try to manage me. He knew I was a manager and gave me my rein to do what I needed to do. I remember when we were trying to find a makeup artist, I went in to Bob to talk about Michael Westmore, and Bob knew him by reputation, because he won the Oscar for *Raging Bull*. Bob said, "Michael Westmore? Yeah, bring him in!" That was the way Bob did it. He had confidence I wasn't going to bring him schlumps. He was a great boss. I worked with Bob more than I did with Rick [Berman]. Bob was more of the production guy in that regard.

DOUG DREXLER

I remember I had come out to visit Bob Justman when they were still planning the show and building the sets. We exchanged letters back and forth. His letters were all just as charming and funny as his memos were. One of the letters I wrote to him said, "It would be the thrill of a lifetime to come and see the sets," and he wrote back, "We want to give you the thrill of a lifetime."

ROBERT H. JUSTMAN

To me, it was the same show. Yes, it might look better and sound better and move better, but it was the same show and only the faces were changed. You'll notice that we didn't attempt to duplicate any of the original characters in any way, shape, or form. We did what we wanted to do and proved to Trekkers that there's lots of room for disparity in the universe; there are a zillion ways of telling a tale, but this was the original show, only done much better.

DAVID LIVINGSTON

These guys not only came up with these wonderful creations in sets, costumes, hair, set decorating, visual effects, but they did it on a television schedule, which is amazing.

RICK BERMAN

Visual effects for many decades were done with live-action models and stop motion. To do it digitally was just too expensive. When we first started *Next Generation,* almost all the ship shots you see are, in fact, models; meticulously painted wooden models that are photographed and made to look like they're doing all kinds of exciting things. By the second season, our postproduction supervisor, Peter Lauritson, realized that we could afford to do certain shots using computer animation. As the cost of computer animation came down, the percentage of [such] shots ended up getting greater and greater.

By the time we finished *Next Generation,* we were doing 100 percent of our work with digital compositing and with computers. Each year the price came down, so our animation and our special effects just got better and better as we went along. You have to give credit to Paramount. They very well could have given us a budget like other syndicated shows that existed. Instead, they gave us a budget that was equivalent to the big network series, which enabled us to use pretty classy effects.

HERB WRIGHT

There was nothing like that show on TV. That's the number one thing, so right away you're doing something different. Second, since you're doing something in the twenty-fourth century, you have this unique opportunity to explore all the stories that impact on what's going on today from the advantage and "safety" of the future, which is remarkable. Third, because of the incredible success of the former *Star Trek* and the movies, Paramount really bellied up like no studio I've ever seen before to make this the best-looking, the best-produced series ever. There were no more cardboard walls or rubber monsters. They were spending the time and money to do it right.

TRACY TORMÉ

But we were barely scratching the surface of its potential. The format of *Star Trek* opens many of those creative doors, but it's up to *Star Trek* to be bold enough to do something challenging. Having the opportunity doesn't mean that you're going to fulfill it. There was a conservative approach taken of not rocking the boat too much, not taking too many chances. I'm the one person who tries to push to do unusual, unexpected, or, hopefully, progressive things on the show, but there always seemed to be resistance. It always seemed to be a struggle to do something that's groundbreaking. That's because the show was such a success that the attitude had become "Why take risks?"

HERB WRIGHT

Paramount was making a fortune, and the pickup for a second year came way early, so they were sitting pretty. They only had to do one thing to make this stuff continue: keep turning out the show. That, unfortunately, was the catch-22 that Gene Roddenberry sat directly on top of, along with his attorney. They had a real problem, because one executive told me that they'd gone three months and had not gotten a single call from any agents and outside writers wanting to write for the show, either on staff or for stories. The news about this show was out.

ALL ABOARD

"I KNOW YOU HAVE YOUR DOUBTS ABOUT ME, ABOUT EACH OTHER, ABOUT THIS SHIP. ALL I CAN SAY IS THAT ALTHOUGH WE HAVE ONLY BEEN TOGETHER FOR A SHORT TIME, I KNOW THAT YOU ARE THE FINEST CREW IN THE FLEET."

One thing everyone involved with *Star Trek* could agree on was that the casting of the new series was of paramount importance, pun intended. A large part of the original series' enduring popularity stemmed from the perfect marriage of actor to character and for *The Next Generation* to endure, the creative team would need to be equally lucky for the new show. Hiring Junie Lowry-Johnson as their casting director, the producers proved that lightning could indeed strike twice.

But the look of this new *Trek* ensemble could have been considerably different if the stars had aligned differently. Among those being considered for the pivotal role of Captain Picard included Mitchell Ryan (who would later play Riker's estranged father in the second season's "The Icarus Factor"), Roy Thinnes (of the popular sci-fi series *The Invaders*), and Belgian actor Patrick Bauchau, who was a front runner for the role.

Perhaps the most intriguing choice of all was the strong interest the studio had in African American actor Yaphet Kotto, who had previously starred as the villain Kanaga in the James Bond film *Live & Let Die*, as well as a space trucker who meets an untimely end in Ridley Scott's *Alien*.

RICK BERMAN (executive producer, *Star Trek: The Next Generation*)

The fans of the original series already had a somewhat jaundiced eye when it came to this new series, because they felt, how can you put a new captain at the seat of the *Enterprise*? Bill Shatner, that's Captain Kirk. And when they heard it was going to be a forty-year-old bald Englishman, they kind of went nuts.

ROBERT H. JUSTMAN (supervising producer, *Star Trek: The Next Generation*)

My wife and I were attending a UCLA extension course on humor, and one night there were going to be two actors who were going to read from Shakespearean comedies and Noël Coward. There was a woman and a man, and the man was Patrick Stewart. My wife and I were sitting there, and Patrick looked familiar, but I hadn't placed him as Serjanus from *I, Claudius* or from *Tinker Tailor Soldier Spy* and shows like that. Patrick sat down, pushed up his jacket sleeves to display his massive forearms, and commenced to read. He spoke a few sentences and I was thunderstruck.

I turned to my wife, Jackie, and I said, "I think I found our new captain!" I'd been back at Paramount preparing the show for a month or two at the most, but I was so impressed with what I saw and heard that night, the next day I called SAG and found out who Patrick's agent was here in town, because he was over from London just for this, and I got hold of the agent and made arrangements for Patrick to visit with Gene and me at Gene's house the following Monday. Patrick came in his rental car, and we sat around for thirty-forty minutes, and then he made his good-byes and left to fly back to England. After he drove away, Gene closed the door and turned to me, and I will quote him exactly. He said, "I won't have him."

RICK BERMAN

I met Patrick Stewart and said to Bob Justman, "We have to convince Gene to use this guy," and Bob said to me, "We can't. When Gene makes up his mind, it's a waste of time to try and change it." But in my case, ignorance was bliss. I didn't believe that.

ROBERT H. JUSTMAN

No matter what I said, he was adamant, and the reason was because the character he had created in his own mind was a very hairy Frenchman, so we embarked upon a campaign that lasted for some months, and when Rick Berman came on the show and became supervising producer with me, Rick jumped all over it, too, and said, "He's perfect!"

RICK BERMAN

I was the guy who basically bugged Gene into realizing that Patrick was the best Picard.

GENE RODDENBERRY (creator, executive producer, *Star Trek: The Next Generation*)

Bob Justman, who has been with me since day one, suggested Picard's identity. He had gone to UCLA and had seen this man he wanted as Picard. He presented him to me, and my first reaction was, "Jesus Christ, Bob, I don't want a bald man." In his wisdom, Justman kept his mouth shut and let me grow accustomed to him.

ROBERT H. JUSTMAN

Our casting director was for it, everyone was for it, except Gene. We went through everybody in town and in foreign countries trying to find the right person to play the captain, and couldn't. Finally, our last candidate came in, read for us and left, and we were sitting there—the casting director, Rick, Gene, and myself—and he finally turned around and looked at us and said, "All right, I'll go with Patrick," and that was it. It was so right, I've never been more sure of anything in my life, at least in the business, than casting Patrick in that role. He was everything that a captain ought to be.

RICK BERMAN

He finally agreed, though he said, "But when we bring him to the studio for the final audition, I want him to wear a wig, because I don't want this guy going in bald." So Patrick made a phone call to London and got a very, very good wig made by one of the best theatrical wig makers in England. And he had the wig sent over.

DAVID LIVINGSTON (supervising producer, *Star Trek: The Next Generation*)

Patrick Stewart is the most consummate, professional actor I have ever met. If anyone would captain a starship, it would be him. He would never blink. Only when he was off-camera. If you watch him on-camera, I defy you to find a time he was blinking, because of the intensity of his captain. I remember the first time I met him, I was alone in the trailer, he comes into the trailer, and he had a box in his hand and asked where he could find the makeup and hair people. In his box were his wigs, because they wanted to see what he looked like in them.

RICK BERMAN

Patrick came in, and somebody was there to help him put on the wig. We brought him to read for John Pike at the studio. It was Patrick and Stephen Macht. A very good actor, but not in Patrick's league for this role. They both read, and at the end Pike said, "Go with the English guy, but lose the wig." And that was the best three words we could have heard. He knew that Patrick was bald, and he had seen all the photographs of him, and we had played him a tape of Patrick's clips. That was the greatest sales point for *The Next Generation*.

STEPHEN MACHT (actor, *Cagney & Lacey*)

Probably the biggest professional mistake I ever made in my life was turning this down. A pivotal figure, whom I'm still in touch with, is D.C. Fontana, whom I met in 1975. She called me in 1986 and said she wanted me to come in and meet Gene Roddenberry. She told me he was the writer of *Star Trek* and she wanted him to meet me. So I went in, I sit down opposite him in his office, and D.C. was with me. He said, "D.C. has brought me clips of everything you've done since you've been in Hollywood. You are my next *Star Trek* hero, Picard." And I'm full of piss and vinegar at that time. I was forty-two and doing well. I said to him, "I've seen these things, and I don't want to do them. I don't want to speak to guys with six heads for the rest of my life." He said, "It's not about that, Stephen. They're morality tales. I want you to do it. You just have to come read for the studio head." "I don't want to read. You want me to do it? Offer it to me. You know who my agent is."

Now, I've had a long time to think about this. When any moment comes in an actor's life, your intellectual, your emotional life, has to be under control for you to make enlightened decisions, and you can't be all ego. I *was* all ego at that time. Which was both my strength and my weakness, because it covered my fear of failing. I had not gone up for a lot of pilots, I didn't want to do a series. I was one of those actors who thought he was going to come to Hollywood and become a movie star. I just was not ready. I would be now, but I wasn't then. In the intervening years, of course, after so much experience, I found that there are so many layers to who I am that I can reveal slowly and that would have made a TV series like *The Next Generation* more appealing.

Looking back at it, I thank Dorothy and Gene for a marker in my life that I can really think about in terms of seeing what the trajectory has been over a whole period of years. I'm choosing to see it that way, because I'm a deeply faithful man who believes in the true growth of the human being. Had I known then what I know now, I would have knocked the shit out of that role.

Prior to assuming the captaincy of the starship *Enterprise*, Patrick Stewart appeared in a number of well-regarded BBC productions, including *I, Claudius* and *Smiley's People*. On stage he won the prestigious London Fringe Award for Best Actor for his performance in *Who's Afraid of Virginia Woolf?* and an Olivier Award for his performance in Shakespeare's *Anthony and Cleopatra*.

The actor, who plays a Frenchman on the show, grew up in the small English town of Mirfield and for twenty-five years was an Associate Artist of the Royal Shakespeare Company. His film credits include David Lynch's *Dune*, Tobe Hooper's *Lifeforce*, John Boorman's *Excalibur,* and the role of the Duke of Suffolk in *Lady Jane*. Since assuming the role of Captain Picard, Stewart appeared in Steve Martin's *L.A. Story* and later helped define another franchise by playing Professor Charles Xavier in the *X-Men* movies while continuing to star on stage in a one-man version of *A Christmas Carol*.

PATRICK STEWART (actor, "Captain Jean-Luc Picard")

As a friend of mine put it when I accepted the job, how do you think it will feel playing an American icon? It did make me a little uneasy, so I'm happy that people accepted the captain as a non-American. The other thing that pleased me is that people said, "You are the crew of the *Enterprise* and we believe in that crew." They refer to the vivid contrast between the previous captain and myself, not in a competitive way, but in that they are so different there isn't any sense of overlap.

BRANNON BRAGA (coproducer, *Star Trek: The Next Generation*)

So much of the success of *Next Generation* was Patrick Stewart, quite frankly. We always used to say the guy could read a phone book and we'd watch him. He just was so good. I always said a *Star Trek* series is only as good as its captain, and Picard was pretty fucking great.

THOMAS DOHERTY (professor of American Studies, Brandeis University)

In early episodes there seemed to be some pretense of a tripartite sharing of power on the Enterprise deck, perhaps because hierarchical military structures were considered an unenlightenened holdover from the late twentieth century (hence, the three command chairs sharing center stage). But Captain Picard—he of the balding dome and clipped accents—blossomed as the unchallenged power, the series' pivotal character and controlling force. Ensemble sensibilities aside, the writing staff conceded the obvious—that a strong central protagonist is as necessary to drive the narrative as command the Enterprise. In Shakesperean actor Patrick Stewart, the new crew found a perfect tribal patriarch. Stewart exudes authority and presence, consistently keeping the proceedings away from *Space Patrol* kitsch. Even in a dumb costume, declaiming deep-space doubletalk, he brings a kind of Elizabethan stature to his role.

PATRICK STEWART

I am truly interested as a human being and as an actor with the use of power. How it is acquired. How it works. I've always been quite a political person, and I've always been fascinated with the use of power in politics. It was always important to me to try and establish and affirm the quiet, but absolute authority he has on the ship, and that seemed to be successful.

SUSAN SACKETT (assistant to Gene Roddenberry)

I love Patrick. We were both on an airplane in Canada, and it was snowing, and they were deicing the wing, and I was really nervous. I looked across the aisle and there's Patrick Stewart, as calm as can be. I said to him, "You look nice and calm." And he said, "I'm terrified."

PATRICK STEWART

It's been my lot for years to play a whole list of national leaders, dictators, kings, princes, and party bosses, and I've never found that tiresome. If you play a king, you get to sit down a lot when the other people are standing. In *The Next Generation*, I tended to be on my feet all the time.

DAVID LIVINGSTON

It was a delight to direct him. The only run-in I ever had with him, I was on the set as a producer and I thought I heard him say a line wrong, and the director said "cut, print." I told the director, I think Patrick got that line wrong. Patrick said, "No, I didn't." The director said, "It sounded fine to me." I had the sound man,

Alan Bernard, play back the take, and I was right. They did the line over again, and Patrick said thanks. That was dangerous. I could have kept my mouth shut, but I had a responsibility. That seems like a minor thing, but when you tell Patrick Stewart he went up on a line and nobody else heard it, that's dangerous.

For other roles, Bill Campbell, who had starred in *The Rocketeer* and Michael Mann's *Crime Story,* was Roddenberry's preferred choice for Riker, although *Aliens'* Michael O'Gorman was also considered a front runner for the role, along with Jeffrey Combs, later to be a familiar staple of the *Star Trek* universe as Weyoun on *Deep Space Nine* and Shran on *Enterprise*; and Ben Murphy, who had starred in the short-lived seventies sci-fi series, *The Gemini Man.*

RICK BERMAN

For the role of Riker, we cast an actor named Billy Campbell, who later did a bunch of other good things, and [John] Pike didn't like him. He didn't feel he had a sense of command. He wouldn't follow this guy into battle. I think it was really more that he didn't audition that well for the part, and that's when we went to our second choice, who was Jonathan Frakes, who turned out to be a terrific choice.

JONATHAN FRAKES (actor, "William T. Riker")

I auditioned seven times over six weeks for this part. Unlike anything I have ever had to fight for before. The last few auditions, I would be sent to Gene's office prior to going to whichever executive needed convincing on this particular audition. I kept going up the food chain. In Gene's office, Gene would give me a pep talk, and Corey Allen, the director of the pilot, was there. Gene believed that in the twenty-fourth century, as he used to say, there'll be no hunger and there will be no greed, and all of the children will know how to read. He was able to convey his passion about the future and this optimistic, hopeful, gentler, more thoughtful future that we all wish we could live.

Gene believed that in his core. It not only was expressed in his writing, it was expressed in how he described the show he wanted to make. As a young actor, eager and willing, I really got caught up in his vision. Patrick and I both have said we wish we could be as articulate and rational as Picard and Riker are when they're in conflict or have some sort of problem to solve. The characters are so smart and so thoughtful and so loyal. This is all part of Gene's vision of the future.

RICK BERMAN

As far as the other characters, they were far more the selection of Bob Justman and mine than they were of anybody else. Gene basically approved, like the studio did, the people that Bob and I chose. Gene was not all that involved in it.

> In the case of the android Data, Mark Lindsay Chapman and Eric Menyuk, later cast as the Traveler, were well liked, but the part ultimately went to Brent Spiner who, in his own way, proved as memorable in the role as Leonard Nimoy was as Spock.

RICK BERMAN

There's a reference in the pilot to Data being like Pinocchio. He is a character that had no emotions. And because he was not human, he served a purpose similar to that of Spock. Data had no human emotions, but in fact was the most emotional of the group. And he was a little like the characters in *The Wizard of Oz*. He wanted to be a real boy, like Pinocchio, but he also he wanted to have a heart, wanted to have a brain. Brent was so good at it that all the writers felt a great desire to want to write for that character, which is the best thing that can happen to an actor.

BRENT SPINER (actor, "Data")

It was incredible for me, because initially when I took the part, my biggest fear was that it was going to be the most limited character, not only on the show but on television, because the canvas on which I was being allowed to paint was such a narrow one. Ironically, it turned out to be just the opposite.

It wound up being completely unlimited, and if I could have chosen anything to do on a television show that ran as long as this one did, it would have been to have played as many different characters as I could. I just lucked into a part that turned into the most unlimited role on television.

MELINDA SNODGRASS (story editor, *Star Trek: The Next Generation*)

I've always used Data as the child. Data is exploring what any child does as they grow up. You can allow Data to make a mistake, learn from it, and rectify it in a way that if you have someone else to make that mistake, it seems unbelievable because these are such highly trained professionals.

BRENT SPINER

I've been a professional actor since 1969, and it wasn't until I got this job that I didn't have to worry about how I was going to make my bills. That was an incredible luxury and it relaxed me a great deal. There's the tension that so many actors are under to just get a job and express the talent inside of them, but the practical reality of making a living is so intense for most actors and it was for me as well. It's the money that's made the difference. Otherwise, I don't think I've changed a bit as a result of this experience. It was a wonderful job. The performing arts are just filled with great people to come into contact with, and I have had wonderful opportunities, and this was just another one, the longest one, and it was a great experience of who I've gotten to meet and become friends with.

> For Tasha Yar, *Enterprise* head of security, Julia Nickson, who would later be cast in *Babylon 5*, was well liked, as was Rosalind Chao, who would later earn a recurring role on the series as Keiko O'Brien, the eventual wife of Chief Miles O'Brien. The role would ultimately go to Denise Crosby, whose previous credits included *48 Hrs.* and *Curse of the Pink Panther*.

SUSAN SACKETT

I remember there was a character that was in *Aliens* that was the tough chick, and they wanted to name a character in *Star Trek* after her. That ended up being the part Denise Crosby got. It turned out not to be Macha Hernandez, which was the original idea.

DENISE CROSBY (actress, "Tasha Yar")

They originally envisioned Tasha as more butch. In the sixties, there really weren't too many roles like that. There were things, for instance, like *Julia*, in which Diahann Carroll played a single working mother living on her own, and I think that was revolutionary.

If you look back at that, it was amazing, because women were very much struggling with being pregnant in the workforce, and trying to raise kids, as they still are. What I liked about Tasha is she's strong physically and direct and is comfortable with who she is. I envisioned Tasha as what I brought to it. I sort of like the quality that she could be attractive and sexy and still be able to kick the shit out of anyone.

My grandfather [Bing Crosby] was a Hollywood legend. Growing up with that wasn't exactly normal or typical, and I think that helped me understand Tasha's imbalance and insecurities.

Ironically, the helmsman of the new *Enterprise* was Geordi La Forge, who happens to be blind. He is, however, able to see via a hi-tech prosthetic device. Among those being considered for the part were Tim Russ, later cast as Tuvok in *Voyager*; Kevin Peter Hall, and, perhaps most amusingly in retrospect, Wesley Snipes. In the end, the part went to LeVar Burton, at the time best known for his role as Kunta Kinte in *Roots*.

LEVAR BURTON (actor, "Geordi LaForge")

Bob Justman produced a television movie that I was in, *Emergency Room*, and when it came time to cast *Next Generation*, he made sure that I came in. I liked the old show an awful lot and when I heard Gene Roddenberry was also doing this one, I knew the show would be done with dignity and taste and integrity. That's the sort of projects I've tried to do in my career. It's in keeping with what I want for myself as an actor.

I have always, above all else, wanted to do good work, and *Star Trek* certainly represented an opportunity to do good work. I like Geordi for a lot of reasons. First of all, his energetic attitude is much more loose than that of a lot of other characters. He has a sort of cynical sense of humor, and I like that about him. I liked the opportunity to play a character who is handicapped, yet that handicap has been turned into a plus for him, and there are all the emotional issues that go along with that.

DAVID GERROLD (creative consultant, *Star Trek: The Next Generation*)

At one point Gene said, "I want to have a disabled crew member." So I prepared a memo listing various disabilities. A guy in a wheelchair, mentally retarded with an electronic brain as a prosthesis, blind . . . things that would be visual, yet at the same time would give us something that would be an identifiable disability. Gene focused on blind. I envisioned Geordi La Forge with some kind of eye treatment; maybe just a couple of enlarged lenses that you put over the actor's eyes.

GENE RODDENBERRY

[It's] a prosthetic device which gives only fair eyesight, but results in telescopic and microscopic vision. More than that, it gives him some "sensor" abilities not unlike what the tricorder gave our people in the first series.

DAVID GERROLD

They went with the air filter look, which I totally did not like. You cover up too much of an actor's eyes and he's got nothing to work with. Then I suggested that he be named after George La Forge, who was the fan in the wheelchair with muscular dystrophy. Gene thought that was a terrific idea, and then I suggested that we didn't have any black people on the ship in terms of our regular characters, and in keeping with the ethnic character of the show, and if neither the captain or the first officer were black, then it was perhaps Geordi who should be black.

LEVAR BURTON

I loved the opportunity to do these stories with this group of actors, producers, and writers, and to provide entertainment that makes you think once in a while. That's what I built a career on, and I was really happy to be able to do it in this framework. I appreciated Gene Roddenberry's approach to science fiction. Gene's vision of the future has always included minorities—not just blacks, but Asians and Hispanics as well. He's saying that unless we learn to cooperate as a species, we won't be able to make it to the twenty-fourth century.

> In an attempt to differentiate the core group of characters from *The Original Series*, one of the additions was the empathic ship counselor, Deanna Troi, the half human/half Betazoid who would gradually come to serve as the conscience of Captain Picard. Cast in the part was British-born Marina Sirtis, who had, prior to the show, made a number of television episodic guest appearances and appeared in the Cannon Films cult classic *The Wicked Lady*, which is best remembered for its campy topless whip fight between between Sirtis and Faye Dunaway. Originally she had auditioned for the part of Tasha Yar.

RICK BERMAN

In the case of Marina Sirtis and Denise Crosby, we selected them for the opposite roles, and Gene said, "I want Crosby to play Tasha and I want Marina to play Troi."

DAVID GERROLD

Bob Justman and I spoke about a person aboard ship who serves the function of an emotional healer. Not a chaplain, because we have moved beyond mere ritual, but someone who serves as a "master." His/her job is to support those aboard the ship in the job of being the best they can be. That would eventually become Deanna Troi.

MARINA SIRTIS (actress, "Deanna Troi")

This is the kind of life you dream of as an actor—to be on a show that gets so much publicity and attention. The bad part, which is outweighed by the good part, is that you're following a legend, so it suddenly hit me a week before the pilot aired that if it didn't work out, we were going to be destroyed. Fortunately, that didn't happen. If I had sat and thought about it logically, I would have known that wasn't going to happen. But if you look up "actress" in the dictionary, it says "insecurity," so that was basically what it was.

The characterization and look changed after the pilot; we felt the character was a little bit too intense and there wasn't enough range in Troi. Basically, we were concentrating on her Betazoid abilities; I worked more on developing the human side of her, which is far more interesting to play. It was difficult to watch the pilot with my hands over my eyes; I didn't feel it was working really well. Personally, knowing what I can do as an actress and seeing what was up there, I wasn't happy.

DAVID A. GOODMAN (consulting producer, *Star Trek: Enterprise*)

The Next Generation did make therapy palatable for a whole new generation, too.

BRANNON BRAGA

A therapist on a ship full of characters that supposedly had gone beyond human foibles and no longer succumbed to petty jealousy and anger? Why is there a therapist on board?

NAREN SHANKAR (story editor, *Star Trek: The Next Generation*)

I couldn't understand it, especially coming from an immigrant family where no-body talks about their problems, ever. The notion of having an onboard psychia-trist was so weird. I was, like, "What does she do all day? I don't understand." She could look at the guy on the viewscreen who's angry and go, "I think he's angry. He seems angry to me, Captain." Poor Marina, we really tried to help her in the last few years of that show.

MARINA SIRTIS

There wasn't enough range in Troi. All she seemed to be feeling was a lot of an-guish. In the first couple of seasons the [writer] turnover was so immense that I don't think they could ever get a hook. They were here for ten minutes and then they were gone, which wasn't really long enough to kind of establish any kind of continuity or character development in their scripts.

TRACY TORMÉ (creative consultant, *Star Trek: The Next Generation*)

I'm not really sure that the Deanna Troi character ever fully worked for me. I liked Marina very much as a person, but that character was a little soft for me and touchy-feely. I thought there was a little too much of that in the show, in general.

MARINA SIRTIS

If you go back to "Encounter at Farpoint," where I was dressed in the cosmic cheerleader outfit with the ugliest go-go boots ever designed, I was about twenty pounds heavier. Imagine a potato with matchsticks sticking out of it, and that was my shape. After the first episode, they decided the outfit didn't suit Troi's charac-ter, because she was cerebral and kind of elegant. They decided they would design something more flattering, so they came out with the ugly gray spacesuit, and they put a belt in a lighter-colored fabric exactly where my fat was.

Unfortunately, what happens if the girls have cleavage, they cannot have a brain because the two don't go together. So when I got the gray spacesuit and got cleav-age, she lost her brain matter. That was a shame, because originally Troi was not supposed to be the chick on the show. Gene [Roddenberry] said she was intended to be the brain on the show, which you would never know from watching it. She was supposed to have equal the intelligence of Spock.

DENISE CROSBY

We were the weird stepchild of Paramount Studios. I used to steal food from the set of *Cheers* and bring it over to the set of *TNG* during the first season. We were working these twelve-hour days. *Cheers* was rocking at that time. They had all the good stuff—we had the crap leftovers.

MARINA SIRTIS

I lost weight over the years, and in the second season they made me the maroon outfit. How much cleavage I showed depended on which one I wore, since they were all cut differently and some were lower than others. And then we got that green dress, the one you wanted to straighten out the neckline on all the time. I wasn't crazy about the dress, because you had to take the whole thing off to go to the bathroom. But the underwear was fabulous.

I had to wear a corset like a merry widow, and then we had what I like to call the industrial-strength, Starfleet-regulation brassiere. This became the standard uniform for every woman on *Star Trek*, and that's because the women saw me as me and then they saw me as Troi, and they went, "I want a bra like that," because it adds inches where there really are none. It is kind of depressing at the end of the day when you take it off.

Meanwhile, actress/choreographer Gates McFadden beat out sci-fi favorite Jenny Agutter (*Walkabout, Logan's Run, An American Werewolf in London*) for the role of Dr. Beverly Crusher, the starship's newest chief medical officer.

DAVID GERROLD

One day during lunch I kept talking about Beverly Crusher, who was the ship's schoolteacher, and in the middle of this I said, "We don't have a ship's doctor yet, why don't we have Beverly Crusher be the ship's doctor?" I wish I'd recorded the conversation, because everybody said, "Nah, that doesn't work," and then they started discussing it.

Eddie Milkis said, "You know, that saves us a character. If Beverly Crusher is the ship's doctor, then we don't have to create a ship's doctor." Then Bob Justman said, "No, that makes it harder for the captain to have this relationship with Beverly Crusher that we want to have. On the other hand, the fact that it's harder to have this relationship puts more tension . . . You know, Gene, that's not a bad idea." And then Gene started discussing it. By lunch, Beverly Crusher was the ship's doctor.

GATES MCFADDEN (actress, "Dr. Beverly Crusher")

It is an ensemble show, and I liked the other people who were cast. I felt the producers really wanted me to be a part of it, and it was nice to be wanted. I was also impressed with Gene Roddenberry. There were some philosophical points of view presented and that was always going to be a part of it. It wasn't just another evening soap.

Comedy is my favorite thing to do, and I auditioned for the part thinking it was a very funny part because they gave me "The Naked Now," and I thought she was going to be a hilarious character, and I ended up with the straightest and most serious character of all.

In the case of the divisive role of precocious teen genius Wesley Crusher (son of Beverly), *Stand by Me's* Wil Wheaton was the front runner with J. D. Roth the runner-up. The character was *not* a popular one, a point driven home by audience frustration that Wesley managed to save the ship more than anyone. Wheaton's early enthusiasm for the role waned over the years, given how the character developed . . . or didn't, as the case may be.

WIL WHEATON (actor, "Wesley Crusher")

I was a Trekkie. Not in the sense I could say what in episode thirty-three, in the fourth hour, in the second minute, Spock's fourth line was, though. I loved the show, but I never sat there and thought that someday I could be on it. They called me and said they'd like to see me for *Star Trek*. It was sort of like the kid who always wanted to be president and is in the White House and gets to meet the president. I justified my purchases of any *Star Trek* items as a business expense, researching my character. Thank you very much . . . write that off.

SUSAN SACKETT

They wanted to have a young person, and that ended up being Wesley Crusher, who was originally Leslie Crusher. She was going to be a girl, and then they thought she'd just come off as dumb, so they changed it to a boy.

WIL WHEATON

Wesley was a teenager with the intellect of an adult, and it's not his fault. He doesn't try to prevent his intellect from showing. A lot of the time he comes across as a smart-ass. He doesn't mean it. The viewers could feel for Wesley because he comes onto a Galaxy Class *Enterprise* with all this incredible stuff, and you walk onto this ship and go "Wow!" When people came on the set I'm, like, let me show you my ship, like I'm showing off a new car.

LINDA PARK (actress, "Hoshi Sato," *Star Trek: Enterprise*)

I was in junior high school when I watched *The Next Generation* and I had a crush on him.

WIL WHEATON

When I was still working on *Star Trek*, we had finished the season, and we were on hiatus when I was cast by Milos Forman to be in his film *Valmont*. The shooting schedule for that movie would have run over into the first week of production on *Next Generation,* which wasn't going to be a problem because, for whatever reason, we were shooting that season out of order and we were shooting the second episode first.

One of the producers told my agent that they could not write me out of that episode because it was a Wesley-focused episode, and I couldn't go work for Milos Forman in Paris. He called my house and told me, "It's a Wesley episode, and I'm writing a scene with you and Gates that's going to move your mother-son relationship forward, and it's really important to the series," and he just lied to me.

TRACY TORMÉ

There was definitely a sense that they were probably going to not stick with Wil. The fans were always sniping about the Wesley character. They just didn't like it. I even had a show where there's some unbelievable scientific problem and they go to him and people criticized me for it. Why would they go to a kid? It *is* kind of ridiculous.

WIL WHEATON

I was really upset, because I was excited to have the opportunity to work with this amazing director in an amazing movie and in an amazing role that I thought really would have solidified my credentials as a young actor. I was really disappointed. A few days before we began production on that season of *Next Generation,* this producer wrote me out of the script entirely, and it was appalling to me. The message was very clear—we own you—and it was a move to sabotage my career.

Years later, Marina Sirtis told me that they knew that if I had done this film, I would have been a movie star, and it would have been harder for them to deal with me. I felt so betrayed by that, and I was, like, "Fuck you guys, I am now doing anything I can to get off this show. Because I can't believe you would treat another person like that." That led me to wanting to leave *Next Generation.*

DAVID MCDONNELL (editor, *Starlog* magazine)

I don't believe the producers anticipated the hostility poor Wil Wheaton would face because they wrote his character so he'd be perceived as the "Wesley saves the ship" teen annoyance.

Before *Next Generation*'s premiere, publicists assured me that two of the ensemble would certainly be the show's breakout characters: Captain Jean-Luc Picard, which turned out to be, of course, correct, and Lieutenant Tasha Yar, which didn't, and Denise Crosby, for her own reasons, soon exited the program. It was Picard, Data—that android Pinocchio archetype imported from Gene Roddenberry's long-ago TV movie pilot *The Questor Tapes*—and Worf—who brought in all the fascination with that alien warrior race—that made *Next Generation* a real hit with *Trek* fans and more mainstream audiences. Stories that primarily involved them—and gave a lesser focus to Riker, LaForge, Deanna Troi, and the Crushers—seemed to work better

WIL WHEATON

When I finally did leave *Next Generation* when I was eighteen, for the first time in my life I didn't have to be going to the set every morning at six and I didn't have to wear a haircut I didn't want and I could have a life of my own. And I really *wanted* to live a life of my own. I had this opportunity to go and work for a computer company, so I did, and then I sort of missed acting and came back after a couple of years. I'm, like, "OK, I'm ready, let's go," and the entertainment industry is, like, "I'm sorry, who are you?"

MARC SCOTT ZICREE (author, *The Twilight Zone Companion*)

Wesley was fifteen and going out and playing ball with blond aliens and falling in the bushes—they were writing him like he was five years old. He should be looking to get laid instead of playing ball. Then he falls in love with that girl and they share chocolate mousse—give me a break.

WIL WHEATON

My favorite episode of *Next Generation* is "Tapestry" and it's a really great example of how everything that happens in our lives, even the shitty things, help shape us into the people we are. There's a really good chance that I never would have found out that I actually needed to be a writer if I had stayed on *Star Trek*. I would have cashed all the checks, and who knows what would have happened? I probably wouldn't be a fully formed human being, because I never would have learned what it means to be a fully functioning adult.

> Although not a member of the weekly cast, equally important was the casting of John de Lancie as Q, the devilish, omnipotent prankster who provided a recurring foil for Picard throughout *TNG*'s run, bookending the series with appearances in both the premiere and finale, "Encounter at Farpoint" and "All Good Things."

RICK BERMAN

[Gene's attorney] Leonard Maizlish had seen an actor named John de Lancie do something, and everybody said we don't want his creative input—but he was completely right. De Lancie came in for the pilot to play the role of Q and he was just perfect; he's a wonderful actor.

JOHN DE LANCIE (actor, "Q")

Gene Roddenberry said I had no idea what I was getting into. I say those words with a sense of pride and a bit of glee in the same way he said them to me, but of course, I had no idea at the time. I was not a *Star Trek* fan. It was never my cup of tea when it comes to SF. I've always enjoyed a darker, much more bleak kind of SF. I'm not a great one for cautionary tales and things like that, but the irony is that as a kid, I always wanted to be involved in SF, but it took me a couple of years to realize I *am* involved in SF, it's just that it's so different than what I had anticipated.

LES LANDAU (director, *Star Trek: The Next Generation*)

He took a role, which, granted, was an exceptional part, and made more of it than was on the page. He made himself a recurring character. He's a dynamic personality.

MELINDA SNODGRASS

I always think of him as Loki. He's chaos. Maurice Hurley always thought Q was here to teach us a lesson, to guide and instruct us. I can understand that to some extent, but I really see him as a mischief maker. He really just wants to foul Picard's head.

> The *Next Generation* ensemble would not have been complete without the casting of Michael Dorn. Originally conceived as a recurring role, Dorn's Klingon character, Worf, in fact proved so popular that not only did he join the weekly ensemble as a series regular, but his tour of duty was extended to include *Deep Space Nine* following the end of *The Next Generation*. The irony of the situation is the fact that initially Roddenberry was completely against the idea of including the Klingons at all.

DAVID GERROLD

Early on I suggested a Klingon first officer.

ROBERT H. JUSTMAN

We would portray the character as loyal to the Federation, but subject to some suspicion by certain of the other crew members. If the Klingon were part human, he—or she—might suffer emotionally because of this unfair prejudice. Perhaps the audience might also wonder if there is, in fact, something there that doesn't quite add up. This character might possibly have afforded us the air of "mystery" which always was part and parcel of Mr. Spock.

DAVID GERROLD

Gene was adamantly against this. He said, "Nope, I don't want to do anything with Klingons," so I dropped the idea.

DOROTHY FONTANA (associate producer, *Star Trek: The Next Generation*)

Roddenberry just felt that Klingons were totally black hats, the development coming from the way they were treated in the movies. He didn't like that, but then suddenly there was a Klingon on the bridge.

DAVID GERROLD

Gene vetoed it for four months until Dorothy said that we need someone to take command when the saucer separates, so let's have a woman commander, and Gene said, "No, let's have a Klingon." He'd rather have a Klingon than show a woman in a position of power. Gene had been badly burned by women. He had a bitter divorce and she wanted half the money of *Star Trek: The Next Generation*. He tends to generalize. If most of the women you meet are mean to you, you will get a feeling that all women are mean, even though it's not true. Maybe you just attract mean women.

RICK BERMAN

Originally Michael Dorn wasn't even guaranteed all episodes in the first season, and I feel that Michael as an actor and the character of Worf grew more than any other one of our characters or actors. It's a shoe-in character; what's more delightful than a Klingon on board the *Enterprise*?

MICHAEL DORN (actor, "Worf")

I used my voice a lot. It got a lot deeper and became deeper and deeper as the shows went on. It's funny, when I got the job and before I started filming, I went up to Gene and I said, "What do you want from this character? I mean, what do you envision? Who is he?" He said one of the smartest things you can say to an actor: "Forget everything that you've seen or heard or read about Klingons and just make it your own." I said, "Great. That's like nirvana, to be able to just go ahead and build a character from the ground up."

RICK BERMAN

There was an actor named James Avery who I thought would be great for the role, but Gene wanted the Klingon to be black and very young. Of all the good black actors, the youngest one and the best of the young ones was Michael Dorn, who got that role.

MAURICE HURLEY (coexecutive producer, *Star Trek: The Next Generation*)

Worf is the warrior. He's easy to write for. He deals with what the warrior has to deal with, which is not the external enemy, but the enemy inside.

JERI TAYLOR (executive producer, *Star Trek: The Next Generation*)

Worf is the person to whom you can give some prejudices and attitudes and mis-understandings, because he comes from a culture that is so different. Every series needs that, and on *TNG* Worf was that person.

MICHAEL DORN

Klingons weren't exactly evil as much as they were totally aggressive. I approached the role initially with that attitude. They likened it to after World War II and how the Japanese and the Americans worked so closely together after being bitter enemies.

THOMAS DOHERTY

The Klingons are very Japanese, and their culture is Bushido Japan, a warrior culture. The Klingons are incorporated into *TNG* with Worf. One of my friends is the best historian of the Pacific war, a guy named Richard Frank. He was telling me about this book about the events leading up to 1941. There's a scene where the Japanese have just taken over Singapore and there's a print of *Gone with the Wind,* this American movie, they're going to show to the general staff as a lark.

They start showing the film and you can hear this murmur in the audience. "Fuck, we just declared war on these people. They can make this movie. It's so far above anything that can happen in Japan; the expense, the special effects, the orchestration of thousands of people." There was a silence in the projection room after the first act with all these Japanese officers when it's dawning on them what they're up against. We were saying, if we had only released *Gone with the Wind* in 1940 in Japan, World War II could have been avoided.

MICHAEL DORN

What they did when they hired us is they hired eight really creative and strong-willed people. A lot of times you want to go "Why isn't it like this, why don't you do that?" but that's par for the course. We do the work and do it the best we can, and along with the writing, I think our performances made the series successful. Working with these actors has been just a catharsis for me. I've taken something from each actor, something I admire and that's really cool, and you really sort of can't help meld into one.

LARRY CARROLL (coproducer, *Star Trek: The Next Generation*)

The actors were quite admirable. We had the highest regard for them being consummate professionals, because quite often they got pages at eight thirty at night with a five thirty A.M. call, and they got to the set and knew their lines and were ready to go. We tried to avoid that, but it was often unavoidable.

JONATHAN FRAKES

One of the reasons this show didn't take the dive we all feared it would in the back of our minds, in comparison to the old show, is because the characters were so well thought out ahead of time. I don't know how they cast it so well. We still went out to dinner after fourteen-hour days. They hired actors who like to act instead of hiring movie stars or models.

MARINA SIRTIS

Brent is such a superb actor. We were on the floor. He is so funny.

JONATHAN FRAKES

Our show was abnormal, in the camaraderie level. Especially after a few seasons, we would work all week and then we'd go down to a bar on the Paramount lot. We'd get together after work and have a drink or we'd get together on Saturdays and have dinner together. It was ridiculous. Our wives thought we were insane.

MARINA SIRTIS

We always had fun. All the directors said they've never worked on such a fun set. It's incredible to have actors get along so well. It's so cliché, but we were all so happy to be there. We point our phasers and nothing happens. When you see it, this magic blue light comes out. They tried to shove some props at me, but I said, "I'm the mental character. I don't use all that stuff." I don't like using it, because if you can drop it or break it, I will drop it or break it.

I'm not adept at the shaking, either. I thought everybody shook better than me. I can't take it seriously. Maybe it's because I'm British. The Americans shake and do it really well, and I'm on the floor doubled up with laughter. If my drama teachers could see me, they would die.

ELIZABETH DENNEHY
(actress, "The Best of Both Worlds")

When the ship gets hit, they give you a cue, "one-two-three," and you have to move and throw yourself. I felt like I was doing a silent movie. It was so funny; it was hard to keep a straight face. The cast has it calibrated. They ask, "How do you want this, a three?" They all know the difference between what a three and a six and a nine is. Then they have to decide "Do we go left-right-left or right-left-right? It's one of those situations where you think, "This is my career and I'm playing cowboys and indians."

DENISE CROSBY

We all pretty much gelled right off the bat, except Patrick. He was still very, very serious. He was not quite getting the sense of humor that the whole rest of the gang sort of have, especially Jonathan.

PATRICK STEWART

Early on, my fellow actors would frequently make each other laugh on the set, and I couldn't understand it. I would get rather stern in my response, and Jonathan would say, "Patrick, we're just having fun." I responded, "We are here to work. We are *not* here to have fun." Can you *believe* what a pompous ass I was?

JONATHAN FRAKES

He's the real Number One. Patrick became silly, which is his great Americanization. There are some shows where you need levity. When the show is light, you play it in the scenes. But I remember how silly we had to be when Denise's character got killed off. Patrick ran across the field singing "the hills are alive . . ." That's an episode where we were all crying as our characters and ourselves. I was the morale officer. Sometimes I'm guilty of being an asshole on the set, and then I'd see someone else misbehaving when I'm directing, and I say, "Oy, Frakes, you've dug your own grave."

DOUG DREXLER (special makeup effects artist, *Star Trek: The Next Generation*)

Patrick couldn't help it! Look who he was on stage with. First of all, Frakes is a maniac. He's totally funny, a jokester, a prankster. Every rehearsal is silly. They make up their own dialogue. But then, when they had to do the line, it was right there. Michael Dorn was funny as hell, Brent Spiner was a nut. They used to sing songs on the bridge and stuff. There was no way Patrick was going to stay that guy for very long. He looks back on it now and says, "They taught me how to enjoy myself."

PATRICK STEWART

I just wanted to do the best job I could, but oh no, no, no. With them, it was always party time. And, you know what? I liked it.

JONATHAN FRAKES

It was such a dysfunctional, wonderful family, both in front of and behind the camera, on the show. By the time I directed on the third season, we'd all been together for three years. It was for ten months a year, so everyone knew each other and, generally, really loved each other. The cast was wonderful and hysterically funny and I was given a big bullhorn by the sound department. It was a very happy time. They all took the piss out of each other, and people were refusing to do what I asked. Everybody behaved exactly the way you'd want them to.

DOUG DREXLER

The *Next Generation* cast was the most fun of all of them. I had never had so much fun on a soundstage before. They all really did like each other. You hear about the originals liking each other, and then find out a lot of them *don't* like each other. These people adored each other.

JONATHAN FRAKES

I realized, as I directed more and more episodes, how difficult and insane we, as a cast, are to work with. We're like herding cats! Part of being prepared was a lot of this kind of mad freedom to rest between shots, rest up until somebody called "Action." Brent was the leader of the pack. The bridge was his biggest stage. He would sing and do impersonations. Michael Dorn and Patrick would perform professional wrestling, Gates would dance. It was just insanity. And when you yell "Action," then everybody shuts up and goes to work.

A MATTER OF HONOR

"IF YOU CAN'T TAKE A LITTLE BLOODY NOSE, MAYBE YOU
OUGHT TO GO BACK HOME AND CRAWL UNDER YOUR BED.
IT'S NOT SAFE OUT HERE. IT'S WONDROUS, WITH TREASURES TO
SATIATE DESIRES, BOTH SUBTLE AND GROSS.
BUT IT'S *NOT* FOR THE TIMID."

While the inspired casting of *The Next Generation* ensemble proved to be a form of alchemy with a group that exhibited not only incredible chemistry on-screen, but off-screen as well, the behind-the-scenes atmosphere on the show early on remained extremely tumultuous.

RICK BERMAN (executive producer, *Star Trek: The Next Generation*)

Any dramatic television show has a set of rules that you've got to follow. On the other hand, with *Star Trek* you've got two sets of rules. A set of rules dealing with physics and astrophysics and astronomy that we follow or try to follow as accurately as we can, and then you've got a set of rules that have to do with *Star Trek*, which are made-up rules. They're not real.

There's no such thing as a dilithium crystal or people transporting. There's no such thing as warp drive and Romulans and Ferengi and Klingons. These things don't exist, and as a result, it's fantasy, but these established rules have to be followed. So you've got the rules of science and the rules of *Star Trek*. Writers have to be willing and able to follow both sets of rules, and it's difficult.

HANS BEIMLER (coproducer, *Star Trek: The Next Generation*)

On *Next Generation,* my argument with Gene Roddenberry was that he felt we were going to solve too many of our problems. Human characteristics like greed and that kind of thing were going to be gone. Captain Picard doesn't have any deep, dark secrets or fears. I always said to Gene Roddenberry that Shakespeare works three hundred years later because the things that motivated human beings then, still motivate us today. That's still going to be true in fifty, a hundred, or two hundred years.

JONATHAN FRAKES (actor, "William T. Riker")

They were deathly afraid of conflict and that's the heart of good drama.

MICHAEL DORN (actor, "Worf")

Worf did bring the conflict; everything isn't wonderful. It isn't so together and so cool, and he loves everyone and everyone loves him. It kind of snuck up on the producers, too. They expected Worf to be this enigma, and he turned out to surprise them where they found there was a whole wealth of stories there about the guy. It's not the same old love story. If you look at it, they had a baby out of wedlock, she didn't tell him, he doesn't like her . . . he loves her, but they fight all the time, and now there's this kid. It's not the usual thing.

RICK BERMAN

Television has grown up a lot. The cynical element of television. Our show was a lot more believable than the old show, and that's due in large part to the creator of the old show, too, because it was Roddenberry who was very vehement when we created *The Next Generation* that it had to be believable. That it would not deal with swords and sorcerers or be melodramatic. The old *Star Trek* had people who wore togas standing under arches, and our *Star Trek* is much more contemporary and believable.

DAVID LIVINGSTON (supervising producer, *Star Trek: The Next Generation*)

There're still cardboard rocks. The creative people on the show were so talented that they're able to make cardboard rocks that are still all fake into a reality. After all, as one of our coordinators said, the *Enterprise* is just plastic on a stick. The only time you are ever disappointed is when you know that you've had to cut the money and, in our minds, we knew that it could have been substantially better.

LARRY CARROLL (writer, *Star Trek: The Next Generation*)

We had what David [Carren] and I have come to call the "M" effect, named after the Fritz Lang film, *M*, where he did everything off camera with Peter Lorre.

People pitched these stories with these fantastic things we could never begin to produce, and it's simply because this show is so well produced and so well thought out that they don't miss those things and believe they're all part of *Star Trek*. And they don't realize how incredibly sophisticated, lean, and spare the storytelling is.

While Stages 8 and 9 provided the *Enterprise*'s standing sets, including the bridge, shuttle bay, sick bay, transporter room, and engineering, across the lot on Stage 16 was the infamous Planet Hell, a sprawling soundstage which would stand in for various planetscapes and alien civilizations. As a swing set, it would almost never be the same set twice, although the production team became adept at repurposing parts of sets for reuse to save money.

DAVID LIVINGSTON

I originally knew [production designer] Herman [Zimmerman] on a Catholic television network for about six months at Raleigh Studios. He was building sets for priests to come in and talk, and I was the production supervisor for this thing. I come to *Star Trek* a couple of months later, and he has three soundstages full of the most unbelievable sets you could imagine. So it was quite a jump for both of us.

He was incredibly creative and a master builder. How he could come up with designs on a little more than a weekly basis was extraordinary. Another gift was how he could recycle them. He would constantly use elements over to reuse sets. It would save an unbelievable amount of money. It saved time, too. The bones were there so you didn't have to knock it down and build it again. His other skill was to revamp sets and use them again, and nobody ever knew.

HERMAN ZIMMERMAN (production designer, *Star Trek: The Next Generation*)

The bridge was large. Perhaps larger than it needed to be, partly because Gene wanted the viewscreen to be very large. It's considerably more advanced-looking than the original *Enterprise* viewscreen, and it lends a great deal of dramatic impact to the shows when you can see the face of Q, for instance, nine feet high in front of Picard, who is standing there a little more than half the height. The construction of such a large viewing screen demanded that the rest of the bridge be built to a scale which would be compatible with it.

The bridge, in fact, was the same width as the original *Enterprise* bridge, thirty-eight feet, but is two feet longer. The height of the ceiling, which was never visible in the original series, is fourteen feet. The descending ramps leading from the rear of the bridge to the helm lend the illusion of even greater height.

DAVID LIVINGSTON

Every year I asked [Paramount] for more money, and every year they gave us the extra money. They asked some questions, but basically we got cost of living and some extra bumps where we needed it. We analyzed previous years' production costs, and it was a true anomaly in terms of episodic productions. Usually, as a show gets more successful, they want to cut your pattern budget. If the show is doing fine, they usually cut your budget by a hundred grand. They never did that.

TOM MAZZA (executive vice president of current programming and strategic planning, Paramount Television)

At the time, it was one of the most expensive television shows—and not because of inflated salaries, but because it was an expense to produce all the special effects and go to planets to visit. We took up three feature-sized soundstages when we ran both *Deep Space Nine* and *Next Generation*. We were the largest tenant of the Paramount lot for many years.

DAVID LIVINGSTON

The challenge was always the money. That wasn't a problem with Paramount. They gave us the money we needed to do the project. I've been on lots of productions where we've been promised money, but we always have to end up cutting down the budget. The way the pilot was written, we didn't have to make substantive changes to make a budget. We didn't film a budget, we filmed a pilot. From a production manager standpoint, that's an anomaly. Paramount was trying a whole new template, being in first-run syndication, revising a famous brand, and they were smart enough to say, we're going to hire the right creative people and let them do what they see fit.

ROB BOWMAN (director, *Star Trek: The Next Generation*)

I spent about twenty days before my first episode walking through those sets, and on Saturdays and Sundays, eight hours a day, just sitting and looking.

MARVIN RUSH (director of photography,
Star Trek: The Next Generation)

Prep is a chance [for a director] to sit and think and ponder, and I have very little pondering time when I'm lighting a set [as DP]. It's mostly, make a quick decision and execute and then move on to the next quick decision and execute that. There's a certain amount of planning, but with the nature and speed of production there's an awful lot of just go with your first thought. With the director, he has seven days [of prep], and with the weekends, you ought to be able to come up with something and have a good plan.

DAVID LIVINGSTON

I loved location work. I wish we could have done it more, but people don't build twenty-fourth-century office buildings. You get cabin fever working on those stages. No architecture exists that worked for us. We had to create it on the stage and in matte shots. We found some, but that's tough. Basically, we were a three-stage production.

DENISE CROSBY (actress, "Tasha Yar")

Every planet in the galaxy is smoky, by the way. They would smoke up the place, but they were using some kind of oil-based chemical. After about seven episodes of being smoked by oil, we were coughing, getting bronchitis, and saying, "You gotta change it." They can't use it anymore, so all the actors that came afterward, we took a bullet for you.

WINRICH KOLBE
(director, *Star Trek: The Next Generation*)

The moment you go onto Planet Hell, it's a different ballgame. It never looks the same. We usually used 75 percent of the stage, including the pit. It takes an endless amount of time to light, and the moment you have to deal with smoke, there is a problem because the smoke has to match from one shot to another. Ultimately, it's a lot of waiting around.

DAVID LIVINGSTON

It's called Planet Hell because they're usually big swing sets that aren't permanent that you can turn around into something else. We had to work the bugs out. They're harder to light, because they're weirder. Usually planet shows deal with aliens and action, stunts and explosions. It's more complicated shooting, so the long hours can really get arduous on that set.

MAURICE HURLEY (coexecutive producer,
Star Trek: The Next Generation)

There's an enormous amount of production value in the shows. *Star Trek* never had problems with money. The problem was, we only had two soundstages, so what you wanted to do was give them time to build the sets, and there's never been a luxury of time for anyone to do that kind of work. They're always running behind, getting a script three or four days late, a week late, and they have to go to the soundstage and construct something very quickly.

The set construction on that show was astoundingly good. If Paramount had not put up the kind of front money that was necessary, the show would never have gone anywhere. It would have looked like it did before—cardboard rocks and funny old sets.

TOM MAZZA

We were constantly having to navigate launching the show with a big episode and then over the first few episodes do what we call a "ship show," and all of a sudden there's a disease spreading on ship and you notice for forty-four minutes we didn't go anywhere. Those are what we called "bottle episodes." You can get away with it sometimes to offset some of those higher costs [on the bigger episodes].

DAVID LIVINGSTON

We had to do ship shows for cost. We tried to balance that and save enough money to do the big shows like our season finales. To me, the two most important parts of spending the money on the shows are the opticals [visual effects] and construction. It does cost an awful lot of money to build those sets, but the goal was not to have the show take place on the ship all the time.

MARC SCOTT ZICREE (author, *The Twilight Zone Companion*)

When I was thirteen, I went on the set of the original series. It was the last episode they ever shot ["Turnabout Intruder"], and it was just wonderful. You got that same feeling on the new sets—except you felt a bit more like you're in a Ramada Inn, which is the way it looks, but it's still a thrill.

> While Gene Roddenberry's inviolate edict remained that there would be no conflict on-screen between the characters, behind-the-scenes remained an entirely different story. Throughout the first three seasons, *Star Trek*'s revolving door for writers became legendary, with a succession of staff writers and even showrunners jockeying for power on the show as Gene Roddenberry was sidelined from day-to-day showrunning duties due to age and health issues. The production team was able to realize the vision of the writers in turning their words into television, but getting shootable stories to the page proved the continuing challenge for the writing staff, which would include the additions of Sandy Fries (albeit, briefly) and the team of Hans Beimler and Richard Manning as coproducers.

GENE RODDENBERRY

I brought in people like Gerrold and Fontana because I knew them. But eventually we ended up with a new show and a new group. Some, like Bob Justman, had been with me since day one.

DAVID GERROLD (creative consultant, *Star Trek: The Next Generation*)

Gene is not a nice man. The fact of the matter is that you have to work with other people, and Gene's pattern is that he doesn't work well with anyone. If he can't be the boss, he doesn't want to work. He doesn't know how to bend. He never learned that trick, because he's always been the boss. He's never ever been an indian, he's always been the chief. You know what you get when you get people who have always been chiefs? You get spoiled brats.

DOUG DREXLER (special effects makeup artist, *Star Trek: The Next Generation*)

I know those first years were shaky. Both those guys were getting old. Gene wasn't in the best of health, they had the writers' strike going on, and, of course, the other thing is, I hear so much crap. I like David Gerrold, I like Dorothy Fontana, but they've always got something bitchy to say about those first two years. I find it disturbing and really kind of unprofessional—especially when Gene's not around anymore to defend himself. I think that they don't realize it, but they look bad. Not Gene. At least in my eyes.

ROBERT H. JUSTMAN (supervising producer, *Star Trek: The Next Generation*)

It wasn't a battleground littered with bodies of directors, not at all. The directors were no problem, but there were a lot of writers throwing up and carrying on and going crazy. Luckily, I didn't have much to do with that.

DOUG DREXLER

It comes with the territory. If you're involved with the show like Gene and Bob, they are the bosses. I've always known that. How come I know that and they don't? I've always treated my bosses like they're in charge. I never held anything against anyone, and if I ever criticize them in public on my Facebook page, I always say I understand how things are.

Things get changed for different reasons that are beyond my control. That's the way it is. It's going to go through a whole approval process. You're going to have different people looking at it. They're going to put in different comments. Sometimes people make comments off the cuff just passing through a room that completely change what's going on. If you're going to be so sensitive that it's going to haunt you for your entire life and you can't shut up about it, I'm sorry.

RICK BERMAN

It's so easy for the scripts not to be believable and to make them contrived and make them fantasy-like; to make the scripts hokey and illogical and muddled. The writing of the show at every level—the story level, the structural level, the dialogue, and the polishing—is so tricky. It's so difficult for writers to write dialogue that's not contemporary and also not sword and sorcery. Gene, in the first year, was incredibly particular to the point where the writers hated it.

HERB WRIGHT (producer, *Star Trek: The Next Generation*)

It was like Vietnam; you didn't want to get close to the other writers because you knew they wouldn't be there very long; Johnny Dawkins, Sandy Fries. They'd be given a script to write and direction and before they could learn what the show was about, they'd be torn apart by the staff and thrown to the wolves. Or Gene would just say "I hate them" and they'd be out the door. It was very strange. I remember Sandy Fries thought he was king of the mountain for five minutes. He went home and had champagne and a big party and Monday morning he walked in and he was fired.

HANS BEIMLER

Ricky [Manning] and I were brought in for the last twenty weeks of the first season, but everybody else was almost gone. There was a long list of people already fired. And every time we went in there for a meeting or something before we were hired—we went there a couple of times—there were always different people there. We actually started a wall of shame, a chart of all of the writers who were hired and fired. We had that in the bathroom. Our first office was Gene's old office on the fourth floor of the Hart Building. Ron Moore eventually took over that office.

At the time, we just sort of buried our heads and wrote scripts as much as we could. We liked it, but it *was* war. We didn't know any better. As far as we were concerned, this is the way it's supposed to be. We had a trial by fire where we had to write a script over a weekend. It was prepping on Tuesday, so we had to turn it in by Monday morning. Like I said, a real trial by fire. We used to lock ourselves in our office and open the transom door and throw scripts out. They'd come back marked up by somebody and we'd take those notes and do them as best we could and hand it back over the transom.

RICHARD ARNOLD (*Star Trek* archivist)

The craziness that went on with the hiring and firing of writers during the period leading up to and during the first season of the show—and to an extent the second season—can be boiled down to one thing: Gene was not about to have anyone tell him how to make *Star Trek*. Not writers, not producers, and certainly not studio executives. The second it became obvious to him that somebody was not going to work with him the way he wanted them to, they were out.

HANS BEIMLER

It was tough, because Gene was very tough to get a story by very often. Gene kept thinking that these were better people; his view of the world was, this was a better world and these were better people than we are. And that was a fundamental problem. You have a show where you travel at the speed of light, you can beam people off and on planets, and you've got the power to destroy planets. So the first part of the story is always trying to disable things. We had so many ionic storms, because it was the only way to get to the story. You had to break down the transporter and take away the *Enterprise* in some way or hobble it a little bit, so that they could be in trouble.

So you spend a lot of time with nonsense. It also belied the principle that we firmly believed, which is people are *not* going to get better. Many times Gene would blow up a script because he said, "We wouldn't do that, because we need to be better than that." And that was always a frustrating wall to run up on. It was a wall that sometimes wasn't always there, and that also made it difficult because it was inconsistent.

MAURICE HURLEY

When they called me, my first reaction was, "There must be another Maurice Hurley around here," because I do hard action. In my stuff, twelve people are killed by the end of the teaser. But I was intrigued by the request to talk to them, because *Star Trek* has such a legend attached to it. You can't think of many shows that have that kind of legendary quality, so I went over there and had a meeting with Gene. In that meeting, I told him that I didn't think I could do a science fiction show, because it wasn't something I was steeped in at all, but if they wanted to hire me on that basis, I'd take a chance and see how badly I could fail. As a writer, you have to have that kind of attitude, otherwise you don't have a chance to stretch.

No doubt one of the most appealing aspects of Maurice Hurley to Gene Roddenberry must have been his diverse range of experience prior to becoming a writer. After serving in the United States Air Force, Hurley did everything from being a rancher to selling shoes to producing documentaries and industrial films (something that endeared him to Rick Berman, a former documentarian himself) before making a decision to become a screenwriter at forty-two years old.

Hurley, who began his entertainment career as a story editor on *Miami Vice*, segued to supervising producer on *The Equalizer* before being hired as a co-executive producer on *Star Trek: The Next Generation*.

RICK BERMAN

Maury was there season one. He was one of the numerous writers who were hired and who went through the writing hell of a first-season show. Especially a show with a showrunner like Roddenberry, who was so demanding and was very locked in his ways. Gene was not an easy person to write for. And [Leonard] Maizlish was always sticking his nose into things. Bob Justman and I were in charge of everything having to do with production and postproduction and casting, and we were asked to give notes on scripts.

At one point, and I've never quite understood why, Gene came and said, "I'm going to divvy up the responsibilities of Justman and Berman." And he basically gave me all the good stuff. He gave me casting, he gave me postproduction, he gave me art direction and costumes and all of that. Basically, what he gave Justman was more of the financial and budgetary elements of the show. We both gave notes on scripts and things like that.

At the end of the first year, Hurley was one of the few survivors. Herb Wright had left. Dorothy had left. There were a lot of writers who left, and in the case of Dorothy and David Gerrold, there was a lot of animosity. In season two, Justman also left, and I was left running everything but the writing staff. Gene was still involved with the writing and Maury kind of became like Gene's right-hand man in the writing area. During that second season, Gene started stepping back and it was pretty much Maury and me.

LARRY BRODY (writer, *Star Trek: The Animated Series*)

Next Gen was an interesting experience. Roddenberry called and said he wanted me to be the writer/producer on the show. This was before the days of big writing staffs and half a dozen or more writer-producers per series, and Gene said very clearly that I'd be his guy. I went to Paramount to meet with him and encountered David Gerrold and a few others who already were working on the show and thought, "Hmm, more than one story editor for me to work with. Cool."

Gene sent me home from our meeting with the bible for the series, and I read it as soon as I could—and was floored because it was the same bible he'd had for *Genesis II* [a futuristic pilot he had produced years earlier for CBS], except that it had been translated into the *Star Trek* universe. Same characters, same personalities, problems, etc. The dude really was an expert at going back to his well. A few days later, Gene called me to say that he'd discussed my writer-producer gig with the studio and they wanted me to write an audition script, which is to say that he was going to give me a script assignment so that the execs could see how perfect I'd be for the new show. He complained bitterly about their lack of foresight and how insulted he felt by the way they weren't respecting his judgment.

After some heated discussions with my agent, I got back in touch with Gene and told him I wouldn't be able to write the script because I was taking another offer. During the next several weeks, I encountered several other writer/producers and was pretty surprised—and angry—to learn that Gene had also offered the producing gig to them with the same audition script proviso. That was pretty much the end of my relationship with Roddenberry for a while.

RICK BERMAN

Gene had to create a new television show from twenty-five years of mythology that had grown up over an old one, and he had to do it all out of whole cloth. You have to understand what it's like to write a stylized twenty-fourth-century script and know what words can be spoken and what words can't and how to go about all of the things we do to create this television show as opposed to if you were creating *MacGyver*.

He also had a lot of people who felt they knew more about *Star Trek* than he did, and he had to get pretty tough about it, and we had a group of writers that came in and didn't have the benefit of someone as strong as Mike Piller.

People had no idea what *Star Trek: The Next Generation* was going to be about. Gene felt the obsessive necessity to put his own imprint on everything to get the show going, and I applaud him for that. By the time I was sort of in control of the series, in the second year, Gene had pretty much cemented his idea of what the show was going to be about and it was my job to continue, to keep it going and not to formulate it, because he had done that.

GENE RODDENBERRY

When they say on a show "created by" anyone, like "created by Gene Roddenberry," that is not true. I laid out a pathway, and then the only thing I will take credit for is I surrounded myself with very bright people who came up with all those wonderful things. And then you can appear very smart.

TRACY TORMÉ

There were various people who, for brief periods of time, were being thought about by the people at the very top as potential showrunners and they soured on them.

The word would get out, it's not going to be so-and-so, not going to be Lewin, and they seemed to settle on Maury. I honestly remember very clearly that he was considered the farthest thing they wanted for a while. The running joke was he can't get a script done. But maybe he was the one that Berman thought he could work the best with, out of all possibilities. I think Berman made a very calculated decision that this was the person he would have the least amount of problems working with.

MAURICE HURLEY

Star Trek is not like any other show, because it is *one* unique vision, and if you agree with Gene Roddenberry's vision for the future, you should be locked up somewhere. It's wacky doodle, but it's *his* wacky doodle. If you can't deal with that, you can't do the show. There are rules on top of rules on top of rules.

RICK BERMAN

Hurley was the head writer, and I was in charge of everything else. Gene, for some reason, put me in a position slightly over Maury, although we looked at each other as pretty much equals. And we got along. He was a very strange guy. He was a golfer and he had done a lot of television writing. He was an unusual character. He didn't suffer fools gladly. He found Roddenberry a pain in the neck most of the time, but he knew how to deal with Gene so that Gene was not unhappy with him.

The thing I remember that stands out more than anything else is our walks. He would call me up and he'd say, "Meet you outside," because we were in buildings right across the street. I would go outside and we would walk for an hour around the lot talking about a story and trying to break through problems with the story that somebody had presented to him or something he or I had thought of. We did a lot of our talking about story problems while walking around the lot. I have very fond memories of doing that. But by the end of the second season, he pretty much had had it.

TRACY TORMÉ

Rick is a very smart and savvy guy, and I think Rick always saw that someday he would be running the show, and what's the best path to get there. And Hurley was the least worst of all the alternatives.

RICK BERMAN

The people who survived on the show are the people who were comfortable with the concept of what it's all about. First season there were a group of writers who had friction with Gene, but it was not personal. It was over how people wrote the show. There were some personality conflicts, but no more than there are on most television series. It was all blown a little more out of proportion than I thought it deserved to be.

HANNAH LOUISE SHEARER (executive story editor, *Star Trek: The Next Generation*)

I was always a fan, though not a Trekkie. My feeling is that the great success of the show was in creating the same feeling with different people. They had so much to overcome. Thematically, it was uneven, as is any new show.

ROBERT LEWIN (producer, *Star Trek: The Next Generation*)

It all came out of the blue. I got the call, and Gene asked me if I knew much about *Star Trek*, and I said no. He asked me if I was interested in it, and I said, "Yes, it's a new thing. Let me think about it. I'm interested in it, but I can't explain why." I went home and the next morning I called him. I said, "I'm just flooding with ideas," so he said he was very anxious to hear them. I went back and we talked for a long time about what my concepts for the future were and that kind of thing. The next thing I know, I got an offer.

JIM LEWIN (son of Robert Lewin)

I was very proud of him, because he hadn't done anything that big in a while, and that was a pretty high-profile show. Also, I was a stoner in my twenties, so me and my friends would sit around and watch *Star Trek* and it was kind of fun. I think he was hired to help with the character development and the dramatic underlying stuff. My dad went to Yale and was a classic drama writer, so he was surrounded by these Trekkie sci-fi buffs. He was brought in to be the old-school guy who made sure the storylines and the character development were interesting enough to keep people interested in the show.

But he was constantly frustrated that the storylines got convoluted and those elements that he was there to do were always challenged. He felt he wasn't really able to do that, because there were too many cooks in the kitchen, and there were too many interests that were pushing scripts to go one way or the other for different reasons, so the stories got watered down.

It was like, let's get one of these old writers from the golden age of Hollywood to make sure we've got some dramatic development here. And he was also there to do that for the overall arcing stories going through the series, like Picard and Crusher, which was something that was going to play out over a year or two. He was there to make sure that from episode to episode that it had the serial feel. There were these two different directions going already, there was some really high-quality stuff that was getting better and better, and there was also this push to do the lowest common denominator, which I think resulted in *Survivor,* and the other resulted in *Breaking Bad.*

TRACY TORMÉ

I was set to do a [new] *Twilight Zone* with Paramount, and I always wanted to do a *Twilight Zone. Twilight Zone, The Outer Limits, Star Trek,* and *The Prisoner* were my big four. I met with them and I picked an old episode that I was going to remake, and then it got canceled. Very shortly after that, they approached me and said they're bringing *Star Trek* back and they wanted to send me a bible. I read the bible closely and I thought there were a lot of interesting things in it, so I went in for a meeting with Bob Lewin and he was such a gentleman. He was a great guy, so easy to talk to, and we just hit it off. He liked me right off the bat, and I had gone in with a story about addiction inside the Federation ["The Dream Pool"]. I pitched it to Lewin, and he liked it, and he asked if I would be willing to come back and tell this to Gene, and I said sure.

So a few weeks later, I was in Santa Barbara with my fiancée when word came out, Roddenberry is in town in Los Angeles and he would like to meet with you today. Can you just drive in and meet with him? I literally left my fiancée behind and jumped in my car, drove back down to L.A., and walked in and there was Gene. I remember thinking how tall he was. He had kind of an intimidating air about him. The very first thing I remember him saying to me was, "So, what exactly is it that you want to do with *my Star Trek?*"

LARRY BRODY

Gene called my agent and said he was in a bind and needed a quick script from me, one that could be written and ready to produce before an impending writers' strike. He was stockpiling scripts in case we were out for a while. I was worried about stockpiling enough money to keep paying my new, high mortgage with, so I agreed to the "quick draft" thing.

I went in to see Gene, and together we worked out an idea. I was surprised by how much older he looked than he had the last time I'd seen him, but we concentrated on the task at hand. I wrote the outline in a couple of days, but instead of hearing directly from Roddenberry about it, I was called by Maurice Hurley. He called me in to meet about the story to get his notes about going to script. While I was there, Roddenberry's office buzzed Hurley and asked him to send me over to see Gene when Hurley and I were through.

When I went to Gene's office, I was surprised by how vague his conversation was. His energy was gone and he had trouble focusing on things. He was holding my outline, but it became clear that he hadn't read it and, in fact, had no idea what the premise was, even though we'd worked it out together. For about ten minutes he talked to me about the title and about how meaningful it was because it was all about being a dreamer and wasn't I, Larry Brody, quite a dreamer? Weren't all writers? The meeting was cut short. I don't remember why. It turned out to be the last time I saw or talked to Gene.

TRACY TORMÉ

I was, like, "Oh geez, I better not misstep here and say the wrong words." So I pitched my addiction show, and Gene said, "I really don't want to open up that can of worms of addiction, but I like the way you think, and maybe if we have an opening somewhere and the right thing comes along, would you be interested in doing a freelance for us?" I said if the right thing happens I'd be interested, because that's all I was intending to do in the first place.

LARRY BRODY

I went home and wrote the script and then turned it in. I didn't hear anything further about it until a few weeks later, when the writers' strike everyone had dreaded was well under way. That's when I received a copy of a final draft, revised by Maury Hurley . . . and with the title changed. It was pretty damn clear that something was up. That became even clearer when Bob Justman, the line producer of the show and a guy who was closer to Gene than anyone, sent me some memos he'd written about the script, detailing what he thought its strengths were. Along with the info that it was being shelved for reasons he couldn't give.

JIM LEWIN

We were kids growing up in the 70s that kind of partied too much and spun out. We actually did okay until my sister finally got pretty bad a few years ago and OD'd, but before that even happened, I went back and watched the *Next Generation* episode "Symbiosis." That episode has a lot to do with my dad struggling to help his kids *not* be addicts. That's the emotional underlying content of the show, because I recognized it when I saw it. I was, like, "This is my dad not knowing how to help me and my sister." That's what that show is about.

TRACY TORMÉ

That might be why Bob liked my addiction script. My addiction show was kind of like the cocaine allegory show that sweeps through the Federation.

JIM LEWIN

By now, most of us have had to face the frustration of having an addict in the family and not being able to help and watching them drive off a cliff or something. You try to help with tough love and you try to help with nurturing, but there's just no way to help someone who is not going to help themselves, and that is what that episode is about.

In some ways, I missed a lot of these details at the time because I was partying too much. Maybe to try to not help them get their drugs, you're not going to help him fix his car to go to the drug dealer's house. I told my sister about it, and I said, "You have to watch this episode, it's about us. This is Dad trying to process his helpless feelings and the generation of parents who didn't know how to save their children who had drug problems." It still makes me cry when I think about it.

TRACY TORMÉ

Robert Lewin was the guy who shepherded me the whole time. They had a script "Love Beyond Time and Space" and they liked the idea, but the writer [Lan O'Kun] was not really getting it, so they pretty much left me alone to go off and write "Haven" for them. They weren't sure whether it was a comedy or a straightforward show, and they really didn't know what they wanted, but they showed it to me and said that I had carte blanche. I focused on turning it into more of a comedy. I knew they were looking for something to do with Majel [Roddenberry], so I created the Lwaxana Troi character for Majel and sort of inserted her into the bare bones of the story that they were working on.

MARINA SIRTIS (actress, "Deanna Troi")

It was very funny—when I read the script, I said to Gene Roddenberry, how did you know all this about me, because this all happened to me in real life? An arranged marriage situation. That was the background of the story, and being Greek, my parents tried to do that to me once. The relationship between me and Majel was so similar toward the feelings I had toward my own mother. It was wonderful to do. There was a feeling about that episode where you could hear a pin drop on set.

JOHN D.F. BLACK (story editor, Star Trek)

I really didn't go pitch Gene Roddenberry. He called me and told me they were going to do my "Naked Time" again, and there wasn't a damn thing I could do about it, so what else could I say. He was right, they owned the rights to my story. Dorothy rewrote it, and it was a bizarre circumstance all the way around.

PAUL LYNCH (director, Star Trek: The Next Generation)

We had to do "Naked Now" in six days, because there was a pending Director's Guild strike. I lived on the lot, because we were shooting eighteen-hour days to make the six days before the possible strike. It was, like, for six days I was in space. I arrived in the morning, in blackness, and I left at night to go to a little room, so it seemed like I never left the spaceship—but it was a nice place to be.

DAVID GERROLD

We were in a story meeting with John D.F. Black, Bob Justman, and Eddie Milkis. We're sitting around and John D.F. Black is pitching "Justice." His story is very simple. The computer on this planet periodically says, "This place for this amount of time . . . if you are caught committing a crime, no matter what it is, you will get blown away." That's all the story was. We said, "Wow, that's great." We realized that the point of the story is that this justice system works. If we come here and try to judge that this justice system *doesn't* work, we're putting our justice system on trial. Gene said, "That's really got to be it. The climax of the story has got to be this courtroom thing where our people and our concept of justice is on trial, not theirs, because theirs is a peaceful planet."

Black brought in a first-draft outline on that, which did not work. He did not address the core issue of the story, and it was a very weak outline. We all did memos about it, and Gene's memo addressed what he really felt was necessary for the story, and I felt that Gene had really hit it in that memo. What happened is that Gene and John D.F. Black got into a disagreement. John's theory was that if you were a witness to a crime, if the bus driver was speeding and you were a passenger on the bus, then you got wasted, too, for not stopping the crime. Gene said, "No, I don't want to do that mayhem. Just one crime." What we eventually saw in the episode was Wesley's accidental crime of falling on the flowers, and he was sentenced to death. It was really stupid, because we didn't get to see a real crime.

When we saw the first-draft script, somebody said, "There's no excitement here. It's a cop-out ending. Nothing is at stake." That one totally got rewritten and John D.F. Black got totally cut off, because he wanted all the mayhem and Gene didn't want it. I sided with Gene on it, that the mayhem wasn't the issue. The issue was the justice issue. John got cut off because of that disagreement. That was the core of it, because they went back and forth on it for the bulk of the meeting. John D.F. Black was the story editor on the original *Star Trek* for the first thirteen weeks. Gene said, "Well, John just couldn't handle *Star Trek* and we had to let him go."

MARY BLACK (assistant to John D.F. Black)

To this day, we don't know what the hell happened there. John was called to come in. Bygones be bygones. Fine. It's a gig. Terrific. And he had experience with Gene, and he pitched a story, which they bought, and from then on out it was a kind of ambiguous direction from the office and just completely unpleasant. John was completely bewildered. Even sweet-natured Bob Justman gave a comment that had nothing to do with critique or guidance and just said "your script sucks," which is not a critique you know what to do with.

DAVID GERROLD

What John says about the thirteen episodes [of the original *Star Trek* that he worked on] is that Gene Roddenberry could not keep his hands off the scripts and that's why he left. I feel it was terribly unfair to cut off John D.F. Black. What we should have done was restructure the outline for what we wanted, and then handed it to him to write, because we knew this was an important *Star Trek* writer, and he was a friend of Gene's, and you don't treat him that way. This was one of the first signs we saw of Gene starting to lose friends from the show.

MAURICE HURLEY

When *Star Trek* is hitting its stride and doing what it's supposed to do, it can be very provocative, but because it's reaching so high and trying to live up to its own expectations, it fails more than most shows. Mediocrity in *Star Trek* is a failure. It's a tough show and a bitch to write.

TRACY TORMÉ

I did one, and they came back and asked if I would do a second one. I'd been interested from the [series] bible about the holodeck and I realized they hadn't really done anything yet with that. That's where "The Big Goodbye" came from. I'm a huge Raymond Chandler fan, and I thought it would really be fun to do a classic film noir and, of course, "The Big Goodbye" is a combination of *The Big Sleep* and *The Long Goodbye*. There's also a lot of Dashiell Hammett's *The Maltese Falcon* in the story as well. It was a very magical script for me. It was very easy to write; it went through very few rewrites and changes and was not messed with by anybody. They left it alone.

THOMAS DOHERTY (professor of American Studies, Brandeis University)

What puts so interesting a spin on the holodeck episodes is the metaphysical content. The personalities inhabiting the imaginative universe are so lifelike that they raise a question of mortality and reality: the computer-generated models may or may not be alive. When Picard and Number One left their respective holodeck worlds and abandoned their fictional companions to an uncertain existential fate, the effect was quite poignant, a rarity in any television drama.

BRANNON BRAGA (coproducer, *Star Trek: The Next Generation*)

The holodeck is one of the most imaginative, maybe even underappreciated inventions. This cyber-reality, forward-thinking idea, at least for TV, was fantastic. Very early on in the series Gene had Picard and Data playing Sherlock Holmes characters. They were recreational, they hung out whether it was the holodeck or the poker game. I don't think that special camaraderie would have evolved without it—I think eventually Picard and Data would have a special bond, as did Picard and Worf, and the characters start to click together. Everybody had their thing.

MELINDA SNODGRASS (executive script consultant, *Star Trek: The Next Generation*)

If the holodeck were really *this* untested and prone to malfunctions as it was on the *Enterprise*, they would have shut down every one in the fleet.

MAURICE HURLEY

Gene sees this Pollyanna-ish view of the future where everything is going to be fine. If we keep going in this world the way we're going, there *is* no future, and the idea that humanity is going to go from its infancy, which is what he currently considers it to be in, to its adolescence in the next four hundred years, I don't believe. But *he* does, and that's why *Star Trek* is a success. It gives the audience a sense of hope. I don't believe it, but you have to suppress all that and put it aside. You suspend your own feelings and your own beliefs, and you get with his vision . . . or you get rewritten.

TRACY TORMÉ

I remember Susan Sackett calling me one morning in my office and saying "Oh my God, I have the most incredible news for you: 'The Big Goodbye' just won a Peabody Award. It's the only one in science-fiction history." It was absolutely out of nowhere. To this day, I'm grateful for it, but have no idea why it happened. And then Gene, Majel, Rick Berman, and I, and the director, Joseph Scanlan, flew to New York to spend the weekend in New York. I was given the award and had to wear a tuxedo. The show was really struggling at the time, it was actually not getting a lot of great response and word had gotten around about a lot of the turmoil on the show, so it was a big shot in the arm for the show to get the Peabody Award. It seemed to justify *The Next Generation*.

The Peabody Award-winning episode featured a great Sydney Greenstreet-infused guest performance by hardboiled actor Lawrence Tierney, who had starred in the classic film noir, 1947's *Born to Kill*, and later would wow audiences in Quentin Tarantino's debut feature, *Reservoir Dogs*, in 1992.

TRACY TORMÉ

Lawrence Tierney caused a lot of turmoil. He was a drinker and he broke down. They wouldn't let him on the lot one day, and he drove through the gate that was blocking him and was chased by security guards. There was a lot of stuff—I'd heard he was kind of a piece of work, but it was great to get him.

MAURICE HURLEY

Star Trek has absolute rules that cannot be broken and nobody knows that until they get into it. It's a problem that *all* writers have had for the most part. My ability comes from character and action, so what I thought they wanted from me was character and action. They didn't want that. They wanted writers who could take the *Star Trek* parameters—Gene's vision—and put a shine on it, button it, and *not change anything.* That's a hard lesson for writers to learn, especially those writers coming in with bona fide credentials and a lot of ego. Some people thought they had a better idea, and God love 'em, they may have, but that's not the point.

TRACY TORMÉ

I was very friendly with Maurice Hurley, and he had admitted to me that he'd been struggling for a long time with this one script he was supposed to write. He told me very frankly he didn't get this show. It wasn't his cup of tea, and he didn't really get science fiction or Roddenberry, who was confusing to him. He said, "Well, I know he's like a bigwig in the business, but I just don't get it." He was already talking about leaving and he was going to try to finish this one script and split. He was very close with Bob Lewin at the time, and because I liked Lewin so much, I liked Maury. Maury also had an interracial marriage, which I respected a lot, and I liked his wife.

MAURICE HURLEY

If you have a form and it works, you have parameters and you must paint within the lines. If you start to go outside the lines, the show loses its definition and people lose interest in it. *Miami Vice* went out of the lines, and after the first year it broke its own rules and started to fall apart. That's a lesson I'll never forget. *Star Trek*, to me, was like trying to paint a landscape on a postage stamp, and you have to be able to see a boat in the middle of the lake and a man fishing in it. Now, if you can paint that landscape on a postage stamp, you can do the show. That's the kind of mentality you have to have.

JONATHAN FRAKES

Maury Hurley took me to lunch. We went to the track together. I really liked him. He was the first one that actually tried to infiltrate Riker with a little bit of Frakes. I thought that was a very clever thing to do. He did it with all the actors who would sit down with him. It was helpful. That's where the trombone playing comes from and the interest in jazz.

At some point Roddenberry gave up on the concept that Riker should never smile, which was part of why I looked so incredibly stiff for about three years in the beginning of the show. It was trying to consciously serve the boss, to create a character that I wasn't that physically comfortable doing. It was quite obvious on camera, I thought. When Riker loosened up a little bit, it certainly got better for me, and the character became a little more. That . . . and the beard helped.

GREG STRANGIS (executive producer, *War of the Worlds*)

I developed *War of the Worlds;* we shot a presentation reel for syndication. You didn't have to go through the whole pilot process, you could do things in short-hand. So now there's a period of waiting, and I was invited to come into *Star Trek* and work as a story consultant. They'd been through a lot of writers, and I was curious about how the show was developing. Rick [Berman] and I had lunch. He didn't give me a lot of information, but I knew a little bit about what was going on. I was seeing writers coming and going. Their offices were right down the road from me.

So I was invited to come on board. There was one writer under Gene who would have been considered the showrunner—although Gene was the showrunner—whose only bit of advice for me was, don't be the lone ranger. Which was his warning to me, don't be too clever. I understood that. Didn't change my behavior any. I knew who not to sleep with my back to.

MAURICE HURLEY

When I became co-executive producer, I became more Catholic than the Pope, and I refused to allow *any* rules to be broken. If somebody said, "The captain of the *Enterprise* does this," I would say, "No he doesn't." "But I need it for the drama." "Sorry, he doesn't do that." I just refused, and Rick Berman was the same way. Even Gene, on occasion, would want to break the rules, and we wouldn't let him.

GREG STRANGIS

In total, I was there for about six episodes. There was a script that was in horrible shape and was supposed to prep the Monday after Thanksgiving and I inherited the rewrite of that. I spent all Thanksgiving working on this script. It was a page zero rewrite. It didn't make any sense. I wasn't even sure how to make it make sense. I dug in and gave it my best. Essentially, it was a four-day first draft. But at least it would have given production something to work with. I got the script in, and about midway through the day I got a call to come down to Gene's office. He threw the script across the room and said it lacked passion. I sat and listened and didn't debate it. You can't change an opinion. It's totally subjective.

And Maizlish was there. He was *always* there. I think he was supposed to take the first blow to the face. He was the secret service to Gene Roddenberry. When someone went to throttle him, Leonard would throw his body across the room and save his meal ticket. I wasn't even sure he threw the right script. I think he was actually referring to another script that hadn't been rewritten. I don't think he would have been clear-eyed enough to read my script, it had just gone to typing and printing and all that other stuff in the morning. So I walked out and went to my office and called my agent and said, "I don't care what you have to do, I'm done with this show. "

I had spent years working with wonderful people like Lee Rich and Peter Roth; phenomenal people who are smart, clever, and creative, and don't have high blood pressure and hyperbolic explosions. Two weeks later we got the pickup for *War of the Worlds,* and I ran into Gene going into the commissary, and he said, "How's it going, Greg?" and I said, "Fine." "Greg, we'd really like to have you back on the show." "Gene, I couldn't be more flattered, but I just got my own show picked up so I don't think I can do it." "Hey, congratulations."

Maurice Hurley's strong-arm tactics were continuing to alienate a number of writers still on board, including executive story editor Hannah Louise Shearer, who ankled at the end of first season, and Tracy Tormé. It was only with the support of Berman, Justman, and Roddenberry himself that Tormé was able to have his script "Conspiracy" produced over the vocal objections of Hurley, who was opposed to the graphic violence and decidedly downbeat tone of the episode, in which parasites invade the bodies of the heads of the Federation on Earth, and the *Enterprise* is brought home to combat the menace.

TRACY TORMÉ

I felt that the biggest weakness of the show was that everybody liked everybody too much. I thought it was very in need of some kind of conflict. One of my main arguments for that was that even the Klingons are big lovable teddy bears now. I'd recently seen the movie *Seven Days in May* and I decided to do sort of a *Star Trek* version. I wanted it to be controversial, I wanted it to have an unhappy, disturbing ending where everything isn't all tied together.

When I was eighteen, I'd seen a double feature of *Three Days of the Condor* and *The Parallax View,* which to this day remain two of my all-time favorite movies, and I thought, "Why not do that kind of a show on *Star Trek*?" So I wrote a detailed treatment, and somewhere during this time period the show had reached such a crisis place where it was either in danger of shutting down for a few days because there was no one running the ship, or it actually did shut down for a few days. I remember it cost a lot of money and there was a big question of who is really going to take the reins and take over. It sort of turned out that the lesser of all evils became Maurice Hurley, and very surprisingly, he went from a guy who couldn't complete the one script he was working on to being king of the hill. And I was happy, I liked him, I thought that was great.

MAURICE HURLEY

I did a page-one rewrite of "Where No One Has Gone Before" and they absolutely hated it. I said, "Wait a minute, I'm used to writing from the point of view of vulnerability. I just write the most outrageous shit in the world, and then we all sit down and work it out, but don't attack it and don't attack me." And that's what happened, so I took it and started rewriting it some more, and it eventually turned out to be a show I liked a lot. But it was during the process of doing two or three rewrites on that script that I started to understand what *Star Trek* was all about.

After fourteen episodes, I was given control of the scripts and the stories and was moved from the corners into the light. The first thing I said was "No memos." The whole system changed. If anybody had something to say about a script, they could come into my office, sit down like a human being, and we talked. We dealt with it as fellows, not adversaries. As a result, the show itself changed.

TRACY TORMÉ

The first sign that anything was up was that one day he came into my office after I had submitted "Conspiracy" and said, "I have to tell you, this is not *Star Trek*, it just isn't *Star Trek*. I'm just letting you know now we're not doing this episode, and so if you've got another episode to do, start again, since we don't have a lot of time." And I said, "No, I've really been zeroing in on doing this," and he said, "You have to come up with something else, because we're not doing this."

Later that same day, I walked into the elevator, and there's Maury, and he's got kind of a strange look on his face. "Well, what can I say, I've been overruled." He said, "Everybody else loves this thing. I don't get it." He seemed very uncomfortable, and from that moment on my relationship with him was never the same.

JIM LEWIN

The political bullshit on *Star Trek* was much more extreme than ever before. Mostly I remember my father saying positive things about Roddenberry. He told me that he had been a cop and that he admired the way he had turned that into a writing career and had this utopian vision for the show that he had developed while working as a cop when he decided he wanted to reinvent the world. He had frustrations with Roddenberry, but it was more the people around Roddenberry who really fought with him.

TRACY TORMÉ

I just don't feel Lewin was treated with respect, and I thought it was all a case of Maury wanting to establish that he was now on a higher level, and I just really hated that. I can only tell you he was a real power monkey and he certainly had not been that way when he was first there. He was a kind of a charming guy with a good sense of humor and kind of soft-spoken, and he really changed.

I realized a little way into the second season that I didn't have any allies on the show. I had never worked on anything in the past where I had been in conflict with anybody. I had always gotten along with everyone I worked with, and all of a sudden I realized that there's nobody on this show who is an ally. I'm a lone wolf, really, and the fact that Lewin and Gene are talking me up was offensive to people. I was pretty young and was naïve to a certain extent, and wasn't really aware that all that was going on, but I do think that was creating an atmosphere that wasn't really helpful to me that I wasn't fully aware of.

HERB WRIGHT

It was so bizarre. Gene was bringing his attorney to staff meetings and he was giving us notes on scripts and secretly rewriting them at night and taking people's names off and putting other people's names on. He would call up writers at home, freelancers, ask them what was going on, how they were doing. It was horrible, one of the principal reasons I left. And Hurley was the last straw for me. He was basically playing drinking buddies with Gene.

WIL WHEATON (actor, "Wesley Crusher")

The ways that Hurley fucked writers could fill a building. Ask Tracy Tormé about Maurice Hurley someday.

TRACY TORMÉ

I finally went to Gene and said, this guy hates me. He's out to get me, he's going out of his way to screw my scripts into the ground. And Gene just looked at me and said, "I really think you're overreacting. I can't imagine that someone that works on the show would want to personally sabotage something." And I said, "Gene, I'm telling you that's what he's doing." "I don't accept that and I think you should take another look at this. Maybe you two aren't the best of friends, but I certainly don't think he's trying to destroy your episodes." So I didn't get anywhere.

JIM LEWIN

Oh yeah, my father said he felt betrayed by Hurley and it was unfair. He felt Hollywood was really getting bad at the end of a thirty-something-year career. He started on *Gunsmoke* in the very early sixties and managed to stay in that world all that time, but he never worked in TV after *Star Trek*. He continued to write some movie scripts, and he wrote up until the day he died, but he didn't work in television after that. He wasn't really allowed to have the satisfaction of doing a show, following through with a script the way a writer usually envisioned it. It always had to be changed around and watered down, and by the time it came out, he was never really happy with the way they ended up.

MAURICE HURLEY

I came on about a month before they started shooting the pilot. I was vilified for the first four or five months of my job on *Star Trek*. I was treated like the worst stepchild you've ever seen. At one point, Rick Berman, who became the co-executive producer with me, said he didn't think I could possibly go through airport security because of all the metal I had stuck in my back. I was coming in with big credentials: *Miami Vice* and *The Equalizer*. I had credits that others didn't have. I don't know if David Gerrold had those kind of credits or Dorothy Fontana, either. Herb Wright kind of flowed in and out and Bob Lewin had a lot of old credits. I had heat. I guess I was viewed as a possible threat or something.

TRACY TORMÉ

I had really come to resent very heavily the way Hurley was treating Bob Lewin. I thought it was terrible and I'd seen the way he'd become like a little mini-dictator. All the writing was on the wall, and I didn't like him at all at that point. I remembered how he had handled trying to kill "Conspiracy" and had never really owned up to it with me, and he'd actually been very cold to me after that. I thought, why is he cold to me? What have I done to him?

ROBERT LEWIN

What I wanted to do and did best was character. Gene was determined to keep it an adventure show rather than a personal show, and that is eventually the reason I didn't want to return. I really wanted to do stories of greater depth and more personal material.

ROBERT H. JUSTMAN

I was suffering from hypertension, overwork; I wasn't as young as I had been, and I was still working sixteen-hour days, and it was taking its toll on me. My blood pressure rose, because I was having problems with Gene's business manager, who was interfering in what Rick and I considered to be our producer functions, and it just drove me crazy. It was the only time I ever had harsh words with Gene.

One day, I drove over to his house after Leonard Maizlish fell asleep in the middle of a casting session, right in full view of the actor who was reading for us. I was furious, and I stopped the casting session, jumped in my car, and rode over to Gene's house and screamed at him. It wasn't long after that I decided, I can't let this happen. I knew the show was going to be successful, it was a terrific show, but I was lucky that I didn't have to remain at work there.

As the saying goes, I had "fuck you" money. I gave away a lot of money by not coming back, but I also kept some hold of what little sanity remained to me, and physically, it was my salvation. I just decided to be happier and have less.

ROD RODDENBERRY (son of Gene Roddenberry)

I got to know Justman as my father's friend before I even had any idea what he did. I only remember they were friends. He spoke well of my father after my father passed, but then he put a foreword in a book that kind of slammed my father. My mother was really pissed at him and then, I believe, he came and apologized to my mother about that. Everything that I've heard and seen and read, I think he was a really good guy.

DAVID LIVINGSTON

After the pilot, and after I did a couple of episodes, I was going to go in and tell them I was leaving because I didn't want to be a television production manager. I wanted to do movies and pilots. I go in to quit, and they ask if I want a better job. They said Bob [Justman] was leaving and they need a line producer. I asked if I had to do both, and they said no, so I told them we had a deal. I had less work and more money and a steady job. I saw the writing on the wall that this thing could go for a long time, and it was a no-brainer. Going in to quit, I ended up staying.

> There were, however, many people who did not, most notably Robert H. Justman, Herb Wright, Robert Lewin, Greg Strangis, Johnny Dawkins, Eddie Milkis, Sandy Fries, Dorothy Fontana, and David Gerrold, to name only a few.

BURTON ARMUS (producer, *Star Trek: The Next Generation*)

Lewin got fucked; he was a nice-enough man. A lot of people got fucked over there that were not treated fairly. Okay, maybe we get paid too much to be treated fairly, but how about treated nicely? You can fuck me, just be a gentleman about it. They were not nice people. The system is not nice and the system fell apart with Gene and went right down to Berman. That's where it all festered and everybody was offended by their insecurity. A lot of nice people were hurt for no reason. Fire you? They have a right to fire you, but they do it badly. The first year was a bloodbath there.

Maury got the second season because when everybody else was chewed up by

Roddenberry, he was the only one that could spit *Roddenberry* out. So when they were killing everybody in the first season, Maury just got his fucking Irish up and shoved scripts down their throat. He kept pushing them down their throat and forced them to shoot them, so the show stayed alive. He knew how to handle Gene. He bullied him, he yelled at him, or threatened him or intimidated him. Whatever he did, he would finally get the script out of Gene's typewriter and into his own. Then he got it over to production and they filmed it. That doesn't mean he's the greatest of anything, just that he could get that shit out of Gene's hands and into production.

> In most cases, that "bloodbath" (or as one writer dubbed a particularly brutal series of axings one week, "The Friday Night Massacre") was the result of politics from Roddenberry and Maizlish, which followed verbal abuse, a shift to increasingly worse office spaces, being denied parking spots, and worse. Fontana described these politics as "patterns of what would evolve over the course of" her employment on *Star Trek: The Next Generation*.

DOROTHY FONTANA (associate producer, *Star Trek: The Next Generation*)

One, Roddenberry and Maizlish lied in an attempt to get me to do what they wanted. Two, they laid off blame on the studio for the situation. Three, if I didn't do what they wanted, I would be punished. [Also], during this period, Leonard Maizlish became firmly entrenched on the show, though he had no official capacity on it. He was given an office, he sat in on all staff meetings and, if Roddenberry was not there, he would lead them on Roddenberry's behalf. His memos and his preferences for stories/scripts could make or break an assignment, a cut-off of story, the shelving of a script. Roddenberry constantly gave Maizlish's comments on a story or script far more weight than any comment from the writing/production staff.

On October ninth [1987], I concluded my contract with *Star Trek: The Next Generation*. Throughout I was subjected to personal harassment, to sexual discrimination, and to personal discrimination. With other writers on staff, my work was interfered with by Leonard Maizlish, a non-WGA member. In fact, a non-writer. Early on, I was asked to perform services for which I was not contracted or paid, i.e. as story editor, and which were against Guild rules. When I refused to go against my principles and the Guild's rules, I was punished with the killing of my novelization contract [for "Encounter At Farpoint"] and also punished with harassments in regards to parking, to my office, and to my work. All of the above appeared to stem from Leonard Maizlish, although Roddenberry himself was not innocent by any means. Without his approval, Maizlish would not have been able to gain so much power and would not have been able to act as he did.

DAVID GERROLD

Gene still saw me as the twenty-year-old kid that he *let* come aboard *Star Trek* twenty years earlier. He didn't realize that I was older then than he was when he created *Star Trek*. Prior to that, the man had been kicked off two TV series. He had no credentials. The only success he'd ever had in his entire life was *Star Trek*, and he liked being the Great Bird of the Galaxy. He believed his own publicity.

The fact of the matter is that I was qualified to be a producer on *Star Trek*, and should not have been asking for the job of executive story editor. I should have asked to be a producer, and so should have Dorothy Fontana. The two of us should have been given the responsibilities of Gene L. Coon, but we weren't allowed to. Gene is like the rich kid down the street who says, "Come on over to my house and we'll play," and you know he's got the $9,000 electric train set. You say, "Oh, boy, this is going to be neat. This kid has got all these great toys to play with. We're going to have a lot of fun." You go over there and he says, "Don't touch that. It's mine." He runs the electric train set and all you're allowed to do is say, "That's neat." *That's* the way Gene ran *Star Trek*. He's going to take credit for everything.

> Gerrold's conflict with Roddenberry—and Maizlish—came to a head over a script he had written for the show—an AIDS allegory titled "Blood and Fire." After turning in a draft, the rewrite was handed off to Herb Wright, which he did (turning it into "Blood and Ice," the focus now on a zombie-like plague on a starship). For Gerrold, it was the last straw and the beginning of the end of his involvement with *Star Trek*.

DAVID GERROLD

What I had done was decide that I was going to be a solution to the morale problem, not a part of it. So no matter how bad things got, I was always trying to find the good part. I thought, "All right, I can walk away from this place and call it a victory. And I could feel good about the show." So about a week later, I'm wrapping up some loose ends before my contract ends. I stick my head into Herb

Wright's office and he says, "On top of everything else, they want me to rewrite your script." I said, "Jesus, it doesn't need a rewrite." "Well, they decided it needs a rewrite."

DOROTHY FONTANA

"Blood and Fire" had a lot going for it, but Leonard Maizlish took a dislike to it. Maizlish's particular protest was that the theme was "aesthetically displeasing." David delivered his final-draft script and took off for an appearance at a *Star Trek* convention cruise to the Bahamas. Lewin, Wright, Hurley, and I all made enthusiastic comments about David's script. Roddenberry made a point of finding out how to get a cable to David on the ship that Friday to congratulate him for doing a fine job. On Monday, Roddenberry's attitude had changed to "It's a piece of shit." In the four weeks between delivery of "Blood and Fire" and his contract's end, David was not asked to rework the script. He was told to stay in his office and write evaluation memos on other writers' scripts.

DAVID GERROLD

I said to Herb, "I wish I was still here, I'd do the rewrite for you." He said, "I wish you were still here, too. David, go downstairs and ask Gene if you could do the rewrite, because I want you to do your own rewrite." I said, "I'd love to do it. You're overworked and have got other scripts to rewrite. Let me do this for you and take the load off. It's my script, I've got it in my computer, and I'll do the rewrite." He said that was fine with him.

So I go down and ask Gene. I say, "Herb's overworked, let me help you guys out on this. Let me be a friend to the show here."

And Gene, the great silver-tongued bird of the galaxy, has his eyes light up and he gives me the famous Gene Roddenberry smile and says, "David, you're my old friend. I can always count on you to come through in the pinch. You're always there when we need you." And he goes on and on . . . and I got sucked right back into it. You know, "Maybe there's still a chance to keep the script honest." Finally he says, "You have to ask Herb for permission." I said okay, because I already knew Herb wanted me to do it. I go up the stairs and walk into Herb's office, and he's on the phone. He gestures for me to sit down and not say anything. He says, "Okay, Gene. Sure, Gene. Bye, Gene." He hangs up and says, "That was Gene. I want you to know something. I don't lie for anybody. Gene told me that I should tell you that it's *not* okay with me for you to do the script."

Gene laid it off on Herb that he should take the blame. That was the day I fell in love with Herb Wright. There was a man whose integrity could not be compromised. And I thought to myself about Gene, "That goddamned lying, hypocritical, deceiving, thieving son of a bitch. That bullying bastard." *Everything* that I had been pretending was not true for twenty years just welled to the top.

I walked out of there and said, "That man can never again call me friend. He's a user." I went home and the first thing I did was pick up the phone, call Harlan Ellison and I said, "*You were right.*"

By the time second season was ready to go before the cameras, it was already late into the production year due to the prolonged writers' strike, forcing the writers to dust off "The Child," an old script intended for *Trek*'s aborted 1970s revival, *Phase II*. Substituting Troi for Ilia, they fine-tuned the premise for *The Next Generation* and launched into the first couple of episodes of what proved to be an abbreviated season necessitated by the late start in production.

ROB BOWMAN

Knowing it was the season premiere, I thought it was too soft. We had an audience we had to show some great things to. People had been waiting around all summer watching reruns, waiting for a new episode, and now they wanted to see something new. The first shot in "The Child" was this huge Louma Crane shot that started on Data, which took three hours to shoot—and, boy, were they all over me. It was taking too long. It was the first shot of the season and we were already behind schedule, but I said the fans deserve this for the wait and they will appreciate it.

JONATHAN FRAKES

The writers' strike happened second season, and I hate to shave, so I let the beard grow. During the strike we had a meeting with Roddenberry and Berman and Hurley, who was the producer at the time, and Roddenberry kept looking at me and said, "I really like this, it looks nautical." What ensued was this bizarre executive beard trimming contest. It became absurd in terms of the length and the shape and everything else. Gene wanted the beard to be decorative and it stuck and I'm very glad to have it. Fortunately, my wife liked it, or else I'd have had real problems.

RICK BERMAN

We did four episodes less than we had wanted, and the twenty-two that we did do were very rushed. Obviously, it was a problem. It was very frustrating. We didn't have the time we needed. The quality of the first several episodes suffered in that we did not have the time that we would have liked to develop and polish the early scripts.

MAURICE HURLEY

We had a ship dead in the water and we had to try and get it up again, and it was like restoking the furnace. The second season didn't jump off to the right level the way it should have. We didn't have the chance to have the right kind of meetings with the right kind of writers to get things moving and take the momentum after the first season. That was a real killer.

SCOTT MANTZ (film critic, *Access Hollywood*)

"Q Who?" and "Measure of a Man" were the only standout episodes. Season two of *Next Gen* was season three of the original series. In fact, it was worse.

BRYAN FULLER (coproducer, *Star Trek: Voyager*)

You get caught in the parameters of what a *Star Trek* show should be, and then once you've sort of done that and fulfilled your predetermined ideas on what it needs to be, you burn through quite a few formats in terms of how you're telling the story. So you have to start doing things differently to keep it creatively fresh for yourself, and then when you do do something that lands, you're, like, "Oh, *this* is the show." Oftentimes, it's the show telling you what it wants to be. That's absolutely the case for *Deep Space Nine* and *Voyager* and *Next Generation*, whereas *Star Trek* sort of arrived fully formed in many ways. The original series grew more dense as it progressed. But *Next Generation, Voyager,* and *DS9* all found their voices in episodes, and then you saw course corrections along the way.

I look at "Measure of a Man," which was a huge turning point for the series where they were, like, "Wait, we can tell stories like this?" And it changed. It was really very satisfying, because you're seeing an orchestra find its rhythm and synchronize.

DAVID CARREN (writer, *Star Trek: The Next Generation*)

There's one basic thing that never really changed, and part of that evolution was the new *Star Trek* finding its way to being a family. The old show worked because it basically was a family. It was more like Kirk was a big brother than a father figure and everyone else was kind of his siblings, and Spock was the wise uncle. There were all kinds of interesting dynamics to their relationships.

The family [on *Next Generation*] didn't really gel per se on this show until deep into the second season or even third, where it really came together. Ten-Forward was an important part of that. It was like that family milieu, and all those elements fell into place and you saw there's Picard and he's the father and here's the rest of the members of his family.

> That family went through some significant changes. First, there was the departure of Denise Crosby's Tasha Yar, who was unceremoniously killed by what was essentially a "sadistic oil slick" (as *TV Guide* described the villainous Armus) in "Skin of Evil." The story for the episode had been written by legendary *Outer Limits* producer and *Psycho* screenwriter Joseph Stefano.

HANNAH LOUISE SHEARER

There had been two or three drafts and everyone seemed to have a different feeling about how it should go. I had to refashion it in a way I could live with and Tasha could die with. The most important thing was the opportunity to kill a main character in a series. That doesn't come along very often, and I wanted to see how it affected the other people involved. Gene wanted an episode that dealt with sudden death; that it's dangerous in space. So rather than making a big thing out of the death, he felt it was important that it just happen as part of a mission without any great cataclysm, because space is dangerous and they don't live in a world that is as technologically secure as it may seem.

JOSEPH SCANLAN (director, "Skin of Evil")

I don't think the death of Tasha Yar made any difference to the show. Denise wanted out, for one thing. She was never well written for, which they all, including Gene, would agree to. If you have too many regulars and you're not running good stories around them . . . well, that's never a way to handle it. Denise was in such good spirits during the show, and worked very hard on the final funeral scene where she's left a holographic message for the crew. Everybody thought that scene was very nice, *except me*. Going in to it, I was uncomfortable with it, but I thought she pulled it off very nicely. We had endless discussions on where she should be looking. Is she looking into a lens? Is she looking at somebody? There's no real connection. *And* I thought it was interminable.

THOMAS DOHERTY

The manner of Yar's termination wasn't very prejudicial: she was zapped quickly and bloodlessly by what *TV Guide* rightly described as one of the most ridiculous monsters in SF history, a psychologically disturbed tar baby. And, save for a maudlin pre-taped farewell, the breast-beating and gnashing of teeth was minimal. But whatever the motivation and manner of execution, greasing a regular cast member is unusual enough to deserve praise.

HANNAH LOUISE SHEARER

I wrote the hologram at the end, and the act of writing that was a great catharsis and a great opportunity to identify who the other characters were through Tasha's eyes, and it was a very powerful scene to do; I enjoyed doing it and people really seemed to enjoy it. We, of course, had major arguments about it, but it pretty much stayed from my original draft into the end, which was very unusual and very lucky for a writer to have. There were a few lines that I argued about that the actors kept in and the producers took out at the end. I was very pleased with the way it turned out. It touched people and it gave her a good send-off and it talked about what happens when someone you work with and love dies, which is not dealt with very often.

The other thing was dealing with a character of pure evil that Stefano had created. I got sick when I wrote the script, and it was very difficult to deal with a creature of pure evil. Gene and I had agreed that the crew of the *Enterprise* has no right to make judgments about other creatures out there and kill indiscriminately because of what they do, but it's a very fine line when you're dealing with self-defense. So the job was to make the character of Armus believable, evil, and give it a base for its horribleness that was understandable in a way, not to destroy it. But to sentence it to a kind of karma that it deserves. I used the word karma, Gene didn't. That was the task at hand, and it was not easy.

JOSEPH SCANLAN

I think the producers wanted him to be so evil that you'd say, "Leave him there, Riker, alone on that planet. Fuck him." But, of course, it never happened that way. He's a poor son of a gun howling like a cat in a back alley, "Don't leave me." There was no way to avoid empathy for it, in my opinion.

JOSEPH STEFANO (writer, "Skin of Evil")

I don't think I've ever said this about something I've written before: no comment.

> Starfleet more or less revoked Dr. Beverly Crusher's medical license as actress Gates McFadden was abruptly let go from her contract to the show at the end of season one and replaced by Diana Muldaur as Dr. Katherine Pulaski. The actress and character quickly earned her fair share of disdain from fans who rejected the acerbic doctor who would continually admonish and torture the innocent android Data in much the way McCoy belittled Spock in the old show. But while Spock could easily defend himself and often got the last word with as little as a raised eyebrow concealing a sinister devilish Vulcan smirk, Data was like a child being abused by his foster parents. Pulaski also held a thinly veiled contempt for the scrambling of her molecules on the transporter pad, a trait which had been best known to belong to another of the *Enterprise*'s chief medical officers, Leonard "Bones" McCoy.

SUSAN SACKETT (assistant to Gene Roddenberry)

I don't think she [Gates] and Patrick worked well together. It was mainly his request. There were some acting conflicts. Some actors work better with other actors. Then they tried Diana Muldaur, but she couldn't remember her lines because she had a lot of technical things to say, so they brought back Gates. Gene had worked with Muldaur, so he was fond of her and thought she'd do a good job, but this wasn't the right role for her.

RICK BERMAN

Patrick had absolutely nothing to do with it. Maurice *hated* Gates. He disliked the whole character of Dr. Crusher and he wanted to get rid of Gates and replace her. He didn't like her acting and he didn't like her. He went to me at the end of season one, and I said I thought it was a bad idea. Then he went to Gene and he managed to convince Gene. It was all part of the fact that he was the last man standing at the end of the first season and he was going to be moving into the second-biggest chair over in the writing area next to Gene. This was a request he was making, and Gene decided he would honor it. So, Gates was let go and we went through a whole casting procedure and ended up with Dr. Pulaski, who was played by Diana Muldaur.

TRACY TORMÉ

I started to work on a new character to replace the doctor, who I'd heard was leaving. I thought of an alien doctor who comes from a planet where the ultimate devotion is to 100 percent truth, 100 percent of the time. The idea was that even if you were treating a patient and found out that they were terminal, you would just say, "You're terminal and you're going to die soon," and that's the way they live. I thought that would be a way to create some conflict on the show. I worked on that for a while, but they already had an idea to bring back Diana Muldaur who, by the way, was the guest star of one of my absolute personal favorite all-time [original] *Trek,* "Is There in Truth No Beauty?" That's an absolutely underrated episode.

DIANA MULDAUR (actress, "Dr. Katherine Pulaski")

Everyone welcomed me on the set, but I was making more money and had better billing than the rest of the cast. You just feel it from people who really hadn't done anything else who were a little insecure. I did everything I could to make everyone feel secure and work well. I'm a very nice person, I'm probably too nice. I take it on the chin. I found on Broadway there to be no tension; everyone there was good, worked hard, and everyone made a product, whether it went on well or not. Off-Broadway, there were stabbings, knifings, it was totally different. You had to go to the right school, you had to study at the studio to get a job, you had to be part of a group.

The original *Star Trek* felt like doing a nice Broadway play. And *Next Generation* was Off-Broadway, it was everyone trying to be somebody, rather than just letting it all happen and letting it go and just being there and acting wonderfully. If there was any tension, it had not to do with me, it had to do with them. My favorite show was the one we did with Sherlock Holmes. It was fun to get out of the spacesuit and be someone else. That was heaven.

PAUL LYNCH

Diana Muldaur was a lovely lady. She did have trouble remembering her lines, though. We solved it by putting them on cue cards for her.

DIANA MULDAUR

It wasn't working out at all. It had nothing to do with me. I wouldn't have stayed. There was a lot I loved about it, but it was not what I thought it was going to be. You go into something with a good group of people, but it wasn't a great, creative, wonderful world, it was all tech. There was no humanity in it, there was nothing to get my creative juices going whatsoever, and that was a waste of time to me, so my leaving the show was very mutual. The directors were all kids, who had just come over from the old country, and didn't know what they were doing. It was not a great creative mix of people and directors. But it was fun, none of it is regretted. What's happened since then is they pretended I wasn't in it and that I was just a guest person.

TRACY TORMÉ

Pulaski was supposed to be abrasive. That lasted about two shows. "People aren't going to like her," they said. "We better make her lovable."

RICK BERMAN

There were a lot of fans who didn't like the fact that Gates had been let go. The reason that was told to the public was one of those kind of classy, she's going off to pursue other endeavors. At the end of the second season, Hurley had left the show and I didn't feel that Muldaur was working out at all. So the question was—do I pick a third doctor? Do we have three doctors in three seasons? Or do I bring Gates back? I decided it would be healthier for everybody involved to bring Gates back; which we did, and she remained our Dr. Crusher. When Hurley left at the end of season two, the very first thing I did was to rehire Gates. I mean, literally the day Hurley left, Gates was rehired.

DIANA MULDAUR

I loved being part of it. From there I went to *L.A. Law,* and there was a lot of snobbery there, like, "How could you have done something like that?" They would be so jealous now if they knew the residuals I made on *Star Trek: The Next Generation*, which paid beautifully. I'd much rather do *L.A. Law* at the time, so I never thought of it as being sent packing. I went right into *L.A. Law* and was very happy over there, and then was sent down the elevator shaft by David Kelley when he left. He wanted me in *Picket Fences* and didn't want anyone else writing his character, but CBS said no. So they cast my cousin, Kathy Baker.

Despite returning to the show in the third season, McFadden's Dr. Crusher would rarely get a chance to shine, however, and was infrequently prominently featured in an episode and, more egregiously, in any of the films.

GATES MCFADDEN (actress, "Dr. Beverly Crusher")

When I came back, I thought that the character had lost all of her positive qualities. She was written like she was at least ten years older. It was odd. I didn't like the way my relationship with my son was going. I felt like Donna Reed, worrying about his lunchbox. Every time Wesley was in trouble or needed guidance he went to a male figure, which I found a bit insulting, considering how many single parents there are in the world.

When I came back I thought it would be just as it was, which is part of why I came back. I was disappointed to see it wasn't that way. Perhaps I had unrealistic expectations as well. You can only write for so many characters. The year I was away certain decisions were made and that was the season where the three men became the focus. I didn't know that had happened, and it was news to me. But that's the way it goes.

In season two, there was another addition to the *Enterprise* family, the "crazy aunt," Whoopi Goldberg, who joined the show as the enigmatic Guinan, bartender in Ten-Forward, a new lounge set that was built for the show's second year.

RICK BERMAN

Once it was announced that Gates McFadden was leaving, we got a call from Whoopi Goldberg's manager saying that she wanted to have lunch with me and Gene. We met her for lunch and she was a huge fan of the show. She asked, "Have you recast the role of the doctor?" But Whoopi wouldn't have worked as the doctor, so we said to her, "What if we create another character?" Because after the first season, the show's popularity had been kind of blossoming, and the studio came to us and very generously said, do you want to add any new sets? Which is very expensive. The one set that I really missed was a place where the cast could be when they were off duty, so we decided to create a bar. And someone came up with a name, that it was going to be on Deck 10 Forward, so it was going to be known as Ten-Forward.

We built this big bar, and that was all occurring at about the same time that we had lunch with Whoopi, and we thought it would be great to have her play this alien character; kind of a Yoda-like character with great wisdom who's really very, very old and comes from some world far, far away. She would be our bartender and could give bartender-like advice. And she agreed. She was terrific, and she was involved all the way through the movies.

WHOOPI GOLDBERG (actress, "Guinan")

Gene Roddenberry is Thoreau. I met with him and Rick [Berman] as I begged to be on the show. They thought I was kidding. I said, "No, you don't understand. We're talking about *Star Trek*. I really need to be part of this." They thought it was very interesting and Gene wanted to know why. When I explained to him that this was the only vision that had black people in the future, he thought that was very bizarre. I guess he didn't realize that nobody else saw us there. This is what drew me to this show and this man. He was a man who was able to reach out through my television and explain to me that I had a place in the world and in the future.

LES LANDAU (director, *Star Trek: The Next Generation*)

She will not settle for second best, she is a perfectionist. There were times when I have seen what to my eye works and she has come up and whispered in my ear, let me just try something different, and invariably she is right. That little nuance, that little touch, that little affectation makes all the difference in the world. After all, Guinan has been around for hundreds of years. Whoopi is the perfect embodiment of what *Star Trek* is. She's an all-listening, yet all-knowing representation of people in the future. She is the representation of a character in the future that is as important to her in the context of *Star Trek* as any role that she has or will ever appear as.

TOM MAZZA

Star Trek always made stars. That's what that show did. The character of Q, for example, was a fabulous character that was created and brought back, and I liken that to Whoopi's character. Whoopi was great in the role that she was in, but do we need a Whoopi for that? In some ways it falls back to the traditional "let's get in a star and see if it boosts ratings." I'm not sure it boosted ratings, but it was fun, it worked. It's stunt casting. We did it, but we did it in different ways. What happened was, characters that were created became stunts themselves, like Q and the Borg.

DAVID LIVINGSTON

Whoopi wanted to do the show because Nichelle Nichols inspired her as a young girl. She was a pleasure to have, she brought something new to the show, and her energy was just extraordinary. The set lit up when she was there.

The show took on a darker tone under showrunner Maurice Hurley, who, although adhering to the strictures of Roddenberry's universe governing the interpersonal relationships of the characters, was quick to emphasize that space was not always a happy and cheerful place to be. In the second episode of the second season, "Where Silence Has Lease," the *Enterprise* is turned into a floating dissection laboratory by a curious alien creature who brutally kills the first red-shirted security guard of the new series on the bridge.

If Roddenberry's stock-in-trade had been judgmental God like beings, Hurley's take was slightly more malevolent. In "Loud as a Whisper," three ambassadors are killed; in "A Matter of Honor," Riker finds himself unwelcome aboard a Klingon ship as part of a Federation exchange program; "Contagion" highlighted the dangers of technology when a computer virus results in the destruction of an entire starship; and in "Time Squared," the *Enterprise* is faced with destruction when a Picard from the future warns of the ship's impending demise.

Joining the show second season was Melinda Snodgrass, a popular fan writer, whose *Tears of the Singers* had been a bestselling *Trek* novel for Pocket Books. Snodgrass's "The Measure of a Man," which was sold on spec to Hurley, was one of the standout episodes of the season.

Eventually opting out of the series was Tracy Tormé, whose second-season scripts, "The Royale" and "Manhunt," had, according to the writer, been so mutilated by Hurley that he had to use a pseudonym on both works. Tormé, who had served as a creative consultant in year two and had once been groomed to take over the reins of the show, was not prepared to carry on meaningless assignments. Nor would he allow himself to suffer through the endless divisive rewrites that had characterized Hurley's tenure on the show, leading to such producers as John Mason, Michael Gray, Leonard Mlodinow, Robert McCullough, and Scott Rubenstein fleeing the show, sometimes after as little as one episode's work.

An addition to the staff was producer Burton Armus, a twenty-year veteran of the New York City police force before he decided, much like Gene Roddenberry thirty years earlier, to give TV writing a try. His writing/producing credits prior to *Next Generation* included *Airwolf, Street Hawk,* and *Knight Rider.* After his tenure in the twenty-fourth century, he produced *NYPD Blue* and *Acapulco H.E.A.T.* Although Armus worked on numerous episodes, the clear standout in the second season was "A Matter of Honor," in which Riker participates in a Starfleet/Klingon exchange program that puts him on the bridge of a Klingon cruiser.

BURTON ARMUS

Maurice Hurley asked me to join the show. It was the first offer after the strike, and I took it. The idea was that I would come over to *Star Trek* and bang out scripts with him, hire writers, supervise writers, and produce.

I went in knowing there were certain problems going on, knowing that they always had problems keeping people, but also knowing that they never really had A-people. They had a tendency to hire people in need rather than people who could do the job. I felt that maybe they were going in another direction and we could knock out a pretty good show for a year or so. I never thought I would do it for more than one season, and neither did Hurley want to do more than that season.

MAURICE HURLEY

You don't look at the ensemble as characters on the show. The ship is a character, the ensemble is a character. It's a strange way to look at it when you write the show. You don't, for instance, find one of the characters in violent verbal opposition to another character on what they're seeing or what they're doing. And you have to write it that way, because that maintains the unity and integrity of the crew, which is critical.

The show's been criticized by writers because there are no internal conflicts. Riker does not want Picard's seat, Geordi does not dislike Data because he has this advanced intellect, etc. If you were to say "I think I can do better," you probably can, but it's not *Star Trek.* If you're going to do *Star Trek,* these are the rules you have to go by.

MARC SCOTT ZICREE

On the original series, Roddenberry had that basic kernel of an idea, which is that the *Enterprise* is one big happy family. He and Harlan Ellison had all those enormous arguments, because when Harlan wrote "The City on the Edge of Forever," he had drug dealers and all that on the *Enterprise* and Roddenberry took it all out. In retrospect, you see Roddenberry was right and that's why you've got all these Trekkies dressing up in their uniforms and dreaming of being on the *Enterprise*. At least he had the wisdom to realize there should be family spats, because that's realistic, but by the time he got to the new show and he was pushing seventy, I guess he wanted lukewarm farina and wanted there to be no conflict ever.

TRACY TORMÉ

One thing that happened was very exciting. They came to me and said, "We think we can get Leonard [Nimoy] to do the opening episode of the second season, and we want you to write it. Would you come up with something that you think would be really cool for him?" So I cooked up a sequel to "The City on the Edge of Forever" and I called it "Return to Forever." They were going to go back to what was now the most forbidden place in the galaxy, which was that time portal, and they were going to have to actually violate the rules about non-interference, and it was going to create a Pandora's box with a whole terrible, unforeseen thing which only the Spocks from the two different time periods coming together could actually fix.

I worked out a way where classic Spock and the Spock from the *Next Generation* would actually both end up together at the same time by using the portal, and they would both be on the episode together, and that was the twist to it. I was very excited about that and got going on it and was off to a very fast start. I was really looking forward to showing it to everybody, and then the word got back to me that the deal with Leonard fell out, he's not going to be doing it. I was very crestfallen, because I thought that would be a really interesting show.

> The subject of revisiting "The City on the Edge of Forever," the original series episode which is considered the greatest *Star Trek* episode ever produced, would come up again later in the show's run, when Michael Piller was running the show, with Jeri Taylor serving as an executive producer.

HARLAN ELLISON (author; writer, "The City on the Edge of Forever")

I had been asked to write a *Next Generation*, so Jeri Taylor [future *TNG* executive producer] was a friend of Kathryn Drennan, who was married to [*Babylon 5's*] Joe Straczynski, and she was an intern at *Star Trek*. She suggested me, and I talked to Michael Piller. I called him up, and Jeri had set this thing up. I wasn't really interested in going anywhere near *Star Trek*, but if I could find something to do I would be interested. The idea was this: *Back to the Future II* uses *Back to the Future*, except you see it from a different angle. Using the original "The City on the Edge of Forever," you have the people from *Next Generation* going back to the same time, the 1930s, because what was changed [on *TOS*] was okay for their time when they did it, but two hundred years later during *The Next Generation*, or whenever it was, the changes have been disastrous, and they have to set things back the way they were. Edith Keeler's got to be left alive. Everybody who was alive in that show is still alive, but you didn't have to have any of the original characters. All you had to use was preexisting footage. Put it in the background and put your characters from the new show acting and doing what they have to do, so what looks like her being killed, for instance, isn't.

I said, "What a great idea." I did up a small treatment, a page or two, and here's what Piller said: "Dear Harlan, it is a splendid script, you don't have to be told that. It is a rare pleasure to read writing like this, but I just can't get behind the notion of revisiting the story with *TNG*. Even though there are elements that never made it to the original show, the episode is held so dear to fans that I think it would be a mistake to tamper with it. It would seem like we were trying to do the original recipe one better. It could also be interpreted as a slap to Gene. I would be delighted to get you in here to do an original premise if you have something else you would like to do. Most cordially, Michael."

In fact, what he said to me over the phone was, "We don't want to do this kind of thing, because we just had Leonard Nimoy do a guest shot; we don't want to do too many of them." In fact, the telling line there is it would seem like a slap to Gene, who was still alive at the time.

RICK BERMAN

After the writers' strike ended, we didn't have the time we needed. The quality of the first several episodes suffered in that we did not have the time that we would have liked to develop and polish the early scripts.

TRACY TORMÉ

Gene used to say to me a lot, "Majel is driving me crazy, when are we bringing back Lwaxana Troi? You'd really kind of actually do me a favor to write something else with her," and I didn't really want to do anything else with that character, but I finally caved and I put her in my last episode.

MAURICE HURLEY

The second half of the first season was great. It was just rocking, too much fun to believe. There were problems, people yelling and screaming, but it didn't matter. We were all pulling on the oars and driving for the same goal. Everybody was busting their butt and it was great fun. If we had been able to kick in and keep going second season, there would have been no telling.

We had a lot of things we wanted to do. I like to move a character from one point at the beginning of the season to another at the end of the season, and one of the problems with *Star Trek* is the characters never change. If you look at the old series, they go through all these incredible adventures and they are still the same characters at the end that they were at the beginning. That's not the way life is. I wanted to arc the characters through the second season, but we didn't have the time to build the foundation. That was disappointing.

MELINDA SNODGRASS

I'm a novelist. If I want to smash galaxies, I can do it, but on *Star Trek*, whatever I put down on the page, they had to try and build, if they could afford it. You ran into a lot of budgetary problems—how big this set can be, how many guest stars, how elaborate the special effects are—constraints that often pull a show back from the grandiose vision of what you want it to be.

MAURICE HURLEY

I saw three episodes of the original. That's all. I only watched them because someone had told me we had plagiarized a story that I had liked, and I said, "Wait, I didn't know that." It was a story somebody was trying to sell us, and I thought it was great. They said, "Yeah, it was great in 1966, too."

Indisputably, Hurley's most important contribution to second season was the Borg, a race of omnipotent, cybernetic super foes, who appeared invincible in the dark and threatening "Q Who." In that episode, the all-powerful prankster Q transports the *Enterprise* into the far reaches of the galaxy where the crew must confront the unstoppable Borg ship as Q issues dire warnings against Picard's complacency.

MAURICE HURLEY

The Ferengi, who were introduced in season one, were a waste of time. We had lots of arguments about them from the beginning. I was the lone voice screaming in the wilderness. Listen, if somebody's interested in gold, they're not much of an adversary. If we can make gold in our replicator, and we can, then it's like sand at the beach. They want gold? Here, take a truckload and get lost. But, if you noticed, when Hurley became the co-executive producer, good-bye Ferengi. They're out of here. Bring on the Borg!

MELINDA SNODGRASS

It was thought we needed some kind of new threat that we could take seriously with the Klingons as uncomfortable allies. The Borg are in many ways Maurice Hurley's. It was his script, and he was coping with creating this new villain. We kicked around a lot of different ideas, and I realized that what we were really kind of describing was cyberpunk, so I talked a bit about that movement in science fiction. The idea of augmented humanity. We felt we wanted to come up with a villain you just couldn't reason with.

ROB BOWMAN

It was a very abstract script. There was a lot of controversy between Maurice Hurley and everybody. I know Patrick Stewart was personally offended by some of the themes in the script, and so it was hard to get behind the story. It was a day-to-day struggle to believe in that material. But it seems Maury was right in the end. It was just the kind of uneasiness, getting that leg kicked out from underneath you, that you needed to make the crew realize we do have to look for impenetrable foes.

Conceptually, it was a brilliant idea. During Picard's whole speech in the fourth act about "What do you want?" to Q, Patrick could not figure out what to do with it. Before we rolled on the master [shot], he even got a bit hostile at some of us who weren't taking it seriously enough, and he was right. We were a bit too jokester at the time.

DAVID A. GOODMAN (consulting producer, *Star Trek: Enterprise*)

That ending speech by Picard is where they find the show. This guy is not Kirk; he's got the ability to apologize, which shows he's mature. An amazing episode.

MAURICE HURLEY

What we really wanted to do, but couldn't because of money, was a race of insects. Insect mentality is great, because it's relentless. They don't care. They have no mercy, no feelings toward you. They have their own imperative, their own agenda, and that's it. We needed a villain who could make you dance, and the Borg could do it.

ROB BOWMAN

I'm not one for depression. Life is depressing enough. Our job is to entertain, but it was a good idea. At the time, we thought we just pooped a blunder with the episode and we'd just air it last, but it was really superb. We didn't know day to day if we were making a stinker or a winner.

JONATHAN FRAKES

The Borg were the greatest invention we had on the series.

DAVID LIVINGSTON

I love Maurice Hurley. He was outside the box. He marched to his own drum and that was good in my mind. He was a bit of an outsider, and he brought a different perspective to the show that I thought was good. Especially the Borg. Without the Borg, we would have never gotten to the point we did. He's always played it really close to the cuff. I was very fond of him. He always seemed like he had something going on in his head that he wasn't going to share with anyone else, but he did it with a smile.

DENNIS RUSSELL BAILEY (writer, *Star Trek: The Next Generation*)

I thought that the second year of the series, in general, was a year in which they had some real writing problems. There were some really good episodes, like Melinda Snodgrass's "The Measure of a Man," which is probably the best episode of the series, but in general I thought they had a real writing problem, and they were going around forever blaming it on the writers' strike, which was nonsense. Every show on television had to deal with the writers' strike that year, and it wasn't easy for anybody, but they recovered.

BURTON ARMUS

The bottom line is this: When left to our own devices, Hurley and I would have made sure that all the scripts had balls. But then you start to get into the inner circle of *Star Trek,* which is Gene. Gene had a proprietary attitude toward it. If it's different, and he didn't think of it, it's wrong. If you can write the show and make it work, he doesn't want you, because nobody can write *Star Trek* but him.

RONALD D. MOORE (producer, *Star Trek: The Next Generation*)

The second season was pretty shaky. I didn't think it was a rip-off as much as I thought it didn't quite know what it wanted to be. It seemed to lack focus and coherent storytelling. And there were episodes I hated. That episode with the Irish, "Up the Long Ladder," I *loathed*. I remember feeling like the show didn't know what it was. I was afraid it was going to get canceled, because I thought it was kind of weak, but it didn't, obviously, and kept chugging along. I was looking forward to it getting better. The first two seasons are kind of unwatchable.

BURTON ARMUS

The only reason that *anything* got done is because the machine needed scripts so fast. So you had this situation where the machine is eating scripts, and Gene could only slow it down so much. Then the *money* of it become so precarious that you've just got to shoot film, so he accepted these scripts with reluctance. And those scripts that he accepted with reluctance, he forced a schedule and rewrites on, so Maury is working all night with a lot of infighting.

I'll give you an example. On "A Matter of Honor," when I wrote the first draft of that, I had used the word "execute," as in a member of the Klingon ship executes the person above him. And Gene said, "This script won't work." Hurley and I said, "Why not?" He said, "Well, they don't execute their superiors." Well, they *do* execute. That was in his format. He said, "No, I said 'assassinate,' so it doesn't work." So we said, "That's easy. We'll change the word from 'execute' to 'assassinate.'" Again, no. He says, "No, it doesn't work. You wrote 'execute.'" He would get his teeth into something like that, and it became a battle to the point where you just say, "Fuck it. What do you want it to say?"

Look, Roddenberry can't write very well. He came out with a concept that suddenly got hot, so he moved his house into this spaceship and he lived on it for the rest of his life. But he's *not* a writer, so when he sees things in a scene and writes them, they don't work. After he does his rewrite, he disappears. Now you have to take it and try not to offend Roddenberry and rewrite it to make the scene work. So Maury was left with letting Roddenberry fuck up the existing script, then taking that and bringing it to some sort of balance between what was good and what Roddenberry said was good, and yet bring it to a production level. Roddenberry at no point was an asset to what we had to shoot, so his rewrites would simply cost you three days, because after he did it, you had to redo it. *That* was the situation there.

> A bit of a triumph for Armus was his script for "A Matter of Honor," which was an atypical episode of the series' early years—dark, taking place largely on a Klingon ship, and rife with conflict.

BURTON ARMUS

It's because I forced them. Once I took them out of the spaceship, once I forced them out of the *Enterprise,* they had to fill a story. I took them out of their comfort zone. I shoved it down their throats and did a fucking story where they were *not* in their element. And there was no way they could make me pull it, because there wasn't time. But that's the thing: every day was a fight. It was never done with comfort. No, they made it very difficult for me and for Maury.

MELINDA SNODGRASS

We seemed to find a direction second season. At about the time I came on board, there suddenly seemed to be this climate of discussion among the writers about what we wanted to do with the show. My impression was that this was a new phenomenon. We were a little bit more on the same wavelength.

TRACY TORMÉ

Gene Roddenberry was very kind to me personally. I'm grateful for that. *Star Trek* was very good to me. I have a lot of great memories and I liked the opportunity it gave me. I'm not going to lie about it. But there was a lot of backstabbing and skullduggery going on, and that's just the way it was.

BURTON ARMUS

Tracy was young. He felt he had a handle on the show, and yet Maury's the boss and he wants it done his way. Now you have a battle of egos. There's two sides to it. Tracy has a handle on that show, which is his. Maury is executive producer and has a responsibility to the show that he feels is his, and it would be Maury's way because he was the boss. I don't mean this to be in any way insulting to Tracy, because he was a good kid, but when Maury says, "This is the way I want it done," and it's not done the way he wants it, he just puts it in his fucking computer and writes it the way he wants it, because it's faster than sitting down and trying to explain what wasn't done. So it became offensive to somebody who was rewritten by Maury, and Maury, not being very political or diplomatic in his manner in many cases, offended people.

MAURICE HURLEY

Two years was enough time in space for me. I did some good, some bad, some mediocre, but it's not a show that I could continue to do. It's not where I come from. The second season became a hassle where you were hassling for mediocrity. You weren't hassling for excellence, and that's always a debilitating kind of feeling. That's not a lot of fun. I told Gene at the beginning of the second season that I was only doing one more year. I couldn't carry on and started disengaging probably around the middle of the year; just started to pull back. It wasn't going the way I wanted it to go, and there was no point in fighting because I was leaving anyway. There's no real overall umbrella philosophy of what I wanted to do. Just the edges, the surprises. Just the kind of things where there was a little more to it, so that it's not just another mechanical god coming in to manipulate things.

MELINDA SNODGRASS

I learned a lot from Maurice Hurley. He was great, because he always let me make my own changes. If he didn't like a scene, he would tell me why and talk it over. But he always let me go away and fight with it. It was painful, but I really learned a lot about screenwriting in the crucible of a fast, hard apprenticeship.

JIM LEWIN

My dad [Robert Lewin] was in the den of sharks for thirty years, but I guess things were changing in the business and were getting even more brutal. He thought

Gene Roddenberry was really interesting. He didn't always like him, but mostly he had good things to say about him. At his memorial service there was definitely some love there from the people who showed up. Maurice Hurley was there. When he showed up at my dad's memorial there were no hints of their problems.

Michael Mann from *Miami Vice* showed up, and he talked about how he really didn't follow through and thank my dad enough, because there was a tradition with those old-school writers where they would help each other get into the business and help each other figure out how to write TV. They would take on a mentor and the mentors would take on kind of an intern, and my dad did that a lot, kind of to the frustration of his ex-wife, my mom. He was kind of a workaholic and he spent a lot of time doing volunteer stuff. He would teach writing at a prison, and he would spend a lot of time bringing up these young writers. That was what they did in those days.

With Michael, he used to spend hours working on scripts with him back when Michael was trying to be a writer. Michael got up at the memorial and said, "I was working in the shoe department in Sears and I wanted to be a writer, and I remember just hating myself and hating my life for not doing anything with it." My dad liked Michael and took him on as a young upstart and worked with him for a year or two, helping him rewrite his first scripts and helping him find places to submit them. And Michael went on to huge fame and power as a movie director.

When my dad was alive, I used to ask about him, because when I was a kid we hung out at their house and they were kind of hippies: his wife was Summer, and they had a little kid and a hermit crab. We would goof around while they were in the backroom typing and talking. Later, I remember asking, "Whatever happened to Michael and Summer?" And, he was, like, "Oh, Michael. He never has time for me. Every once in a while I'll see him and he would be, like, we should have lunch sometime. But we never did. Michael never came back around and gave me time, even as a friend. He didn't do any professional favors for me, and he didn't even make time for a phone call."

But Michael, I think, understood that, and he got caught up in work just like humans do. He probably had the best intentions, but didn't make it happen. And then, at the funeral, he was weeping, saying, "I wouldn't be here if it wasn't for Bob Lewin, and I didn't really give back."

BURTON ARMUS

Let me explain Maury's personality and you'll probably have a clearer picture. Maury is a workhorse. He finds it easier to do it himself than to have somebody else do it. His concentration is very centered, so when he does it, he just fucking does it and he doesn't care whose toes he steps on. He had a tendency, in that pointedness, to offend a lot of people around him. And then to cover up that "maybe he's wrong," he has a "Hey, fuck it—it's done" attitude.

MAURICE HURLEY

Because of the way I am, I put people's noses in it a lot. That means I can be difficult to work with, so that with the kind of personality I have in a working situation—there's a tendency to look and see if there's a way to get rid of me, which people would, if they could. But since I can put it on the page, they suffer me. No matter how rank your personality may be, if you can dance, they're going to keep you around.

MAGIC MIKE

"DO NOT KNEEL BEFORE ME . . . I DO NOT DESERVE IT."

The third season of *The Next Generation* is widely considered one of the best seasons of any *Star Trek* series ever produced, and signaled a dramatic change from the policies of the first two years. When Maurice Hurley announced he was leaving the show, Gene Roddenberry and Rick Berman brought aboard a science-fiction veteran, Michael Wagner. Wagner had headed the writing staff of the short-lived ABC series *Probe*, inspired by science-fiction author Isaac Asimov. Wagner came aboard in hopes of charting a new, smoother course. But soon after joining the staff as a co-executive producer, he departed as did so many writers had before him.

RICK BERMAN (executive producer,
Star Trek: The Next Generation)

Maurice Hurley got really tired of it all at the end of the second season and he pretty much had had it. Gene and I started talking about a replacement for him, and Leonard [Maizlish] was involved in all that, too. Gene was looking for someone from the outside, and we found a fellow named Michael Wagner, who was hired as the co-executive producer along with me. He was a very lovely guy, but just could not deal with Gene's rules.

MICHAEL PILLER (executive producer, *Star Trek: The Next Generation*)

It was complete turmoil there at the time. *Star Trek: The Next Generation* was considered the worst place to work in Hollywood, and the reason for that was that Roddenberry had very strict rules. His vision was sacrosanct, and he didn't care about excuses or explanations. He didn't want to argue about it. He just wanted you to do it his way, and a lot of writers couldn't see his future his way. Gene really didn't want any conflict between human characters, so the problem that Mike Wagner was having was the problem that every writer on staff was having. They felt that they were suffocating within this box that Roddenberry had created.

RICK BERMAN

I remember the three of us sat down in a meeting and Gene mentioned something Michael Wagner had written, "You have an alien here that just with the power of his brain can destroy a planet." And Wagner went, "Yup. Right." And he said, "We don't do that on *Star Trek*. People don't have that kind of power." And Wagner said, "Why not?" And Gene said, "Because I said so."

I don't remember exactly what happened after that, but shortly thereafter Michael Wagner came to my office, I'll never forget it, he was literally crying. He couldn't take it. He could not take the fact that he couldn't dot an *i* or cross a *t* without Gene having some comment about it, and he resigned because he could not work for somebody who was as locked in about his ideas and his rules as Gene Roddenberry was.

Wagner, who had toiled on the final frontier for only three weeks before quickly departing, was replaced by Michael Piller, a former journalist, TV executive, and television censor, who had worked briefly with Wagner on *Probe,* and who had also contributed to *Miami Vice*. Fresh from a four-year stint on *Simon & Simon*, Piller embraced the idea of reinvigorating the sputtering starship. It was his strong conviction, in fact, that *TNG* already ranked as one of the best shows on television. The irony is that the science-fiction genre was *not* one he was ordinarily drawn to.

SANDRA PILLER (wife of Michael Piller)

He kind of fell into sci-fi. Even when he got on *Star Trek*, he said, "I don't even know how to write this stuff," but Rick Berman told him he would just have to talk to the tech guys and they'd tell him what to put in. So his feeling was he was writing about the human condition; he realized that people are people, even in the twenty-fourth century.

The classic *Star Trek* had not survived its third season. Piller understood that its successor would have to last at least four for it to be profitably stripped in second-run syndication. The writer/producer was therefore anxious to put his own imprimatur on the show and break with the sins of the past.

Helped by now-veteran *Trek* hands Richard Manning and Hans Beimler, who had worked on the show's first two seasons, and by Melinda Snodgrass, who had been honored with a Writers Guild nomination for her "The Measure of the Man" script, Piller and his staff began to craft some of the series' finest episodes, ones that remain standouts to this day.

With Hurley's exit, Berman also further involved himself in the writing of the show, bringing Piller under his administrative and creative aegis. Berman asserted his newfound authority subtly, at first ordering costume changes and replacing several key below-the-line production crew members. Berman was seeking a new and more distinct look for the series.

Piller, meanwhile, complemented Berman with a keen eye for strong spec material, opening the floodgates to unrepresented writers who were willing to sign a release form to have their material evaluated by the *Star Trek* staff. This helped pave the way for the hiring of some of the series' most talented writers, people who would subsequently go on to run and create their own series, including Ronald D. Moore (*Battlestar Galactica, Outlander*), René Echevarria (*Dark Angel, Castle*), Naren Shankar (*CSI: Crime Scene Investigation, The Expanse*) and Brannon Braga (*Flashforward, Salem*).

In a sense, the origin of Piller's professional writing career can be traced to the day he found himself discouraged from being a writer by the instructor of a creative writing class at the University of North Carolina at Chapel Hill, his alma mater.

MICHAEL PILLER

I was a fairly successful high school writer, and then you get into college and start finding new challenges and sometimes over-challenge yourself. To be very fair to this professor, I was not writing well in college, but the class that I was in was one in which he opened the class by saying, "There are enough bad writers out there; I really have no interest in sending any more bad writers out into the world, so if I think you're a bad writer, I'm going to do everything I can to discourage you from becoming a writer." Unfortunately I was one of those people that he decided didn't cut it.

I was living in the 1960s when everybody was doing a lot of drugs, and I wasn't, and everybody had this new consciousness and open liberalism. Although I was liberal, I was a Kennedy liberal, so I was trying to stretch my writing into directions that I knew nothing about. I learned the hard way that when you start writing about the horrors of war and don't have anything but old war movies to draw on, you're not going to be able to bring anything new to the table. I always tell writers, write from experience, but the bottom line to this story was, by the time this course was over, I was emasculated as a writer.

SANDRA PILLER

This instructor not only discouraged Michael from being a writer, he *humiliated* him in front of the class. So Michael went into journalism and news.

MICHAEL PILLER

I went into journalism, but I had a religious experience when I went to see a performance of the show *A Chorus Line*. There's a song by the character of Morales, which is called "Nothing," and it's about her struggles to become an actress. She sings that she went to this school, and the teacher in this course basically told everybody that they had to feel the wind on the toboggan and feel the snow, and she didn't feel anything. The teacher said, "If you don't start feeling something soon, you're going to be transferred," and she goes on to talk about feeling frustrated and lost and confused, and how this teacher kept telling her she was no good, and she went to pray for guidance.

I'm sitting in this theater, surrounded by hundreds of people, and I'm saying, "This is my story," and what possible answer could she get? She goes to church to pray for guidance, and Santa Maria speaks to her and she says, "This course is nothing. This man is nothing; go out and find a better class," and I thought, "Why didn't I think of that?" So from that day forward, I started writing again, and of course eight years had passed and I had much more life experience, and was a little more confident. It wasn't like things happened overnight, but in time I found my voice, and to make a long story short, I found what I was meant to do in this life.

SANDRA PILLER

Writing was a very Zen thing for Michael. He would give all of the writers on the staff of whatever show he worked on, *Zen and the Art of Archery* or some sort of Zen book, because that always got to him. So he did enjoy the writing; he would hear those voices. He got to know the voices and it would just start coming out. He'd start writing early in the morning. Before computers, we had an old typewriter and, let me tell you, he'd be typing early in the morning, *click-clack, click-clack* in my brain. He was *very* passionate about it.

Although under Piller and Berman *Trek*'s ratings (and quality) improved, harmony did not always prevail behind the scenes, as the revolving door for writers continued to turn. Story editor Richard Danus barely lasted a month, and Trekkies Hans Beimler, Richard Manning, and Melinda Snodgrass, responsible for some of third season's most distinguished episodes, quickly found themselves at odds with Piller, who had his own ideas about running a starship. By the end of the season, all were gone.

Joining the staff, however, was producer Ira Steven Behr, whose credits included *The Bronx Zoo,* the TV version of *Fame* (where he had previously worked with Beimler and Manning), and *Once a Hero*. Although no one realized it initially, Behr would play an integral role in *Star Trek*'s future, most notably with the evolution of *Deep Space Nine* years later.

MICHAEL PILLER

I was very interested in *The Next Generation*, not because it was SF, but because it was good. I remember very distinctly being a fan before I even thought about writing for it. My family and I watched the first two seasons together, and it was something we *could* be together for. Every once in a while those two seasons would put a gem of a story in place, like "Measure of a Man," and you just got blown away. I happened to have lunch with Roddenberry and Rick Berman and Maurice Hurley the week after that episode ran. Now, I did not get the job that I was after on the writing staff, because they hired my old friend Mike Wagner, whom I'd worked with on *Probe*.

RICK BERMAN

When Maurice Hurley left, there was basically a weeding-out process by trial and error, trying to bring new people on board. *Star Trek* is not an easy show to write. There are some people who could be Emmy Award–winning writers on a lawyer show or a police drama who just can't grasp what it is to write for a somewhat-stylized twenty-fourth-century world where the conflict between characters is very, very subtle. Because of the way our people treat each other, there are a lot of writers who just don't get it or who have a lot of difficulty at it. It's nothing to do with how smart they are, but how they fit into writing *Star Trek*. So you end up getting turnover.

MICHAEL PILLER

I didn't save *Star Trek*. I think the show would have survived, but I take a great deal of pride in bringing a creative focus to the characters and doing as challenging material as I could help find. We did do some very special things the third and fourth seasons that set a standard and made *The Next Generation* a must-view weekly experience for a lot of people.

IRA STEVEN BEHR (producer, *Star Trek: The Next Generation*)

We were still getting the comments that Picard isn't Kirk, Data isn't Spock, and Crusher isn't McCoy. We were getting mostly negative feedback, and that's why it's so amusing that the perception is that that's the year it turned around. That's obviously hindsight with the smoke having cleared and the bodies buried. The decisions and opinions are formulated. But, at the time, that's the last thing we were thinking. We were trying to do good shows, but the feedback was thin.

MICHAEL PILLER

The odd thing is that I wasn't really a Trekkie. I did not watch it while I was growing up. It was wonderful to discover the show as a new, fresh, and totally original piece of material.

TOM MAZZA (vice president of current programming and strategic planning, Paramount Television)

Michael had a very strong creative sense and a very strong creative point of view. But at the same time he was very open and very collaborative. I never felt uncomfortable with him, as opposed to others, disagreeing about an area we needed to make a change in. He fought for his principles, he fought for what he believed, but at the end of the day he was absolutely pragmatic. He understood financial limitations, but creatively he had a very good sense of it, and he had a good relationship with Rick. And Rick was an incredible asset to him. They were a great team.

RICK BERMAN

Michael Piller came and met with Gene and I, and the three of us talked. We liked him very much. He seemed to know how to run a writing staff in a traditional fashion. Breaking stories, having a board, having the production assistant write the board, giving out script assignments and assignments for rewrites. We had never had that. Gene certainly didn't work that way and Hurley didn't work that way. Wagner didn't have time to put together anything. Michael was hired and that kind of ended two sort of tumultuous years.

MICHAEL PILLER

I came in with the attitude of "Look, Roddenberry has obviously done something right, because *Star Trek* has lasted three decades. I'm not here to do the Mike Piller universe, I'm here to do the Gene Roddenberry universe."

HANS BEIMLER (coproducer, *Star Trek: The Next Generation*)

What Michael Piller did, for right or wrong, is he came with some decisiveness. [Writer] Robert Wolfe's father was a green beret in Vietnam. He said that his father would say, "It's important when you're leading men in battle that you have to give them orders. The orders don't necessarily matter what they are. Just give them orders and execute them." The worst thing you could do is let the people that are depending on you for information, for direction and for guidance, wander around without any of that.

RICK BERMAN

I've read a lot of stuff about people talking about how horrible the first two years were, but they were horrible for people like Herb Wright and a bunch of others who kind of felt the wrath of Gene and ended up either quitting or getting fired. People who had been on other TV shows, who knew the way it was being done first by Gene and then by Hurley, felt that it was wacky and not at all the way it was traditionally done. But, at the time, I believe that we *did* produce some very good episodes in the first two years and the show was remarkably successful. All my fears about it being a science-fiction syndicated sequel went out the window. Things settled down a great deal more when Michael Piller arrived.

DAVID LIVINGSTON (supervising producer, *Star Trek: The Next Generation*)

Michael Piller was an incredibly compassionate and beautiful man. I'm a big fan. I didn't have a lot of interaction with him, because he was the head of writing staff for a lot of years on several shows. My main thing with him was for "Piller Filler." The shows would inevitably run short, and I tracked them every day, because we did not want to go into post-production knowing we're going to have to go back and shoot additional photography. I would tell Rick we're going to need two more minutes, and they would write to that time we were supposedly going to be short. The term for this was "Piller Filler." Sometimes it was wonderful; sometimes it was stuff they wanted to originally include but felt they didn't have the time for. So they were able to enrich and expand on the episode more than just filling a hole.

BRANNON BRAGA (coproducer, *Star Trek: The Next Generation*)

Initially I think the show was a little clinical, but the show was finding itself. I really do credit Michael Piller with turning the tide on that show and humanizing the characters. You can see it happen from the moment he came in and wrote his first episode.

CHRIS BLACK (coexecutive producer, *Star Trek: Enterprise*)

Michael brought updated storytelling to the series. We can't do reboot episodes of "Mudd's Women." Those were not the stories that were going to fly for a show that's being done at this time.

BRANNON BRAGA

Not only did he turn the show around, but he gave it a new voice. He did have a knack for hiring good people. Michael Piller was a really smart, brilliant man. Very warm and caring, but socially awkward at times. He was very blunt in giving notes or criticism. I think he deserves sainthood for putting up with us young writers. I realize, being a showrunner now, what a nightmare it must have been for him. I have him to thank for my career completely.

BRENT SPINER (actor, "Data")

I'm not even sure which one he is except that he wore a baseball cap.

NAREN SHANKAR (story editor, *Star Trek: The Next Generation*)

Michael didn't want that interaction with the actors. He didn't really care for it that much.

BRYAN FULLER (coproducer, *Star Trek: Voyager*)

Michael Piller is so much the voice of the new *Star Trek*. What was great about what Michael Piller did is he set up an environment for writers like Ron Moore and Brannon Braga and René Echevarria and Joe Menosky to come in and bring a freshness to the science fiction. So you had the classic sense of heroic storytelling and the human philosophy that Michael Piller was adamant had to be the primary ingredient to these shows. And then Ron and Brannon and Joe and René all came in and had different spins and turns where each of them brought something so unique. René's sense of a rich emotional tapestry with Ron's honorable sense of the hero's journey, and Joe's philosophy of what it is to be alive and to be sentient, and then Brannon Braga's twists and turns where he brought *The Twilight Zone* to *Star Trek* in a fantastic and organic way. I look at those writers as champions of science fiction.

MICHAEL PILLER

As soon as I started, I said, "I need to see every script, every abandoned story, and every submitted piece of material that's sitting around, because I have to have something to shoot next week." Somebody gave me a script called "The Bonding," by a guy named Ron Moore who was about to go into the Marines, and it was a very interesting story about a kid whose mother goes down on an away mission and gets killed. The kid is obviously torn apart by the death of his mother, and seeing how much he's suffering, aliens provide him with a mother substitute. The writing was rough and amateurish in some ways, but I thought it had real potential to tell an interesting story.

I went to Gene and pitched him the story, and he said it didn't work. I asked him why, and he said, "Because in the twenty-fourth century, death is accepted as a part of life, so this child would not be mourning the death of his mother. He would be perfectly accepting of the fact that she had lived a good life, and he would move on with his life."

I went back to the writing staff and told them what Gene had said, and they sort of smirked and said, "Ah-ha, you see? Now you know what we've been going through." I said, "Wait a minute, let's think about it. Is there any way we can satisfy Gene's twenty-fourth-century rules and at the same time not lose the story that we have to shoot on Tuesday?" I finally said, "Look, what if this kid has in fact been taught all of his life not to mourn the death of his loved ones, because that's what society expects of him? He's taught that death is a part of life, so he loses his mother and doesn't have any reaction at all.

That's what Gene is telling us has to happen. Well, that is freaky, that is weird, and that's going to feel far more interesting on film than if he's crying for two acts. What if the aliens who feel guilty about killing his mother provide him with a mother substitute and the kid bonds with this mother substitute, and it's Troi who goes to Picard and says, "We have a problem? The kid is not going to give up this mother substitute until he really accepts and mourns the death of his real mother, and we're going to have to penetrate centuries of civilization to get to the emotional core of this kid in order to wake up his emotional life."

So the show becomes a quest for emotional release and the privilege of mourning. Well, Gene loved the idea. It respected his universe and at the same time turned a fairly predictable story on its ear, and it became a far better story and episode than it would have if Gene had simply signed off on the original pitch.

SANDRA PILLER

It was so hard for people in Hollywood to figure out Gene Roddenberry's universe, but somehow Michael was able to do so. The turning point for him was "The Bonding."

MICHAEL PILLER

From that experience, I learned that Roddenberry's "box" forced us to be more creative and to tell stories in more interesting and different ways than we would have in any other typical universe, so I loved that box. Ironically, I became dedicated to preserving the box as much as I possibly could, and as time went on it sort of became Piller's box.

BRANNON BRAGA

There were times where we got really mad at Michael. I remember one time in the writers room at the end of season five, we were all gathered and someone asked him what plans he had for changes for the next season, and he said, "I'm hoping to find some real writers." He didn't mean it, but what he meant was we were kids and he wanted some more high-level people with experience, because when that happens you don't need rewriting. Piller would rewrite us from time to time, less so as time went on.

I know what he meant, but at the time we were appalled. That's not a criticism, that's just how it was. There's one thing I admired about Michael, he was just a very honest person and a good guy. If he were alive today, he'd still be doing shows. It's a shame. I think with so many scripted dramas on the air today, this would have been a great time for Michael.

ANDRÉ BORMANIS (science consultant, *Star Trek: The Next Generation*)

Michael was a very thoughtful guy, kind of cerebral. Michael was really interested in baseball, but I know nothing about baseball, so it was awkward to try to connect with him on any level. I remember I was in Phoenix visiting my parents and Spring Training was going on. Michael Jordan was playing for some minor league team at the time when he briefly went off to try and play baseball, so I thought I'd go check that out. He hit a solid double and it was kind of fun. I hadn't been to a baseball game in years, and I don't know if I've been to one since then, but I saw Michael in his office and told him about it. I brought him a poster or something, and it's, like, "Yeah, okay." It's weird, because on some level it's like you know you're sucking up and he knows you're sucking up, but it's understood that is what people do. And you're trying to get somewhere in your writing career and all that stuff.

BRANNON BRAGA

Michael Piller really thought of it as a drama and, by the way, his thinking of it that way made the show better. He focused on the humanity. I always saw it as a crazy sci-fi show personally, and as a result, my episodes seem to be bereft of any so-called character development.

MICHAEL PILLER

We had a process that we call "breaking a story," where we put all the writing staff in a room and we look around and whatever the writer came in with serves as only a starting point. Everybody sits down and we go to a board and break it down into acts and scenes and we try and see how the show is going to lay out. I told everyone that in this room it is a safe environment and that they are to speak out with whatever ideas they have, even if it's stupid or wrong, because it may spark an idea in someone else that leads us to the solution of a particular problem in a script.

IRA STEVEN BEHR

In season three, we were behind. We were a writing staff in a deep hole that we never really pulled out of. It's the fear of all the writers on a show to have the production team prepping off of outlines instead of scripts, or scripts coming late. I spent that whole season worried we were going to have to shut down. I have never been on a show that shut down before, and I kept swearing to myself I'm not going to let it happen, but it gave me sleepless nights. The first time it ever happened to me that I spent all night lying in bed without once falling asleep was on the third season of *TNG*. Thinking how the hell are we going to do this? How the hell are we going to keep this train moving? It just seemed like there were too many obstacles. We were rushing, but not seeming to go anywhere. It was terrifying. I remember watching the darkness slowly fade away into light thinking, "Fuck me. I've been up all night thinking about this goddamn show."

NAREN SHANKAR

Michael was a really good boss in all the important ways. He gave people a process, he was quite disciplined, smart editorially, in terms of story, and he would tell you what he would think. I think that his basic process, the detailed room break, structure on the boards, that was what he had brought to the show, because the show had very little process and very little structure before.

That was an incredibly important discipline to bring to it. On the downside, I didn't find him to be a warm guy. Weirdly enough, my wife, who was my girlfriend when I was on the show, he was super-charming with her. We were at a party together and she started talking to him and he just kind of lit up. I was, like, "Who the fuck is this guy and why wasn't he here the rest of the time?" I don't know if he just kept a little distance between himself and the younger guys, but there was a little bit of coldness to him, and I think that warmed up over the years. He took great pride in seeing everybody kind of go on and do well, and I think that Michael's coaching tree sort of speaks for itself in the sports metaphor.

IRA STEVEN BEHR

Michael kept wanting to keep things in the pipeline, and so we would have these pitch meetings, because those were the days when freelancers still pitched and no one pitched more than at *Star Trek* where freelancers came in all the time. It became a thing where we never knew what the outcome of a pitch session would be, because Michael could sit there, and no one did any talking. Occasionally, I would say something, but most of the time everyone left it to Michael to see what Michael would do. Some poor guy or girl would come in and pitch a bunch of stories, and Michael would buy it, and it would be, like, "Really?" And he'd say, "I think there's something in that." He'd send the writer off without much direction and it would be, like, it's going to take a miracle for that to happen.

MICHAEL PILLER

I was more dedicated to bringing in new and untried and untested freelance writers than any other show in the history of this town. No other show except the *Star Trek* series has opened the portals to access scripts by amateur freelance writers, as long as they were willing to sign releases for their material. Once we saw good material, I insisted to my staffs that they take pitches from freelance writers day after day. And they *hated* it, because most of the pitches were bad. But maybe one out of a hundred would turn out to be something, and I felt freelance writers brought fresh voices to the show.

IRA STEVEN BEHR

One infamous time, somebody came in and Michael bought multiple stories from this guy, and you knew it was going to be a mess. What would happen is, it would always get dumped in our laps to then try to make this thing work. It would be a story that you didn't necessarily approve of or like, and it did not seem to me the best way to do it. But, Michael just felt, or seemed to feel, that we were so far behind we just had to keep things going.

MICHAEL PILLER

The alternative is that most television shows rely on staff writers to write the entire season. You want to put the best writers you have on staff on it, but I think you have a better assembly line if you have writers inside *and* outside working on product. However, with the open-door policy, I basically said to these people, "Look, you have an opportunity and access here, and I will let you take this story and/or this script as far as you can by yourself. If you can do the whole thing, that's terrific. I'll probably hire you on staff next week, because that's generally how I hire staff. But if you can't and I have to do the work that you couldn't do, I have no hesitation about asking the Writers Guild for recognition for what I achieved in the rewriting of that script." I love to find that new talent and give them an opportunity, but the rate of success is maybe 10 to 15 percent. By the way, that 10 percent includes René Echevarria, Ron Moore, Ken Biller, and Brannon Braga, so is it worth it? Yes.

IRA STEVEN BEHR

On occasion you'd get "Yesterday's Enterprise" or something, although that came from in-house, because Eric [Stillwell] worked on the show. But it made me feel bad. Both for the writers and for us. And ultimately for Michael, because Michael spent most of the time in his room at the typewriter or the computer doing rewrites. Toward the end we switched off episodes in terms of who was in charge of it. That was just faith that he showed in me that I wasn't sure where that was coming from. Which is why I wrote only one episode of my own that season, because I was just so busy rewriting other shows. And, at the time, that kind of annoyed me a little bit.

MICHAEL PILLER

It was Gene Roddenberry's *Star Trek* and it was my job to execute it. You could probably say I wrote almost the whole year third season, because the other people here, with the very clear exception of Ira Behr, were so hostile to me and to Gene and they just couldn't find the freedom to write.

IRA STEVEN BEHR

I did three years on *Fame*, which was a lot of fun, and was also in syndication, and we had no one looking over our shoulder. *Star Trek* wasn't something I was looking for. I hadn't been watching *The Next Generation*. I watched part of the pilot and then turned it off. Someone at Paramount had read a proposal I had for a science fiction show, believe it or not. I got a call to meet with Maurice Hurley during the second season. I went in without any judgment. I didn't know much about what that universe was like, but I got an earful from Maurice, who did not seem tormented. He seemed actually quite neutral about it. What he was telling me was just nightmares in my mind. Stuff like, writers aren't allowed to go down to the set, you can't talk to the actors, there's no conflict on the show, you have to be careful what you write. All stuff that we now know was going on back then. As was my wont, I pretty much said "No, thank you." And that was it. It did not sound like anything I wanted to be involved with.

As often happens, the people on the field changed and suddenly Hans Beimler and Ricky Manning, who I had worked with on their first job on the final season of *Fame* and who I got along with very well, were there.

HANS BEIMLER

On *Fame*, Ira really taught us how to break a story. He was our guiding light. He's such a natural leader. We used to come in and we'd have these beautiful boards and different scenes, in different colors and different storylines. And he'd come and look at them and say, "That's the most beautiful board I've ever seen, but it doesn't work at all." He'd erase it and we'd rebreak the story from scratch, and we *really* learned how to break a story. Then *Star Trek* happened.

IRA STEVEN BEHR

I had never worked with Michael Piller, but I had met him when he was a censor for CBS. We talked movies a lot, and even though we were incredibly different people, in a lot of ways I always liked Michael. I got Michael. A lot of people did not get Michael. I got Michael and he seemed to get me and he was in trouble. Season three was already in disarray when I got there. Michael Wagner had quit, but they were very much behind and I kind of said yes. My first day, I say hi to Ricky and to Hans and I meet Melinda and Richard Danus, who was on the show at the time, and Piller calls me into his office. I hadn't seen an episode and he literally said, "OK, here's what I need you to do. I need you to write act three of 'The Hunted.' Just go off and write it and have him run through Jefferies Tubes."

I come out and I go into Hans' and Ricky's office, and they were in the middle of a rewrite, and I said, "What's a Jefferies Tube?" They were so miserable by that point, they basically just blew me off. So, luckily, this guy, Richard Danus, who I didn't even know was about to be fired in a couple of weeks, sat me down and gave me a quick overview of what I needed to know. I wrote that act that day, scared out of my mind. Thank God it was a chase act and there wasn't tons of dialogue. So, I handed it into Mike and I figured, "This is it. I'll be fired." Of course, I had already heard about all the people who had been fired. He read it and he said, "Great. Terrific." That was my first day. It was successful, but the pressure and the sense of falling down the rabbit hole was so extreme that I can't say I enjoyed it so much. And little did I know that from then on that would be considered one of the few good days. When you were *just* terrified, that was a good day.

Hans and Ricky and Melinda and Richard Danus, to an extent, were beaten and broken and cynical and angry and despairing and we all got along great. We were a tight little group. Ron [Moore] came in and Ron was the new guy. He was Alice in Wonderland, he was just so amazed to be there that he had a different vibe, because he had nothing to compare it to and was *such* a fanboy.

RONALD D. MOORE (producer, *Star Trek: The Next Generation*)

It was tense. Ira was the cheerleader. But Hans and Ricky and Melinda definitely had chips on their shoulders coming out of the second season. One of Piller's saving graces was that Mike was guileless. He wasn't a politicking guy, he wasn't working for different agendas. But the downside of being guileless is that you say shit that pisses people off. Piller at one point wrote this memo to the staff. It was literally how to write for television. Stories have a beginning, middle, and end. Characters should not say what is on their mind. It was a three- or four-page memo to the whole staff, and I'm reading it in my office going, "Oh. Here's a memo on how to write for television."

Meanwhile, there's this explosion down the hall. I go down there, because I hear shouting, and Ricky is ready to quit and Hans is throwing things and Melinda is upset and Ira is trying to calm them all down, because they took it as a huge insult that they had to be told how to write for television by this guy who just showed up. Ira had tried to tell Piller not to send the memo, because Piller was a network executive and he was used to doing stuff like that. Writing memos on how to do things . . . his social skills were somewhat lacking. So he sent this memo that really pissed off everybody, and they all just wanted to kill him. They just didn't like Michael, and they didn't respect him on some basic level. Michael was trying to sort of wrangle the show and wrangle the writers and it was very difficult.

IRA STEVEN BEHR

We'd go to lunch and go down the stairs and I would croak out this song called "Defeated," which was a song by The Fugs. All I remember is the first verse, which included the lines "Defeated, defeated, you know I am defeated. Defeated, defeated, you are defeated, too." And we would come down the steps saying, "Defeated, defeated, you know I am defeated. Defeated, defeated, you are defeated, too." So, that was kind of the vibe. But, we laughed. At times people would shut down. Rick would clean the keys on his keyboard and turn his back to the room and just shake his head.

RONALD D. MOORE

Gene was still directly involved and Gene would throw out scripts that he didn't like. Rick was not really in charge yet, the writing staff had a lot of resentments and there was a lot of politics in the first couple of years. So, when I came in third season about a third of the way into the season, everything was chaotic and crisis. It was just all crisis management, because you had no scripts ahead. You had stories; you had scripts that were in bad shape and things that were going to get thrown out. You were taking pitches and it was just hand to mouth. You were constantly trying to catch up.

NAREN SHANKAR

It was my first job in the business, so I had nothing to compare it to. I learned later, of course, that this was highly anomalous. In reality, you really aren't supposed to let junior writers take pitches. That's kind of a no-no and we sort of treated it with a certain level of disdain ourselves. We had the dry-erase board in my office where we tallied up all of the pitches, and they were categorized, like "Holodeck breaks." Everything was neatly boxed, because the show was that way. You could literally pick "Data Falls in Love," and there were seven of those.

IRA STEVEN BEHR

There was a show, "A Matter of Perspective," written by Ed Zuckerman. Ed Zuckerman was a comedy writer, and clearly when he went off and wrote it he realized that the story wasn't working. Nothing was working. When the draft came in, we all sat around because we were desperate at the time for something to come in that was usable. It was the hardest I had laughed on a TV show. He had turned one of the characters into this Columbo-type character. He wrote this detective who sounded totally modern. One of the character's names was Manua. The spaceship was a giant cigar.

   Whatever it was at the time, we needed a laugh, and it was the laughter of the condemned. We were literally rolling on the floor. Then we brought Ed Zuckerman in to give him notes, and he literally got on his knees and begged us to fire him, and we said, "No, we don't have time! We're too busy rewriting other shows. You have to take another pass at this." So, that was fun, but it was gallows humor most of the time.

RONALD D. MOORE

By the end of the year, they all left . . . except me. I was the only one from third season who stuck around in the fourth. I was really hoping that Ira was going to come back, and Hans and Ricky, too, but I really liked Ira. Michael really wanted Ira to come back, too, because Ira had that ability to get along with anybody politically. He could figure out how to deal with Piller, later he would figure out how to deal with Rick Berman. He was that guy. He could get a show broken and he could take everybody out to lunch and make them feel better and be a cheerleader for them.

HANS BEIMLER

Things were better in season three, but it was still very frustrating, because we'd break a story and have it really well done, and then we'd get nailed by something Gene or somebody—it was Gene, mainly—would object to. We couldn't do the things that we wanted to do when we wanted to do them.

BRANNON BRAGA

Next Generation had to have had an impact, because what makes me freak out about being older but is also heartwarming is meeting younger writers like [*Lost*'s] Damon Lindelof or [*Family Guy*'s] Seth MacFarlane, who grew up on *Next Generation* and were influenced by it. In some small way *Next Gen* and *Star Trek* in general paved the way for genre TV being accessible and in the mainstream.

> One undeniable contribution that Piller made in season three—which would carry on in subsequent seasons and literally have a long-range impact on not only *Star Trek* but the television landscape itself—was the aforementioned open-script submission policy.

NAREN SHANKAR

Michael did an extraordinary thing. In an era where there were a lot of television writers, journeymen, freelancers, Michael recognized the value of fandom and its connection to the show, and he solicited fans to send in material. It's like if you really look at the breakdown of our staff, Brannon was an intern, Ron was hired off a spec, René was hired off of a spec, I was a Writers Guild intern. That door to create a staff was super-unusual and that was Michael saying, "No, I want this to be the way we hire people. I want this to be the way we find talent." I'm not even sure that's repeatable.

That's how Ron got in the door. Ron hadn't seriously been considering being a screenwriter as a career. He was a natural writer, but that was his window into the business. That was that little crack that allowed you to get in.

RONALD D. MOORE

I'd flunked out of college, I'd moved to L.A., I was living with my ex-roommate in Studio City, sleeping on the floor and trying to be a writer. I had been working for a few months at the animal hospital on Ventura Boulevard, and as part of trying to get into the movie and TV business, I used to walk across the street to the gas station where they would have *Daily Variety* and *The Hollywood Reporter*. I would go in and buy the trades to read up and understand the business.

I remember picking up *Daily Variety*, and there was an article that said, "Trek Beams Back to TV," and I was thrilled and excited. From that moment, I wanted to write an episode for that show. I sat there the night it premiered, and when it said, "Space, the final frontier," I remember tears came to my eyes. I thought, "It's back. It's really back," and that was an amazing experience.

NAREN SHANKAR

When Ron and I were in college together at Cornell, we would, late at night in our fraternity, go down to the TV room and we would watch old *Star Trek* episodes and we would race to see who could identify them first. Weirdly enough, for some odd reason or another at Cornell, McDonald's was doing delivery, so for one glorious summer we could order hamburgers late at night, but they wouldn't deliver fries because they couldn't be delivered hot enough. So it was like either Domino's Pizza or McDonald's hamburgers and watching *Star Trek* late at night.

We had a friend of ours who had decided that he was going to go out to Los Angeles and break into the movie business. Ron was vaguely ROTC, I was an engineer. Film business? What the fuck is that? Well, a year later this friend came back and said, "You hate school. Come on out to L.A. and be a screenwriter." Ron basically took him up on the offer. And then a couple of years later, when I finished my doctoral thesis and I decided I didn't want to be an engineer and didn't know what I was going to do, Ron literally said, "Come on out to L.A. and be a screenwriter," and I was, like, "Sounds good."

RONALD D. MOORE

I would tape *Next Generation* every week on VHS and watch it, and told myself someday I'm going to write for it, but I was still sort of at ground zero in terms of actually having a writing career. I was working a series of odd jobs in L.A.; at an animal hospital as a receptionist, I was a messenger, and I did contract administration. Along the way I started and stopped scripts. I wasn't really pursuing a path to get me through the doors of Paramount, which is so odd in retrospect. I was just kind of being a young guy in L.A. and telling myself I was going to write for the show someday.

It wasn't until I had started dating this girl who noticed I was wearing a *Star Trek* pin when we met and said, "Oh, you know, I used to work at *Star Trek* and I still know some people there." Early in the relationship, she said, "I can probably get you a tour of the sets. They have a regularly scheduled tour of the *Next Generation* sets." To her surprise, I didn't know, and I said that'd be amazing. She made a call to Junie Lowry, the casting director she had worked for, and got me on a set tour.

It was going to be in about six weeks or so, and it was only at that point that I decided I'm going to write a episode, take it with me, and see if I can get somebody to read it. I knew that was taking a chance since that wasn't the purpose of the tour, but I didn't know that it was really crazy to try and do that. I had had an idea kicking around in my head about the *Enterprise* and the families aboard the ship. One of the things that I was interested in in the first season was they said all these families are aboard. They had played it a couple of times that Picard would get in trouble and "Our families are our strength." But it just felt like they weren't doing very much with the idea of what it really meant to have thousands of children aboard a starship like that, which, frankly, I thought was kind of a crazy idea in concept. I didn't think it made sense. How often was the *Enterprise* about to blow up? Really? They are really going to put families on this thing? But, once they had done it, I thought, "OK, I'm interested to see what they are going to do with it," and then they didn't seem to do much with it.

When I started thinking about what episode would I write, it was, I'll do one about what happens to a boy when his mother dies and he doesn't have a father. What do they do aboard the *Enterprise* when there's a kid who is suddenly orphaned? I thought, that's an interesting show that I'd want to watch.

I had a copy of the script for "Encounter at Farpoint" so I could see the format, and I just started typing away on my Mac. I didn't have a scriptwriting program, so I just sort of did it all with tabs inserted and copied the format as best I could. I didn't do a lot of rewriting on it and that was the copy that I took with me. I went to the set. It was the first time I ever drove up to the Paramount lot and there were the big gates. I parked in the tank in front of the big, blue sky and walked to the Hart Building.

I went upstairs and there was [archivist] Richard Arnold and a handful of other people on the tour that day. Richard was chatty and very personable and nice. I'm sitting there with this thing under my arm and eventually he noticed and he was, like, "What's that?" I said, "Oh, this is something for you for later." He's like, "Hmmm." He knew right away it was probably a script. He was, like, "Yeah, you know, I can't really read that." And I was crushed. I just wanted to leave it. And he said, "Well, we'll talk about it." He was trying to be polite more than anything else, and then we went out on the tour and I left it at his office.

I was still a little distracted about what I was going to do about my script, but I do remember walking onto the soundstage where engineering was. I walked around the back and saw all the sets were made of wood; you could see all the wood framing on the outside of the corridor. Then we walked into engineering and the big console was covered with a plastic tarp and the engine light was off, but it was still clearly engineering. I was, like, "Oh my God, I'm here!" We walked a little bit further and went into the hangar deck and they were doing a scene from "Time Squared," where Picard was getting out of the shuttle. We left the soundstage to go walk across to the bridge, and I remember as we walked out of the soundstage, going, "I'll be back."

We went back up to Richard's office, and on the way back to the Hart Building is when I start chatting him up a little more. I think he was, like, "OK, I shouldn't do this, but I will take a look at it." He read the script, and then he said, "You know, this is actually pretty good. You got some of the formatting wrong, we actually have a five-act structure now and this is four, but it's pretty good." I was a little embarrassed that I hadn't picked that up, so I rewrote it into five acts and gave it to him again a few days later. Then he said, "You need an agent to submit it to the show." I said, "I don't have an agent." He said, "Well, I can put you in touch with my agent."

Richard had an agent to represent him for things like the *Star Trek* calendar he did and stuff like that. He negotiated literary deals. I said, "That'd be amazing, because I've been trying to get an agent for a couple of years with no success." So he put me in contact with Sherry Robb who, at that point, was a literary agent who wanted to represent television clients, so it was sort of a good opportunity for both of us. She took the script, formally submitted it to the show, and then it sat in a slush pile for, like, seven months.

Every once in a while, Richard would touch base and say, "You know, some-body looked at it today" or "No, they haven't looked at it." I just waited, but I still had this innate faith that they were going to read it and then buy it. It's weird, look-ing back, but I do remember that feeling.

What I heard later was that Richard kept putting it at the top of the slush pile. Eventually, Melinda Snodgrass, who was on staff, was the first one to read it. She liked it enough to give it to Michael Piller, who had just come aboard as the new executive producer and head of the writing staff at that point. Piller read it and I got a call. I was in my office doing contracts for a very small international distributor of films, when I got the message that somebody named Michael Piller was on the phone. He said, "Well, I read your script and I enjoyed it and I think we're going to buy it." It was an enormous moment. It wasn't that I had forgotten about it, but it had been seven months and, even though I never really lost faith it was going to happen, I wasn't thinking about it that week. I was just doing my job and I got this call out of the clear blue sky and it just changed my life in a moment. "We're going to produce it and I'd like you to come down and pitch us some ideas for another one."

I was thrilled and I scraped together a bunch of concepts for another pitch. I didn't even know how to pitch . . . or what a pitch even was. I had a yellow pad full of ideas, and in a week or two I found myself sitting outside Michael Piller's office in the Hart Building. I went inside for the pitch and there was the whole writing staff. It was Ira, Hans [Beimler] and Ricky [Manning] and Richard Danus and Melinda [Snodgrass] and Michael. I proceeded to pitch them stories, and they were sort of loglines, and they pretty much shot them down one by one. Some they'd already done or some they'd rejected, but what was interesting is that they were enthusiastic. I remember Hans saying when I went through them all at the end, "Is that it?" and I said, "That's about it." And Hans was saying, "I can't wait to hear the next five, because those are great." It was like I was in the groove of what they were doing.

Michael just said, "Yeah, let's do this again when you're ready. You'll come back in and pitch another group, and meanwhile your show will be in production in a few weeks and you're welcome to come to the set." So, of course, I went home and I was disappointed I didn't sell one, but I was happy the door was still open. I cobbled together a second group, went in for a second pitch, and didn't sell any of those, either. But then a morning meeting ran a little late, and Michael said, "Why don't you come with us, let's go eat lunch together and we can talk more there." So, we all went to the Paramount commissary and I had lunch with the staff for the first time. Over lunch, we kind of went through whatever was left of my story ideas and they were all rejected again. Then what happened was we started chatting and they were talking about the show, and Hans started talking about still wanting to do a Romulan show this year. Somebody said, "I don't know, maybe it's a hero or a villain or a Romulan defector." I just sort of seized the moment and went, "You know, actually I've been thinking about a show about a Romulan." And they went, "Oh really?"

I just sort of started riffing in the moment and talking about Romulans and defectors and it could be a Cold War thing, and then Piller went, "Hmm, well, that's kind of interesting. Let's do that." Suddenly, I had sold a story. The next time I was there I came to see them shooting my episode. Richard took me down to the set, and they were filming a scene, and Patrick [Stewart] was there, and, at one point, Richard called Patrick over and introduced him to me and said, "This is Ron Moore, he wrote this episode."

Patrick said, "Oh, lovely to meet you. It's a marvelous script. Just so delighted. So are you writing another one for us?" And I said, "Yes, as a matter of fact I'm writing one about this Romulan defector." And he said, "Oh, just marvelous, can't wait to read it. Just bear one thing on mind: The captain doesn't do nearly enough screwing and shooting on this show."

Another major talent that was discovered through the open-script submission process instituted by Piller was René Echevarria, who would go on to work on *The Next Generation* until its conclusion. He later became one of the most accomplished writers on *Deep Space Nine* before running such series as *Dark Angel*, *Castle*, and *Teen Wolf*, which he developed for MTV.

RENÉ ECHEVARRIA (supervising producer, *Star Trek: Deep Space Nine*)

My father was a doctor, and I come from an immigrant background. My parents were from Cuba, and there was really no choice in the matter. I was going to be a doctor. It was the only thing you could do to protect yourself from the vicissitudes of life, because you never know when you might have to pick up and move. I was a good student but, at the same time, my father said, "If you ever want a book, I will always buy it for you." And that ended up costing him, because I was a big reader. I read all the Tarzan books, and there's like twenty-two of them. We bonded over *The Three Musketeers* and books like that.

In fact, I didn't want to become a doctor. I was squeamish and didn't like being in a hospital. I was at Duke majoring in history with the aim of being a professor, and then I fell into the theater department. I moved to New York after graduation and floundered a little bit. When *Star Trek* came out in '87, I was, like, "Oh, a new *Star Trek*." That was the first time I'd ever conceived the idea of writing for the screen at all—and even more specifically for television. Nothing had interested me before that. I didn't even know that it was a job you could have.

TOM MAZZA

Star Trek was a unique animal unto itself. It told moral tales, it told ethical stories, all wrapped around a science-fiction storyline. And on top of that, you had to have the jargon, the ability to write technobabble, and it's easier said than done because you have got to do it and make it sound like it's got some credibility and that it makes sense. And then, of course, the next level is there has to be some scientific logic to it. All of that needs to come together.

We used to get a lot of spec scripts that were great attempts, but never really could put it together. And so we were always reading. And we actually got a plethora of them. It wasn't so infrequent as you think, but there were few that actually made sense and worked. One of the spec scripts that I remember went well was from René Echevarria out of New York, when he was living there. René was really special. You could tell that, and we had read it and sent it over to Rick. Rick really responded to it and the rest is history. He started writing scripts and ended up on staff.

RENÉ ECHEVARRIA

It was a rocky start for me. I started writing a spec script, I believe it was a little bit like "The Enterprise Incident" from the original series. That somehow we were in a shuttle that almost starts a nuclear war. At the time, Reagan's Star Wars was very much in the news, the discussion about nuclear missiles and space defense shields, and it was all about that. I thought it was going to change the world. But I don't know if I was ever able to get it read. I didn't know you could send a spec script in. At that point, my friends were starting to worry about me.

I kept sending these scripts to Paramount Pictures in an envelope and then never hearing back. Eight months went by and, unbeknownst to me, I was lucky enough to get caught in that sieve that Michael Piller had started of reading fan scripts, and one day after about eight months I got a call from this guy: "Hi, I'm Michael Piller from *Star Trek*. I really like your script and we want to do it. Can you come out here next week?"

Michael had only been on the show for a few months, so I didn't recognize his name. I remember having this whole conversation and then going, "Can I ask you one more thing before we hang up? What do you do on the show?" And he kind of chuckled and said, "Well, I'm the executive producer and the head writer." And I'm like "OK! So, are you guys going to get me a plane ticket?" And he says, "No, you need to get out here yourself." "Can you recommend a good hotel?" He's like, "Kid, do you know anybody out here that can help you? I just need you here on Thursday!" "What should I wear?" He's like, "I can't talk to you anymore. Here's my assistant."

RONALD D. MOORE

I wrote my second episode, "The Defector," and interestingly enough, especially now knowing what I know, we didn't break the show. I didn't meet with the staff and go through the whole process, Piller just sent me off to write it as a freelancer, so I wrote it and I struggled with it. It was a harder script to pull off, and I turned it in and waited a week or so, and then I remember on a Friday I got this call from Piller saying, "Well, I got it and frankly I'm a little disappointed. Not really what we had in mind. It doesn't feel like the writing is quite there so I think this will probably be it. And we'll take it from here." And I was devastated. I was like "Should I come up with some other ideas?" And he said, "No, I think we're pretty much full for the year." And that was it. I was really crushed, because then it felt like the door had suddenly slammed shut. They didn't like that script and they didn't even want me to come in and pitch more.

I called Melinda, because she and I had become somewhat casually friendly, and I asked her what had happened. She said, and I will always remember her quote, "I guess you want blood, right?" I said "Yeah." And she said, "You need a little more maturity. The voice isn't quite there and it just felt like a very green writer. And I'm sure you'll do better and you have a lot of potential." And that was it. I spent that weekend just really depressed and my agent, Sherry, was saying, "Oh don't worry about it; there's plenty of other TV shows and you have two credits now, so you're on your way." I just didn't care. I was really shocked. And then Monday came around, Michael called again, and he said, "Well, you know what? I read it again over the weekend and it's got some good stuff in it. It's not that bad. Why don't you come in, and we're going to re-break the show with the writing staff, and you can be a part of that process. And maybe you can write one of the acts." I went in, and this time I was there for one of my first formal break sessions with the whole writing staff, and we broke the show. It was the first time I'd ever seen that or participated in it, and I gave my thoughts. I was willing to argue the point when I thought somebody was wrong.

We broke what became "The Defector." I bonded with the staff and had a great time. I went out and then I think I wrote one of the acts, and it was a gangbang. That was the term we all used whenever the entire staff was working on the script; Piller would sew them all together in the end. So I was part of the gangbang. The script came together, and it was much better received, and it went right into production, because they were so tight on time and they were just desperately trying to keep ahead of the shooting schedule.

Then after that was done, I got another call from Piller, and he said, "Well, I just let a writer go today. I just fired a story editor." I knew it had to be Richard Danus. And he said, "I need a staff writer. Can you come down and start working tomorrow?" I just showed up, I didn't even negotiate a contract, and started work as a staff writer. I met with Michael in his office, and he said, "We're going to see how this goes. There's no guarantees. It's going to be a week-to-week contract. If it doesn't work out, don't feel bad. It was just something we tried and we'll do it as long as you can. Just so you know, you're walking into a very demoralized staff.

I've just taken a script away from Melinda and she's not speaking to me and Hans and Ricky are in a bad mood. Ira is trying to keep everybody together, but he's not having much success, so there's a lot of animosity up there on the fourth floor."

The week-to-week contract went on for quite some time, because people just kind of forgot about it. Piller kind of forgot about it and nobody mentioned it again. But that was my contract. It was week to week. So what would happen is, every Friday I would wait for somebody to tell me, like, "Oh, you've been officially picked up another week," but they never did. Not even the first week. I just came back on Monday, but I would walk through the hall on the ground floor with this sense of dread. If I could make it to the elevator that was a good thing. Eventually it came to a head at one point when we were doing the script for "Yesterday's Enterprise" and we were gangbanging that one. Everybody took an act and for some reason Michael couldn't do one, so he said, "OK, somebody needs to do two acts. Who's going to do it?" And I just said, "I'll do it." And they all looked at me like I was crazy, because we were all so tired and strung out and everybody was working lots of different projects at that point. And he went back upstairs and Ira turned to me and said, "What are you doing? Why are you volunteering for work?" And I said, "Well, I'm not like you guys. I'm here on a week-to-week contract. I have to prove myself every day and I have to do more." And they all looked at me, again, like I was crazy. You're going to what? I said, "Yeah, I'm just here week to week." And he shook his head and went to talk to Piller and the next thing I know they gave me a contract as a story editor after three months.

RENÉ ECHEVARRIA

I got out there and came in. Unbeknownst to me, there had been a lot of turnover in the staff, a lot of people had been hired and fired. In a bathroom in Ron Moore's office there was this *Star Trek: The Next Generation* memorial wall with all the names of writers who had been hired and fired. Ron himself was a nervous wreck. He was on a week to week, because Michael wasn't sure about him. Like me, he had written a spec script that got made and then he'd been asked to stay on staff. Frankly, I don't think liked me being there.

Michael Piller was new, and he was bringing a different kind of storytelling discipline to the show, which had really moved it away from the sort of allegory of the week. He just had this insistence it has to be about one of these people and they had become real. You could see it as a fan. I credit so much of the success of the show to that discipline Michael brought. But, it was a big adjustment for the writers. I remember there was a big controversy going on. They were all very upset, because there was a Data episode where Melinda Snodgrass really wanted him to feel something, to have an emotion. I walk into this meeting to discuss "The Offspring" and I can't believe I'm there, and everybody is, like, "Data is a toaster!" I'm like, "What does that mean?" "He's a toaster, he's a refrigerator! Got that! So good luck, kid! Good luck writing an episode about a toaster having a baby!"

They were all kind of upset because this lovely story had gotten shot down because ultimately Gene, who was still somewhat involved at that point, had said, "Data is a character on a quest. Don't let him reach the end of it. So, him falling in love is a misstep." And, ultimately, in the long term he was right.

NAREN SHANKAR

Ron had slept on the floor of this friend of ours for weeks when he came out to Los Angeles, and when I came out, I slept on Ron's couch for a couple months. I had written a *Star Trek* spec because he said to do that, and Ron had gotten it to the gang, and they read it and then I got an internship on the show.

And in the makeup department, another super fan was about to arrive aboard the *Enterprise* as well. Doug Drexler had just finished work on Warren Beatty's *Dick Tracy*, which would eventually land him an Academy Award for makeup, but his real dream job was to work on *Star Trek*.

DOUG DREXLER (special makeup effects artist, *Star Trek: The Next Generation*)

I knew that as soon as *Dick Tracy* was done I wanted to go right over to Paramount and beg Mike Westmore to hire me to work on *Star Trek*. Which is exactly what I did. Mike and I hit it off immediately, we were fast friends and he's like family to me now. The Oscar happened while I was on *Star Trek*, which was even more amazing, because I remember Mike saying, "Why do you want to do television?" And I'm, like, "Mike, this is it for me, right here. I don't want to be anywhere else. This is where I want to be."

RONALD D. MOORE

I didn't have a lot of interaction with Gene. You'd see him in the corridor; you'd see him at events and Christmas parties. I only really had one creative meeting with him. I was a new writer and I had been there for a week or two, and they said, "Gene wants to meet you." So I went downstairs and into his office and met him.

It was the only time I was with him one on one. He was a big bear of a guy and he smiled. He had this gentle warmth to him. You liked him immediately and he was very welcoming. He was, like, "Oh, enjoy it. I'm so happy to have you. I think you're a great writer." I don't remember most of the conversation, because he just kind of talked a little bit and welcomed me aboard. I shook his hand and walked out. I felt like a million bucks, and pretty much after that, I'd see him in the corridors, he'd always have his little can of Coke, which had bourbon in it, of course. It was a running joke for all of us. You'd see him coming into the Hart Building. He'd be at meetings now and again or Christmas parties. His health started to fade in the fourth season.

First season he was still the guy, and he didn't have a cane, and he was more notorious for throwing out this or throwing out that. There was a story that Hans and Ricky had that we all got really excited about. It was about the *Enterprise* pulling up to some planet, and it was something like they were Nazis or some genocidal thing with an alien race destroying them. There was a Prime Directive issue, but Picard decided he had to intervene and stop this genocide from happening. Gene threw the story out and literally said that if the *Enterprise* came to a planet where they were shoving Jews into ovens, the *Enterprise* would have to leave. We freaked out and we were so upset. We were, like, I don't care about the Prime Directive. At a certain point this violates the whole concept of this idealism. Kirk would never do that. Kirk violated the Prime Directive all the fucking time. We just couldn't believe it. But Gene was running this much harder line on stuff like that.

He just wanted the show to be more about a utopia of the future rather than a TV series, really. So you ran into those kind of problems, and so he was kind of known for being a pain. He was a problem in the third season. There was a point where he did a rewrite of "Ménage à Trois" and there was a scene where Troi and Riker are down on Betazed having a picnic and Mrs. Troi is there. We were reading the scene descriptions out loud, because in the script it said something like "Mrs. Troi picks up a long cylindrical-shaped fruit with a tip and veins running down its sides and hands it to Riker." It was *overtly* sexual.

It was funny. I remembered there was a memo on "The Defector" he wrote, which was Gene's reaction to the story outline. Somewhere in the comments was Gene saying, "What's Romulan sex like? Maybe Beverly should have sex with a Romulan. I bet their sex lives would be amazing. It probably is quite violent." It was like a paragraph and I was just, like, "*What*?"

IRA STEVEN BEHR

Gene was involved. Not on a daily basis. He didn't always come in. When he came in I'd see him in the hallway. He was always very nice. He seemed a little unsteady on his feet. He was not in good shape. My one real face-to-face sit-down discussion with Gene Roddenberry was on "Captain's Holiday." It wasn't pretty. The idea that I came up with was a story about a Picard who is overworked, he's stressed out, and he goes to this pleasure planet called Risa. But, it's not to get laid, as it turned out. It was just to relax and take it easy. And there was a kind of a holo-suite on the planet where you go in and face your deepest fears.

So he thought he would have an entertaining adventure and go off and kick some butt and have a good time and kind of have a, dare I say, Captain Kirk–like adventure. And what happens is he goes there and the holo-suite program plays a scenario where he's been made an admiral. He's no longer going to be the captain of the *Enterprise*. Riker has taken over as the captain. And it's about looking at middle age and all that stuff. His fear was one day he'd have to step down. And we were all really excited about it. Ron thought it was great, and I pitched it to Michael. Michael loved it. Everyone was, like, "Yeah, this is the kind of story we have to do."

Then I had a call from Rick saying you've got to meet with Roddenberry. Roddenberry wants to meet with *me*? He hardly notices me. So, I go in there, he was behind his desk. He's very nice and then we get into the story and he goes, "We're not doing this story." And all I have heard so far were positives, so this blanket negative really took me by surprise. Why it should, given all the stories I had heard, I don't know. But, to be a writer in television you have to be an optimist. Maybe you have to be an optimist to be a writer to begin with, but on some level you have to believe that it's going to work out.

He said, "We're never going to do this story. Picard would never, ever have these self-doubts or concerns. This is the twenty-fourth century, we're all perfect human beings. We're emotionally stable." And then he said the words that really cut to the heart of it all for me. He said, "Jean-Luc Picard is John Wayne. And John Wayne has no fears." And I said, "Whoa! Hold on a second." Now you're on my turf, because I've been watching and studying John Ford and John Wayne and Howard Hawks and John Wayne movies since I was a wee little kid. And let me tell you something, you're talking about John Wayne the icon, the perception in the media. But if you're talking about his movies, and then I talked about *The Quiet Man* and I talked about *The Searchers* and *She Wore a Yellow Ribbon,* which was a perfect example. It's all about a man who has to retire after being in the army all those years. What he said is just not true. That's *not* John Wayne.

If you want Picard to be John Wayne, let him be John Wayne. But an interesting John Wayne. And it was absolutely not. "There is no way we're doing this story. But, I like this idea of the pleasure planet . . . come up with a story where he's stressed and overworked and he goes down to this pleasure planet, and I want to see in the background women holding hands with other women, and men walking, holding hands with other men. In scenes in the background I want to see women kissing other women and men kissing other men, and then in the background I want to see orgies." "Orgies on *Star Trek: The Next Generation?*" "Yes, I want to see orgies. I want this to be an erotic episode where the captain gets to indulge his erotic nature." It just went on and on and I'm thinking, someone pinch me, someone wake me up, because I have literally gone into a Philip K. Dick alternate reality. This can't be real. So, I go back and I say to Rick, "Rick. Orgies. Men and women and cumming and sex." And he goes, "Oh, don't listen to any of that. Forget all that, just get Picard laid."

So then we had to go back and come up with this asinine story, which was like *The Maltese Falcon* with the Vorgon and the Tox Uthat and that stuff. Mike asked me to put a Ferengi in it, even though I wasn't happy about it, because when I looked at the Ferengi episode it was not good and I was not happy. Then I get a call, Patrick Stewart would like to have lunch with you at the commissary. It's like, "Really? Patrick wants to have lunch? He doesn't know me. Can they send someone else to be me? He won't know the difference." So, I go in and Patrick is the nicest man you'd want to have lunch with. We order and we talk and we chat and then he goes, "There is a rumor going around there is this episode being considered where the captain has fears about growing old. I have to tell you that there is no way I would do that episode." And it's, like, Gene Roddenberry just killed this episode three days ago. What the hell?

He gave me, "The trouble with the show is the captain doesn't get to fight and fuck enough. That's what it needs more of. It doesn't need this kind of 'Am I getting too old for the job?' If they gave the job to Number One, I would say, 'Good job, Number One, congratulations!'" That was that lunch. It was like killing a flea with an elephant gun.

I wrote the script and everyone seemed to like it. We filmed it and then I created this character of Vash and we had the big hot scene on *The Next Generation,* which is Picard and Vash in a cave, where else? We're watching dailies and they start kissing and suddenly Ricky Manning is no longer cleaning his computer keys, he's staring at the screen with his mouth hanging open going, "Are they swapping spit? They're really going at it." The next thing we hear is they're a couple and he's left his wife. So because we didn't do "the captain has fears about becoming an admiral," his marriage went south and he got himself a new girlfriend.

Despite Patrick Stewart's concerns that the captain didn't "fight and fuck enough," by mid-season the new show was sufficiently secure with its place in the *Star Trek* pantheon to reintroduce Sarek (Mark Lenard), Spock's father from the original show and feature films.

IRA STEVEN BEHR

When we did the "Sarek" rewrite, the fight over the word 'Spock' was insane. I was absolutely not allowed to use the word 'Spock.' Rick [Berman] made a big issue of it and said we can't do it. There's no way. We did it once. We had McCoy show up at the beginning, but no more. No references to the original series. I said, "It's Spock's father, we're already in that territory." He said, "Absolutely not." About a week later, I was up in his office discussing something else, because there came a point where he only wanted to give me notes or have me there when he was giving other writers notes, so I had to be the one there all the time as he went through the script and went over his little red changes. We were talking about something, and it was kind of benign, and I just suddenly said to him, "Rick, tell me again, why can't we say the word 'Spock'?" And his whole body language changed, he leaned back in his chair and flung his hands up behind the back of his head, and I could tell he did not want to have this discussion again. But he couldn't think of a reason at that very moment, and he just said, "OK, you can say it *once*." It was ridiculous.

Patrick came up and didn't want to do the mind meld scene, which we thought was a terrific scene. He had a big problem . . . I wish I could remember what it was. He just didn't like it. He wanted to cut it. We wound up cutting a line or two and then he was fine. That was another one of those "have I gone down the rabbit hole?" moments. That was a fun scene to write. I felt I was having interesting ideas that were met with disapproval.

MARC CUSHMAN (writer, "Sarek"; author, *These Are the Voyages*)

I pitched to Gene Roddenberry between the first and second seasons of *Next Generation*. Actually, I suggested three or four stories, but the idea of a Vulcan going through senility was the one that caught his attention. It grabbed him instantly. I felt like I barely got the pitch out before he was responding and asking questions. And once Gene liked an idea, he would start discussing it with the writer and the story would develop. I'd heard this from others who had pitched to him and then experienced it myself. He was a very creative writer, but, by this time, he also had a lot of rules about what emotions could or could not be explored on *TNG*. He felt humankind would have evolved beyond the primitives of *TOS*. And that took some of the fun out of it.

I asked Gene how old a Vulcan could live to be. He said they had never locked in an age, but he figured three hundred to four hundred. I said, "Then Sarek would likely still be alive. And Mark Lenard is still acting, and you wouldn't even have to dye his hair this time. It's gray now." Gene liked Mark, and so seemed okay with the idea. However, after I turned in a first draft, he had second thoughts. He felt it was too early in the series to be bringing in characters from the original *Star Trek,* so asked me to make it a different Vulcan . . . or even someone other than a Vulcan. And that broke my heart. Eventually the story was turned back toward Sarek, but that was a year or more later, and I don't think it was Gene's idea. I think Rick Berman or Mike Piller wanted that.

Meanwhile, the mood turned dour on set, and that would infect the tired and weary ensemble for the rest of the season. Cast and crew were burned out by the prolonged shooting schedule necessitated by second season's Writers Guild strike and anxious for summer hiatus.

IRA STEVEN BEHR

The third season was such a demented time. It was so difficult for everyone involved, including Michael [Piller], to get it all together. The show had fallen way behind because of the things that happened in the beginning of the season, and it was a long and unpleasant season. It was a time when the pressures of doing television were getting to everyone, and they aren't a lot of fun to begin with. On the third season on this show, it got ugly. I'm just talking about the pressures, and I think we all reacted in ways that did not show anyone at their best. That's totally understandable, and if it happened all over again, I'm sure no one would act any better. It was just a very difficult situation.

DAVID CARREN (writer, *Star Trek: The Next Generation*)

There's an English television writer who said that in England TV shows are written and in America they're assembled.

WIL WHEATON (actor, "Wesley Crusher)

Midway through the third season, I was beginning to feel like a day player who was just doing a lot of consecutive days. Around the time I turned eighteen, I really felt I was stagnating, until I said I wanted to leave and do films. Then they started writing great stuff for me. If they had given me stuff like in "Final Mission" and in the two or three shows that led up to that episode, I would have never left. I could go around and say "Aye, aye, Captain," for another year or I could go. I asked to be let go.

LISA WILKE (writer, *Star Trek: The Next Generation*)

I had gone to the sets a year before and [Michael Piller's assistant] Eric Stillwell told us, "Bottle shows; all they want are bottle shows. Don't go to another planet, make it as cheap as possible and maybe they'll buy it."

ROB BOWMAN (director, *Star Trek: The Next Generation*)

For some reason *Star Trek* gets away with it more than any other show would. There is an impression we are on a ship in space, so there's really no place to go. Can you imagine a cop show where you're in the squad room the whole time? How come we don't go out and catch some bad guys?

DENNIS RUSSELL BAILEY (writer, *Star Trek: The Next Generation*)

I wanted to demonstrate that we could turn in work they could use. The upshot of this was that they had reached a point third season where they really needed an extra show. Michael Piller and the rest of the staff were pulling stories out of nowhere and making them better than had been seen first and second year. Piller and the people he handpicked turned the show entirely around, and they were up against the wall every week.

They wrote "Yesterday's Enterprise" in three days with five writers, and it came out wonderfully. There came a point where we were told they wanted a script that was ready to shoot, so they could spend more time working on the scripts they thought had a lot of potential and needed rewriting, and they had no expectations they could find a script out of nowhere.

> Few shows did more to cement *The Next Generation*'s reputation as a worthy sequel to the original series than "Yesterday's Enterprise," a dark, fatalistic alternate timeline story in which history is changed as the *Enterprise-C* arrives through a time disturbance and changes the timeline so the Federation is now losing a prolonged war with the Klingon Empire (and Tasha Yar remains very much alive). To this day, "Yesterday's Enterprise" remains widely viewed as one of the best episodes of *Star Trek* ever produced.

MICHAEL PILLER

That's a classic episode, but it had *so* many plot holes in it. I'm not sure we ever plugged them all. It was as entertaining and unique a time travel show as you'll ever see, but, hell, Picard sends five hundred people back to their death on the word of the *bartender*.

RONALD D. MOORE

I'd heard from time to time, I wish you'd do some war stories, but this is the reality of war. It's not a pretty place. But it *was* a lot of fun to watch that ship move and see Picard biting off Riker's head. I wrote a couple of different story outlines on it. Somewhere during the course of that, I came up with the idea that the alternate universe would really be nasty and awful and militaristic and that we're losing the war with the Klingons.

ERIC STILLWELL (writer, "Yesterday's Enterprise"; assistant to Michael Piller)

Trent Christopher Ganino and I were inspired by "The City on the Edge of Forever" and "Mirror, Mirror." It started out as two different stories, one that Trent had written about an *Enterprise* from the past traveling through time, but no alternate universe scenario, and a story I had been developing as a Sarek story involving "The City on the Edge of Forever," which was also an alternate history story. Coincidentally, I had seen Denise Crosby at a convention in San Jose, and she had expressed interest in coming back to the show, and said, "You should write a story for me." So Trent and I started tossing around ideas to bring back Tasha using a variation of the alternate universe idea I'd been working on.

The story was pitched and Michael Piller called Sarek and the Guardian "gimmicks" from the original series that he wanted to avoid at the time, but he was aware of Trent's spec script about an *Enterprise* from the past and asked us to combine the two stories.

IRA STEVEN BEHR

Even though the episode came out well, it was a miserable experience. It was Michael having you bring a writing staff in over the Thanksgiving weekend to break the story for "Yesterday's Enterprise" and having really unhappy writers in that room. I was the one who had to crack the whip. I wasn't too thrilled about that.

RONALD D. MOORE

That got past Gene, because it wasn't really the characters, it was like doing a "Mirror, Mirror" story, in essence. You had an alternate universe. At the time, though, we thought it was a disaster. The script was in pieces. It was a spec originally and then I wrote an outline of how to rewrite it. I decided in my version I wanted to change the way the bridge looked. They were all armed and it's darker. It was gang-banged around Thanksgiving, and I remember having to be there on the Thanksgiving holiday, and all of us unhappy about being there. Ira cheerleading us all and then scolding us, like, "Hey guys, this is the job, so get over it, crybaby. We've got a fucking job to do here."

It was chaotic and expensive with big effects and redoing the sets and uniforms. It was going through so much churn and turmoil that we thought it was going to be an epic flop. It wasn't until we started seeing dailies and we saw how cool it looked on camera that we started to have some hope that it might turn out to be okay. That was the best we could hope for. We had no hope that it was going to be one of the great episodes of the series.

ERIC STILLWELL

When all is said and done, I think the story resonates with the fans for the same reasons that "Mirror, Mirror" and "City" resonate with *TOS* fans. That partly comes from the fact that Trent and I were true and genuine fans and that came through in our story ideas.

I loved how the episode turned out, thanks to Ron Moore, Ira Behr, Hans Beimler, Richard Manning, and Michael Piller, who all worked together to pull a rabbit out of a hat when the script development was accelerated to make it possible to have Whoopi and Denise available on the same week.

DOUG DREXLER

I was working on the *Enterprise-C* bridge on "Yesterday's Enterprise" one day after *Dick Tracy* came out. I was at the craft service table and one of the A.D.'s [assistant directors] came over, and it was pretty early, not everyone knew me, and said, "Are you Doug Drexler?" And I'm, like, "Am I fired?" She goes, "No, Mr. Roddenberry would like to speak to you." Holy crap! She took me on the *Enterprise-C* bridge and Gene was sitting in a tall director's chair. He just wanted to tell me what a great job we did on *Dick Tracy*. I was blown away that he would even take the time to do something like that.

By the time Oscar time rolled around, I was part of the family and everyone was so excited about me going to the Academy Awards. They were shooting while I was there, and everyone on the ship, the crew, all stopped and gathered around the TV to watch us get the award. Every time I'd run into LeVar Burton, it didn't matter where we were, he would stop whatever he was doing and turn to everyone and say at the top of his lungs, "Ladies and gentleman, Academy Award–winning makeup artist Doug Drexler!" And one day I'm in Studio City walking down the street, and this guy comes running around the corner and runs right into me, and it's LeVar. He looks at me, and he turns to the entire street and yells it to everybody on the street. It was really great.

Also throughout the third season, the character of Worf became a more pivotal and multidimensional character, including in "The Enemy," which puts the Klingon Starfleet officer in the unwelcome position of being the only one on board who can give a vital blood transfusion to save a dying Romulan's life.

BRANNON BRAGA

Michael Piller really started to push the boundaries third season. In "The Enemy," where Worf refuses to give his blood to a Romulan and the Romulan dies and Picard flips out on him, I thought that was great conflict because it came out of a situation. I think the basic tenets of Gene's vision for humanity is an appealing idea: No matter who you are, you belong and have a purpose, and people aren't bickering. We're past all that shit.

MICHAEL DORN (actor, "Worf")

I've always had a good time. I've never really had major problems with what they've done with my character and everything they've done has been positive and wonderful. Even some stuff I didn't want to do turned out great. A good example is when Rick Berman wouldn't let me save the Romulan in "The Enemy." I had a little trepidation about that, because he's a Starfleet officer, and if he lets a guy die, everybody is looking at him like he's an asshole. But I think it worked, and that's the way it was for seven years.

MARINA SIRTIS (actress, "Deanna Troi")

In the original draft of "The Enemy," which I happened to read, it was Troi and Geordi stranded on the planet, and because Geordi was blinded by the electromagnetics preventing his VISOR from working, when we came across the Romulan, it was actually Troi who incapacitated him. I felt very excited about this. I finally got to do something interesting and different and, of course, when the final script came, not only was I *not* on the planet, but I had one line at the end of the show—and that was actually cut. That's the kind of thing that happened.

> By the end of the series, Ron Moore, who had become a staff writer, became known as the go-to "Klingon guy" or, as Brannon Braga would later label him, "The Margaret Mead of the Klingon Empire." It's not a moniker that Moore sought out, but one he nonetheless was well equipped to realize, dating back to his childhood fandom.

RONALD D. MOORE

There was a *Star Trek* novel written by John M. Ford in the early to mid 80s called *The Final Reflection*. It was a unique *Star Trek* book at the time, and probably still is, because it was written from a Klingon point of view. It was essentially from the perspective of a Klingon who was an orphan, and told of his training as a warrior and growing up to join the fleet.

It was just a really interesting book I was fascinated with, and I read it a few times. I remember one thing in particular, where he said Klingons liked pastries and sweet juices. I loved the idea. I think as a kid, or a young man, just the notion that these big burly, crazy warriors had a sweet tooth, and that was just part of their culture, was great. I always remembered that. Worf's love of prune juice was a direct callback to that. That book cemented in my head certain concepts of how to think of that culture.

I kind of got handed the two scripts that became "Sins of the Father" when I first joined the staff. They were Klingon stories and had to deal with the Klingon homeworld and Worf and his brother and father. I combined them and, after doing "Sins of The Father," I became known as the Klingon guy as a result. It really wasn't a dream come true as much as it's the way it turned out.

As the tumultuous season began to wind down, the insatiable appetite for scripts by production continued, and Piller and his staff turned back to several of the freelance writers who had come through for them earlier in the season.

RENÉ ECHEVARRIA

I had gone back to New York after "The Offspring" and Michael called me a couple of weeks later saying he had a story that was dead in the water. It was a premise they had bought involving us finding some crashed ship on a little moon, and there's a man whose basically dead, and we use miraculous twenty-fourth-century medicine to bring him back to life. I thought about it for a while and came up with the basic idea for "Transfigurations"; that someone was evolving out of their human form into an energy being. We've seen both of those stories before, but we've never seen the intermediate step.

Michael went for it and commissioned a story. I came out and did a break and wrote the first draft. That script also was the second-to-last episode of the season, so there was a huge time constraint. After the first draft, I went back to New York, and he called me and said come back and help do the polish and the rewrite. It was broken up by act and everyone on staff at the time wrote an act. Then it was all put together, and Michael did a polish on it.

Next, Michael said he wanted to do an environmental story, and I came up with something for which I wrote many, many drafts, but it never got off the ground. Toward the end of that process, he said he had a script that he wanted me to write. It involved every environmental story that people had done and seemed fairly obvious. They, in fact, commissioned a teleplay that was literally smokestacks. It would have been very obvious to the audience that it was the cause of the blindness and mutations in a tribe that was kept on a little island called the Island of Tears. They were kept there, hidden from view, so that the rest of the society could maintain its mode of production, which was highly exploitive and environmentally unsound. The audience would have guessed at the end of the first act what was going on.

MICHAEL PILLER

I had argued when we were having trouble finding good Picard stories and doing character stuff that we should marry him off. Gene felt that was a mistake and, in retrospect, I think he was right. I was delighted to have the permission to have one of our crew get married and have that on a regular basis to play with, so we did that with O'Brien. He's an important part of the ship.

> As the long season wore on, it became clear the show's lead was unhappy with his role. On the original series, Shatner had asserted the predominance of his character, excluding his supporting cast from most seminal dramatic scenes and episodes, but Stewart simply wanted a "piece of the action," pointing out that Riker and Data seemed to be receiving the most attention.
>
> Distressed, Stewart felt Picard talked too much and that when anything happened, he was invariably left on the bridge while his subordinates got the call to action. Watching Picard is like "visiting a social worker," concurred right-wing science-fiction writer Ben Bova at the time.

MICHAEL PILLER

Patrick came to me in the middle of the season and said, "I'm bored. You haven't given me anything interesting to do," and he was very unhappy about it. He was upset with the way Picard was being treated and he had every right to be. But third season we basically were just trying to keep our head above water, because we didn't have anything in development.

TOM MAZZA

It's hard when you have a seven- or eight-person ensemble. You think about Patrick Stewart not being more involved as the captain, and think about how Number One wasn't. When you really start taking each of the actors, how many pages do they have in a seven- or eight-day episode? The problem with a one-hour series ensemble like that is you have so much downtime. And downtime is always a dangerous thing, because you just obsess over "I could do more! I'm just sitting here!" Yes, you could.

We had to address Patrick's concerns like we addressed all of them. Avery Brooks had his questions on *Deep Space Nine;* Kate Mulgrew had her questions on *Voyager.* That's part of what we used to do a lot. I don't want to say handholding, but I guess in many ways it was. We just kind of had to walk them through it.

> Piller was responsible for one of the most seminal episodes of the series produced, "The Best of Both Worlds," in which the *Enterprise* confronts the Borg, only this time Picard is abducted and transformed into a Borg, Locutus. When

the Borg attack the *Enterprise*, Riker refuses to be assimilated and proves resistance isn't futile. In addition to providing the first *Star Trek* cliffhanger since *The Original Series*' "The Menagerie," it also gave the producers an out in the event they were not able to sign their unhappy star for a fourth season.

RICK BERMAN

I'm not a big fan of the Borg. I find them very two-dimensional, in a way. They are faceless characters without personality and without specific character traits. They're sort of a one-beat group of bad guys to me, and in "Best of Both Worlds" they represented a threat as opposed to characters, but that was a great episode. My only interest in Borg is when they're used off-center in other than the way they were originally conceived.

MICHAEL PILLER

People here felt they were boring, because there was no personality you could sink your teeth into. Because they are all "one," there is no spokesman or star role. To me there was something special and frightening about the Borg that their lack of character brought. For a show that dwells on and specializes in character, to be challenged and possibly destroyed by a characterless villain seemed, to me, to be a special kind of threat. But when we started talking about the cliffhanger and the Borg, we really did talk about who was going to be the "Queen Bee."

That "Queen Bee" obviously turned out to be Picard himself. However, early drafts had both Picard *and* Data being abducted and combined into a Borg.

MICHAEL PILLER

Someone asked, "Why would they do this?" We didn't have a good answer, so we dropped that. Good writing usually draws upon something that is meaningful to the writer. At the end of the season, I had decided not to return to *Star Trek*. Rick and Gene asked me to come back because things were going very well, but I had many other things I wanted to do. I wanted to write features and create my own shows. I had always told myself that I wouldn't commit long-term to anything.

But as I was sitting writing this script, I found myself in the position of Riker, who was trying to decide whether he was going to leave the ship or not. Much of what happened to him in "part one" was about what was going on in my head. He comes to the realization that ambition isn't everything. If you're happy and comfortable and find the rewards in the people you work with, that's something that counts for a great deal.

We push ourselves and push ourselves and sometimes it's good to do that. It has certainly been healthy for me all my career. But there are also times when you sit back and enjoy your success, and being with the people you love. That was really me speaking through Riker.

RONALD D. MOORE

We were just desperately trying to get the script done. And it was Piller. He just did it without a break. None of us broke it. He just said, "I'm going to do it," and he just went for it. I remember him talking about the fact that he saw himself as Riker, so he wanted to write it from that perspective. He identified with Riker and he wanted to stay.

He had a particular take on that episode. And he deliberately said, "We are not going to break this. It's a two-parter, and *Trek* hasn't done that and had a cliffhanger. And I don't know what the second half is and I don't *want* to know. We'll figure that out later." So he just wrote it as "part one." But we were so in the weeds at the time. I was doing a rewrite of "Transfigurations" or something, and Ira and the staff were just so exhausted and so tired. We were all just trying to get to the end, and Piller is going to do this episode off on his own.

The cliffhanger ending we all knew was kind of bullshit, because nobody believes Picard is really going to die, but it was that summer while we were working on the fourth season that I remember we started to pick up stuff in the press. In those days, they would always send out these Xerox copies of press clippings from newspaper articles, magazine articles, and they would distribute them to everyone. You would get this big thing of publicity material every once in a while, and buried in there were all these articles and mentions of "Best of Both Worlds." And "Can't wait to see what happens!" Must-see TV kind of stuff. And it started to pick up a little bit of a buzz.

DAVID MCDONNELL (editor, *Starlog* magazine)

From my perspective, the fan response to *The Next Generation*'s first season was promising but muted. It really didn't explode in popularity till partway through the second season and then especially in the third.

RONALD D. MOORE

That was when we started to realize, "Hey, people really responded to that episode, that's kind of cool." When we were working on the show that third season, we were very aware of the fact that the fans had not really embraced us yet. They *were* watching the show. The numbers were out there. Ratings were strong enough to keep the show going, but in a lot of critical fan mail and critical reaction in fan circles we were the bastard stepchildren. We were not "real *Star Trek*" at that point. But with "Best of Both Worlds," that was really the pivot of when we became the real *Star Trek*. Then we were accepted and the conventions were different. It all turned on a dime.

DAVID MCDONNELL

A show's creators may initially intend—or expect—certain elements to be important, but it's the series itself and its audience that really determine what works, what doesn't, and what we'll see more of. A perfect example is "Encounter at Farpoint" and the antagonist the producers expected to recur, a character so uninteresting I can't recall his name now. No, it was that same episode's other frenemy, Q—so deliciously portrayed by John de Lancie—who became the guest star we most looked forward to seeing. And it was just so obvious when you watched "Farpoint."

RONALD D. MOORE

It wasn't as big a phenomenon, but it *was* similar to the "Who shot J.R.?" moment. It's a great cliffhanger that got people talking, and then everybody wanted to see how it was going to resolve. It opened you up to people who stuck around to keep watching the show.

RICK BERMAN

When we finished the first half, we had no idea what the second half would be. With a little help from me, Michael Piller resolved it.

MICHAEL PILLER

It was after my contract was signed. I never try to think of these things until I have to. I'm a very instinctive writer. The people I don't work well with are the people who need all the answers laid out before they start writing. I find the discovery process is what the life of scripts is about. You need to have the broad strokes and a direction so you know where you're going. Television is too expensive and proceeds too quickly to run all the way down the road only to realize you don't have anything when you get to the end. But I honestly believe that you let the characters take you. Just listen to what the voices are saying when you write a script, because, ultimately, you'll find wonderful things. The danger, of course, is when you get a block. You can't figure out what the hell they're trying to say.

ELIZABETH DENNEHY (actor, Commander Shelby" on *Star Trek: Deep Space Nine*)

Nobody knew who was going to come back. They had to go through all the contract negotiations and people kept thinking Patrick was leaving and Jonathan was going to take over.

BRENT SPINER

We had no idea what was coming, and we didn't even have an idea if Patrick was coming back the next year, which I think was one of the reasons they set up cliffhangers to begin with. To hedge. Generally someone is in jeopardy and we find out whether they're going to make good on their contract next season. That's the *real* reason for a cliffhanger.

RONALD D. MOORE

It was incredibly difficult. The break session I remember is us breaking the second part with a new writing staff. It was just, who knew what this is going to be? Piller himself didn't have an idea. You're starting from zero. It was thrilling on some levels, because you're really working without a net. It fell down a little bit and the technobabble overwhelmed the solution, and that sort of faded the end a little bit.

NAREN SHANKAR

Michael really gave a lot of people their first opportunities. He came from a slightly different era of television, but he knew what the show wanted to be and what it needed to be and made it that. We really did create the modern franchise. It's kind of interesting many years later to see how many people say, "Oh my God, you were on *Next Generation*? I loved that show."

Maybe it's just because I'm old now, but people who watched it when they were young are talking about it the way I used to talk about the original series, and that's actually a nice feeling. So Michael gave us all that opportunity and it was really uncommon.

IRA STEVEN BEHR

When I was doing writing that I liked or felt had some quality to it, it was always a fight, it was always a struggle, and the bottom line was the basic tenets of the show just did not speak to me. I hated pretending or forcing myself to say, "Well, it doesn't matter, because it's a job and it's *Star Trek* and it's pretty cool," and all the stuff you tell yourself. I could not see the point in it.

And then they wound up offering me a two-year, pay-or-play deal for a lot more money than I'd been making. I was on vacation in Hawaii and my agent called me and gave me the deal and it was, like, "Oh shit, this is going to be tough to turn down." Then he said, "Rick Berman said you would never ever turn down this deal." And I said, "I'm not coming back. Tell him I'm done." And that was it.

RONALD D. MOORE

Gene had thrown out "Captain's Holiday," and it turned into something else that really broke Ira's heart, and it was a big struggle. He liked *Star Trek* and wanted it to be better, but he couldn't turn it into the places that he really wanted it to go. He really did like *Star Trek* as a show creatively. Loved the original series. I just think he was disappointed and exhausted and a little heartbroken about where it was. So he walked away. But he did like Piller, so when Piller called him years later and asked him to do *Deep Space Nine,* he did come back.

IRA STEVEN BEHR

I forever called *The Next Generation* the Connecticut of *Star Trek* series. Those were my feelings: clean, white, and proper. Nothing messy about the world of *The Next Generation*. It just wasn't the world that I lived in.

Ultimately in terms of staying or going, none of that mattered. I just wanted to be able to sleep through the night. It was weird, because, obviously, Michael valued me a lot. It's not like I felt undervalued, and I also felt in some ways Rick valued me, too. So, it's not like I was feeling beaten or misused. I guess I felt at 50 percent what Hans and Ricky were feeling at 100 percent, which was this is *Star Trek*, it could be so good. It could be so interesting. It could be an amazing show we could all be proud of, and yet here we are and were really *not* proud. It isn't about money and it isn't about a job.

RONALD D. MOORE

Ira was one of the guys I later worked for on *Deep Space,* and I sort of modeled being a showrunner after the way Ira ran shows, because I could see how effective it was. He was smart, and he was a good writer on top of that. Piller really wanted him to come back for the fourth season, but Ira had had enough, and it just wasn't a pleasant experience, and he left. So I was the sole survivor.

IRA STEVEN BEHR

One of my favorite lines of all times is from the Sam Peckinpah film *Ride the High Country* when Joel McCrea's character, Steve Judd, says, "All I want is to enter my house justified." That's been my mantra. That's all I want. It's not about the public perception; it's not even about my family and friends' perception. I have to feel like I enter my house justified. As dopey as it sounds, I felt that on a creative level, right or wrong, I could not enter my house justified and stay on that show. I know it sounds fucking ridiculous, but it's how I felt—and it's how I still feel.

It's how I try to conduct my career. How do I feel? Do I feel good? Do I feel that all the pain and fears and struggles to create something that wasn't there before—a piece of material that you got to pull out of your head—is it worth it? Am I justified?

HUNGRY LIKE THE WOLF 359

"THE FEDERATION *DOES* HAVE ENEMIES!
WE *MUST* SEEK THEM OUT!"

In its fourth season, *The Next Generation* faithfully continued to fulfill the mission of the starship *Enterprise* in boldly going where no man, woman . . . or Andorian . . . had gone before, and, to some, even improved on the quality of its impressive third-season voyages. It also was the first time a *Star Trek* series had made it to a fourth year in space.

MICHAEL PILLER (executive producer, *Star Trek: The Next Generation*)

In the fourth season, I built a staff in the image of what I thought a staff should be. I made it a group of people who really worked together to help one another to make the best show possible. And the quality of the show soared. That's my greatest contribution to *Star Trek*.

With the departure of Melinda Snodgrass, Larry Carroll, and David Carren, Piller was able to finally put his own distinct imprimatur on the show's writing staff. To his regret, he had also lost a disenchanted Ira Steven Behr, who would eventually return to run the spin-off, *Deep Space Nine*. One of his most important hires was Jeri Taylor, who would eventually take over as showrunner and help cocreate *Star Trek: Voyager* with Piller and Rick Berman. Taylor's background included producing gigs on *Quincy, M.E.; Blue Thunder; Magnum, P.I.; In the Heat of the Night;* and *Jake and the Fatman*.

JERI TAYLOR (executive producer, *Star Trek: The Next Generation*)

I didn't feel I needed to come in and fill any sort of vacuum. My tastes were very much in synch with Michael Piller's, and we really perceived the stories in very much the same way. If there's anything I wanted to do more of, it was developing the characters of Crusher and Troi, because I thought they were underused and wanted to flesh them out and make them more rounded and interesting people.

There is a very small way in which I sometimes remind people about the role of women and sometimes they remind me. I'm not saying that this was a staff of men and I had to come in and show them the way, but maybe it was something a little more in the foreground with me than some of the others.

RONALD D. MOORE (producer, *Star Trek: The Next Generation*)

Several writers came and went. There was a guy [Lee Sheldon] I got into a big fight with. He wrote the one where you think Beverly is alone on the *Enterprise* ["Remember Me"]. We were breaking that story, and he and I got into an argument about some piece of logic. I just remember having an in-your-face shouting argument with this guy, who was much older and more experienced than I was. He was treating me like a kid who didn't know anything and kind of said as much. "When you get more experience, you'll know this kind of thing." I bristled at that and shot back at him.

There came a point where Piller had to come in and say, "Enough, enough. This is an extraordinary meeting. Extraordinary." I was really just gunning for this guy, because he was condescending to me like I didn't know what I was doing. But then a couple of weeks later he was fired. We were still in the revolving door.

I had the *Star Trek* writers memorial wall in my bathroom, which I think Ricky [Manning] and Hans [Beimler] had printed up in a big poster that they put together. They listed all the names of the writers who had quit or had been fired. It started at like twenty-five names. Then every time a writer would leave, we would have a small gathering and I would add a name to the board. It was a little ceremony. We would all go in and have a drink of tequila in honor of Hans, who had left a bottle of tequila on my desk on his way out the door. So we always drank from that bottle and put up a new name on the memorial wall.

> Jeri Taylor joined the show as a supervising producer (eventually becoming the show's executive producer and showrunner) after Lee Sheldon left the series over the usual "creative differences," which had sidelined so many of his predecessors.

MICHAEL PILLER

I had to take a chance, because I needed help. It turned out not to be a decision either of us was comfortable with, so that didn't work out.

JERI TAYLOR

I did the rewrite as sort of a tryout. I was second in command, his point man as it were. On our show, our producing chores were somewhat limited. In the past, I've been very involved with all aspects of production, from casting to post to scoring. It was more compartmentalized on *Star Trek*. It allowed us to devote all our energy to turning out the scripts. They're very difficult to do.

RONALD D. MOORE

Jeri Taylor became a very calming presence. She was very maternal and a good writer who managed the room very well. We loved her. She was the only woman. She was our boss and we were her boys. Jeri's boys. She mothered us and scolded us and propped us up when we were depressed. She would fight our battles for us, and she would usually come back and say we couldn't get what we wanted from Rick. And we would rail, "Why couldn't you fight him about this?" She just took it and went, "Well, that's just the way it is, and now we have to get back and we have to do our jobs." She allowed us to vent and allowed us to be upset. She just kept us going and always told us we were doing good work and was very much a cheerleader in the room. A really wonderful woman who had a great presence. That provided a huge amount of stability, and Rick and Mike loved her, so she was a really crucial component as the show moved into the middle or later years.

JERI TAYLOR

Within weeks I had seen every episode of *The Next Generation* and the features. Then I went back and watched every single episode of the original series. It was a fascinating experience. I sort of emerged from my den a month later with my eyes like pinwheels. Doing it so intensively, in such a short period of time, was like being immersed in that universe. I felt like I had a thorough understanding and grasp of the characters, and I saw the differences in the approach to the old series and the new series.

RENÉ ECHEVARRIA (supervising producer, *Star Trek: Deep Space Nine*)

Jeri was like the den mother. She had to put up with all of us. We were young and thought we knew everything, and she would just let us argue and fight and get us where we needed to go.

JONATHAN FRAKES (actor, "William T. Riker")

Jeri at the helm was nothing but delightful, and she kept her writing staff intact, which we all benefited from. She's very bright and cared about actors and writing and all aspects of the show, and she *didn't* have a hidden agenda.

ANDRÉ BORMANIS (science consultant, *Star Trek: The Next Generation*)

Jeri just makes everybody feel comfortable. She is the opposite of intimidating, whatever that word would be. Nurturing, welcoming, open. It was great. I don't know that I would have gotten as far as I did if it hadn't been for Jeri. She was the first person I talked to on the staff when I was submitted for the science consultant job. We had a forty-five-minute conversation; it was when I was still in D.C., and it was just a phone call. That gave me great confidence.

If I had been pitching to Michael Piller or Rick or somebody else, I suspect it would have been a much harder and maybe impossible kind of journey for me, because they probably would have just been very pragmatic. Take it or leave it. She was more encouraging. For me, that makes all the difference. I am the kind of person who needs a mentor. I need somebody who is kind of going to encourage me a little bit more, and Jeri was certainly that person. In terms of running the show, I know that it was necessarily a different style than anybody else who ran the show that I worked with.

RICK BERMAN (executive producer, *Star Trek: The Next Generation*)

The show got better and better each year. We all took it extremely seriously, and that's the only way you can do it, because it's such hard work, and the second you start getting sloppy, the audience sees it instantly. The fact that we kept up the quality and integrity of the show and simultaneously the audience got bigger, is a wonderful achievement . . . and it's wonderfully good luck as well.

RONALD D. MOORE

We were able to get ahead on scripts fourth season. We had a better handle on it going into the season, so we never really got to that scary point where you're madly writing things out on the stage.

MICHAEL PILLER

I don't think there was one clinker in the whole group. Certainly, third season we had some. Arguably you could say there were better shows third season [than in the fourth year], but week after week we maintained a much higher consistency of quality than we had . . . or most shows ever achieve.

RONALD D. MOORE

It was still chaotic, but the ship was righting. You still ran out of scripts and were desperately trying to get ahead, but not quite to the level of the third. The third season was the toughest. It was by far the worst just in terms of organization and pace and workload. It was never that bad again. You're trying to do twenty-six episodes, which now looking back on it, is unbelievable. But, you can only write so much, and freelancers are out writing episodes and those are coming in, but they all need to be rewritten because none of them were good.

Every freelance script we sent out had to go through a major pass in-house. So, that takes one or two or three members of the staff to redo that. You're also generating original material, and there's a show on the stage and there's one in prep. It was just never ending, so you got to places where stories are still getting thrown out and there's huge rewrites and Gene doesn't like this and Rick doesn't like it and Michael doesn't like it. Everyone was giving notes, and the stories and the scripts were constantly in a sense of upheaval.

We'd go to production meetings with nothing but an outline. We wouldn't have a script to prep, which made the production people pull their hair out. But there was *nothing* you could do. It was always last-minute disasters and huge rewrites on something you thought was set. *Or* this story is getting tossed, that show is way over budget so it has to be completely revamped, or a myriad of problems for everything. It was always in a bit of turmoil. But the spirit was better. The revolving door of writers started to spin slower and slower. If you look at a list of writers from fourth season, you'll still see people coming and going quite a bit. A lot of them came and went. But then a core group started to settle in. I was there; Brannon, Joe Menosky. We became settled. Eventually René Echevarria and Naren Shankar. That was the staff that finished out the series.

> Equally important to the success of the show in its fourth year was the arrival of
> Brannon Braga, an Academy of Television Arts & Sciences intern who would, ul-
> timately, go on to write two of the feature films, oversee several seasons of *Voy-
> ager,* and cocreate *Enterprise,* as well as write some of the most well-remembered

and imaginative episodes of *The Next Generation* and become one of the most influential creative talents in contemporary *Trek* history.

BRANNON BRAGA (supervising producer, *Star Trek: The Next Generation*)

I had an internship through the Academy of Television Arts and Sciences, and I found out I was going to be on a show called *Star Trek: The Next Generation*. Although I was not a *Star Trek* fan, I had checked out *Next Generation* when the pilot aired and I watched the first couple of episodes. It wasn't my cup of tea. I thought it was cheesy.

Right around the time I got this internship—I was at UC Santa Cruz—people were saying you should watch *Next Generation*, it was getting really good. The episode I watched right before I started my internship was "Best of Both Worlds." Wow! I thought this show is pretty great. I started my internship and my first day there I walked in to meet Michael Piller, who was my mentor, and he was at his laptop computer saying, "How do we beat the Borg?" He was writing "part two" and struggling with how the hell to end the damn thing. I never could have imagined that fifteen years later I'd be turning the lights out and be the last one in the building.

MANNY COTO (executive producer, *Star Trek: Enterprise*)

There was a great show on the radio called *Hour 25* and, at the time, Harlan Ellison was hosting it. He would come on and rant like Harlan does, but he also promoted the *Next Generation*. He'd have people on and talk to them, so it just built up to this fever pitch. I couldn't wait for it to start. Then I saw the pilot and hated it, thought it was atrocious, hated all the characters. I just saw the first couple of episodes and I said, "I'm done. Bye!"

It wasn't until a few years later that my brother [film director] Carlos [Coto], who is also a *Star Trek* fan, said, "You have to start watching this again, it's really good." Year three and four is when it started to turn around. I started watching it again and kind of fell in love with it, the characters and the stories. From that point on, I was a pretty regular viewer of *TNG*.

After viewers were stunned by the epic scope and high-octane drama of "Best of Both Worlds," the series did something even more astonishing: it told a small, intimate character story about Picard literally coming down to Earth as he confronted the repercussions of having been, for all intents and purposes, raped by the Borg. The episode was "Family," which was beautifully and sensitively written by Ronald D. Moore.

RONALD D. MOORE

It was a big deal. Rick didn't want to do it. I think Gene was against it. The only creative meeting I had with Gene was about "Family." It was Gene, Piller, Berman, and me. Gene didn't like it. His reasons were he didn't like the conflict between the brothers. He thought that said they had had bad parenting, and they weren't twenty-fourth-century characters, because they had all of this jealousy and petty animosity. One point he said is if they're going to fight with anybody, maybe they should fight with his father, who'd still be alive.

We were, like, "We're going to watch Picard fight with an eighty-year-old father?" He didn't like the continuity from "Best of Both Worlds." He wanted to throw it out. We walked out of that meeting into the hall of the Hart Building, and I remember being really shell-shocked, because I thought my show had just gotten tossed. Rick and Mike just said, "Don't worry about it. Go write your show. We'll deal with it." And they did.

I never got the story of what happened, but somehow they went in and dealt with Gene. I think Rick was, at that point, learning how to handle Gene. And he did, because the show was done and produced and I never heard another word of protest, but Gene didn't like it.

It was Piller who drove it, because he felt it was important that after the events of "Best of Both Worlds" there had to be an episode where Picard had to deal with that and heal before he could become captain again. That was really his push. Originally, there was a B-story that involved Beverly alone on the *Enterprise* [which became "Remember Me"], but it just was unwieldy. As you tried to break it, it was clear that you couldn't do this.

The A-story couldn't be this emotional story with the captain while there was this crisis going on aboard ship upstairs. And so Piller just said, screw it, we're going to split that off as a separate episode and "Family" is going to be nothing but characters. No jeopardy, only a character show. And that was a thrill. I was really happy and excited about it. It was the only episode that never went to the bridge. There was no red alert. It was a straight-up character piece. And to be fair, Piller did a significant rewrite on it. I was not at the point in my career where I was finishing my own drafts and doing my own notes. Piller took a big pass on it before it went to air.

LES LANDAU (director, *Star Trek: The Next Generation*)

It was certainly one of my best episodes and one of the best episodes of *Star Trek* ever. It was the perfect follow-up to the Borg shows and the conclusion of that storyline. That opening moment where Picard walks into the vineyard and sees his brother on his hands and knees picking grapes, and his brother doesn't even acknowledge him, gives me chills just thinking about it. It was the first episode of the season, but it was the fourth episode to be filmed, so Patrick had to adjust and relive all the events and make it believable that he had just come back from this incident and was going home after doing two other shows. Everything about that show worked.

MICHAEL PILLER

The normal objections were that we were not serialized. We try to tell our stories in one hour and that's what we do very well. When I got to the end of "part two," we made the decision not to extend it, and I called up Rick and said, "Hey, listen, next week Picard can be fine, but for a show that prides itself on its realistic approach to storytelling, how can you have a guy who's basically been raped be fine the next week? There's a story in a man like Picard who's lost control." Finally, I was persuasive enough to talk Gene and Rick into taking the chance.

Rick said, "I'll let you take Picard to Earth, but I want a science-fiction story going on aboard the ship at the same time. So we struggled for weeks and weeks trying to come up with an interesting science-fiction story that we could match with Picard going down to Earth.

RONALD D. MOORE

We very much wanted to do more serialized storytelling, and we would try to sneak it in whenever possible. You have casual references to other episodes or events or other characters just as part of the fabric of the show, but you had to be careful. The episode that did break that mold before "Family" was "Sins of the Father." Because when we did "Sins of the Father," I deliberately left it open. Worf has lost his honor and leaves. It was pretty clear that eventually you're going to have to follow that story up.

There was a moment in Rick's office when we're working on the script when he said, "So, we're going to have to do a follow-up to this, right?" and I was, like, "Yeah." "Paramount doesn't like that." I was ready for him to say you can't end it this way, but he didn't. He just kind of grumbled and moved on. He wasn't ready to throw the whole ending out. Because of that, you kind of knew you would have a continuing story with Worf, and I went back to the writers' office and it was kind of exciting. We thought now we could do a little bit more continuity as things go on.

BRANNON BRAGA

I was so intimidated as I settled into my eight-week internship. I could not fathom how they did this. They'd sit in the writers room and come up with ideas and Piller would guide things, and I just remember thinking I could never do this. It was a crash course in television, and I was in the right place at the right time. It was basically Michael Piller and Ron Moore after the writing staff had been cleaned out. So I was definitely lucky to be there when Joe Menosky, Jeri Taylor, René Echevarria and all these people started to come aboard to form the writing staff of *Next Gen* for years to come.

BRYAN FULLER (coproducer, *Star Trek: Voyager*)

I didn't sort of fully flower into my *Next Generation* fandom until probably the end of season two or going into season three. I had seen parts of the pilot, and it didn't hook me immediately, because I felt like in the twenty intervening years of television the effects hadn't advanced all that much in terms of we were on a soundstage planet surface and things like that. Initially, I was not drawn into it until it really kind of hit its creative pace with "The Best of Both Worlds." That's when I was, like, "Oh my God, this is real" in terms of it actually taking *Star Trek* to the next level, and it provided the level of stakes and drama that you would get in a *Star Trek* feature film.

Next Gen was at its height between seasons three and five, which is when it was at its absolute sharpest. It was as good as anything on television at that time. It was as challenging and thoughtful as *The X-Files*. It was remarkable television. They really were kind of peeling off, or actually they were crafting a whole new *Star Trek* right in front of our eyes. The show was evolving week-to-week and becoming a very sophisticated science-fiction show.

BRANNON BRAGA

At the end of my eight weeks, I got my big break. I would have been happy to walk away from that internship with the experience of having had it, but my break came when a script called "Reunion" needed a rewrite and Mike Piller paired me with Ron Moore to do it. That's the one where Worf's girlfriend, K'Ehleyr, gets murdered. It was a great experience. Ron and I thought we did a good job on it, and I remember Michael Piller saying to me, "You didn't hurt yourself with that rewrite." Michael never really heaped on the praise, but that was a compliment. I got a freelance script after that called "Identity Crisis," and after that, I got brought on staff and the rest is history for me.

RONALD D. MOORE

We were the two youngest on the show at that point. The other writers were older and more experienced. I had done one season and Brannon had done none. That was our first time writing together and we enjoyed it and had a good time. We bonded and we became friends. We would pair up periodically over the years after that.

BRYAN FULLER

I was fascinated with *Next Generation* and I would have dreams about being on the set. I would have dreams about talking to the actors. I remember one time, I ran into Marina Sirtis in the grocery store and approached her. I asked if she was Marina Sirtis from *Star Trek,* and she absolutely denied it, because she probably didn't want to be bothered. Then I realized she was holding a box of feminine hygiene products in her hand. So here is this geeky twentysomething, while she's trying to buy tampons, talking about how much I love *Star Trek.*

I was kind of vaguely aware of the hyper-connectivity of the fan base at that point, too, because it was really going bonkers in a great new way. I remember around the 1994 Northridge earthquake, they were offering a writing class at one of the conventions in Pasadena on how to write for *Star Trek.* I went to that and had my pen and paper and sat in the front row and asked questions and jotted everything down. As I was walking out of the class, there was an aftershock. So, here I am walking out of the convention center hall, looking up at a couple of tiers of the convention center during an aftershock, and I see all of these people in Starfleet uniforms running and screaming like it was a Borg attack. It was so surreal to be there. I felt like this *has* to go somewhere.

BRANNON BRAGA

I was sitting in a room reading *Next Gen* scripts trying to figure out what a script even was. And trying to figure out the show and watching writers being hired. I became fast friends with Ron Moore and Joe Menosky, because we're similar in age. I didn't meet Rick Berman for a month. He was kind of the mysterious figure across the way. The writers were in the Hart Building at the Paramount lot, and the production staff and Rick were in the Cooper Building, and everyone knew that Mike Piller would go and see Rick and get notes on stories and scripts, but the actual writers wouldn't go. He would give the notes to Michael. The writers were kept very separate; in those early days writers were not allowed on the set.

IRA STEVEN BEHR (executive producer, *Star Trek: Deep Space Nine*)

Either the first day or the second day I decided to walk down to the sets. I had gotten maybe twenty feet from the Hart Building when the unit production manager walked past me. He knew I was the new guy and he said, "Where are you going?" I said, "Down to the set." And he said, "You're not allowed down to the set." My pippy response was "Well, I'm going and they can fire me."

I had my process, that was mine. Part of it was trying to feel a blood-kinship with the show on every possible level. With the staff, with the crew, with the sets. I live, eat, breathe the show when I'm working on it. Much to my family's consternation at times. My kids grew up with me with that faraway look in my eyes over meals. Daddy's thinking again. My wife's talking to me and not getting an answer. It wasn't even a thought process. It wasn't something like I said I'm going to draw a line in the dirt. Nothing like that—I went down to see the sets. No one was coming with me, because there was already a miserable miasma. A cloud hanging over the Hart Building. So, I said okay, I'm going to go down, fuck man, I want to stand on a transporter. I'm working on fucking *Star Trek*. Right away, you get this "you can't." Why not? Am I going to damage something? Am I going to speak insurrection? Am I going to in any way hurt the show? So I went. Nothing happened. It was never mentioned.

NAREN SHANKAR (story editor, *Star Trek: The Next Generation*)

Rick was very jealous about guarding the editorial side of things. I'm not sure what he was so jealously guarding, because the show was quite pedestrian in its editorial style. It's so funny, having run a show like *CSI*, which was literally cutting-edge in looks, style, and cinematography. Which I love. It's actually hard for me to go back and watch the old *Star Trek*s, because I look at it, and the lighting is ghastly, the editing is horrible, and everything about it is safe and simple. What I have to keep reminding myself is that the stories were *really* good.

BRANNON BRAGA

In the beginning, writers were basically told to stay in their offices, we were like caged mice. Eventually, the mice would be let loose, and we nibbled our way onto the set and into Rick's office. By the time we hit season seven, it was a happy family and it was a better-functioning family.

NAREN SHANKAR

The strange thing about it, the thing that was enforced on *Star Trek* that I thought was a really bad thing, was the weird sort of divide between production and writing on that show. I mean, the writers were Michael's, the production was Rick. You'd literally have to walk across the street to go to the production side of things. You had to ask permission to go down to the set. You're not allowed to talk to the actors. Everything was really rigidly enforced and, in a way, that's incredibly bad for real creative expression.

It was actually one of the most interesting things that I learned coming away from the *Star Trek* camp. The next show I went to was run by guys who'd all been in Stephen J. Cannell Productions, and those guys couldn't have been more opposite [from] the *Star Trek* guys. The attitude was so different; the youngest guy, they would toss into the pool. They would take you in the editing room to teach you. They would take you into casting. They would talk to you about it. They showed you every aspect of production, and you learned.

The best thing that happened when I left *Star Trek* was I got exposed to an entirely different level of production experience: editing, directing, all this stuff that happened that didn't exist on *Star Trek*. It was institutionalized to an extent on the *Star Trek* shows that I don't think is healthy. It doesn't generate good showrunners. You were never allowed to go. You had to go and visit and then leave. They would say, literally, I remember it, "Writer on the set!"

MIKE SUSSMAN (producer, *Star Trek: Enterprise*)

My writing partner loved to be on set. It got so bad to the point where I think she was ultimately banned from the set. I didn't go down there too much. It's fun to go down to the set, and everyone wants to talk to you since they don't know if you could be the showrunner in a year or two years or tomorrow. So, people paid attention to you. But, then work stops getting done, so I certainly understand why, and honestly, while you're there you're not in the writers room and you're not writing and you're not generating ideas. It's a wonderful waste of time and there are legitimate times to be down there, but just hanging out for hours, I can't imagine doing that.

BRYAN FULLER

It was always sort of like you snuck down there. It was not frowned upon, but you would definitely get looks like, what the hell are you doing on stage? There was a sense of control about the environment that was not necessarily conducive to a warm atmosphere.

IRA STEVEN BEHR

One of the great things about the franchise, obviously, is those sets were built to last. They're iconic. I could have stayed down there a lot longer probably and been very happy. The one thing I do remember in watching the actors at times is you had to be careful, because the way the actors do their craft and what they need to do in order to do their craft is not that much different from what writers do. But writers talk behind closed doors and actors will talk trash on the set and shit.

I know that they were the happy set and a wacky, swashbuckling bunch of actors with great senses of humor. But I saw a lot of bitching when I went down there. Brent can speak his mind and be sarcastic about the material at times. So, I didn't go down there and say, "Hey, this is going to be a great place to hang." I've been on shows where it's been pretty good to be on the set, but this did not strike me at the time that way.

RICK BERMAN

I'm a little vague on this, but I have reason to believe this was a Roddenberry thing . . . and a Hurley thing as well. It might have been a Berman thing to some degree, but I think nowhere near as big as a Roddenberry and a Hurley thing. I, as an executive producer of the show, should have been on the set a lot more than I was. But I always knew that if I would go to the set, where I would be treated princely, I'd spend an hour there and they'd ask me questions and I'd make a decision about this or that. I'd chat it up with everybody. It would be fun, and I also knew I'd get home to my wife and kids an hour later than I normally would have, because I still had so much work to do.

There were times when Gene went to the set a lot and Hurley would go down to the set and would find both moderate-level and junior-level writers sitting on the stage. Their attitude was, "What the hell are you doing here? We've got a show to write! Why aren't you back in your office?" At one point, somebody, whether it was Gene or Hurley, got pissed off and basically said writers should only go to the set when they are called and asked to go down there, or if their show is being shot. It's not a place for people to go and hang out.

A lot of people think of hanging out on the set as being the fun part of being involved in all this. I certainly was not involved in the official policies of where people went and what they did. I'm not sure if Gene or Hurley had ever made an official policy, but I know that it was a definite attitude and there could have even been a little of Piller in that in season three, which was writers are paid to write and they should spend most of their time doing that.

> But while the writers may not have been always welcome on set, as the show's popularity grew, more and more notable visitors would pay the twenty-fourth century a visit. Admittedly the constant procession of visitors could be a nuisance to much of the cast, particularly Brent Spiner (who once famously kvetched, "How would you like it if people came to where you worked and stood over your shoulder all day?"), there were a few legendary guests that proved electrifying to everyone on set. Among them were former president Ronald Reagan, the Dalai Lama, actress Sharon Stone at the height of her fame and, perhaps most thrilling of all, brilliant physicist Stephen Hawking.

BRANNON BRAGA

We snuck down when there was a special guest; we snuck down to see Stephen Hawking. I didn't really start interfacing with the cast in a meaningful way until season seven. I interacted with Patrick Stewart, because I happened to write the two episodes he directed, so he had to interact with me. I look at pictures of me and him from back then and I think, "Of course he was standoffish, I look like I'm twelve. And I'm writing his shit." The friendliest cast member was Jonathan Frakes. He really liked talking to the writers. I think season five I went to the set to try and hit on Ashley Judd. With zero success.

RICK BERMAN

I got a phone call that Stephen Hawking was outside Stage 8 of Paramount and wanted to come in and see the *Star Trek* sets and was it okay? I immediately said it was okay and went down to the stage. I was introduced and asked him if he'd like to see some more of the sets and he, with that computerized voice synthesizer that he has, said he would. We took him around, and when we got to the bridge of the *Enterprise,* he started punching in something that he was going to say to us.

He just moves one thumb and with it he has a computerized monitor that has basically dictionaries of word groups that he can use to construct sentences, and then they eventually come out as a synthesized voice from the computer. And after about a good sixty seconds of punching this little button, out of the computer came a sentence that I will never forget, and it was, "Would you lift me out of my chair and put me into the captain's seat?"

The people who were there with him did it and he was lifted up and put into the captain's seat. It was a pretty amazing sight to have perhaps the greatest mind of the latter half of the twentieth century in applied mathematics and theoretical physics, wanting more than anything else at that moment to sit in Picard's chair.

The next morning I got a call from Leonard Nimoy, who said that Hawking had mentioned something about wanting to be on *Star Trek*. So I called his people, and it turned out that he was interested, and with the help of Ron Moore, we came up with an idea for a scene in which Data goes to the holodeck to play a little poker, and he conjures up images of Sir Isaac Newton, Albert Einstein, and Stephen Hawking. We told Hawking that we wanted him to give us some notes on the script, and he loved it and agreed to do it.

BRENT SPINER (actor, "Data")

Stephen Hawking, the Hawk I call him. The Hawk is really a fabulous actor in his own right. I don't know that anybody could have portrayed him as believably as he did. He was terrific. I was nervous, because I'm unused to playing scenes with the brightest man in the universe, and he's easily the smartest actor I've ever worked with. Not to say my costars aren't bright, but none of them, including myself, are the most brilliant person in the world. And Stephen Hawking happens to be.

BRANNON BRAGA

He was really cool, and I was a fan of his work. It was the only time that anyone ever played themselves on *Next Gen*. Out of all of the visits we had, that was the one that people got most excited about. I also remember the day the Dalai Lama and all the monks were there, and Data took his picture on the transporter pad with all the monks. It was surreal. We would have shuttle astronauts come. There was one, Mae Jemison, who was the first black female astronaut.

GRANT ROSENBERG (executive producer, *Time Trax*)

The good thing about *Star Trek* was that I'm good friends with Rick Berman and I'd known Mike Piller for years and Jeri Taylor. They're so smart and so good at what they do that it was just a delight working with them. I was a writer/producer under contract at Paramount and I was writing *MacGyver* and various other shows, and Rick Berman called me and said, "We need a *Star Trek*, would you like to write one?" And I said, "I'd love to." They said do not come in with ideas. The chances of you coming in with a fresh idea that we haven't heard or rejected or done is slim.

JERI TAYLOR

There are some series where it's easier to develop ideas, like a contemporary show, where you can just devise a location and say I think we'll have it take place at the ballet and you set a murder mystery there. We didn't have that option, we don't have a ballet or a rodeo. Every story needs to be unique with a science-fiction phenomenon and have an emotional base and all those kinds of things, and when you've done as many as we have, they get harder and harder to scratch for.

It's true of any series, you can never stay ahead of it, because production is like this giant maw that just eats scripts. We fantasized that during the summer hiatus we'll get ten scripts done, but they're treated with such tender loving care that you can't just churn them out. Each one is molded carefully and scrutinized line by line, and it's just such a careful effort that the time it takes doesn't allow you to accumulate a trunkload of scripts ready to go.

BRANNON BRAGA

There was a list of rules about writing: Gene had instituted no time travel, no dream sequences, and a host of other things. We would all eventually break those rules. And me in particular—all I did was dream sequences and time travel—but Rick Berman was this scary, Darth Vader–type figure. I remember meeting him for the first time and getting notes on a story, and I was extremely nervous. He would eventually become a very close friend, but I think in those early days I just spent a lot of time in the writers room with staff and watched a lot of really incredible episodes get written.

JOHN WHELPLEY (writer, *Star Trek: The Next Generation*)

You take a Zen approach to it all. You've heard the story about the guy who traveled over hill and dale and climbed up to the highest temple, and he got there and had his mind open to the great wisdom of the temple, to be truly close to perfection, and he is handed a broom and a shovel and is told to clean out the stables. He says, "Wait a minute, I come all the way out here for enlightenment and you tell me to go clean the stables?"

The whole idea was you've got to clean the stables once in a while, but the Zen approach is to make it the cleanest and best stable possible. Whether you're sitting down to do a *Baywatch* or if you have the opportunity to do a *Star Trek,* you just do the best you can do, so if you take a Zen approach as a freelancer to episodic television, you can survive it.

IRA STEVEN BEHR

After leaving *The Next Generation,* I sold a feature to Joel Silver and was working with Harrison Ford and trying to get this movie made. Mike called me said, "We're back in that place and I need some help. Would you write a script?" I didn't want to say no to Michael, because I had already felt bad that I left him in the lurch. That's the biggest regret I have in a way. We still had a friendship.

He called me up and they were doing this Q episode, "Q-pid," and it was going to be about Robin Hood. So I was the freelance writer. I was waiting to do a rewrite on the movie and I wrote an entire episode of *Star Trek and* I went to the set to watch some filming while I was *still* waiting for notes on the movie. That's the difference between TV and film.

> To end the fourth season, the writers decided on another cliffhanger, "Redemption," this one involving a civil war within the Klingon Empire. It also carried forward the narrative strands of Worf's excommunication from the Empire in "Sins of the Father." But writer Ron Moore didn't realize the biggest threat to the Klingon warrior would come not from the Empire, but a far more unlikely source.

RONALD D. MOORE

I was with Rick, and he said Gene wanted to throw the script out. I couldn't believe it, and Rick said, "Well, Gene doesn't think that Worf is a major character on the show. In Gene's mind, Worf was a character that he put on the bridge just to put into the background so that you could comment on the fact that the Klingons and the Federation were at peace now. I know we all see it differently, but in his mind Worf is not a major character in the show. Gene doesn't want to do a whole cliffhanger about him." I was, like, that's crazy! And he said, "I know, I know, but that's how he feels. I'll go talk to him again and we'll figure it out." And Rick figured it out and I never heard about it again.

But it *is* crazy. Whether Gene felt that all the way through or that's just what he was saying at that point is the question. Certainly there had been episodes about Worf before that, so he wasn't a glorified transporter chief. He was on the bridge, he was in the cast photos for God's sake. How strongly Gene felt that is open to question. So, you heard those kind of rumblings and there'd be comments from him on various scripts, but it was definitely on a downhill slope.

René Echevarria, another writer who had distinguished himself with several freelance assignments, would finally have the opportunity to join the staff, while Naren Shankar, who had been the show's science advisor, would find himself moving toward a bigger role on the show as well.

RENÉ ECHEVARRIA

At the end of fourth season, Jeri Taylor had called me and told me they were going down to Mexico to brainstorm and that it was an ideal time to send some ideas along. I sent three ideas, "The Perfect Mate," being one of them, which changed quite a bit, and "I, Borg." They called me back and said they were going to buy two of these stories. *That* was a great day. "I, Borg" was the first one I started to work on since we decided to use Guinan, and her availability was very limited. Even though it wasn't produced until very late in the season, I still had to write it in two weeks. I turned that in and everybody seemed pretty happy with it, and it was the first time I was able to take an episode through the process: two drafts and a polish. I had gotten notes from Rick Berman for the first time in addition to Michael and the staff, and that was the first time they had the opportunity to see I could bring a script through the process.

NAREN SHANKAR

After my six-week Writers Guild internship, they kept me on as a science consultant, because I had my engineering Ph.D. and Gene had always wanted *Next*

Generation to be on a more solid scientific foundation than the old series. It kept me around to pitch stories and I got to continue working with the writers. Brannon hates technobabble, so he loved having me around to do the science and tech stuff.

I remember one night in the fifth season I got a call from Brannon and he said, "You have to come right now," and it was late at night. So, I come to the lot, and I remember they were filming *Patriot Games* in the main parking lot, which was flooded and there were all these wind machines and lightning, and, as this was happening, I was walking into the Hart Building. Brannon was in his office with crazy Herb Wright, with his crystal blue eyes and mad look, and they were arguing about a script, and the only reason Brannon had called me there was he had wanted somebody to witness that Herb was insane.

I was, like, "What the fuck is happening?" and he said, "I just wanted you to see that this is crazy. I want to go on record as having a witness." But it was so surreal to walk across the lot at night with lightning flashing and wind machines and coming in and hearing Herb just go on about his crazy fucking ideas for a show. That was the joy of that series, coming to the Hart Building and dealing with that kind of craziness.

FRED DEKKER (consulting producer, *Star Trek: Enterprise*)

It was really cool to have an office on a classic Hollywood lot. The stage that our ship was on, the NX-01, was the stage where Hitchcock shot *Rear Window.* I found that out the first day of shooting. It takes away a lot of the sting of what was disappointing. The same place as *King Kong, Citizen Kane, Gone with the Wind.* The history is magic to me.

NAREN SHANKAR

You would enter the studio through the old Desilu Studios entrance, and I loved it, because you would walk in and they have this big, beautiful picture of Lucille Ball. You'd walk through the door and the first thing you'd see was the Paramount water tower, and I was, like, "This is like the most awesome job ever."

I just loved coming to work at the Hart Building every day. It was really the nice thing about *TNG;* it was a really great environment. Even when you were working hard or working late, you liked everybody. The people were nice. It wasn't mean or nasty politics.

ANTOINETTE STELLA (supervising producer, *Star Trek: Enterprise*)

The Hart Building is very, very old and very, very haunted. What we did late at night when we were hanging around before we were let go for the day is we would tell each other whatever story we heard about the Hart Building being haunted. Supposedly an actress had thrown herself off the top of the building years ago. Somebody said that Lucille Ball's makeup person haunted it. I don't know why she haunted it. There was apparently a writer who, late at night, went into the bathroom and saw somebody looking back at him in the mirror, and then screamed and had a meltdown.

NAREN SHANKAR

There are no ghosts in the Hart building! There may have been people who were wasted or drunk in the Hart Building who thought they saw ghosts. The most horrifying thing in the Hart building was the fucking elevator.

ANDRÉ BORMANIS

I spent many years in the Hart Building. Never once saw a ghost. I think it's a matter of susceptibility. If you believe in ghosts and somebody tells you a building is haunted, you're probably going to see a ghost at some point. And if you don't, I'm pretty sure you won't. I spent a lot of weekends and late nights. I even spent New Year's Eve in that building and never saw a ghost.

> Perhaps the origin of the ghost stories developed from the way many of the writers came up with some of their more creative ideas: smoking pot on the roof of the Hart Building overlooking the Melrose Avenue lot.

TRACY TORMÉ (creative consultant, *Star Trek: The Next Generation*)

That was right above my office, and we'd go up on the roof and look at the studio and smoke weed, very true. There was a ladder on the side of the building, and you climbed up, and then you'd find yourself on the roof, and the roof was a tremendously cool place. It was literally right above my office, so when people would go to do that, they usually dropped in or stuck their head in and let me know that was what they were doing.

NAREN SHANKAR

It was the building where Orson Welles and [Herman] Mankiewicz wrote *Citizen Kane,* because it's part of the old RKO Studios on the edge of the lot. The old RKO globe was still on the top. Even though I had the shittiest office on the fourth floor, it was kind of an amazing introduction to Hollywood.

A SEVEN-YEAR MISSION

"LET'S SEE WHAT'S OUT THERE."

The fifth season was a significant year for *The Next Generation*. It was the first time a *Star Trek* series actually survived to travel the cosmos for a five-year mission. In addition, relative stability amongst the writing staff was uncharacteristic for a series that had been relatively tumultuous until then. Dramatically, it also proved to be yet another strong year for the series as well.

RONALD D. MOORE (producer, *Star Trek: The Next Generation*)

Ironically, the final seasons of *Next Gen* were characterized by stability among the writing staff, which bred a consistent level of quality among the episodes. I think the shows were better. There was more of a family feeling to the crew, which is reflected because there was more of a family feeling on the staff.

BRANNON BRAGA (coproducer, *Star Trek: The Next Generation*)

The writers all brought their own perspective to things. Ron Moore and René were really big fans of the original. Ron was what we called the Margaret Mead of the Klingon Empire—he was great with the social and political aspects, and he was our resident Klingon guy.

NAREN SHANKAR (story editor, *Star Trek: The Next Generation*)

Ron and Brannon and René were my mentors, although you could make the argument that we all self-mentored. I think that Jeri was a very smart manager, because she knew she had a very high-spirited staff of really young guys who were just starting out, so she just kind of let us run wild and understood that that was the best way to get stories done. Michael was a great editor who would come in and give us comments that were usually quite insightful, and then he would leave and we would bitch, "Oh God, he was such a pain in the ass." It was like the kids bitching about Daddy.

That was the normal dynamic, and then you're faced with the constraints of the show, which are always kind of a pain in the ass to deal with, because it was a little bit straight-laced and kind of like writing in a box. But that was largely the dynamic. Jeri kind of let people go really nicely in the best possible way and weighed in when she needed to, but she guided us really, really smartly. It ended up giving everybody a lot of confidence, and that was part of the joy. We all hung out together and we took vacations together, so it was a lot of fun and it was a great environment to start in.

Those first experiences when you're on the show are very, very, formative. If you end up in bad rooms with bad people, you get bad habits. And those really chase you for a long time and you perpetuate them, but I think with *Next Generation* everybody came out of a great "speak your mind—best idea wins" kind of situation, and I still say that today.

BRANNON BRAGA

To me, the show was an anthology show like *The Twilight Zone,* an opportunity to tell the kinds of stories I was really into, which were mind-bending things. This was a show where you could do anything. You could warp reality, you could tell stories backward, you could do whatever the hell you wanted, and that made it plausible. It was great fun. It really was a very creative time.

We were trying stuff out that in retrospect was very experimental for the day. When I think of the show, probably the most famous episode I worked on was "Cause and Effect." It had a repeating loop of time, and when we aired that, people were calling in because they thought something was wrong with the broadcast: it kept repeating. That kind of storytelling was new. We were doing some pretty cool stuff that had never been seen. *Next Gen* is still loved for its characters, but also for its storytelling. It was a fertile time for us.

PETER ALLAN FIELDS (executive story editor, *Star Trek: The Next Generation*)

Star Trek: The Next Generation is what it is. It's a science-fiction show. It doesn't mean illusion or fantasy; I think the audience expected things with a science-fiction twist to them that doesn't make them less believable. The best kind of science fiction is rooted in your own life, what can happen now and is a reasonable extension. To do a character story and blend it with science fiction is the pinnacle we reached for.

BRANNON BRAGA

I did an episode about quantum alternate realities, the multiverse. I read a physics article about where there were possibly branching realities which were not really in the mainstream consciousness. "Parallels," where a character is jumping across a couple of universes, was mind-bending. Now, of course, that kind of storytelling is old hat. But at the time, I remember when I would pitch an idea like that, people would look at me like I was nuts.

The "Cause and Effect" episode Michael Piller kind of tolerated as a strange idea, but then I remember I came to his office one day and he said that's one of the most popular episodes we've ever done. It's really not your typical television series, and I do believe that it's one of the reasons the show was really engaging. There were episodes that were just straight-up drama and so it was a good mix. Each week you didn't quite know what you were going to get on that show.

> But as Braga made the high-concept sci-fi story his stock-in-trade, Piller and Jeri Taylor continued to search for the same allegorical storytelling that had been a bedrock of the original *Star Trek* and helped cement its place in popular culture and television history.

BRANNON BRAGA

At the time *Next Generation* was tackling certain issues, torture was not on the tip of everyone's tongue, neither was gay rights. These were things that *Next Gen* was in a position to tackle metaphorically as *Star Trek* always did, and it was very effective, I thought. "Chain of Command" got everyone talking. Everyone remembers the four lights.

> In "Chain of Command," a powerful mid-season two parter, Captain Picard is captured by and violently tortured by a Cardassian interrogator while the *Enterprise* is assigned a new captain, Captain Jellico, played by a potent Ronny Cox.

RICK BERMAN (executive producer, *Star Trek: The Next Generation*)

Money and creativity have never really gone hand in hand when it comes to *Star Trek*. Episodes like "Measure of a Man" was one of our cheapest episodes and one of our best, but an episode like "Yesterday's Enterprise" was quite expensive and it was wonderful. "Chain of Command" was a very inexpensive episode and was one of the greats.

MICHAEL PILLER (executive producer, *Star Trek: The Next Generation*)

Ultimately, the victory for Picard is just surviving. We made the decision early on that we couldn't say that Captain Picard was such a great man that he would not break under torture because that would be doing a great disservice to everybody in the human rights struggle who has broken. Nobody can resist torture. Anybody who wants to get you to speak, *will* get you to talk if they're willing to do the hideous things necessary.

There had to be a different kind of victory. I can't imagine a better show than "Chain of Command, Part Two" and it had no tricks or whizbang stuff. *And* it was one of the least expensive shows of the season. David Warner was sensational and Patrick Stewart was even better. I don't think there's been a better show in the history of the series.

RICK BERMAN

It showed Patrick off at his best, and David Warner is someone who I've always been a huge fan of. I remember Patrick introducing me to David Warner at a party at Leonard Nimoy's home once, and it was great to bring them together. We had something to say about man's inhumanity to man, and we got a lot of criticism for it being a little bit too graphic. I think we kept it from being as graphic as it could have been. It was a wonderful piece of television.

> In the wake of fourth season's "The Host," in which a male Trill ambassador who falls in love with Dr. Crusher is killed mediating a dispute and the parasitic symbiont inside is eventually transferred to the body of a woman, thus ending their affair, the closest *Next Generation* came to tackling LGBT issues was in "The Outcast." In that episode, Riker falls in love with a genderless alien who risks serious consequences for carrying on a relationship with a human male.

BRANNON BRAGA

It's one of the most outstanding episodes we've ever done. Being in love with someone is not very fresh. Having the parasite as the real intelligence and the body as the host is. It was not pitched as a love story, it was pitched as a squirmy worm who's really the intelligence. What's ironic is that the most repulsive story ever pitched to us ended up being the most touching love story and that's why this show was so unique.

MARVIN RUSH (director, "The Host")

Most of the people that I have talked to thought the show worked pretty well and were entertained. Some commented that they were unhappy with the ending. I felt that it was more about the nature of love, why we love and what prevents us from loving. To me, the best analogy is if your beloved turned into a cockroach, could you love a cockroach? It's the same person with the same personality, but can you get past the outside shell? Gates, in her last scene in "The Host," talks about maybe someday our ability to love won't be so limited and says mankind may one day be able to deal with this, but I can't. To me, that is about the nature of love. I think it's an interesting, worthy discussion.

JERI TAYLOR (executive producer, *Star Trek: The Next Generation*)

"'The Outcast" is still the show I'm proudest of. I asked to write that episode for that reason, because it was something that I felt. Although I am not gay, I am a female, and I know some of the feelings of what it is like to be judged on a basis other than for what and who I am. So that message about the importance of tolerance was very important to me.

MICHAEL PILLER

Jeri did a marvelous job on the script, and to me this was the turning point of the season. This was where I thought we started doing excellent television again. We had been the target of a concerted organized movement by gay activists to put a gay character in the show, and what it came down to was Roddenberry had been barraged by letters and had discussed with us before his death the possibility of having two men hold hands in some scene, which was totally irrelevant to the issue of homosexuality. I didn't think, nor did Rick, that was an appropriate way to do a story that addressed the issues of sexual intolerance, which I felt was really what the broader issue was really about.

ROD RODDENBERRY (son of Gene Roddenberry)

I really like the answer my father gave when people said, "Why aren't there any gay people on the *Enterprise*?" It was a bit of a cop-out admittedly, but the answer was in the future it's a nonissue. You know? People don't do the stereotypes. They're not wearing the rainbow flags, they're not skipping through the hallways or whatever, singing show tunes. They're not doing the stereotypical gay thing, because in the future it's a nonissue. It doesn't matter. That's the future that my father envisioned, that's the one that I want to live in. That's the one that I think everyone wants to live in, at least people who follow *Star Trek*.

BRANNON BRAGA

Very rarely did we start thinking about an episode in terms of an issue. "Let's do a show about AIDS, let's do a show about terrorism." We usually thought in terms of neat science-fiction twists, and that's what sends us in the direction of what the story's about and who's in it.

RONALD D. MOORE

When we have started by saying, let's do a show about terrorism, you get things like "The High Ground," which is an abomination. It's our one terrorist show. We didn't have anything interesting to say about terrorism except that it's bad, and Beverly gets kidnapped—ho, hum. They take her down to the caves, and we get to have nice, big preachy speeches about terrorism and freedom fighting and security forces versus society. It's a very unsatisfying episode and the staff wasn't really happy with it. It's just an example of what happens when you start at the wrong place.

With the end of the show's wildly successful fourth season, Rick Berman turned to a writer from *Star Trek*'s troubled early years to rejoin the staff for the fifth season. The hope was to infuse more veteran talent to a staff that, with the exception of Piller and Taylor, was largely comprised of novice writers. And so Herb Wright, who segued from *Star Trek* to Paramount Television's *War of the Worlds* five years earlier, returned to duty to hopefully juice up the science-fiction content of *Next Generation*. He would depart several months later over creative differences in the show's direction with Michael Piller. Despite their problems, Wright found when he returned to the series that it had changed dramatically, both on-screen and off.

RICK BERMAN

The first year was very chaotic. But the second year Gene stepped away and Maurice Hurley and I took the reins and there was additional shakedown, but things smoothed out a little bit. In the third year Piller came, and it was shaky at first and then started to stabilize and it was very stable ever since.

HERB WRIGHT (producer, *Star Trek: The Next Generation*)

Fifth season was no comparison. People were so much happier and calmer and quieter and really helping each other. It was a kinder, gentler place to be. The first year I was the kinder, gentler guy, and the fifth year I came back and I was suddenly the hawk. In story meetings people would say, "In this scene let's kiss the baby" and I'd say, "Bullshit, let's kill the baby," and everybody would look at me and wonder what was wrong with me. I was the kid on staff then. I came back and all of the sudden I was the old man.

BRANNON BRAGA

Once I was hired on staff, it was a crazy time because as we entered season five, the show was enormously popular, the staff was set, and it was a very young staff. I was twenty-five, for fuck's sake, and Ron was twenty-six, and Joe [Menosky] had to be in his late twenties.

HERB WRIGHT

It was radically different, not only in content, but in the makeup of the staff and the way it's put together.

RONALD D. MOORE

Herb was a little crazy. He was funny, and I liked him, because he was a sort of bigger-than-life person with sort of an old pro attitude. You enjoyed him, but he was a little insane. I remember he put up this picture of the face on Mars on his bulletin board, and he was telling us all about how it was real and it was important and we should do a show about this. There are really people on Mars that did this. Picard could discover it. And we were wondering whether or not he was kidding.

He would also tell stories about Leonard Maizlish and how he had a big fight with Leonard about something, and then he was leaving for Christmas vacation and was at LAX and taking off when the plane turned around and came back because there had been a bomb threat and his whole vacation was destroyed. He went back into Leonard Maizlish's office and told him about it, and Leonard looked at him and smiled. He says he was convinced at that moment that Leonard had called in the bomb threat to keep him from going on vacation.

The fifth season also marked the introduction of a major new character, Ensign Ro Laren, played by Michelle Forbes (*Kalifornia*, *Battlestar Galactica*, *True Blood*, *Powers*), who would recur throughout the rest of the series. Due to her popularity with the fans, the producers had planned to include her in the spin-off *Deep Space Nine*, but Forbes, reluctant to commit to seven years in space, chose to pursue a short-lived feature career instead, leading to the casting of Nana Visitor as Kira Nerys. Despite her reluctance to get typecast, Forbes made a notable impact on *The Next Generation* even though she only appeared intermittently throughout the remaining seasons.

MICHAEL PILLER

There was no plan at all for *Deep Space Nine* when Ensign Ro was developed. What was in the back of our minds was the need for a character, and we thought we needed another woman on the show. When we talked about what kind of woman we would want, we thought it would be nice to have someone who had a little backstory and somebody we could use to create a some conflict. So Rick and I worked on the concept of Ro, and it was a show I was very satisfied with.

MICHELLE FORBES (actress, "Ro Laren")

I've become very attached to *Star Trek*. It's a wonderful place where imagination just runs wild, which is rare and a lot of fun. It's really nice to know that if something is going to be around and if your committing yourself to celluloid history, it's *Star Trek*.

MICHAEL PILLER

It's one of the fifth season's greatest accomplishments—and not just by Rick [Berman] and I, but by the acting of Michelle, who is just a wonderful performer—to create a new character on a series where you don't just throw in new people, because this audience is really particular about who they're going to make part of the family.

> Fifth season also marked the return of Leonard Nimoy as Spock in a two-part episode, "Unification," whose main goal appeared to be promoting the release of *Star Trek VI: The Undiscovered Country* in movie theaters.

RICK BERMAN

It came out of Frank Mancuso, the chairman of Paramount at the time, who said to Leonard when they were planning *Star Trek VI*, why don't you figure out some way to pass the baton. Maybe you could make some elements of *Star Trek VI* that reflect on *Next Generation*, and work with Berman to make *Next Generation* reflect *Star Trek VI*. I sat down with Leonard and Nick Meyer, and we discussed elements of our show. Mike and I spent a lot of time kicking things around, and finally we came back to Leonard with an idea he didn't particularly like. We made a big change in the room and he loved it.

MICHAEL PILLER

It's no secret I was disappointed by my own work on it more than anything else. I thought it was a historic opportunity, and I don't think we delivered what the potential of it was. I remember watching it for the first time cut together and saying, "This is dark, it's flat, who cares, it's talky." I'm a writer who depends a great deal on his instincts, and they almost always lead me in a good direction. This time I don't think they did. It was our feeling if you're going to bring Spock out of retirement, it needs to be something of cosmic significance.

> Unfortunately, fifth season was also the year when Gene Roddenberry would tragically pass away after years of alcohol, drugs, hard living, and even more hard work took their toll on the legendary Great Bird of the Galaxy. He died on October 24, 1991, at the age of seventy.

RONALD D. MOORE

There would be longer absences, and nothing really was said, but you noticed he wasn't around as much. You would hear he wasn't feeling well. He started walking slower. He wasn't in production meetings or story meetings with us.

There were parties every year that we all went to. We all went to the Halloween party and the Oscar party at Gene's house. Gene was at the Christmas parties and the wrap parties. So, you saw him at gatherings more than you saw him day to day on the show.

CHRISTOPHER KNOPF (friend of Gene Roddenberry)

I really loved Gene, he was so damn bright—one night he and I and my first wife, Betty, were all going out to dinner. On the way back, it was a wet night, and as we pulled up, there was a motorcycle in his driveway. And I said, "When did you get that?" He said, "Let's go for a ride." So there we are in our suits, driving down Beverly Glen. He turns right and we skid right into a rosebush! Our knees were all smashed up and everything else, and he said, "You'll probably never do this again."

ADAM MALIN (cofounder, Creation Entertainment)

In 1991 I became aware that Gene had taken ill and, simultaneously, this was the twenty-fifth anniversary of *Star Trek,* and so we decided to do a tribute to Gene that would feature the entire cast of *Star Trek*. We booked the Shrine Auditorium, and the entire cast agreed to come and be at this event. Unbeknownst to me there was some bad blood, and there were some challenges getting some of them to be on stage together with Roddenberry. Much to my consternation, what I thought would be the end flourish of the event, I didn't discover wasn't going to be possible until the actual event day itself.

But even more dramatically, as a prelude to this event, in the weeks before the event, I had received a letter in a very clichéd form, which looked like a ransom note where each letter was cut out of a newspaper and pasted to form words of a sentence. The letter said, "If you put that Jew Shatner on stage, we will blow up the Shrine." Getting that letter was really intense. We had police presence and metal detectors for everyone coming into the Shrine, so we had six thousand people ir-ritated to no end who waited two or three hours extra to get in, and they blamed me for it, but I couldn't tell them what was really going on. I can kind of look at it now and laugh, but they didn't know what a bad situation it was. Of course, no threat ever presented itself and no doubt it was a crank, but we took it very seriously. In any event, the thing went off beautifully once it got going, each member of the cast got up there and said a few things about Roddenberry, about *Star Trek*, and they were wonderful.

I do remember when it was finally Bill's time to get up and speak, he seemed to run a little long with his speech, and then out of the blue DeForest Kelley comes running on stage with a big hook to pull Bill off the stage. Anyway, finally we had that iconic moment, the entire classic cast on stage together. It was the first time they ever appeared all together at once, and the only time they would share a stage the same day with Gene Rodenberry. Then Gene comes out, and he was in a wheelchair, and he delivered a heartfelt, brief thank-you to the audience for everything they had done to support him and support *Star Trek*. He told them that he loved them, and it was very sincere, and, for me, it was one of those amazing moments in my life and it was the end of an era and the start of a new era. I remember being very emotional about it. It was one of the best moments of my career.

CHRISTOPHER KNOPF

Gene just lived on the edge. I remember when he was so terribly sick, and we were at Sam Rolfe's house for dinner one night, I asked Majel how he was, and she said, bad. She was very angry. He would not quit smoking, he would not quit drinking.

SUSAN SACKETT (assistant to Gene Roddenberry)

On the day that Gene died, Michael Piller called everyone into the office, and we didn't know what it was about. He made an announcement that Gene Roddenberry died. I thought that was very insensitive. This is not a thinking or sensitive person. I found that very, very annoying and saddening, and I felt like he had socked me in the face.

HAROLD LIVINGSTON (writer, *Star Trek: The Motion Picture*)

Susan was a nice woman, but she was in love with Roddenberry. I sold a novel to a publisher, and it was called *Wind Jammer*. It was science fiction. And a character was a Roddenberry-like character. It begins with him in a whorehouse, getting the shit beat out of him. So, when he dies I have his secretary running down the aisle saying, "They killed him! They killed him! The studio killed him." Somebody told me that's what Susan did. She was madly in love with him.

CHRISTOPHER KNOPF

He had a supreme ego and I'm sure he enjoyed all the success. I do know that Majel, right till the end after he died, would give parties. They would have twenty Christmas trees in their house, there was a band, there were singers, there were magicians, there were painters who would paint portraits, there was caviar, the food was so lavish. It was incredible.

ROD RODDENBERRY

I was pretty isolated. You know, Shatner and Nimoy or any of the actors for that matter really didn't come over to the house. I've seen old film footage of my father and James Doohan on a boat together and stuff. He was friends with DeForest Kelley and James Doohan, but I don't remember a lot of Hollywood parties. I wasn't completely oblivious to *Star Trek*, but I just wasn't watching it.

CHRISTOPHER KNOPF

I was one of the eulogists for Gene. It was a huge turnout. They had planes flying overhead with the missing man formation, and Patrick Stewart spoke, too. I miss him. He and I had a very special relationship. It wasn't a professional one, it was a personal one.

NAREN SHANKAR

I was thrilled to meet Gene. The only time I had any real interaction with him was at my good-bye party as an intern. I think he was there largely because there was champagne. As you know, Gene liked to drink—as do I.

BRANNON BRAGA

In a blink of an eye they were all gone: Ernie the limo driver, Susan Sackett, Richard Arnold. There were political and personal dramas going on that I was not privy to. All I know is we heard Gene died and suddenly they were all gone after an hour or two.

RICHARD ARNOLD (*Star Trek* archivist)

After Gene died, everyone who had worked for him was fired, most of them the day he died, especially in Susan's case. But I was working not just for *TNG*, but for four divisions of the studio, who all still wanted me there. The exception was Arthur Cohen, who was the senior VP in charge of the merchandising, and with whom Gene had had terrific battles for the last couple of years. It was at Arthur's insistence that I was finally fired, nearly a month after Gene died. The actors and people I had worked with on the lot for some fifteen years were all very supportive, but my employment at the studio was over.

RICK BERMAN

It was devastating. We all knew that Gene was ill, but not critically ill. He died very unexpectedly. Oddly enough, he was at a doctor's appointment with his wife. He finished the appointment and got back into the elevator and just collapsed and died. I got a call from Majel and I went down to the set and I pulled Patrick aside. Patrick was not only the captain, whose character was the captain, but he also was sort of the unofficial leader of the cast and they all looked up to him and respected him. I told Patrick and then we sort of gathered the cast and crew around and everybody was pretty shocked.

Gene got in his golf cart virtually every day and went down to the set to visit. Everybody was extremely fond of him. He was the father of this whole thing. It was very upsetting to everybody.

JONATHAN FRAKES (actor, "William T. Riker")

We were on the bridge and the news came to us. Berman came down to tell us and said Gene would have wanted us to keep working. Patrick and I looked at him and said, "Bullshit. We should go to a bar and have a little wake is what we should do."

NAREN SHANKAR

I was a technical advisor, science consultant at the time, and Ron called me and he said, "Hey, Gene died today," and it was really sad. As a guy who created something that was a big part of my childhood, it was really sad.

With the death of Gene Roddenberry, a chapter of the *Star Trek* saga forever closed. And a new era—captained by Rick Berman, who would remain the steward and new Great Bird of the franchise—would begin, lasting a decade and a half until the cancellation of *Star Trek: Enterprise*.

BRANNON BRAGA

Rick Berman started to open up more after that. He got the keys to the kingdom and he suddenly started to interact more and more with writers and became a bit more of a friendly guy, which was a transformation for him. That was a big thing I noticed. We were all really sad, but we did start to push the boundaries a little more when Gene left.

RICHARD ARNOLD

At no point ever, at least not until after he died, did I ever hear anyone say that Rick Berman was Gene's personal choice to succeed him. Quite the contrary, his first impression of Rick was that he was some studio suit that they had sent to spy on him. Rick was only a supervising producer when the show began . . . he was not the cocreator nor the executive producer of the series. As Marina Sirtis pointed out, Rick didn't so much carry on the torch as he pulled it from Gene's still-warm hands.

BRANNON BRAGA

Rick was not as nice or accessible when I first started. He was feared, and to some degree resented because he could throw things out. And he wasn't a writer, he wasn't a part of the writing staff. Eventually, from my perspective, I came to know him as a very talented writer, and I would end up writing a lot of scripts with him. Maybe he felt more insecure when Gene was there.

DAVE ROSSI (assistant to Rick Berman)

While Rick may not have been a writer, he did know the studio system and how to play that game. In many ways he was the last of his kind; an autonomous showrunner that the studio left alone. That's unheard of today. We never got notes from the studio, the networks, executives . . . none of that. We were free to craft the show the way Rick saw fit and, again, that is unheard of today.

He also employed co-showrunners, like Michael Piller, Jeri Taylor, Ira Behr, who did run the writing staffs. While Rick had ultimate say, it's not like he simply made sweeping declarations. There was a process and meetings and discussions and, on the occasion Rick wanted something a certain way, well, he was the boss. It was completely fair to the process in my eyes.

IRA STEVEN BEHR (executive producer, *Star Trek: Deep Space Nine*)

One of the things that struck me was at Gene's Halloween party Mick Fleetwood was walking around in a goddamn Starfleet uniform. I hadn't been on the show long and I didn't know many people. So, I'm looking for Mike and Rick there.

I walk over and say hello, and Rick is in Rick mode. He's not happy and he's edgy. Mike isn't coming. And he goes, "Can you believe it? Mike's not showing up." And to me, I had no opinion. And he looks at me, "You know, how would you like it if I made you king?" And it was, like, "Huh?" So, Mike doesn't show up at a Halloween party and you're offering me his job. It was showing who's boss and also wanting to see my reaction.

Now, I think Rick knew I was friends with Mike, so there was no real reaction. But it just struck me as being weird. That was a strange beat in this journey. I'm sure in Rick's mind it was a joke and meaningless, but, you know, nothing is meaningless.

RICK BERMAN

I don't believe I was intimidated, because Gene had stepped back really close to two years earlier. After the first season he stepped back, and after the second season he pretty much was out of the picture. He just was sort of ill, and he had a lot of wonderful people involved with the day-to-day work on the shows.

Rick Berman had already absorbed many of Gene Roddenberry's responsibilities, including becoming the final arbiter for stories and scripts. And after Roddenberry's death, Berman would continue to enforce posthumously what he perceived as Roddenberry's rules governing *Star Trek,* as well as cocreate the spin-off series, firmly placing his distinct imprimatur on the franchise forever.

BRENT SPINER (actor, "Data")

Episodic television is not particularly inventive. If you look at all the great directors like Hitchcock and Ford and Allen, they really set the tone of the production. Television really is a producer's medium.

CHRIS BLACK (coexecutive producer, *Enterprise*)

Rick Berman was very ambivalent about *Star Trek,* in my opinion. He took his role as the steward of the franchise seriously, but had complete contempt for it at the same time. You could never go in and reference anything from the original series. At the same time, he would tell you that in terms of the storytelling, we had to endeavor to preserve that ethos.

I remember pitching for *Enterprise,* and Rick had a problem doing anything that had a conflict within the crew. His argument was that in Gene's universe these conflicts between Starfleet officers don't exist. I think that is demonstratively not true. How do you tell stories? Drama is conflict, and if you're being told that your lead characters can't have conflict between them, and you're giving the central conflict to the guest actors, it seems like a poor way to write a television series.

RICK BERMAN

I believe that for the purposes of our show, Gene's vision of the twenty-fourth century is dramatically correct. I don't think we're going to be living in a *Blade Runner* society, but I think we'll be living in a future which will be very similar to the world we're living in now. Then again, the show had nothing to do with *my* vision of the future. I became an expert in Gene Roddenberry's future. It's like learning a language, and I'm fluent in it and could protect it and police it and nurture it in the same way that Gene did.

JONATHAN FRAKES

I know people who want to have Rick beheaded. I see their point of view about him in terms of his arrogance with the system, with the family. With the keys to the car. I don't know why he's disliked in the fan community. What happens with anything is you start off really successful, but as anything just drifts away and falls apart, you start blaming the person that kept it going for a long time. Suddenly they're an idiot because they can't keep it going anymore. I'm not saying they are an idiot, I'm saying that's the perception, because if you think about it, the way *Star Trek* dwindled away with *Enterprise*'s ratings dropping and *Insurrection* and *Nemesis* bombing, it was like *Star Trek* was dying before their eyes, and who are you going to blame for that? The guy in charge of *Star Trek*, right? Rick Berman.

BRENT SPINER

Rick in particular was always fairly dedicated to staying within Gene's vision. There were things we'd do that we'd say, if Gene was still alive we probably wouldn't be doing this; occasionally religion raised its ugly head on the show, and Gene was totally opposed to any kind of reference to religion. He wasn't particularly keen on mythology; science fact was sort of his thrust and, for the most part, the show stayed within his idea.

NAREN SHANKAR

You would go in and talk to Rick and he would mock you with, like, a line of dialogue that he found particularly shitty. He would tell you, like, six hundred times how shitty it was.

RICK BERMAN

We had to manufacture our conflict from other than interpersonal conflict among our characters, and that does make it very difficult to write. The language has to be stylized; we don't know how people are going to speak in the twenty-fourth century and so we have them speak in a sort of stylized generic fashion. It's not twenty-fourth century, it's not contemporary, and on the other hand, it's not medieval, either. We had to deal with science fiction, and a lot of people don't understand what sci-fi is. A lot of people are interested in dealing with fantasy, and the writers have to deal with a lot of technical elements.

DAVE ROSSI

I don't think people understand what it must be like to protect someone else's dream day in, day out for eighteen years. That's a testament to Rick's dedication and his appreciation of Gene's vision of the future, which I might add, I don't think he shares. I know there are stories out there, many of them secondhand, that talk about Rick being mean or cruel, but I never saw that. I found that he respected anyone who would stand up to him, even though there weren't many that did. Rick ran the show and that was that. Yes, he could be very tough sometimes, but I imagine the same could be said of any executives in high positions, and being tough shouldn't be misunderstood as being mean.

RICK BERMAN

I read something recently where one of the writers from *Deep Space Nine* said that they wanted to get rid of the technobabble, but that Rick Berman insisted on leaving the technobabble in, which is comical. I would fight tooth and nail with Gene and with others to get rid of technobabble. I thought technobabble was always overdone to a comical degree. *Deep Space Nine* writers didn't like getting notes from me. They just found it offensive in some way. My notes were probably a little bit more picky than they should have been, which I will take responsibility for, but it was probably one of those situations where it was a line of technobabble that I said we should leave in. Somehow that grew into Berman insists on technobabble.

NAREN SHANKAR

The thing about Rick was he really did take very seriously maintaining Gene's legacy. Maybe it was also a cudgel he used to shut you down when he didn't want you to do something, but I think he did take it seriously. He did care about the show quite a bit.

BRANNON BRAGA

One aspect the writers never got involved with was editing. Rick Berman was in charge of postproduction, so very rarely would we get called into the editing room. If Rick ran into a huge problem, he'd come in and say, "What the fuck is this?" I wish we'd been more involved with that, because *Next Gen* had some great shit going on in post. We were the only show that used a full orchestra. It's unheard of these days.

RON JONES (composer, *Star Trek: The Next Generation*)

[Composer] Dennis [McCarthy] did the pilot a week and a half after I did "The Naked Now," so I had all the pressure. I had all the gray suits from the executive offices at Paramount coming around and watching my every move. But after they figured out I knew what I was doing, I got to do pretty much whatever I wanted to the first year.

LUKAS KENDALL (editor, *Film Score Monthly*)

Rick Berman, to his credit, realized that the new *Trek* could not be scored with 1960s television conventions—it would be laughable. In fact, it was dreadful when Fred Steiner scored "Code of Honor." As Berman solidified control, he ordered his composers to systematically eliminate anything necessary for interesting music—themes, rhythm, varied orchestration. He wanted the cultural legitimacy that a traditional orchestra provides, but playing a kind of droning non-music— just the way the technobabble was non-dialogue, and for that matter a lot of the characters were non-characters. It's a shame: the show robbed itself of one of the great tools of cinema that could have elevated the storytelling and done exactly what Berman probably wanted—enrich the literary values and emotion without coming off as cheesy TV music.

RON JONES

Bob Justman would just come in and be a cheerleader and say crank the music up.
    Meanwhile, there were all these indicators from on high that everything wasn't necessarily the way they wanted it to be. I felt like at first that I was being guided very gently in certain ways away from doing things more dramatically and being forced to mellow out. But I saw the episodes as needing certain things dramatically, and I tried to do what I could. I really saw the series more like a series of movies, and I thought people would appreciate that approach after we got done with the series. That they would sort of stand on their own more.

LUKAS KENDALL

Ron Jones wrote brilliantly shaped and evocative music, but he was let go for making a pest of himself; he tried to replace the strings with a Synclavier on "Brothers," the equipment crashed, and it was a fiasco. From that point on, he was a dead man walking. Dennis McCarthy and Ron's replacement, Jay Chattaway, didn't have Ron's death wish for bucking authority. At the scoring stage, they would be instructed by [postproduction supervisors] Peter Lauritson or Wendy Neuss to remove anything even remotely provocative. I saw it happen; it was bizarre. McCarthy wrote a fine score for *Generations*, and Chattaway's source music for "The Inner Light" is so good, fans asked to play it at their weddings. That could have been the music for *Star Trek* every week—but the postproduction bureaucracy took the boss's pet peeve about cheesy TV music and turned it into a crusade. It was very unfortunate.

RICK BERMAN

I have read time and time again I fired Ron Jones because he was too good, his music called too much attention to himself, and I wanted mundane boring soap opera background kind of music. That's something that not only have I read—it's even been on my Wikipedia page! It's very far from the truth. Peter Lauritson was one of the most important people in *Star Trek* and a person who gets very little attention. He selected all of the composers and I would approve them. We had numerous composers over the course of all of the years, with Dennis McCarthy being one of the two main composers. Ron Jones came in, he did a number of episodes for us. Both Peter and I, who worked very hard and had a hand in both selecting and deselecting composers, felt that Ron's music was not working for us. We didn't have to necessarily explain ourselves.

I could say that there were times where it called attention to itself a little bit too much. That was one thing that Peter or I may have mentioned at one point to somebody, and I have been chastised in print and at conventions over the years for firing this "genius" composer, because he was too good. Which is just another one of these things people say about you that is just nonsense.

DAVE ROSSI

Rick, through letting actors and crewmembers direct episodes, helped kickstart a lot of careers in the field for many people, and yet he never receives credit for it nor asks for any. Likewise, when actors had chances to do other projects while still under contract, Rick would bend over backward to accommodate, altering our shooting schedules to allow it. I think it's easy for people to revisit hard feelings, especially if they've been festering for years, but you need to paint the whole picture as you're talking about a whole person. Rick has his faults, just as you and I do. Ultimately, though, he's a good man, loyal friend, and he had a career anyone would envy.

RICK BERMAN

It fits into the category of no good deed goes unpunished. Jonathan Frakes came to me after a few years and said, I really want to direct. Jonathan and I were quite close, so I said, "Okay, but first you have to go to school." He said, "What do you mean?" I said, "I want you to spend the next two months shadowing directors. I want you on the set all day long whether you're working or not. I want you to sit in the cutting room and watch the shows being edited. I want you to come to production meetings. I want you to come to preproduction meetings. I want you to come to visual effects meetings. I want you to learn the art of directing from the show that you're costarring on backward and forward." Jonathan was a mensch. He was absolutely terrific. He did exactly what I asked him to do. After X number of months I gave him a directing assignment ["The Offspring"]. He did a great job, and then he did God knows how many episodes, two of our movies, and a number of other movies. He is still directing.

JONATHAN FRAKES

I went to Berman and said I'd like to do a show, and he said you have to go to school. I spent about three hundred hours in the editing room and on the dubbing stage and learning about that side of directing. Naturally, I looked over the shoulders of all our regular directors and took some seminars and read textbooks and, finally, I didn't go away. Rick was kind enough to give me "The Offspring," and I was thrilled, because I got a Data show and those always work.

RICK BERMAN

Jonathan started this ball rolling, and all of sudden other people started making the request. My feeling was that this was a gift and not something that, as far as actors are concerned, that I owed them. There were some actors during the course of the four series who were not necessarily perfectly behaved in terms of being prepared, being on time, not giving grief to various people that they were working with on the set. I had no interest in giving those people the gift of a directing assignment, but there were others like Gates [McFadden], LeVar [Burton], and Michael Dorn who did direct.

On *Deep Space Nine,* a lot of people wanted to direct. And it kept going. Sometimes it was very hard because one of our finest actors, and I'm not going to say who, did a very mediocre job at directing and, in fact, there was more than one. There were maybe two or three actors over the course of the shows who didn't do a great job of directing, and I had no interest in giving them a second assignment. Which was very hard, because these were people I was working with and dealing with on a daily basis.

JONATHAN FRAKES

I thank Rick for giving me the opportunity, which I'm sure he regretted since everyone in the world beat down his door. He's given editors, a.d.'s, actors their shot, and it came back to haunt him. I heard the caterer was looking to direct an episode.

RICK BERMAN

When it came to some of our production people, an assistant director, like a Les Landau, these were people who were completely qualified to direct. Giving them directing assignments was no big deal. People like [line producer] David Livingston, who came and asked to direct, was incredibly knowledgeable and incredibly studious and did a wonderful job. There were times where I felt with people like Jonathan [Frakes], and Roxann [Dawson], and Robbie McNeill, where I felt really proud of having given them assignments and seeing the remarkable work they did. And there were times where I wished I had never done it and it came back to bite me in the ass.

MANNY COTO (executive producer, *Star Trek: Enterprise*)

I really loved Rick, I got along great with him. A lot of other *Star Trek* writers had their views, but I really had a great time with him. I thought he was funny, I enjoyed meeting with him. He and I had the same sort of sarcastic outlook, so we had fun together. The guy I saw was someone who actually was very insistent that it be good; he didn't want it to be cheesy, he wanted it to be as good as can be. He gave very specific notes. You give him an idea and he would say, "No, that's terrible." By the way, many times he would come up with great ideas and save our asses in story. He was a great idea guy. There are some writers who feel anybody who has a different opinion, who's at the top, they immediately assume he's a villain.

They think "I've got to protect my integrity" and all this stuff, and some of it *is* well-founded. But sometimes it's a little bit of posturing, like "I'm a creative genius and how dare you interfere with my words?" Not everybody deserves that. This is a collaborative industry, and I've found most of the writers who tend to be like that are the ones who are the most problems. There's always an exception, there *are* geniuses. But most writers in this business who think that their words are dictated by God are usually the ones who need the most help. Rick was very supportive of everything we did in season four of *Enterprise* and was open to it. Sometimes we had to convince him, but very often he would come around. I found it to be a very good relationship.

DOUG DREXLER (special makeup effects artist, *Star Trek: The Next Generation*)

Star Trek was micromanaged by Rick Berman. We all knew it. I was in a production meeting when Herman [Zimmerman] made a suggestion about one of the stories, and Rick literally called Herman an idiot. "What? Are you writing the show now?" On *Battlestar Galactica,* Ron Moore knew a good idea when he heard one. He didn't care where it came from, and we were always free to change things. Ron's *Galactica* is very much a descendant of *Star Trek*. It's more a descendant of *Star Trek* than it was the original *Battlestar Galactica*.

Ron Moore had lived through *Star Trek,* and he wasn't going to let it be that way on *Galactica*. We had an amazing give and take between the departments. The art department and the visual effects department worked hand in hand like we were the same department. There was never any competition or ego.

ROD RODDENBERRY

I've heard such horror stories about Rick, and I'm sure a lot of them are true, but the way that he presented himself, what he said about taking over after my father weighing on him . . . I guess what kind of affected me the most was the stuff he read on the Internet. He acknowledged that he's read all the slamming that goes on. He made a comment to me that "when my kids see that, I have to explain it to them." It kind of made him human to me in a way instead of this evil bad guy. I'm not saying I don't believe the stories, I don't think he's a bad guy. I can't even tell what it's like to be in his shoes at that time. Insecurities, ego, fear. I'm very forgiving. He wasn't Gene Roddenberry. And neither am I—and neither is J.J.—and none of us ever will be.

DOUG DREXLER

I'm not going to say I don't like Rick Berman. I actually love Rick Berman. He did a lot for *Star Trek*. Some of the best years were run by him. He gets a bad rap. On the other hand, he did a lot of things I definitely don't agree with, and I thought that it was a very fear-run type of thing. I used to see it with Peter Lauritson that he was afraid of Rick Berman. He wouldn't show Rick everything that came from the art department, he'd only pick out the things he thought Rick wouldn't explode at. We found out later that he didn't see half of the designs. So, while I have some bones to pick with Rick Berman, on the other hand I feel like he made the show a success.

TOM MAZZA (vice president of current programs, Paramount Television)

Rick and I talked every day, and part of what we had to do at the studio was to oversee the production finances, production and creative. So, if we needed to spend twenty thousand more on a particular guest cast star and we thought it would be a good choice, "OK, fine." Where are we on the budget? Rick was always true to his word. If I would say, "Rick, we're over budget on this episode," he'd go, "I got it. I know where we are going to save it. We've got something coming up." And that's all I needed to say. Very rarely do you get to do that. That kind of trust is rare. I've never had that kind of a relationship with a showrunner.

BRENT SPINER

We didn't see Rick on the set very often, but, by the same token, after watching the MGM documentary, [Irving] Thalberg didn't show up on the sets very often, either, and I think I'll leave it at that.

JONATHAN FRAKES

Rick Berman was definitely in control of the show . . . he would have it no other way.

TOM MAZZA

For me, working with Rick on all three series was remarkable. There wasn't a day hat Rick and I didn't speak, if not once then three times a day. I will never forget e days. We were just making a great and fun television series. There was no nce. We had to report to our bosses, but we had good support all the way

DAVE ROSSI

Rick Berman was entrusted with another man's dream and legacy and preserved both. In my experience, Rick always operated under the premise "What would Gene want to see here?" And he did that for eighteen years. I understand people have criticisms of some of the creative choices made, but no one can ever fault Rick for always putting *Star Trek* first. I hope that's what his legacy is: that *Star Trek* inspired and thrived under his leadership, which I think is what Gene would have wanted for it.

BRANNON BRAGA

People would test boundaries. There was a script that Gene really took offense to when Gene was still giving notes. Those rules were really followed by Rick Berman after Gene passed away—but things did loosen up. I remember when I did "Cause and Effect," I had found a way to do time travel that wasn't really time travel, it was just a time loop, so it was okay. It wasn't about going back and preventing Abe Lincoln from being shot. It was something new, so I was able to get away with it, and that's kind of what started to happen.

We started to push boundaries in different ways. Ron was always pushing for more conflict between the characters, I was pushing more conceptual boundaries, and others were doing other things, but I would say that, personally, I never took issue with the non-conflict rule. To me, that was one of the premises of the whole damn show. It was at this point in *Star Trek*'s history that people didn't have that petty shit going on, it just didn't exist, and the conflict came from outside, and I was fine with that.

RONALD D. MOORE (coexecutive producer, *Star Trek: Deep Space Nine*)

There were all these dictums that we'll never bring back original cast members or do alternate timelines or time travel shows, and people had sort of forgotten the reasons for those dictums. The show really began to evolve, and by sixth season we were really taking a lot more risks; the show found its strength and just sailed.

BRANNON BRAGA

There was no reason for us to tell a mundane story. We could do anything. The frustrating thing about it was we desperately wanted science-fiction elements. It's hard to come up with those vital science-fiction twists.

JERI TAYLOR

When you deal with time travel, I can't tell you how complicated it gets trying to figure out what to do—and arguments and discussions about different timelines and alternate universes.

BRANNON BRAGA

We all feel like we know how time travel works—and it's an imaginary concept. Ron has his conception and Jeri has hers and I have mine and it's a matter of consolidating all of those ideas. The conversations would frequently descend into bizarre, ludicrous realms of time theory, which frequently happened on that show.

RENÉ ECHEVARRIA (producer, *Star Trek: Deep Space Nine*)

It prompted very hilarious arguments about time travel and how it worked— "That's not how time travel works, you idiot!"—with huge accusations and people falling back on primary sources like *Bill & Ted's Excellent Adventure*— "That's the way it works, you can *so* meet yourself"—and all sorts of preposterous stuff.

BRANNON BRAGA

You have to keep in perspective that what you're talking about is imaginary, but at the same time as a staff it was our ability to be able to imagine things like time travel as real phenomenon so completely that we believe it that gave us the ability to write the show at all. There have been writers on the show who didn't believe, and they didn't work, and they could never get it. I think you have to be a little bit schizophrenic to be able to embrace unreal concepts as reality and explore them.

As the series entered its sixth year, Frank Abatemarco was brought on staff during the summer hiatus by Piller. The writer/producer, who had worked on such shows as *Simon & Simon*, had been hired for a variety of reasons–most of all to give support to Jeri Taylor, who Berman and Piller were unsure would be able to ＋ through the season on her own without another veteran writer on staff while ʰer producing duo were busy with films and spin-offs.

MICHAEL PILLER

Jeri was going into the season with a bunch of young people, and Ron and Brannon had not been asked to step up and take responsibilities that they evolved into. I wanted to give her someone strong so she didn't feel like she was out there alone. Frank had been pitched to us for a number of years, and I sat down and had lunch with him. I was just terribly impressed with his philosophy and attitude. I said to Jeri, "I know you're going to hate me for saying this, but go have lunch with the guy and see what you think."

RENÉ ECHEVARRIA

Michael was passionate about the show, but he wasn't the greatest people person. He put up with us. He would tell us he needed a real writer in the room, someone with experience, but those guys would always come and go through the revolving door. They never lasted. It didn't bother me, but I think it did Ron.

MICHAEL PILLER

The hardest thing there is in this business is to find people who can write *Star Trek*, but as so often happens when we hire a writer without trying him out on a script first, it did not work out. Frank was not getting to the bottom of the characters, it was just not reading like *Star Trek*, and we tried to give him feedback. Jeri was working with him far more than I was, but the bottom line was he wasn't getting done what needed to get done, and so we just decided to go separate ways. He left with a great deal of bitterness and there was a very uncomfortable scene between him and I before he left. I regret that, because I still respect his work and it's just a shame, but it was something Jeri felt very strongly about and I backed Jeri up 100 percent.

BRANNON BRAGA

A lot of good writers don't get *Star Trek* and have a difficult time with it. Frank was an intensely personable fellow and from what I've seen of his work, a superior writer. What I sensed was that he wasn't getting *Star Trek*.

A highlight of the season would be the return of James Doohan as Scotty in the Ron Moore-penned "Relics," in which the *Enterprise*'s former chief engineering officer—found preserved in a transporter loop—proves vital in saving the *Enterprise* one last time from destruction inside a Dyson sphere.

MICHAEL PILLER

When I came on board, you could not mention the old *Star Trek* in an episode, you couldn't make a reference to a character without major problems. But at this point, because we were firmly established, I think everybody felt a bit more comfortable that we had proven ourselves. We don't owe anything to the old *Star Trek*, except like the guys who went to the moon, the Mercury guys had to go up there first and we respect them for that.

RONALD D. MOORE

I think in the earlier seasons of the series we felt like this show had to go and prove itself, and we made the decision very early on that we weren't going to pick up any old plot lines and we weren't going to talk about those guys and we weren't going to have their sons and daughters on the show. And that philosophy drove the show for quite a while. "Sarek" was the first time that it felt comfortable enough to sort of start to acknowledge its history a little more, and then after "Unification," I think they sort of felt, "Well, okay, that wasn't so bad, we can do this without really destroying who we are, and we can do shows that make references to the old series without destroying our own." So when "Relics" came around to do, there wasn't a big cry and debate about it.

ALEXANDER SINGER (director, *Star Trek: The Next Generation*)

I had never worked with Jimmy Doohan, and I felt that potentially the show was a kind of classic, and I understood exactly what I had in my hands. I did not know physically what shape Doohan was in. There was a lot of dialogue, and I don't think he ever did a show in the old *Star Trek* where he had this much drama and this many notes to hit. By the time we came to the scene on the old *Star Trek* deck, he was not only the center, but he had to support a very powerful dramatic scene. It's a scene that, in reading it, I choked up. Part of me is very hard-headed and realistic and then part of me is very romantic and very sensitive and I was deeply moved by that story.

wanted to meet him first so we didn't meet on the set, and he came in graciously, and we talked, and his delight in doing it and his manner reassured me enormously. I think that he wanted me to be comfortable, and he wanted me to have a sense that he could indeed carry this load, and he convinced me. And subsequently there was only one day, one scene, where he had a very technical page of technobabble, and he was utterly exhausted at the end of a very long day, that we had any problems whatsoever. For the rest of it he was a delight to work with.

JAMES DOOHAN (actor, "Montgomery "Scotty" Scott)

It was terribly easy to do, because they treated me like a king, and if they had been Japanese, they'd have been bowing all over the place. It was just a marvelous experience, and everybody treated me so well.

RONALD D. MOORE

I set out to do a show that was nostalgic and sentimental and that would resonate with what people cared about. Originally, Troi was going to ask Scotty if he wanted to know what happened to his collegues aboard the *Enterprise*. There was a line in a scene that got cut out between Troi and Scotty where she said, "Would you like to know what happend to all your friends and family," and he said, "No, I'm not ready to hear that." That was the closest allusion we were going to make. My thought is it would clutter it up a little bit to make direct references, since once you bring up Bones and say that Mr. Spock is James Bond now and underground on Romulus, you have to talk about everybody else, and we didn't want to say what happened to everybody else because we didn't want to lock ourselves into it.

With *Next Generation* having lapped the original series and become a critical success in the process, the writers began to take more risks. One of those risks was "A Fistful of Datas," a holodeck western directed by Patrick Stewart, who had helmed "In Theory" the previous season and was anxious to get back behind the camera.

RICHARD JAMES (production designer, *Star Trek: The Next Generation*)

Patrick and I were standing there [on the Universal Studios Western Street] together talking about the episode, when one of their Universal Studios trams came by. I was laughing because Patrick had his back to the tram, but the tour guide was pointing out something, and all these people recognized Patrick and were taking pictures. I said to him that he had been recognized and he said, "You know, Richard, twenty years ago I was one of those people on the tram."

DAVID LIVINGSTON (supervising producer, *Star Trek: The Next Generation*)

Patrick did a wonderful job. He had a great time. He was Sergio Leone out there or Clint Eastwood, and Brent chewed every piece of scenery in sight and there wasn't any left by the time he got done. I think he played more characters in that than he ever played, because he was *everywhere*.

JERI TAYLOR

To think that someone from Great Britain would direct the quintessential American story, which is a western, seems a little oddball, but I think that might have been the happiest thing that happened, because Patrick was thrilled at this. He went out and rented every classic western and immersed himself.

You could always tell what western Patrick had seen the night before, because he would come in and have a new idea, and it would be a new idea that came from *The Man Who Shot Liberty Valance* or *High Noon*—and so he just piled all of it in there and it worked gloriously. It was a tough production, we had to go on location and he had a lot to do out there, but it just had a smashing look and it was tons of fun.

NAREN SHANKAR

Patrick did a wonderful job directing, which I think is hilarious. The funniest thing is Brannon didn't know anything about westerns, either, so he was writing a western directed by an Englishman.

BRANNON BARGA

I've seen very few westerns, so it was ironic that I was handed this, not being familiar with the western genre, and Patrick Stewart, who was even less familiar, was going to direct it. It brought a freshness to it, and I think this show was more fun to write than any other show. I really enjoyed doing it.

The first draft, which was written by Robert Wolfe, didn't have a solid western story, and it needed one, so I watched *Rio Bravo* and that's the story I decided to kind of utilize for the holodeck fantasy. I became a lover of the western genre and watched dozens of them, and my favorites were *The Outlaw Josey Wales* and *The Searchers*.

BRENT SPINER

I would have liked have done a show "For a Few Datas More."

Perhaps few shows on the series are more beloved than "The Inner Light," in which Picard experiences an entire lifetime while unconscious on the bridge. To this day, most fans consider "Inner Light," named after the B-side of The Beatles' single "Lady Madonna," another of the series standout episodes. Rife with emotional turmoil and pathos, "Inner Light" is one of the most finely textured and moving hours of the show as well as boasting one of its most intriguing sci-fi high concepts.

Originally pitched by writer Morgan Gendel, a former NBC programming executive and showrunner for the Pamela Anderson series *V.I.P.*, Gendel receives story credit along with a shared credit on the teleplay with former *TNG* executive script consultant Peter Allan Fields.

MORGAN GENDEL (writer, *Star Trek: The Next Generation*)

My original idea involved this ship that would zap this interactive thing into your mind and puts you in a different place. Instead of advertising "come to Maui," you find yourself on a beach somewhere else. That was my original thought. I really liked the notion of an alternate reality, so when I went in to pitch a probe zapping their brains, I came up with an antiwar message.

I thought, what if some civilization had been through some terrible war and didn't want others to repeat it? So Picard and Riker are hit with the probe and find themselves on a planet with stormtroopers coming and they had to finish the story to get back to the *Enterprise*. It seemed entirely real to them while they were there, and they had to escape these marching soldiers and a war, which was leading up to a nuclear holocaust. Meanwhile, aboard the ship, they're in comas. What intrigued the staff was this idea of an alternate reality, that you're lying there on the ship while experiencing something else.

I pictured the movie *Zardoz* and something in the pitch hit that note with Joe [Menosky], and he latched onto that and really liked it. At that point, we were going to put Ensign Ro in there and Picard was going to have to marry her in this alternate reality. Michael [Piller] knew immediately it should be Picard alone. That's where the heart of the story was, with him leading this other life. Michael rightfully said, "We're not going to need to cut back to the ship that much. The story is going to be with Picard."

MICHAEL PILLER

I remember putting all these lines on the board with each one creating the connections and relationships for Picard in this other life, so that by the end of the show, when they die or they are lost, there is an emotional impact that the audience should be absolutely heartbroken that he's lost. I actually had tears in my eyes when we were breaking this story.

PETER ALLAN FIELDS (executive story editor, *Star Trek: The Next Generation*)

Morgan wrote the story, and the first draft as well, and when I started work on the premise and the structure from the story, I made up my own sort of relationships. I felt it was an opportunity to give Captain Picard an entire lifetime, which was the antithesis of the kind of life he had always lived aboard the *Enterprise*. I understand Patrick enjoyed playing it very much, and it was a delight to be able to write it. Interestingly, Picard doesn't change. Even though he's not the captain, his personality doesn't change. He has now had a life he's never had; he has love, a home, marriage, and a family, which he never thought he needed before. He not only has them, but he loves them and is used to them and loses them. It turned out pretty darned well.

RICK BERMAN

"Inner Light" is one of the best episodes we've ever done. It allowed us to bring Patrick and a wonderful group of guest actors together and create a world. It was a challenge, and we see Picard at half a dozen different ages, involving prosthetics, and a man's entire lifetime in the course of an hour. It's quite dramatic and well written, and Peter Lauritson did a lovely job directing it.

> One of Gendel's biggest regrets is a sequel story he pitched that was never produced. In the proposed storyline, a starship would encounter another probe from Kataan and summon the *Enterprise* when they find it holds three people in cryo-stasis. One of those aboard is the scientist who played Eline in Picard's probe fantasy.

MORGAN GENDEL

Picard was married to this woman, made love to her, and grew old with her, so it's not like a dream. It's real to him, and now his dead wife has come back to life, which is a really powerful thing and made more so by the fact she doesn't know who the hell he is. *And* she's married to one of the scientists also on board the probe. I have a personal attachment to this episode, and I thought my passion for that would get it through. The idea is so powerful. His whole family has been destroyed in a natural holocaust, a nova explosion, and now he finds out his wife is alive. I pitched my heart out, but they thought it was best not to tamper with the memory of "Inner Light."

> This was only one of many ideas that never made it to the screen. Some concepts were just too outlandish—even for the out-of-this-world series that was finally willing to push the envelope even further than it had in the past.

JERI TAYLOR

We wanted to make Geordi an alien. He was going to discover that his father was not who he thought he was, and his mother had an almost *Rosemary's Baby*–kind of thing and had been impregnated by an alien. As a result, Geordi was actually half alien and now, at his present age, his people were coming back to get him. I thought that would have given Geordi's character a lot of elaboration.

Another even more audacious idea was the discussion of killing Commander Riker in "Second Chances," an episode in which the *Enterprise* discovers a doppelganger of Riker, Thomas Riker, that was created in a transporter malfunction on an Away Team mission nearly a decade earlier.

RENÉ ECHEVARRIA

We wanted to kill Riker and replace him with Tom Riker. We thought it was a great idea and no one could tell us different, but Michael knew it was wrong. As I've gone on to run other shows and sat in that chair, I could see he was right, and sometimes you just have to say no.

JERI TAYLOR

Maybe we were trying to rock the boat a little *too* drastically. My original idea, which we thought was very bold and surprising and would energize the seventh season, was to kill our Commander Riker and let Lieutenant Riker come onto the ship as a rejuvenated, energetic, driven, ambitious character. He wouldn't be Number One, he would be at ops and have to prove himself and build his career and get into conflict with the others, because he had these rough edges from having lived that arduous experience. It gave it a wonderful life that would energize the seventh season with everyone in a different place and a new character, and yet our same character there, and I was very, very taken with that. It was just too bold.

RICK BERMAN

That was one I basically said no to, but it gave me a lot of pause. My initial knee-jerk reaction was no and then I became a little bit more willing to say yes, but there were other problems it created. Once I started leaning toward yes, we started looking at what that would do and how it would fit into the movies and how it would fit into a lot of the different relationships. Basically, you're putting a character on the ship who has not experienced anything of the last six years and doesn't know any of the characters. How would it affect the movie and other variables? I ended up feeling rather strongly I didn't want to kill off Riker, and I didn't get any major arguments about it from Michael or Jeri.

MICHAEL PILLER

It's a fascinating premise. The most interesting part of it is Older Riker vs. Younger Riker, and that changed along the way since they were the same age. I had two very strong feelings about this story. The premise of this was that this was going to be the season cliffhanger and that the new Riker would come on board and during the course of the episode the Riker we've come to know and love would be killed and the young Riker would take his place as a lieutenant on the ship. Rick and I both did not like this idea, Rick more than I. Riker has always been a difficult character for writers to write, and they said, "Let's get some conflict, let's get some excitement and energy," but the fact is he's a pretty darn good character. A character that I related to a great deal.

JERI TAYLOR

We were going to have a very sort of bittersweet, deathbed poignant scene, and ultimately Michael said, "No, don't kill him, it'd be more interesting to know there are two of them out there and maybe they'd come back." We said terrific, let's go for it, and we'll end it with two Rikers somewhere in the universe, Will and Tom.

MICHAEL PILLER

We struggled long and hard to decide if we wanted to do a cliffhanger sixth season, because I felt if we did a lousy cliffhanger it would put a bad feeling on the season. I did not want to force ourselves to do a cliffhanger if it didn't work. It has become something of a tradition, but I didn't want to do it because it was a good story. I killed two or three of them, and Jeri came up with "Descent." It was not a Borg show to begin with. It was a show that had to deal with an invasion of space creatures and they turned out to be working for Lore [Data's evil brother].

I wanted to do it as a cliffhanger involving *Deep Space Nine*, a crossover, but Rick did not want to do that, so we left it to the *Next Generation* to do, but without having the crossover between the two casts. There was still a concern there was not really an inherent interest in a new set of space monsters, so they came up with an idea that had been tossed around since we did "I, Borg," which is what happens when Hugh [a Borg separated from the hive] goes back and chats with the other Borg.

Other concerns revolved around the future of the show, with rumors once again running rampant that Patrick Stewart would not be returning for a seventh year given his continued unhappiness. That displeasure directly resulted in the atypical episode, "Starship Mine," which has been pejoratively referred to as "Die Hard on the *Enterprise*," in which a phaser-carrying Picard has to save the ship from alien terrorists who have taken over the ship. Yippe-kay-yay, indeed.

JERI TAYLOR

It was a strange kind of premise for *Star Trek*, but we really hadn't serviced Patrick well in the beginning of the year, and I think Patrick was beginning to feel that. There were a lot of episodes that didn't really focus on him, and when you have someone like Patrick, that's not a good idea.

> "There was concern, but I think we all felt they were going to do features and that was a big carrot to get him to commit to another year," offered one member of the writing staff at the time. "When we were doing 'Chain of Command,' that's when the first inkling that Patrick might not be coming back was. Bringing in a new captain in part one, you could see how that could give the show a really fresh start if you could find somebody good. Frankly, we were more concerned that Brent wasn't going to come back, because Brent is irreplaceable. You don't just bring on another android or cart out a Vulcan or something to fill his role. You have to have a captain and there was, in fact, some enthusiasm about the possibility of getting someone new. We were talking about bringing a woman in."

JERI TAYLOR

As far as I know, that was completely informal. There were for thirty minutes or so some real concerns Patrick wouldn't be back. Most of the people felt in all probability he *would* be back. The negotiations were difficult, and had he not come back, then the door would have been wide open.

> One other thing that didn't change on the show was the abundance of technobabble, the *Next Generation* mumbo-science that continued to populate virtually every script. With the show's previous science consultant, Naren Shankar, now on staff, André Bormanis was charged with creating the science that made *Star Trek* sound real.

NAREN SHANKAR

I learned very quickly that the job of a science advisor was not about science, it was about maintaining the fake science of the *Star Trek* world. That's really what the job was about, and doing what I called "spray-on science fiction." Like giving it a little bit of terminology that made it sound official.

The guy that they had before me as the science consultant was a real stickler for details and he would always rag on them, like, "This is not real. You can't do this!" and I think they got fed up with it, they just wanted somebody to say, "Just make something that sounds good and sort of is right, we don't give a fuck about the science. Make sure the photon torpedoes work the same every episode." And so I understood that that was my position. It's not *Cosmos*.

ALEXANDER SIDDIG (actor, "Julian Bashir," *Star Trek: Deep Space Nine*)

They have a sadistic love of technobabble, but I actually quite enjoyed it. It's the nearest thing to Shakespeare. Stretching the mind to get your tongue around it and make sense of it when you talk. I actually quite enjoy trying to see if I can make something of it without making it sound flat. That's part of the lie of trying to make it sound like I'm actually a doctor or a science officer. Data on *The Next Generation* was an unbelievable robot because he did it flawlessly.

BRENT SPINER

Leonard [Nimoy] asked me how I could remember all this technobabble, because he said if the series hadn't been canceled after three years, his mind would have turned to mush. I said that's because he started out with a mind. My problem is that I can't just go in having some idea what to say. Since I'm playing an android, I have to know *exactly* what I'm saying and have it memorized.

MICHAEL PILLER

The actors used to call it Piller-filler, which is unfair since I know less about technology than anybody.

BRENT SPINER

That was one of my big complaints. Gene always said technobabble should be used as a spice and not as the main course.

With smooth sailing through season seven, *The Next Generation*'s final year presented the show's staff with some of its greatest challenges, becoming one of the most difficult seasons for the writers who were charged with creating another twenty-six hours of engaging television viewing while its producers continued to expand the franchise in new directions.

JERI TAYLOR

I'm not sure how everyone got everything done. Rick Berman not only took on developing a new series, *Voyager,* but also continued the development of a feature film. We were all kind of pushed to our limits, and there were several things that made the season uniquely difficult.

RENÉ ECHEVARRIA

I did a lot of writing seventh season. I went from one teleplay to another. By the end of the season, I literally went from finishing an episode to doing a rewrite of another episode in five days to starting an episode that was due five days later. I wrote three episodes in the time you ordinarily have to write one. I was writing ten pages a day to get it done.

JERI TAYLOR

The poor cast was exhausted. Patrick, who directed "Preemptive Strike" just before the finale, was in every scene of the final episode and was really going on adrenaline. Everybody was stretched thin, but nobody slacked off.

While it's a *Star Trek* cliché that "Spock's Brain" is the worst episode in the history of the franchise, one episode that certainly gives it a run for its money is season seven's "Masks," in which the *Enterprise* is transformed into an ancient temple and Data is possessed by the spirits of an ancient alien civilization. With Brent Spiner completing work on "Thine Own Self," the previous episode in which Data was heavily featured, the actor was surprised to be handed a teleplay for the very next show in which he would play multiple characters.

BRENT SPINER

I got the script for "Masks" on the night before we shot it. I was finishing "Thine Own Self" the midnight before, so I didn't have the time to even absorb the script and digest it and figure out who these people were that I was playing. You could look at it as an opportunity—and I would under normal circumstances. I think I said to Jeri at the time, "Give me six months and I think I could get all the characters," but as it was, I didn't know who these people were, and so I was doing instant acting and just coming up with whatever I was coming up with, because we had to put it on film.

JERI TAYLOR

Brent was very nervous about doing all of those parts. He said, "Dustin Hoffman had a year to figure out how to do *Tootsie* and portray a woman, and I don't have that kind of time." I said, "You don't have to portray a woman, just portray a leader." He ended up carving out four unique, distinct personalities, which is very, very tough on an actor, especially given the time constraints.

RONALD D. MOORE

I remember seeing the initial story [by Joe Menosky] and saying, "Jesus, what is this?" It was pretty out there, and then the script came in and we all sort of scratched our heads and looked at each other and went, "What is he smoking out there in Alps?" But when we started to examine it and get into it a little more, we saw what he was doing. He has some really interesting ideas and he approaches things from a fresh angle. It was a fascinating episode. It was just full of wild concepts, and from that angle alone it was worth doing, because sometimes you have to take those risks and really go out someplace and do something bizarre.

NAREN SHANKAR

Everybody pretty much would agree that the seventh season got off to a bit of a rocky start. A lot of it had to do with the fact that we went out of the sixth season on a real roll and it was creatively very exhausting. Unfortunately, we never really got a break between seasons. René managed to get away for a couple of weeks, but I had less than a week of vacation to get back. Ron and Brannon went to Hawaii and wrote *Star Trek: Generations* and came back immediately and we just jumped right in. As a result, I think the beginning of the season shows a little bit of exhaustion and it's unfortunate. You never sit down and say you want this season to suck.

In the heavy-handed "Force of Nature," an allegory for pollution and climate change, the Federation is forced to set warp speed limits as high warp speeds are damaging the fabric of space itself.

RONALD D. MOORE

"Force of Nature" was something I fought for early on and went to the wall for. We had a big meeting with Rick and Mike and Jeri and we all got on our high horses and we went in there and said we felt strongly about the episode, saying, "We want to do this, we want to make a statement, and we want to change the *Star Trek* universe forever. This is important and this is right and we should do it!"

Now, I'm just going, "What was I thinking?" It was such a great idea in concept. We always said that dealing with the environment on this show is incredibly difficult. It's hard to do a show about the ozone, because the ozone is huge and impersonal, and hard to make dramatic. We thought we had found a way to personalize it and make it our problem and it became "Force of Nature."

BRANNON BRAGA

That's an unsuccessful *Star Trek* episode. It was an analogy for pollution or global warming. The reason that that episode is a bore, in my opinion, is that there is no allegory. It is on the nose. It is a fastball down the middle, and it feels preachy. Suddenly, you're not deriving the meaning from the episode, the meaning is clobbering you over the head.

MICHAEL PILLER

The truth is, I spent so much time on *Deep Space Nine,* particularly at the beginning of the year, that my involvement with *The Next Generation* was that of a Monday-morning quarterback. It made me feel uncomfortable at times, sort of being an absentee landlord coming to collect the rent. I would come in to check the stories and read the scripts and give notes, but I felt seventh season my influence was beginning to lessen.

It was almost two years since I had been in the room with the guys breaking stories, and these are very good people who deserved to be able to try the things that they always wanted to do. "Force of Nature" certainly inspired us to have several long meetings on where the season was going. I felt we were letting it slip away.

NICK SAGAN (writer, *Star Trek: The Next Generation*)

Despite the people who say *Star Trek* is science fiction and not a serious drama, we were able to really get into some very deep human emotions. That's one of the things I love about the show. I had run into Gates McFadden and I thanked her and she thanked me. It was a really nice conversation. I told her she made me look really good, and she said that I had helped turn the season around for her. She had been kind of down on *Trek* after doing it so long, and my episode ["Attached"] and then "Sub Rosa" and her directing really turned everything around.

MICHAEL PILLER

The problem was that we didn't have a lot of ideas. We had to go with the best ones we could come up with, and then within each one of those execute it as best we could. I was unhappy with the first third of the season, but then I thought we really hit our stride. I was mostly inspired by the emotional impact on myself and others of the Beverly/Jean-Luc "Attached" episode.

That episode did not work in a couple of ways, but the way it did work was to fundamentally go to the heart of the series and force two characters who had a subtext of a relationship burning for some seasons to finally confront those feelings. I found the emotional resonance so affecting and meaningful that I said to Jeri, let's spend what little time we have left really working on tying up some loose ends. That really inspired much of the last half of the season.

JERI TAYLOR

Each year it got harder and harder to find things that haven't been dealt with before. I talked to Patrick and Brent at one point and asked if there was any facet of their characters that they thought we hadn't explored yet. Both of them turned to me and said, "Nope." They couldn't come up with anything.

MICHAEL PILLER

There were about five episodes in the middle of seventh season that were as strong a group of episodes as I have ever been a part of, going from "Parallels" to "Pegasus" to "Lower Decks," which was really one of the wonderful shows of the year. I also thought that the Beverly Crusher romance with the ghost ["Sub Rosa"] was a very well-executed show. It was a terrific group of episodes. I thought we were doing as well as we possibly could. But the appetite of the season begins to gnaw at you, and finally you say, "We have to do a show next week. What are we going to do?"

RONALD D. MOORE

The final year we thought the magic formula was just to break the rules, based on the success of the sixth season, and then we started hunting for something to do differently, like introducing warp drive limitations and stuff like that. Then we started to realize: so what?

Another low point in *TNG* history was "Aquiel," in which the episode's antagonist is revealed to be a shape-changer which has taken the form of a dog.

NAREN SHANKAR

It always comes back to that fucking dog! Truly a low moment. It was really bad. What am I least proud of? It's probably a lot of things, you know, but honestly, even as bad as a moment as that moment in "Aquiel" was, it wasn't coming from a place of "How do we make the shittiest episode ever?" Nobody was saying that. What people were trying to find was a surprise.

People were trying to find something that you were not looking for, a real twist that was internally consistent in the piece, and it fell flat on its face and it was horrible. But when you don't fall flat on your face, I don't think you're trying hard enough. Part of the joy of working on a show like *Next Gen* was, I think Ron used to joke, "We could put a fucking test pattern up and get a thirteen rating" at the time, because the show was doing insanely well. And his point was that we weren't trying hard enough to stretch the medium, and he was right.

If I had an issue with the show overall, over all these many years later, I would say we played it safer than we had to. I wish that we had had the ability to uncork a little bit, because when the show was at its best, it was really good. "Inner Light" is a beautiful piece of material. There are shows like that that you can just find all the way through the run of the show. So, the ability was there, it was just hard to get them through. Had we had the constraints opened up just a little bit, the show would have prospered as a result. You can't fix it when you're on the bottom end of the totem pole, and we were all very junior at that point. I wish that had been possible.

In "Journey's End," Wesley goes off with the Traveler, who was first introduced in season one's "Where No One Has Gone Before," ultimately boldly going where no brilliant, bratty teenager has gone before. . . .

GENNIFER HUTCHISON
(supervising producer, *Better Call Saul*)

I always had this thing about Wesley Crusher and his character being kind of not the most interesting character on the show. He had this evolution from the whiny kid to the best ending on that show. He becomes a time traveler, and he could go anywhere he wanted, anytime, and that's sort of my dream. It would kind of piss me off that this whiny kid ended up with the best fate out of everyone on the show.

Among the more radical ideas incorporated into the narrative tapestry of seventh season was the Worf/Troi romance, which first blossoms in "Parallels," Brannon Braga's story of an alternate timeline in which the two officers are married.

JERI TAYLOR

This was something we had been talking about for quite a while. "A Fistful of Datas," for instance, was an effort to gradually bring Worf and Troi a little closer together. Their romance just sort of erupted into bloom at the end of this season, and it gave us some very nice moments. It was unexpected and not what the fans predicted, and I think that that's good. I probably got more antagonistic mail on that than anything.

RENÉ ECHEVARRIA

We were talking about how we wanted to marry Riker and Troi, and we thought the fans would love that. Michael and Rick didn't care for the idea. Michael wanted to explore the Worf-Troi relationship. The actors were not happy about it. Marina has always maintained that Riker is her Imzadi.

MICHAEL DORN (actor, "Worf")

I think it was a coincidence, because I did lobby for it for a long time at conventions. I would talk to the fans, and they would love the idea. They really are a cute couple. They are beauty and the beast. It's an interesting triangle, because Worf is interested in Troi because of the way she handled his son and that relationship, and he's grown to admire and respect her and, of course, respect is a big thing with Klingons.

The thing between Riker and Worf is interesting, because they have a great relationship, and my line at conventions was that Worf would come up to Commander Riker and say, "Excuse me, but are you through with Counselor Troi?" After all, you know how guys are.

RENÉ ECHEVARRIA

I thought if the series is ending, we don't need to have Riker and Troi free to fuck space bimbos. So why not have her marry Lieutenant Riker? One of the biggest regrets I have is the impression we've given that time and time again none of the characters is capable of having a genuine relationship. It is something that the fans are aware of and are disappointed by, and I think it would have been the right thing to at least bring one of those relationships all the way home.

MICHAEL DORN

I had one complaint about the seventh season, which is I wish they had taken the last six episodes or even the last four episodes and made it more about us rather than just a regular season episode. Talking about Troi and Worf is something they didn't deal with in the movie, so it's kind of wasted. I would have liked the last four episodes to be about all our characters; Riker, Data, Dr. Crusher. That's my only regret.

Marrying Troi and Riker was only one of the many ideas that never made it to the screen seventh season (although they would finally tie the knot in the tenth feature film, 2002's *Nemesis*). Several other concepts were also vetoed by the executive producers, including an Alexander show which predated "Firstborn," in which the young Klingon is transformed into a twenty-five-year-old warrior, having lost his childhood.

BRANNON BRAGA

There was also a Barclay show that was not done. There was a Q episode that Ron, René, Naren, and I came up with on our brainstorming trip to Las Vegas, during which not a lot of brainstorming went on. The story was Q went insane and some of the Enterprise crew found themselves unwittingly in a reality that was completely twisted. They come to realize that something's not right, and it turns out that Q has gone insane, and somehow he folded the laws of physics and the universe into his insanity. In this bizarre reality, where different time periods converge, Q is this homeless person going on and on about how he used to be a super-being. It was kind of our homage to *The Prisoner* and it didn't get approved. That could have been a classic.

Other stories included a gay-themed episode in which Wesley becomes romantically entangled with a beautiful alien woman whom he later learns changes sex; an Ensign Ro story in which the murder of a Cardassian is blamed on Ro; a new Moriarty episode in which Sherlock Holmes (and Picard's) arch-nemesis discovers he is trapped in a virtual world and entreats Data to enter with a distress signal; as well as an abortion show that was, er, aborted.

RENÉ ECHEVARRIA

Michael didn't feel that it worked. He was very concerned with it being too pro-life, and though it was ultimately pro-choice, the basic idea we came up with was that we have an alien on the *Enterprise* that has been on there for years, and some super alien species comes aboard and says, "This is our fetus and it is time to make it either be born into one of us or abort." The alien never had to feed and never understood why. It took in nutrients through its parents, these energy beings, so there was this dependence, and they had the right to terminate the dependence of the fetus, but Michael was concerned that our sympathies would be with the fetus and it would come off as being too pro-life.

NAREN SHANKAR

I was working on a Chekov story where he returns as a prisoner of war from a planet where he was imprisoned for many years and finally released. Now he has come back as an ambassador to help the Federation to open up diplomatic relations—like Vietnam, essentially. The story was going to be about Worf and Chekov, because they are both Russian, and Worf has heard about him and they kind of strike up a relationship together. Throughout the course of the negotiations with these people, it appears as though Chekov is sabotaging them and ultimately it turns out is he is essentially plotting to use the *Enterprise* to lay waste to their capital for revenge and to screw things up for the Federation, because he feels that the Federation abandoned him and let these people torture him.

BRANNON BRAGA

I thought that was a very good story. The idea of Chekov returning and being evil was one that I was quite fond of.

NAREN SHANKAR

You know when people start talking too much about people's long-lost relatives, it's like it's time to fucking go. People suddenly have brothers and sisters and fathers and mothers that you've never heard of and it's, like, "Oh *there* they are!" You can tell the writers are out of ideas. But we had one of those really good series finales. "All Good Things" was great.

Seven years of starship voyages finally came to an end in the beloved series finale, as Captain Picard confronts a juxtaposition of time periods in an attempt to solve a puzzling galactic mystery which Q threatens will lead to the destruction of humanity.

In the two-hour finale, Picard travels through three time periods: the past, the present, and the future, twenty-five years hence, in which the show successfully re-created the "Encounter at Farpoint"-era *Enterprise* as well as current and future iterations of the iconic starship. Picard ultimately learns that Q is responsible for his time slipping and must go on to confront a deadly threat to humanity in the form of a temporal anomaly.

BRANNON BRAGA

Ron and I were working on the movie for a year; the script "All Good Things" we cranked out in three weeks. It was amazing, and if pressure makes diamonds, well, there you go. I remember vividly working on "All Good Things" and the movie at the same time, and we really cranked it out between the office and at Ron's house in Burbank. Ron and I were in a real groove as writers and we were able to crank a lot of pages out in a day.

RICK BERMAN

Unlike a movie, where you have six months to write something, a television episode—you've got eight days to write it. And they came through. Brannon and Ron and I had just written the movie and they were absolutely wiped out. And *then* they came up with this wacky idea of the show taking place in three time periods and seeing our characters in the sort of collision of time. It was just amazing, because these two guys wrote this episode in a week. And it was a big production challenge, because it was a very, very complicated show. It was just a very, very exciting and emotional episode of the series.

RONALD D. MOORE

The toughest thing was getting approval on the story, because everyone wanted the story to be really, really special and good. There was a good week where we kept trying to get it approved. Time was running out and it was just really frustrating. It was made more difficult by the fact that the final episode, ironically, was going to go into prep before the second-to-last episode, so there was even less time than there normally would be for the season finale, which drove everyone crazy. The director, set designers . . . *everybody* really had to go for it on this one.

JERI TAYLOR

We knew since the beginning of the season that that episode was coming at us and would have to be done, and it was intimidating. Any final episode of a series is unique and important. For a series like *Star Trek,* which has cut such a niche in the American consciousness, the expectations are really very high. Brannon originally came up with the idea of time slipping, which he pitched as an episode idea.

Michael seized on the idea as having the scope and epic qualities that a final episode should have. When we started breaking the story, we were really flying by the seat of our pants. It seems that some of our best work gets done under pressure, because the adrenaline starts running and we just started brainstorming.

RONALD D. MOORE

Michael Piller had some ideas we talked about early on. I had originally mentioned that Q should be in the final episode in a different context, and Michael liked that idea and hung on to it. He said, "I think you should have Q, it should focus on Picard, and it should have some time travel elements in it." Then it was just a matter of trying to bring those ideas together.

BRANNON BRAGA

Once we had the initial concept of time shifting and Q's involvement, it became a great struggle again for us, because there was great scrutiny by everybody since it was the last episode. It just took a lot of work. The main problem is we didn't have a lot of time left to do it, and so we were rewriting stories in one day, and that was kind of tough.

RONALD D. MOORE

Once you know that the show is going to wrap up in the seventh season, then you just start talking in very casual terms about how we might do it. Everyone kind of quickly came to the idea that it would be a Q show and that we knew we kind of wanted to bookend the whole series with it. That Q should show up in the last one like he did in the beginning. So that gave you kind of a general direction, and if you were going to bookend it would be nice if it had some relevance to the "Encounter at Farpoint" story.

That's about as far as it went for a long time. It would come up every once in a while in discussions in the writers room, but it was never really discussed at length. Brannon and I never thought for a minute we were going to write it. Everyone just assumed Piller was going to do it, because that was his prerogative and he ran the writing staff. And Brannon and I were going to be with the movie anyway. It just wasn't on the table for us, so we didn't need to think about it very deeply.

And then Piller just surprised us, because he was busy with *Deep Space,* and asked Brannon and I to do it pretty late in the game. We were already almost a year into *Generations.* And then suddenly it was, "Okay, we're going to do this." We wrote that script start to finish in, like, a month. We had no time. We did an outline rather quickly, Michael gave notes on the outline and then we went straight at the script.

BRANNON BRAGA

There was only one thing Michael Piller wanted us to put in: a storyline about Pilgrims. There was a socio-political aspect to the story that Michael had put in that Ron and I squealed about; there were some Pilgrims who were being damaged by the rip in time, or what I call the anti-time fracture. This put added pressure on Picard, something I really felt quite strongly was unnecessary, and that no one would remember. I sure as hell don't remember, and I wrote it. It reminded me of what Piller did in "Best of Both Worlds." Does anyone remember Shelby's and Riker's dilemma about whether to take a promotion? Did *anybody* fucking remember that? By the way, it occupies an enormous amount of screen time and it's comparatively a mundane story, with all due respect to Michael. What everyone remembers is the Borg. There was a component of that to "All Good Things."

Actually, there were going be two paths we were going to play out, including part of the plotline in "Best of Both Worlds" in which Hugh is aboard to save Picard. It would have been great to see that episode start to play out differently, but they felt it was just too much story and we'd better have only three time periods.

RONALD D. MOORE

At the outline stage, Piller said, "No, no, lose the Locutus story. This should be three stages of a man's life. The past, present, and future." It simplified the whole concept and we kind of focused in on it from there.

JERI TAYLOR

We wanted to tell a story in which we realized that all the parts of a person's life contribute to making them what they are. Their past informs the present, the present informs the future and determines what they will be. That was the underlying kind of thematic material that we addressed in the context of an epic action/adventure story, which was *still* laden with a rich character story that, we thought, would leave no one disappointed. It has scope, it has action, it has humor, it has mystery, and it's all packed into two romping hours. It's the quintessential final episode.

BRANNON BRAGA

We knew we wanted it to be special and the culmination of everything that makes *Star Trek* special. It's really a combination of two premises. Ron had a premise floating around for the final episode where Q comes back to put us on trial again, and I had an idea about jumping through time. It actually began as an Alexander story. I had this idea where Alexander, Worf's son, would experience a time slip and trade places with his future self twenty-five years in the future. The future self would have come back to the past, and we would do a story that intercuts between the past and future. It was just a Worf/Alexander story, but Michael Piller liked it so much he said, "If you combine this with the Q idea, I think we may have two more episodes." And what eventually happened was it became a story about Picard time-slipping through the past, present, and future, and Q's involvement in that and the destruction of humanity.

Structurally, it was the most ambitious episode we've ever done. Telling a story that takes place in three different time periods and trying to tell a unique storyline in each with unique characters in each and showing how the characters change in each and yet having the stories, ultimately, all have to relate with each one, was a tremendous challenge.

JERI TAYLOR

Ron and Brannon didn't start writing this two-hour episode until nine days before the prep date. Poor production was behind right from the get-go, because, of course, they could not finish writing the two hours in that time. We had a production meeting on the first hour, then we had a production meeting on the second hour, then Michael and Rick Berman felt that the story wasn't working in the second hour, so we had to go back and rebreak the entire story all over again. The production people were magnificent in terms of rolling with this really severe punch, being flexible and good-natured and understanding. We were sort of all in this together and somehow we all pulled together and made it happen.

BRANNON BRAGA

We broke and rebroke that show and ended up having very little time to write it and then very little time to rewrite it. The most anxious time was when we had to do a page-one rewrite on the first draft in one week. But somehow it was appropriate that this happened on the final episode.

DAVID LIVINGSTON

They began combing the prop department for some of the things we had seven years earlier, including the reclining chairs on the bridge. There are many things that had already been tossed out and we had no way of getting back, so we had to re-create the same feeling as the pilot.

The courtroom set was a very complicated and time-consuming set, originally in the pilot, and we simplified it and worked out some of the kinks that existed previously in terms of working off the crane. I think [director] Rick Kolbe solved the problems quite cleverly and made it look very interesting.

The different timelines—past, present, and future—were tough, because we had to come up with makeup and wardrobe that were appropriate to those periods. *And* determine how much we wanted to re-create the original pilot. For instance, Michael Dorn's makeup has changed considerably over the years, and one of the questions we asked was whether or not we wanted to go back and re-create exactly what he had looked like in the past. We decided it wouldn't be appropriate, because his facial structure has changed.

RONALD D. MOORE

There were some things we just couldn't physically do, which we talked about in production meetings. They promised they would do everything they could to re-create the "Farpoint" look on the *Enterprise,* but there are certain built-in limitations because some of those things just don't exist anymore. The way the viewscreen looked around the edges is a little different and the cost was just too much to make a whole new viewscreen. We recarpeted the *Enterprise,* but who cares about that?

Also, in the old days, the ops lounge and the sickbay were physically the same set, which was just redressed. Now, they're different, so there were certain things where we said we'd just shine them. Do the best you can. Do the things that are going to be what your eye will visually go to, like the costumes, putting the gold ships back on the wall in ops.

DAVID LIVINGSTON

The script was in continual rewrites, and we had a major rewrite right before going into production. It put all the pressure on the director, and Kolbe is a director who does immaculate preparation—which he was *not* permitted to do because of the time constraints. He was always having to spend an extraordinary amount of time just keeping current with what was going on as well as contending with the schedule, which was an extraordinarily difficult schedule. But he is a man who exists with grace under pressure. He was a point man in Vietnam, so I guess after that nothing's going to rattle him too much.

WINRICH KOLBE (director, "All Good Things")

The show changed quite a lot from the original script to the final shooting script. Unfortunately, for most of us it changed too late. I think, out of the fourteen days of preparation I had, I sat around for nine days, and the last five days were just a frantic struggle to get it all together. The show basically was rewritten. The general idea was there, but scenes were completely rewritten. The problem for me was that these scenes had to be tied together very carefully. There were transitions in there that were given in the script, and I was expected to continue these transitions so that if Picard made a particular head move in the past, the moment we switched over, that head move would pop up in the present or future. All of these things had to be choreographed.

MICHAEL PILLER

I got more involved in this than I had on any show on *The Next Generation* for two years. I actually went into the room with the guys and we rewrote the story, because it wasn't working. This became controversial, because for the first time in four years, Patrick Stewart called me up after seeing the first and later drafts and said, "I'm terribly unhappy with the changes made in the script."

The problem with the first draft was that the guys were trying to bring as much character interplay into two hours as they possibly could, but there was no plot as

far as I was concerned. They were on their way to something until act nine in a
ten-act structure. I knew in my gut that act nine had to be moved to act six. Instead of it being a romp with very schticky things that people loved, I wanted it to
end with an adventure and a mystery.

BRENT SPINER

The first draft that Ron and Brannon wrote was extraordinary. It would have easily have been thought of as the greatest *Star Trek* episode of all time. Michael came
in and added a few thousand words of technobabble to it and took out some of
the character scenes, which he is not keen on. There were moments when I read the
first draft that my heart jumped into my throat, because I was so excited. There
were some wonderful moments between Picard, Geordi, and Data. Nonetheless,
it's still a very good episode.

BRANNON BRAGA

In the future, they went to the Starfleet Museum where the *Enterprise* is with a
bunch of other ships and they get a guided tour. The tour guide doesn't even know
who they are and they have to commandeer the *Enterprise* to go on this crazy mission Picard wants to go on. But just as they're about to go, Admiral Riker comes
in with a bunch of security people. They end up going anyway, of course, but to
me that was a lot of fun.

There was a lot of good character work that was lost. Did we need Geordi's
VISOR to hold the key to the mystery? We've seen that about twenty-five times
in the show. Do we really need his eyes to be getting younger? Would it have
been better to have more character at the risk of meandering a little bit? Yes, I
think so. But that's just my opinion. Michael Piller's opinion is probably just as
valid and I believe the show works either way. I'll tell you, it was a lot more fun
to write the scene of the crew stealing the *Enterprise* than it was to write tech
about people getting younger, and I believe what's more fun to write is more fun
to watch.

RONALD D. MOORE

We talked about it, but there wasn't much we could do about that, so we figured it
was only seven years. It wasn't like asking the original series actors to try to portray themselves in the sixties. I thought the audience would basically accept it,

and we were fortunate in that the "Farpoint" story happens to take Riker out of the picture, because we weren't going to make Jonathan shave his beard and make him look younger. Fortunately, we found a clip to use with him on the monitor talking to Picard.

DAVID LIVINGSTON

The last show was an incredibly ambitious show, in terms of scope and in terms of recapturing the pilot. I was directing an episode of *DS9* when Rick Kolbe started shooting, so I didn't have a lot of advice to offer based on my experience working on "Farpoint." But I *did* tell him the courtroom set was a very complicated and time-consuming set originally, in the pilot, and we simplified it, and we worked out some of the kinks that existed before in terms of working off the crane. Rick Kolbe solved the problems quite cleverly and made it look very interesting.

WINRICH KOLBE

When I finally got the script, I said to myself: Do I want to spend my time on the set trying to figure out how I'm going to shoot everything? Or do I start prepping from the outside and eliminate some of the logistics, eliminate some of the staging; try to figure out what is happening in a scene and hope that I'm right? If I don't really understand what's going on, I've got Patrick, I've got Jonathan. I've got everybody else who's been doing this for years. They'll help me. Well, it almost worked out that way. But, unfortunately, tensions were rather taut on that episode.

RONALD D. MOORE

There was a lot of danger involved in trying to find the right balance of how much of a sci-fi mystery should it be, how much should it be a valentine to the characters, how funny should it be, how much action? What will the Q part of it be? It was certainly the first time that we have dealt with a two-hour piece of the series where we didn't feel like we had to pad at some point. Usually, at some point those two hours feel like we didn't have quite enough story to keep going. This one had *so* much story going on, that trying to keep it all together within two hours was a bigger challenge.

BRANNON BRAGA

For me it evolved and, as any show, it came into its own. With Michael Piller and Rick Berman's guidance, we really fashioned a show where the characters became more three-dimensional, the stories became more confident, although there were some turds here and there. I just really think if you look at the final two-hour episode, you're just seeing the show firing on all cylinders, you care about the characters, a sentimental bond occurred—we as writers bonded with the show. So when we have a tear in our eye at the end of the final episode, it's more likely the audience will.

I often think to myself, with all due respect to the cast of, say, *Voyager,* which I worked on, had some of those *Voyager* episodes been *Next Gen* episodes, I think they would have been classics. There was some fantastic storytelling going on in *Voyager,* and it had its own vibe, but Picard and Data and the gang had a particular chemistry and I don't think any other show has quite captured it since.

MICHAEL PILLER

The episode is a true *Star Trek* adventure that works on a metaphorical level and deals with the human condition and talks about all the issues that I think *Star Trek* really speaks to. There are some wonderful performances and [Winrich] Kolbe directed it terrifically. The goal of the episode was not just to speculate about how families change, but also talk about how it takes a lifetime—or many lifetimes— for a man or mankind to create the problems that he has to deal with in this existence. It also takes a lifetime for him to solve and address the issues and problems that he has created.

BRANNON BRAGA

Imagine it done on a movie budget. If it had been the *Next Gen* movie with feature quality, I think it would have been a damn good movie. It's always ranked as one of the best final episodes ever, along with M*A*S*H and *Newhart,* and I think that's where it belongs.

MICHAEL DORN

It was brilliant. I wish they had filmed the final episode as the movie, because it was really good.

GATES MCFADDEN (actress, "Dr. Beverly Crusher")

This last season was my best season, which was nice to end on a positive note. The high point was directing "Genesis," but "All Good Things" was great. Jeri Taylor was always in agreement that we should do more with Crusher and Picard and pick up that thread. I liked that they were married and divorced. I thought I should have his fish in my ready room skewered or the Shakespeare text ripped in the settlement.

RONALD D. MOORE

The poker game that ended the episode, and the series, has become the signature of the show. It was a great idea that brought the crew together in a social situation. It's something we've always played through the years, and it seems like them at their best, sitting around, off the bridge, just interacting with each other. Rick Berman's big note on the script was that he wanted the end of the series to have a sweet, nostalgic feel, and he wanted everybody to walk away with a warm fuzzy feeling.

That was his dictum to us. We wanted it to be something sweet and sentimental and we wanted the whole family there together, and we did *not* want to do it on the bridge. We thought it was the most obvious thing to do. The bridge is kind of cold and it's not very personal, and we wanted to do one last poker game and end it there with the whole family in a quiet, intimate setting.

PATRICK STEWART (actor, "Jean-Luc Picard")

I was, at times, anxious as to whether I would get through the end of the season. I'm not being melodramatic. The producers had, once again, been very generous in allowing me to go off and do my *Christmas Carol* one-man show. This time I had done it in London for my entire Christmas holiday, which is the one substantial break we get in ten months. I was on stage doing a solo show, and I flew straight back and went right back into production and, of course, they had saved up a lot of heavy episodes for me.

I still had one show to direct, and I wasn't sure that I was going to be able to stay upright long enough to do so. They found one for me, and it turned out to be a show that I was very [performance] heavy in, which had never happened before. This was followed then, immediately, by the final show, in which I was in every single scene of the episode and shifting between time periods. It was a difficult time for me.

Toward the end, I got so tired that things got a little rough and raw for me. I know that there were all kinds of rumors circulating; all of them, for the most part, exaggerated my bad behavior on the set. It was entirely due to the fact that I was trying to do the best job that I could and, at the same time, there were a lot of people with other needs and demands and I found it all a bit distracting.

JOHN DELANCIE (actor, "Q")

The last scene of the last episode of the show that we shot, and it was out of sequence, was the primordial Earth scene. If truth be told, Patrick was involved in the emotionality or the significance that this was the last episode of this seven-year show they had done, while I was much more involved in—since we were up on a twenty-foot platform with a guy who was holding a bucket of goo beneath me—whether I could drip the goo on the top of his head during the scene without him laughing.

For me, it was perfect, because it was the kind of naughtiness the character would have. I can't say that I was all choked up about the fact that it was the last scene at one o'clock in the morning. We were just at different spheres at that point, but for me, I saw the opportunity of being a little naughty, and it worked, because when I turn to Patrick and say, ". . . in this goo," and I have that little flash in my eye, it had much more to do with the guy whose face was dripping with goo and couldn't say anything, because he was standing on a twenty-foot ladder, than it had to do with Patrick.

PATRICK STEWART

John was the first of the actors in the series with whom I had any kind of close acting relationship with, because of the nature of his role in "Encounter at Farpoint." I felt so much at home with him, because I thought I was working with a man who spoke my own language, who had a theatrical background, who had a very theatrical side, and it was a treat. There was a lot of electricity between us and, I think, a lot of respect.

JOHN DELANCIE

So much of what happens on a show the audience doesn't need to know. It takes away from the show. I worked on a show for months where every night, they would say, "Oh, what a marvelous group you are, it's so clear that you all loved each other and had a wonderful time out there and were so supportive," and what they didn't realize was that when one of us would go up, the other person would say, whispering, "Oh, get out of it!" because we all hated each other's guts. The audience didn't need to know that.

As long as there is tension, the audience is happy to interpret that in the direction that the play is going. It's when there's no tension that it isn't any good. I'm a great believer that any tension is good, and there was tension to burn on this one.

WINRICH KOLBE

Even though there was going to be a feature film, mortality was rearing its ugly head. The actors might say they're glad it's over; I'm sure they all had ambiguous feelings. That's what created the tension during the making of the episode. Yes, we want it to end, because we have done it and we're bored with it.

On the other hand, it's security, it's safety, we don't have to sell shoes. Unfortunately, the movie was there at the same time and everybody, especially Patrick, was involved in the moviemaking, the script conferences. There were all these problems and those problems took away from attention being given to this particular show. So the best laid plans of mice and men began to crumble rather early in the shooting, and we had to struggle. There was a lot of tension. There was a lot of fun as well.

It's a show that I would never want to do again and would love to do again. I think that's the feeling we all had. I'm very proud of what we did. It's a good-looking show, we gave it a dignified ending, but, boy, what a pain in the ass it was to shoot.

MICHAEL PILLER

The day I went down to say good-bye to Patrick on the stage, I felt a loss. It's the loss I felt from missing a character that I've really become attached to. I think Picard is a remarkable character, and Patrick Stewart made him that way. I'm [singling] out Patrick, because he is a special talent. It was five years of surprises and delights, and you can't imagine how rare it is in television to have the pleasure of working with talents like these people. So I really felt sad the last day when they were shooting the last shot, because it was the perfect teaming of writers and performers where we were able to say something through television in an entertaining fashion.

MICHAEL DORN

I miss the laughter and the fun we had more than anything else.

BRENT SPINER

It was good television, which is a rare animal in itself. I think we satisfied the entertainment angle and, to a large extent, we made allusions to the world we live in. I think we could have been more hard-hitting. I think we waffled on a few issues, because there were so many rules that were attached to world of *Star Trek*. It would have been nice to break some of those rules and stretch the envelope and go beyond what we did do with this wonderful format. How our writers cranked out twenty-six episodes, period, much less some really good ones, I don't know.

> For others, the significance of the end of the *Next Generation* television era came when they received their invitations to the show's wrap party. An invite which depicted a stark picture of an empty bridge reading "1987–1994."

RONALD D. MOORE

It was like a funeral notice. You just kind of go "Oh man, it's really ending." And that was the first time it really hit me. Even writing the final episode, it was just a project that we had to get done.

BRENT SPINER

It was Gene's concept from day one that Data would begin as a blank tablet and, from being around humans, he would absorb their qualities and idiosyncrasies through osmosis. By the end of the entire experience, he'll be as close to being human as possible—and still not be one. I think we've been successful at that. If you ran the whole series from day one to the last episode, you would see that occurring naturally. Maybe it would occasionally slip once or twice, but for the most part it was a clean arc toward Gene's idea.

TRACY TORMÉ (creative consultant, *Star Trek:*
The Next Generation)

It still feels kind of sterile and stiff, which is one reason I thought it may not catch on, but I can't really judge it because I haven't watched them. I still feel the old show has more life and is more fun to watch, but I think I'm probably getting to be in the minority in that. *Next Generation* is a very professionally produced show with a great cast, and I'm glad I worked on it. I'm proud of my time there and I wouldn't have created my own show [*Sliders*] if I hadn't been at *Star Trek* first.

JONATHAN FRAKES

It's a show that I've been very proud to have been part of, other than the time a fan raised his hand at a convention and asked, "Mr. Frakes, does Riker have hemorrhoids?" They're convinced my walk came from that. I think it's because I screwed up my back carrying furniture for so many years as an unemployed actor in New York.

BRANNON BRAGA

The show grew in popularity with each season, and by the time season seven rolled around, it was a really popular show. By the time we did the movie *Generations,* we hit an apex. The apex was when Kirk and Picard were on the cover of *Time* magazine. *Voyager* was on the way, *Next Gen* and *Deep Space Nine* were on the air, and *Next Gen* was going to the movies. It was truly at an apex, and it never really hit that again. It sustained itself for a while and then it tapered off.

TRACY TORMÉ

The Next Generation will probably be what everyone thinks of when people think of *Star Trek.* Given the direction the world is headed in, you're going to see a lot more of *The Next Generation* and a lot less of the old show. It's an unqualified smash success. It's going to live on.

BRENT SPINER

We were looking to find the show in the first two years and what worked and what didn't. What seemed to be appealing and what wasn't. The powers that be seemed to make their decision about the format and what worked and what didn't work, and kind of went with that. I'm not sure that's as exciting to work on in a creative aspect.

To me, it doesn't feel like a particularly creative process as much as a re-creative process. That's not to put down the efforts of our writers and producers, because I think they've done a miraculous job, and it's very, very difficult to turn out twenty-six quality episodes every year. I do think they managed to get a goodly number of quality episodes on the air in a very short amount of time, which is difficult. But for an actor, I think the fun is exploration.

BRANNON BRAGA

I've never really had as exciting and primordial experience since those days, and we were really the only kids on the block science fiction–wise and genre-wise on TV. I don't think we got a lot of respect for a while, at least not until we got an Emmy nomination for Best Dramatic Series in season seven when we finally got some kind of acknowledgment that we even existed.

NAREN SHANKAR

It sputtered a little bit, because people were really tired. We had a great run in season six, it was a really strong season. People were fatigued at the beginning of season seven, but then I think we caught a sort of wind and it would have been nice to have season eight. We had ideas for it, but it was the right time to go.

DAVID LIVINGSTON

Feature division trumps television, and they wanted to do *Generations,* so we had to stop. It was nominated for an Emmy for Best Dramatic Series. It was at its pinnacle and they pulled the plug.

BRENT SPINER

One hundred and seventy-eight hours of anything is just about enough, and it was a brutal sort of seven years of work. I was glad not to have to get up at five o'clock in the morning anymore. We were really almost all ready to stop doing it. Maybe a couple of people would have been interested in doing an eighth season, but not many of us, really. We felt, "Yeah, we have done this now for seven years, and with luck, we will get to come back and do it every couple of years," which we did.

JONATHAN FRAKES

I only wish we'd found a way to have the irony and tongue-in-cheek banter of the triumvirate of the original. Picard, Data, and Riker should have that. We had our own relationship, but there are moments between Kirk, Spock, and McCoy that I've always envied. That's a small complaint in a show that I was very proud to be a part of.

ANDRÉ BORMANIS (science consultant, *Star Trek: The Next Generation*)

People criticize some of the spin-off shows. We never did an episode as bad as "Spock's Brain." I think people forget how bad some of the original series episodes really were.

BRENT SPINER

I'm not nervous about how I'm going to make my rent payment anymore, and that's a big deal. I've been a professional actor since 1969, and it wasn't until I got the job that I didn't have to worry about how I was going to pay my bills. That's been an incredible luxury and it's relaxed me a great deal.

RONALD D. MOORE

By the time *Deep Space Nine* ended, I had a ten-year career, but it was all *Star Trek*. I had a wake-up call. When my agent and I started talking about getting on another show, he said, "Well, why don't you write a spec script?" And I said, "What? I have, like, fifty credits! And fifty more I didn't even take credit on. I've got plenty of script material to show people." And he said, "No one in town will read a *Star Trek* script. They don't think they are legitimate and they don't understand them. So what about a *Desperate Housewives* or something?" You've got to be kidding me. I've got to write a spec? I didn't, but I was just appalled at the idea that I was a ten-year professional writer who had risen to a co-executive producer and had cowritten three feature films at that point, and it was as if none of that counted to the rest of the television community because it was *Star Trek*. It was insulting and there was a lot of anger in my life. That was a reality check, and I had to start over. My first gig was as a creative consultant on *Good vs. Evil*. Then I got to *Roswell* and things started over for me. But, it was really kind of a shock leaving the cocoon.

And because it *was* a cocoon, I didn't have to deal with a studio and there was no network. Just being on a show that might get canceled was a new game, because on *Star Trek* we never worried about getting picked up for the next season. It wasn't even a conversation. It was an assumption you were going to get a next season and you planned accordingly. The show never really shut down. The machine was always in motion, because you did so many episodes. Twenty-six a year. There was never a point where *Star Trek* was not in production at all. And suddenly I go to *Roswell* and this show is on the bubble. It's fighting for its life, and that was a weird moment—"Whoa, what do you mean? Really? What's this strange cancellation thing? Who are you network people that want to tell me what to do?" Welcome to television. It was the real world that everyone has been working in.

NAREN SHANKAR

When [TV writer] Javier Grillo-Marxuach was an executive at NBC, he loved *Star Trek,* and he felt the problem with *seaQuest* was that they didn't have any of *Star Trek*'s disciplined storytelling behind it. So he sought me out and he strongly pushed me for the show. With the next few shows that I did, which were all genre shows, the *Next Generation* credit was very significant for that era of television. The room break process, the way we looked at stories, all of those things were incredibly valuable on the shows that I went to subsequently.

JAVIER GRILLO-MARXUACH (creator/executive producer, *The Middleman*)

Naren's comment is completely accurate. One of the big frustrations of working on science-fiction shows—both as a writer and as an executive—in the nineties was that networks and studios had very strong institutional prejudices against writers who came from genre shows, or who genuinely wanted to do genre for the sake of genre. As a result, you had a lot of science-fiction shows staffed by people who primarily did ten o'clock cop/doctor/lawyer shows. The networks truly believed that non-genre writers would somehow "elevate" genre material . . . and that resulted in a lot of really tone-deaf and asinine science fiction.

When I was hired at NBC and became one of the executives working on *seaQuest,* I made it a mission to find writers like Naren, and I remain, to this day, infinitely grateful that he took the job . . . especially because, right after he was hired, I quit the network to go write on *seaQuest*, and he essentially became my boss and mentor.

NAREN SHANKAR

I remember years later when I was in the middle of *CSI* and the Bruckheimer guys were looking for writers for one of their procedurals and they said, "We need one of those *Star Trek* guys!" What they were saying was "Those guys have really great room discipline, they knew how to break stories." It was an amazing turn-around from just a few years earlier when nobody would have said that, because the view of what science fiction was changed a lot. Genre wasn't a bad thing anymore.

BOBAK FERDOWSI ("Mohawk Guy," Jet Propulsion Laboratory)

TNG took two elements that were present in the original series and really extended them into serious elements of the show itself. The first was the question of what it meant to be human, which Data exemplified. And the second was science as a character in the show. Science drove many of the plots and possibilities of *TNG*, especially when you consider an episode like "All Good Things."

TRACY TORMÉ

A lot of the positive legacy of *Next Generation* comes from the quality of the acting; Patrick definitely brought a sort of Shakespearean presence, LeVar is as much of a pro as you'll ever find, Brent is great and had a very difficult job to try to differentiate that character from Spock. The quality of the work that the actors did, always being on top of their game, knowing their lines, bringing their own nuances, was impressive.

GLEN C. OLIVER (film and TV critic, *Ain't It Cool News*)

I didn't mind the show's reinvention of the nature of *Star Trek* stories it wanted to tell, and I didn't mind that it was clearly interested in conveying such stories differently from its predecessor. What I didn't embrace, however, was the overall execution of the series. It often felt muted. A tad soap-operatic in its staging and execution. Aesthetically conservative. I often cared less than I should have for the people with whom I was traveling on the *Enterprise-D*. *TNG* felt like a tremendous notion which never fully committed, whether this was due to a conservative overall vision, budgetary restrictions, a lack of clarity behind the scenes regarding what the show was and could be, or some combination therein. I was always very glad

TNG existed, and did warm to it over the years, but it never spoke to me in the way *The Original Series* had.

NAREN SHANKAR

It's a lot of years later and people are coming up and saying, "Oh my God, you were part of that, that was so amazing, I loved that show." That's really nice, because I remember saying those same things to Peter Allan Fields. He was one of our writers, and it's just, like, "Holy shit, this guy wrote on *Rat Patrol* and *The Man from U.N.C.L.E.*," shows that I had watched when I was a kid. I thought that was the most awesome thing ever, so it's nice to be part of that chain. That's kind of cool, and I feel like it's rare when you get to be part of the show that is a cultural touchstone, and *Next Generation* was one of those shows.

RENÉ ECHEVARRIA

When we were working on *Next Gen*, we thought no one would care about *The Next Generation* in a few years. *Deep Space Nine* had all the money and the incredible sets. We thought *that* would be *Star Trek* from now on.

NAREN SHANKAR

It was really sad. I was actually very disappointed, because the last year of *Next Generation* they had launched *Deep Space Nine* and they were about to launch *Voyager*. Ron and René were going to *Deep Space Nine,* Brannon was going on to *Voyager,* and Michael just didn't think I was ready, so I was kind of cut loose. I remember getting a call from Jeri [Taylor] who was, like, "I tried really hard, but Michael doesn't think you're ready and we're just gonna do a small staff." I was really devastated.

I was the most junior writer on the staff of Ron, Brannon, René, and me. I felt it really sucked, but in retrospect, it was a really good thing, because I got out of that cocoon very early. I got a much bigger and broader view of the industry and the filmmaking process than I think I ever would have if I had stayed there fifteen years.

ROD RODDENBERRY (son of Gene Roddenberry)

That's the show that spoke to me. That was my generation, that's what I grew up with, and I became a genuine fan of that show. I would much rather be on a ship with Picard as the captain than Kirk because I think I'd live longer. The messaging in my opinion is far more powerful in *Next Generation*.

RICK BERMAN

I'm very proud of the show, and I think that a lot of our actors should have gotten a lot more acclaim than they did. The fact that not one of our actors from Patrick Stewart on down ever got nominated for an Emmy is criminal. And when I see Roxann [Dawson] and Jonathan [Frakes] doing some remarkable directing, or so many successful writers like Rob Doherty [creator of *Elementary*] or Ron Moore, it's wonderful.

We gave the first acting jobs to people who became movie stars, like Tom Hardy, The Rock, and Ashley Judd. Tom Hardy had never had more than one or two lines in a show or movie before, and we gave him a leading role. He is now one of the top movie stars in the world. Even Patrick Stewart, who was certainly not a household name at the time. A lot of them have gone on to do great things.

GLEN C. OLIVER

TNG set the stage for a long run of *Star Trek* projects which never felt as fully realized as they might've been . . . as they should've been. And it's hard not to wonder how the franchise might've alternately developed if *TNG* had established, and adhered to, a standard for a bolder, more energized storytelling and presentation and thematics. I'm pretty sure post-*TNG* history would've unfolded very, very differently.

RICK BERMAN

I would say my favorite series was *The Next Generation*, simply because it was the one I cut my teeth on. All of the actors from *The Next Generation* are still very close friends. I can't say that about any of the other shows. We all started in this new *Star Trek* world together in 1987 and we had seven very successful years. We got nominated for Best Dramatic Series. We went and did four movies together, we went four times to London for command screenings and numerous locations around the world, including Japan and Germany and South Africa. These actors are the ones that I feel the most connection to. It was very special for me, because it was the beginning of it all.

JERI TAYLOR

I wouldn't presume to say how this series will be looked at years from now. What we tried to do is put out the best possible product we could week after week with respect to telling good stories and making statements about truth and humanity. We dealt with issues that are current, contemporary, and profound, but we always did it in a somewhat oblique way and came at it from an angle so that it's not right on the nose.

For us to have the same kind of place in the popular culture as the old series does, it's going to have to go through the years of repeats and the coming of age of the young people who watched the show. The public determines what they will seize onto and how they will respond to it and history will judge. I suspect they will judge us kindly.

THE NEXT GENERATION MOVIES

MOVIES

(1994–2002)

GENERATION NEXT

"RISK IS PART OF THE GAME IF YOU WANT TO SIT IN THAT CHAIR."

To say that November 11, 1994, was a day being looked forward to with great anticipation by *Star Trek* fans is an understatement of dramatic proportion. From the moment the trailer for *Star Trek: Generations* began unspooling in theaters—playing in front of Paramount's *Clear and Present Danger*—audiences had been primed for the release of the first of the *Trek* movies to feature the *Next Generation* crew, brought to the big screen by most of the same creative team who had shepherded the weekly episodes to the small one.

It seemed easy enough to take the award-winning TV series and create a new movie franchise perennial for years to come. After all, such a metamorphosis was not without precedent. The original crew of the starship *Enterprise* piloted one of the most successful series in cinema history, so why shouldn't *TNG* be able to find equal, if not greater, success on the silver screen?

By mid-September 1994, it appeared everything was on trek, er, track. Despite a tight shooting schedule (still a walk in the park compared to the nearly round-the-clock shooting schedule of the *TNG* finale "All Good Things"), no one had any reason to suspect *Generations* would be anything *but* a box-office smash.

That all changed one Tuesday night on the Paramount lot when a recruited test audience viewed a rough cut of the movie. Although it was missing many of its completed visual effects and had only a temp music track using scores to previous *Star Trek* films, by the time the comment cards were collected, it became clear that, without changes, *Generations* was *not* going to be the massive success the studio expected. The film reportedly scored far less with invited audiences than the 80–90 percent studios covet for their blockbuster releases, and *Generations*, until then considered the heavy hitter of the holiday movie season, was tagged as a film in trouble.

With plans afoot for secret reshoots to bolster the film's final fifteen minutes, which test audiences rated as "unsatisfying," the press began circling like piranhas. Allegedly spurred on by a variety of sources, ranging from disgruntled ex-employees to Universal Studios (which was hoping to shift attention away from its own troubled big-budget production, *Waterworld*), the man who found himself in the crosshairs was *Star Trek* executive producer Rick Berman. The executive who assumed Gene Roddenberry's paternalistic oversight of the franchise had inevitably, like Roddenberry, made many enemies during his seven-year tenure as the chief engineer aboard the seemingly unstoppable *Star Trek* flagship. Auteur theory aside, it was Berman's movie, and success or failure would rest on his shoulders.

The story of *Generations* began in February of 1993, when Paramount first approached Berman about stewarding the *Enterprise-D*'s journey to the big screen. The studio had signed most of the *TNG* actors through a potential eighth season, but the promise of ending the show after seven years and transitioning directly into motion pictures was seemingly enough to lure back Patrick Stewart to Starfleet duty for a final year, the biggest holdout for season seven.

RICK BERMAN (producer, *Star Trek: Generations*)

When I was first asked to do this, I was not asked to do anything with the original series characters. Paramount wanted a *Next Generation* movie. I went to them and said, "I would like to integrate the characters from the original series, do you have any problem with it?" Sherry Lansing and John Goldwyn, the people I was dealing with in the motion picture division, said, "Great. Contact Bill and Leonard and see if they have a problem with it," and they did not. The plan was, I would write two stories with two separate writers, and that I would be involved with selecting which one was the best. One writer for the film was [former *TNG* coexecutive producer] Maurice Hurley, who worked with us before, and the other was the team of [then current *TNG* writers] Brannon Braga and Ron Moore.

RONALD D. MOORE (writer, *Star Trek: Generations*)

We thought we were being fired. Rick said he wanted to meet with us and didn't tell us the reason. Brannon was sure the series was being canceled. We finally got over to Rick's office and we were both pale and he said, "I've just completed two months of negotiations with the studio and I've been asked to produce the next two *Star Trek* movies. I want you boys to write one of them." We just sort of stared at him, dumbstruck. It was completely out of left field. He said there's a possibility the original cast might be involved. He told us not to say anything to anyone until it was official. We walked out of his office going, "I can't believe this." We flipped out.

MICHAEL PILLER (executive producer, *Star Trek: The Next Generation*)

I rejected an opportunity to write a script for the seventh *Star Trek* film—the first one to star the *Next Generation* cast. Rick had been hired to produce the movie, his first. The studio wanted to prepare two separate scripts. The best script would be filmed. From the studio's point of view, it made perfect business sense. Rick was a first-time feature producer, this was the studio's most lucrative franchise—why take a chance on one writer; why not have two scripts written and pick the best one? But from a writer's standpoint, there's something deeply discouraging about knowing that you're writing *against* someone and that one of you is wasting his or her time. Having guided the stories and the scripts for *The Next Generation* for five years, I found it very difficult to participate in a contest and turned the offer down.

BRANNON BRAGA (writer, *Star Trek: Generations*)

Rick eventually would ask us to write the first movie, although there were some complications there—we weren't his first choice. Paramount had a process where they wanted two scripts developed simultaneously so that they could pick the better one. Maurice Hurley was chosen for the other one, and to my recollection Piller really chafed at this. He said, "I'm either writing the script or I'm not." So Rick went to Ron and me and said, "Will you write the first movie? And by the way, there's another script being done jointly." And Ron and I, we could care less, it was going to be our script, of course, and it was. But that's how that went down.

> While Moore and Braga worked on their story treatment, in conjunction with Berman (who receives a story credit on the final film), Maurice Hurley, the veteran *TNG* producer from seasons one and two, was hard at work on his own treatment for the film, in which the *Enterprise* encounters a destructive inter-dimensional phenomenon that prompts Picard to re-create Kirk on the ship's holodeck.

MAURICE HURLEY (co-executive producer, *Star Trek: The Next Generation*)

There was basically a fold in space and an adversary who had been in a battle was blown through it into our universe. It is trying to get home to save its species, but in order to do that—and in order to get home—it has to basically destroy us. You can compare it to a parent in a schoolyard with his two-year-old child, with the parent on one end and the child on the other. The child is in a dangerous situation, about to die. You rush across the schoolyard, stepping on toes, knocking down children, breaking bones, and smashing heads to get to your baby. Then you save your baby and you look back at all the mayhem and chaos and blood that you have caused among all these other two-year-old children. You could have killed one of them, but it wouldn't have made a difference to you until after the fact when you looked back and said, "Oh my God, what did I do? I'm sorry, but I just didn't have a choice." *That's* the story. These other people who are here and are about to destroy us are basically saying, "Sorry, but there's nothing we can do about it. You're all going to have to die."

BRANNON BRAGA

I don't think he ever finished the script. I read parts of it and it wasn't going very well. That's what leaned Rick to our script, although our script had its share of problems, God knows.

MAURICE HURLEY

My story was a chance to put these two classic characters—Picard and Kirk—and two really good actors together and let them bang on each other. Picard realizes there's no subtext to the attack. In a battle with a Klingon or a Romulan, there's a subtext. Romulans want to kick your ass and, in the process, they want you to know how damn smart and superior they are. These people have no subtext and Picard begins to investigate. What he finds is that the only other time on record that this has ever happened, and the only person who witnessed it was Kirk. Picard attempts to get a point of view from the Kirk character that is different from what he's getting from pure facts. But that's not enough, so he starts manipulating the image, which produces a couple of bizarre scenes between Picard and Kirk—and they get pretty confrontational at certain moments. You want to bring back Kirk and *not* have it get confrontational? Kirk will get confrontational with anyone. In *Star Trek V,* Kirk got confrontational with God.

RICK BERMAN

We spent early spring of 1993 writing both stories, and by the late spring the studio and I agreed we wanted to pick the one with Brannon and Ron involved.

BRANNON BRAGA

We knew it was wide screen and everything had to be bigger. We knew it had to have action, a villain, humor, and less internal character scenes and less *Star Trek* lore. It had to be a film that someone who has never seen *Next Generation* in their life could sit down and enjoy.

RONALD D. MOORE

We sat down and watched the first six films several times. We watched *IV* closely. We watched *The Wrath of Khan* several times, because it's my favorite of the six films and the best as far as the story level and execution. We just sort of looked for how they handled some things. We didn't really say, let's make this like the other ones, but we wanted to get a feel for how *Star Trek* translated to the big screen and what the action sequences were like.

For instance, we got very, very used to writing tightly controlled space battles on the series where there were only one or two phaser hits and you shake the camera a lot. To break ourselves out of that, we watched the *Reliant* attack on the *Enterprise* in *Wrath of Khan* and how they really milk it.

BRANNON BRAGA

Undoubtedly the two best films are *Wrath of Khan* and *The Voyage Home*. *Voyage Home* was laughs. It's the most fun, it's the best movie, I think. But *II* was wonderful because it had a very serious undercurrent, and Khan was a great villain. We were hoping to capture the best of both worlds. Ron and I both were after the right mix of humor, action, and character.

RONALD D. MOORE

Writing the film had a different set of requirements than the series did. It had to appeal to a different audience, in a sense. The studio told us that we couldn't assume that everyone going to this movie was familiar with the television show. It couldn't be a story that depended on the TV series and was mired in our back stories. We also didn't want something incredibly technical. We wanted something that was broader and had more action and adventure. We also wanted something with a lot more humor than we normally do on the series. We had a lot more money, so we could do more yet not have it feel like "Oh, gee, they got loose in the candy store and really just gorged themselves and it became stupid." It was a fine line.

We realized later that we sort of shot ourselves in the foot to a certain extent, because we, on a weekly basis, delivered a series that had almost feature-level production qualities to start with. You look at the original *Star Trek* series and look at the movies, and there is a *vast* difference. The original series didn't have much money at all, so it was a very cardboard kind of look. But *Next Generation* and *Deep Space Nine* looked like mini motion pictures every week. So there's a certain logic to the studio saying, "Here is three or four times that much money; you should be able to give us something that we can put in a theater and be proud of." We already had a lot of standing sets, we had a lot of special effects work, and we already had a cast. I didn't have a sense of getting shafted by them and I don't think Rick did.

BRANNON BRAGA

For some reason, writing this series was easier than writing a movie. I don't know why. I realized that writing a movie was a little more meticulous, because it was a different medium. It was the big screen.

RONALD D. MOORE

We started talking right from the start about how to integrate the two crews, and to what extent. The image that Brannon and I were most in love with was the idea of a movie poster for the film showing the *Enterprise-D* and the *Enterprise-A* locked in combat, shooting at each other. If you could have a situation where you had the two ships coming to blows, that would be really cool. It quickly became apparent that finding the motivation for the two to be at such odds and then keeping them both sympathetic and heroic was going to be a real tough sell. It was going to be too much trouble to get to this one cool scene at the end of the film. We knew that we didn't want to do a time travel story, and we didn't want the original crew to all be ancient like McCoy, who was in the twenty-fourth century in the *Next Generation* premiere, so Rick came up with the idea of a mystery that started in the twenty-third century and picked up seventy-eight years later in the twenty-fourth century. We knew that everyone was going to want the two captains to meet, since they had never met, and that led to a discussion of having them meet somewhere other than the twenty-third or twenty-fourth centuries, in a place where time had no meaning. That led us to the Nexus.

RICK BERMAN

The studio embraced the story very quickly. By the late spring, we started writing the script, and the first draft was ready by the first week of June 1993, after about six months of rewriting and polishing. We spent the fall working on it with Patrick, Shatner, the studio, and [director] David Carson.

He was my favorite director by the time we got to the end of season one. I knew he was a television director, but we had asked Leonard Nimoy, who had said no. I selected him, the studio saw his background and looked at some of his stuff, and they approved David to direct *Generations*.

The resulting script chronicles the *Enterprise* crew's attempt to stop an alien scientist—Dr. Tolian Soran—from destroying the populace of an entire star system in order to complete an experiment that will allow him to return to an enigmatic "Temporal Nexus," where life is apparently like being "wrapped in joy." The screenplay underwent several substantial rewrites as it evolved, needing to satisfy the tastes of many masters, not only the writers, but the studio, the *Next Generation* cast (contractually wielding considerably more clout than on the TV series), William Shatner returning as Captain James T. Kirk, and Rick Berman.

WILLIAM SHATNER (actor, "James T. Kirk")

I've never liked the science-fiction game of time travel. It seems to me to pull the plug on any tension, besides which it stretches the imagination. It's hard to imagine it being at all possible, so from both those points of view, I have never liked the idea of time travel. We used it, in effect, with this movie, and it's used with great effect . . . with good effect . . . it serves the purpose.

RICK BERMAN

The developmental stages of writing the film and being involved with Ron and Brannon was the most delightful part of the making of the film. It was a very creative time. On the production part of it, there were a lot of budgetary battles that had to be fought in the early stages and a lot of tremendous problems negotiating with the actors. All the actors wanted to do the movie and there was a 130-page script with characters they were playing, which put them in a very good negotiating position in terms of the pressure that went on between the actors and the studio.

BRANNON BRAGA

I'd be the first to tell you that the first draft needed work. It was the first draft of the first movie, and we needed input very badly on some particular elements.

There were some painful notes and the script was long, and we had to cut out a large part of the storyline, but, guess what, that helped the movie a lot. There was a whole thirty-page section we took out, and suddenly the movie worked for the first time. Was it work by committee? No. It was notes from people who were very passionate about making it the best movie it could be.

RICK BERMAN

On the movie, I was dealing with studio executives who didn't necessarily know me enough to trust me, and we didn't get a lot of notes, but I have to say that most of the notes we did get were very productive. When you spend a year writing a script, rather than three weeks, you get very close to it, and it's great to have perspective from others.

RONALD D. MOORE

It was very different from what we dealt with on the show. On the show, Rick was God. Rick was the final word. This was different. The relationships changed. Our relationships with the actors changed. They didn't have to do the movie, and they had the ability to walk away. So we had to talk to them more, and their opinions weighed a little heavier than they did on the next episode just coming down the pike. The studio was also much more involved in this than they normally were on a television show.

RICK BERMAN

Paramount made it very clear that they had originally wanted to have it out in March, then they said Christmas, then they said Thanksgiving. Every month the release date just kept creeping up on us.

> Also impacting heavily on the final draft of the script were the wishes of its stars, Patrick Stewart and William Shatner. In Stewart's case, Picard's story involving a tragic personal loss was deepened at his own request.

PATRICK STEWART (actor, "Jean-Luc Picard")

Primarily, my interest was in creating a storyline for the captain which had something more than the narrative sequences in it. One of the things I found most pleasing about the movie, which we developed through meetings and discussions with the writers and producers and director, was a B story for Picard which is very personal, private, intense, and emotional, and which runs parallel to the main action story. For me, that was the most satisfying and successful part of the preliminary work on the movie.

RONALD D. MOORE

We wrote that Robert [Picard's brother] just died of a heart attack in his vineyard, and there was a nice line for Picard where he says he wears this uniform and there are risks that go along with being a starship captain, which he accepts, but Robert walked out to his vineyard one morning and died of a heart attack, and his only enemy was time. That brought home a certain realization: "I can fight off the Klingons, and I can do this and do that, but there is one enemy out there waiting for me that's going to get me eventually. It gets everybody, no matter what kind of job they have." So that we liked, but Patrick felt that he was missing the element of continuation of the family line, the tradition, and that this means a lot to some people.

Patrick wanted more of that sense of family, and once we heard that, we realized that could give us some interesting beats to play in the Nexus. At the end, it was Patrick who was the one who said, "And it should be a tragic, horrible death. If the captain is going to react in a way he's never reacted before, this one better really hit him between the eyes. You know, burn him to death."

PATRICK STEWART

One of the strands of mortality is, of course, your immortality through your progeny or family. You don't have many movies about mortality or death. It's one of the great things that *Star Trek* is able to do; it's able to take an enormously grand theme and play variations on it. Kirk's variation was different, Picard's was different, Soran's is different. But they are all variations on that theme. Everything has to do with death and rebirth, some way or another.

RONALD D. MOORE

From the get-go, Rick said he wanted to do a Data arc as well as a Picard arc for the first film. Data was a very popular character and there was a lot to mine there. We agreed that the movie was the right place to take him to the next stage, and that's where the idea of his emotion chip came in. One of the things we kept saying was this is the movie, it's not the series anymore. It's a different place. We can do different things, we can take bigger risks, we can move characters in directions we couldn't do on the series.

BRANNON BRAGA

A lot of people related to Data's arc in a very basic way, though it supplies more than anything the comic relief in the movie. It's also a very poignant storyline, a very touching one.

BRENT SPINER (actor, "Data")

It seems that the character went from being childlike and naïve in the series to being a different kind of child in *Generations,* because of the newness of the emotions and the inability to control them and know exactly how to handle them. He was a child with emotion, and the obvious place to take the character is into gradual maturity—an emotional maturing. What I was hoping for was a deepening of emotions and the subtleties of emotion and how to deal with them.

> By the time the writers had returned from a Hawaiian "vacation," during which they finished work on their first draft of the script, many of the original cast members were balking at participating in the film, which was heavily skewed toward the *Next Generation* cast. With the exception of Kirk, all of the characters would only appear in the opening sequence on the *Enterprise-B,* captained by John Harriman, during a sequence in which Kirk would seemingly die while saving the ship.

JAMES DOOHAN (actor, "Montgomery 'Scotty' Scott")

I was very disappointed in the whole idea [of *Generations*]. If they were going to split it properly, why didn't they plead with the two top actors Bill and Leonard to appear in it, even if it was going to be for a little less money than on the other films? I wish they had done that . . . got them all straightened out one way or the other . . . and then written the script, because I think it was just terrible not to have Leonard and De on there or Nichelle and George. But I'm not going to turn down money because of what they did. The way it went, if Leonard had said, "Yes, I'd be delighted to be in that movie," I probably wouldn't have been on it. As it was, they made a big boo-boo and had to pay me forty thousand dollars more, because I had a previous engagement, so they screwed up on that one.

BRANNON BRAGA

I would say hindsight is 20/20 about *Generations*. I was a minor voice in the chorus there. I was writing it with Ron, and you had Patrick Stewart and William Shatner, and you had the studio, and you had a director who was initially Leonard Nimoy.

Nimoy read the script and *hated* it and felt the only aspect of the script that was interesting was Data's emotion chip story, but he hated everything else. By the way, he probably wasn't wrong. Rick and Leonard were very good friends, but he refused to direct the picture without a rewrite, and Rick said no, and they never spoke again. They were both pissed at each other.

RICK BERMAN

[Paramount studio head] Sherry Lansing had suggested that I ask Leonard Nimoy to direct the first movie. We had kind of a pretty big disagreement in terms of Leonard, who had read the script. It had gone through a lot of rewrites and the studio loved it and they basically felt it was a shooting script. When Leonard read it he said, "This needs a page-one rewrite." I told him that that was not the way we were planning to do this and that's not the way it was scheduled, and we parted ways. I think a lot of that had to do with my inexperience in this genre. It was very unusual for us to write a script with no director involved at all. And it was also unusual for us to go through all the approval stages and the rewrite stages with the studio. There were a lot of people at the studio involved: Don Granger and John Goldwyn and Sherry Lansing, and Mr. Nimoy was probably right in that he should have had a pass at the script, but I was not experienced enough to actually know that. If he had suggested that he wanted to work on the script it would have been one thing, but he kind of had a page-one rewrite sort of attitude. I had a meeting with him and Brannon and Ron, and it ended up just not working out.

LEONARD NIMOY (actor, "Spock")

Bill's picture, *Star Trek V*, had its own built-in problems—or at least the story did— which he was never going to be able to surmount. Bill's picture was a kind of ride, and it just sort of petered out. It had no way of resolving successfully. But *Generations* bothered me. My God, what are they doing? Why that scene? What's this scene about? Where are they going with this? That was the reason I wasn't involved in making it, though it was offered to me to direct.

PATRICK STEWART

It had been an argument of mine that the film should include as many of the original *Star Trek* members as we could get. For the most part, I was alone in this feeling. Most of my colleagues didn't share this point of view and felt, since this would be a transitional movie, we should just cut the original cast off. I felt having members of the original cast would provide the opportunity to present something really intense and dramatic. I was thrilled and relieved when offers did go out to the original cast, and it saddened me when only three of them were in it. I was particularly saddened that Leonard and De were not in it. I felt they would have made a marvelous contribution. But critical to all this was to have Bill. I felt that having the two captains share the screen space was something audiences would enjoy seeing.

RONALD D. MOORE

We knew that as soon as everyone sees that Patrick Stewart and William Shatner are in the picture, they're going to wait for the scene where these two guys say "hi" to each other. And what are they going to say? What are they going to do? It was a real tough thing to crack.

BRANNON BRAGA

One thing cannot be denied. When Shatner plays Kirk, he *is* Kirk. It is magic.

RICK BERMAN

We spent about six months rewriting and polishing it and working with Patrick and Shatner and the studio.

LEONARD NIMOY

My feeling about *Generations* is very negative. *Star Trek* seven was a media event. *Generations* . . . two captains meet at the Nexus. Okay. Something to sell. And they sold very hard on it. The campaign was a slogging campaign—get it out there, talk about it, sell it. But I don't think the picture was very good.

WILLIAM SHATNER

I tried to get Leonard and DeForest. They weren't interested because there was so little for them to do. Both of them separately expressed themselves the same way. They preferred to be remembered for *Star Trek VI* and not go out in some smaller thing.

BRYAN FULLER (coproducer, *Star Trek: Voyager*)

The opening had the entire crew of the original *Enterprise* saving the *Excelsior* and all the transplants from Guinan's race. So, you had Uhura there working the con and telling somebody that you have to treat it like you're going to treat a woman. So there's all the sort of fun, anachronistic charm of that crew. And then, of course, that got reduced to Shatner. But when you see Spock and Uhura and the entire crew sitting on the bridge of the soon-to-be *Next Gen* era, the connective tissue, it was pretty exciting to read.

LEONARD NIMOY

There was a character called Spock who had a dozen lines you could easily assign to anyone else, which they did. I felt they needed to rethink the story, and the response was "We don't have time." So I said bon voyage, good luck.

DEFOREST KELLEY (actor, "Leonard 'Bones' McCoy")

When they sent me the script, I thought we appeared throughout the film. When I read the script and saw we were only in the first ten minutes, I thought it was best to pass and go out with *VI*. At the time, I didn't know Leonard had passed as well, and I certainly wouldn't have done the film without him in it.

GEORGE TAKEI (actor, "Hikaru Sulu")

Sulu only had three lines and, to boot, he was back to being a helmsman on the *Enterprise,* so I let them know that I wouldn't be interested. I guess they decided they didn't want to subject themselves to another rejection, because Leonard walked out on them and then so did De, so they didn't offer me the opportunity to pass on it.

RONALD D. MOORE

Everybody has their take on it, and we can't make everybody happy. There were choices that had to be made.

WALTER KOENIG (actor, "Pavel Chekov")

According to Rick Berman, Paramount didn't care if anybody was in it besides Shatner.

RICK BERMAN

This has nothing to do with Leonard. The other characters all had relatively minor roles. I wouldn't call them cameos, but they were only in the first fifteen minutes and that was it. In the case of Bill, it was a whole different story. His part had a great deal more depth to it.

DAVID CARSON (director, *Star Trek: Generations*)

George Takei in a way was in the film. I thought having Sulu's daughter on the bridge of the *Enterprise-B* was a wonderful way of continuing the generations and speaking about mortality. It was more important for us, I think, to deal with our theme, which is about mortality, the handing on of torches, the passing from generation to generation. To have a child of one of the originals on board the ship actually makes a greater point than producing everybody from the last series. To have the entire old cast makes it become a little bit like an old boy's club instead of telling the story. We wanted to have a point. It wasn't a lark and romp in space.

RONALD D. MOORE

The idea of making the original cast glorified cameos was shortsighted on the studio's part. They were overthinking that they had to present the idea that it's the *Next Generation*. They were really caught up in the idea that this was going to launch a new movie franchise and we didn't want to be tied into the old. We wanted people to come to the movie and not feel like they were watching the old *Star Trek*. They just had overthought it and talked themselves into this idea, and then they likewise talked themselves into the idea that a successful *Star Trek* film had to have a villain like Khan in it. "Who's going to be the Khan in this movie?" We were asked it over and over again. And if you watch the subsequent *Next Generation* films, they are all trying to do another *Khan*. It's just like an obsession, and Khan was really an exception to the whole franchise. There aren't many characters like that for a good reason. He's singular. There's not a lot of other characters that lend themselves to performing that role that was both big villain and had a very personal connection to the captain.

The irony was, of all the original series movies, *The Voyage Home* was the one that made the most money and it didn't have a villain at all. Somehow they all just wrote that off, which is crazy because if they were just dollars-and-cents people, it would be, "Give us another *Voyage Home*." But, no, they all wanted another *Wrath of Khan*. When we did *First Contact* we didn't have any of those parameters. We weren't given a laundry list; it was "Do whatever you want." So then we could kind of come up with something from a fresh start.

> In the end, the script for *Generations* was rewritten to feature only two members of the original cast alongside Shatner: James Doohan and Walter Koenig, who were on stage for the film's first week of shooting on Paramount's Stage 8. At the same time, the *Next Generation* cast enjoyed a brief respite between the end of their final season and the start of shooting on the feature.

WALTER KOENIG

The bridge we worked on was similar to ours, so it did feel like *Star Trek*. On the other hand, like Bill says, I felt like a guest on the show. I didn't feel like we were really part of it. As secondary as I felt on our own series, this one felt *really* strange, because I knew that this was, at most, a preamble for a story before they really got on their way with *The Next Gen*.

However, like their classic counterparts, many of the *Next Generation* cast felt slighted over what they perceived to be a Picard film, which left many of them playing what they regarded as cameo roles themselves. Marina Sirtis reportedly approached Shatner in the Paramount commissary and commented on the brevity of her role, allegedly prompting Shatner to quip, "You're lucky you're in the movie at all."

MARINA SIRTIS (actress, "Deanna Troi")

Generations is a transition movie and consequently had William Shatner and members of the original cast. However, we as a cast always got much more to do on the show than the original Gang of Four did. They were really supporting actors. On our show, Patrick and Brent were the main characters, but Worf got a hell of a lot, and I got four or five scripts a season based on my character. Gates got storylines. LeVar had much more to do than Jimmy Doohan did as chief engineer. So I don't think we were as excluded as much as they were.

GATES MCFADDEN (actress, "Beverly Crusher")

It's a small part. I don't really want to comment on it.

MICHAEL DORN (actor, "Worf")

Worf finally gets a promotion. Besides that, there isn't much for me to do.

JONATHAN FRAKES (actor, "William T. Riker")

The script changed *so* much between drafts, and we were really cut out of the other part of the story. Worf and I ended up with the "B" story, whereas originally we were tied in a little bit to the Nexus story. In the end we no longer were. It's like a big Picard episode with the "B" story being those on the Away Team. That's what it all comes down to, but, hey, it's a great job. My attitude was, maybe I'll have more to do in the next movie. I'm not one to complain.

MARINA SIRTIS

In hindsight, it was my own inexperience in filmmaking in Hollywood that messed me up. In England it's very different. There you get a script and you shoot a script. In America, that isn't the way it works. Rewriting is happening up until the day you shoot it. When we were approached about doing the movie, we were reading the first draft. The first draft bore no relation to the final draft.

RICK BERMAN

This was a movie that had fifteen roles in it that had already been cast before we wrote the movie, so you are not dealing with actors who read for a role and get it and are happy just to get it. You have actors who have the role already, who feel they know more about the character than you do, and who undoubtedly feel underpaid and under-used. That is something you've got to deal with very sensitively. We had seven characters from *The Next Generation,* Whoopi Goldberg is eight, three characters from the original series makes it eleven, and a couple of others. So you've got, like, fifteen characters, but you can't have fifteen stars. As this story evolved, we ended up with Kirk and Picard and Data having the three major arcs in this film, and Soran, our guest villain.

PATRICK STEWART

There had been all kinds of legends about what Bill's attitude toward *The Next Generation* was supposed to be, that he was opposed to it and that he was not happy that there was another *Star Trek* series, but I was lucky enough to spend some time with Bill and I found out what kind of man he is. When it came time for us to work on the film, we worked very well together. The two captains have always been of interest to me, given that Gene was responsible for casting both of us. We had a lot of fun and a lot of laughs. I know that Gene had many ambivalent feelings about the history of the first series. I hope that Gene would have been happy to have seen Kirk and Picard sharing the screen together if he's looking down from the great writers' building in the sky.

WILLIAM SHATNER

The tabloids had all of these rumors about how Patrick and I didn't get along. They're so mean-spirited that they would prefer to tell a lie, a total fantasy about two people disliking each other, than to tell the truth about something as equally interesting: that two people *did* like each other. It seems to me that the audience would like to hear that the two actors playing the parts had an instant liking and respect, and here are the games that they played, and the laughs they had. Why wouldn't that be just as interesting as the fantasy of us fighting on the set, which is ludicrous? It is such an instance of what the tabloids do and we, in the eye of the public, are besieged by those kinds of lies. People read it and think that it's probably true.

RONALD D. MOORE

We had a meeting with Shatner after he read the script, and he had problems with it. He was very quiet, very soft-spoken, listened a lot. He used the Kirk voice once. We were sitting there talking, and Brannon was explaining something, and he didn't feel he was integral in the first draft, and we were explaining why we felt he was integral in the script. Shatner was listening and he said, *"Well—he's not—in fact—integral—to the script."* Brannon's head kind of snapped back because it was suddenly "The captain had spoken." It was a funny moment.

Once he explained his reasoning for why he didn't think Kirk was integral to the script in the first draft, we understood what he was going for. He was looking for a deeper kind of character problem with Kirk, which we were surprised at, because we didn't know how big of a part he wanted Kirk to have in the first place. He actually wanted Kirk to be more angst-ridden. He wanted Kirk to be questioning his fundamental decision about going into Starfleet, which is a pretty big thing for that character. Once we got that note, we kind of went, "Whoa, all right, we can do this. We can dig deeper if you want us to dig."

WILLIAM SHATNER

The script wasn't quite ready and we met several times and gradually it changed. The beginning changed to where it was more active and the end changed where it was more meaningful. By the end of the creative process, and before we went on camera, I thought that what I had to do, which was somewhat limited in the film, was as good as it was going to get. I then brought to the part, and especially the ending, some thoughts of my own that I hope were effective.

Two significant aspects of the plot for *Generations* dealt with the unwavering attempts of Soran to get back to the Nexus, and Data, via an emotion chip, trying to cope with human emotions for the first time and not really being able to do so effectively. Playing Soran is Malcolm McDowell, whose many credits include *A Clockwork Orange* and *Time After Time*.

BRANNON BRAGA

We tried to craft a more multidimensional villain and a formidable nemesis for Picard that, in a way, had never been done in the series. In movies you seem to need a bigger villain. Soran is obsessed with time and time running out and time as a predator stalking him. He's desperate to get back to the Nexus and cheat death. Yet he's a villain who's suffered a personal tragedy as well. The Borg killed not only his family, but his entire world, and in the Nexus he believes he could get it all back. We hoped there would be a sympathetic element to him. At the same time, you're appalled at what he's doing to get back there, while you can totally understand why he wants to do so. I don't think he's your typical cardboard cutout bad guy.

DAVID CARSON

In the end, once we knew who we were going to have from the original series, we were able to concentrate on who was going to play Soran, which was a very difficult part to cast. You've got Captain Kirk. You've got Captain Picard, and you've got all these other people like Riker and Data and Worf on one side of the scales, between good and bad. And then on the other side of the scales, you lump this poor, innocent—well, perhaps not innocent—person. We met people from Europe and America and we settled happily on Malcolm. We're used to seeing Malcolm McDowell as this off-the-wall villainous type, but this is a performance that he hadn't given before.

MICHAEL DORN

I hate to say this, but when you work with us, you have to kind of sink or swim. If an actor comes on the show and is very serious, that's fine. It's not going to be like we are going to ostracize them, but it's just that when you start working with us, you're going to have to kind of jump in there in order to get the best out of the whole experience, because we have been together for so long and are very brutal with each other. If somebody's ego gets out of control or if they give a bad performance, we'll say it. But we respected Malcolm and he jumped right in there. He said he had a wonderful time and that doing the film was as much fun as he's had in a long time. That's one thing about us, we do have fun. We really wouldn't enjoy doing this stuff if we couldn't have a lot of fun.

MALCOLM MCDOWELL (actor, "Soran")

He's obviously a very strange man, and there's a bit of a poet in him as well. Of course, he *does* have his dark side, but I never play villains as if they are villains. I play them as quite normal people doing quite nasty things, although there's a reason for everything. Nobody is just black or white; there's always those gray-shaded areas, and those are the most fascinating to play.

I read the script, and I didn't really understand a word of it with all that Nexus stuff. I didn't know what the hell they were talking about, but I thought there was a glimmer of a part there. A glimmer of something that could be fun. So they asked me for a meeting, and I went into a meeting with them, and they asked me to read for it. I said, "No, I won't." It was ridiculous. What do they think it is, Shakespeare? So I wouldn't read it, but I had a very good meeting with Rick Berman and David Carson and I got the part.

DAVID CARSON

I consider Malcolm McDowell to be a key to the movie, believing that if the villain isn't satisfactorily frightening and powerful in a *Star Trek* vehicle, the story quickly flattens out. McDowell's wonderful—we were very lucky to get him. Like all the *Star Trek* villains, he has to go up against everybody, so he carries half the movie. He sits at the same level as Picard and Kirk, and he does very well. He's especially equipped to be a *Star Trek* villain, because he is such an incredibly talented performer, an instinctive actor who can also handle words, which people on *Star Trek* need to be able to do.

Beyond Soran, I was intrigued by the idea of what he was after: The Nexus. It's something that affects you like a drug, therefore it's something that is desirable, not unlike a hallucinogen into which you can sink and be happy within the confines of. You really need to be able to find the strength to deny it. From the craving that the addiction can breed comes the behavior of someone like Soran, who is trying desperately to get his fix, no matter what the cost and how many lives it takes.

MALCOLM MCDOWELL

That's what I played. I enjoyed finding the character, because it really wasn't on the page of the script. I really—in my mind—had this idea that this man was like a drug addict who had to get a fix and wouldn't let anything divert him from that. He was a very concentrated man. I really liked Soran as a character.

> For his part, Carson had directed a number of *Star Trek* television episodes, including *TNG*'s "Yesterday's Enterprise," and the ambitious (and expensive) pilot for *Deep Space Nine*, "Emissary."

DAVID CARSON

I think everybody at Paramount was pleased with the pilot of *Deep Space Nine*. When it was decided that Rick was going to produce the movie, everybody thought it would be a good idea if I directed it—keeping up the partnership with him, as it were. It also has to be said that I would be cheaper, which I know had *nothing* to do with Paramount's decision.

It really was Rick's choice to give me the movie, and it was potentially a big risk for him. I acknowledged that was a big risk and also acknowledged that I was flattered by his ability to entrust me with it.

MARINA SIRTIS

David is one of those rare breed who is an actor's director and a technical director. *Star Trek* needs someone like that. We had directors on the series who were very good with the actors at bringing out the motivations, but when it came time to make the show look interesting, they fell flat on their face. Or we had the opposite, where they were moving the camera around and had these great action shots, but when it came time to say "Why should I be here?" the answer was "The camera's there, that's why." So he's the rare combination of the two.

BRENT SPINER

The only real difference in the collaboration with David Carson was the luxury of time. Generally, on the series, we were shooting between eight and ten pages a day. On the feature we were doing between two and three pages a day. That afforded both David and the cast the opportunity to try more and to actually get it right as opposed to just get it. But as a director in general—and I was more aware of it on the film because in the episodes David directed, I never had that much to do—I found him really, really bright, prepared, and whenever I would be at a loss of where to take something, he had a real clear vision on where it should go.

I found him enormously helpful, and I admired his sort of digging his heels in, because, as always, there are time and monetary constraints that the studio has to be concerned about. But David made his primary concern to make a good picture and just basically refused to be budged on that notion. He would just dig his heels in and say, "I don't want to just make a movie, I would like to make a very good movie, if possible," and he stuck to that all the way through the final day of shooting.

DAVID CARSON

When you work on television, you are a guest of the production, the producers, the writers, and the actors, and you try to serve the production the best that you can within the parameters and guidelines of what everyone is doing on a regular basis. When you do two-hour movies or pilots, then the same team structure applies except that you are in on the ground floor and you can work more or less on an even footing with the producers and the writers. Then again, you have to be aware that if you're doing a pilot, as I was with *Deep Space Nine,* all of these people are planning for seven years of work. You're doing two hours of material, but after those two hours, it's "Thank you very much. Good-bye." Therefore, they have to make decisions which affect your two-hour show, because they are making their decisions for the future of the series.

When you come to a movie, everyone starts with their delineated roles. In Rick's and my relationship, we had worked closely and happily together on episodes of the series and the pilot of *Deep Space Nine,* but within the parameters that I described. Therefore, when we came to do the film, our roles did not change automatically. What happened was that Rick gave me the space that a film director is normally accorded, which was extremely generous of him, because he was working with the same people he had worked on the series. And he, as producer, is accustomed to having the last word. But he handed me the baton, as it were, to conduct the orchestra, and I conducted it.

RICK BERMAN

There were a lot of problems with David directing *Generations* because he went from being a television director to being a movie director in personality and approach very quickly. He fell behind schedule very quickly. Oddly enough, I think some of this had to do with the cinematographer that he had selected, John Alonzo. Alonzo pretty much took David under his wing and said, "Look, you're the director, you can do whatever the hell you want to do." And David took that to heart. If David had fourteen setups for a certain day and he would get seven of them done, his attitude was, "Too bad. I'm going at the pace that I want to go." And the studio started going apeshit. They got very upset at him. I remember there were people flying into Las Vegas where we were shooting out in the desert and insisting on him speeding things up because we were falling behind.

The film's early drafts, which traversed a vast canvas—including two major scenes which never made it to the final draft: a battle at the Armagosa Observatory with Romulans and a confrontation—after the *Enterprise* crash-lands on Veridian 3— with the Klingons Lursa and B'Etor (who have been working with Soran) around and inside the crashed saucer section of the starship.

BRYAN FULLER

It's interesting, because a lot of those *Next Generation* films were still produced like television shows. I thought the finale of *Next Generation*, "All Good Things," was a far superior film to *Generations*. But if you read that first draft of *Generations*, which I did, it was a different movie. It was a bigger movie. It was a very exciting movie. But it was over budget and they slashed the budget. So many things that they were going to do that would have been mind-blowing and exciting got boiled down to "Let's produce it like it's an expensive television show." And it took some of its big-screen appeal away.

When they are sailing on the ship and they get the distress call that a science outlet has been attacked by Romulans, in the original draft they're in the middle of a battle. They come and they battle it out with Romulan war birds, and there's a huge battle. And then in the new one they come, the battle has already happened. It's all past and it's boring, comparatively. And then when they crashed on the planet, it was significantly different. Data had to open negotiations with Lursa and B'Etor, essentially by Deanna Troi sensing that they're in need, and so Data has to go in and power-fuck the both of them into opening negotiations. And then the Klingons and the crew of the *Enterprise* are working together to get people off the planet. It was just bigger, it had more ideas, and all of that came crashing down when they were, like, "Okay, let's produce this like a television show."

RONALD D. MOORE

The genesis of the saucer crash was in a story called "All Good Things," which was not the series finale, but a story that was going to be a cliffhanger for the sixth season of *Next Gen*. Brannon and I had come up with a story where Starfleet recalls the *Enterprise* home and is going to split the crew up. The *Enterprise* is going to become the *Queen Mary,* basically, and on the way home, the characters all decide what they're going to do with their lives. But in the course of returning home, there's a big battle and the saucer separates from the battle section, which explodes, and the saucer crashes on the planet's surface. The producers hated that story for the cliffhanger and we tossed it aside, but when we were doing the movie, the crash of the saucer was one of the first things Brannon and I came to Rick with.

We crash in the jungle and we know that Soran is going to extinguish that star pretty soon—and when he does, the shock wave is going to destroy the planet. So they are going to evacuate the children [in the one surviving shuttlecraft] and are leading kids out across the destroyed hull of the *Enterprise,* when all of a sudden these laser beams come out of the jungle and pin them down. It turns out Lursa and B'Etor have survived with a few of their men. There is a standoff and a mediation that takes place in Ten Forward, which has been completely trashed. It was fun stuff, but the script was 140 pages, and at some point it had to go. David Carson said, "Cut it all," and we said, "But it's got our favorite stuff." When we took a hard look at it, though, we realized he was right. The first draft came in and they budgeted it at some ridiculous figure.

BRANNON BRAGA

Look at the crash sequence that *is* there. It's great. It's something we always wanted to do on the series, but didn't because saucer separation was very expensive and elaborate. But we always wanted to crash that sucker. Come on, we'd been with that same starship for seven years. We needed a new one!

DAVID CARSON

It's interesting that you have a battle in space where you have a winner and a loser, in this case the winner being the *Enterprise*. But as a byproduct of winning, you find that your ship is in trouble. So, no sooner do you have a chance to celebrate your victory than your ship hits the rocks, as it were. You generally believe, I think, like all the good guys, that the *Enterprise* is going to make it. Well, we have a small problem in the warp core, we evacuate the ship, do the separation sequence, the damn thing blows up, and off we go back on the roller coaster again.

The action sequences inside the ship are very, very exciting. You have battle scenes and suddenly you've got a disaster movie like *The Towering Inferno,* with all these people being moved out of the ship and scurrying into different areas. It's sort of like getting ready for an earthquake. You know it's going to happen and everyone's preparing for it. Everything's getting worse, and then the crash happens and it just goes on and on. It was, I hope, a very frightening and terrifying sequence that takes you just beyond the battle and puts everybody into a *major* jeopardy situation.

HERMAN ZIMMERMAN (production designer, *Star Trek: Generations*)

The shattered bridge was very interesting from the point of view of the people who had worked on the show for all those years. The *Enterprise* never looked so good as it did at the beginning of the movie, but it was for only about three days until we started tearing it apart. It's very ironic that I got a chance to do things I didn't get a chance to when I first built the bridge for the show. I beefed up the ceiling, put in some other computer terminals, changed the colors to more realistic—for the big screen—colors, and I raised the captain's seat up six inches, giving him a little bit more of a commanding presence, and getting Worf in particular closer to Picard. As soon as everybody saw it, they said, "Oh God, this is *so* nice," and then we started destroying it. Soon the *Voyager* set was sitting in that location.

BERNIE WILLIAMS (executive producer, *Star Trek: Generations*)

The studio said, "Bernie, if you can't make it at $30 million, it's not going to get made." They said, "For every dollar you go over, we're going to cut it out of the script. We're going to cut even more of the shooting schedule, because the director has to understand—right now—that we're the seventh movie along. It's a risk movie and we have to have this movie for a price." We had ten million dollars above the line for actors, so the biggest problem I had was walking into a movie that was budgeted at $42 million and supposed to be shot in Hawaii.

They can tell you how much the film's going to gross, domestic and foreign. They can tell you the cable and video almost to the dollar, and what they do is work back from their profit and say, "Well, we're going to have to spend X amount of dollars on print and ads." Working backward, we then say, "Well, that leaves us $25 million to make the picture," which is scary. So I ended up walking into this forty-two-million-dollar movie that could not be made, because they told me I had to make it for $25 million. And I told them that the last movie cost $32 million, so how the hell was I supposed to make a more complicated movie with more action and, in my opinion, a better quality movie, two years later, for seven million less? They said, "Well, that's why we've got you in here. Figure it out."

Among the first budgetary decisions Williams made was that the film's action, set to be filmed in such exotic locations as Hawaii and Montana, would instead be filmed closer to home. Scenes involving Picard and Kirk meeting in the Nexus on horseback were filmed in nearby Simi Valley on the Noah Beery ranch instead of on the wide-open plains of Montana. The film's climax, on the jungle world, originally to be filmed in Hawaii, instead ended up being shot in the Nevada desert's Valley of Fire.

DAVID CARSON

Now, in hindsight, a jungle in Hawaii is very Earth-like, it's not much like some other place, especially since we all know and love it so well from *Jurassic Park*. The Valley of Fire, however, was highly unique. It was wonderful because you could stand on top of the peak and could look for 360 degrees and not see civilization. It is an extraordinary landscape, which looks like some weird planet with these extremely blue natural lakes with deep red rocks, which are the result of a volcanic seabed in the Mesozoic Era. It was spectacular.

JOHN ALONZO (director of photography, *Star Trek: Generations*)

It was very, very difficult physically for everybody to climb. The temperatures were 110, 115 degrees in the sunlight, and we had to climb a mountain to go to work every morning, stay up there, and climb down again. It was possibly the most physically difficult part of a picture that I've ever been involved in.

DAVID CARSON

The Valley of Fire was very difficult for different reasons. The incredible heat made life very difficult but, more than that, the location was about a quarter of a mile across the desert floor, so we cut out a road through the desert. Once we were up there, we had to climb up to the plateau and up to the top of the rock on which a lot of the action happened. And every day the cast and crew had to walk up there and stay up there in the blistering heat. Every night, the valuable equipment had to be taken down and stored—and carried back up again the next day. It was a very tough part of the shoot.

> In order to reduce the film's budget further, the shooting schedule was cut to a mere fifty days, a tight schedule for a visual-effects-heavy, major studio release in the pre-CGI era.

DAVID CARSON

That's extraordinary for a huge epic movie. People trim things and you have to pull your horns in a bit. I immediately think of the next creative solution. One can't afford to sit around and think, "I lost all this money, what do I do about it?"

JOHN ALONZO

It is a total departure from the kind of things that I've shot before. I thought I could bring something to it and I found [director] David Carson to have a vision for this film that I had not expected. It was not a TV box vision, it was something with grand scope, and he fought very hard so we could shoot the film in Panavision. There's also a message, and a very superior performance level to the previous pictures. I think the main challenge was to keep the integrity of Gene Roddenberry's universe and not tie it into the TV series. We tried very hard to tell ourselves that this is an entirely original project which needed to be action packed and still have something to say about the condition of mankind. This was the first movie as far as I was concerned.

DAVID CARSON

I didn't approach it as one of a series. I approached it as the first feature for the *Next Generation* and also my first feature. I didn't think of it as having a set style as there is in television where the producers don't want you to be changing their visual style. I didn't look on this as a continuation of a series, nor did I have any allegiance to what had been done before. We tried very hard not to call it *Star Trek VII*, but *Star Trek: Generations*.

I was very fortunate to have John Alonzo as the cinematographer, because as well as being a brilliant cameraman, he is also a very sharp. He was able to achieve things in a short time that very few other people can because of the experience that people on the film had of not just doing features, but also working in television. And particularly telling a story with the camera; we just rose to our game and decided we'd make it absolutely the best movie, in spite of the fact we only had fifty days to do it.

BERNIE WILLIAMS

David [Carson] would always look at the producer as "He's taking away from me." But I never took anything away from him. What David felt he deserved more of was shooting time. The whole point of giving a television director a break was that, if you make these [television] shows in eight or ten days, fifty days should be enough to make this movie. So, we gave him fifty days and he struggled through it, but it was fine. He turned in a very good movie. I've worked with Kubrick, David Lean, and Fred Zinnemann, and if David has a problem, that's *his* problem. I don't give a shit. I'm very experienced and I can't kowtow to the whims of a director who wants, wants, wants. Thirty million dollars for this movie was enough. Understanding budgets means, if you don't think it's enough then you don't take the job. But don't take the job on and then start complaining about it.

DAVID CARSON

When I was a theater director, I always said if you're any good at your job, you ought to be able to take a budget of five hundred dollars or a budget of fifty million and do a good job with both. Neither one should faze you. You should simply embrace the limitations of the one and not go crazy with the excesses of the other. Just try to hold on to your creative spark, whatever that is, and be true to it.

HERMAN ZIMMERMAN

I'm afraid Bernie has a small mind. Bernie is doing what Bernie thinks is a good job. I believed he was more of a hindrance than a help on the picture, and I wish that somebody else had that job. I don't dislike Bernie, but I think that his point of

view was "I'm gonna make it the way I want to make it, regardless of what anybody else says," and he couldn't do that from his position. He wanted to be the director as well as the unit production manager/producer. I'm afraid he didn't
cooperate with David on things he could have cooperated on and, frankly, got in
everybody's way.

DON LEVY (unit publicist, *Star Trek: Generations*)

On the first day of shooting, the cast were blocking a scene on the bridge, and all
the actors fell into their positions as it was for the TV series, in which they stood
very close together. John Alonzo reminded them to spread out, that the film is
widescreen and you don't have to stand right on top of one another. We have a big
screen to fill and you can open yourself to a more natural position to play the
scenes. That was one of the goals we had in the making of the film. On the bridge,
for instance, we added ramps, some coloration, changed some videoscreens, and
added some new computer screens.

Star Trek: The Next Generation has always been blessed in the financial sense;
they always had a little bit more money to work with than your average action-
adventure hour on television, but on a film, you have even more freedom to take
advantage of a bigger budget both in terms of set design and special effects, making it a little bigger and a little broader.

> All of which, in a sense, merely served as a prelude to the main event, which
> was, of course, the meeting between captains Picard and Kirk. As established
> in the film, the Nexus brings you into the world you most fantasize about. In
> Picard's case, it's finding himself celebrating Christmas morning with the wife
> and children he never had; and in Kirk's, it's living a simpler life, settling down
> with a woman he loves (the unseen but heard Antonia), but had forsaken in the
> past.
>
> This whole sequence of events serves as a means of Kirk accompanying Picard
> back to the "real" universe so that, together, they can stop Soran from carrying
> out his plan while, in the process, giving the former captain of the Enterprise the
> chance to "make a difference" one more time.

SCOTT MANTZ (film critic, *Access Hollywood*)

Antonia?!? Who the hell is that? Why didn't they make that Edith Keeler from
"The City on the Edge of Forever"? Can you imagine Joan Collins in there? What

the fuck is happening? Imagine the poignancy of Kirk being on a farm with a horse and Edith Keeler?

RONALD D. MOORE

We talked about having it be Edith Keeler, but, again, that got into the fact that the studio was so worried about continuity with the TV show. They didn't want it to be a "fan movie," whatever that meant. Things have changed since then. At that point in time, on the television level there was still a great fear of any kind of continuity or serialization and a worry that the audience would be lost. They had the same fear about feature films. "People would be lost. They won't know who Edith Keeler is or care. They barely know who Kirk and Spock are."

The studio had this attitude that the audience is just kind of dumb. The people that buy the tickets, that go to the features, in their minds were people who didn't know what the hell *Star Trek* was. There was this weird audience out there somewhere, this feature audience, that was going to show up and watch this movie and they had never seen *Star Trek* before. I'm in my head going, "Who *is* that? Who's buying a ticket to this film that doesn't watch the show?" It just didn't make any sense to us, but that was their perspective.

DAVID CARSON

In the Nexus, each character discovers why it is they are where they are as they go through their scenes, more specifically Kirk, who discovers what's happening. Which actually makes the themes interesting from the audience's point of view, because it pulls you along a storyline that the character is discovering within himself. You see what the temptation is and why he doesn't want to go anywhere else. So it's quite an interesting and seductive thing to do to an audience at that stage of the movie.

PATRICK STEWART

I was told that cinema audiences cheered when Kirk says to Picard, "Don't you talk to me like that. I was out saving the galaxy when your grandfather was still in diapers." It's a funny line and, of course, it reverberates in a multitude of different ways, too, because it's not only Kirk speaking to Picard, but it is the actor Bill Shatner speaking to Patrick Stewart. I thought that was charming.

RONALD D. MOORE

What *I* remember is the struggle of getting it done and how hard it was. And how determined we were to make it work. Then watching it and feeling that our reach was exceeding our grasp and it wasn't going to quite come off. But you were really hoping, "Ahh, I'm just too close to it. It's better than I think and I hope it's going to be great." It got a big box office number when it premiered, so that was great, but now I feel like it's a miss. We didn't succeed in achieving any of our goals on that. I feel like we were so hamstrung by the list of requirements that had to go into it, and we had to construct this story around those elements. So, as a result, the movie kind of looked like that. It looked like a movie that was trying to hit a bunch of different points and deliver a bunch of different themes, and it doesn't feel like it has an organic life to it.

Part of it was just the fact that we went straight in from the series. There was only a week break or something, and they just started shooting the feature immediately. So, I think there was an exhaustion factor. We didn't have the benefit of having time to look back and think a year later, "Hey, let's put the gang back together, and what do we think about the show now? What do we want to say?" There was no sense of reunion. We were not re-gathering this cast and crew and putting them back together and enjoying the moment. It was just another day at the office for us, and I think part of that quality showed, too.

While the torch of *Star Trek* may have figuratively been passed in *Generations*, a passing of a more literal nature occurred at the November 17, 1994, premiere of the film on the Paramount lot. Standing behind a podium prior to the unspooling of the film, then-Paramount president Sherry Lansing singled out the film's producer Rick Berman as "continuing the legacy of Gene Roddenberry." As Berman basked in the glow of the evening's festivities and the positive news coverage the movie was now receiving (including cover stories in *Time* magazine and the *Los Angeles Times* Calendar Section), all the sturm und drang of the film's tumultuous birth seemed to fade into the background, obscured by the glare of the klieg lights. And yet, only a few weeks earlier, the prospects for success had seemed very much in doubt as the crew trekked *back* to the Valley of Fire to reshoot the film's problematic dénouement.

DAVID CARSON

We thought that there was some work that needed to be done in the balance of the last fifteen minutes of the movie. We could see that toward the end, the balance between the humor and the action wasn't quite right.

BERNIE WILLIAMS

The *Enterprise* crashes in this movie, which is a million-dollar sequence in itself, and that's a big high for the movie. So once that ship has crashed, where do you go from there? I got a feeling the ending of the movie was a little flat.

HERMAN ZIMMERMAN

The ending wasn't bad by any means. The ending was fine. It was just that the rest of the footage was cut together in such a brilliant way that the ending . . . wasn't up to the rest of the picture.

MALCOLM MCDOWELL

The screening went extremely well, but, in fact, even when we were shooting the end of the film, we always felt it was anticlimactic, which is what the audience intimated. They were rather silent and quiet. People *should* have wanted to cheer when I got killed, and they didn't. Remember in *Blue Thunder* when I got killed? Everyone cheered. Kirk's death happened too quickly.

RICK BERMAN

We knew that we had less time to shoot the ending than we wanted. This was at the very end of the shoot and we were running out of time—and we didn't have the time to do it properly. When we came back and screened the film for a test audience, we had a wonderful reception to the movie, but the test audience—and, more important, all of us—saw the six and half minutes involving Picard, Kirk, and Soran, and felt that it was not as exciting as it could be. We were blessed in that Paramount said to us, "If you want to go back and redo it, go back and redo it." So there was a part of us that kept moaning about the fact that we would have to go back to that dreadful mountain in Nevada, but we did. We went back and reshot that six and a half minutes and made it better.

In the film's original ending, Picard and Kirk return from the Nexus, allowing Picard to reach the launcher containing Soran's sun-destroying missile while Kirk battles Soran atop one of the bridges spanning the desert mesas. As Kirk turns to see if Picard has been successful, quietly murmuring, "The twenty-fourth century isn't so tough," Soran looks up from a nearby precipice and shoots Kirk . . . in the back. Soran then forces Picard away from the launcher and prepares for the Nexus to arrive. As it looms ominously overhead, the missile veers off course and explodes harmlessly nearby. Picard has successfully reprogrammed the missile's course. In the final showdown, Picard kills Soran and then stands over Kirk as he dies, with Shatner exclaiming, "It was fun," before dying.

WILLIAM SHATNER

I wouldn't have chosen it. But rather than dwindling out, it's a nice ending to a long-term character that I had the chance to play through every stage of his adult life. I don't know whether it's ever been done before. There was definitely a conscious effort along the way to take the aging into consideration as well as the changes in psychology. While it was extraordinary to play a character over the course of thirty years, it wasn't thirty years for me. It's been intermittent. After three years of making the series, ten years go by, and then there was a movie we shot for a couple of months, and then it disappeared for another two or three years. It was very intermittent, although the *Star Trek* comet trails the people in it. But to have people think of the character as an entirety and to mourn the death as though it was a real person, that's a wonderful feeling.

For playing that scene, you can only perform, you can only read the lines as a result of your own experiences. I can't read a laugh line or a line of love the way you would, because I don't have your experience of it. I only have my own. So, my coloring of a line is based on my experience. As a result, playing the death scene required me to look at what I would feel like if I were to die, and we all avoid looking at our own death. We all wear rose-colored glasses, not on life so much but on the absolute certainty that you are going to die. For all intents and purposes, your life is meaningless, because you have lived and died and who remembers? So, all those thoughts that we avoid completely and only in the most stressful moments do we think of, and then avoid thinking about them again until the next stressful moment, I had to think about it because I wanted to play the death of the character as honestly as I could. I required myself to look at what I would feel like if I was to die and how I would like to die and what it was like to die. *That's* what I played.

It was odd, and it grew to be more and more odd and stranger as the time to shoot it approached. But I believe you die the way you live. Captain Kirk lived pretty much the way I wanted him to live. He was a distillation of all that I would like to be: heroic and romantic, forceful in battle and gentle in love, wise and profound. The ideal soldier/philosopher.

RONALD D. MOORE

As a writer, I was drawn to telling it, because there is something inherently dramatic about writing a character's death. You always have that going for you, and this would be one of the most dramatic deaths of all. So you want to do it if someone is going to do it, but I was interested in making the character real, as strange as that sounds. The fictional character never dies. James Bond never dies. You just keep telling another story and another story and you're recasting. As a result, he's bigger than life, so he's not a real person. I wanted Kirk to be a person and a person has an ending. He has a mortal life, and I wanted to complete that. I didn't want him to be just a character that was forever sailing the *Enterprise* unto the stars—as romantic as that was, that makes him not real. At that point in my life, it was important for me to complete that circle. You want Pinocchio to become human, and when it becomes human, it becomes mortal.

BERNIE WILLIAMS

I didn't understand the philosophy of why he died in the first place.

RONALD D. MOORE

That was an early creative decision that we made on our own. We said, "What if Kirk dies at the end of this picture?" And we sat there and said that it could have a real emotional impact if we could justify it. We thought, *Star Trek II* handled Spock's death pretty well, except for that little coda that tells you "Hey, wink, wink . . ." just when you were drying your eyes. But we wanted to do it and it seemed the right thing to do. There wasn't a big debate.

BRANNON BRAGA

I know it sounds corny and pretentious, but when we wrote that line, sitting in a condo in Maui, we kind of sat there for a moment, a little shell-shocked. Ron especially, because he had been a big Kirk fan most of his life. So it was weird. We knew that he was imaginary, yet this moment would be meaningful to a lot of people.

RONALD D. MOORE

Writing it was hard. Emotionally for me, personally, because of what he meant to me, and trying to then focus in on the actual moment. In your head you couldn't help comparing it to Spock's death in *Wrath of Khan*, so you always have that looming. You didn't want to have to try and top it, but you sort of felt like you had to in some way. Looking for some twist. I was an advocate of the idea that he got shot in the back by the bad guy, because I thought there was something ironic and wistful about that. Instead of him going out with guns blazing on the bridge, which is what everyone thinks is going to happen, to go this other way.

When we were writing it, we said, "When he dies, we must somehow have resolved his story arc by that point. Kirk must die saving the galaxy one more time, in conjunction with Picard. He must go out the hero we always knew him to be." But it was very weird. We were writing that scene in Brannon's condo in Hawaii. He was sitting at his computer and I was standing and talking, and I got to that moment and said, " 'It was fun' and then Kirk dies." And I just had to sit down, I had tears in my eyes. Emotionally, it really hit me. I thought, "Wow, I've really done it. I've killed my childhood hero."

MALCOLM MCDOWELL

It was actually funny being there for that moment. There was this actor who had been performing this part for thirty years. There was the usurper of the crown, and there's the guy, me, in the middle who's about to kill him. It was kind of weird. Of course, he refused to die. It took him days and days and days to die. He didn't want to go. The scene seemed to go on forever, and I can understand why after thirty years.

RONALD D. MOORE

It was sort of like *Sands of Iwo Jima*. John Wayne is there, and they're taking the island and they're winning, and the flag is going up and he's there with the guys, and he's shot in the back by an off-camera sniper. It's this horrible tragic thing, and I was kind of looking for something similar to that. You would just shock the audience and make them feel the impact of the death.

DAVID CARSON

"It was fun" was really simple and doesn't get too maudlin or too meaningful. Kirk's been meaningful about how important it is to make a difference, and the bad boy in him, the naughty schoolboy, is twinkling, because the odds are against them and it sounds like fun. It sort of has an irony to it. An enjoyment of life that's important for the Kirk character, and rather than quoting Shakespeare, Peter Pan, or something pretentious, like the other movies have given him to do, to make it very simple and moving was the best way to approach it.

RONALD D. MOORE

The test audience *hated* it.

WILLIAM SHATNER

Somehow everybody lost sight of the fact that I was being shot in the back and the whole ending kind of slipped away. They wanted more and they were going to change the shot in the back, but the dialogue remained the same. So, yes, I had to go back and die again, but by that time I had worked out the performance, so I didn't need to look at it with the clarity of what it's like to die. I had already done that, so the second time I knew the performance.

DAVID CARSON

The idea remained the same in both versions, that Captain Kirk gives his life for 230 million people; that he dies trying to save the universe and dies with Captain Picard. The challenging thing about it is not that he dies, but *how* he dies and the expectations of everybody who had been with him in his various mythical exploits over the previous thirty years.

RONALD D. MOORE

We shot it again and did the whole thing with the bridge falling down, trapping and crushing Kirk. I never thought it was that great. But when we did that reshoot, we were really boxed in because then you had to have something that worked within the story and the plot and the date. You were locked into that location and all the other pieces of the movie that it had to fit into, so it was really hard to figure out some other method of killing him. Or another moment. It was a misfire; it was too bad.

BRANNON BRAGA

Kirk should have died on the bridge of a ship, not *under* a bridge. It was terrible. The film not only went through rewrites and reshoots, the film suffered from Ron and I being novice screenwriters, but also too many cooks in the kitchen. If you look at "All Good Things," it's obvious we can write a two-hour movie, but *Generations* was kind of a mess. It *wasn't* a *Next Generation* film.

MALCOLM MCDOWELL

I freed Shatner up to go on *Boston Legal* and we became great friends. He's hilariously funny. When we finished his death—which I thought was rather meek, actually—I said, "Good God, you've been with this thing for thirty-odd years, they couldn't send you off in a better way?" So we sat down and he got out a little tape recorder and he says, "Do you mind if I tape record this?" And I said, "What's it for, Bill?" He says, "I'm going to write a book about it." And I said, "Jesus, we just shot it five minutes ago," and he said, "Yeah, I want to do it while I still remember what happened."

I said, "It's fine, anything you want." "Okay, what's it like to have killed an American television icon?" I'm thinking, You've got to be kidding. I'm not saying it. But then I said, "Well, Bill, I'll tell you what it's like: it's like half the world is going to totally and utterly hate me, and the other half is going to be so happy." He goes, "Oh yeah, who's going to be happy?" And I went, "The ones that have had it up to *here* with you, Bill, after thirty fucking years." True story.

BRANNON BRAGA

It went through many rewrites. Too many rewrites. I always thought the poster for that movie should have been the two *Enterprises* locked in battle, a battle between Kirk and Picard, and by the end they end up working together to defeat a common foe. You had to have these two captains go at it, and instead they ended up cooking scrambled eggs. It was never what I wanted, but I had to go with the flow. I'm not laying blame, I'm just saying I know what the movie *should* have been, and even the time travel I found lackluster; it wasn't my brand of time travel, it was a special anomaly that could basically do whatever it wanted to, so the film had terrible flaws.

DOUG DREXLER (special makeup effects artist, *Star Trek: The Next Generation*)

I remember Shatner went flying against a rail in a scene and it broke and he went down. I was there for that. He tells the story later that one of the young pretty things ran up—"Oh, Mr. Shatner, are you okay?" And he's, like, "I still got it." And she helps him to his feet, and she goes, "You know, for a man your age to fall like that. . . ." And he was, like, "Hmmph."

SCOTT MANTZ

The first scene of that movie is great, but you can see why Nimoy and DeForest Kelley didn't want to do it, because they just gave their lines to Scotty and Chekov. That's embarrassing. But, I'll tell you, when they're on the bridge of the *Enterprise-B* and all hell breaks loose, Captain Harriman says he is going to run down to engineering. Kirk sits in the command chair, but then he goes, "No, your place is here," and *he* sets off to save the ship. *That's* Kirk. Perfect. And he goes down and he just fixes it and goes, "That's it! Let's go!" Kirk to the rescue.

Seeing Kirk and Picard together was cool, but it felt too gimmicky to me. Listen, I'll take Shatner in a bad movie over no Shatner. I really will. That's how much Kirk means to me. But I saw the original ending when he got shot in the back. Yes, they fixed it and they made his death more heroic, but it didn't improve the film at all.

WILLIAM SHATNER

The film has some good points about it, but I thought it was a little disjointed, a little slow. It lacked an emotional cohesiveness. I was aware I brought something to the film. You know, it's a delightful character to play. And I'm very fond of everyone I worked with, particularly Patrick Stewart.

Meanwhile, Patrick Stewart's inauspicious final shot of production involved a visual effects shot in front of a blue screen at Image G for a bit that would composite him with Soran's missile launcher.

RONALD B. MOORE (visual effects supervisor,
Star Trek: The Next Generation)

When we finally wrapped, it was an emotional moment, but Patrick seemed to be taking it very well. He got out of his costume, walked down a hallway to leave the building, and walked straight into a plate glass window. He almost knocked himself out cold.

MAKING CONTACT

"THE LINE MUST BE DRAWN HERE! THIS FAR, NO FURTHER!"

Given the $120 million worldwide gross of *Generations,* it should have been apparent to Paramount that there was still life in big-screen *Trek.* Nonetheless there were still a few unanswered questions, primary among them being whether the film was actually a successful transition of *The Next Generation* from television to the movies, or if the audience was coming first and foremost to see William Shatner play his final scenes as Captain James T. Kirk. Believing the latter, Shatner felt he had a chance at convincing the studio to go with his scenario for a sequel that would allow the two captains—Kirk and Picard—to interact one last time.

Ultimately published as a novel entitled *The Return,* Shatner's tale had the Romulans and the Borg using advanced technology to resurrect Kirk. By the end of the novel, Kirk is reunited with the now elderly Spock and McCoy and, together with Picard and his crew, they travel to the Borg home world where Kirk—in a far more effective and heroic moment than the one afforded the character in *Generations*—sacrifices himself to end the Borg threat, hopefully forever.

WILLIAM SHATNER (actor, "James T. Kirk")

I'd been asked to do a trilogy of *Star Trek* books, so I fleshed out an idea that I had after I finished shooting *Generations.* I expanded that idea and then sold that to the publisher. I turned around and gave that synopsis to [Paramount studio chief] Sherry Lansing and Rick Berman, and they both loved it.

I thought my fantasy was coming true, but then I read in *Variety* that the next film was going to be a *Next Generation* film completely with no members of any other crew in it. It wasn't a change of plans on their part, because they never said they wanted to do it. I told Leonard I was writing this and I was writing Spock with him in mind. He seemed very doubtful as far as he was concerned that he would come back as Spock. I took that to mean that it would have to be awfully good a role for him to come back and play the part. I thought that the studio would jump at the chance of seeing Kirk and Picard together again.

RICK BERMAN (producer, *Star Trek: First Contact*)

Bill talked to me a lot about taking advantage of what happened in the last movie and reviving Captain Kirk, but we did kill him twice in *Generations,* if you think about it, so we had to leave him dead for a little while. The overall feeling was that although it was an interesting idea, it was not really the direction we wanted to go at that point. We wanted to do a film that was pretty much isolated to the *Next Generation* characters.

BRANNON BRAGA (writer, *Star Trek: First Contact*)

It would have been *disastrous* to kill Kirk in the first movie, and then bring him back in the second. It would have just been chintzy and would have taken away any kind of credibility we'd tried to establish. I don't think that film would have done very well.

RONALD D. MOORE (writer, *Star Trek: First Contact*)

The writing of *First Contact* was a very different experience from writing *Generations.* With *Generations* there was a laundry list, "Here's what the movie has to have in it," and it *was* a list: "Original series cast, but they can only be in it for the first ten to fifteen minutes at the most. Then you can have Kirk in it later on at the end. There has to be a strong Picard story. There has to be a Data B-story that's kind of funny. There has to be a big villain that's sort of like Khan, and an element that's something like time travel, but we don't have to have time travel per se. Also, we'd like to have Klingons in it, because the Klingons are the most popular characters. Probably Lursa and B'Etor, because they were the best two Klingons. And there has to be a big action component. And the stakes have to be enormous. So go write that." It was, like, "Uhhh, okay . . . ?" You are just trying to check those boxes. How the hell are we going to do time travel without time travel? Suddenly you have this thing called the Nexus.

BRANNON BRAGA

Generations was actually very successful despite the mixed reactions to it, so we started work on the next movie pretty much immediately. After *Generations* was released, we started talking about what the next one would be.

RONALD D. MOORE

When we did *First Contact,* we didn't have any of those parameters. We weren't given a laundry list. It was more like "Do whatever you want." So then we could kind of come up with something from a fresh start. *That* was fun. We said, "Let's enjoy this one. The first one was all about death and mortality. This one is about adventure."

RICK BERMAN

We held back in certain action sequences in *Generations* that we should have fought a little harder to get. More important than that, we did a story that was a little too dour. We did a story about a very serious Picard who was mourning the loss of his brother and nephew, and it was quite ponderous and sad. It was time to move to something that was a little bit more action/adventure. Something that the fans could have a little bit more fun with. That was one of our major goals. This was going to be a reeling and rocking adventure movie with a lot of fun to it and a lot of great action sequences that turned Picard into kind of an action hero rather than a brooding intellectual. These are things that I don't regret having done in the first film, but once we did them it was good to go a new route.

PATRICK STEWART (actor, "Jean-Luc Picard")

There were aspects of the previous movie that had left me feeling a little uncomfortable when we'd finished. It was interesting to have that thread in there about the brother and nephew's death, but it added a slight shadow to Picard over the whole movie. If you're going to satisfy the function of a character like this, essentially what he has to be first and foremost is heroic. That was in everybody's mind when this script was in development. You've got to put Picard back on the bridge of the *Enterprise* and have him leading the troops and not somebody having to deal with all kinds of psychological issues.

Of course, it then became a Borg story and the demons were immediately present.

BRENT SPINER (actor, "Data")

Generations is a film that definitely has problems, as most movies do. One of the problems with *Generations* was that they had to accomplish so much with it that a lot of stories got short shrift. Instead of doing one story and exploring that in detail, they had to do all sorts of things to handle the passing of the torch experience and all of that. When I first saw it, expectations were high, and I was slightly disappointed by it. In retrospect, after having seen some other movies that were breaking box office records, I think *Generations* is a better film.

RICK BERMAN

In the first film we had a single villain—a human, single villain. We felt it was time to bring back some great old meanies; to get some bad guys that had more of an alien bent to them, which led us quite quickly to the Borg, who had always been an adversary that people seemed to find spooky and one of those groups that people loved to hate, like the Klingons. The problem with the Borg is that by being this sort of assimilating cooperative of mindless, obeying characters, you don't have anything personifying them. No single voice. Because it was very hive-like, we came up with the idea of a queen bee. The Borg are very curious, mysterious, and thus, very frightening to people. We'd used them sparingly on the series and it was time to come up with a way to use them in a feature film. We also had the money to develop the way they looked, the way they were made up, and the way their costumes worked in a manner that we couldn't afford on television.

HERMAN ZIMMERMAN (production designer, *Star Trek: First Contact*)

Alien certainly featured the quintessential monster. What I think is different about the Borg as antagonists is that they once were human or humanoid organisms, and the monster from *Alien* was always a creature of an entirely different species with no concern about human values of any kind. The Borg have had humanity or humanoid origins and are now assimilated into this machine culture. In a way they are more scary than something that tears you apart, because they *don't* tear you apart. They make you over into something you don't want to be. To me, that's much scarier than just being killed. That's the kind of nightmarish bad guys we were creating.

ALFRE WOODARD (actress, "Lily Sloane")

I can imagine our preoccupation with our bodies here and now as a forewarning of Borg-dom. It's like we pinch and we pull and we tuck. People with perfectly fine noses get new noses. You can take a picture to a surgeon and say, "I want to be her. I want to be him." Once it becomes easy to do plastic surgery and it's fail-safe, I imagine for my children's children it'll be very normal to go, "You know, I want my head pointed. I want this, I want that." If my arm was bionic, if there was a machine in there where I could throw a ball harder, all I'd have to do is put a couple of little nuggets and transistors. I could just see us, eventually, in an effort to make ourselves perfect, going past humanity and into machinery.

BRANNON BRAGA

I was eager to do time travel again, because I was stinging from that Nexus crap in *Generations*. Also, we were waiting for *First Contact* to really dip back into the Borg. But I have to say, our initial ideas for the movie were pretty lame. We were talking about the Borg traveling back to medieval times, the 1500s. It was just insane. We talked about that for a few weeks, and Patrick got wind of it through Rick, and he refused to wear tights on the big screen. That was his quote. But it was a dumb idea to begin with.

RONALD D. MOORE

We went through a variety of time periods during the development process, from the Italian Renaissance to the present to the Civil War. Nothing really got that far, but we talked about a lot of different periods in terms of what would be interesting, where the Borg would go and why, and what we could do there. We realized fairly quickly that there's been a lot of time travel done. Almost any period you go to has been done in one way, shape, or form. Then we came up with the idea of doing the near future and to involve what is essentially the birth of *Star Trek*.

RICK BERMAN

I had somebody make a little list of things that happened before the original *Star Trek*, and they are not just various little backstory pieces that get glued together over the years. There's kind of an odd period in there where there's a holocaust of sorts on Earth. A third world war. And soon after a guy named Zefram Cochrane, who appeared once in the original series, created warp drive. In a relatively short period of time you went from this post-apocalyptic depression into the renaissance, in a sense, that became the *Star Trek* era. It was a fascinating idea. How do you go from the dark ages to an enlightened time in such a short period?

BRANNON BRAGA

We eventually landed on the idea of what I called the *Star Trek* nativity scene—the birth of everything; the birth of *Star Trek*. The three wise Vulcans who arrive on Earth and step out of their ship for our first contact with an extraterrestrial species. And the Borg were going to prevent that from happening, which really struck a bull's-eye for me, because it would allow non–*Star Trek* people to understand why *Star Trek* matters by putting the crew and the Borg back in that time frame. I thought it would appeal to a larger audience. *Star Trek* itself was at stake in that movie, and that was supercool to me.

RONALD D. MOORE

Interestingly, the *Star Trek* universe has a continuity that somehow still holds together and, lo and behold, Zefram Cochrane invented the warp drive and in turn made first contact with an alien race. We combined the two adventures and that became our story.

RICK BERMAN

Gene Roddenberry, when he created *Star Trek*, was very big on aliens being good guys. That can get kind of boring real quick, so he invented the Klingons and the Romulans and all of these alien bad guys. What we chose to do here is to say that the Borg go back into the past to change Earth's history. We could have had the Borg attacking Earth and blowing the hell out of it, but it seemed much scarier and more interesting to have them take over the ship deck by deck, knowing that once they did we were in a lot of trouble and so was mankind if we couldn't stop what was happening.

Now, people brought up potential paradoxes in history when the *Enterprise* went back in time. If you look at *Star Trek IV,* which the fans adore, Kirk and company have to travel back in time to get a whale. What they do is sort of say, "Let's just slingshot ourselves around the sun," and they're back and then it's, like, "Well, what we have to do is slingshot ourselves around the sun in the other direction." I don't think that caught a lot of criticism from people. The same can be said about *Terminator,* the same can be said about any one of them. H.G. Wells developed a little machine with dials on it.

The biggest problem with time travel is the paradoxes you run into when you're writing it. We had these sort of temporal directives not to mess around with things in the past, but in this instance we sort of had to because the Borg had gone back before us and messed things up. We had to go back and try our best to straighten things out. We had to go back and find a Cochrane who wasn't much of an admirable character to begin with, and who had lost any of what he had when the Borg started blowing up his ship. We had to get him back on track a little bit and help lead him in the direction we knew that history had meant for him to go.

BRANNON BRAGA

The initial couple of drafts actually did not have the Borg Queen in it, and also did not have Picard on the ship. Picard was on Earth having a Frank Capraesque adventure with a photographer, which was bizarre, and Riker was fighting the Borg. That draft of the script got to Patrick, and I remember we flew to New York where he was doing a play. We sat in his apartment and he was very nice, but he was, like, "This shit ain't gonna fly. I have to be on the bridge fighting the Borg."

PATRICK STEWART

Everyone realized that was somewhat absurd. If you're going to do a Borg movie, then Picard has got to be at the heart of that Borg world. In effect, Jonathan Frakes and I ended up changing roles. We made a deliberate decision to activate Picard more for this story. I wanted to put him in the trenches, in the front line. I wanted him to lead from the front. When the Borg became our principal power in the story, it was critical then that you bring Picard as close to the action as possible.

There was a history that we really shouldn't overlook, so we went for that historical connection with the Borg. And it paid off. I was very happy seeing this man who was feeling strongly, expressing his feelings strongly, was intense and active and mixing it up with the villains. Many comparisons have been made between Shakespeare and *Star Trek* over the years, and quite authentic ones. It's larger than life, it's epic, there are heroic figures, and even the language of *Star Trek* is not totally a naturalistic language.

BRANNON BRAGA

We did a substantial rewrite. Also, it was Jonathan Dolgen at the time who ran Paramount, the biggest cheese there was, and he was also a ravenous *Star Trek* fan.

Rick and I used to go into his office for meetings all the time, and he would say, "Oh, I really like this episode and that episode." I think he was the one who said the Borg are boring, they're just zombies, you need a voice. We thought, "Shit, okay, it's like a hive. Like a bee colony. Let's make a queen," and it was probably the best invention we could have possibly come up with.

I don't think anyone realized by shuffling Picard and Riker around it would change things so monumentally, but I'm glad it did. Because it was the next movie, and it had been two years since you had last seen Picard, you kind of wanted to do big things with him. You wanted to have him fall in love and take a woman with him at the end. Actually, it was a good instinct on Patrick's part, because you want to see these characters in new situations. But this is an action movie. A romance? What a stupid idea. In the rewrite, the Borg meets the captain and he's our action hero.

RONALD D. MOORE

That shift was probably the biggest change, and that changed the emphasis of the film, because where Picard goes, the rest of the film goes. The planet stuff got smaller and the *Enterprise* stuff got larger as a consequence. That was a good choice, because the planet stuff could carry more humor. That part of it is the more fun adventure of the two, with James Cromwell as Cochrane. That became a lighter storyline. The *Enterprise* storyline, because it's more action-oriented and more deadly, becomes the more driving storyline.

BRANNON BRAGA

Interesting side note is that *MAD* magazine came out with a parody, a satire of *First Contact* when the movie came out, but the satire they did is based on the first draft of the script. It's completely different from the movie. Mort Drucker drew it, but he has got Alfre Woodard playing a photographer on Earth. The whole storyline is different—they obviously got a copy of the script to get a jump on it, but it's not the movie.

PATRICK STEWART

I had my head in the scripts from day one of the series. That's the way I've always worked. I come from a background where you can speak up at any time and talk about the creative process of the work that's being done. I remember saying to Gene Roddenberry, "I'm going to be involved in this. I'm not an actor who learns his lines, hits his mark, and draws his paycheck. I like to get hands-on." Rick and I spent many nights on the telephone. I would get home, look at the draft of the next day's work, and get on the phone and talk to Rick. The great thing was that over those years, he always took my call. I like that. I think we worked together very well. The same thing with Brent, too.

BRANNON BRAGA

There was a really dicey moment in the writing of the movie where Patrick Stewart had a clause in his contract that he could bring in a writer of his own, which Ron and I really learned about late in the game. Indeed, I think Patrick thought in his mind, God bless him, that Tom Stoppard would come in and write a *Star Trek* script or something. Unlikely, man. At least he saw his involvement in a loftier light, but he brought on a screenwriter who I believe had done the movie *Rush Hour,* named Ross LaManna. So he came in to do a character pass for Picard and Alfre Woodard's character, Lily.

RONALD D. MOORE

Patrick wanted a rewrite on *First Contact.* It had something to do with his motivation or relationship with the Alfre Woodard character. Rick just called us over and he was sort of nervous and embarrassed. He told us they were bringing in this writer and that hopefully it would still come back to Brannon and me.

BRANNON BRAGA

Ron and I were appalled and insulted, because we thought the script was really good and they brought in another writer to do a pass.

RONALD D. MOORE

At that point, Brannon and I were tired. We were so deep into the process at that point and had done so many drafts, and we were working on *Deep Space Nine* and *Voyager.* So there was a part of us that was kind of relieved as we walked out. At the same time, we were obviously kind of crushed and disappointed to be taken off the movie, which in the feature world is completely normal. It happens all the time, but it was *our* first encounter with it. We kind of went on our way and swallowed it and dealt with it, and then at some point later the writer did the draft and turned it in and they wanted to bring us back.

BRANNON BRAGA

What happened then was, in my humble opinion, it sucked. And Rick said to me and Ron, "Come back, we need you two back on the script; we have to fix this," but Ron refused. He was *so* mad.

RONALD D. MOORE

I took it personally. It was on the day that we were told that they were replacing us, I had run into Patrick on the Paramount lot, just by happenstance, and I said, "Hey, Patrick, how's it going?" and he didn't say a word to me. Then I walked to Rick's office and was told that Patrick told us to come in and that's what pissed me off. I took that pretty personally, which in retrospect I probably took *too* personally. So then later when they asked us to come back, I didn't want to do it. I was in Rick's office with Brannon and Rick said, "Now we'd like you to come back. This draft didn't work out, it had some problems, and we're starting to shoot. We need a rewrite." I was, like, "I don't give a fuck. Fuck him. Patrick can go stick with that other guy." Like I said, I took it very personally.

BRANNON BRAGA

It was the only time Rick ever yelled at us. He brought us into his office and yelled at Ron for being stubborn and yelled at me for not getting my friend in line.

RONALD D. MOORE

Rick got upset and walked out of his own office, leaving Brannon and me there. We kind of looked at each other and were, like, "Should we go? I guess we should leave." Brannon and I literally walked around the Paramount lot and eventually came around and cooler heads prevailed.

BRANNON BRAGA

Ron and I just looked each other and said, "Let's just do this," and we went back on the project. I think we kept one line of dialogue from him, which was Lily's "watch your caboose." As *Star Trek* writers, we had never been rewritten, so it was vaguely traumatic, but fortunately, we regained control of the script.

RONALD D. MOORE

We came back and I went to the location with Brannon and Rick and met with Patrick and went through his notes on the new draft. There was a moment at the beginning of the conversation where Patrick just kind of said, "I hope we can let everything go. This happened before now and let's just try to make a good movie." And I took that as enough of an apology, because I didn't need anything else, and we just moved forward. Looking back now, I took it way too personally. I personalized what was just a business decision. But at that point in time I was so close to it. We were much more optimistic about *First Contact*. You felt it was a better film, it was going better, we were having more fun. We knew this one was going to fix all the problems that we'd had in the first one. So to be taken off of it hurt even more.

In the final version of the script, the *Enterprise* pursues the Borg to the twenty-first century, and an Away Team consisting of Picard, Data, Geordi, Troi, and Crusher beam down to Resurrection, Montana, where they see that Cochrane's ship, the *Phoenix,* has been damaged. There they meet Cochrane himself (in a fun twist on *The Man Who Shot Liberty Valance,* the legendary space pioneer turns out to be nothing like they would have expected) and Lily Sloane (Alfre Woodard), who is injured and beamed back to the *Enterprise.* Picard gives the order for Riker, Geordi, and Troi to help repair the damage to the *Phoenix* while he, Crusher, and Data beam back to the *Enterprise* with Sloane.

Once back on the ship, they learn that members of the Borg collective are aboard and have begun assimilating part of the vessel as well as members of the crew. It is up to Picard (who has been seeking vengeance for all the Borg had done to him), Data, and Worf, along with Sloane, to combat this threat before a signal to the Borg's contemporaries lead them to Earth of the twenty-first century for planet-wide assimilation. In between, Data is captured in engineering and "seduced" by the Borg Queen (Alice Krige), who promises to make him more human. Picard must stop the onboard threat while Riker works to ensure that Cochrane keeps his date with destiny.

BRANNON BRAGA

There was a glow around the movie. We just had a good feeling about it, and there were no troubles. There was some additional photography that happened to show more of the assimilation process, and to put a few scares in there, but other than that it was an effortless process and a lot of fun to make.

RICK BERMAN

At the time of *First Contact,* we found ourselves in a situation where people were going to films like *Independence Day,* which had come up with new techniques of putting what used to be impossible amounts of visual effects into movies. But you get to a point where you can only do so many booms, so many explosions, and so many ships blowing up. Instead, you want to try and come up with some unique things. For me, *Independence Day* was a movie that just had a lot of overkill to it.

If you want to see the Empire State Building blow up, you can do it with two explosions or you can do it with twenty explosions. *They* did it with *eighty* explosions. A lot of films forget you have to deliver a story, you have to have some heart and humor to a movie to make it work. *Star Trek* stories are all grounded by the characters and driven by the characters. The space stuff is an addendum in a way. It's not really what it's about. You can't tell stories about rocket ships. It gets very boring. You've got to tell stories about people.

BRANNON BRAGA

Part of the movie is about the journey of Picard and the ultimate recovery from all he went through with the Borg, but at its core it's a story of vengeance with Picard dipping down into a twentieth-century kind of mentality. Lily Sloane is making him realize that he's taking too many risks. In many ways, he's acting like Captain Ahab with his obsession and quest for vengeance. The Ahab quality is subtle, but it's definitely there and becomes worse and worse as the movie goes on. You definitely see a very interesting arc for Picard in this movie. He still harbors a lot of profound anger toward these creatures he hasn't met for a while. Patrick really did some amazing things in this movie.

PATRICK STEWART

At the time the script for *First Contact* was in development, I was in *The Tempest* on Broadway, and there was an intriguing blending of the two characters. They were definitely parallel stories. Much of *The Tempest* bled into this story—the whole idea of a man who has stored up unexpected fury, murderous rage, because of a wrong done to him, which was done to both Prospero and Picard. It just happened to bleed across into this script, too, but in a way that is filled with action and not with a psychological trauma that incapacitates him. Instead, the crew is largely *restraining* him from action.

RONALD D. MOORE

Data's arc was a little tougher to crack, because the character fulfilled his primary quest in *Generations* to gain human emotions. We didn't want to irrevocably change the character again. Giving him the emotion chip was a pretty big deal. We wanted to explore something different with him, but not change the character permanently. Just keep moving him along the spectrum of discovery.

BRANNON BRAGA

We didn't want to worry about Data until it came naturally, which happened very late in the process. Once we invented the Borg Queen, we realized that Data being seduced in some way by her would be very interesting. It is the most provocative and strangest experience he's ever had, and he does come very close to physical existence thanks to the Borg. This is actually a romance. It's a sick and perverted romance, but it's perfect because it represents many things, including temptation, seduction, and romance, but all filled with Borg perversity.

BRENT SPINER

It was a really cool arc and a logical extension for the character, because it's been an ever-evolving process. The last film dealt with him getting emotions and not being able to control them or deal with them, because they were new. In this film he's much more in control of the emotion chip in terms of how and when he uses it. But the seduction of the flesh is the obvious next step for him. In a way, it's the darkest and most psychologically disturbing part of the story and the film.

One of the most surprising aspects of *First Contact* was Rick Berman's choice of director: *Next Generation* cast member Jonathan Frakes, who had helmed numerous episodes of *TNG*, *Deep Space Nine*, and *Voyager*. Berman had actually been interested in veteran *Trek* director Winrich Kolbe helming the sequel, but

Patrick Stewart reportedly put the kibosh on that as the two had gone toe-to-toe a number of times during the tumultuous shooting of the *TNG* finale, "All Good Things."

RICK BERMAN

There were a lot of problems with David Carson directing *Generations*, so when it came time for the second movie, I knew I needed to go elsewhere, and I had very strong feelings about Jonathan's talents and about Jonathan's work on both *Next Generation* and, at that point, *Deep Space Nine*. We hired him to do *First Contact* and he did a remarkable job. The first movie was, I would say, a little disappointing. It did better than the studio expected it to do. We had comically low budgets. I was very proud of everything in *First Contact*.

I believed, as I did on *Generations*, that it's important that a person understand *Star Trek* to be able to direct one of these films. There are just too many *Star Trek* elements that need to be understood to bring someone else in from the outside. Of the people who were available who were directors, who really understood *Star Trek*, Jonathan was one of the best. A lot of major film directors who are big fans of *Star Trek* wouldn't dream of directing one. If you think about it, one of the charms and challenges of directing a movie is creating the characters and bringing them to life. You don't do that in a *Star Trek* movie. The characters are all there, and the look is pretty much pre-set.

The truth is, Jonathan is a terrific director, someone who's a close friend and someone who has always had the ambition to direct. His desire to direct both television and features had been paramount in his mind for years. I knew him well enough to know that he would commit himself to this in a way that was necessary, which was to just be completely absorbed in it for a good six to eight months. With his understanding of *Star Trek* and his relationship with certain crewmembers and all of the cast members, I knew he was going to be a major plus. I was proven right. He did a great job.

JONATHAN FRAKES (director/actor, "William T. Riker")

It was kind of thrilling and certainly daunting to have this as my virgin outing as a film director. It was sometimes overwhelming, exhausting, exhilarating, and terrifying, but I'm thrilled at the product. It was a great gift, and I thank Rick Berman publicly for trusting me to do this script. Fortunately, it happened to be a wonderful script, and my job was not to screw it up, because the script holds up far better than any of the other *Star Trek* movies. It also holds up as a movie that just happens to be a *Star Trek* movie, which we were all hoping would be the case.

PATRICK STEWART

Jonathan brought a history to the film in a way that no one else could. In fact, the first day he walked on the set as a director during the making of the series, everyone knew he was, indeed, a bona fide director. Jonathan had a knowledge of the actors not only in terms of what they can do, but what their *potential* was as well. The energy he brought to it, the good humor and fellowship, were exemplary. It's thanks to Jonathan that throughout production our spirits were high and positive. We had the reputation while doing the show of being the nicest show to guest on, but also the most undisciplined. That's a very happy combination.

MICHAEL DORN (actor, "Worf")

Jonathan is like my big brother in real life. He's very nurturing, he listens, he allows you to do things, he realizes that sometimes actors have great ideas—it *can* happen, you know! But he'll also pull your coattail if he thinks you're stinking it up. He has all the tools. He has an eye for drama, an eye for the camera. I was actually very impressed with the things that he did and the way that he kept it going. I didn't have a moment to roll my eyes and say, "Why are they still on this scene?" That's the big difference between what we're used to seeing in *Star Trek* and this movie.

The previous movie was about a lot of things in front of the camera and behind the camera. It was about transitions. You had Whoopi, Shatner, and Patrick—three very forceful personalities in one movie. It became about a lot of things, and I think that's why I felt that it was only okay. As a whole this movie probably didn't get self-indulgent or dwell on things that were uninteresting. It was about something and we never lost sight of what it was about. Once a movie starts straying in different directions, it loses its strengths. This film had a point to make and it made it, and I have to give a lot of credit for that to Jonathan's direction of it.

JONATHAN FRAKES

Obviously I was familiar with the gestalt of *Star Trek*. I also think I had an ease with my comrades, which allowed them as actors to feel comfortable enough to try things that they might not try with a director they don't know as well. We also have a great sense of fun on the stage, and if we were able to inject some of that into the film, that's great. One of the treats, of course, was having the time to actually rehearse a scene, which you don't get on television. And some pre-production time where you can plan some shots and actually go to the producers and cameraman and say, "Can we get a crane for this shot?" and instead of them saying, "Frakes, get out of here, we don't have the time or the budget," they say, "Yeah, that'll work." More people said "Yes, we can do that" than I had dared hoped for.

ALFRE WOODARD

There was a confrontation between Picard and Lily that took three days to film. It was a very intense, confrontational moment. It was so cool because it was just us and Jonathan Frakes, so we got Jonathan's undivided attention. It was meaty. There were things to do, and you're there with a partner that you know can run the relay with you. It's like crewing and everybody being in top, top form on the boat. Jonathan, whom I'd known for twenty-one years, is the kind of director that does direct you, but because he's a good actor—and good actors don't always make good directors, which is something that has to get through to people—he does have everything that makes for good directing impulse. The language is there immediately and it's fabulous. Those days we had the drama, the intensity of yeah, yeah, we're kicking ass; this is so great, but at the same time, in between takes we were laughing about whatever we chat about—politics, life, dirty jokes . . . whatever it is. It was like partying all day.

JONATHAN FRAKES

I think my strongest suit as director is allowing the heart of the scenes to come out. I like the acting scenes; the scenes where the people share their emotions. Where you can build the arc of the scene and feel the tension, and it seems to me that's what made this movie hold up as more than just an action piece.

At the same time, I looked at both *Alien* and *Aliens* when I was prepping—more than once. I thought both Ridley Scott and James Cameron have a wonderful eye for action and suspense. They also made it clear that when it comes to villains, the more that's *suggested*, the scarier they are. I tried to get that with the Borg.

BRENT SPINER

Jonathan did a fantastic job, and we certainly knew he would. But he handled areas of the picture that we didn't think he was going to be able to do. We thought he could comfortably let us take care of the acting and grapple with the size of the production, which was formidable. He managed to do that and stay on top of everybody about their acting. There was nobody in the film that Jonathan wouldn't have adjustments for. Every single take was followed by him coming up with an adjustment for us, and they were always very intuitive and very smart and eye-opening for us.

Also eye-opening about *First Contact* was the fact that LeVar Burton's Geordi La Forge *finally* got rid of his VISOR, which many compared unflatteringly to an automobile air filter over the years.

LEVAR BURTON (actor, "Geordi LaForge")

It was time. Eighty percent of my vision was cut off when I wore that thing, and it physically hurt, which was one of the more important reasons I wanted to get out from underneath it. We held on to it for so long, because, as Rick says, it was one of the ways that we established in the minds of the audience the technology of the twenty-fourth century. On the series it became problematic because it was cost prohibitive.

We were never able to show the audience what Geordi saw, because it was too expensive and we were on a tight budget. So it became a barrier to storytelling, physically painful for me, and on a spiritual level, it's really just a sin to cover an actor's eyes. I wasn't really aware of how much of a barrier it had become until we shot this movie, and in the absence of the VISOR, I noticed that the other actors were relating to me very differently. They were engaging me in a way that they never did in scenes. So the visor is dead; long live the visor!

Prior to *First Contact*, Alice Krige (the Borg Queen) was perhaps best known for the 1981 film *Ghost Story* and numerous television episodic appearances. James Cromwell (Zefram Cochrane), who longtime fans remember as Archie Bunker's friend Stretch Cunningham, at the time of *First Contact* had starred in *Babe* and, a year after the *Trek* film's release, the critically acclaimed *L.A. Confidential*. And then there was Alfre Woodard (Lily Sloane), whose credits in the 90s include *How to Make an American Quilt*, *Gulliver's Travels*, *Mission to Mars*, and *Primal Fear*.

BRANNON BRAGA

There was talk of Tom Hanks for Cochrane. I remember Anjelica Huston being mentioned for the Queen, and in fact she *was* interested, but we felt it was too similar to the role in the Michael Jackson *Captain Eo* thing, which was kind of Queen-like, actually. I was always a fan of Alice Krige in the role, because I remembered her from *Ghost Story* and she was very sexy creepy in that movie, and that's what the Queen had to be. I thought she would be perfect and, of course, she was.

JONATHAN FRAKES

This also happens to be the best guest cast of any *Star Trek* movie ever, with James Cromwell, Alfre Woodard, and Alice Krige. They're prestigious and wonderful actors cast against type. Alfre is an action hero for much of this movie, which is a part you never see her in.

BRENT SPINER

It was really nice having actors of the caliber of Alfre and Alice and Jamie Cromwell in this picture. It was a real tip of the hat to us that they were willing to be in a *Star Trek* movie, because a lot of people pooh-pooh the idea of being in one of them. They also recognized these were delicious roles to play. *Star Trek* does afford the actor a level of performance that you don't get ordinarily in a picture. It's a heightened style of playing that you can go further with than you can with most material. And it's fun. It's a credit to them that they recognized that opportunity.

ALICE KRIGE (actress, "Borg Queen")

For the first time in my working life I didn't construct a backstory. I made, however, a decision about who I thought she was. No one ever asked me what I thought, so I hope I'm right. I came to a conclusion that she is pure intelligence and that she just colonizes physical forms when she needs them. She takes what she needs and moves on. She just takes over people's brains.

BRANNON BRAGA

The Borg Queen is the strangest Borg we've ever seen. She's pretty weird and the most elaborate and creepy Borg ever. She does speak in a more human way, but that's probably because she knows she needs to. We get close to her in a natural state, which is pretty bizarre. There is also an interesting relationship between her and Picard that's revealed at the end.

ALICE KRIGE

The Borg Queen wanted Picard, but ultimately wasn't in love with him. Brent pointed out to me, and it was very useful, that at the end of the TV episode where Picard is being taken over by the Borg and he's fighting valiantly to attain himself, the one who actually cracks the code and sort of accesses the Borg to release Picard, is Data.

JONATHAN FRAKES

We saw almost a hundred actresses for the Borg Queen, but nobody was able to nail it, because the language was very difficult, stilted, metaphoric, and not very conversational. So it's very tough to act. It was tough because we needed this character to be dangerous and sexy and strange. Alice brought all of that into the room. When she walked in, Rick Berman and I both breathed a collective sigh of relief that we had found an actress who could play the part.

We had to redesign or rethink the look of the Borg Queen, which we had been working on at the same time, and we assumed we would have some similarities that the Borg drones have with the eye and tubes and all that stuff. But then we thought what a mistake it would be to cover Alice's beautiful face up, which is how we decided to pull most of that stuff back. We attached some stuff on her neck, so we wouldn't cover up her beautiful mouth and eyes, which were mesmerizing. It would have been a shame to lose that behind a mask. I've worked a lot with aliens over the years and one of the problems is that the actor sometimes gets buried behind the prosthetic. We didn't want that to happen with Alice.

ALICE KRIGE

When they were designing me as the Borg Queen, they used something on my head that I hope to never encounter again called Gafquat. It's a concentrated hair spray and they put it on with a spoon and it gets so hard that it's like you've got a saucepan on your head. It comes off very easily, but when it's on it's completely rigid—it keeps the hair out of the glue, so I guess there's compensation. I'd say from the neck up it took about six hours a day to make me up, and then it took about an hour to get into the suit. Then it took another two hours to get out.

The people who suited me up every day were an interesting group. Scott Wheeler created the head, and Todd Masters, who has a workshop, created the body. They were all actually fine artists in their own right. They were sculptors or painters or potters. I guess you don't get to be part of the *Star Trek* team unless you have a slightly wacky imagination. So we had a lot of fun. I have enough dirty jokes to last me a lifetime; they told me *so* many jokes sitting there.

BRENT SPINER

Alice Krige is remarkable, because even with all that stuff on, she's pretty sexy. She's a really gorgeous woman. In that stuff, she was just sensational. There is something disturbing and peculiar about the romance, which is exactly what I think it needed to be. It's almost like a David Lynch romance. It couldn't be just a simple love scene, it had to be heightened. Data is the only character she could have had that romance with and have it work. Anything else might have been gross.

ALICE KRIGE

The idea of power and sexuality and where they interface is interesting. And she uses sexuality very, very skillfully; very powerful. Which is kind of an interesting area to explore. I also found interesting the fact that she is part human and part not. There's a moment when I blow on Data's arm and ask, "Was that good for you?" We had a lot of fun. Brent Spiner is lovely to be around, and he took my breath away that after nine or ten years of playing the role, he should still be actively pushing out of the envelope for the character. Still looking for places for Data to go. I fell in love with the character of Data. That innocent, naïve personality was totally endearing. He made me laugh a lot. That innocence is very sweet and funny and kind of unexpected.

BRENT SPINER

There's something about these two mechanical beings engaging in romance that is fascinating. It worked really nicely, actually, and Alice is the key to it, because the Borg Queen is clearly the most difficult role in the film to play. It was the one role on the page when I read it that made me say, "I don't know how someone is going to play this," but Alice came in with a plan and executed it perfectly. She brought so much to the film and managed to not only be evil, but also truly seductive.

ALICE KRIGE

Really what the Queen meets in Data is an intelligence as formidable as her own. She's fascinated by it and she knows that Data's Achilles heel is his desire to be human. I guess she kind of reels him in with a taste of human sexuality, which is kind of compelling. But she gets hoisted on her own petard because she kind of gets fascinated by him. And lets down her guard in the process.

ALFRE WOODARD

Lily Sloane is a very earthy, realistic, grounded woman, so I basically was doing the same thing in fantastical situations. I think she takes a present-day audience along onto the *Enterprise-E* just in that way, because even if you've been watching *Star Trek* for a long time, you go there because you've been taken to that world with Lily; you walk from where you are onto the *Enterprise* with her.

JAMES CROMWELL (actor, "Zefram Cochrane")

The *Star Trek* company happens to be very guest-friendly. They're known for that. They include you, they make sure you're comfortable and that there's a lot of input. But television is quick and dirty and everybody tries to do their best despite the limitations. You're basically there to keep an audience captive until the next commercial comes up. There is not the time to develop a story as fully as you can in a film. The difference is that a character like mine can really spread out. He's not lost, he's not jammed in somewhere. One of the things that I liked about the character is that in some ways he sends up *Star Trek*. The last thing you expect is this irreverent, wasted maniac who's a scientist.

BRANNON BRAGA

Zefram Cochrane is a drunken lunatic in the film. He's an eccentric, crazed person. Brilliant, but not quite what our twenty-fourth-century heroes expected. It's kind of like going back in time to visit a historical hero who is credited with changing mankind, only to find out that he's an asshole.

JAMES CROMWELL

When we were shooting in Angeles National Forest, it was *freezing*. Everybody was cold *except* me, because I had this great coat on. Also, I had to play the drunk scene. Now, I'm not a drinker, so I got myself a bottle of Irish whiskey and every time I'd go back to my trailer, I'd take a shot. By the time I got back to that scene, I really wasn't acting. I had a great time. When I saw it, I laughed, because it's hard to create that kind of timing.

> An additional new "character" was the *Enterprise-E,* constructed to replace the previous ship that had been destroyed in *Generations*.

HERMAN ZIMMERMAN

The *Enterprise-D* was a wonderful design for seven seasons on the TV show and one of the feature films, and it was a good idea to put a fresh ship on the drawing boards. This one had a longer profile, while the mass is probably smaller than the *Enterprise-D*. If it owes any genealogy to anything, it's more homage to Matt Jeffries' original design for the 1966 series than it is to Andy Probert's design for the *Star Trek: The Next Generation* television series.

It's not to say that they aren't of the same lineage, because they definitely are. We just had a ship in *First Contact* that is more fighting machine than Hyatt Regency. The *Defiant* [on *Deep Space Nine*] was definitely the prototype for a ship capable of combating a threat as serious as the Borg, but the new *Enterprise*'s technology was built on that experience as well.

> After going through a succession of title changes which ranged from *Star Trek: Resurrection* to *Star Trek: Borg,* the studio finally settled on *Star Trek: First Contact,* which was released on November 22, 1996, and ultimately grossed over $146 million, handily beating *Generation*'s box office receipts of $120 million. Virtually everyone agreed that it was not only superior to that film, but had a crossover appeal that the franchise hadn't enjoyed since 1986's *The Voyage Home.*

JONATHAN FRAKES

Generations had two separate stories going on. *First Contact* has an A, B, and C story, but they intermingle and cross paths and then come back out. It's structured more sexily than the previous movie. We also had more laughs. Humor and play-fulness between the characters is an essential part of *Star Trek*. It's one of the great charms of the original show, and that's something we went back to for this film. At the same time, while some of the adventure in the past is very humorous, some of it is very serious.

BRENT SPINER

Star Trek is, in kind of a Joseph Campbell way, a modern mythology. Mythology is always based on the hero going out in search of something to bring back to his people—a weapon or enlightenment or medicine. We weren't heroes in the pre-vious movie, and that was a serious element that was missing. In this film, every-one had a heroic moment in the movie. As a result, it was much more satisfying.

JONATHAN FRAKES

First Contact still holds up. It's a great action-thriller-horror movie. Thematically it's interesting, with an incredible guest cast. It's a very successful movie that just happens to be a *Star Trek* movie.

HERMAN ZIMMERMAN

Generations was a fine picture and a passing of the baton from Bill to Patrick. As much as *Generations* was the end of one era in the *Star Trek* universe, *First Contact* was the beginning of another.

SCOTT MANTZ (film critic, *Access Hollywood*)

First Contact was *Next Generation*'s *Wrath of Khan*. It's another Moby Dick story. You've got time travel and you've got their best adversary, the Borg. It felt cinematic.

JONATHAN FRAKES

I got a phone call from DeForest Kelley, whom I had only met for a day or two once when he was on the *Next Generation* set. I had also seen him at a convention and had dinner with him and his wonderful wife at Berman's house. So I had met him probably three times. *First Contact* opened on a Friday, but on Saturday, while I was in Great Barrington, he called to congratulate me on the success of the film. And to tell me how pleased he was that the franchise was in good hands. Oh, man, it was the most thoughtful, unnecessary, pleasant surprise. De Kelley of all people! I *adore* him. He was my favorite, and probably the best in the entire *Star Trek* family in terms of who he was as a man.

LOVE IS THE DRUG

"CAN ANYONE REMEMBER WHEN WE USED TO BE EXPLORERS?"

With the success of *First Contact*—both critically and commercially—it seemed that *The Next Generation*'s transition to the big screen had been successfully achieved, the future for the new incarnation of the big-screen franchise ripe for exploration. But, as time would show, what appeared to have been something of a renaissance for *Star Trek* actually turned out to be the demarcation point for the franchise's imminent decline as the twentieth century was coming to a close.

The first indication came with the 1998 release of *Insurrection*, a film that had originally been conceived as a futuristic take on Joseph Conrad's *Heart of Darkness*. Instead it became a morality lesson about the pursuit of youth at all costs. To many, it may have been too "soft" a follow-up to the Borg. It certainly was for Paramount, as the film grossed $112 million worldwide (on a $58 million budget) compared to its predecessor's potent box-office of $146 million.

BRANNON BRAGA (writer, *Star Trek: First Contact*)

After *First Contact*, which was so successful, I remember how proud I was of everyone involved when I just looked at the newspaper ads. It was around Thanksgiving and it was such a happy time. I was young, successful, and I had this movie with all these great reviews. *And* Siskel and Ebert reviewed it, which was my dream come true, and they *loved* it. They said it was the best movie so far of the entire series, and I was, like, "Wow!" I grew up with them in the late seventies, and that was a great moment. Then the movie did huge business, and Rick came to me and said he wanted me to do the next movie. There was talk of me even having a producer credit, because essentially I was a producer with *First Contact*; I was involved in the redesign of the Borg. I was on the set every day, I was very much at Rick's side for the entire production of that movie and they were dangling a producer credit in my face.

RONALD D. MOORE (writer, *Star Trek: First Contact*)

Rick came and asked Brannon and me to do the next movie very shortly after *First Contact* came out and had done well. Paramount had approached him to start working on the next one, and he asked us. I think Brannon might have done it, but I was out. I said, "I'm done." I wanted to end on a high note. I was proud of *First Contact.* We'd overcome the obstacles and other elements of *Generations,* and I just didn't want to do another one. Let's walk away now with our heads high and leave it to somebody else. Rick was very disappointed, and Brannon was kind of disappointed, but went along with it. My attitude was "Let's not just keep doing this."

MICHAEL PILLER
(writer, *Star Trek: Insurrection*)

Rick Berman wasn't sure that I'd want the job. The first thing he said when he came into my office was "Don't say 'no' until I finish talking." And when he finished talking about his hopes for the next *Star Trek* movie, he asked me if I would be interested in writing it. I surprised him by saying 'yes.' It may seem odd that anyone would even consider passing on a chance to write a feature film, but Rick knew I'd been moving away from the *Star Trek* franchise.

BRANNON BRAGA

This was, without a doubt, the hardest moment of my fifteen years with *Star Trek,* because I was being offered the next film. But I had also just been promoted to showrunner on *Voyager,* and this was truly the most agonizing decision probably of my career . . . and probably the worst decision I made in my career in retrospect. But at the time I was really worried that we didn't have a good creative direction for the next film. Rick was thinking of doing something more of a romp, like the whale movie. I liked the idea, but wasn't quite sure. I was fearful since I would not be working with Ron.

Quite frankly, I honestly did not think I could run *Voyager.* I'd never run a show alone before. And to do the movie at the same time seemed impossible, so I turned Rick down. He didn't speak to me for two months, he was so pissed off at me. By the way, I don't blame him and it sucked. I would get notes from him on scripts sent over, but he wouldn't talk to me. It took a while for him to talk to me again. I know Rick went to Michael Piller, but the film suffered from Michael wanting him to do a really serious meditation on morality for Picard and Rick wanted to do a romp.

As a result, it was a strange movie and not really successful. I wish I'd done it. I would have made a better movie, but on a personal level I do feel like I let Rick down and shortchanged myself in the process.

RICK BERMAN (producer, *Star Trek: Insurrection*)

Both Brannon Braga and Ron Moore, who I worked with on the previous two movies, were critically involved with the two television series, *Voyager* and *Deep Space Nine,* and I didn't want to have to wrestle them between the two, which we had to do during *First Contact.* So I went to Michael Piller, who I had worked with for ten years, and we sat down and decided we have to do something different from *First Contact.*

MICHAEL PILLER

The timing was right for me. It had been two years since Bill Dial and I had created the series *Legend.* Since then I'd written a feature script that Sydney Pollack had optioned, a cable movie script, and a couple of television pilots. And *none* of them had been made. I was in a place known in this business as "development hell." So, Rick's invitation to write a *Star Trek* movie was like a visit from an old girlfriend after you haven't had a date for a year. I was awfully glad to see him.

> At about the time Piller had accepted the assignment, he had had a pilot he'd written rejected by ABC due to the fact that its perceived demographic would be too old.

MICHAEL PILLER

I was in front of the bathroom mirror cursing to myself about the network's youth obsession as I sprayed Rogaine on my bald spot, when my mind made an unexpected jump to the *Star Trek* assignment. We're obsessed with youth, I thought. Looking young, feeling young, selling to the young. When was the last time anybody did a fountain of youth story? I couldn't remember. And I smiled.

> That smile didn't last very long. Piller came up with a treatment in which Picard is sent out to stop a former friend who has seemingly gone rogue, and the pursuit leads him to a planet that serves as a fountain of youth of sorts. As such, it allowed the writer to explore a sci-fi take on *Heart of Darkness* while discussing themes of recapturing lost youth. In a meeting, Rick Berman read aloud a passage from the treatment, noting, "We begin to realize that Picard is getting

younger, first psychologically and then gradually physically as well. We see that swashbuckling spirit of an earlier era revived in his heart."

MICHAEL PILLER

Rick looked at me and said, "In other words, Picard's an old man who doesn't get to buckle his swash until the planet makes him young again. But he's our hero. When the movie's over and he's back to normal again, he needs to be a vital man of action. Patrick will hate this. He'll never do it." "But he didn't have a problem with a fountain of youth concept," I said. "He will when he reads this," said Rick. "You're telling our star he's an old man." I sputtered, looking for words to argue, but I couldn't find them. "If it's a fountain of youth story, he's got to get younger," I finally said. "Then maybe it shouldn't be a fountain of youth story. I won't be able to sell this to Patrick."

From there, Berman suggested that the person Picard be pursuing is Data and that it could be a battle to the death (with the promise of Data's resurrection, given the fact that he's an android).

MICHAEL PILLER

Once we put Data on the planet, he would become a wayward son. It would become a story about the *Enterprise* crew's commitment to him, defining the crew as a family and emphasizing its importance to the franchise. Rick assured me that there might be a way to keep the planet a fountain of youth. "Maybe it just affects the aliens, but not humans," he said. It didn't make much sense to me. The fun of a fountain of youth story is seeing your heroes change. Several days later we jettisoned the whole fountain of youth theme.

RICK BERMAN

The key thing that we started out with is not wanting to duplicate what we did on the last one. And in this case, the last one had a lot of terrific elements in it. *First Contact* has us trying to save mankind, which is a biggie. We had great villains in the Borg, we had time travel. All very cool sci-fi things to work with. On this film we didn't want to duplicate any of those things. We came up with, I think, a more thoughtful approach with a story about a moral dilemma that Picard finds himself in.

MICHAEL PILLER

In this film, Patrick wanted his character to be a plain and simple hero. In *First Contact* he had been driven for vengeance. In *Generations,* Picard was full of self-doubts because his only family had been killed. Patrick did not want to be "haunted" in this next film. Keep it light and simple this time, he was saying.

PATRICK STEWART (actor, "Jean-Luc Picard")

From the very earliest we had talked about finding a different tone for this movie. We never wanted to stand still with *Star Trek,* never wanted to repeat what we'd done before. *First Contact* was really quite good, I think. We could have done that movie again, but why? This group of actors, this ensemble of actors, has terrific range. They can do anything.

RICK BERMAN

It was a story about questioning certain members of the hierarchy of the Federation who may be starting to turn a blind eye to certain principles that they have always upheld. There was that *Heart of Darkness* idea of the *Enterprise* going off into a strange inhospitable part of the galaxy to find somebody. That somebody started off as one person, became somebody else, and finally became Data.

LEVAR BURTON (actor, "Geordi La Forge")

I felt very strongly that if we were going to do another one of these after *First Contact*, that it needed to be different energetically. Upon reading it, I was relieved to discover that it was in the best tradition of *Star Trek* in that it was *about* something.

RICK BERMAN

Don Granger was the vice president [at Paramount] who was sort of in charge of our projects. Don was a huge *Star Trek* fan and knew as much about *Star Trek* as anybody, and the notes that came from John Goldwyn and [studio chief] Sherry Lansing were very reasonable. They were big notes, like Piller wanting to do a movie where Patrick Stewart got into a downward spiral and ends up losing his position at Starfleet, losing the Enterprise and his friends. All he had to hold on to was his dignity, and he manages. It was sort of a very dark story. I think he probably saved the universe at the end, as always. But, in the process, it was a very dark series of events that leads him to where he ends up. The studio just could not believe that. They almost thought we were joking when we gave them the first story outline.

MICHAEL PILLER

In the first draft, Picard and Data are brutal, bitter enemies. In the film there's a wonderful moment where they battle in a dogfight while Picard sings Gilbert and Sullivan. That used to take seventy pages, and in that battle Picard was ultimately forced to kill Data. That was all very interesting, but by the time you had Picard go down to the next planet, you basically had a miniseries worth of plot. Neither side of it was good enough to support the elements.

It was Patrick, frankly, who said, "This is dark and dreary and it's not fun," and he was the one who put us back on the fountain of youth course that ultimately really leads the story to its current state. So we stripped away the *Heart of Darkness* aspect and went with the other plot, using the *Heart of Darkness* elements as a tease to the other plot.

RICK BERMAN

It was really not Patrick who put the kibosh on the story, it was the studio. And I think to a great degree they were right. They thought a *Star Trek* movie should be up and fun and exciting. And those were not words that really fit into Mike Piller's vocabulary. Exciting maybe, but not fun. But that was like the biggest note that we really ever got.

The errant behavior of Data on an alien world in which the Federation is secretly monitoring a race known as the Ba'ku leads Captain Picard and the *Enterprise* there to stop him by any means necessary. What unfolds is a conspiracy in which members of the Federation (most notably Anthony Zerbe's Admiral Dougherty) are covertly working with the Son'a (particularly F. Murray Abraham's Ahdar Ru'afo) to secretly remove the Ba'ku from this world so that they can claim it and its mysterious youth-instilling properties. Along the way Picard connects emotionally with the apparent matriarch of the Ba'ku (Donna

Murphy's Anij) as he grows determined to reclaim the moral foundations on which the Federation was built.

RICK BERMAN

The whole idea of a place where people never get old—the fountain of youth, a *Lost Horizon* idea—and how that could play into both the moral dilemma of Picard as well as something that could give us some romance and some humor . . . all of that came to the foreground.

MICHAEL PILLER

The idea of trying to out-Borg the Borg as villains was doomed to failure, so we really had to come back with something that was lighter, more character oriented, something that would provide the opportunity for humor and, perhaps, romance. I think romance was a strong wish on Patrick's part.

PATRICK STEWART

For long periods of time, it appeared as though there was a romantic relationship with Beverly Crusher which would be revived, but from time to time the producers would bring to the show some old love—you know, someone he knew as a student, somebody he knew when he was first out of the Academy, and so forth. So there was always a rather wistful, sad sense of what might have been about him. There's a feeling that Picard actually does have a hole in his life that should be filled by someone else.

GATES MCFADDEN (actress, "Beverly Crusher")

I certainly think it spoke well of my character in this film that she didn't show any jealousy. I don't know whether that's because we've all been in love with a million aliens in all those years. I had questions about it, but what are you going to do? I didn't get into it this time, and you know why? You read this script and you're intelligent enough to know there is only so much time. What is the movie about? Unless you're going to deal with it in a certain way, it's fine. If it had been the first time I'd seen the captain gaga over somebody, that would have been one thing, but it *wasn't* the first time. It makes a difference.

RICK BERMAN

There was a little romance cut out of the final film: a couple of kisses. And there were some heated debates as to whether the kisses were in the right place. Those who were against the kisses were against them primarily because the first one was during an altered reality sequence where the water slows down and the humming-bird slows down. There were those among us who believed that we were right in the middle of this exodus, there was a lot of action going on, and for those two characters to start making out seemed to not necessarily be appropriate at that moment.

The second kiss took place at the very end of the movie right when Picard says, "I've got 318 days of shore leave coming," but without the first kiss, the second kiss seemed very odd and out of place. There were a lot of discussions with the studio people and the final decision ended up being to take them out. It would not have made all that much of a difference one way or the other, and I don't think that the kisses would have done any damage to the story. Nor do I think their absence was all that missed.

PATRICK STEWART

In *First Contact* there had been the character of Lily played by Alfre Woodard, whom I also kissed and which also got cut out of the movie. There must be something they don't like about my kissing. It's the oddest thing. With the kiss with Alfre, it was on the cheek, but they took it out. So when it came to Donna and something a little more intense . . . it's gone and it's very irritating.

DONNA MURPHY (actress, "Anij")

There was a whole sequence, a portion of which is still in the film, where I'm leading Picard through this altered reality, stepping inside a moment and kind of suspending time. It was more kind of a sensual exploration, a heightened sensory response to different ways of touching each other, and that led into this kiss. When I saw that that was cut, I thought that it may have been to give a greater payoff to a kiss that was at the end of the movie. And when I saw that *that* was cut, I was surprised.

I initially had a negative response to that, because you shape performance thinking that there are certain pieces of the puzzle that are a given, and if you take those pieces out you might have chosen to shape the performance differently if you knew that those pieces were not going to be there. Patrick and I played that relationship as if there was an intimacy that had taken place at a certain point. I was told it was a studio decision that the kisses were not necessary.

JONATHAN FRAKES (director/actor, "William T. Riker")

I never knew firsthand why directors got so furious with their movie. You read about that all the time, how directors react, but I've always been such a company man until this. You turn in what's called a director's cut, which is the movie that you want everybody to see. But they paid the money to make it, so it's really *their* movie. The cut that Rick and I turned in had maybe five or six more minutes. A couple of other things were cut, but nothing as significant as the kiss.

MICHAEL PILLER

Somebody at the studio said, "What you really want to do is [second season *TNG* episode] 'Measure of a Man' here, to do that kind of thoughtful story,' and very often, *The Voyage Home* was raised as a comedy relief kind of situation, so Rick and I were basically telling each other, and the studio was very much in concert with the idea, to do a change-of-pace movie. Then somewhere around halfway through the process, fears began to rise that it wasn't going to be "big" enough.

RICK BERMAN

The script evolved and we played with it for four months maybe, and then we got Patrick involved and he had some thoughts and the studio people had some thoughts, and Brent Spiner had some thoughts. The stories flip and flop until you get it right.

JONATHAN FRAKES

Patrick was distinctly involved with *Insurrection*, because I don't think he was as excited as he was about *First Contact*. And then Brent was feeling his power and popularity, because they'd paid him his number. He kept renegotiating each film individually, so he was feeling very powerful.

MICHAEL PILLER

Jonathan Frakes was constantly part of the revision process as we went through the drafts. We sat in a room with Rick, Jonathan, and me and beat by beat set out the outline for the new draft on whiteboard with marker. By the time we were finished and before I went to write, all three of us felt that we knew very much what the movie was going to be. Having the director committed to that vision before you start writing is a wonderful feeling. When he finally read the finished script, he was just delighted and he respected my work and gave it the greatest attention as it was translated into the movie. I couldn't be happier with my relationship and what I was allowed to do with Jonathan.

JONATHAN FRAKES

I was not involved in the development of the script as Piller seems to remember. I was brought in after they made a deal and the script was in place. I was there for all of prep, but certainly not in the development of the script. Rick is very exclusive with whom he develops the script, and there weren't a lot of changes in prep.

BRENT SPINER (actor, "Data")

I get the scripts, and then there is an open-door policy when I can come in and debate the script. Usually I spend somewhere between eight and twelve hours arguing points in the script. Some of them I win and some I don't, and then I just forget about it and dive in, because it's only in the preparation that I can sort of debate the points. Most of the time if they're really firm about something they want, I'll do it. I can generally find a spin on it that makes me comfortable in the performance of it. But, in general, I win maybe 10 percent, I guess.

MICHAEL PILLER

Patrick rejected the first draft I had written, and, let me tell you, that was a very dark day. At the same time, and I mean this sincerely, it wasn't the script he was reacting to, but the first story. And he was right. No writer likes to hear that, but I can say without hesitation that the conflicts with Patrick, and although he was right about the story, the direction we took from there we had a great deal of conflict over regarding his character. I felt they were points I had to win to make the script work.

We had long and difficult conversations, letters and meetings, and without a doubt that script is far better as a result of that conflict. It certainly is important to realize that from conflict with people who really care about the material, and are really smart, good results can come. The result here, I think, is one of the most interesting roles that Picard has had to play in a *Star Trek* story. He is fighting for the principles he has fought for his entire life, because the Federation seems to have abandoned them.

At the core of the film is the issue of morality in how some great nations can mistreat minorities in the pursuit of the greater good. The point I'm making is that our history is filled with injustices to minorities who have been murdered and forcibly relocated and kidnapped and moved because the technology or the march of time or progress demanded it. And their presence wherever they were was inconvenient. This is a story that resonates with the history of both the United States and man. It's really getting to a fundamental issue of morality and, ultimately, to ethics as Picard has to decide: does he follow orders or not?

JONATHAN FRAKES

That element sparked a lot of discussion behind the camera. People saying "What would *you* do?" It became a very interesting, philosophical debate. Anthony Zerbe's character of Admiral Dougherty came down on the side of "Fuck 'em, kill six hundred people. It's for the best." And Patrick came down on the side of the Federation. It was quite interesting to hear the dialogue in front of the camera and behind it. It's Bosnia or Zimbabwe. It's where they sacrifice the few for the sake of the many, because the many happen to have bigger guns or more money or whatever the hell they have. It's unethical, it's immoral, it's racist, and it's all the things that we in *Star Trek* are against.

F. MURRAY ABRAHAM (actor, "Ru'afo")

It's not only political, there's also a humanistic overtone to all of the *Star Trek* films. They're trying to teach certain basic principles, and in this one the idea of technology being more important than the natural world. There's a tension which we experience now in our society, in our world, where the technology is practiced to such a degree that you begin to forget it's human beings that are involved. What we *shouldn't* do is say that the natural world is more important and we should get rid of technology—that's absurd. Technology is too useful not only medically but in many ways. The trick is to achieve a balance between the natural world and the technological world.

MICHAEL PILLER

We wanted to have the picture being about more than just political principles. It seemed like there was a trap for me as a writer, because in the last movie Picard was sort of misguided in terms of his motives, because he was seeking vengeance against the Borg for what they had done to him. In the movie before that, he was questioning his life choices after his family died. Here, I felt the need for an emotional journey for Picard, but it was very difficult for me to find where to start without finding a flaw in the Picard character that needed to be resolved.

What it finally evolved into for us was looking at contemporary life, as many of us know it: our lives are not unrewarding and we're not unhappy with what we're doing. If somebody came up to us and said, "Are you a happy person?" Yes, we are. But what our lives have been cluttered with are details and job and more things than we can handle. Data overload became the theme of the next decade. What we find at the beginning of this picture is Picard caught in an avalanche of details. His arc, his journey, is that by going to this planet and finding a group of people who worship each moment of life, he learns a little bit—this is lightly handled, it sounds heavier than it's portrayed—and he finds a way to look at life in a slightly different way than he came. And ultimately as the movie ends, he plans to bring that appreciation to the Federation Council and tell them to slow down a little bit.

> The Data arc in the film was even more difficult to realize as Piller was more interested in returning the character to his more innocent ways as depicted in the *Next Generation* series, while Brent Spiner viewed such an approach as a regression.

MICHAEL PILLER

Brent had a very strong feeling when he read the script that I was treating his character as though the last two movies didn't exist. To be honest, he was right. Jonathan Frakes and I were determined to bring back that Pinocchio quality from the series. My argument to Brent was that the big-screen audience had never had an opportunity to see that quality of the character Data that we had all fallen in love with in the first place. The discussion continued until the very last day of shooting.

BRENT SPINER

You can't keep beating something over the head. In the last two films we dealt with Data's emotion chip, and the feeling was enough is enough.

MICHAEL PILLER

I have always been afraid of the "Rhoda Effect." There used to be a show called *Rhoda,* featuring a character named Rhoda, which was a number-one-rated series for a couple of years. The key to Rhoda's character was that she could never find a man. Then she found one, Joe, and married him, and it was the highest-rated show in television history up until that time. But the moment she found a man, Rhoda was over, because everything that defined her character had been lost. I feared that giving Data what he always wanted, or a lot of what he wanted, was hurting the character in a way that lost that wonderful Pinocchio-like quality that defined him in the first place. The only way to maintain that was to work around the emotion chip, which, as I said, was like Joe to Rhoda.

BRENT SPINER

Part of what brings people into a *Star Trek* movie is that it is familiar territory, not the unknown. There are certain slight variations from film to film, but they're not all that different. None of the nine are remarkably different from any other of the nine or any of the hundreds of episodes. There's a real similarity to them, and that's what brings people back.

At the same time, Data has certainly changed from the first episode of the series, but that was a design built into it. Gene Roddenberry wanted this character to start as a sort of blank tablet, and his idea was that by the end of the day he would be as close to being human as possible . . . and still not. That's the way it's been written all the way down the line. They try to have Data experience or grapple with every aspect of the human condition. In this particular film he's dealing with locating the inner child. That's a part of the human condition he hadn't dealt with yet. This one went in a certain direction with the first two films where Data changed by virtue of having an emotion chip. Some people liked it, some people didn't. I don't really care.

> As was the case with *First Contact*, the attempt was to strengthen the *Insurrection* ensemble by ensuring solid actors were cast in the "guest star" roles. For Ru'afo, Academy Award–winner F. Murray Abraham (*Amadeus, Scarface, Inside Llewyn Davis, The Grand Budapest Hotel*), and Tony Award–winner Donna Murphy (on stage in *Passion, The King and I,* and *Wonderful Town*) as the Ba'ku's Anij.

JONATHAN FRAKES

My biggest fear was that after James Cromwell, Alfre Woodard, and Alice Krige in *First Contact,* this would be a letdown. But we had as interesting, if not more interesting, guest stars. One of the things about *Star Trek* is you can hire a wonderful actor who can't get a performance through the prosthetic makeup. Murray did not have that problem. I took great pleasure in seeing how much he could act through the rubber. He said something wonderful early on about working with Patrick. He came up to me and smiled a Machiavellian smile and said, "I get the feeling we're both meat eaters." I'm not quite sure what that meant, but it certainly inspired him.

F. MURRAY ABRAHAM

The makeup process was four and a half hours long. If you smile, there are about 135 muscles that go into making a smile. And it affects the eyes. If you're going to make a proper mask and not just a mask but a makeup, you have to get little tiny thin pieces of latex and lay them in to follow all of the muscles so that when you smile, it smiles. Otherwise it's just a flat mask. That's why it takes so long. So I would wake up at three in the morning and do a big workout. It's important to be in good shape for this kind of sitting. Then I would go to the studio and would start makeup at four thirty and then, four and a half hours later, I would begin the day. That's when the day would begin for me as an actor. Then at the end of the day, it's an hour to remove the makeup.

There's something about masks that empower people. I think it's mystical. It's magic. You can compare it to primitive cultures who, before they go into battle, put paint on. What does the paint stop? It cannot stop a bullet; it cannot stop an arrow or a spear. But it gives you magical power to go forth. You are not a warrior until you put this on. I feel the same way about masks. There's something that happens when you hide behind the mask. It opens a little valve of some kind. It gives you a new kind of energy. It's very mysterious, and it's very good, because there's no control over it. To me, the expression of art does not involve control. It involves discipline, of course. And the background, but it's not all control.

DONNA MURPHY

In trying to play a character who was three hundred years old, I tried to think of it as sort of multiplying the layers of my own life. In the short amount of time that I've been on Earth, there have been many chapters to my life. So I just thought of sort of multiplying the layers of my experience and trusting that she's a woman who's sagely arrived at this place of center and acceptance. She wasn't born that way. She's had a lot of time to get there. That's how I chose to look at it, and I did a lot of reading about Eastern religions, which was also helpful.

PATRICK STEWART

I had seen Donna Murphy on stage in her Tony-winning performance in *Passion* and her Tony-winning performance in *The King and I*. So I had sat there as an admirer in the audience, never thinking that we would one day be colleagues.

JONATHAN FRAKES

Donna Murphy found a character that had the potential to be boring, because she's so delicate and so fragile, and it could have been too new-agey, but she somehow kept it interesting.

DONNA MURPHY

Jonathan as director makes the set like summer camp. He keeps it very light, because they're long days, and he had a lot of people that he was shepherding. He keeps it light, and then when you're doing the more intimate stuff you can take the time to sort of talk to an actor—first of all, a fellow actor, because he's been on that side of it, obviously—to work more on the intricacies of the scene.

F. MURRAY ABRAHAM

Jonathan is from the theater and is a baritone singer. My background is the theater, so when we would have maybe a little bit of a problem or a hiccup, he'd suddenly burst into song. He'd start singing, and I'd start singing with him because I knew most of the songs he did. Here's this guy in the makeup and him singing this duet from *Oklahoma!* It was really fun. He just wouldn't let things drag. This can get very highly technical, but he didn't let it stop us.

JONATHAN FRAKES

I was less neurotic on *Insurrection* than I was on *First Contact*. I slept at night. The first time I didn't; I shot all day and then stressed all night about what the next day would be and whether I got all the coverage I needed. I was actually able to go home, and when my kids allowed me to, I was actually able to get a couple of hours of sleep. But I enjoyed it more as a result. Also, we were outside, which is great. We were outside for weeks. And it was glorious.

DONNA MURPHY

The cast is so close-knit that I was nervous, because I knew they probably had a shorthand. I had a ten-minute break with them and was reminded the banter among them is just boom, boom, boom. So there were moments that I couldn't help but feel a little outside of it, but it's not a negative thing. First of all, they are *very* entertaining, and second, they were very welcoming and really went out of their way to try to make me feel comfortable as quickly as possible. But since the character I played was somebody who was of another world, feeling a bit separate at times was okay.

F. MURRAY ABRAHAM

Humor is the essence of my life; it's the thing that keeps me going from day to day. By the second day, after the formalities were taken care of, they began to start each day with a joke from me. Jonathan Frakes would say, "All right, stop work, everyone. It's time for Murray's joke." I would tell a joke and then we would start work. They were wonderful. I have never experienced anything like it in my life in a film. I'd made over fifty films and this was absolutely the best experience of my life. When I left, when I was told I was wrapped and finished, I almost wept. I hated to leave. I had the time of my life.

While there had been some exterior sequences in *Generations* and *First Contact, Insurrection* stood apart from its two predecessors in that it was largely filmed on location at Lake Sherwood, located outside Los Angeles. Production designer Herman Zimmerman had to create a village for the Ba'ku that represented their anti-technology approach to life.

JONATHAN FRAKES

We were all a little sick of that ship-bound thing. Bad guys on their ship, good guys on our ship, and they go out and face off. There was a little more going on in *Insurrection*. Plus, so much time on location can change the whole gestalt of duty. A lot of wider-angle shots, a lot more crane work, a lot more lyrical camera movements. All of which made it a lot more interesting to me.

HERMAN ZIMMERMAN (production designer, *Star Trek: Insurrection*)

We had to create a village that you could believe six hundred people lived in. On a movie with budget concerns, that's pretty hard to do. There's nothing about the village that's computer generated. It's all a real place that we really built in what looks like stone. There's no glass, there's no steel. There's copper, wood, and stone, and lush landscaping. There's not a separation where you feel like you're not a part of nature. That's all part of the spirituality of the place.

JONATHAN FRAKES

Herman Zimmerman, our production designer, at his finest hour. Everybody walked in and said, "Is this a resort? What's the deal here?" It was exquisite.

PATRICK STEWART

As an actor, I've always loved going on location. It always seems to me that there's a certain amount of vacation time about it. We all feel very blessed at those times.

We go to these places and they bring along a catering truck and a comfortable trailer. And they pay us for doing it, too.

JONATHAN FRAKES

One of the great ironies in the movie is that the place that we found as Shangri-la or the fountain of youth looks so much like Earth in the twenty-fourth century. It's also a place that's chosen to reject technology. They bury their guns and put their computers away. It's subtle yet sort of ironic. Especially since at that time the millennium was coming and it felt appropriate to think maybe all technology isn't good just because it's faster or bigger or stronger. To the film's credit, there's a lot of what *Star Trek* has done that is in it where it has a little moral or message, or an ethical point of view, without browbeating you.

As was the case with *Generations,* reshoots were done on *Insurrection* to bolster the ending after test audiences reacted with what can best be described as apathy over the film's climax.

JONATHAN FRAKES

What was always there at the ending was the bit with Beverly and Deanna coming back down the hill, Patrick and Anij having their little walk, and Brent and the boy playing in the haystack. Prior to that it was just Murray and Patrick mano a mano, and the collector. But the collector didn't blow up, Riker didn't come and save the day with the *Enterprise*, Worf's ship was not retaken by the bad guys.

To the studio's credit, they said, "We'd like to see more action here at the end, because the audience expects more." And instead of just having two guys fight it out to the end, we were able to weave three stories, with the collector blowing up, the *Enterprise* going back—everyone wants to see the *Enterprise* save the day—and the bad-guy ship is involved. We got Worf in one ship, Riker in one ship, and Picard about to give up his life. So the stakes went up a lot and it really improved. There were definitely a lot of ups and downs during the making of this film.

MICHAEL PILLER

I've written a whole book about the writing of *Insurrection,* which unfortunately Pocket Books chose not to publish after a barrage of telephone calls from the studio. The irony is that the people at the studio who complained about it hadn't read it. The book is not a "burn bridges" book, it doesn't put anybody down, it's basically a book that was meant for young screenwriters as a textbook. It's something that I don't think was ever done—how an idea turns into a movie and all the changes that you go through, and all the problems a writer has to confront, and the notes from Patrick Stewart and the notes from the studio, and a first draft of the story that we threw out and started over again, and then the first disastrous draft of the script, and dealing with what went wrong and going back and getting a new vision.

It really turned into a fine script, and then, of course, all the changes that are made before it goes to the set, and the final version of it. And then, of course, what happens when you go through the camera and the editing room. It's really a wonderful book, by the way, and everybody who's read it agrees with that, but unfortunately, the studio felt it was not a comfortable situation for the studio to let people see behind the curtain, if you will. I can only tell you that I have mixed feelings about the way the picture ended up.

ANDRÉ BORMANIS (technical advisor, *Star Trek: Insurrection*)

I can't say I'm a big fan of the movie. There was a lot of technobabble in it. In fact, I went to the premiere and I was there with a woman whom I wanted to impress. And Michael Piller said something, which at the time I thought was a great compliment. When I introduced him to my date, he looked at her and pointed at me and said, "He wrote half this movie." "Oh, thank you." Then I saw it and I wasn't so sure I wanted that credit. My actual credit came somewhere between the dog trainer and the hair stylist.

JONATHAN FRAKES

I always thought the F. Murray Abraham story was the most exciting part of *Insurrection,* as opposed to the benign Ba'ku, which, in retrospect, looks like a good Aryan race. I had a friend on the set, who's no longer with us, who said, "I was the only Jew Ba'ku; I was the bagel maker." And LeVar used to say, "Are there no black people among the Ba'ku? It's the perfect world and there's no black people in it? What's up with this?" Somehow that eluded us during the development of the script. That's pretty naïve for three liberals like Piller, Berman, and me. It's a very interesting and embarrassing oversight.

The description of the film as being too soft is legitimate. Much more like one of our episodes as opposed to a film. What I thought was soft was the Data and the kid story. While somewhat emotional, between that storyline and the Donna Murphy/Patrick storyline, those are two of five or six storylines, both of which were somewhat soft. It was beautiful and emotional and soft in a way when Geordi was able to see for the first time thanks to the effects of the planet. Those were beautiful moments, but certainly not horror movie stuff like we had with the Borg. Overall, there were highs and lows. Loved the acting, loved the fountain of youth story. But the Ba'ku were a . . . gentle people.

RICK BERMAN

Both Patrick and Brent managed, in their contracts for the third movie, to get a little more say—I think that's the best word—in the writing and directing. When it came time for *Insurrection*, I wanted to use a director we used on the series named Jimmy Conway, but Patrick thought it was time to get a big-time feature director. Of course there were no big-time feature directors who were interested and we eventually decided that the best thing to do—and Patrick agreed—would be to go with Jonathan again, which we did. And there were writing changes and arguments and things that went on in *Insurrection* having to do with the actors getting involved in that process. There was some unpleasantness, but not major ones.

In the end, there were so many rewrites and so many conceptual changes based on the fact that the studio was looking for a Marvel kind of movie and Michael was looking for a *Heart of Darkness* type of movie, and we ended up somewhere in between. It was a *strange* process. The movie was injured by all of the different conflicting attitudes about what direction it should go. It was damaged before we got to the stage.

SEND IN THE CLONE

"I ASPIRE TO BE MORE THAN I AM."

Over the years, the big-screen adventures of the *Enterprise* have run the gamut from the exceptional to the awful. One of the biggest clichés surrounding that series is that the even-numbered films (*The Wrath of Khan, The Voyage Home, The Undiscovered Country, First Contact*) are the strongest entries, while the odd-numbered adventures (*The Motion Picture, The Search For Spock, The Final Frontier, Generations, Insurrection*) stand as the weaker installments in the series. But anyone who subscribed to this axiom would have been shocked to discover that the tenth silver screen voyage, *Nemesis,* a so-called "even numbered" Trek, may be the worst film of the bunch.

Released in 2002, the film, written by Academy Award–winning writer John Logan (*Skyfall, Gladiator*) and directed by Stuart Baird (*Executive Decision, U.S. Marshals*), was budgeted at $60 million and pulled in a paltry worldwide gross of over just $67 million. Along with *Star Trek V, Nemesis* stands as the true box office dud of the long-running film series, and the grosses of *Nemesis,* coupled with the eroding ratings of the fifth and final Berman-era live action television series, *Enterprise,* seemed to indicate that the star trek may have finally been over for the *Enterprise*. It would be seven years before another mission would be attempted under a completely new creative team.

RICK BERMAN (producer, *Star Trek: Nemesis*)

The head of the studio had really tried to convince me to do a movie without the *TNG* cast. The feeling was, "These guys have all gotten kind of older. It's time to introduce some new, fresh blood." There was an attitude that I should go out and find a new Tom Cruise. I felt strongly against that for two reasons. One reason was that when we were developing this movie, the *Enterprise* series was coming out, so the *Star Trek* audience was about to get introduced to a whole new cast of young characters on television. For us to simultaneously introduce them to a whole new cast of young characters in a movie seemed to be insane to me.

The other reason was I felt that after a four-year absence from the screen, the fans really wanted to see Patrick, Brent, Jonathan, and company again. I could have been wrong on one or both of those beliefs, but I felt strongly it should be another *TNG* movie.

BRENT SPINER (actor, "Data"/"B-4")

I didn't care for *Insurrection*. I just didn't think it was a very interesting story and it didn't show us at our best. There was a germ of an interesting idea that didn't get realized. It just wasn't ready to make. There may have been a very good film potentially there, but it was rushed into production.

RICK BERMAN

Michael Piller's idea was, let's go with a more thoughtful, more Gene Roddenberry–like story. The film was *not* greeted quite as well. It was profitable, but it was not greeted with the excitement of *First Contact*.

BRENT SPINER

Insurrection wasn't wildly successful, and I don't think it seemed worth the effort to the studio to make another. Paramount may have felt that we'd had our day. When we did end up doing *Nemesis*, we did take less money. That was part of the deal—to make it cheaper.

PATRICK STEWART (actor, "Jean-Luc Picard")

When we finished *Insurrection*, which I think everybody's acknowledged we were disappointed in, I felt it might be time to hang up my space suit. But I would have done it with a certain amount of disappointment. A feeling that we had gone out with a bit of a whimper, and perhaps wished that *First Contact* had been the end.

RICK BERMAN

A number of years went by after *Insurrection,* and both Patrick and Brent had an attitude of "We don't know if we want to do another movie." They certainly weren't in a rush to do one.

PATRICK STEWART

I was a passionate advocate that if there was going to be a tenth movie, that we should let a little more time pass before we rushed into production with something else. Just let everybody mull over what we had done and then, of course, decide if we even wanted to do something else.

RICK BERMAN

At one point, one or both of them said, "We'd be interested in doing a movie if you work with this fellow John Logan." And John had this incredible résumé. I met with him and we discussed a story that he had already cooked up with Brent. We decided to go with not rewrites, but reconceptualizations about what exactly the story was going to be, but it was still Mr. Logan's story.

PATRICK STEWART

John Logan was the first really significant step for this film. Also, Brent Spiner taking on the role that I had in the previous two movies, formally becoming involved with the development of the film.

JOHN LOGAN (writer, *Star Trek: Nemesis*)

My agents said, "You want to do what?!?" The whole thing for me is that I'm a life-long Trekkie, and utterly proud of it. My sort of obsession or fascination with *Star Trek* began with Captain Kirk on his original mission. Even as a kid, I was, like, "This is extraordinary." The chance to be a part of that story was just too exciting to even think about logically or in any other way.

I would like to say I kept some objective distance, and viewed this as a professional writer being well paid for this experience, but most of the time I was this wild fan, because I was there all the time during filming and had the exact same experience. I'm, like, "Oh my God, I'm on the bridge of the *Enterprise*" or "There's Patrick Stewart," whom I've known now for a long time, but he's walking in in his uniform and suddenly he's Picard. For a fan who spent so much time living and thinking about that world, to see Brent Spiner and Patrick Stewart doing a scene that I had written and realizing that that was going to become part of this ongoing story was hugely thrilling.

BRENT SPINER

John is such a huge *Star Trek* fan; it was almost as if he had been writing *Star Trek* his entire life. The first draft that he sent read like a *Star Trek* movie. It wasn't something that was completely alien. He certainly knew much more of the history of it than I did. Despite the fact that I've acted in all of those episodes, I never actually had a chance to watch them. I'm sure there are fans all over the country and all over the world who know way more about it than I do. And remember it way more than I do. I mean, my thrust was trying to memorize the dialogue and figure out how I was going to do it and portray the character the next day. So I didn't really watch and absorb the nuances of the episodes. John did. We were just very lucky that an A-list writer also happened to be a *Star Trek* fan and really wanted to write a *Star Trek* movie.

RICK BERMAN

Rather than going with someone like Ron Moore or Brannon Braga or Michael Piller, who'd been involved with *Trek* television for so many years, here we had a fresh, A-list Hollywood writer who happened to be a gigantic fan of *TNG*.

JOHN LOGAN

At the time, I'd never done a franchise movie before, so I didn't know the parameters. A friend of mine who had written a James Bond movie said, "Look, the only thing about a franchise movie is that when you take the toys out of the toy box, you have to put them back in the same way. You can't mess anything up." Which is absolutely *not* what we were doing with *Nemesis*.

It was to Paramount's credit that they agreed that we should make a strong statement with this movie and recognize that there is a continuum with these characters. We were moving on with them, and we should underline that at certain points. My personal favorite *Trek* film is *Star Trek II*. That's the one I looked back on and studied. The smartest thing ever done in a *Trek* film was in that one when Nick Meyer gave Captain Kirk glasses. That said, "These characters are getting older, they're moving on in their lives." In this movie, we acknowledged that as well and celebrated the fact that life is moving on for these characters.

And what makes a good *Trek* film is what makes any good adventure film, which is a really strong adversary.

BRENT SPINER

It's a film about nature vs. nurture. It's about family. It's about change. It's about all sorts of things.

JOHN LOGAN

In any story, if there's a personal connection between the hero and villain, it gives you more opportunity for drama. The dramatic possibilities here were all the better because the villain not only is equal to Picard, he *is* Picard.

BRENT SPINER

How do you come up with another story after you've done 180-odd hours? Actually, John Logan and I came up with a story that it turned out had already been done on *Deep Space Nine,* and neither of us had seen that. Rick, being there all the time, knew the story very well and said, "We've already done it." Then the three of us sat around together and thought about what would be interesting. We tossed around ideas and finally something stuck, and it evolved from there.

JOHN LOGAN

What I did try to do is say to myself, "What makes a great *Star Trek* story?" All the elements that excite me about my favorite episodes or my favorite movies, I tried to reflect in *Nemesis* in various ways. For example, *Star Trek II* worked so well because of the relationship between Kirk and Khan. It was a tense relationship so I thought, "Okay, we need Picard to have an intense relationship with a villain, whoever it is."

An episode like [*TOS*'s] "Arena" or the last half of *First Contact* worked so well because it is men in battle. I thought, "Okay. I want to write a war movie." I tried to take things that spoke to me personally about the best of *Trek* and tried to reflect that in *Nemesis.*

It was all about keeping focused on our crew, which is why I essentially wrote a bottle show saying: We're on the *Enterprise.* We're not dealing with Starfleet. We're not going to Earth. We're dealing with these characters in crisis, and kept the focus on the primary characters, particularly Picard and Data because they're the most important.

In *Nemesis,* Picard battles someone who is, literally, every inch his equal—a younger version of himself, a clone, Shinzon, created by the Romulans to bring down the Federation. Guest stars include actor Tom Hardy (best known at the time for *Band of Brothers* and *Black Hawk Down,* but whose subsequent credits include *The Dark Knight Rises, Locke, The Revenant,* and *Mad Max: Fury Road*) as Shinzon, and Ron Perlman (then known for *Quest For Fire, Ice Pirates,* and TV's

Beauty and the Beast, more recently for the Hellboy films and the television series *Sons of Anarchy*) as Shinzon's sinister right-hand man, the Viceroy.

PATRICK STEWART

The film was about longtime superpower enemies fighting together against lone
hostile forces, which is very applicable to current affairs. This was a very appropriate way to bow out.

JOHN LOGAN

I wanted to keep the focus on action and adventure and military protocol. The *Trek*
that I love most is not the whimsical *Trek*. It's the bottle shows I love: The Romulans are here. The *Enterprise* is there. What's going to happen? Rick Berman was
shocked during my first pitch when I said, "I think this script has one exterior action sequence and everything else is on ships or on planets. I think it's a very
tightly contained story about the individual characters we're choosing to play
with." So, for me, the villain and the action are important.

TOM HARDY (actor, "Shinzon")

I don't think anyone playing a villain thinks of themselves as being a bad person,
just a product of society. I'd look at pictures of Napoleon and Hitler and think,
"Why are these people monsters?" I'm not one to make any political comment,
because it's just about human beings. I don't think the baby comes out of his
mother's womb and is evil. So, what is evil? What is villain? It's a human being
that's been through a sequence of circumstantial situations and it's attracted
baggage, both genetic and through his observations and senses, that leads them to
commit acts of an atrocity that can be deemed as, and *are,* evil. However, you don't
go out there and play Camp Villain.

RON PERLMAN (actor, "Viceroy")

Jonathan Frakes and I worked on a play together many years ago when he got the
Star Trek series. In fact, he got that series the same day I got the Beast on *Beauty
and the Beast.* Even though we hadn't seen much of each other over the years, there

was a great fondness and a real enthusiasm that we were working together—and beating the shit out of each other.

TOM HARDY

Ron Perlman is a splendid man. His acting is fine and it was brilliant to work with him, because he's such a kind and generous and funny bloke. My first thought was that if Shinzon was a Napoleon or Hitler-y type—a spoiled bastard in a way, the right-hand man, the Viceroy, has got to be big and mean and hard and scary. I saw Ron Perlman's photo and I thought, "Oh, he's not that scary. He's got to scare me." On set one day I saw him from the back. He turned around and had these yellow eyes in and *Geez!* I was *really* scared. I couldn't look at him.

JOHN LOGAN

The actual relationship between Shinzon and Picard is much less important than what it in fact signifies, which is a father-son relationship. That to me was always the significant part of it. That Shinzon, having grown up without human beings and not knowing human beings, desperately wants to know from an older man what it is to be human. That became important to me, the actual MacGuffin of it, if you will, was relatively unimportant.

A central question was, how can Picard have an intense relationship with the antagonist? We considered any number of ways to accomplish this. I knew I wanted sort of a young male, sexy, villain, because we'd never seen that before in *Trek*. I thought that it would be really cool to have Patrick Stewart playing off an antagonist who is young and vibrant and very much like he is, and from that came the obvious connection between them. We played around with a lot of different avenues before we got there. We played with the idea, is this his long lost son he never knew he had? Or is this a son he knew he had but no one ever knew about— but that just ran so contrary to the *Trek* canon that we sort of didn't want to go there. Finally, it was Rick who came up with the idea of, what if he really is Jean-Luc Picard?

Immediately, I thought, oh, God, of course, it's the mirrors. The dark mirror. What a great way to show Picard grappling with where he is in his life now, look-ing at a sort of a younger distorted version of himself. For drama, it was just so much fun because the challenge was you had to create a character as good as Picard, whose language was as vibrant, as intelligent and as interesting as Picard's, so they could mirror one another.

PATRICK STEWART

In a slightly bizarre way Picard suddenly becomes a father; a father with a brother and a young man who is deeply troubled. So it raises questions of how much can we depend on simply our environment to make us who we are? Could all of us with a minimum provocation become extremely violent or extremely compassionate? How strong are the bonds that hold us back from extreme behavior at different times? And because it's *Star Trek*, and because this is the way we have always worked on *Next Generation* in particular, we can never just tell a story.

Every aspect of that story overlaps and interconnects, so that an issue was seen to be discussed from many different points of view and, in this case, what is the nature of a creature and how much is he influenced by his environment? How much of it is genetic? How much of it can he change? How much control do we have, in fact, over our lives? Is it possible for a human being to turn himself around, or herself around, and become a different person? Or are we for all time trapped, caught in being whatever our early experiences have made of us? It's an action movie and yet, because it's *Star Trek*, it has all of this, which, let's face it, a lot of action movies simply don't.

For the cast, the appeal of *Nemesis* was the opportunity to deepen the bond between the ensemble of characters, beginning with an early sequence in which the romance between Riker and Troi—first established in the original *Next Generation* pilot, "Encounter at Farpoint"—culminates in their long-overdue nuptials.

MARINA SIRTIS (actress, "Deanna Troi")

I'm glad the film began with the wedding of Troi and Riker, thanking God that it wasn't Troi and Worf. I would have killed myself. I *never* liked that relationship. We pretend that it never happened. Michael Dorn was subtexting his ass off, but a lot of it ended up on the cutting room floor.

LEVAR BURTON (actor, "Geordi La Forge")

One of the things that really works in this franchise, and in *Nemesis* and what the *Next Generation* has become, is the interpersonal dynamic of how these folks relate to each other. We tried to go back to who these people are and what they mean to each other.

PATRICK STEWART

All of us were anxious that the *Star Trek* family should be at the center of the film.

BRENT SPINER

Data's quest to be human is something we've covered so much from the series through the films. *Nemesis* was about family and about his need for family and to feel that he is not alone in the universe. Suddenly the opportunity arises where he finds a brother and is disappointed in who his brother turns out to be, for a whole different reason than he was disappointed in Lore, his other "brother."

JONATHAN FRAKES (actor, "William T. Riker")

It's a very interesting theme explored in the film, which is what makes each individual different? Heightened by the android's story, what makes an android's experience different than a human's experience? What about Picard is attracted to, and what is Picard terrified of, with Shinzon, his clone?

JOHN LOGAN

The real driving human core of the movie is a question that Shinzon asks Picard, which is, what is it to be human? It's a question that Data has grappled with his entire life, that Picard has grappled with in various ways, and now really has to grapple with it with Shinzon. What Picard finally comes to recognize and celebrate is something Data says to him, where he says, "I aspire to be more than what I am." The B-4 does not, nor does Shinzon. What Picard gets to, is to be human is to dream, is to hope, is to make yourself a better man. The tragedy of Shinzon is that he is incapable of doing that.

BRENT SPINER

For the record, I didn't write much of the Data stuff in the movie. Really, John Logan wrote most of that. We sort of conceived it together, but he really wrote it. My contribution was mainly in action beats. Literally, John would call me and say, "Okay, I'm up against it. Where do we go now? We've got to have an action beat that gets us out of this moment." And that's what I would do. It was fun coming up with stuff like that. I have worked in the action genre for a while now, so I had more knowledge about what we'd done and what we hadn't done. What we kept trying to come up with is stuff we hadn't done and hadn't seen.

RICK BERMAN

When it came time to find a director, Sherry Lansing said to me, "Would you be kind enough to hire Stuart Baird to direct?" And I said, "Who's Stuart Baird?" He had done two feature films. Big feature films, but he was known as an editor. And not only an editor, but the kind of editor that would come in and save a movie that was in trouble. He had done that for Paramount on the Lara Croft movies. I think somebody thought they owed him a favor and they hired him to do this movie.

STUART BAIRD (director, *Star Trek: Nemesis*)

I was brought on by Paramount asking me if I'd be interested in doing it. I wasn't sure, because I hadn't seen it. It wasn't that I wasn't a fan, it's that I just hadn't watched them. Then I read the script by John Logan, which was a really solid story, very interesting, with the intricacies of meeting yourself as a clone and the dark side and how you cope with that. And Picard's going through a life change anyway, and he's been confronting himself in other ways. All of that was interesting.

MARINA SIRTIS

It was different with Stuart Baird, because he wanted to make it his own and we kept saying things like, "You know, we wouldn't do that, because in the series . . ." And it's kind of hard for him, because he was approaching this like it's the first *Star Trek* movie. We had to make compromises of not necessarily referring back to what we would do, but letting him tell us, "Do it like you're doing this for the first time."

STUART BAIRD

I had seen a few of the TV episodes some years before in England, and I had seen one or two of the films, but I could not be called a Trekkie by any stretch of the imagination. I read the script and thought it was a very good script. I thought that maybe a fresh look, a fresh person in there, would give another dimension or another perspective to it. The story was good and I think of myself as a storyteller, so I treated it like an ordinary movie, except that it has a very great following. I was careful to follow some of the guidelines and, of course, Rick Berman and the cast steered me in the right direction if I was veering off too violently.

PATRICK STEWART

Without a doubt I think Jonathan had done a terrific job with the previous two movies, particularly *First Contact*. It had such a strong script, less strong one for *Insurrection,* but he had done well. For Jonathan as well as for us. But I think it was a sensible move not to go to him again for this.

Stuart Baird was a case of another outsider—but a *real* outsider, because he pretty much had to be entirely introduced to the world of *The Next Generation*. But he was a man with outstanding credits as an editor, particularly as an action editor, who had already directed quite successfully two movies. And he was very, very energized and enthusiastic about being involved with this one. He brought a different tone to the film, a new sort of intensity. Although at times we would say to him, "But, Stuart, you don't understand. That's *Star Trek*. You can't do that," or "You've got to do this, it's *Star Trek*."

RICK BERMAN

Stuart Baird's a very smart guy, but he knew nothing about *Star Trek* and he managed to get up on the wrong foot with a lot of people. He would call LeVar, Laverne. A lot of problems with Patrick. Not problems, but attitudinal things. And the fact that he didn't know *Star Trek* and didn't really care to learn that much about it, made it a difficult time. There were budgetary problems as well.

But early on the thought was "This is great. We're going to do a movie with an outside director, with an outside, top, A-list writer and one who really knows and loves *Star Trek*." So it was the writer who knows *Trek* and the director who doesn't know much about *Trek,* but knows a lot about action. A script was written and it was too long and *way* too wordy. It was always a bit too Shakespearean. The idea of the story went from Picard's son to a Picard clone that was the same age as Picard, where Patrick would play both characters.

PATRICK STEWART

I felt that the idea of a child was territory that had been covered before, rather regularly, and that it might lead to a somewhat sentimental or emotionally inappropriate development. Then the notion of the clone was suggested and I thought that was brilliant, because all the same connections are there, except they're even more intense. You're not just looking at somebody who is genetically similar, you're looking at yourself. Or rather as you might have been had circumstances been different for you.

RICK BERMAN

The story ended up being the Tom Hardy character was a clone of Picard, but not a look-alike. There was a lot of suspension of disbelief in the choice of actor. Obviously Tom didn't look exactly like Patrick, so that was kind of hard to buy. But we worked very hard.

STUART BAIRD

Shinzon was a multidimensional villain, and I liked the idea of discovering an actor, because, when I read the script, I knew it had to be someone who wasn't known, who was twenty-five and looked like Patrick Stewart and could go head-to-head with him, which was a challenge. I think Tom delivered in spades. I had seen hundreds of tapes. I'd heard about Tom Hardy and seen a picture. I thought, "Oh yeah, that may work," but he was doing a picture in Morocco. I sent the notes out, pages out, and he came back with none of those pages done. He made a little film himself. He had an attitude. It wasn't what I wanted, but it was an attitude.

TOM HARDY

When I arrived in L.A. to do the screen test, I got very nervous and I ballsed up the audition really badly as far as I was concerned. I left them with a tape I made at the hotel, which is what I tend to do for jobs if I really click with something and I want to do the job. The audition circuit can be so nerve-wracking, so I put myself on tape doing the scenes or working a line or working on a character, so I have homework to give them when I get there. If my audition goes badly I can say, "Here's some homework I did. Something I prepared earlier."

STUART BAIRD

He had a street quality about him, which was good. I didn't want somebody like Patrick Stewart now. I wanted Patrick Stewart or Picard under other circumstances.

Casting Tom was a risk, because he hadn't done a lot of stuff, but he had sex appeal, which is huge. There was another actor I liked, maybe a more experienced actor, but he didn't have the same sex appeal. That clinched it. I said, "This is the way I'm going to do this movie."

TOM HARDY

In approach to the character, Paramount was not tight in any way regarding the source material that they gave me to look at Patrick and to study his character, his movements, and his nuances. I had lots to work with. What it came down to is the fact that I had to find an essence as one would do with any character, to find the *human* essence of this person and then hang his nuances, his movements, his characteristics on that central issue, or as close to the center of Picard as I could get.

JOHN LOGAN

It was very important for me to recognize the mirror, how they were alike and how they were not alike. Literally, when I wrote Shinzon's dialogue, I counted out the meter of the beats to make it sound like Picard's dialogue. I knew how Patrick spoke, I knew how Picard spoke, and I wanted Shinzon to mirror that. Sometimes very technically I would try to mirror the actual language they used.

Certainly their experience shows they're both powerful leaders, both very eloquent, both able to surmount challenges, both men who are able to dream. The truly compelling thing about Shinzon is that he's a very poignant character and, in ways, very sad and very sympathetic, because as anyone from Hitchcock to John Ford to Shakespeare will tell you, the more complex your villain is, the better your story is.

PATRICK STEWART

I knew that Tom was nervous at the beginning. This was perhaps the largest screen role he'd had. It's not just that it was a large role, but he had to carry the weight of the antagonist in a *Star Trek* movie. Major scenes of dialogue, complex emotions. He was a young man with really extraordinary ability and personality. I felt, as I would anyway with any younger actor, that it was absolutely essential to try to create the best atmosphere in which he could be relaxed and do his best work.

TOM HARDY

In creating Shinzon, I had to use imagination and realize that in order to make this gentleman three-dimensional, as opposed to one-dimensional, I had to find a human issue on him. That means that I don't have to copy or mimic anything that Patrick does, which is very freeing, because suddenly you have a foundation to develop character, and then proceed to the question: "Why would he walk like that? Why would he wear these rubber teeth?"

STUART BAIRD

One of the strengths I was playing on was that the young Tom was slightly intimidated by Patrick Stewart, because he respected him so much. That played on the vulnerability side of it. I kept saying to him, "Look, who is this guy, Picard? He runs one lousy little ship somewhere in the universe. You, by your own power of will, with a bit of help from your friends, have become Napoleon, so you look down on this. You are contemptuous of it. You are angered. Also, he's two people. He's this hugely self-confident grandiose figure, and yet the other side is this maladjusted adolescent, right?"

PATRICK STEWART

I never socialized with Tom, even though we were months filming this. I felt that keeping some distance between us was proper. I wanted our life to be a life in front of the camera, apart from the small talk of sitting around waiting to work, of which, even then, there was very little. If there was an edge in the relationship, I wanted it to be visible when the camera rolled. To that extent, I think both of us were cautious of the other one.

JOHN LOGAN

We never wanted to make a one-dimensional villain that we hated. We wanted to make a really interesting, complex, serpentine character with Shinzon. I give so much credit to Jack Sowards and Nick Meyer for *Wrath of Khan*. It was absolutely my model because it worked. Every cylinder was firing perfectly. There wasn't a moment of that movie that was flabby or that wasn't involving, engaging, or exciting. We were influenced by certain elements from that movie, the primary one being these people are getting older. Time is moving on and they are dealing with that fact, which became central to *Nemesis*. It was the first thing I said to Rick when I met him for the first time. I said, "You know, when they gave Captain Kirk glasses on his birthday in *Wrath of Khan,* that's what I want to do in *Nemesis.* I want to say time moves on. Life is moving on for these people. Let's let them grow up to a certain extent."

BRENT SPINER

What was most interesting is that Data is searching for a family, and Picard actually has that going on with Shinzon. Even though Shinzon is a clone of him, he's still almost like a son in a way. He wants to appeal to his better instinct, what he knows is inside of himself, but I think where they all come to finally is that the core for all of them is themselves as that group of people.

JOHN LOGAN

As soon as we decided that Picard was going to be providing a clone, we thought it would be nice to do something similar for Data; to throw him into a situation where he had to deal with something that was very much like him, but wasn't him exactly. Since I believe the theme of *Nemesis* is family and this family in particular, for both Data and Picard, to have them meet family members they didn't know existed and in fact were adversaries of them, I think was just a really exciting opportunity.

PATRICK STEWART

I think the range of mood is one of the great things about this film. It's light and frivolous at times; playful and quite shockingly disturbing and dark at others. When I saw the film, I watched it with a handful of people who sat through the last twenty to twenty-five minutes with tears in their eyes. I actually saw it with my agent, who's a very sophisticated and worldly man, and about twenty minutes before the end of the movie he grabbed my arm and said, "You're not going to die?!? You're not going to die, are you?" I don't think he was just thinking of his commission, either.

Actually, that element of the film—clearly borrowed from the climax of *The Wrath of Khan*—has Data sacrificing himself to save the *Enterprise* just before the dying Shinzon can unleash an ultimate doomsday weapon that would destroy all life aboard the *Enterprise*. And *then*, in a moment perhaps paying homage to the ending of *The Search For Spock,* Data's doppelgänger, B-4, implies that there's a good chance that Data still lives on within him. The seeds for Data's death actually preceded *Nemesis* and had been planted early during the development of *Insurrection.*

BRENT SPINER

I said no to the first film [*Generations*], and then we got into negotiations for it and they created an attractive enough reason for me to do the first one. The second one [*First Contact*] I wanted to because I liked the script; I liked the idea. And as soon as it was presented to me, I thought it was a great idea.

Insurrection I was less inclined to do, but, again, a really good point was made to me by my girlfriend, which was: "You're going to hate it when it gets to be time to shoot this film and all your friends are there doing this movie and you're not going to be there." And I thought, you know, it's really true. Also, the fact that *Star Trek* is different from other films I do, because they asked me to do them. I don't have to win a contest in order to get the part. They call, they offer me a part, they offer me a handsome salary to do the part, and it's a good part. *And* I get to hang out with my friends and play for three months. It's an attractive proposition, always.

With *Insurrection* I had reluctance. I hadn't read the script yet, so it wasn't the script. It was the idea of doing it again at that moment. I was in the middle of a nine-month run on Broadway and I was going to have to leave the show to come back to L.A. to do another *Star Trek* movie. When I called Rick from New York, I told him, "When you write this script, consider killing Data at the end of this film." And he said, "For what reason?" and I said, "A: it will create a really interesting scene in the movie and we can count on that. And, B: the studio won't have to negotiate with me again, which is never a pleasant thing. And, C: when you get ready to do the next movie, you won't get caught off guard with whether or not I'm going to do it. You'll already know I'm not going to do it, because I'm gone and everybody will be let off the hook in a really gentle way." And he said, "I'm going to go into a meeting with producers and all and let me think about that." I said, "Okay." So about two weeks later I got the script and there was a note attached to the script from Rick that read, "Sorry. Kill you next time."

JOHN LOGAN

I think it's the best performance Brent's ever given as Data, and his name is on the movie as one of the authors. He was involved in the movie from day one, and I think he has a sense of authorship about it. All three of us working together was one of the things that made it so happy an experience. We worked together as a unit on every single element. There's nothing in *Nemesis* that wasn't the result of all of us.

RICK BERMAN

From the very beginning, John Logan and I and Brent all agreed that this story was going to end with the breaking up of the group to some degree, and with a story where Picard is undaunted by these losses and will have the spirit to carry on. That was a given. It wasn't like we were three-quarters of the way through the story and then said, "We'll kill Data!"

JOHN LOGAN

You can't do anything blithely. Every decision Rick and Brent and I made when we were coming up with the story, when Patrick became involved, when Stuart Baird became involved, we thought very seriously about and how it would refract off the entire *Trek* journey. Nothing was done lightly, that's for sure. I was so concerned with how once we made the decision for Data to sacrifice himself for Picard and the crew, how we did it because I wanted Spock. I did not want Kirk because I found that inglorious death inappropriate to the character.

JERI RYAN (actress, "Seven of Nine")

When they were shooting *Nemesis*, Paramount called Rick Berman and said, "Put Jeri Ryan in the movie," which is very nice and flattering. And I was, like, I did four years in a catsuit on *Voyager* and I just got on a David Kelley show, which was my one chance to break out of *Star Trek*, which was still a fear that I had that I wasn't going to be able to escape that. Why would she be there? It was just odd. It wasn't the right thing to do. They understood, but then Rick was, like, "Do you want to do a cameo at the wedding?" And I was, like, "No! I don't know these people, I don't want to go to their wedding!"

> The release of *Nemesis* was met with indifference, raising the question of whether or not *Star Trek* had reached a saturation point in popular culture, or, more significant, whether the idea of a morality play in the modern age of Hollywood was simply out of place.

MICHAEL PILLER (writer, *Star Trek: Insurrection*)

There's a new kind of action writing in Hollywood that I simply don't know how to do. It begins—even before a word is put down on paper—with identifying "set pieces," big self-contained action moments that are thrilling and memorable, and then finding some way to string all your set pieces into a coherent narrative. The theory is that audiences are really coming for the "eye candy"—to see how we've filled the screen with awesome visuals and special effects. Set pieces sound great in pitches and make for good coming attractions, but in my opinion, this approach almost never results in a good movie, because it abandons the fundamental demands of storytelling.

DAVID ROSSI (production associate, *Star Trek: Nemesis*)

Star Trek works best on TV. We had, relatively speaking, very small budgets for those movies, so they relied on storytelling rather than effects and action-driven plots. There's an expectation that when you see a space film, it's going to be epic in scope and the movies following *First Contact* didn't quite achieve those expectations.

JONATHAN FRAKES

I've always said this publicly, that part of the problem was the greed that drove Paramount, after the success of *Next Gen*, to develop *Voyager, Deep Space Nine,* and *Enterprise*. What they've done now, wisely, is *not* develop any television and take time between movies so that there is an appetite for that first weekend again.

RICK BERMAN

John Logan has gone on to win Tony Awards, he got nominated for Oscars, he writes James Bond movies—just a remarkable talent. And he wrote a very classical, almost Shakespearean-like *Star Trek* movie. I was very surprised at how it did both critically and financially. I don't want to say poorly, because it didn't lose money, but it didn't go anywhere near as well as anyone had hoped. And everyone was quite disappointed. I, for one, believe it's not a bad movie, but there are thousands of people who disagree with me about it. John has gone on to write one brilliant movie after another, he had the best play on Broadway with *Red*. Stuart Baird has basically gone back to being a top-notch editor.

There were a lot of people who blamed the opening date when you're sort of wedged between two huge movies—one of the Lord of the Rings movies and then a Harry Potter film. But I don't think you can blame that, because if that were true, the film would have done a different kind of business overseas where it wasn't positioned in that way. I don't know what went wrong. One could blame it on franchise fatigue again.

GLEN C. OLIVER (film & TV critic, *Ain't It Cool News*)

This would've been the perfect juncture for the Powers That Be to kick some ass and reacquire the attention of audiences that had drifted from the fold. Instead, *Nemesis* comes along, and felt like a tired movie from its very earliest promotion. Much like 2015's *Fantastic Four* movie, *Nemesis* felt completely unconvincing *as a movie,* regardless of its subject matter, from our earliest sense of the picture. It felt completely uninvested in itself and its creative potential. More like a knock-off than many people were comfortable with. It felt like . . . more of the same.

BRANNON BRAGA (writer, *Star Trek: First Contact*)

It seemed like the characters were going back to the first season. I didn't know if the people cared about the "Imzadi" stuff between Riker and Troi. I think a franchise is definitely showing its fatigue when you do an evil twin story. It's hard for me to say, but I think Rick's heart was in *Enterprise*. It was kind of the last nail in the coffin for the *Next Gen* crew. I don't even think Paramount wanted to do a *Next Generation* movie. They were ready to do a new crew, and Rick very wisely said that although a good idea at first glance, we have a new crew coming into *Enterprise*; do you really want to introduce a new crew in the movie, too? That's too much to ask of the audience.

JOHN LOGAN

The first cut of the film was something like two hours and forty minutes. To which my response was, "And this is a problem?" One of the ironies is I felt a responsibility to all the characters to really give them something to do, or to do my best to give them storylines and little arcs that the audience could follow. At the same time, we introduced a very complex villain, a whole new race, a very complex situation with Romulus and Remus and the empire, which took up a lot of screen time. It was always a very delicate balancing act between how much we could afford to pay homage and spend time with the characters we like, and also tell this story that involves people we don't know at all. At the end of the day, we ended up cutting a lot of stuff I was really fond of.

MICHAEL DORN (actor, "Worf")

When it was over, it wasn't like "Oh my God!" *Nemesis* was a tough shoot. I didn't think it was as much a sense of finality as it was . . . odd.

BRENT SPINER

I never think about *Star Trek* when I'm not doing it. I only think about it when I'm working on it. And I do think there is a sort of negative wish fulfillment that goes on for anything that has success. The American way is to put something on a pedestal and do your best to knock it down. We've done that with every sort of icon we've ever had in America. We love seeing success, but it'd be an even sweeter taste to watch it fail. I think it's a peculiarity of America. It's the whole reason for celebrity, frankly. We create celebrities just so we can destroy them.

JONATHAN FRAKES

With *Nemesis* it was as if the Fates stepped in. We had John Logan, who's an A-list writer. We had what was a great company back together again. Tom Hardy was a brilliant guest star. My take on it, though, was that there was not enough of the family. It was a little too much of Shinzon and not enough of Picard and Data. The first weekend people came to see Bones, Kirk, and Spock, or Picard and Data, you know what I mean? The story of *Nemesis* was very much a story about the obsession of Shinzon, Tom Hardy's character. The front end of the movie with the wedding of Riker and Troi, and which was so charming, just got cut to bits. We originally had Whoopi and Wil Wheaton and all of these Easter eggs in there, and Brent sang. It was a big deal that got cut up to nothing.

LEVAR BURTON

The whole shebang was lacking in a vision that was appreciative of the field of play. Mr. Baird didn't get *Star Trek* and Mr. Baird didn't appreciate *Star Trek,* unlike J.J. Abrams, who was excited to get his hands on the franchise.

GLEN C. OLIVER

At any other juncture in time, *Nemesis* might've been forgiven—and further *TNG* movies, or a miniseries, or something, might have been generated to make up for it. But *Nemesis* came at a critical moment in which *Star Trek* needed to make a statement of some sort. It needed to scream *"I'm still here! I still matter!"* But in concept and execution, *Nemesis* . . . was an argument against continuing *Star Trek*, instead of championing its cause. And, even more dangerously, it felt this way from its inception. Fans, purposefully or not, reacted in the only way they knew how: by asking, "Why should we support a franchise which isn't even acknowledging its own best interests?"

A waning and increasingly skeptical fan base, unwavering oversight that was loath to take any chances to correct the course of a franchise that was very much adrift, a director who did not appreciate or understand *Star Trek*—and wasn't even a terribly capable director at that—awkward pacing wrapped in murky photography backed by inconsistent visual effects, all conveying an insular concept which was difficult for broader audiences to access? It was a *perfect* recipe for failure, and that's exactly what came out of the oven both perceptually and artistically.

MARINA SIRTIS

To have someone who comes in who's never, ever seen *Star Trek* before, and when you say to him, "You know, my character wouldn't do that," and he says, "I don't care, do it anyway." First of all, you want to punch his lights out, but, second of all, he is the director and you have to do what he says, because he just keeps making you do it over and over again until you do. It was like you had to kind of go with it and say, "Okay, I'm just going to see what happens and try and make this work."

JONATHAN FRAKES

It didn't help that Stuart Baird was trying to reinvent the wheel, but I don't think you can blame the director for *Nemesis*' fate. At the same time, I remember calling him and saying, "If there's anything I can do to help you, I've been around these people for all these years." And I think in the same phone call I said, "We're really here to help. You'll find that we're a very strong team and we know how to do this and we're really happy to help make the best movie you can." And he didn't pick up either of those offers. In retrospect, it seems like arrogance. Why *wouldn't* you accept that kind of offer?

MARINA SIRTIS

The director was an idiot.

PATRICK STEWART

I will say that at the end of the film I'm saying good-bye to Riker and I found myself completely caught up in the moment. I broke down. Out of the clear blue sky, my emotions overwhelmed me. I collapsed in Jonathan's arms and felt such a fool. The entire crew watched me cry and then started muttering, "What's going on? Has he been drinking or something?" But in that moment, absolutely everything coalesced—the feelings that I had for these people over the years. Saying good-bye was absolutely terrifying and agonizing for me.

You know, when I finished shooting *X-Men* in Vancouver, I spent three days driving back to Los Angeles, stopping at small motels in Washington and along the Oregon coast, eating in truck stops. I was quite outside the Hollywood–Los Angeles–New York world, having encounters with ordinary people in areas where they don't expect to run into someone like me. I was continually touched by the strength of feeling that people have about *The Next Generation*. It's something quite profound—and it's very gratifying, because when I started as an actor, I had no ambition to reach an audience in that kind of way.

When the history of popular culture in North America is written, I do think *Star Trek* will have to play a very significant role. From the sixties with Bill Shatner and Leonard Nimoy to today, it has had *such* an impact on popular culture.

JOHN LOGAN

I felt things were left really nicely in terms of the characters moving forward with their lives and finally achieving their proper destiny. Meaning, Riker and Deanna get married and Riker gets his own command and he's going off in his own ship. The idea that Picard has dealt with this tormented part of himself, his past, and dealt with it both in terms of physical losses and the loss of people that he works with, and has worked with for fifteen years, and yet still is excited to go off where no man has been before or woman has been before. I think it leaves on a very sort of positive note in terms of saying good-bye to these characters. We did it with dignity in a way that is appropriate to them.

RICK BERMAN

The ironic thing is that everyone from the studio to me thought we'd crafted a really good movie. And *nobody* came to see it. It wasn't even a question of not getting good reviews. Any *Star Trek* movie opened and it would have a huge opening weekend, but this one didn't. Now, why? I understand and appreciate the criticisms of the production or script, but, to this day, I have some difficulty understanding why it met with such a poor reception. John Logan has gone on to write huge movies, but the movie backfired and there's certainly a lot of room for discussion of why. It was sad and a little baffling to me.

DEEP SPACE NINE

(1993-1999)

FAR BEYOND THE STARS

"I DON'T BELIEVE THE FEDERATION HAS *ANY* BUSINESS BEING HERE!"

Somehow, through all of the chaos and his own diminishing health, Gene Roddenberry had proven his critics wrong: He *could* do it again and *did*. Lightning had indeed been caught in a bottle a second time with *Star Trek: The Next Generation*, elevating the franchise far beyond its already august accomplishments. So when word filtered out from the final frontier that there would actually be a third live-action series, the question was whether or not it could work, since this time it would be created without the involvement of Roddenberry, who had recently passed away.

In developing a sister series to *TNG*, cocreators Rick Berman and Michael Piller, who would bring aboard that show's season-three producer Ira Steven Behr as an integral part of the staff and the show's development, realized that they would need to address the liabilities of a universe in which interpersonal conflict was anathema. As a result, that show, ultimately called *Deep Space Nine* and set on a space station of the same name, became a place populated by races from across the galaxy, only some of them members of the Federation. The world they inhabit is gritty and alien, unlike the sterile and utopian confines of a starship inhabited solely by Starfleet officers.

RICK BERMAN (cocreator/executive producer, *Star Trek: Deep Space Nine*)

When you create a premise pilot, which is what we did with *Deep Space Nine*, you create a two-hour show where you have to set up an entire world and an entire group of characters and what brings them together, and at the same time tell an entertaining and meaningful story. You have a big job cut out for you. Michael Piller and I started creating the premise for this show and the backstories for the characters and the relationships these characters were going to have and what sort of story would unfold, spending months working on it. What the *Next Generation* pilot "Encounter at Farpoint" and five and a half years of *Star Trek* at that point did was allow me to know what was possible and what wasn't. What our visual effects guys could give us and what they couldn't. What sets we could expect, how much we could expect to get done, and what was pie in the sky.

Michael and I talked about *Star Trek* spin-offs and we talked about a lot of other shows as well. There were many series we discussed. The only one that was really a spin-off was *Deep Space Nine*.

MICHAEL PILLER (cocreator/executive producer, *Star Trek: Deep Space Nine*)

We pretty much knew that there were only three kinds of series that you could do in space. One was going to be on a ship, one was on a space station, and one was on a planet's surface. We talked about the planet's surface for a while, doing a Wild West town, but we realized that we were going to wind up having to shoot on location up in the mountains above Hollywood and thought that was untenable. We basically turned our attention to the space station idea. So then it became, where do you put the space station? The idea of putting it at Gibraltar, or a key critical spot in the Roddenberry universe where there was danger and threats and things like that, seemed to be a logical extension. Then you had to figure out what was in the Straits of Gibraltar, what made it such a strategic location.

RICK BERMAN

I went to Gene and mentioned we were thinking about a spin-off, and he said, "Great," and that we should talk about it some time. Unfortunately we never did, because he was not well then and he got worse and worse.

MARINA SIRTIS (actress, "Deanna Troi")

The truth is that if Gene was alive, *DS9* would have never been made, because he absolutely said no to it when it was presented to him. He said *Star Trek* is about exploring space, it's not about a hotel in space. So it would never have happened.

ROD RODDENBERRY (son of Gene Roddenberry)

I'm very . . . I keep using the word "forgiving," but I don't think it's the right word to use. "Accepting." I don't think they represent the Roddenberry ideology that well. They're fine, they're *Star Trek*. They're a little bit more *Star Wars*. They still had messages. I'm proud of Rick and the entire team for what they did. I'm not a basher; I don't hate it, I just never really got too into it. [*Star Trek* archivist] Richard Arnold said one thing that stuck with me, which was, "*TOS* and, especially, *Next Gener-*

ation had a humanity that was a better humanity. And in *Deep Space Nine*, specifically, that was us today. They were dealing with the same sort of issues we were dealing with today, our petty issues of selfishness, and so it wasn't necessarily that intellectually evolved humanity." Not as much as *Next Generation* was. *Next Generation*, we were already better than we are now. With *Deep Space Nine*, we had taken a step back to our little petty squabbles and things like that.

RICK BERMAN

I got a call from [former NBC network president] Brandon Tartikoff, who had just been made chairman of Paramount Pictures. Brandon was one of the biggest names in television. I went up to his office and he said to me, "I want to do a new series, I want you to do it, and I want it to start next year." What I learned later is this was a traditional fashion of Tartikoff's, and he said, "My idea is *The Rifleman* in space . . . a father and son out in space." He didn't know anything about *Star Trek*. So, I got together with Michael Piller and we started thinking about a father and a son in space. That was the beginning of *Deep Space Nine*.

SUSAN SACKETT (assistant to Gene Roddenberry)

Gene had not approved *Deep Space Nine*. He *hated* it and he did not want them doing it. A week after he died, they took it and ran with it, and that's not something I was happy about. "Gene's gone, now we can do *Deep Space Nine*." They did not hesitate. Within two weeks, they got a green light on it. When he was alive, he said, "You can't do it. I don't approve of this." I think it was the premise and the characters. Gene had an ego, so maybe it was because he wasn't involved in creating it and felt it was too soon. I know he did not want it or like it. And they lied and said Gene approved it.

> This assertion is vehemently disputed by Rick Berman, who publically commented, "Michael Piller and I pitched our ideas for *DS9* to Gene and he gave us his enthusiastic approval." As always, there are multiple sides to every story. Berman clarified these remarks for this volume.

RICK BERMAN

Gene was very ill. Most of the encounters I had with him were at his home in Bel Air. I specifically remember going to sit with him and Michael in his kitchen and basically telling Gene that the studio had asked us to develop a new show and that we were working on it. I can't say he was excited about it. Nor was he in any way upset about it. He just kind of nodded and said it was really interesting and he'd love to know more. It was discussed vaguely with Gene, who never seemed extremely enthusiastic nor in a way problematic with it. This was at a very early stage and he really wasn't interested. I think it maybe wasn't a question of disinterest. I think it was more a question of he was not very well at that point.

Michael Piller and I were both very close to Gene, and Gene learned quite early in the *Next Generation* process that we could be trusted with *Star Trek*. When we developed this new series, every step of the way we had Gene sitting on our shoulders. And many things were rejected, because "Gene wouldn't buy that." I very much believe that Gene would be very pleased with the way that show went.

MICHAEL PILLER

The philosophy of Gene Roddenberry guided us. He didn't have any exposure to the specifics of this series, but he was with us in anything having to do with *Star Trek*. We had learned from him and from experience that stories that combine science fiction with philosophy with optimism, with a comment on social issues and an exploration of human values, are the stories that work for *Star Trek*. Those are the stories that worked for us.

RICK BERMAN

I felt a responsibility, especially after 1991 when Gene passed away, to try to keep *Star Trek* as close to his vision of what it would be. I wanted to be able to bend the rules but not break them. I always thought that was a very important element of one of my responsibilities for the show. In terms of conflict, I think in *Deep Space Nine* we found a way around that.

IRA STEVEN BEHR (executive producer, *Star Trek: Deep Space Nine*)

There were plenty of people around—Richard Arnold and those people—who were clearly shaking their heads and whispering amongst themselves, thinking that Gene would disapprove. I could tell right away that it might turn out to be a disaster, but it would be a different type of disaster. And I was much relieved by that feeling.

I've given many statements over the years saying that if he had lived, I can't believe that as the show went on he could have remained as negative about it as he might have allegedly been at the start. I'd like to think that as a creative human being, he would have come to appreciate it. But, the more stories I hear about Gene, I'm not so sure that would have happened. I know his little posse *hated* the show; they were *not* fans.

DAVID LIVINGSTON (supervising producer, *Star Trek: Deep Space Nine*)

Well, it wasn't *Star Trek*. It was a grounded piece that made it a character piece. The characters on *Deep Space Nine* were strong, grounded, and diverse. That's a gift that Ira and the writers brought to it.

BRADLEY THOMPSON (writer, *Star Trek: Deep Space Nine*)

Ira always said it's all about character. This is not about whether the "freck screen demodulator is capable of being realigned with other technobabble."

MICHAEL PILLER

Rick didn't come to me, I went to him. The truth is, I had been bugging Rick for probably two years to get the studio to consider a spin-off of *Star Trek* and to create another series. I came out of the network world, and when you had a huge phenomenal hit like *The Next Generation,* you did another show. There's no question in my mind that the audience was ready for another series.

Rick agreed with me and went to the studio. It was either [Paramount TV executives] John Symes or John Pike who said, "We will never do another *Star Trek* series at Paramount. We are still negotiating the contracts with Roddenberry's lawyers, and we've got ten lawyers assigned to *Star Trek* now; we're not going to do this again!" And then something fundamental changed and that was the leadership at the head of the studio. Brandon Tartikoff came in and took over Paramount and the first thing he said when he sat down was, "I want another space show."

RICK BERMAN

Brandon Tartikoff, who was running Paramount at the time, said that he and Kerry McCluggage, whom he had just brought on board to take over the television division, wanted to do another series to coincide with the fourth season of *Next Generation*. He said he wanted a science-fiction show and I said, "You mean a *Star Trek* show?" He said, "I don't care if it's *Star Trek*. I want another science-fiction show I can say is being created by the guy who's been bringing you *Star Trek: The Next Generation*."

The one idea he suggested to me was, "Let's do *The Rifleman* in space. A father and son going around righting wrongs." And when I went back and discussed that with Michael, who I had asked to develop this with me, it didn't seem like the kind of thing that we really wanted to do. But we did end up taking elements of it, because *Deep Space Nine* would have the lead character have his son with him when they arrive on this space station. I went back to Brandon and told him that I had been working with Mike Piller on a number of ideas. It was one of those, "Oh, and by the way, I just happen to have one right here."

MICHAEL PILLER

We decided on *Deep Space Nine* in a very fledgling stage, and we went to the studio guys and laid out a pretty general idea. They said go and work on it, and we spent a number of months coming up with the premise before the story was written with the earliest bible of the show: what the location would be, what the backstory would be, and so on.

RICK BERMAN

We must have had fifty meetings before we felt comfortable with what we had come up with. The premise of the show grew the way a child grows from something that is young and simple to something that is more complex. The premise never made a major left or right turn. The characters and the premise became more focused, as did the settings, the people and the interrelationships.

Mike and I knew that if we were ever going to do another *Star Trek* show, it would have to take place somewhere where adventure could come to us as opposed to us going to adventure. It was very important to us that *Deep Space Nine* had to be different, because it was going to be on the air for three years along with *Next Generation,* so we really couldn't plunk seven people on another spaceship and have it plopping around the galaxy. It just didn't seem right.

We had structured into *Next Generation* a conflict between the people living near this wormhole, the Cardassians and the Bajorans; the Bajorans being the kind of sweet, good people and the Cardassians being the militaristic creeps.

This was a Cardassian space station that was very cold and inhospitable and that we were asked to take over, because of the political unrest in the area.

MICHAEL PILLER

It's conflict on every level we could find it. They are in conflict with their environment. They are in conflict with each other, because the *Enterprise* had had everybody with the same agenda. Everybody was basically on a mission and they all got along very well. Here, they're thrown together with aliens, different species, and all have to coexist on the same space station. All of them have different agendas and goals. The character of Quark wants to fill his pockets, and the character of Odo wants to catch him.

Right there, you have conflict. We had Major Kira as our Bajoran liaison, and here again is a very deliberate tilt. We made the Bajorans a very mystical, spiritual people, as different from the humanist, logical humans of the twenty-fourth century as we could. While we protected the vision of humanity that we inherited from Gene, we put that in direct conflict with a very different kind of people. So those people are in conflict on every level.

RICK BERMAN

Gene Roddenberry was a great believer in not wanting any conflict between the characters on the *Enterprise,* which was very frustrating for us because that's what good drama is born from. And we didn't want to break Gene's rules, and in so doing there was not a lot of conflict between Starfleet officers; that's why we developed the concept of the environment and put our people into an environment where there are a lot of characters who are *not* Starfleet officers, and that enabled us to develop that conflict.

MICHAEL PILLER

Gene also believed a great deal in the diversity of species, and there was room for all these different species in the universe. We had just not made them regularly a part of the show. Gene would be the first to tell you it doesn't matter what alien race you're talking about, how hideous they seem to be. There are no bad aliens; each of them has a culture that must be defined, recognized, and appreciated for what it is. With the Bajorans, for instance, we simply created a new alien race with a new set of circumstances and didn't change Gene's vision of what humanity is in the twenty-fourth century. We were simply showing how we are affected by conflict with that alien race.

For instance, Bajoran spirituality does not go against the atheist beliefs of Gene. If he were still with us—and he was on our shoulders as we thought about these conceptual issues—I don't think it would bother him one bit. What he felt very strongly about is that humans, and to some degree Federation members, had a humanist attitude. His humans do not overtly celebrate religious beliefs. What we had simply done in creating an environment that brings conflict to our people, which we desperately wanted to do, is to put a group of people with a group of aliens that are different than we are, who had a difference and a conflict with our humanist beliefs.

Giving them strong spiritual mystical orbs and prophet worship forced our humanist people to deal with another alien race that is as different from us as the Klingons are.

IRA STEVEN BEHR

One night Michael Piller and I went to a baseball game and, without any preamble, he said, "I want to talk to you." I thought we were just going to a ball game, but he starts talking about a new series coming along. I'm, like, "Okay, interesting. Congratulations." In the very first discussion about it, he said, "I'm going to give you the bible." The script had not been written yet. It was just the bible. He said, "I want you to read this and I want to tell you that if you decide to come back and do the show with me, it's a show that's going to reflect your sensibilities a lot more than *The Next Generation*. And if you come back, after two years I will hand you the show."

Shocked is probably the accurate description of how I felt, because Michael wasn't a bullshit artist, so if he was saying it, he meant it. Part of the shock came from the fact that if Michael Piller had been working for me on a show and then in the midst of the absolute hell season that was going on, and knowing that there was another hell season coming up, and he had bailed on me like I bailed on him after the third season of *Next Generation*, I'm not sure I would have forgiven him so easily, to be honest. I take that shit very seriously. But it never seemed to affect our relationship one iota. He told me it was on a space station and he kept saying that what happens on the show is going to have consequences. I went back home and I read the bible and I saw certain things in it that, if I allowed it to, could speak to me: the captain who had suffered a great defeat and a great loss. The isolated shape-shifter sheriff, even though at the time he said I should think of it as Clint Eastwood; the young doctor.

Basically, I kept thinking of the frontier. You know, "We're on the edge of the frontier. No one knows what's behind the wormhole. There are these wormhole aliens. There's this Bajoran culture." I can't say I fell in love with it or anything that romantic, but I was certainly interested in it. My wife was *not* surprised for some reason that Michael would do something like that. I talked to my sister and said, "Hey, you're not going to believe this . . . ," and she said, "Who gets a second chance like this? It ended so badly on *Next Generation* and left such a bad taste in your mouth. Why not say yes?"

MICHAEL PILLER

I credit Ira with the ultimate long-term success of *Deep Space Nine*. Those represented a great couple of years for me, because at one point I had *Deep Space Nine, Voyager,* and *Legend* on at the same time. But I felt it was not fair to the show or to Ira to maintain a control and take his title of executive producer on *Deep Space Nine* while my attention was really focused on the other shows. It's just one of those things that you know is going to be in good hands. Eventually, a lot of the cast was concerned when I was basically turning things over to Ira, but I also told them that I would not turn the show over to somebody I didn't have an absolute, fundamental trust in. I would say a year or two later they didn't even remember I was still alive. Ira loved the pilot and really thought we had created the circumstances to do something special there.

IRA STEVEN BEHR

Mike said I should meet with Rick, who I imagined was probably not too thrilled . . . or at least I could say that, rightly, he would say, "This guy jumped ship once before. How do we know he's going to come back and stay?" So we had a meeting in the commissary and I could tell—or I felt I could tell, because I don't know what's on Rick's mind—that he was sizing me up to see if this was just some kind of a wacky Michael Piller idea or if I really had the wherewithal to make a commitment. I guess it was the commitment that they wanted. The meeting went fine.

HERMAN ZIMMERMAN (production designer,
Star Trek: Deep Space Nine)

From my point of view, Gene Roddenberry created, without being maudlin, an eternal idealization of the future. The characters that he created came out of his imagination pretty much from whole cloth. You could compare "The Cage" to *The Sign of Four,* which was written by Arthur Conan Doyle. Sherlock Holmes and Watson and Moriarty and Lastrade and the Baker Street Irregulars each have a charm and an identity that is immediately discernible from that very first novel. Seventy years later, a fellow named Nicholas Meyer can take the same characters and write a very believable Arthur Conan Doyle story, maybe even better, using all those same characters and ideas and call it *The Seven-Per-Cent Solution.*

Gene Roddenberry created Kirk and Spock and McCoy, Uhura, Sulu, Chekov, Picard, Riker, Troi, etc., and when they were first introduced to the audience, just like those characters from Arthur Conan Doyle, they were whole. They haven't changed, although they may have grown. They've been interpreted, and that's the beauty of Gene's vision, from his positive view of the future to his ability to mix and match personalities that play well together. I think any good director, writer, producer can take those criteria, those characters, that idea, that vision, and make it work. Within that we have the grittiness that Nicholas Meyer prefers, the Hyatt Regency approach that Gene liked in *The Next Generation,* and we have the bizarre, darker alien version of the stories in *Deep Space Nine.*

RICK BERMAN

When people referred to the show as dark, to me the connotation was of the show having a bleak or eerie quality to it, which I don't believe it did. Our series was designed to have the same uplifting messages—and would deal with the same metaphorical way of approaching the future that both of Gene Roddenberry's series did previously. I didn't think it was going to be "dark" in terms of a dark outlook toward the future, and that's where I think it was misunderstood.

DAVID CARSON (director, *Star Trek: Deep Space Nine*)

One of the things they were striving for is to look at the people in the twenty-fourth century who are not as much at peace with themselves as the crew of the *Enterprise* was in *Star Trek: The Next Generation.* In *The Next Generation,* it was always a big thing when a character went through an emotional or personal crisis. The stories usually end at peace with hope, not only hope in society but hope in the behavior of people, who most of the time behave in an exemplary manner.

I have a feeling that the darker, grittier tone is one of the reasons they wanted me to direct the pilot. They wanted my experience with grit in *Star Trek.* This was a much grittier environment than the *Enterprise,* which was part of the attraction.

MICHAEL PILLER

I had gotten a letter from, like, twenty-five grade school children in the middle of the country saying, "We've read"—this was before the show premiered—"that this is going to be a dark new series," and, with their teacher's help, they were saying, "Please don't do this. We use this as a tool of hope, of teaching potential, and so forth. Don't change the vision." That's what scared us when the misinterpretation was put to the word "darkness." See, in conflict there's also humor. That's the secret of all situation comedies, that you have an enduring conflict. In our case, we found that the kind of conflict on this show also yielded a certain kind of humor within the context of our kind of drama.

This may be a strange analogy, but there's an analogy between *The Next Generation* and *Deep Space Nine* and two popular comic book superheroes. *Next Generation* is like Superman and *Deep Space Nine* is like Batman. Clearly, the complications and the psychological underpinnings and the quality of the storytelling and the angst is greater in Batman, but they both exist in the same DC Comics universe and they occasionally meet. The point is, if you think of all of the pale imitations of Superman, they have all gone out the window. But Batman has endured because it touches people in a certain, specific way. It is a more adult comic book, and somehow we managed to do that with *Deep Space Nine*.

BRANNON BRAGA (coproducer, *Star Trek: The Next Generation*)

When Michael Piller went to do *Deep Space Nine,* he essentially left *Next Gen.* He would give notes on scripts and stuff, but he was not involved in the day-to-day writing of the show. Jeri Taylor took over, and Ron Moore and I and the other writers really started to spread our wings. I'm very proud of the work we did in seasons six and seven; there was some cool shit. But there was a moment, some time in season six, when Michael came to me and asked me to come to the writing staff of *Deep Space Nine.* I'll never forget sitting in his office and him saying, "You would be the staff's secret weapon." I don't know what he meant by that, but I kind of liked the idea of being a secret weapon. Then again, who wants to be a secret?

I really was tormented by the decision, because there was something cool about *Deep Space Nine,* but my main reason for turning him down was because I really wanted to see *Next Gen* through to the end. Maybe I knew there was greatness to be had at the end of the road—and there was. I do not regret the decision, because I ended up doing the *Next Gen* series finale, "All Good Things." I gambled with staying on *Next Gen*; I didn't know there would be a *Voyager* at that point. He was disappointed.

IRA STEVEN BEHR

We didn't really know what the show was yet at that point. At the time it was myself, Peter Allan Fields, who turned out to be one of the most interesting people I've ever known—Pete's a pistol that not everybody gets, and Pete doesn't give a fuck whether they get him or not. Just a brilliant man. Self-destructive in certain ways, but still a brilliant man and a friend of mine. It was just the two of us for a while, and then Robert Wolfe came on. Nothing was written in stone yet, so I felt that I could contribute pretty much from the beginning.

PETER ALLAN FIELDS (producer, *Star Trek: Deep Space Nine*)

I was on *Next Generation* in the fifth season, and at the end of that season Michael and Rick were off writing the pilot for *Deep Space Nine*. Michael said to me that it was in the contract that if *Deep Space Nine* was a go, they had the right, if they chose, to move me over. I was delighted when Michael called me and said that's what he was doing. I did not know a lot of *Next Generation* or even *Star Trek*. At least with *Deep Space Nine* I was going to be in on the ground floor and have an equal chance for survival.

At that stage in the season, the writers are the ones who do shape it. The executive producers are the ones who have an idea about what the characters should be like, and the idea can change from episode to episode. In the beginning, though, I was the only one there. Michael and Rick were somewhere over in the other building writing the pilot, and I was sitting there, wondering what I was supposed to do. I remember saying, "Geez, we now boldly sit where no one has sat before."

Deep Space Nine didn't go anywhere and the pilot kept changing, which was pleasing because everything was developing. Then Ira came in and for a while it was just Mike and Ira and I, and we had a great time. I'd been writing for something like twenty-eight years, and the most fun that I have ever had in this profession was the first four or five months there. It was very hard work, but Ira and I were working together. He's clinically insane . . . and I love him very much.

IRA STEVEN BEHR

I came on *DS9* on June 8, 1992, and a week later Mike was still doing the pilot and the show hadn't been cast yet. We were functioning totally in the dark. Peter Allan Fields and I sat down for about five days and we just came up with story ideas. One of them was "Dax," one was "Babel," one was "Captive Pursuit," one of them did not fly, but it was one of the proudest moments we had together, because here we were, I'd never met Peter before, did not know much about *DS9*. No one did at the time, although I knew more than most people, but we came up with all these little stories and most of them actually got made.

ROBERT HEWITT WOLFE (producer, *Star Trek: Deep Space Nine*)

I had sold the story for "A Fistful of Datas" to *Next Generation*. What happened with *Deep Space Nine* is they had an outline, or a story doc, for "Q-Less," and it didn't work. There were a lot of issues with it. It's tough when you're a freelancer and the show is not on the air yet to figure out the rhythms of the show and what you're writing toward. So they showed it to me and asked me what I thought. I sort of said that the whole final ten minutes as proposed wasn't necessary. The story ends with this alien egg going into the wormhole. There was a whole second half of an adventure when they were off the station, and Q was less involved. I was, like, "No, this is about *this* segment. This is the sweet spot of the story." They thought that was smart. I think Ira and Michael liked that and they brought me in to write the script and then they liked the first draft and hired me onto staff.

IRA STEVEN BEHR

What we wanted to do was give the series an identity, something I never really felt that *TNG* had, except in the most cursory way. We wanted to say, "Okay, this is *DS9*, this is what *DS9* can do, this is a different series, a different kind of *Star Trek* series," and that's what we wanted to do. Look, I didn't create the fucking show, I didn't create these major characters; they were dumped in our lap, almost from day one.

Mike was off doing pilot rewrites on *DS9* when I was off with Pete Fields trying to get freelance writers to write the first episodes. We were thinking about what the hell the series is going to be, and that's all we'd ever really done. What is the series? Not what Mike and Rick thought it was going to be, because to tell you the truth, I think they were trying to get a pilot onto the air and struggled to come up with something different. But they hadn't a fucking clue what was in the Gamma Quadrant or what the Gamma Quadrant meant or what was through the wormhole, or how the show was going to be told.

RICK BERMAN

The story for the first episode was forty pages long and extremely well-defined when Michael sat down to write the teleplay. He wrote a first draft and then he and I spent about a month working on it. We discussed it, we made changes, draft after draft, and finally we got it to a point where we were pretty happy with it. But no one had seen it except the two of us. We had worked on it for a few weeks and Michael then became unhappy. We were looking for a direction and, as is typical of Michael, he was frustrated and felt that something wasn't working. He did a rewrite that was not a major rewrite at all, but it was a rewrite that brought into it the ideas that we had discussed all along that had to do with the 1992 Los Angeles riots; the idea of people rebuilding and of people living in an area that had been damaged and had been violated. And the *spirit* that goes into the rebuilding of it. It was a good change, but not a major change. More important than being a good change, it was a change that made Michael happy.

MICHAEL PILLER

When I looked at the teleplay, I was really troubled, because I was not falling in love with my own dialogue and my own characters, and I was extremely critical. Rick will tell you that throughout the process he had said to me things like "It must be terrible waking up every morning and being as negative as you are." But I felt very strongly—and Rick will agree that I dragged him into this rewrite kicking and screaming—that the first hour was flat, nothing happened, and that it was basically doling out the characters for everyone to see.

I said, "Sisko's not a hero. Sisko's got to come in and have something to do and have a problem that he has to deal with as a hero." While our mystery is unfolding, which would ultimately blossom in the second hour, Sisko must take this situation by the hand. In the first draft of the script, our guys essentially come to the Beverly Center mall in Los Angeles and decide to stay. I thought that was great, and the studio said, "We want to open with a shot of the Promenade and people gambling."

So I wrote it that way, and I realized it didn't work. Sadly, though, while I was going through this agonizing process, we had the riots in Los Angeles, and both Rick and I wanted to somehow say something in our show about humanity coexisting and coming together. And we wanted to build this into the alien interaction that we had in the second hour of the script. I had also started thinking that it was not a dramatic situation for a man to come to the Beverly Center. It's not very dramatic for someone to go to their favorite mall and decide to stay. *But* for a man who goes to South Central Los Angeles and finds it in ruins and decides to stay, *that's* dramatic. I argued with Rick that we should come to a space station that's in ruins and that Sisko must begin the rebuilding process in the first hour in order to be driving the story.

IRA STEVEN BEHR

What we were trying to show without really articulating it while we were doing it, was to demonstrate that Sisko's job is, in a way, more important, or certainly more complicated, than Picard's or Kirk's, because they're explorers and he's a builder. What he has to do is basically build an alliance and build a relationship. It's a different thing than they get to do. They get to have fun. He gets to have fun, too, but he has to make sure that his fun doesn't come and bite him on the ass three episodes down the line. There was a whole bubbling cauldron that seemed to take on some new heat, at least for the writers, and we realized we were on a unique show with its own identity.

MICHAEL PILLER

I was listening to the radio on the anniversary of Martin Luther King's birthday—a man who stood firm on the subject of violence—that violence is not the answer. And it didn't matter what anybody promoted him to do—whether you were black of white—he refused to find a violent solution to the problems, the very severe problems of this country. As I wrote *Star Trek*, there was no greater responsibility than to continue to tell that message in any way that I could. So when you see Captain Picard or Commander Sisko decide that logic, reason, and communication are the way to solve problems and not turn to violence, then we were telling something to our audience that needs to be said on a regular basis. It's very important.

IRA STEVEN BEHR

The ideas that had been thrown around since the beginning of the series were definitely shots in the dark about what the series was going to be, because I do think there was a kind of nervousness about it. Even with the creators. "We're doing something different, which was good, but how different dare we be and what exactly do we want to do with the series?" It still had to be *Star Trek*. And then Peter and myself and Wolfie [Robert Hewitt Wolfe] and the guys who came later said, "Well, I don't care if it's *Star Trek*."

I once made an offhand comment to Mike Piller, and he got *very* worried about it, because I basically said, "I don't care about the franchise, I just care about *Deep Space Nine* and making that the best show possible." It wasn't really in those words, it was more inflammatory, but that's what we were trying to do. We were trying to define the series and not listen to anyone else, and for the most part, given the fact that it is *Star Trek* and it carries all that goddamn baggage attached to it, Paramount and Rick and Mike were very supportive. We were able to push it as far as the shackles of the franchise would let us go.

Whereas most of the spin-offs from the original *Star Trek* took place on a starship (whether it be *The Next Generation, Voyager,* or *Enterprise*) and represented variations on a theme of "boldly going," *Deep Space Nine* and its setting required an entirely different approach to create a working and living environment.

DAVID CARSON

The space station was designed in such a way that is completely different from the ship, so it does have a different feeling to it. It's sort of like a town, in a funny kind of way. A town in terms of its social setup. I suppose a good analogy would be on the *Enterprise* we very rarely leave the officers or people who are driving the ship and that side of things, but there are hundreds of other people on board the *Enterprise* doing whatever it is they do. One of the things *Deep Space Nine* did was expand its frame of reference from not just the officers that deal with the space station, but to the other people whom we rarely see.

WINRICH KOLBE (director, *Star Trek: Deep Space Nine*)

Deep Space Nine is *Gunsmoke*. It's the town that everybody comes to. Get the characters in there. That's actually the selling point, and because of its setting, it became more of a character show. We had people in there that represented the different opinions. We didn't have to schlep through some deserted canyon in order to get there, they had to come to us.

DAVID WEDDLE (writer, *Star Trek: Deep Space Nine*)

This genre does have a lot in common with westerns. I didn't realize it when we first started on *Deep Space Nine,* but I came to realize it because I brought up westerns all the time in the writing room as analogies for whatever we were working on. And the fact is that they are both allegorical forms of storytelling. The American westerns, they exist in a sort of imagined world. It's not exactly what the West is like. They're mythic storytelling, and it's very much like outer space, because you have people going across an uncharted wasteland where there is no rule of law, no civilization, and they have to face existential choices about what choice am I going to make here for myself? What am I going to decide is right or wrong? And there's no authority to tell me or guide the way. They're stripped-down morality tales.

BRADLY THOMPSON (writer, *Star Trek: Deep Space Nine*)

By the decisions you make in the show, whether or not it's by space or horses, that is how you define yourself as a human being.

HERMAN ZIMMERMAN

In designing Deep Space Nine itself, the first thing I had to do was find out what the scripts were going to be like, and there was some hesitation about that. I spent quite a few weeks working without any script, just story ideas and what we thought the exterior of the station would look like. The producers were so heavily involved with the tail end of the fifth season on *Next Generation* that I was pretty much left to my own devices. I probably have seven inches of single-spaced paper stacked with drawings that never came about; ideas that came and went as we got closer to an agreement on what the show should be about and what the station should look like and what sort of people we were going to put into this environment. Some of the ideas from the early days were useful, and quite a few of them were not. It was an interesting and creative time for me.

RICK BERMAN

I knew I wanted to bring Herman into this from the start, and the exterior of the station was something that we spent a lot of time on. There were dozens of designs, most of which I didn't like. Some of which Michael liked and I didn't, others I liked and Michael didn't. Finally, we came up with an idea that worked nicely and constantly changed.

HERMAN ZIMMERMAN

The exterior of the miniature of Deep Space Nine is composed of three concentric horizontal rings. The outer ring is a docking ring, the middle ring is an environment and cargo ring, and the center ring is the Promenade and the power core of the station. The operations center is on a pedestal that's attached to the center of the power core. The Cardassians like things in three, according to our philosophy, so there are three concentric rings, and on the outside ring there are three vertical pylons that are docking pylons. The vertical pylons are also docking positions. At the very end of each of the pylons are weapon banks, phaser and photon torpedo locations, which are arranged mathematically in such a way that they make a very pleasing exterior shape when seen from a distance. Any fan should be able to recognize the shape of Deep Space Nine the way they recognize the exterior shape of the *Enterprise*.

ROBERT LEGATO (visual effects supervisor, *Star Trek: Deep Space Nine*)

The Deep Space Nine model is a wonderful amalgamation of everyone in the art department. The basic configuration was Herman's idea, and everyone extrapolated from that. Designers Nathan Crowley and Joe Hodges set the standard for Cardassian architecture, which is a wonderful mixture of pseudo-fascist and crustacean. The way we thought of it was that the Cardassians are really bad guys, so fascist architecture—real serious and dark—was called for. It's like looking at an insect. There's a shell on top of it, and if you pull off the outer shell there's some really cool intestines on the inside of the insect.

HERMAN ZIMMERMAN

For the interior, we went through a number of ramifications. At first, Berman and Piller thought the station should be falling apart and in a very bad state of disrepair, showing the effects of time and neglect and so on. But as we started developing sketches for what that kind of a station would look like, none of us liked it. We were saying to ourselves, this is space. The final frontier, four hundred years in the future, and we should be as high-tech and slick and believable in scientific terms as possible. We did a fairly sharp one-eighty and went to another concept.

The Cardassians as a race had been seen in *Next Generation*. Their makeup and their costume had already been developed. Costume designer Bob Blackman's costumes showed a kind of chest-plate armor that looked like a crustacean. Taking off from that very fundamental idea, we decided the Cardassians like structure and they'd like to see the structure on the outside instead of hiding it inside the walls. The station itself and all the exterior sets are designed so that you can see the support columns and beams and the skin of the station applied to the structure rather than the skin covering up the structure as you would in a Beverly Hills mansion.

It's a design that is at the same time honest and a little bit awesome, because of the size of the beams that support everything. The size of the windows, the shapes of the doorways, and the way the doors operate are all very intimidating. They're not user-friendly in the way the *Next Generation* sets were user-friendly, and that was intentional. The idea of the creators of the series was that our Starfleet people would never feel exactly at home; they would never be terribly comfortable and always aware it was an alien environment in which they were working.

ROBERT LEGATO

I'm most proud of the interior of the station. It was very important to me, because when you sit down and think about it, you're setting a design standard that will last the life of the show. People around the world saw the model for Deep Space Nine, and I can say I helped design that model. I'm proud of that. I'm also proud of the operations center, ops. That's a *really* cool bridge; I don't know how anyone could be disappointed walking onto that set. You're expecting the bridge of the *Enterprise* and you don't get that at all. Boy, that thing is big. The third thing is the Promenade. To my knowledge, that has to be the largest set ever constructed for television. Walking through and seeing all the shops, Quark's bar, the versateller [ATM] is really enjoyable. A little bit of trivia: I was the one who came up with the sketch for the versateller on the Promenade—and they built the thing. It wasn't in the script, but I sketched it out and the next thing you know, it's lit and a Ferengi bank is running it. And there are all kinds of logos on it, including a Romulan logo.

MARVIN RUSH (director of photography,
Star Trek: Deep Space Nine)

The requirement was to make this show look different. It was a conscious choice. Obviously the fact that it's a meaner-spirited place is reflected in the architecture— it's got a lot of hard, angular edges. If you think of the Federation as being normal looking, *Deep Space Nine* has got a very different geometry to it, and the color scheme of the walls is much darker. The feeling of the set is more foreboding, which played into the lighting style for me. One of the techniques I used was to make sure the show had more contrast. If you compare them, the bridge of the *Enterprise* has a big soft white dome over it and it creates an office-building kind of feel to it, like any conventional interior today. When you see that, you pretty much have to light it that way because it drives the choices.

ROBERT BLACKMAN (costume designer,
Star Trek: Deep Space Nine)

I loved the fact that we created twelve Cardassian costumes for the pilot of *DS9* and then we got to use eleven of them on *Next Generation*. There are aliens walking around on the Promenade that gives the notion of this floating hotel, this United Nations in space. Unlike *Next Generation*, where it was primarily humanoids with a small smattering of aliens, on *Deep Space Nine* it was the reverse, with a small smattering of humans constantly facing one kind of alien after another.

MARVIN RUSH

On the *Deep Space Nine* set, we used much darker and more sinister lighting. We used harder, less diffused light. There were more areas where light was lower and people could come in and out of the light. Overall, it was more contrasty. All of these things created an additional sense of contrast and more tension. As we went along, the station became more familiar to our audience and also to our cast, so ops became a little less contrasty. In the pilot, it was broken down and wasn't working. Ops was a little bit more elevated in terms of lighting. When there was jeopardy, you wanted more contrast to give a sense of danger.

ROBERT BLACKMAN

The Starfleet uniforms went through a lot of changes, most notably a reversal on *Next Generation*. Starfleet has a very dignified kind of appearance, with that vertical, perfectly done military-esque kind of structure to their outfits. In *DS9* we took it in another direction. It's very utilitarian. It's a cross between a NASA jumpsuit and a mechanic's jumpsuit. They're very loose-fitting, and they have those T-shirts, and some people roll up their sleeves so they look like men at work.

There's something about the dignity, which is just wonderful in *Next Generation*, but there's a kind of propriety about it. Now these were the guys who kind of opened their jackets and their shirts and pushed their sleeves up and got down to it. It was a very hands-on existence and was fascinating to me.

One of the most memorable aspects of the pilot is the sensational opening teaser, which offers a glimpse into *Star Trek* history by depicting the Borg battle at Wolf 359, whose aftermath is only glimpsed in "The Best of Both Worlds, Part II."

MICHAEL PILLER

It's a great backstory for our hero, and it's a piece of action that our audience has heard about and heard on the sound monitors and never seen. It was, of course for me, who wrote the original Borg two-parter, a great opportunity. To go back and do some more was just too irresistible. You want to desperately open your show with a bang, and what could be a better way to open the show than to have Jean-Luc Picard as Locutus on screen saying, "You will surrender, resistance is futile"?

Even with Piller's teleplay completed weeks before production began, shooting the pilot was an incredibly arduous affair. Things were complicated by delays in casting and set construction, which made it a far more difficult shoot than "Encounter at Farpoint," the *Next Generation* pilot that was shot six years earlier but still loomed large over this latest *Trek* effort.

MICHAEL PILLER

There's a great deal about the structure that's similar to "Encounter at Farpoint." One of the tricks I learned from watching "Farpoint" again was that they didn't introduce Riker and Geordi and Beverly until two or three acts in, and I said to Rick [Berman] when we were structuring the pilot, let's hold off the arrival of two of our regulars late enough that I can do something with the other characters. My first suggestion was everyone was there and they're working and it wasn't as effective.

The other thing that comes out of "Farpoint" is a vision of Roddenberry's where we have Picard arguing for the future of mankind representing the advocate of humanity to this Q who puts humanity on trial. That's an extraordinary philosophically ambitious idea, and it really helps to define why *Star Trek* is what it is. Without that it would have been spaceships and monsters and special effects.

DAVID LIVINGSTON (producer, *Star Trek: Deep Space Nine*)

I had the same anxieties and hesitations about even wanting to do "Emissary," because I knew what a struggle it was going to be, and the pilot *was* hard. Fortunately, I didn't have to deal with the day-to-day minutiae of a production manager and I could sort of sit back a little bit. Bob Della Santina is the wonderful production manager I hired to do the job who took care of everything for me. It was tough and I told everyone it was going to be tough. It wasn't like just doing another episode or a double episode. It's doing a whole new thing again. It was a pilot, and we had all forgotten what that was like. We had the life of Riley on *The Next Generation* for five years, and I said it's all going to change—and that was true. It did. It was very difficult, because there were so many dynamics working: building all these new sets and a whole new cast and new wardrobe. Michael Westmore had to create a bunch of new makeups, including Odo's, which was very difficult. All of those dynamics made it very, very difficult.

ROBERT BLACKMAN

They cast early, but we couldn't get them [for fittings] until one week before the show started shooting. The principals arrived pretty much at the same time, but for an episode where there was a lot for them to do and a lot of multiple costumes, it was difficult. Sisko had six or seven outfits to wear in the pilot. As we get a board with a shooting schedule saying the first week you'll be shooting this and the second you'll be shooting this and the third and so on, that's how we build, in that kind of order since everything is made to order. We had a lot of the background costumes started, but the shooting schedule started changing when they didn't have Dax cast. The more they would pull stuff up from the fifth week of shooting and stick it into the first week, the more you're completely unprepared. It was amazing, but we pulled it off.

MICHAEL PILLER

Rick said the first day we sat down to meet about this that somehow this story must have the philosophical ambition that the "Encounter at Farpoint" script had and that *Star Trek* represents. Ultimately, what we created was this interaction and confrontation between alien and human that is not so different from "Farpoint," but, of course, on a weekly basis we were exploring issues and philosophies through encounters with aliens.

With the concept of the show and the aesthetic of the Deep Space Nine space station coming together, attention turned toward casting. That ensemble, of course, would have to be anchored by someone who could bring this show's commanding officer to life in the way that William Shatner had James T. Kirk and Patrick Stewart had Jean-Luc Picard. For *Deep Space Nine*, that character would be represented by Commander (later Captain) Benjamin Sisko. The role would ultimately go to Avery Brooks, who had made an indelible impression as Hawk on the ABC detective series *Spenser: For Hire,* based on the popular book series by Robert B. Parker, and the character's short-lived spin-off, *A Man Called Hawk.*

MICHAEL PILLER

Our commander is somebody who's lived a life of tragedy, in essence because when Picard was with the Borg as Locutus, and led the Borg on their attack, Sisko was a commander on one of the ships destroyed. He lost his wife and now he's raising his son by himself, and he hasn't really been able to go on with his life since he lost her. One of the arcs of the first story is some conflicts with Picard and how he gets by some of those things.

DAVID CARSON

When you have somebody like that who leads the story, he has to come to terms with what has happened to him, otherwise he spends his entire time in a bitter rage, which he doesn't. This was a buried part of his psyche, but it was nonetheless there.

WINRICH KOLBE

Anybody who saw the pilot has to be aware of the fact that we had an unwilling leader of the group. Now *that* was intriguing. If he was unwilling once, even though at the end he said he's going to fulfill his obligations, there could have been a time bomb in that character. He wasn't the character who would say, "I'm loyalty above all and I'm going down with the ship." There was a possibility that he might do something different, totally unexpected.

RICK BERMAN

The key word is "presence." We needed someone who could match or hopefully exceed the sense of presence that Patrick Stewart exuded on a pretty regular basis as Captain Picard. We didn't want to go backward, we wanted to go forward in that. We were looking for a good actor, but more than anything we were looking for someone with that sense of commanding presence, which this guy gave us.

DAVID CARSON

We decided that the role could be played either by a white man or a black man, or, as in the case of Picard, by an American or Englishman, or Belgian or German. In fact, we did interview a Belgian actor and a German actor who came over from England. What race or creed he was, was very important, but it was never a question of whether or not there was opportunity for everyone, every type of person to play the role. In the end, even though you would expect us to say this, I think all of us can truthfully say that we were able to come down to who we considered to be the best actor for the job.

Avery Brooks is a phenomenal actor. I've rarely come across an actor with a combination of his incredible depth of ability to portray emotions and feelings, but also his extraordinary technical skill in front of the camera and an amazing strength of performing with the lens. He was a real joy to work with. And the way he senses out a character . . . He developed his character into a very subtle blend of types of feeling with which he handled himself in different situations. He's extraordinarily deft and constantly interesting, and I think the character gave him much more ability to have these differences in his psychological makeup than Picard, who was a very much more straightforward character you could probably predict would react in a certain way in different situations. It was very difficult to do with Sisko, and Avery played those opportunities with delight.

DAVID LIVINGSTON

The show was very introspective, thanks to Avery. Sisko defined the mood of the show, which was a lot darker and which made it more compelling and interesting. When they were discussing casting for *Deep Space Nine,* Michael Piller was looking for an African American to play the commander, and I recommended Avery. [Casting director] Junie Lowry said she'd check him out, but it turns out he was on vacation. I said, "Send him the script on his vacation," which she did and the rest is history. If I'm responsible for anybody being hired on *DS9,* I was responsible for at least getting him in the door. He was unbelievably wonderful in the part. He defined the whole milieu of the show.

AVERY BROOKS (actor, "Benjamin Sisko")

The casting process happened very quickly for me. I was in the Caribbean, actually, and I talked to my agent, and he asked me if I was a fan of *Star Trek*. I said,

"Well, I watch it, of course," but he said I have a script you might want to read. I read it and I was thrilled about it. The writing was extraordinary, the story very compelling, and so I pursued it. And then—this is actually true—I was on my way to lay down something on tape in New York and my car started to slip out of gear. I called my wife and said, "I don't know if I can make it," and so I called the people frantically and said, "I don't think I can make it in." But they let me do it again, and then I was out of town again. They said, "We need you to come to California now." I said, "I'm in Atlanta." So then I flew out to Los Angeles and it all happened very, very fast and I was thrilled.

Very quickly I realized that, production-wise, it was very different from the on-location shooting of *Spenser* and *Hawk*. It was a different kind of rhythm. Working inside requires that you not lose your energy and your focus and your concentration, because it's easy after twelve or thirteen hours to realize you've been working that long and your body says "I want to go home."

MICHAEL PILLER

We knew we had found our Sisko. We had been looking for a quality that continued with the heroic leadership potential, but we knew that very big boots had to be filled. We had two great stars in the leadership role in the past, and it was very difficult to find someone who really impressed everybody in the room with the presence of command that Avery did.

AVERY BROOKS

I wasn't worried about typecasting, because I had been blessed with a thunderbolt artistically before that moment. I'd done a myriad of things. For example, I'd been doing Paul Robeson for a decade, and those kinds of things I would do to separate myself from the Sisko character. We all hope that we are able to do anything, so sometimes I'm Sisko and sometimes I'm not.

IRA STEVEN BEHR

Making Sisko a commander is one of the tragic mistakes of *DS9*. I'm sure it seemed like a good idea at the time, but what a mistake. To the fans, the hero of *Star Trek* is the captain, and if you're not a captain, there's got to be something wrong with you—you're the star of the show and you're not a captain *and* you're a man already in your forties? If he would have been in his early thirties, like they had said he was going to be, it would have been a different matter. Avery didn't give off that youthful feeling. I remember when they told us they were going to cast Avery, Pete and I looked at the audition tape, which I think I still have somewhere, and said, "Boy, this isn't what we thought. Why is he a commander? What happened to the younger guy who was going to have all these doubts and feelings of defeat?"

A key factor in the success of the original *Star Trek* bridge crew was the inclusion of Mr. Spock, an alien who could provide a unique perspective on humanity. That same function was fulfilled on *Next Generation* by Data and, then, on *Deep Space Nine* with shape-shifting security chief Odo, played by veteran actor René Auberjonois (best known at the time for his role as Clayton Endicott III on the long-running sitcom *Benson* as well as for his role in Robert Altman's film *M*A*S*H*).

MICHAEL PILLER

Odo was the security chief assigned to the space station when the Cardassians were there. We inherited him because he was very savvy about the goings-on of the Promenade. But he was a guy who had his own way of doing things and would take the law into his own hands to make things the way he wanted to. He also happened to be a shape-shifter and had a very interesting backstory.

WINRICH KOLBE

I did a show where Odo is trying to discover where he came from, but he unfortunately ends up with somebody he doesn't believe. He doesn't believe anybody to begin with, but this guy he *really* doesn't believe. When this guy suddenly begins to tune in on Odo's shape-shifting capability, he says, "Maybe I know something that might be intriguing to you." And then Odo says, "Forget it, you're a liar and a thief and I can't trust you," but then follows him anyway.

It's intriguing because here is a person who's very, very distrustful, which makes him the perfect sheriff. He pushes the envelope of what the police should be. The police should be trusting *nobody,* and Odo's philosophy of arrest first, ask questions later was an intriguing aspect of his profession which obviously put him into conflict with Sisko. We were talking issues about society. We were talking about the death penalty, the Napoleonic Code versus the Anglo-Saxon code. Are we guilty until proven innocent or innocent until proven guilty?

RICK BERMAN

René Auberjonois is another phenomenal actor who we were so lucky to get, extremely talented, who had to put on two hours' worth of makeup every day and act through this mask. And he was *terrific*.

IRA STEVEN BEHR

When we saw René's tape and compared him to the way the character of Odo had originally been described, the reaction was *"He's* Clint Eastwood? *Really?"*

DAVID CARSON

Like Avery Brooks, René Auberjonois has this extraordinary classical background. Both of them come out of this tradition of performance. So to have the luxury of having had someone like René playing a shape-shifter was quite extraordinary, because he isn't really first and foremost a TV actor who came out of *Benson*. He turned that character into somebody absolutely fascinating. And the fact that he is classically trained made him particularly able to work with the mask-like thing that's on his face. He's an actor who learned how to work and perform through a mask, because he's trained with masks and trained other people to act with masks. You get much more richness and depth out of somebody like him than somebody who doesn't have that depth of experience.

RENÉ AUBERJONOIS (actor, "Odo")

When I was cast as Odo, I didn't study Spock or Data any more than anybody in the audience watching the show does. There are certainly similarities, but the differences are more striking. The thing about Odo that I find fascinating is that there is a kind of pain in him, because he is forced to take on a humanoid shape, which is unlike those other characters. He is in a position, especially early on, where he is observing humanity, but he is not wishing he were human. He wishes he could find out exactly who he is and where he comes from, and if there were any others like him in existence.

Odo, in terms of who he was and his incredible dignity and sense of justice, was very appealing to me. He was sort of a curmudgeon and he was a very rigid man. He was uptight, but he's also got a wonderful deadpan kind of humor. In terms of

Odo's shape-shifting and dealing with the fact that his transformations would happen in postproduction, it's just the nature of being an actor. For people who are not professional actors, the easiest thing to do is just to remember what it's like to play house. I remember as a kid there was a place in the attic where my brother and I used to go to pretend to be scientists. It's just this willing suspension of disbelief. There was something wonderful about Odo, because I turned into all these different things. We shot things where I just sort of stand there, and I know that I'd just turned back from being a rat, and it was magical for me to see that.

ROBERT HEWITT WOLFE

René brought a tremendous sense of longing and this sort of pathos to Odo that wasn't necessarily there originally, just from his looks. I don't know whether he was acting it or it was just a moment in the room, but his attraction to Kira was something that came more from the way the characters interacted and seeing the dailies and realizing, "These guys are great together. We should make it so that he has a thing for her." That *really* came from performance.

> Following in the steps of Doctors Leonard "Bones" McCoy and Beverly Crusher is no easy task, but that's exactly what Julian Bashir was attempting as chief medical officer of *Deep Space Nine*. The role would ultimately go to Siddig El Fadil (later known as Alexander Siddig).

MICHAEL PILLER

Julian Bashir was a young, ambitious, wet-behind-the-ears, thinks-he-knows-it-all young man who had just graduated from Starfleet Medical and came out here because this is where heroes are made and this is where the adventure is and this is the wilderness. He had a lot to learn.

RICK BERMAN

The one casting credit I feel I can take and am very proud of is Siddig El Fadil as Julian Bashir. I had seen him on public television and I sought him out and had the Paramount people in London find him. He read for us in London, and he's someone no one would have ever considered. He was an extraordinary actor. The original idea was to put a Hispanic character onto the original group of people on

Deep Space Nine, and our original name for the doctor was Dr. Julian Amoros. But we just had trouble finding the right person and when we met Siddig, we decided to change the character to someone with an Arabic origin.

MICHAEL PILLER

Rick discovered Siddig on a PBS show, *A Dangerous Man,* a prequel to *Lawrence of Arabia,* in which he played King Farouk and was very good. We'd been looking for Sisko from here to eternity and we told our casting people in Europe to find this fellow. We brought him in and we looked at him and he just jumped off the screen. He was just delightful. We had not met Avery Brooks at that point, and we asked ourselves, "Could Siddig possibly be Sisko?" And we found out he was twenty-five years old, and that was too young. But there wasn't another doctor candidate. . . .

ALEXANDER SIDDIG (actor, "Julian Bashir")

My agent gets in touch and kind of talked out what my audition potentials were. She tells me, "It's Wednesday night, off you go. It's *Star Trek,* you've got this scene. Learn it. Do a good job. See you later." And this is in London. So I thought it was for *Next Generation,* and I was wracking my brain, because I knew the show. I thought maybe it could be for Deanna Troi's brother or something. I had no idea whether or not she had a brother, but it seemed that might be a fit—I was a quite pale young Arab at the time. And so I went along and did my few lines and was astonished to find out that they wanted to see me again. I had no thought at the time about how potentially big this was or that it was a big deal. Turns out I was kind of a shoo-in at that point. I didn't realize it, but looking back I see that Rick Berman had already approved me for a role, so I just came and took it.

What trickled down to me is that Rick Berman saw me do a movie called *A Dangerous Man* with Ralph Fiennes. It must have been 1991. I looked a little older than I was, and he thought that I might make an interesting captain. Kudos to him, because he was already thinking multiculturally for the lead. And so he asked me along to see him. Somewhere along the line someone told him—I think it was Junie Lowry, who was the casting director at the time—"This guy's a kid. He's not going to be a great captain." So he said, "Okay, let's look for another part." And when I first received the script, the part that I was doing was actually Amoros and he was Hispanic.

Then they switched that to Bashir to suit me. And because Rick had already anointed me, my audition was just a formality. I just had to come in and say a couple of lines. I didn't realize that until just after the audition and some bigwig came out and said, "Well, I think you're really going to enjoy it here." I was, like, "What do you mean?" So I kind of knew everything by inference right there. The moment I got off the plane and went to the studio—which is all pretty intimidating, because there are twenty people in the room—they came up and patted me on the back and welcomed me to the family. Which is lovely, my goodness. That never happened again.

ROBERT HEWITT WOLFE

Bashir was very different from how he was written on the page at the end of the day. He had a different name, he was a different kind of guy, and he was a little more suave, with a little more in the way of personal skills. He wasn't as prone to shoving his foot completely into his mouth as the way it felt when Sid did those scenes, which were great. But it was a totally different guy. The naïveté came through much stronger with Sid than I think the way it was written. The earnestness. He brought such a great vulnerable enthusiasm to the character. On the page he was maybe a little more sophisticated.

ALEXANDER SIDDIG

The characters in the bible really weren't developed. I mean, everybody got like half a page and the Amoros character got like three lines. So he was an unmade-up character at the beginning, and I think that the early shows kind of prove that. He was trying to find his niche, who he was, so I got a chance to put a lot of stuff into it on my own, rightly or wrongly, and the character slowly kind of came out of his shell and evolved.

In the beginning he was very awkward, and I used a lot of information that I was gathering at the time about my experience coming to America. It was kind of perfect: I was a naïve young kid who really had just been acting for two years. Even in England I was pretty innocent. So going to *DS9* was pretty much like going to L.A. As far as I was concerned, everyone was pretty alien there, so it was very easy to break off that chunk of my life and stick it into Bashir. The plan in my mind was to grow him up on screen; there was no master plan beyond that.

MICHAEL PILLER

With the doctor, I wanted to create a character who was somewhat unlikable so we could make him grow into something interesting. So we created this fellow who was rather full of himself, and by the middle of the year we started getting research back from the studio saying, "We've got to fire the doctor; nobody likes him." Well, *that* was the idea. So we prevailed in saying, "We're not going to fire the doctor," but we probably softened him up a little bit.

ALEXANDER SIDDIG

You jump ahead several seasons to the Dominion War, and you see how strong he became; that he's learned to do the right thing. He learns how to be the cowboy that everyone wanted him to be at the beginning. But at the beginning, you're not even sure of his sexuality. Then they throw the Cardassian Garak in the mix at a very early stage, and it's *not* subtle. There's a kind of quivering sexuality going on there, which obviously doesn't come home to roost, but it's hero worship. I had fun with that, and I know that Andy Robinson, who played Garak, did as well. Andy just changed my game for me. He gave me a direction to go in, and I began to understand what was going on with the character once I got to talk to him. It was pretty much the only talking I did. The Terry Farrell/Jadzia Dax infatuation thing just didn't work.

ANDREW ROBINSON (actor, "Garak")

Bashir is really good-looking, so as a character choice I thought, "What the hell? Why not go for it?" There is a close-up of Garak where it looks like he could eat him alive. And I'm sure that's why I got the job.

ALEXANDER SIDDIG

I gave Garak some of the best years of my life.

Acclaimed actor Colm Meaney had served aboard the *Enterprise* on *The Next Generation* as O'Brien, a nameless character in the show's premiere who gradually was elevated to a more prominent position as transporter chief, and then joined *DS9* as the station's chief engineer while continuing to work as a much sought-after character actor in myriad independent films.

RICK BERMAN

Colm is probably my favorite actor on Earth. He is truly a remarkable talent, and he shows up now in movie after movie, and he's one of the great Irish actors, I believe. I have met some pretty impressive directors, like Stephen Frears and Alan Parker, who would corroborate that, because he's been in a lot of their movies. Colm, in the pilot of *Next Generation,* played an unnamed character. We had something called "the battle bridge," and he steered the ship from the battle bridge when the ship separated, which it didn't do very often.

Eventually we gave him the role of Ensign O'Brien. I named him after my nephew, whose name is Miles O'Brien. We wanted a little crossover, so we had him become a regular character on *Deep Space Nine.* It was amazing, because he constantly was being asked to do movies with wonderful directors and I could never say no to him. So we would always have to juggle the schedule around or have O'Brien off visiting his home or something like that in order to allow him to go and shoot a film. He worked on a film with John Huston, and he was just always getting wonderful roles in movies. So that was a delight.

IRA STEVEN BEHR

We knew we wanted to do something with O'Brien. Colm is a really fine actor, and he had limited chances on *The Next Generation.* On *DS9* he was a lead, and we were always trying to find new things to do with him. If I had gone back to *TNG,* I was going to give O'Brien a lot more. I thought he was the most human character of them all, and I really wanted to explore that character, so I was very happy he was a part of *DS9.*

DAVID CARSON

I'd worked with Colm before on *Next Generation* and he's tremendous. Very wonderful, warm, interesting, varied actor, and I think it was an interesting choice to have him come over from *Next Generation.* He wasn't prominent over there and to have suddenly revealed him was a good way of linking the two series without doing it heavy-handedly. That was a really good choice.

COLM MEANEY (actor, "Miles O'Brien")

I was in New York for a year with *Breaking the Code* and that was the year of the writer's strike, so *Star Trek* didn't get going again until September or October of 1988. When I came back to *Next Generation,* they brought me on as Chief O'Brien. For the first five or six shows that I did, he just kept cropping up and I was transporter chief. Then a script arrived and suddenly he had a name.

IRA STEVEN BEHR

One of the things we did was team O'Brien up with Bashir in a certain way. In those early days, Bashir saw O'Brien as kind of the old pro from Dover, the guy who's done it all. The way I saw O'Brien was as the workingman's hero, and so did Bashir. Bashir wanted to be like him and wanted to know him and emulate him. O'Brien looked at this young kid from the Academy with that English, upper-class accent and it was, like, "Go away, kid, you bother me." It was fun, because you don't usually see that. We shot a scene where Bashir was talking, talking, talking, and he turns to O'Brien and says something to him, and O'Brien just gives Bashir a look, with not one line of dialogue, that was, again, "Get the hell away from me, kid." It was funny and it was character.

COLM MEANEY

They were looking for a way to get me off the *Enterprise*. Over the first four years there was more written for me on *Next Generation*, but obviously with the cast set over there, there was only so much room for the development of every character. Then this opportunity came up. Obviously, in one sense, a bridge between the *Enterprise* and *Deep Space Nine*.

O'Brien is someone who's more human. He obviously liked his job, but he also had other aspects to his personality. He didn't have the element of being a fearless superhuman.

MICHAEL PILLER

We tried to tell stories about a married couple between Keiko and O'Brien, and some people found the arguing between them and the stress of the relationship crossed the boundary and got into personal conflict that Roddenberry wouldn't like, so we pulled back on that.

The greedy, large-eared Ferengi were introduced on *Next Generation*, and it was decided to include a member of the race as the owner of the bar on *DS9*'s Promenade. Although plenty of humor was mined from the character, he would prove to be far more multidimensional than the silly way in which Ferengi characters had previously been portrayed. Armin Shimerman (the TV series *Brooklyn Bridge*, *Beauty and the Beast*, *Alien Nation*, and later, and most memorably, Principal Snyder on *Buffy The Vampire Slayer*) was no stranger to Ferengi, having been among the first to play one in the *TNG* season-one episode "The Last Outpost."

RICK BERMAN

Armin Shimerman was just a wonderful character actor and incredibly funny.

ROBERT HEWITT WOLFE

Armin brought a dignity to Quark. Quark could have easily just been nothing but a comic character. Armin is a Shakespearean, very well-trained actor, and he brought, for lack of other words, a humanity to the character that wasn't always there on the page, and a dignity and a pride. Like a real person, he was proud to be a Ferengi, and you bought it. It wasn't a joke when he said those things. When he criticized humans, it was coming from a place that he understood who he was and what he was and where he was, and it was just something really great.

DAVID CARSON

Armin and I worked together on *Alien Nation*. He's terrific. Like René, he took to the mask completely and developed the character wonderfully well. Unlike some of the Ferengi characters there have been, Quark was not quite so silly. He had a much more malevolent presence, which I think is very good because it added to the drama.

ARMIN SHIMERMAN (actor, "Quark")

They remembered me from five years before as one of the first Ferengi. I think what Rick said to me was they remembered how strong a Ferengi I was, because they wanted that for Quark. He also had to be able to play chess with Sisko—that kind of quality to him. I did not have to audition as many times for a series regular as I would if they had not seen my work and kept me in mind. The first time I had a callback, and usually there are a number of actors sitting there, it was only me and Max Grodénchik. He'd played a Ferengi before. At the final audition, it was just me. They gave me the impression after I was cast that they had indeed written the part with me in mind.

Working in the mask was a little frustrating. Every actor would prefer that all of his face was shown. I would be a fool to say otherwise, but I think the mask worked really well, and the combination of the mask and whatever inflections I gave to my voice and my eyes came across quite well. It meant working a little harder and being a little big bigger. I was used to playing roles where it's very low-key and underplayed. I tried to teach myself to do that for years. Then I was being asked to overplay a little. It was just a new challenge.

MAX GRODÉNCHIK (actor, "Rom")

I got to know Armin a bit during the audition process. He had so much more history with the show. I'd be lying if I didn't say I was disappointed that I didn't get the role of Quark, but it made me feel better knowing that Armin landed the role. I thought it was fair, and I also felt he was a better foil for Sisko, since I watched some of his old episodes and thought he could play very strong emotions very well. When they asked me to play his brother, Rom, I was thrilled. I had no idea that it would turn into such a recurring role, so I don't think things could have worked out better even if I had gotten Quark.

MICHAEL PILLER

In the pilot, Sisko threatens to incarcerate Quark unless he stays aboard and helps in the rebuilding process as a "community leader." In that scene where Odo is watching Sisko in action and Sisko is doing this number on Quark, I suddenly found myself writing these asides between Odo and Quark. Quark is saying, "What do you want me to stay for?" and Odo says, "I'm a little mystified myself, Commander. The man is a gambler and a thief," and Quark comes back and says, "I am not a thief." Odo says, "Yes, you are. You're a thief," and suddenly these two guys were going at each other. I realized there was magic there. There was a relationship there. They get off on this trying to one-up each other, and there's a love that comes from within for one another between the good guy and the bad guy, and we really explored that. *That's* the discovery of character and interaction Rick and I wanted to have. It was a conflict that was fun and restored to *Star Trek* something that hadn't really been in evidence since the original show.

RENÉ AUBERJONOIS

That love/hate relationship was very dear to me. Our characters were sort of the antithesis of one another. He is a con artist extraordinaire and I am a man who just sees black and white. Something is either just or unjust. A very complex relationship, and although we were always bickering and I was always after him, I think we forged quite a friendship.

ARMIN SHIMERMAN

What I think they found in the early episodes was the great comic potential between Odo and Quark. There was this sort of Mutt and Jeff relationship that both René and I savored a great deal.

IRA STEVEN BEHR

Michael and Rick realized that this was a learning process of finding out together who these people were and then, of course, you cast the goddamn thing and the actors make it who they are. Then you sit back and say, "Okay, maybe that's not what I had in mind exactly," but it worked, and so all the best-laid plans went out the window the second the cameras started to roll. What I found interesting and fun about the show was not so much each individual character, but how the characters began to interact.

Making Odo and Quark this kind of twosome was something we knew would have juice for ages, because Odo was a repressed, haunted figure and René really played the makeup to a certain extent in that he's a man alone, which you didn't see a lot of in the twenty-fourth century. And Quark was a Ferengi, but not your typical cringing Ferengi. He was a Ferengi with a little edge to him. Their comic relationship, I found, was something that was a lot of fun.

At the same time, in seven years Armin—even though I love him and he's one of the actors I'm closest to now as a person—and I never really got on the same page totally with Quark. But that's not the actor. That's just a difference of opinion.

Cirroc Lofton made his television debut as Jake, the son of Commander Benjamin Sisko. Having lived on four different starships and been stationed on two planets, Jake yearned to return to Earth rather than be forced to live aboard *Deep Space Nine*. As the show would progress, the relationship between Jake and his father would become one of the strongest on the series as well as one of the deepest depictions of a single African American father and his son on television.

MICHAEL PILLER

When we came up with the character of Jake Sisko, it had nothing to do with the Wil Wheaton character of Wesley Crusher on *Next Generation*, which was a supergenius who seemed to save the ship every week. This was a kid who is growing up in his life with his dad. The two of them struggled as fathers and sons do every day in our lives. This kid did not have any great technical skills, he was not going to save the ship. He was a kid. The bottom line was that this hero, this leader, our star, had to be different. He couldn't be Picard, he couldn't be Kirk. He had to be Sisko. And to me, and to Rick, we felt giving him a son as an added burden enriched his character and the opportunities to see him on a personal level that we rarely got to see Kirk and Picard on.

DAVID CARSON

He was a very, very talented young man. He had minimal drama training, according to his mother, and for a boy who had so little training, he was really quite good. He was way and above the best actor that we saw for the role, and we saw many, many actors. I think he had a refinement of manner and a refinement of feature as well, which made him just that little bit set apart, which I thought was very good for Sisko's son. His family comes from Ethiopia, and I suppose his background had some effect on him, his bearing, and how he looks.

ROBERT HEWITT WOLFE

Cirroc brought a slightly haunted quality. He was a kid who lost his mom and was living in this strange place, but also a kid who was fundamentally a really great kid who had been raised by a good father. He and Avery bonded in a really special way. They still talk about that; it was a real father-son relationship that developed there. For Michael, that was always the intent. He always wanted the single father raising a son on the frontier and saw it as central to the premise of the show. What was wonderful was how real it was between the two of them. You could feel it and see it in every scene they did together.

MICHAEL PILLER

Frankly, I think anything we could do to provide a role model for kids and parents is a good thing. "Family values" has become a curse word in some ways, but it's important that we, as writers and creators, continued to provide strong role models on television for parents and for television.

IRA STEVEN BEHR

I really liked the Sisko-Jake relationship from the beginning, but as Cirroc grew, and boy did he grow, he was able to take on more weight for the stories. Obviously, there was some talk during the first season that we didn't want Jake to be Wesley Crusher, so that was always in my mind. We had to make the audience care about him. Another thing that happened, and I don't know if it was first season or not, was his relationship with Quark's nephew, Nog. It was just great seeing two kids hanging out, being in this amazing place but seeing it from the eyes of kids who see the Promenade as the place they hang. I liked the friendship thing.

As originally conceived, the first officer of *Deep Space Nine* would have been Ensign Ro, a Bajoran character introduced on *The Next Generation* and played by actress Michelle Forbes, but those plans were scrapped when Forbes passed on the role. Fortunately, Forbes' departure came at the same time Piller was working on a rewrite of the pilot to strengthen the first act, which meant changing the character of Ro to another Bajoran with a new and different backstory. This, he soon discovered, proved advantageous for the new series. Eventually cast as Major Kira Nerys was Nana Visitor, late of the TV version of *Working Girl,* among others.

MICHAEL PILLER

Michelle Forbes is a wonderful actress, and her character of Ensign Ro created the entire canvas for this new series. It had always been assumed that she would be one of the people spun off and moved over to *DS9,* but she wanted to be a feature actress.

I found there was a great deal more conflict in having the Bajoran *not* be Starfleet. Immediately you have different priorities and agendas, and the two people immediately have a conflict with each other the moment they step onto the station. The one between Sisko and Ro would have been a much different one, because ultimately she's Starfleet and has to do what the boss says. Kira Nerys could do things that are not appropriate Starfleet behavior. We created this character, and it was really a matter of rewriting two or three scenes that defined where she was from and a couple of speeches in other scenes, which were mostly action-type scenes.

WINRICH KOLBE

There's a confrontation in the pilot between Sisko and Kira in which he warns her that if she ever goes over his head again, he'll serve hers on a silver platter. I love that. That, to me, is more human, it is more contemporary. Sometimes we have to work with people with whom we occasionally disagree and have differences of opinion, yet—despite that—they are capable of fulfilling their jobs. In the pilot, I think Sisko said, "I want you because you're Bajoran." He could have had any one of a million Bajorans, somebody who would say, "Yes, sir, whatever you want." He wanted somebody who comes from the background of Kira, who was in the underground against the Cardassians. A nationalist, so to speak.

It intrigued me because I felt that, yes, we are changing, but we are not necessarily becoming more advanced. There's nationalism two thousand years from now, and it will always be there, because it's something genetically inside us. Like racism, which is something that's always coming out. We only *seemingly* live in a better social society if we are able to combat it, but the moment we let our guard down, bingo, there's the conflict. I like that in *DS9* when it came down to the Kira/Sisko conflict. It's politics, but it's the politics of Starfleet, of the larger unit that says, "We want to expand our influence," and the small unit, which is the planet Bajor, which says, "Hey, it's all very nice, but you're taking over. We don't want you, either."

DAVID CARSON

The casting of Kira was difficult, though no more so than when you're setting up something completely new, because on these television things everything is done by committee. So you're juggling three million opinions at the same time. It's sort of a different world from the one that I'm used to in that sense. You feel as though you're walking through a minefield as you struggle toward the final choice in television, it seems to me, because there are a whole mixture of opinions to be taken into account, some informed and some uninformed. Sometimes, as we all know, terrible mistakes happen in casting. I think, though, we were extremely lucky this time and everybody had the necessary patience to not say yes because we had to start shooting. In fact, some of the roles weren't cast until we were three weeks into it. We had to change the schedule around to accommodate it. With a show like this, getting a good cast was really so important.

NANA VISITOR (actress, "Kira Nerys")

I watched *Star Trek* when it was in reruns. I think I know them all from cooking dinner in my brownstone in New York. I was a fan of the quality of the show, but

I was not a Trekkie. I didn't get it and I didn't understand that this was *Star Trek* when I auditioned. I did not understand what I was getting into.

DAVID CARSON

The cast and company were so lucky to have her. She's one of those rare chameleon kinds of actors who is able to assimilate herself into a character and transform it into something you don't expect. She's also very beautiful, and she obviously delighted in playing this role. I was very pleased when she walked into the room, and I think that once she did, she was the only Kira that we thought could play the role. Of course we weren't going to tell anybody that until we'd signed a deal with her. She was and is extraordinary. She was also delightful to work with and able to tune her emotion to the camera. She also had this specific, tangible relationship with the lens, which is delightful for a director to work with.

IRA STEVEN BEHR

The only actor who auditioned that I really bought into was Nana. Even though she modulated that performance quite a bit. But I believed Nana right off the bat. For everyone else, it's like I had all these other pictures in my head of what we had been told, and it was confusing. It was the beginning of the confusion; the first season confusion was in the casting. It all turned out fine, but we had given people the wrong idea going off to think of ideas or to write outlines. It was all wrong. We were sitting there, looking at each other, going, "What the fuck? All of that stuff is going to come in and it's all going to have to be changed."

MICHAEL PILLER

Kira was coming across to us in the early going as a little bit too hard, and I think we moved her into a more accessible kind of voice.

RICK BERMAN

For a first officer, you have two ways to go: male or female. It just seemed making the character female was the right thing to do. I don't think we did it to be politically correct. I don't think we did it to mimic the original *Star Trek* pilot, "The Cage." We did it because it felt right as we were creating the characters.

NANA VISITOR

Kira's forceful presence was right there on the page. That was one reason I was so excited when I read the script and read a woman who was a powerful woman. She was first officer, so she was in command, but she wasn't just politically correct. She's not perfect. She doesn't do everything just right and always knows the right thing to think and do. She makes mistakes, she's not sure within herself. The fact that she is a woman suddenly wasn't an issue anymore. It was a species who had spirituality, who had aggressiveness, who had ideas of her own. She's a truthful, emotional being, and that was very exciting. It was a matter of me filling out the spaces of the character.

RICK BERMAN

Nana says the character was all on the page, but I don't think that's really true. We create characters and then we hire actors to play those characters, and the actors bring, in many instances, as much to those characters as we did in creating them. It's *that* marriage that ends up becoming either a character that works or doesn't. The same thing is true with every other element of the show. It's something that you've got to be very open about and watch evolve, as we did.

NANA VISITOR

I didn't even know I would be wearing a nose. I talked to Rick Berman and he said, "At least the prosthetic is one of the least we have," and I said, "What prosthetic?" And he said, "It's nothing. Just a small elephant nose that you wear." And he had me going for five seconds. But I had no idea. I just knew I wanted to play this woman very badly.

RICK BERMAN

A slightly morbid story is when, during one of the very rainy days here in Los Angeles, Nana slipped on the wet steps of the makeup trailer. Nana is a dancer and she is one of these real "the show must go on" types, but we told her that it was really important that she get to the hospital. So they brought her to the hospital, and she walked in wearing full costume and makeup, and the emergency room doctor asked her how she was, and she said she had hurt her lower back but that she thought it wasn't all that bad, and he said, "Well, in that case, I think we better get you an X-ray right away to check out that broken nose." He was a good emergency room doctor, but didn't know Bajor from Adam.

Introduced on *The Next Generation* in the episode "The Host," Trills are a humanoid species native to the planet Trill, a small percentage of which coexist with sentient symbiotic organisms inside their bodies. The resulting joined Trills retain the personalities of the previous hosts of the symbiont. On *DS9*, the final character to be cast was science officer Jadzia Dax, the latest host of an old friend and mentor of Sisko's, Curzon Dax. Cast in the role was actress Terry Farrell (who had starred in the short-lived evening soap opera *Paper Dolls*, as well as cult favorites *Hellraiser III* and *Back to School* with Rodney Dangerfield).

RICK BERMAN

That role was a bitch to cast. If you need someone who's beautiful and a good actress to come onto a syndicated television series, it's hard to find. Women are either good actresses or they're beautiful. But if you find one that is beautiful and a good actress, they get that kind of monopoly card that says, "Skip television and go right to the movies." We read so many people for that role; it was really difficult. And of all the tall, beautiful women that we read, Terry was certainly the best, and the studio really liked her, so we hired her.

TERRY FARRELL (actress, "Jadzia Dax")

When I was five or six, *Star Trek* was my favorite show in the whole world. In the playground we'd make a big pile of leaves be the spaceship. There was the shortest kid in the class, his name was Grant, and he would be Captain Kirk. I was always the alien from another planet, which I liked very much. The green hair or purple eyelashes or whatever they were doing was always so much fun. I'm not sure what it was, maybe it was the adventure that attracted me to the show. I always liked anything that had to do with spying or espionage. Anything that pulls you into the story of "who did it?" There's an urgency to it all—you have to save the planet or the world or the people. Or the ship. We're going where no one's gone before. I loved that. It was unique. All these people came together and made their own family, and there was something special about that. You weren't forced to be close; you're close because you have so much in common.

MICHAEL PILLER

We were already in production when we cast Terry, and part of the reason that that part was so difficult to cast is because it's a character that's a little hard to define. I could write a book about Trills now, but what does that mean in the day-to-day existence of these people? How do we make it different from Terry Farrell? How do you make it something alien and yet accessible?

TERRY FARRELL

I didn't think of myself as being an "alien chick" when I was playing Dax. Certainly looking back to the sixties' version from when I first got the job as Dax, I think she had much more integrity, and the writers wrote for me with a much stronger voice than the aliens that I thought were so cool-looking when I was a little girl.

MICHAEL PILLER

Terry came in the last day or two of casting for this show, and we had her back a couple of times. We had two or three others that we were very interested in, but truth is, Terry was the only actress who came in to read where Rick and I looked at each other and agreed that she had hit the scenes that she was reading. We had finally gotten to the place where we had to cast somebody. Terry did not have the experience of some of the others, and we knew, and she knew, that there would be a great challenge of acting and performance.

TERRY FARRELL

I was in the last round of people, and they were sort of, like, "We don't think she's right, but we've seen everybody but these ten people. Let's bring her in." I knew that. I don't think they liked me as an actress very much, but certainly there was room to grow. I don't think I was my best at twenty-eight, either, and that was some heavy-duty stuff to throw at someone, that dialogue and everything. It was terrifying, but I was motivated. I hadn't worked for a while because of a relationship and I wanted to get my career back on track. *And* I didn't want to lose my house—that's very good motivation.

IRA STEVEN BEHR

This Trill is supposed to be the wise old man in a woman's body. You meet Terry and she is *so* open and *so* beautiful. You got the feeling that this was not a woman who's holding stuff back. It was hard to see her at first as the Trill, and it took us a long time to do her justice. For a while I felt she was our Troi. Troi had an ability that seemed a little hard to use, which is, you know, "I feel anger." "Well, yeah, he just said he's pissed off." Troi's empathic ability, though it sounds great, I always felt was never used properly, and the same thing with Dax in the beginning. It was only when she realized she could have some fun with Dax that you could see what Dax could be. That having all of these people inside her could make her a bit of a swashbuckling, adventure-loving character. But that took a while to come.

MICHAEL PILLER

There's no question that we had trouble with Dax from the very beginning. I originally called her this Grace Kelly ice princess, but we could not figure out what the voice of somebody who had two entities was. We had a very difficult time figuring out a way to communicate the duality of the nature of the character. It really wasn't until Ira basically turned it upside down and decided to make her a wisecracking Howard Hawks kind of girl that she really found her voice. Originally she was stuck with all the technical jargon, which Brent Spiner used to call "Piller filler," and obviously Terry Farrell was not well suited for that role, so we went off from that.

TERRY FARRELL

It must have been when Michael Piller left and Ira became the head of the writing that I really got to know Ira. And *that's* when my character had a more interesting change. I like to work out and I like to stay active. As Ira got to know that about me, he made Dax more active and used the word "roguish" to describe her. I don't remember what season it was that he came up to me and said, "I think you're going to like Dax next season; she's going to be a little more roguish." And that's when my whole thing with the Klingons started happening. Oh my gosh, I *loved* how they wrote for me. From that point on it was so much fun and I felt like I had a lot more interesting things to play.

PETER ALLAN FIELDS

When Dax came along, this was a different kind of Trill than had appeared in *TNG*, so I just made up my own rules. It didn't mean I could do anything I chose, but we originally started off with the idea that Dax was going to have all these lives and people scrambling around inside this lovely twenty-something-year-old person, who is very often fighting against herself. And she'll even go play cards with the Ferengi, so it's more fun to have all of these people at war inside of her. She is no less competent, she's just more fun.

DAVID CARSON

Most of the time with Terry was struggling to see what in fact a Trill should look like. Together with the fact that she was cast very late, we had all these problems of what should be stuck on her face. There were countless tests and some people didn't like this, some people didn't like that, until eventually she came out with spots. Trills have an established look, which is sort of lumpy prosthetic look on their faces. As you'll notice, she in fact didn't have any. When we first started shooting her, she had these old prosthetic lumps on her face. But frankly they did not add to her undeniable attractiveness, so everybody decided that her face should be left alone and spots should be added, which went under the collar of her costume, thereby being suggestive of where else the spots might be. Not that anybody would ever know.

TERRY FARRELL

She was a strong woman. The biggest part of the appeal, whether it's going to pay for your house or not, is that there has to be something about it that makes you excited. And playing the science officer, which was the role Leonard Nimoy had played on the original series, was the thing for me. I thought my character would be a cool character just because she was science officer. The problem is that I had a really bad time knowing my lines. That was really difficult for me, which was a huge Achilles heel on top of not having any sleep—*not* a good situation. I wasn't sleeping because I was so nervous about knowing my lines that it was causing me not to get enough sleep. And on top of that, I got sick with bronchitis or something and they were thinking about letting me go.

They hired me an acting coach named Ivana Chubbuck, a very good acting coach. Thankfully, she did a lot to help me with my self-esteem, too, because that's a scary place to be when you think you're going to get fired because *they* don't think you're good at what you do. She told me that my biggest problem was I needed someone to just run lines with me, so I would go to someone's house to run lines. But the lines changed so many times that it wasn't super helpful. In the end, though, I got to keep my job.

MICHAEL PILLER

We had very strong women on *Next Generation,* though they were cast and created in caretaking roles. Their characters were caretakers by their jobs. Doctors and therapists are caretakers and they have a very mothering kind of role. The actors would have loved to have transcended that, but the fact is that you have to write the character you've been given by Mr. Roddenberry.

As it evolved through the beginnings, you saw stronger and stronger women on *The Next Generation.* Ensign Ro is the best example of that I can think of. Tasha Yar was created for *Next Generation,* but it was a character that wasn't working and the actor wasn't happy. We went out of our way *not* to make the women on *Deep Space Nine* caretakers, although I think Dax is somewhat of a caretaker—but she is the science officer, so she has a technical expertise to bring to it. There was no question that Kira was always going to be an action hero. We went out of our way to create women who were contemporary and really showed us a full range of female experience.

One consideration Rick and I made was that a woman would be Sisko and the star of the show, and that, too, would have been an advancement for television. It's not that we didn't take it seriously, we just moved in a different direction.

ROBERT HEWITT WOLFE

In the beginning the biggest challenge, which is the same in every television show, is that Michael wrote these characters with very specific ideas of who they were going to be, and then cast them, and a lot of times he just wanted the best actor he could get. He picked a couple of people who were terrific, but they were slightly different than what he'd originally written for the characters.

For instance, Terry Farrell was terrific, but she was not by nature of who she was someone who was going to spit out a bunch of technobabble. She lived and breathed in scenes of comedy. So it was taking this vaguely Taoist, but mostly fascinated by the universe, kind of person and recognizing that the science stuff was not really her strength.

ANDRÉ BORMANIS (science consultant, *Star Trek: Deep Space Nine*)

An important lesson on technobabble came to me courtesy of Terry Farrell. I was at my first *Deep Space Nine* wrap party at the end of second season, and it's the first time I've ever been to wrap party so it was like a pretty big deal to me. I'm walking around and talking to the people I know. And I see Terry Farrell standing off by herself. I'd never actually met her, so I sheepishly go up and introduce myself to her, and I said, "Ms. Farrell, I'm André Bormanis." "Oh, nice to meet you. What do you do on the show?" I'm like, "I'm the science consultant. I'm the guy who puts all that technobabble into your dialogue." And she literally grabbed me by the lapels and lifted me off my feet. She's six feet tall. She's a very tall, striking woman. She's, like, "You fucking asshole!" And she starts shaking me, and I'm, like, "I'm sorry, it's my job!"

She puts me down and starts laughing. But she told me something very important: "If I'm in a scene by myself, and I'm just talking to the computer making a log entry or whatever, running a test in the lab, you can put as much technobabble in my dialogue as you want. But, if I'm in a scene with another actor or two, I have to hit my marks, I have to think about what my character is thinking and feeling in this scene. I have to play up the other actors and how they're playing their characters. In that context it's very hard for me to, like, remember terms in my dialogue that mean absolutely nothing to me." She said, "The less you can do in those situations, the better for me." That's a really good note. I wish somebody had given me that note when I started.

ROBERT HEWITT WOLFE

Her strength was the playful scenes with Sisko. She brought out a really nice note in scenes with Avery. She's much more fun as a lovable rogue and a bit of an unpredictable wild card than she is as the Zen master scientist. That was a big adjustment that we had to make on the fly. So it's stuff like that, or finding a way, for example, to write Sisko that was true to both who Sisko was and what Avery brought to the package. All that stuff. Realizing that there were some kinds of stories that *Next Generation* could do way better than us and finding the shows that we could do way better than *Next Generation*. *That* was the adjustment.

MICHAEL PILLER

I believe that every television show creates an ersatz family. The success of the television shows of worth are those that create families that people want to be part of. In a sense, I think they fill the needs of people in this world that have lost some of the strength of family that we had in prior generations. I believe that any successful family is going to have a strong parent figure. You had that with Kirk and then you had that in Picard, but in the ensemble approach there's a real question mark about how that worked for us in *Deep Space Nine*.

That's the one missing element—that the audience never found "Dad" in that environment. We started playing against that, because it wasn't working the way we intended it to when we created it. It turned out to be an unusual and unique series because of it, but in terms of fundamental success and acceptability of the audience, that's what I always look at and say, "We just didn't have that one character that the other characters all played off of."

> With all of the pieces in place and scripts being written, *Star Trek: Deep Space Nine* premiered on January 4, 1993, resulting in stellar ratings and a first season that began to delve into the characters and the interaction with various alien races. Like its predecessors, the storytelling remained very much stand-alone, although the nature of having as many recurring characters as this show had began to slowly introduce elements of serialization, which was anathema to the studio. Additionally, there were criticisms leveled against the show for its stationary setting and, according to some naysayers, not fitting in with the *Star Trek* nature of storytelling.

RICK BERMAN

I was very pleased with the way the first season went in a lot of respects. First seasons of television shows tend to be potentially very chaotic. The first season of *Next Generation* certainly was. The first season of *Deep Space Nine* was very peaceful in terms of the actors, the crew, the writers, and the budgets. As far as the episodes, there are things about them that I loved and things about them I didn't love. That's the way it is. We were always looking to make things better. What I was most pleased with in the first year was the fact that the concept worked and we managed to create stories that I think all hang pretty well on the armature that we'd built, the backstory and the characters.

MICHAEL PILLER

The eighteen episodes of the first season can be divided into three distinct groups of shows. The first eight to ten were specifically designed to elaborate and expose the audience to each one of the characters. If you went through them show by show, you could see one was an Odo show, another a Dax show, an O'Brien show, etc. We wanted to really define those characters in a way *Next Generation* never did the first two seasons. We wanted those characters known to the audience right off the bat. We couldn't do it all in the pilot. We did Sisko in the pilot, we did some Kira in the pilot, and then each one after that exposed more of the characters.

RICK BERMAN

It was very frustrating sometimes not having the *Enterprise* to be able to take you to warp six and places unknown, but I think, considering what we had constructed and the situation with Bajor and the space station, the writing staff and the actors and everyone involved became more acclimated to it, and it continued to get better. If you go back to look at some of the episodes of the first season of *The Next Generation*, you'll see actors who weren't all that familiar with their characters, and characters who weren't familiar with their relationships with other characters. These things grow.

MICHAEL PILLER

The next group of shows was trying to show two things: how the ensemble will work together and how far the series could stretch its wings. Then you have a third part of the season, which is paying the cost for the first two-thirds. The shows at the end of the season were not bad shows by any means, but were designed specifically to pay back some of the bills that we owed.

IRA STEVEN BEHR

We kept getting the same old complaints: "It's not a family." Well, it *is* a family— sometimes a dysfunctional family, but we had much more of a family like the original series than *TNG*. Spock and Bones may not get along, but they love each other. These characters care about one another; Odo and Quark, Bashir and the Cardassian tailor Garak, Kira and Dax, Dax and Sisko, Odo and Kira. I couldn't believe it was such a hard concept to grasp. There were no unlikable people. I saw that men were threatened by Kira and they said they didn't like her because she's too strong, but that's because we live in a screwed-up society, not because she's a bad character.

MICHAEL PILLER

We did politics awfully well. The problem with that is there may have been something to the fact that people would rather watch space monsters, enigmas, and anomalies than politics. But one of the things I was proudest of with *Deep Space Nine* is that I began to realize that it takes a great deal more courage to stay and deal with problems that don't get solved than it is to go in, meet somebody, change their lives or have them teach us something, and then zoom out to the next person.

IRA STEVEN BEHR

Robert Wolfe, our story editor in first season, explained it best: *DS9* was unlike *TNG* and the original series, where you go out into the great void and explore and map and meet people and have adventures and then you leave. We knew every move that Sisko made, every thought he had, every action he took, had repercussions that we could go back to and work on and play with. That's why we had the best supporting characters on television. From Dukat to Garak and Rom and Winn and all these wonderful people that we can continue to explore, because they didn't go away. We could leave as much as we wanted to, but we always came back and the station was still there.

ROBERT HEWITT WOLFE

One of the things that we figured out very quickly was if you have someone do a great job and their character popped and they were interesting . . . well, we're a fucking space station. We could see them anytime we want. The first time we realized it was with Garak, also with Winn and Rom and a whole bunch of the Klingons, Martok, eventually.

The episode "Duet"—which focuses on Kira and a Cardassian war criminal (played magnificently by guest star Harris Yulin)—is generally considered the standout show of the first season. It was followed by the season finale, "In the Hands of the Prophets," focusing on an ideological division between members of the Bajoran people and others on the station.

MICHAEL PILLER

We had to come up with some very creative ways to do shows that did not cost a lot of money. "Duet" was pitched to us by two of our interns, who wanted to do something about a war criminal. In the context it was pitched, it didn't turn me on. The idea of a war criminal found aboard *DS9* seemed to me to be an interesting concept, but at first it seemed to me to be a *Judgment at Nuremberg* court show. We had done "Dax," which was a court show, and didn't want to do another. Ira Behr gave us the twist that gave it *The Man in the Glass Booth* kind of feeling, where the guy isn't who he says he is but is doing it for more noble reasons. The writing is really quite powerful.

ARMIN SHIMERMAN

I've always been a big fan of Harris Yulin. We were acquaintances years ago when I first met my wife. We were all doing Broadway together. It's a fascinating episode dealing with Bajor and nationalism and with Cardassian war crimes. I love these kinds of scripts, because they deal with social issues placed in the context of space.

NANA VISITOR

The action comes out of big issues on this show. There's action and intrigue, but the writing really lets us deal with issues we're not embarrassed to commit ourselves to as actors and people. On a sitcom, very often it's "Should I let Johnny stay out after midnight or not?" It's an important issue, but not quite so much as Holocaust victims and facing evil in one person and how you deal with that, which is one thing that I had to deal with in "Duet." It was kind of harrowing to have to deal with that subject matter every day, but the harder it is, the more rewarding it is.

IRA STEVEN BEHR

On one level, you could just say that with "In the Hands of the Prophets" we were doing *Inherit the Wind*, but I think it enabled us, as a specific television series, to explore the Bajoran spiritual life, which we hadn't done too much of. It's one of the things we'd talked about, which is the rational, scientific bent of the Federation versus the Bajoran spiritual outlook on life, which is a clash that gave us episodes for quite some time.

MICHAEL PILLER

The episode is really the showdown between the humanist ideals of the Federation and the religious spiritual philosophy of Bajor. It provides a bookend to the season that has a confrontation that seems to have been coming all along when we met these people and found out what their lives were like. You start to deal with religion in school, school prayer, the Scopes Monkey Trial, and fundamentalism, and it was all very thought-provoking.

IRA STEVEN BEHR

The first season was a toughie. We were struggling, and some episodes were problematic, but it was a whole different thing than on *Next Generation*. With the exception of postproduction—for some reason, Rick felt that was his bailiwick, and you couldn't get involved in post until the end when I finally burst through that fucking glass ceiling—I really felt from the beginning like much more a part of the show. There was a much greater connection and I could give opinions on things besides the writing of the episodes. Even before it was my baby, it was already developing into something special. Yes, the show had a real shakedown period, but I don't recall saying at any point I made a mistake coming back. That's not to say I didn't bitch and moan about some of the episodes we were doing, because I *know* I bitched and moaned about some of those first-season episodes, but it was different. That's normal creative differences.

RICK BERMAN

I believe that because *Deep Space Nine* was a show that is grounded in a space station and is stationary, there are fundamental elements to the show that are going to be less attractive than a show about people going forth and exploring the stars, so the minute you're locked down on a space station and a single spot, it isn't the same thing. I think it's some great television, but I believe to a lot of people it was not exactly what *Star Trek* is. It wasn't like we said, "Hey, I've got an idea, Michael. Let's *not* create a show about a starship."

IRA STEVEN BEHR

We were just doing the best job we could, putting it out there and then whatever happens after that is almost beside the point. We were trying to please ourselves. We were obviously a grittier show and we didn't quite have the rosy outlook of *TNG,* although I think we were a very positive show in our own way. But I'm not talking about what was perceived—and usually what's perceived and what's real are two different things. Right from the beginning we believed that *Deep Space Nine* would be looked at by people as a very interesting take on *Star Trek*. We were getting about as "out there" as *Star Trek* could in terms of what we dealt with and how we dealt with it and the characters that we had.

ROBERT HEWITT WOLFE

From the first season, the creative atmosphere on that show was always the same: very focused, very professional, but never oppressive. It was like professional play. We all loved the show and we loved what we were doing and we liked each other. Even from the very beginning there was always an attempt to do really good television. Ira and Michael were very committed to doing a show that was about stuff and had great characters and fun dialogue that was well written. This sounds stupid to say, because everybody wants to write good television, but they were pros. They knew what they were doing. Absolutely were well-experienced guys who had been on a bunch of different shows and really knew television and really knew what made it work. It was a great learning environment, a very creative environment. It was like everything you wanted to experience, and for a first job I was so blessed.

MICHAEL PILLER

In terms of Sisko, we were having a difficult time matching what our ambitions were for the character with the actor. I've never actually talked to Avery about this, but in the Roddenberry world, race and color really don't play a major role except in terms of whether you're green or an alien, but in terms of humanity, the role of the black man is no different from the role of anybody else. I always felt that was a problem, because I felt a great deal of what Avery had done in the past had used black attitude to define what the roles that he had created and become famous creating were, and there was nowhere to do that in the twenty-fourth century. So there was a certain kind of anger that he carried around with him as a character that was derived from the fact that Sisko's wife had died and that he felt a little bit lost in the universe. It also felt a little bit out of character for Roddenberry's universe, so we were struggling with how to use Sisko in the context of the role of the builder.

Ultimately, I think that worked out all right, but it was a struggle at first. We did have discussions with Avery about that as well. I remember writing a long memo to Ira at the end of the first season saying, "Here's what we need to do with Sisko. Who is this guy, how does he operate as a hero?" and so forth.

IRA STEVEN BEHR

It was at the end of the first season when we received word from the studio where they suggested that we put rockets on the station so it could go off and have adventures. I'm *serious*. And they also wanted us to get rid of Bashir. I don't exactly know why. I just felt that *they* felt the character was an irritant in some way. Which I guess is another way of saying he got on O'Brien's nerves, even though they were friends, and he was a bit of a loose cannon and he wasn't just there to support the captain. He had other things going on, and I don't think they liked that. But we said no, Mike said no, everyone said no. The space station was no and getting rid of Bashir was no.

ALEXANDER SIDDIG

Bashir was *very* unpopular. The audience wasn't used to that kind of character. They kind of like their whiskey straight up, and this watered-down young romantic hunk, which is what I was billed as, was very far from it. I read things like that in the early press releases and thought, "Oh, this is a mistake." I don't think that of myself as a human being, let alone as a character, that I was some kind of dishy hunk served up for the American public; that's just not my thing. So there was a backlash against that. The comments were compounded by the fact that people didn't know what to make of the show, too. There was the first black lead, which wasn't stereotypical. And this was a group of guys in a space station that's not flying around? It was a hard pill to swallow.

Rick Berman actually had to protect me, because they wanted to fire me after the first season. I just wasn't as popular as they wanted and I wasn't fulfilling the demographic duty. I wasn't ticking the box I needed to tick for the eighteen-to-forty-whatever crew.

Deep Space Nine's second season commenced with a groundbreaking troika of episodes that was the franchise's first three-parter, allowing the writers to deal with growing civil unrest on Bajor and a movement to expel the Federation from *DS9*. As such, it was a fascinating, in-depth exploration of Bajoran politics and its impact on virtually all the characters.

An added bonus was the casting of veteran character actor Frank Langella as Bajor's Minister Jaro Essa and the return of Louise Fletcher as Bajoran religious figure Vedek Winn. It was also an effort that flew in the face of the prevalent attitude of the time that everything had to be stand-alone and that serialized storytelling would prove disastrous for future syndication. Unbeknownst to anyone (except perhaps Ira Steven Behr) it also served as a portent of things to come insofar as the series was concerned.

MICHAEL PILLER

The first three-parter that kicked off the season was a commitment to say, "Hey, look at us. Look at what we can do." It was, in a sense, supposed to do for us what "Best of Both Worlds" had done for *Next Generation*. I think that we succeeded. Those three shows really did show the breadth of ambition of storytelling that we were able to do, and the special effects were terrific, the guest stars were great, and the credibility was there.

IRA STEVEN BEHR

Michael, back from his days as a network executive, is definitely a man who is into publicity, and he said, "You know, we didn't do a cliffhanger. Let's do a three-parter. Let's do three and let's jump off from 'In the Hands of the Prophets.'" And since I have to relate everything to either a book or a movie in my life, it seems, I said, "So in other words 'In the Hands of the Prophets' is *The Hobbit*, and now we are going to do the *Lord of the Rings* trilogy." I don't know if he knew what I was talking about, but that's how I saw it.

ROBERT HEWITT WOLFE

The premise of the show is one of serialization. The whole point, and we realized this very quickly, is that the show was about consequences. How the things we do ripple and echo and sustain, and we did not warp away every week at the end of the episode. The premise of "come to a planet, have an adventure, warp away" is inherently an episode-by-episode stand-alone premise. The premise of "come to this place and take control of it and build it into something better" is not that. It is a serialized premise; it inherently lends itself to that kind of storytelling. That is a part of what we were figuring out, but it didn't take very long to figure that one out, to be honest. It was a quick realization.

DAVID LIVINGSTON

It was like doing a movie or miniseries. It had a lot of gunfights and space battles. Piller threw it all into the mix. It was big. We knew we were going to spend a lot of money for the first three episodes of the second season and that we'd have to make it up later, but Rick and Michael just wanted to start off the season with a bang, and I think we did.

WINRICH KOLBE

The metaphor for any artistic endeavor, especially an endeavor that involves time, is Ravel's "Bolero." If you start too fast and too high, you have nowhere to go. If you start too slow, you might never get where you want to go. So it's a very precarious balance. With writing, the longer the writing stretches and the longer the arc of writing stretches, in this case three hours, the more difficult it is not to—pardon me—blow your wad in episode number one and say, "We basically solved all the problems. What do we do for the next two hours?" It's not that extreme, but my feeling was that in "The Siege," the last part, we were really vamping.

LOUISE FLETCHER (actress, "Vedek Winn")

They just asked me to play this outrageous part and I thought it was this one-time thing. Then they kept coming back and asking me to do more. As it turned out, I was available most of the time. You just run over to Paramount, put on the costume, and you try and remember the words, which is not easy. It's a lot of language and it's almost classical. I don't want to say Shakespearean, but Winn did have the tragic flaw of ambition and pride. It's fun to play that high drama. Villains often come across as the nicest people, and that's just pure fun to play.

WINRICH KOLBE

Frank Langella scared the shit out of me. There's a mythology around him. He's a tremendous actor and he's got those dark brown eyes that seem to strip you bare of anything that you're wearing emotionally or literally. When he popped up on the first bit, we started rehearsing, and I figured, "This guy could be trouble," because there's something in him that tells you, "Watch that guy. If you tell him what to do, he might just tell you to fuck off." But he didn't. He was terrific.

Much of the second season was devoted to fleshing out the characters and couching those explorations within high-concept sci-fi stories. It also managed to reveal just how strong the recurring characters were and would continue to be, many of them—such as Max Grodènchik's Rom, Marc Alaimo's Gul Dukat, and Andrew Robinson's Garak—proving as vital to the show as the series regulars. There were moments that celebrated the original *Star Trek*, most notably "Blood Oath," which brought back John Colicos, Michael Ansara, and William Campbell as original series Klingons Kor, Kang, and Koloth (all old friends of Curzon Dax); and "Crossover," a sequel to the "Mirror, Mirror" parallel world episode of the first *Star Trek* that, of course, focuses on that universe's version of *DS9*. Most important, there was the introduction of the concept of The Dominion, a major force within the Gamma Quadrant controlled by the shape-shifting Changelings, known as the Founders, who use the Vorta as their "diplomats" and the drug-addicted Jem'Hadar as vicious foot soldiers. Needless to say, The Dominion was not a benevolent force, and they would become *the* key alien adversary of the show.

MICHAEL PILLER

Ira Behr and Robert Wolfe and the staff worked very hard on creating a new group of aliens that are quite different from the others that we have had before. There is a symbiotic relationship where you have to peel back several layers to understand what they really are. What seems to be the most threatening is not necessarily the most threatening.

IRA STEVEN BEHR

By the second half of the season, things were getting interesting. In season two it was Robert Wolfe, Pete, Jim Crocker, and myself. And as we always did for those seven seasons, no matter who was on staff, lunch played a big part in our thinking about the show. At some point I think we were at a sushi place close to the studio and I said, "Here's what I want to do. I want to come up with three villains. Not one, not two, but three villains. Three new races that will become the antagonists of *Deep Space Nine*." I hadn't talked this over yet with Michael, but this was the beginning of it. This went on over the course of a couple of weeks. Of course we were also discussing what was in front of us at the same time.

At some point we got to the Vorta, and this is a good one just to continue the René–Clint Eastwood comparison. The Vorta were going to be like Brian Dennehy types. That's how that started, that they would be these capitalist, corporate guys who were getting everything set up in the Gamma Quadrant. And the Jem'Hadar were going to be the drug-addicted soldiers, because I had written a screenplay that was set in the future, where soldiers were routinely given this cocktail of drugs before they went into combat. I thought that was kind of a good thing to carry over into this. The big thing, which I wasn't sure how Mike would take, was that the main villains were going to be Odo's people. René Auberjonois said he gave a million interviews where he said we were never going to find out anything about his people. So that was exciting. *That's* when everything started to change.

MICHAEL PILLER

The second season finale "The Jem'Hadar" was a good show, and we had a good look to some of them, but that was only the tip of the iceberg. The Cardassians the first time were very undefined. They had a good look, but it took two or three years before I really felt good about them.

IRA STEVEN BEHR

I said to Robert Wolfe, "Go off and write three documents putting together everything we've talked about these alien races." He went off and came up with the name Jem'Hadar, he came up with the Vorta. He wrote a document that I thought was really good. We presented it to Michael and Michael went for it. Then I figured the coolest way to do this and bring up the Dominion was to just start it in a way that no one is going to know what's coming. So we put it in a Ferengi episode called "Profit and Loss." It was, like, "Oh, this is cool; no one knows but us what's happening."

Then I thought, "Let's do the Jem'Hadar and get these bad boys in here, but let's do it in what seems to be a Jake and Nog story. And people are going to think, 'What the fuck are they doing?'" Unfortunately or fortunately, we rolled quite a bit like that.

MICHAEL PILLER

Deep Space Nine suffered from the middle-child syndrome in its third season. There was *The Next Generation,* which was a media phenomenon—there was nothing like it. When people realized that it sold magazines, the coverage went crazy. *Deep Space Nine* got a great launch, with a lot of publicity, but then Paramount decided that they wanted to do *Voyager,* so the baby came into the family and took attention away from the middle kid. At the same time, *The Next Generation* ended, which got a great deal of press. And since *Voyager* was getting ready to start, people viewed it as *TNG*'s replacement. *Deep Space Nine* just got overlooked. I feel it was treated unfairly for a show of such quality.

IRA STEVEN BEHR

This show is different from the show that came before it and it's different from the show that came after it. Even though people talk about science-fiction fans having vision and being able to embrace the different and the odd and the slightly more esoteric type of show, I don't think that's true when it comes to television. I think people like to find something that's comfortable, and *Deep Space Nine* did not always fit in that way. That made some people uneasy. I really believe there were a lot of people who didn't "get" the show.

   Star Trek is a phenomenon that people have not always been comfortable with, and I think the media waited for what they perceived to be a weak point in the franchise and something they could kind of gang up on. *Deep Space Nine* was an opportunity to do that. The bottom line is we live in a media-haunted society where perception is always more important than reality. Because the show was perceived as a show about people who don't go anywhere, about a space station that is not off exploring the galaxy—which is what *Star Trek* seems to be—that in some way lessens the impact of the series.

MICHAEL PILLER

I would say that *Deep Space Nine* is a much more adult series than any of the other *Star Trek* shows. It's much more psychological and it forces people to confront things that aren't always comfortable.

MICHAEL TAYLOR (writer, *Star Trek: Deep Space Nine*)

It's interesting that all the shows needed a couple of seasons to sort of find their feet, during which time I wouldn't say they sucked, but they weren't as great as they got to be. But they had that time to evolve. At first with *Deep Space Nine,* people are thinking, "Look at these guys, they don't fucking go anywhere. They sit on a space station." The season I came on as a freelancer—it was season four—everything was so different. What is so cool about the show is that it's such a departure from the vibe of *The Next Generation.* It was *dark.*

IRA STEVEN BEHR

Anything we did, six episodes later came back to haunt us. Everything was interwoven and interconnected. This was a very fluid show, which is what I liked about it. Everything—the relationships, the political ramifications—were all very fluid and changed.

I was always aware of the fans and I always wanted to make the show challenging for the fans in what we thought was a good way. Keep them on their toes. We were trying to push the envelope in a way that hopefully the fans would appreciate. We weren't going to give them the same show every week. They had to pay attention. By that point I was fairly obsessed with the idea that we had this great playground, so we had to come up with some new games. What is the show about? How are we going to be different? What can the franchise hold and what can't it hold? Let's not be afraid to fail. Let's risk failure and own the failure as well as the success.

So, anyway, I thought, "Final episode of the season—Jake and Nog? What the hell is that?" And then, bang, zoom, hit them with the Jem'Hadar and pave the way so that people are going to say, "Okay, it's the second season, there is stuff happening here. Can't wait to see season three, because now we're starting to get it." Whether that worked or not, I don't know, but it certainly worked for us.

With *Next Generation* having ended, many of its writers were given the opportunity to work on either *Deep Space Nine* or *Voyager.* In the case of the former, the gains were René Echevarria and Ronald D. Moore, who, together with Behr and Robert Hewitt Wolfe (plus Hans Beimler, who would join the following year) would form the nucleus of the writing staff that would propel the show to tremendous creative heights over the balance of its run. And living up to his earlier promise, Michael Piller stepped back from the show, handing the writing reins to Behr—though a message was delivered to the new showrunner that did nothing but encourage him to truly boldly go where no *Trek* series had gone before.

IRA STEVEN BEHR

At the start of season three, Michael came into my office and said, "Look, Ira. I want you to know I love *DS9* and I think you're doing a great job, but you just have to prepare yourself that *Voyager* is going to be the flagship show of the franchise. *DS9*, no matter what you do, will never be that show. It will always be overshadowed by *Voyager*, because it's going to have the ship, it's going to be on a journey to get back home. It's just going to be way too in the pocket of the franchise for *DS9* to compete."

Well, you can imagine my reaction. My reaction was "Fine. Okay." There was no conflict between Mike and myself, but talk about waving a fucking red flag at a bull. It was, like, "Okay, the Eye of Sauron has moved away; it's looking in another direction. We are going to go for it. Take that as an advantage. Yes, the actors will be disappointed if that's true. Everyone's egos will take a hit." But it was already becoming clear to us that we were our own separate little isolated thing. The bastard child, as the actors still talk about it. But if we were going to be the bastards, we were going to be inglorious bastards!

RENÉ ECHEVARRIA (supervising producer,
Star Trek: Deep Space Nine)

When *Next Generation* was ending, Michael Piller told me I was going to *Deep Space Nine*. But I really wanted to go to *Voyager*, because it was something new and exciting, and I told him that's where I wanted to go. He said, "Well, you're going to *Deep Space Nine*. You can go there or you can leave, it's up to you." Later he told me he thought Ira Behr was a great mentor, a much better mentor than him, and that I still had a lot to learn . . . and he was right.

By the time I became a part of the show, they'd laid a lot of pipe, and I came in at a really great time in terms of a creative flowering. To me, these were really fun characters to write. I found them more real than the *Next Generation* characters, who were almost iconic. They were having a fantasy life where between adventures they would all go to the theater. *Deep Space Nine* felt more real to me in terms of the characters and the setting.

One of the things I remembered talking to Jeri Taylor about when they were developing *Voyager* is that it would be really helpful for the show to have a couple of young guys who are close enough friends that one can drop by another's room, say, "Hey," flop down on the couch, pick up a newspaper and read for five minutes and say, "See you later," and walk out. On *Next Generation* you had to have an excuse for someone to be in someone else's quarters. You'd write a scene, and the notes would say, "Why is Riker visiting Geordi?" There had to be a reason. Thankfully, there was always the crew evaluation report. On *Deep Space Nine* you find people having coffee together or walking along the Promenade. There are so many types of stories you can tell on *Deep Space Nine*. If it wasn't an action-adventure show for young men eighteen to forty, we could have easily done an entire season on life on a station where nothing much happens except everyday life.

RONALD D. MOORE (co-executive producer, *Star Trek: Deep Space Nine*)

In all honesty, when *Deep Space Nine* was being developed and during the first couple of seasons, there was this competitive nature between the staffs. We at *Next Gen* kind of looked down on *Deep Space*. We were the big kids on the block and there was a competitive thing going on. But then you start realizing what they were doing over there, and they started doing cooler things than we could do, and you start getting challenged. It was an interesting evolution of feeling toward it.

In the seventh season I remember I had a meeting with Michael about notes on a script or something, and then the subject came up about the following season and what I wanted to do. I wasn't sure. At that point they were developing *Voyager* and there was something fun about a new show if it was going to be really different. But he said, "I think you might enjoy *Deep Space*. It feels more like your sensibilities. I think you'd enjoy working with Ira again and I think you should think about that. Maybe watch all of the episodes if you haven't seen them."

And from that point I really kind of did shift gears and started thinking more seriously about *Deep Space*. Ira and I had lunch and we talked. By the time *The Next Generation* ended, I'd written those characters for four years. I cowrote the movie; I'd written a lot of shows for them. We knew more about Worf's family than I cared to know. Just moving over to a new series that was starting a third year and looking at these characters made me realize that there were all kinds of possibilities for filling in their backgrounds.

When we were shooting the movie *Generations,* I was there at the beginning of the shoot and then I left for a vacation. It was the end of *Next Gen*, "All Good Things," *Generations* . . . the writing was basically done. Brannon was on the set all the time and I didn't want to be. I just wanted to get away. So I went on a long vacation, came back, and when I came back they were still shooting the movie. The first day I came, I have a picture someplace, I wore a *Deep Space Nine* black T-shirt and a blazer over it and went down to the set. There's a shot of me and Patrick Stewart talking and I'm wearing my *Deep Space Nine* T-shirt. After that I went to the writers' offices and reported for duty. That's how I began *Deep Space*.

IRA STEVEN BEHR

With the end of *Next Generation*, Mike came to me and said, "We're going to make some changes." We talked it over and he felt that Jim Crocker, who I loved, and Pete, who was just having a hard time and for a lot of reasons already started not to seem healthy, had to go. And *then,* after the fact, Mike told me he had fired Robert Wolfe. And Wolfe was devastated, because he had given his heart and soul to the show. I walked into Mike's office and I said he was making a mistake: "I cannot let you make this mistake. Wolfe and I worked a lot together. I worked on his episodes, he worked on mine. I've never had a relationship with any writer where we could get into a room and we just get it done." And he said, "Gee, I didn't know you felt that way. If you feel that strongly about it, we won't fire him." So I went back to Robert and said, "Put on a happy face!" And so, literally, he was fired for fifteen or thirty minutes. It was just so fucking stupid.

But with Pete and Jim, I knew there were other things happening with *TNG* ending and they wanted to find places for René and Ron and Brannon Braga and whoever else would be looking for places. Mike said to me, "I'm giving you Ron and I'm giving you René, even though René wants to go to *Voyager,* but he'll learn more from you. *DS9* will be better for him, even though he doesn't know it." And it was true. René didn't want to come over. He wanted to do the new series, the successful series, the flagship series.

ROBERT HEWITT WOLFE

God bless Ira and God bless Michael, because there's a lot of showrunners who would never have listened to that plea and would have spent the next whatever it was, twenty weeks, trying to prove Ira wrong. Michael was not that guy. Michael was, like, "If you believe it, Ira, I will go with this. And we'll give him more time." That's what they did, and it all worked out. Thank God for Ira's intervention and Michael for keeping an open mind.

IRA STEVEN BEHR

I still remember the day that Michael Piller hugged me for the first time after being in therapy for a couple of years. It was the most awkward hug; it was like being hugged by the Tin Man. But he wanted to show his affection. He had talked to me about how he wanted to evolve. He wanted to become a little more accessible. It was very tough for him. That's not how he was wired, but the fact that he continued to work on himself made him different from a lot of other people. He really looked at himself and saw things that he probably didn't love or wish could be different. I know part of the reason he liked me is because he wished he could be as emotionally open as I was or unfiltered because he was a very filtered guy. Even when I saw things go down that drove me crazy, he refused. He was a gentleman and just wouldn't do it.

ROBERT HEWITT WOLFE

Michael was smart and really knew TV. He could be a little more disengaged on a personal level, because he was so focused on the writing, he was running the show, and there were so many things that he was having to do. So he could be a little less sort of "in" the relationships. He cared, he really did, but he was just a guy who was the most comfortable when he was sitting in front of a computer writing scenes. That's what he loved to do. And he could be a difficult boss, because he had very specific things that he wanted to see happen out of the show and he had a very specific taste. He was very demanding that those things were met, and if he thought you weren't doing it, he would do it himself. But he was really good at giving people a chance and he was, in the end, a very good mentor. What was tough was if you were sitting in a room with him talking about the show—he would much rather have been sitting in a room *writing* the show. That was his thing.

MICHAEL TAYLOR

These guys were like a machine by the time I got there. They were friends, they were all at ease with each other. You could attack an idea or attack each other over an idea as hard as you wanted in the room, but in the end you'd go and get lunch every day and get a drink afterward. It was great.

> Kicking off the third season was the two-part "The Search," which, among other things, gave *DS9* a starship in the form of the *Defiant* and answered one of the show's earliest questions: What race does Odo hail from?

IRA STEVEN BEHR

The major thing we wanted to accomplish in year three was to take the Dominion, which we had been teasing the audience with throughout the last half of the second season, and really bring them to some kind of fruition. We needed to show that there was something worthwhile in the Gamma Quadrant, which for the first season was this big empty piece of space. I think that's what we went off thinking: How do we make this Dominion the next big enemy or antagonist of the *Star Trek* franchise?

A lot of things flowed out of that concept. At one point Robert Wolfe and I were sitting around after the "Jem'Hadar" episode had been filmed. We were looking at dailies and saying, "Jesus, we're blowing up Galaxy Class starships, these guys are tough and all we have are these freaking runabouts that no one likes and are very difficult to shoot in." You had these little piss-ass ships going up against what we were saying were the greatest force of the Gamma Quadrant. We had to come up with a ship to combat them, and that's when we talked to Michael Piller and Rick Berman and said, "We need to build a ship, to come up with something powerful and nasty, something with teeth to it, so it doesn't seem ridiculous that this space station is the only thing between the Dominion and the Alpha Quadrant," and that got us into the first couple of episodes.

RICK BERMAN

For two years we were dying to somehow find a way to get the show to be a little less stationary, and the feeling was that if we could come up with a ship that was slightly bigger than a runabout shuttle, it would give us a little more freedom. On the other hand, it still is not the same thing as being on a starship. If you get on the *Niña* or the *Pinta* or the *Santa María* and go to find the new world, you're an explorer. If you do it in such a way that you have to come back to Barcelona every weekend, it's not the same thing.

IRA STEVEN BEHR

Oh, man, getting Rick to agree to the *Defiant* . . . no ship was better named than the *Defiant*, because it was, like, "This is what we want to do and you have to give it to us." "Well, it has to be small." They didn't want it to be a starship. We said, "Fine, but it will have a bridge and it's going to have weapons. And it's going to be a ship to defend the fucking Alpha Quadrant from whatever comes through the wormhole or what goes through the wormhole." That was a fight, but we stuck to our guns.

ROBERT HEWITT WOLFE

We spent a lot of time thinking about what kind of ship felt like our ship. What kind of ship was like our show? The underdog that people don't always see, but packs a tremendous punch. I think that was a good metaphor for us.

JIM MARTIN (production illustrator, *Star Trek: Deep Space Nine*)

The first concept drawings to come through were these muscular runabout designs. Then it actually grew in size and the producers decided they didn't want something they'd seen before, which brought us to this scooped, *Defiant* look. To begin with, we made the nacelles part of the body and not off of the ship itself; kind of a compact fighting look. The design wanted to be sleek and something with teeth, so we went along with doing some scooped intakes and giving it a smooth, sleek look. Working with Herman Zimmerman and the producers, I'd say we tried a range of looks—things that were sleek, things that were very muscular. We must have done four different batches of designs to give them a broad feel.

From the drawing phase to the model phase, Tony Meininger and company in postproduction really made it come alive. They made that model a fun ship, and Gary Hutzel and his people really photographed it well. I was the first stop in the idea of the *Defiant*, but it was really a collaboration.

RONALD D. MOORE

Everyone acknowledged that with *The Next Generation* off the air, *Voyager* three months away, and *Generations* not due until Thanksgiving, there was a window of opportunity for *Deep Space Nine* to really grab an audience and establish itself. To really say, "This is us, by ourselves, and there is no other *Star Trek* floating around at the moment." We really wanted to do an opening two-part episode that would do a lot for us. We threw the dice and did as much in those two episodes as we possibly could.

IRA STEVEN BEHR

One day Michael said, "I've got a crazy idea. You're all going to think I'm nuts: what if the Founders turn out to be shape-shifters?" We had lunch with René Auberjonois to clue him in, and that's how it came down.

RENÉ AUBERJONOIS

When I first read the pilot script, even though Odo's character was quite sketchy, the fact that he didn't know where he was from and didn't know if there were any others like him was what was most fascinating to me. When they told me we were going to find out, I was concerned about where the character would go. But I must say that I was satisfied by the solution.

RONALD D. MOORE

It was a risk, but less of a risk than doing it with Data. Data's thing is an internal character quest, like Spock's. There's internal conflict all the time as he tries to figure out how to be more human. The Odo thing had a danger of running out of steam early anyway. How many times can you play "I don't know where I'm from, but here's another clue on this planet. Will this show where I'm from? Oh, not this week." I think you would have gotten tired of that after a while, because it was an external mystery and you can only appease the audience for so long and then you start building traps for yourself. It was ultimately a good decision to just go for it, because then we could play all the things with Odo and his people out there who want him back. That's a complex emotion. Who are his loyalties to?

ROBERT HEWITT WOLFE

We just changed his quest a little bit. We took him from someone who wanted to find out who his people were to someone who knew who his people were, but still felt lost. A lot of *Deep Space Nine* was about the quest for self-discovery, and that the truth of the matter is that there really aren't magical answers to the things people are looking for.

But the search continued with every character being explored in different ways, and as the show continued to challenge the notion of traditional *Star Trek* throughout year three, there were many highlights, two of which were the two-part "Past Tense" and the season finale, "The Adversary." In the former, a transporter malfunction projects Sisko, Bashir, and Dax back to San Francisco, circa 2024, where the homeless are imprisoned in areas known as Sanctuary Districts.

The trio has arrived at a precipitous moment in history: A series of events—sparked by the anti-Sanctuary Gabriel Bell—has just begun that will define humanity's future, but Bell is killed while trying to save Sisko and Bashir in a brawl and Sisko finds he must take Bell's place in history or Earth's prosperous future will be lost forever. In the latter, while on a mission aboard the *Defiant,* Sisko and others discover the admiral accompanying them is actually a shape-shifter, culminating in a battle to the death between the Changeling and Odo.

IRA STEVEN BEHR

"Past Tense" was a real highlight of the season. I've always said that I don't like issue-oriented shows, because it's really tough to deal with an issue in an hour; to say something that is worth saying that doesn't just simplify a difficult problem. But Robert Wolfe wanted to do a show about the homeless and came up with all these ways to do it. I had also been inspired by seeing all the homeless people in Santa Monica, who I call living statues, because people used to step over them. They're right there, overlooking the ocean, and people are lying there in the grass. And there are people taking pictures of the ocean and literally stepping over these people.

ROBERT HEWITT WOLFE

My initial idea had Sisko waking up on a Santa Monica beach in 1995, disheveled and disoriented. He knows he's a Starfleet commander, but everyone around him thinks he's crazy. We were trying really hard to avoid time travel because of all of the pitfalls that time travel brings with it, but we didn't succeed.

RENÉ ECHEVARRIA

We certainly didn't want to do a Martin Luther King story, which would have been an obvious way to go. We didn't want to have Sisko leading a march or a protest. That's when Ira came up with the idea of "Past Tense." It was sort of a twist on "The City on the Edge of Forever" where he has to take someone else's place in history. This was not meant to happen, but now that it has, Sisko has to step into history. You don't know what's going to happen, and when you cut to the future you see that history has changed.

RONALD D. MOORE

I liked the idea of Sisko taking Bell's place. It separated him from Kirk and Picard. They always kind of shied away from interfering with the past and being instrumental. We wanted Sisko at the heart of the action.

IRA STEVEN BEHR

When we were developing this, I was struck by memories of the Kent State shooting in 1970. Once they started shooting down American college students, everyone I knew who was still pro-war said, "Maybe we should just end this damn thing." And many of the counterculture kids, ironically, said, "If they're going to shoot us, screw the revolution. Let's become accountants." It had a big impact on me, and I got the idea of doing a combination of Kent State and an Attica/prison-type siege, starting with the question: What would happen if the government started putting homeless people in camps? How would society deal with that or rationalize it? How would the homeless people deal with it?

The frightening thing is that when we started shooting here in L.A., the mayor at the time, Richard Riordan, came out and said something like "We want to take part of the factory district and throw people into camps." That proposal, or re-mark, was on the front page of the *Los Angeles Times,* and everyone on the show went insane when they saw that. Here we were shooting this thing, and it could have actually happened. I don't think we showed anything in that episode that wasn't a very possible future for this country.

RENÉ ECHEVARRIA

Originally we were planning on a big two-part episode to end the season where we go back to Earth—maybe the Academy—and realize that there has been Changeling infiltration. It was supposed to be a big, big show, but we were told we couldn't do this two-part episode. Everybody was very disappointed, though I have to admit that the story we were conceiving was too political.

IRA STEVEN BEHR

"The Adversary" was meant to be a paranoid, tension-producing show and repre-sented an interesting way to use the Changelings, making them more of a threat. The fact is, that show was written in five days after we were told we could not do a cliffhanger. I think it worked well.

One of the most important aspects of this episode was Sisko's promotion from commander to captain. It was about time. We should have made him a captain long ago. It was a mistake to have him be a commander, though it seemed good when the show was created. I would have made him a captain at the end of season one, but certainly by the end of season two we were all feeling we should do it. It was important. We were no longer the junior show. We were as much the fran-chise as *Voyager* was at that point, and we deserved the captain, and he deserved to be the captain. It was a nice way to end the season.

We made a big thing over that promotion, which is what I wanted. By then Mike had stepped away, and if I was going to be executive-producing a *Star Trek* series, I'm going to have a captain. By then we also had the *Defiant,* so many things that had been gnawing at me had been resolved.

There was also an important moment in the second season when we did an episode called "Life Support," and decided to kill Vedek Bareil, whom Mike had always seen as a possible love interest for Kira, but that just didn't seem to be taking hold. I felt it was time to start telling the audience that people, at least recurring people, don't always necessarily make it all the way through to the end. Mike brought Ron and I in there, because Ron was doing a rewrite of what had been his script, and Mike said, "I really don't think you should kill Vedek Bareil. But I'm no longer in the day-to-day ebb and flow of the show. I'm not in the writers room anymore. I'm not hearing how you came up with this stuff and all the different things you tried in the room before you came up with it. I just want you to know, Ira, that this is the last note you're ever going to get from me on the show. Take it or not." I said, "Mike, he's going to die."

Now that doesn't mean he didn't have an opinion on things, but Mike stepped away. He had *Voyager* on his plate, and I'm sure that was more than enough work. And that was it. That's when I really felt completely that the show had passed to me, even though I didn't get the upgrade until the last episode of the season. Avery became a captain and I became the executive producer. We both got the promotion.

ALEXANDER SIDDIG

It clearly became Ira's show about season three or season four. We *did* notice. I mean, Bashir grew up overnight with the James Bond show, "Our Man Bashir." That was the moment where it was, like, "You've been complaining about this guy. Tomorrow you won't." And they were absolutely right; they turned a lot of America's opinion about me on a dime just by delivering that show. It was, like, "Okay, grow up. Be the kind of guy they want you to be." And from that moment on, I was being altogether more serious and more complex and more attractive in an archetypal sense.

ROBERT HEWITT WOLFE

To be honest, Ira was always there, so it was a very smooth transition and Michael didn't just walk away. It's not like a mic drop and exit stage left. It was a transition. It started with Michael running the show. Then they ran it together. And then Michael was still there and reviewing all the documents, but Ira was on point. And then Michael was basically gone and it was all Ira. But it wasn't like everything changed or anything. The show evolved organically and Ira took the reins and it was still true to what Michael wanted. The show was Michael's creation mostly. I mean, Rick did some stuff, I think, but to be honest it was really Michael's show and Michael's baby. And we made it our own, but I don't think we took it out of what Michael ever intended it to be.

Ira deserves a lot of credit. He's a spectacular showrunner and a terrific writer. He's a really good guy and he knows how to run a team and he knows how to create terrific television. And so certainly he did take the ball and he ran with it. He deserves a tremendous amount of credit. But factually it wasn't like everything suddenly changed. The show was moving along, and I think it's fair to say it kept evolving as René and Ron came on. And kept evolving when I left and Hans [Beimler] and Weddle and Thompson came on. The show had its own momentum and I didn't think any of those things made the show radically change at any given time. It continued to grow.

DAVID WEDDLE

Ira Behr was a huge fan of my book *If They Move . . . Kill 'Em: The Life and Times of Sam Peckinpah*. He loves Peckinpah. He loved my book and he invited me to lunch at Paramount. I had lunch with him, and he treated me very well, and then he took me for a walk through all the sets of *Deep Space Nine*. Half of the Paramount lot was *Star Trek* at that time. It was pretty phenomenal.

And being a shameless opportunist, I thought, "This seems like a door opening." So, I asked Ira if I could pitch to his show. I later found out he said to a mutual friend, "Why does this always happen? I have a friend, somebody I like, and then they want to pitch to my show. But then they stop being my friend after I wreck their dreams." But he didn't say any of that to *me*, he just sent a whole bunch of scripts and stories from the current season. [My friend and later writing partner] Brad [Thompson] knew *Star Trek*. I was not particularly a sci-fi–oriented reader. I had sort of an ordinary appetite for it. I saw *Planet of the Apes* and *Twilight Zone* and *2001*.

So, I said, "Brad, I met this guy and he was really nice to me and he sent me all his scripts. Do you want to try and do this, do you want to try and pitch to this show?" Brad said, "Sure." And then we sat down to watch a *Deep Space Nine*. And I was, like, flabbergasted. I didn't know what the hell was going on. What's a Ferengi? What's a Cardassian? I don't understand half the things they're talking about on this show. But we studied it for a month before we went in to pitch.

BRADLEY THOMPSON

David came along with this opportunity, and I was doing educational films at the time. The market was drying up fast, because why would you pay 170 bucks for an eight-minute film about brushing your teeth when you can pay fifteen bucks and have *The Terminator*? So, you could see the writing on the wall for that. So, I was, like, "Okay, let's do this!"

RENÉ ECHEVARRIA

Ira Behr was first among equals, like in the Roman Senate. He would never play the boss, he would let you argue it out and a good idea would win. He would sit down and write with you—he was amazing to collaborate with, and you never felt like the boss was working over your shoulder. And not go in the other room, either: you'd work together.

DAVID WEDDLE

You had to be in the office at nine A.M. on Ira's show. Never been with another showrunner who starts that early. Ira liked to start at nine and be done with all room work and everything usually by six P.M.

BRADLEY THOMPSON

If somebody was writing, they were excused from the room work. But when Ira was doing writing, then usually the room would run and he would write from nine to noon. He would go to lunch, go over the scripts and stuff. And then we'd come back and we would be in the room either fixing that or breaking the next show. And then dailies would come in and we'd all watch dailies together at the end of the day. And then generally you're stuck with being the new guys trying to figure out "Oh, jeez, what is act four of this going to be?" And wandering around till eleven at night trying to solve those problems.

DAVID WEDDLE

It was a super-disciplined room. Very high degree of craft. It was a lot of intense concentration on solving story problems and then, yes, all of a sudden, punctuated by moments of crazy fun.

BRADLEY THOMPSON

Ira would put a mask on and just be sitting there with this thing over his face.

DAVID WEDDLE

And you never knew what color his hair was going to be from one day to the next. But we were working on "One Little Ship" and Ron was writing another episode. We're breaking the episode in René's office, which is on the fourth floor at the top of the Hart Building, when all of the sudden we hear "tap, tap, tap" on the window, and we turn around and there's a little model of the *Enterprise* on a string. Ron had rigged this up and was up on the roof and had lowered it down. There was a lot of discipline, too, and we learned the craft of storytelling from that room from very highly disciplined and talented writers.

IRA STEVEN BEHR

The way I do my job, and I'm not saying it's the right way to do the job, is that I tend to be very open. I say what's on my mind, often to my detriment. I include people; everyone knows what's going on. There are no secrets. The fucking writer's assistant knows as much as the executive producer. I don't hide things unless it's something personal. There are limits, obviously, but what you see is basically what you get. And that is not the way other people work. They have much more of a divide-and-conquer kind of way to go about the business, and it's not my way at all.

MICHAEL TAYLOR

Ira Behr gave me one of my first lessons in showrunning. He said, "I don't know about the rest of you guys, but I was driving home on the highway and I had to pull over to the shoulder because it hit me: What does Odo know and when does he know it?" Or something like that. And I thought, "Holy shit, this is my episode." *I* sure as shit didn't pull over on the highway to think about my episode. I just went to dinner with a girlfriend and had some dinner and fucked each other . . . whatever. But this, it's on his mind twenty-four/seven; these characters all matter to him so much. And that was a lesson in passion and commitment. And you know it's some of the obsession you need to make a show great. So, Ira was awesome. Those guys were all awesome. It was a wonderful experience for me.

RENÉ ECHEVARRIA

I remember Ira was in our office when a call came through from Rick that he's just read the latest draft of a script, and Ira took the call right way. Ira got hyped up: "No! It has to be done this way!" And he marshaled this wonderful argument about how it didn't break the *Star Trek* rules or aesthetics, because of this and this and this and this. It was almost like a breathless rush of intense argument. And then he goes, "Yeah. Uh-huh. Okay," and he hung up and said, "It's staying in." Whatever it was. It was great to be there to watch him make that argument and watch him win it right in our office.

RONALD D. MOORE

Ira's very smart and cunning. He knows when not to run straight at people to get what he wants. He knew how to deal with Rick. He knew how to deal with Mike. He knew how to make his arguments and to make incremental progress and then make breakthroughs every once in a while. But he wasn't always swinging for the fences. He knew he was working a longer game, moving the show piece by piece in certain directions.

He'd start playing character beats with O'Brien and Bashir that, at first glance, are irrelevant character pieces, but bit by bit he's building a web of that relationship, and a deep relationship of these two men and their families and their backstories. And before you know it, you've got this long continuous story of these two characters. How they didn't like each other and how they started hanging out together and then they become buddies and pals and then they become the closest of friends.

That's a complete, long-running arc. He spent a lot of time and energy slowly moving it along the way. When he would fight with Rick, he knew how to fight with him. He knew when to give and when not to. When he could get Rick to back down a little bit by throwing him something else . . . well, he was just very clever about it.

HANS BEIMLER (co-executive producer, *Star Trek: Deep Space Nine*)

It was a continuing battle between Ira and Rick. Rick is not a writer. If you don't think like a writer, you don't think like a writer. Your focus is a different thing. It's much more a director/producer's point of view, and he doesn't see the value of certain things that we, as writers, are going to think are going to make something better. Rick always fought for more money for us when he could. If there was something we thought was really important, he'd go and fight for some money. But that doesn't mean he necessarily understood *why* we insisted on something.

RONALD D. MOORE

Rick can be incredibly charming and funny. You walk into a meeting, and he has that gift that you sit next to him and he's going to start telling you a story or an anecdote and put you at ease. He has that gift of gab. He was very dedicated to the show, but I think on some basic level he was embarrassed that he was there. I don't think that's where he saw his career going. He wasn't a writer. It wasn't his thing. It was Gene's thing and it was *Star Trek*. I think he always had a conflicted relationship with it as a result. He didn't like the fans at all. It was kind of a bad thing to be known as the fan on the production. That was my rep from the very beginning, but even I tried to keep my head down about it. I would put stuff in scripts that were clearly a reference to the original series and everyone would give me a round of shit about it. "Oh, you're putting that fan stuff in the show again." Those of us who were on the show, who were true fans, just learned to keep quiet about it, and Rick didn't like that aspect of it.

He was a very good producer; he knew how to produce a television show on budget and on time. It worked like a machine. All the different parts were running on this very big, complicated endeavor. But his writing notes could be infuriating, because he could get really caught up in making it grammatically correct.

HANS BEIMLER

He would just make you go through hoops. Like he'd get a script, and we were in the final stages of things, once the script has gone through first and second draft already, and Ira and I would take it to the last edit because Ira had me in the room. He did this with Robert, too. We did this to do things faster. And Rick Berman would say he had notes for us. Ira just hated going to those because they were a waste of time. He would have to sit there and listen to Rick Berman's notes, and they were always notes that were to, like, change the word "happy" to "glad." Or there'd be punctuation marks and things like that. Word changes. But the one that was annoying to me and everyone else was when he would give notes on pages that we had already cut out. But he couldn't stop himself; he had to give us the notes. We'd say, "Rick, that's long gone." He'd go, "Yeah, okay, well, I wanted to tell you anyway." And he would have to give the note, because it was the only way he had any power over us. What's the Shakespeare line? "Cloaked in brief authority." We knew that what would get us through those meetings was that that was the only power he had over us.

RONALD D. MOORE

He would give *voluminous* notes, and we started making fun of him, because he would then have to explain the notes to you. He would give you a physical script where he had jotted the notes down in the margin, and each time, he would laboriously explain what these notes meant. You'd heard it a thousand times, but he would put a "B" in the column referring to a line of dialogue. He would say, "Now 'B' means better." And then he'd write "corn," and that means this line is corny. He would write a squiggle and the squiggle means repetitive, you've used a word twice.

And he would explain these notes to you *every time,* and you just wanted to scream, because you've heard the explanation to what "B" means. "I know, 'B' means better! I get it! Just give me the script!" The worst was sometimes he would want to change a line of dialogue, so he would say, "Here's what we're going to do: you read your line and then I'll read my line and then we'll see which one is better." I'm, like, "Oh my God, do I *really* have to sit here and do this?" So I'd have to read my own dialogue for Patrick or something and then Rick would read his dialogue for it and he would have to discuss which was better. And it was, like, "Oh my God, I will cut the line instead of having to sit here."

We were always in Rick's office for hours getting notes on scripts and arguing. I probably argued with him more than any of the other writers, even though we all did. So it was a lot of fighting with Rick and trying to talk him out of things. Sometimes you could, sometimes you couldn't.

ALEXANDER SIDDIG

Ira had such strong ideas and such a firm commitment to them that I don't think anyone was going to hold him back. And Rick trusted Ira; they were strange bedfellows. They're an unusual pair together, and I'm not sure that there's much love lost between them, to be honest. I would be remiss if I didn't point out that Rick was the essential early guardian of the show. He was Roddenberry's man, he was the bearer of the mantle.

RONALD D. MOORE

He took the Gene thing too seriously, in my opinion. After Gene passed away it became Rick's mission to become the guardian of the flame. I just think he didn't really believe in it. It wasn't like he had drunk the Kool-Aid and believed that this is really the twenty-fourth century and this is how people will be. He didn't believe it on that level, but he felt that that's the way Gene said it and that's what we have to do. So, then you had to fight Rick on a note that you *knew* he didn't really believe, but he was doing it because he thought Gene would have given that note, which is really frustrating.

Earth *isn't* a paradise, Rick. C'mon, that's insane. It's insane there's no religion in three hundred years. The religions of Earth have lasted thousands of years. They're not going to vanish in the twenty-fourth century. That's what Gene believed. And you're, like, "Oh my God! How does society function? How does Starfleet function without money? Explain this concept to me! Explain the economics of the twenty-fourth century."

BRADLEY THOMPSON

Deep Space Nine under Ira—remember, I never knew it before then—had the bad boys of *Star Trek*. One of Roddenberry's rules was that we were working for the benefit of mankind. In one episode, Jake wanted to buy something for his father, but he had no idea how to do so. Nog wanted to know why he wouldn't use Latinum. The answer was because they worked for the benefit of humanity. Nog looks at him and says, "What does *that* mean?" He would push against those original rules and concepts to see how far he could go. It was great.

IRA STEVEN BEHR

I barely knew Gene Roddenbery, and I know millions of Gene stories and I've heard people tell Gene stories, but why he got so caught up as a creative human being and allowed himself to restrict his storytelling, I'll never know. I know we need restrictions and being in a box. Like I've said a lot of times, being in a box I have used to my advantage. But to be *that* rigid about it? I always felt that *Next Gen* was meant to be a monument to him. To his future as a futurist. As a man giving hope. I'm not against hope. The fact that there's a show taking place in the twenty-fourth century is pretty freaking hopeful to begin with. And I get that. But I want to understand something: there's no wars, there's no money. Well, if you're going to say that stuff and there's no conflict, you better be able to back that up. I felt the show could never back it up. It was just these rules. They might as well have said the color orange has disappeared. In the twenty-fourth century there's no more orange. I don't know how, but it went with the money. I wish I had the time to sit with him over a bottle of something and—even if it would have ended badly—put him in a position where he would have had to explain it. Not to me, but himself almost. I wanted him to hear it out loud as we went through it piece by piece and validate it, because I can't. I still can't.

RONALD D. MOORE

You have a fight with Michael or Ira, we're all coming at it as writers. We're telling a story. It's a debate about the best way to tell a story. And it's a debate about who the character is. Would Picard do this? Would Picard not do that? Is that really who Worf is? That story is old and tired. You're having a different kind of debate. And with Rick there was some of that, but sometimes it was more dogma-oriented. It was more about what we do and what we don't do on the show. "That's not *Star Trek,* this is *Star Trek.* This is Gene's universe, this is not Gene's universe."

You were having a different creative conversation with the other writers because we know what it is to write a script and we all kind of understand the mechanics of how these pieces fit together. So we're all mechanics, together figuring out how to fix a car. With Rick it's more like you're talking to the guy who owns the dealership. He knows cars and there are cars everywhere, but he's not someone who really actually works on the engines and actually knows why the piston does that.

There were times where you were really mad at him and frustrated and felt like he was the guy preventing you from doing good work, but then again sometimes he was just delightful, and a lot of times you just had a good relationship with him and enjoyed hanging out and laughing with him. You didn't hate him. It was just he was a guy in charge and so your focus or frustration always goes to the person telling you no. There was no studio above him to give notes to us and there was definitely no network, so the buck kind of stopped with Rick. He was the obstacle to letting you do what you wanted to do, whatever it was.

TOM MAZZA (vice president of current
programs, Paramount Television)

There was no network, it was truly a partnership with the studio, so we were on the same team. The tricky part of *Deep Space Nine* was really a matter of what's right for the audience. We were really unable to explore new worlds; new worlds have to come to us. That made it a far more character-driven series, and as a result the characters had to be a little bit more "villainous," because we had to create drama on the set. But that's not something you necessarily go out and know from day one. It evolved over the course of the first two seasons into "This is who we are."

RONALD D. MOORE

It became a more challenging show. The characters could be challenged further. The concept could be challenged further. You could be more ambiguous, you could have harder choices with less satisfying answers. You could see characters evolve and change over time. You had relationships to play with. It was definitely more in the spirit of the original. It was just more of a frontier show. The original series is about the final frontier. *Next Generation* you never quite felt that same sense of living out there on the edge. *Enterprise-D* was a very safe place; they had kids on it. No matter how many times you threatened to blow up the ship, it was still this community with play schools and stuff on it. And *Deep Space Nine* was a rougher and edgier kind of place. You felt like you were on the frontier on that show. And that was definitely in keeping in spirit with the original.

HANS BEIMLER

Ira was continually trying to make it about people. These people had to be real human beings where not everything was explained and not everything was understood about them. But you got to know them on a human level. We never talked about set decorations or anything; it wasn't the way into our story problems. It was always about how to get these people in trouble and what does that trouble bring out in them? How do they react to the outside forces that are being placed against them and how do they deal with it? I mean, that's really the fun of it. When I wrote "The Ship," it was about putting people in a pressure cooker and then turning up the heat until something gave.

The building up of the ancillary characters was something else that Ira was behind. We all were, but he convinced Rick Berman to take that on. Rick did a lot of things I didn't like very much. I never liked his taste very much. I think it was mediocre. But I do respect his desire to make *Star Trek* good and to commit money to it and to fight for more money when we needed it. He didn't want anything but first class. But there was a continuing battle between Ira and Rick.

RICK BERMAN

Ira came in and was very strongly opinionated about how he wanted to start running the show. This was when Michael and I were involved with the beginning of *Voyager*—and even probably before then. I had a lot of disagreements with Ira. I've read a lot of things about the disagreements that I had with the writing staff of *Deep Space Nine* and I think a lot of them are bullshit. Or a lot of them are extremely exaggerated.

IRA STEVEN BEHR

It's the non-writing producer syndrome. The dramatic MB—"Make Better." *That's* a hell of a note. Give that to a writer. Here's the deal and the last thing I really feel like discussing is trying to figure out Rick. Although if there were a novelist writing a novel of the two most interesting characters, it would be Rick and Mike. If a novelist could render them and their many sides, I definitely think they'd be the most interesting characters.

RICK BERMAN

I was in charge of this series and I had the responsibility to keep it *Star Trek*. At that point, the writers became a very tightly knit team. Robert Wolfe and Ron Moore and Ira. They were a little bit resentful about getting notes from me, which I understood. They got a lot of notes about keeping certain things within Gene's way of looking at the twenty-fourth century, which I think they all sort of more than occasionally had problems with.

For instance, one of the big points of contention had to do with the Dominion War for which they wanted to do an entire multi-seasonal arc. I basically said that Gene would be extremely opposed to the idea of a *Star Trek* series being all about a war because this was not what Gene believed *Star Trek* was about. We had give and take and we ended up doing multiple episodes dealing with it but not quite as much as they wanted. More than I wanted. But, all in all, I'm very proud of it. I think there are some great episodes. There were certain tensions on the set between the cast that didn't exist at all on *Next Generation*, but, all in all, it was a terrific television show.

IRA STEVEN BEHR

All I can say is this: on a day-to-day basis, Rick treated me with respect and I treated him with respect. Doesn't mean I agreed with things, but we never had what would be called a really ugly moment. We never got into it in a way that it became personal. I always felt, and certainly by *Deep Space*, yes, we had a world of difference and some of those arguments became what I felt were silly and just a pissing contest. Would Rom lose one leg or two legs in the siege of AR-557? Would we have ten episodes on the Dominion War or eight episodes, and who's going to make that decision? Though he became an advocate finally, can Avery shave his head and wear his goatee?

We had plenty of disagreements, but I think he showed me as much respect as he was capable of at the time of showing anyone who was a writer. I don't know how he worked with Jeri Taylor or anyone else. I never saw any of that, so I can't say, but in that sense I did not feel disrespected as some people felt. Also, he was a bright guy. No doubt about that. Again, like Mike but with less places where Mike and I got along very well. Mike was a close friend. Rick and I were two different people. The way he represented himself and the way he avenged his powers were different than the way I would my powers, let's say.

Major changes took place in season four with the addition of Michael Dorn, reprising his role of the Klingon Worf from *Star Trek: The Next Generation*, as a series regular. It also served as a bit of a shake-up to the *Star Trek* universe as the two-hour premiere, "Way of the Warrior," focused on a breakdown of Federation and Klingon relations, covertly undermined by the Founders.

MICHAEL PILLER

It was very clear to us that the ratings for *Deep Space Nine* had eroded over the second and third season, though we were very proud of the show. Clearly some people had made the decision early on to leave it or not make the time to watch it. We wanted those people to watch again so that they would see what a great show it was. Worf was one of several things we used to say, "Hey, come on back. Check out what we're doing." With a character as beloved as Worf played by as good an actor as Michael Dorn, we thought that would be a nice addition.

IRA STEVEN BEHR

There had been some talk of doing an episode in which the Vulcans pull out of the Federation, which was how the fourth season would have opened. Then I watched the episode "The Die Is Cast" and the line the Founder said, "The only thing we have to worry about in the Alpha Quadrant is the Federation and Klingon alliance, and that won't be a threat for much longer." That just leaped out at me. Suddenly the light went on. I called Ron Moore into my office and said, "You know the line"—which he wrote—"think about it. Maybe we're making a mistake. Maybe the Vulcans should not be the ones leaving the Federation. Maybe it's the Klingons who should break off diplomatic relations. That might have more heat to it."

I brought the idea to Rick Berman and he said, "Bingo! The Klingons. It's gotta be Klingons." We met with Paramount and they said, "It's an okay idea, but you guys don't understand: We want something even bigger than the Klingons."

RICK BERMAN

Our ratings were slipping a little bit and the studio said to me, "What can you do to try to boost them up?" I thought the idea of bringing another character over, because the two shows took place simultaneously, would work, so we assigned Worf, a very popular character, to *Deep Space Nine*.

IRA STEVEN BEHR

I was told that it looked like the addition of Worf was going to happen. We had to go from where we had been tracking through season three with the Dominion and suddenly now we have to deal with the Klingons. Putting Worf into the show as a character was not that big a deal. We knew there'd be episodes where he would certainly be helpful and that he'd be another character that we could explore, hopefully taking what had been done on *TNG* and deepen the character further. So that was fine. It was just the Klingons as a whole became a season-long thing we had to deal with. So that was what was going on behind the scenes. It was, like, "Okay, slow the ponies down, we've got to step back a little bit from the Dominion and what's heating up there and find a way to bring this all together."

I didn't like what the addition of Worf represented. I didn't like the idea that we had to use an established character. See, I loved O'Brien on the show, because I thought he wasn't used all that much in *TNG* in terms of where I knew we could take him. So that was fine. But Worf already had his own storyline, we were trying to establish *DS9* and now there's this *TNG* element—a *strong TNG* element. That being said, of all the characters from *TNG*, if you asked me which one I thought would prosper on *DS9*, it would be Worf. We didn't need Riker, we didn't need the doctor, we didn't need Troi or Geordi or Data, who was *way* too *TNG*. We didn't need Pinocchio—Pinocchio would be killed on *DS9*.

But this wasn't done because we were saying we needed the character dramati-

cally. It wasn't like we were sitting around, thinking that. It was a corporate decision; it was a business decision.

MICHAEL DORN (actor, "Worf")

Rick has a way of making me do things just in the way he asks me. I've got to be
honest, though: when we heard that *Next Generation* was coming to an end, I said,
"I'm ready for it to be over. I'm ready to move on." It was scary in that I was suddenly out of work after seven years, but I was prepared for it. It was truly amazing
that I was back. More amazing is that I wasn't freaking out about it.

RONALD D. MOORE

DS9 is a station of people who are all outsiders coming together. They're all people
who stand alone among their own. That certainly suited Worf. The character dynamic that we went for is, basically, following the destruction of the *Enterprise* in
Generations, his home was destroyed. He had a home and a family there for seven
years and then it was taken away from him, which brought about a reevaluation of
his life. In "Way of the Warrior" he was talking about going back to Boreth, the
place we established where there are Klingon clerics and religious monks. He
wanted to go there to check out his life and see what he wanted to do.

MICHAEL DORN

Inserting Worf into their universe upped the tension level a little higher than it was
before, and it was pretty tense already. The tension that I wanted to insert into this is
the same tension that Worf felt when he first came on the *Enterprise*—a fish out of
water. These are brand-new people, and a lot of them he did not like. But he recognized rank and privileges, so he did not go too far, though he definitely let these
characters know how he felt. That's the beauty of Worf. All of these things he's not
used to seeing, you never know what he's going to do or how he's going to react. His
reaction isn't a lot of words; just let me look at you with that glare. He's *always* pissed.

TERRY FARRELL

When Michael joined the show as Worf, it gave me more confidence, because I felt
like I was doing something I felt I was good at. I feel like I was good at the stunts.

I was good at the action. The whole urgency stuff. Again, just active. When I'm active I'm feeling more confident. And because they liked what they were seeing, they were writing more for me.

RONALD D. MOORE

We could get into darker territory with Worf on *DS9* than we could on *Next Generation*. Some of the fun of that first season was his adjusting to the station, bumping into some of the stranger conventions of *Deep Space Nine*. It wasn't a starship and it didn't run like one. What's with the Ferengi bartender-smuggler-thief-criminal that everyone seems to put up with? Obviously Odo is the chief of security and Worf used to be security. At the same time, there was an interesting contrast between Odo and his notion of justice and Worf, who stands for honor. Sometimes those concepts are closely tied together, but they can also conflict with each other.

MICHAEL DORN

Before, Worf had his comrades around him, he was on the best ship in the galaxy, and he had the opportunity to fight and be honorable. But *DS9* is like a station in Alaska or something. He didn't consider it a punishment, but it wasn't the choicest assignment, either. I think he brought a lot of different things we definitely hadn't seen before. It was very exciting.

RONALD D. MOORE

The Klingon alliance was cool and interesting, because they had been villains on the original series. Well, that alliance had been established ten years earlier. We hadn't seen the Klingons as true villains; they'd gotten sort of defanged. All you could really play with them was the internal politics and the Worf family material. Ultimately, though, they're just great villains, worthy adversaries and very interesting. I think that's why we brought them back that way.

ROBERT HEWITT WOLFE

I wouldn't call the idea of turning the Federation and the Klingons into adversaries again retro *Star Trek*. What Gene wanted to do was portray a better society where problems could be worked out. We were still portraying that vision. The Federation was still the good guys; they were still going to try and find the peaceful solution. But this is history. Our perspective, in a weird way, was that *Star Trek* in particular and science fiction in general is about history. It's showing you what has happened and what can happen again.

In the real world, friends become enemies and then become friends again. Sometimes seemingly overnight. So we took a realistic approach, and the more realistic you can make the universe, the more powerful you can make the message. If things are real bad but there's still a way to work them out, then that makes a more powerful statement. It reminds me of the *Deep Space Nine* manifesto: It's easy to be a saint in paradise, but this ain't paradise. It's easy to be a saint on the *Enterprise,* but it's a little bit harder to be a saint on *DS9.* Our guys still managed it. Sisko was still kind of a saint, but he's a saint that just had to work a lot harder.

IRA STEVEN BEHR

By this time, we had the attitude that we were not going to be stopped. We might have to zigzag. We might have things come up—Worf showing up kind of threw out the season that we had planned and moved it to the following season. But whatever it is, we're going to take it in whether it's a virus or it's positive. We're going to take it into the body of the show and find a way to make it work. Whenever we would get stuck in a story session and realized we had a problem in the flow of the story or there was something we were stumbling on, René Echevarria would go, "Make it a virtue!" And it was, like, "Yeah! That's the fucking attitude! Let's find a way to make it a virtue."

An example of what I'm talking about are the Klingons. There were terrific episodes in *TNG* on the Klingons, but they were episodes. And then you do a whole bunch of other things and then you do a Klingon episode that might or might not have a connection to the previous Klingon episode. Here the Klingons became part of the continuing storyline. We all love to talk about the serialization that took place in season seven, but let's face it: the show was *always* serialized, whether people wanted to talk about it or not. Whether we could do it as fully as we might have wanted to is another story. So suddenly the Klingons are there and there was unity to the stories, there was consequence to the stories. That was interesting and helped that culture, giving it even more specificity.

And it all helped the hell out of the Dax character, for sure, giving her someone she could play off. And that relationship helped Worf's character.

ROBERT HEWITT WOLFE

If we were going to bring on Worf, if we were going to bring on the Klingons, we were going to do them the way *we* do them. We were going to make them a part of the show. It wasn't going to just be a stunt or something that you're popping in and then it goes away and then it pops back in. We wanted to make sure that it was built right into the fabric of the show and was all sorts of strong; that everything built on each other and everything was additive.

And it was a lot of fun. It brought a lot of energy, and the Klingons are just fun to write. It was all good. It was just like throwing in a new ingredient or putting a new item onto our menu that we could serve up. Again, it was not going to be guest-starring Worf; he was going to become part of our family. That was the intent, so that lends itself to a completely different kind of storytelling than if we were just stunting him in for a few episodes.

> The creative dichotomy that is *Deep Space Nine* was probably never better exemplified than at the beginning of season four when it kicked off with the action-packed two-hour "Way of the Warrior"; and *then*, in the very next episode, offered up the intimate and emotional "The Visitor," in which an aged Jake Sisko (Tony Todd) is a reclusive writer living in the backwater of the Louisiana bayou when a young woman visits his home. The woman, Melanie (Rachel Robinson), claims to have been caught in a storm, but is actually searching for advice from the famous author and trying to learn why he gave up a brilliant writing career.
>
> In a series of flashbacks, Jake tells the story of the death of his father, which he wants to share before he dies. What unfolds is that an anomaly has cast Sisko into another dimension in which time moves much slower. Periodically he appears in this universe and is connected to Jake, who is aging normally. Decades later, Jake devises a means for the two of them to get a second chance.

MICHAEL TAYLOR

Sisko and Jake was a powerful relationship on that show. All the characters resonated on different levels. Harry Chapin's song "Cat's in the Cradle" was going through my head when I wrote for them in "The Visitor." I remember sort of blubbering about that and then waking up out of that trance saying that's not my relationship with my dad—but still thinking about that and thinking about this sense of time passing like snapshots, which led me to that whole idea of that story if there was some *Star Trek* anomaly. So maybe it's my relationship with my dad, but whatever it is, it led to my first story for the show.

RONALD D. MOORE

Quite a tour de force. When we were breaking that show, we knew that was going to be a special episode. The format we chose—doing the flashback from the beginning and the old Jake telling the tale to the young writer—was just a great concept, a great idea. It was a departure, which was another thing that was really good for us, because you need to do different things, keep stretching the muscles so the show doesn't get boring. Just a great show and Tony Todd's a great actor.

MICHAEL TAYLOR

Star Trek characters were not lone gunmen. They were not Clint Eastwood riding through town. These are characters who in a way are defined by their connection to each other, to other characters. And when those connections became apparent, when those connections started to feel real is when these shows started to really kick into gear. And that takes time. And maybe it's inevitable that it takes time. Each of these shows gained a real sense of themselves it seems in the third season.

Whether it's *Next Generation* or *Voyager* or *Deep Space Nine,* they had that time to grow. Sisko starts becoming a great character when we realized the depth of the connection to his son. Or the depth of the son's connection to him, because that's the testament to a good father. The son who would change his life, wreck his life, ultimately kill himself to resurrect his father.

RENÉ ECHEVARRIA

The concept was really a challenging one. As Michael Piller would say when you're breaking a story with him, "If you're not crying when you write this scene, it's not working." I'm very happy with the way it came out. In my rewrite, the story didn't fundamentally change except that I tried to give a character arc for the old Jake and Melanie so that that story had some kind of arc to it other than just telling you what had happened in the past. I wanted to give them a relationship.

The other major change is that I had Jake actually write the book about his father. Originally, the way we broke the story and the way Michael Taylor wrote the first draft, Jake never got back to writing, and I realized as I was rewriting it that that was very bitter. In a sense, Sisko had failed as our hero to change Jake's life. So I restructured it and brought Sisko back one last time in limbo, and I had him impact Jake and got him to go back to it. That became his gift to his father, and his gift to Melanie, in a sense. I also thought Tony Todd was just lovely as the old Jake. The show worked on every level.

MICHAEL TAYLOR

I was still in New York playing in a band and temping for money. I remember "The Visitor" came out and I was doing a word processing gig at a big Swiss bank. I heard these two bankers talking about this *Star Trek* episode they saw the night before that they loved. They walked by and I said, "Hey, you know I heard you talking. I wrote that." And they said, "Oh my God! You fucking wrote that? It's so amazing! It's so great! And you're working here?" And I was, like, "Yeah, you know, I still need more money." And they're, like, "God, it's so great. I feel bad about this, but will you proof this document?" So, that's kind of where I was. Betwixt and between still.

IRA STEVEN BEHR

It was another of those *Star Trek* episodes that fans love—a sensitive little episode. The script is terrific, René did a terrific job on the rewrite. He really understood that show. Director David Livingston was really jazzed by that show, and it comes through. Cirroc and Tony Todd did some wonderful things. Avery did some wonderful things. A really good show; a nice, interesting, complicated little tale.

TONY TODD (actor, "Adult Jake Sisko")

As a guest-star actor, I couldn't ask for a better template and will probably never see anything like it again. It was *so* dialogue-driven. Usually they had eight days to shoot an episode, but on this one they had ten; they knew it was a special episode. The last day, I had pieces of the script all over the floor and around the set. There were a lot of words. I didn't have a problem doing it, but we needed to do that so we had something to hold on to and wouldn't slip off the track.

The woman who raised me, my aunt, had passed away about three months before I shot that episode, and I was inconsolable. She was my best friend, she helped me become who I am, she gave me so many virtues, we used to watch *Star Trek* together, and I was depressed. Out of the blue they sent me the script for "The Visitor," and it was like she had reached down and said, "Turn the page, turn the page . . . now fill the page." This was my opportunity to not only bounce back in my life, but to go back to work and try to channel her. The episode is about parental connection, parental responsibility, and what it is to be a genuine person. Older Jake sacrificed his life, his very existence, his future, to bring his father back. It's probably the greatest gift that anybody could give to a family member. If you watch "The Visitor," there are certain mannerisms in older Jake, the way his hands shook, the way he laughed, the way the shoulders were hunched—all of it was completely borrowed from her.

AVERY BROOKS

The preparation for an episode like that is that every day is brand-new. You wake up every day with the full knowledge after you are awake to be grateful for this day, and therefore you go to work or do whatever it is. All I'm interested in is telling the truth. It's so simple in another way, because I loved Cirroc Lofton then and I love him now. Most of what you witnessed in the exchange between us, and indeed Tony Todd in the assistance, most of what you saw was *real*.

DAVID LIVINGSTON

The best script I directed! It was all talking, but emotionally it was profound. About a father and son relationship, and at the time my son was ten, so it really affected me. When I first heard about the script—about Jake and his dad—I just shook my head. I remember when I read the script, I was blown over and thought it was unbelievable. With Ira's suggestion, I rehearsed Tony Todd and Rachel Robinson's scenes at my home in front of my fireplace, because they had to nail that instead of on stage. Tony was great. I had to try to prevent him from crying after every take, because he was crying. He was *so* emotionally invested in it. It was special.

> With all of the action and tension of the season, characters remained at the forefront, with former enemies working together (Kira and Gul Dukat), friendships frayed to the point of breaking but somehow managing to survive (O'Brien and Bashir), characters facing retribution for perceived crimes (O'Brien and Odo), romance (Sisko and freighter captain Kassidy Yates, Kira and Shakaar, Dax and a female Trill), reunions (Gul Dukat and his half-Bajoran daughter, Worf and his brother Kurn) and betrayals (*DS9* security's Michael Eddington revealed to be a Maquis agent; the two-part episodes "Homefront" and "Paradise Lost" in which Admiral Leyton manipulates the Changeling threat to get the Federation president to instill martial law on Earth and give Leyton the power he needs for a more militarily aggressive move against the Dominion, presaging Bush's and Cheney's assertion of WMDs and invasion of Iraq by several years).

And, in the cliffhanger season finale, "Broken Link," Odo is served Changeling justice for having killed one of his kind by being stripped of his shape-
shifting abilities and made human, but not before he learns from his people
that Gowron, the head of the Klingon Empire, is actually a Changeling.

IRA STEVEN BEHR

With "Homefront" and "Paradise Lost," the feeling was that if the Dominion was
going to be such a player out in the frontier, yes, we can keep it to our little special
part of the franchise, which is kind of away from everything else, or we could say,
"No, let's make it bigger than that. Let's say that the stakes are higher." Those were
two big episodes in our thought process in terms of trying to not bring us so much
into the bigger franchise, but to say that *DS9* isn't such an outlier that it doesn't
affect the bigger picture of the Federation itself.

And also, let's face it, it seemed like a smart move on the Dominion's part, and
there's that chilling moment where we find out there are only, like, five shape-
shifters on Earth or something. That was a great moment, because you suddenly
realized the havoc, and now we live in a world where one man, or two men, can
create such havoc if they're willing to go the whole nine yards with suicide bombers and terrorism, and what do you do about it? Do we do martial law and effect it
on society as a whole?

ROBERT HEWITT WOLFE

At what price liberty? If the United States became a fascist state to fight fascism,
would that be worth it? I would say no, and most Americans would say no, and that's
a special thing about the United States and a special thing about the Federation. We
really wanted to explore the idea of whether or not you would destroy the village
in order to save it. We know that the *Star Trek* answer is no.

RONALD D. MOORE

It was a cool idea: a military takeover of a democratic government and how it
would work. What I liked about that episode is that in the first part you're really
on the side of who turns out to be the bad guy. You are with them as they're dealing with these security problems. You think the admiral is on the up-and-up,
and Sisko totally buys into it. It's easy to buy into it. You have a security problem

and you start chopping away at these personal liberties and it all seems perfectly reasonable and rational until, suddenly, you say, "My God, where are we going?" That's what I really liked about part one. You take the audience on a journey and by the end of the episode you've got troops on the street, and you think that's cool, that it makes sense. I thought it was an important show that demonstrated that the best of governments had to be watched. You can't allow our fear or outside forces or interior threats to chop away at our own democratic institutions.

IRA STEVEN BEHR

To a large degree they redid this plot in the movie *Star Trek Into Darkness*. I wish they had done it better, actually. It was too simplified, but it's an action movie and, as Ron Moore says, that's why *Star Trek* films are problematic in terms of the franchise, because they have to be action movies. And *Star Trek* is *not* an action TV series. It's about a lot more than that, and that was a perfect example. All I kept seeing with that movie were missed opportunities, but at the same time I'm not a dope. I realize who they're trying to appeal to.

ROBERT HEWITT WOLFE

The idea of "Broken Link," where Gowron was said to be a shape-shifter, made a lot of sense to us, so we incorporated that into the ending to give the season ender a kick. Every year we sort of managed to end the season with some kind of "Oh shit!" ending. The second season was "Oh shit, the Jem'Hadar!"; the third season was "Oh shit, they're everywhere!"; and the fourth season was "Oh shit, they're running the Klingon Empire and are going to start a war."

IRA STEVEN BEHR

On a certain level it's a strong character piece, and we were a little worried about whether we should go bigger because "Way of the Warrior" had kicked the season off in such a big way and the audience expected us to go out with a bang. Well, we did, but it was a different bang. We wanted to do something that brought the season around full circle.

A notable strength of fourth season was Avery Brooks's Captain Benjamin Sisko, who came to life in a way he hadn't in seasons past. Much of the "new" Sisko could be attributed to the fact that the actor had finally been allowed to shave his head and grow his goatee, thanks to Behr's determination to make the actor comfortable in the role.

IRA STEVEN BEHR

Why *did* we put the guy through almost three seasons of not feeling comfortable? Why? By this point, though, Rick and I were ready to do battle. It was one of those times we were totally on the same page. We got ourselves all revved up. Rick had a cassette with Avery's look of being bald and with the beard. We went into Kerry McCluggage's office, ready for this big fight. Rick puts the cassette in and plays this two-minute thing for them. We're ready for a fight and they said, "Okay, fine."

That was a really good moment, because we were really looking at each other laughing, going, "Wow, don't you feel like there was a fight in your heart that just didn't happen?" We had so many things that we wanted to say that we didn't get to say. I said, "Isn't it weird that it just happened like that?" A quiet victory, but why did it have to be a victory anyway?

ROBERT HEWITT WOLFE

That's what Avery looks like, so why shouldn't you let the guy look like himself? You have a guy who looks in the mirror and doesn't see himself, because that was so much a part of who Avery was. That look, that persona. As a man, as who he was: this sort of unapologetic, strong figure. You put him in the uniform and you take away that look. . . . I don't know if he was struggling, but I would say that it was when we started writing *to* Avery and let Avery look like Avery, the character became a much better character. It let him identify a little more with the character, and the key to a good performance, especially in television where you do it every day, is to be able to really find where you and the character intersect. When you make someone radically alter their appearance in a way they don't identify with, that can be restrictive. It's a subtle psychological thing.

TERRY FARRELL

Avery wanted that look from day one. For us, the notion of the white man "holding us down" is not a thing, but for Avery it *was*. I can't even imagine what the poor man went through with those guys. With Rick Berman. It's like they stripped him of his power. But then as soon as he got to be his physical image and he stopped looking like a black Ken doll—I'm sorry, it's true!—and got to look like his vision of Sisko, it was like night and day. He was suddenly a powerful cat and it was, like, "Whoa, I wouldn't fuck with him!" Before, it was like he was being held back, with them saying, "You can't do this, you can't do that."

J. G. HERTZLER (actor, "Martok")

It felt like Avery had a blanket on before that. They wanted something Middle American when they started out and they finally realized it wasn't right.

HANS BEIMLER

He looked like an idiot before that, but nobody would listen. It was a terrible look, and combined with the uniform, it made him look like an overgrown kid. Hawk is what we needed.

ROBERT HEWITT WOLFE

If an actor brings a tremendous amount of humor to the part, you don't want to write them nothing but straight lines. You're wasting a resource. So Avery's strength and dignity, but also his jazz brain way of looking at the world, his unpredictability—writing to that really helped make the character more than what he would have been if we would have tried to straitjacket him into what was on the page in the initial form.

IRA STEVEN BEHR

As much as he was happy with the beard and the hair and all of that stuff, I think he was fucking thrilled to be made a captain. With all of it he was more in control of his body and his look, and now he's got the authority and he's back in the pantheon of what *Star Trek* is: a captain.

RONALD D. MOORE

There's a scene in "Way of the Warrior" when Sisko is sitting in a room with a Klingon general and Worf. It's a tense scene and they're looking at each other, but you get the impression that *Avery* is the guy in the room you've got to worry about. Sisko, suddenly, is the most threatening presence and the guy who is just going to kick your ass. There are two Klingons with him, and he's just blowing them away. It really gave him an edgy presence, which is great. He was suddenly a comfortable actor and that made a difference.

IRA STEVEN BEHR

One of my great Avery moments is when I was coming out of Rick's office, coming down the stairs. So for some reason, of all people, there's Avery coming up the stairs. I was so jazzed and I said, "Avery, they said yes, you can be bald and have the goat." I just felt like it was a real victory. I felt it was a three-year struggle we had been through together. And he looks at me and he goes, "Oh. Okay." Nods and walks right by. It was, like, "Jesus Christ."

TERRY FARRELL

What I found about Avery is that if you're not willing to talk straight to him about where you're coming from and you're trying to talk around something or put some kind of filter up, he's going to mess with you. That's what I think. My first scene I had with him, I had to pull him aside and say, "Look, I'm really feeling intimidated and I'm supposed to be this old man and I can't." I'm saying it much stronger now than I did then, because I'm a completely different person than I was at twenty-eight talking to him. But I was really nervous and had to somehow resolve this. But that opened up a conversation between us that was just honest and real.

Honestly, he deals with a lot. We were at a convention together and there was a car that we were literally about to step into. Suddenly we get pushed out of the way so Shatner can get into the car and whiz off. It sounds silly, but why aren't you respecting Avery as much? It was *our* car. But if the situation were turned around, there is *no way* they would have ever pushed Shatner out of the way. I know Shatner has been around longer, but it's just glaring. It's not as if anybody came up and said, "I know this is an inconvenience, but we're in an emergency. Would you mind terribly if . . ." No, it wasn't explained at all. It was just completely rude and *that's* the issue.

AVERY BROOKS

The contradiction between what we were playing and reality is this: Oftentimes we worked until two or three in the morning. We're not the only company still shooting, but, yeah, we're late. Cars are going through the gate, the arm comes down. There's a line of cars. Then when I get there, the gate comes down and security says to me, "Open your trunk." I said, "No. Why? All these other cars just . . . Why? What do you think I have in this Volkswagon Rabbit? What's in there, the *Defiant*?" What I'm trying to say is that the contradiction, or the paradox of it all, we can't get away from. You see what I mean? I wish sometimes that were true; that the fact I played Sisko would make some kind of difference on the street. No, only on the screen. The contradictions are evident. They are inescapable in a way.

RENÉ ECHEVARRIA

Between the end of the third and the fourth seasons, I really do believe that *Deep Space Nine* established itself as a legitimate part of the franchise. *DS9* was an imaginative leap almost of the same order as the original *Star Trek*. *Star Trek: The Next Generation* was an evolution of the original series—basically a new *Enterprise* out there having adventures. I think it was an inspired move when they set the show on a space station. People criticized it for not going anywhere, but as we were going into the fifth season, we'd had a solid year where we proved there were many stories left to tell and that continuing storylines could make great *Star Trek*.

IRA STEVEN BEHR

Being a show which is about a family facing the crises they encounter on the edge of the frontier, shares a kinship with Kirk, Spock, and McCoy, which really made that part of the franchise work in the first place. As I've said, we often talked about it being a darker show and a dysfunctional family—which it was on occasion—but we grew those relationships, that sense of unity and the sense of people working together. It's what *Star Trek* is all about. Just working to make something better. At that point, I stopped feeling like the bastard black sheep of the family.

It may have begun in season three, but in season four, the lunatics were running the asylum! The floodgates were open and there was such a feeling of potential. It was, like, Worf comes along, we weren't expecting that, but goddamnit, we're going to make it work. We're going to make everything work. We're going to find ways. It's like this huge canvas, and by that point felt like we were on a roll. We were building on the past and establishing things about the series that made it unique. At that point it was, like, okay, we gave them Worf, forget about the hearts and minds of the fans. They'll come, they won't come, we're the middle child or whatever they want to call us, but we wanted to make the best show that we could. A show we could be proud of. It was a great feeling. A heady feeling.

ALEXANDER SIDDIG

Around that time we became a lot darker. Something left the building and I couldn't put my finger on what it was. The lightness that might have been there before left and it became a darker place. The writing was darker, which must have been part of it. But people's moods had set . . . we were probably negotiating for more money at the end of season three. That made us all grow up, too. We realized Paramount was selling an awful lot of merchandise and not giving us an awful lot of money back. That probably darkened the mood.

There was a perfect storm; there were all sorts of different things that came together to make a different vibe on the show. But that suited me. I could get my teeth into the character in a way that I was kind of ready for by that point. I could darken up, get heavier, become much weightier. We quickly resigned ourselves to the fact that we *weren't* going to be *Next Generation*; that that phenomenon was not going to be repeated. So we had no problem with going with whatever Ira wanted to do at that point.

ROBERT HEWITT WOLFE

The beautiful part of all this is that we were making it up as we went along. That's the secret. There was no vault with five years' worth of stories. It was basically the five of us tap-dancing as fast as we could.

ALEXANDER SIDDIG

The devil was present in the room in a way that it had not been, and I think Kerry McCluggage had something to do with that. His attitude was "I don't know what the fuck you're doing, but whatever it is you might as well have a go. It's *Star Trek*. We can't close you down—that would be too humiliating; that might ruin the franchise. So just get on with it." They resigned themselves to planning their own Paramount network and starting another show that would be the kid they *really* wanted. So they let us get on with it, and Ira benefited from that, because I don't think he would have been very good dealing with the studio and that kind of thing.

IRA STEVEN BEHR

By the time we got to season five, we were able to get the show back in the direction it was headed before we got somewhat sidetracked with the Klingon War, which was to get the Dominion back to the forefront as our enemies. We also had the arc of Kira carrying the O'Briens' baby, which was an interesting character-revealing arc. We were also able to play with Odo's loss of powers for a while, which went fairly well, and continued the developing romance between Worf and Dax.

When we launched season five, we brought back J.G. Hertzler as the Klingon, Martok. He was fine in "Way of the Warrior," and at the end of the fourth season we said we were going to make Gowron a shape-shifter. Then we started to think, "Maybe Gowron being the shape-shifter is too on the nose," so we made Martok the shape-shifter, and then you get rid of him. Plus there was a feeling that the fans were loyal to Gowron, so we made it Martok. Then we watched the show and said, "Gee, this guy Martok is great," so we brought him back on the show as the *real* Martok and he became a recurring character. He's a terrific actor and was a great Klingon. Very charismatic and fun.

RENÉ ECHEVARRIA

Year five was a *really* good year. We had a lot of interesting shows in which we put characters through some rather difficult situations. We did a lot of theme shows; classic themes about violence and how far people will go for their ideals—similar to classic Western themes. There were some stumbles, some shows that didn't quite work, but a lot of good stuff.

RONALD D. MOORE

The quality of the season and the show in general was just a reflection of a really good writing staff who sat around and had fun and really enjoyed the process. We were willing to go through the struggle to make it good each week. We would take it upon ourselves to rebreak stories when we didn't like them and go back to the board if we had to. We just wanted the show to be as good as it could be.

Fifth season brought with it a growing, ominous sense that kept getting worse and worse in the background. The situation with the Dominion just kept getting more dire until the point where you get into an episode like "In the Cards," where you start the show by showing everybody being depressed, which is an interesting way to start an episode. That spoke volumes about where the season had gone by that point.

There had been highs and lows, but this unstoppable march toward war was happening. On *TNG*, the *Enterprise* pulls up to an episode, to a planet, a problem, a character, and then moves on and next week they're someplace else. By the very nature of this show, we're still in the same place and last week's plotline does have to impact what happens here, whether you like it or not. It's hard to get away from that.

RENÉ ECHEVARRIA

Because of the way Ira ran things and because it was so collaborative, we really did dig deep and hard. If I turned in a first draft that wasn't in as good a shape as I thought it was, and then I'd get notes from all these people and realize that I had a huge amount of work to do over the next six days; I was excited about it, because I knew it was going to be better. I knew that the notes I'd been given were good ones, that this was going to be better, and I didn't care how much work it took. One of the great dangers of television is just letting the schedule and everything get you down and doing what you have to do to be done with it.

Probably the worst thing you could say about a plot twist or a story in our room is that it's so TV, so expected, so obvious, such a straight ball down the middle. We were always trying to dig a little deeper, come up with an unexpected reevaluation on a character's part, a more shaded response on the part of our characters if they're confronted with a situation.

We were always looking for stories that put our people in difficult boxes and then really pushed them against the wall to see how far they'd go. There have been a handful of stories where we were seeing people do things that we've never seen on *Star Trek*. We allowed people to fail, to go too far.

The characters were a lot more real and a lot more fun to write. When you sat down to write a *Deep Space Nine* scene, we always tried to get into the scene in an oblique way, not like Counselor Troi would just start talking about her feelings or people who would talk explicitly about their feelings. Ira was always pushing us to try and craft a scene where you got into it in a different way and people didn't say exactly what they were thinking, revealing things more reluctantly or more indirectly. It was a lot more satisfying, as a writer.

ALEXANDER SIDDIG

Ira needed to get political and he had a vision that could be done using *Star Trek* to deliver something meaningful. And credit Rick Berman, kicking and screaming as he was, for letting that happen. He didn't go crazy and he didn't do anything stupid. From my point of view, he was still Rick and he was the titular head of the show, but somewhere along the line there must have been a concession, because I don't think we would have been Rick's ideal.

> The highlight of season five was an episode created to celebrate the thirtieth anniversary of the original *Star Trek*. Entitled "Trials and Tribbleations," it dealt with Sisko, Dax, Bashir, and O'Brien traveling back to Captain Kirk's twenty-third-century *Enterprise* and finding themselves right in the middle of the original series episode "The Trouble with Tribbles." They did so to prevent the physically altered Klingon Arne Darvin from changing history by murdering the starship captain as revenge against Kirk.

IRA STEVEN BEHR

The only thing I would like *Deep Space Nine* to be compared to is—and I know this sounds weird, because so many people, certainly the media, don't see it that way, which is why we try and rub it in their faces with things like "Trials and Tribbleations"—is that even though the two shows are really different, we try in our own way, which is a lot different from a 1960s way, to make this show fun. I don't really think that *TNG* was ever meant to be fun, I just thought it was meant to be serious and "important" on a certain level. I never thought it had much of a fun level to it. They tried in the movies, but that wasn't always successful. I didn't hear a lot of things about *Voyager* being fun. So we tried to be fun. It's a different kind of fun than the Kirk fun, but that's the thing I enjoyed.

There's a bit in "Trials" where some of the characters are talking about how Worf smells. That's the kind of stuff that we could do on *Deep Space Nine*. Those characters know one another. I hung out with a lot of friends when I was growing up, and I'm used to just hanging out with groups of people and having that kind of interaction. We tried to keep that alive. Obviously, that was the best thing about the original series, though it was really just Kirk, Spock, and McCoy. Here we tried to do it over a wide range of regulars and wider range of recurring characters. I think that some of that stuff we did the best, and it made the show unique and certainly made it different than other *Star Trek* enterprises.

ROBERT HEWITT WOLFE

This was the most fun episode of television I've ever been involved with. The most fun to do, the most fun to shoot, and it turned out great. And it was blessed by weird kismet.

We used to go out to lunch every day for an hour and a half. One day we went to Mulberry Street Pizza in Beverly Hills. We were trying to figure out this episode and were talking about it over lunch like we always did, and we realized that the key to the episode was, if we were going to go back in time to "Tribbles," we needed to use the character of Arne Darvin as the Klingon spy. That this character was crucial to the story that we were talking about telling. We were sitting there saying, "We need this character, it won't work without him. Is Charlie Brill still around and is he still acting?"

And Ira said, "Well, I know for one thing he's still alive, because he's sitting right over there." He *was* sitting in the freaking restaurant with us. It was the weirdest freaking thing ever. I honestly can't remember, but I believe we may have walked over to him and said, "Hey, we were just talking about your character in the original series, and we may have a part for you." Which never happens, but it was great. And he did a great job, and it was just one of those things that came together in a magical way.

ALEXANDER SIDDIG

It was such a fun episode and a lovely nod of respect to Gene Roddenberry. We poked fun at ourselves, the genre, and *Star Trek*. And we had those hairdos. Colm and I looked like the Monkees. I loved doing that show, and the guys from the original series came around and they were great. I'm pretty certain George Takei and Walter Koenig were there, just having a laugh. That episode was also the first time I felt a part of history. What's funny is that on *DS9* we had to sullenly fall in line and go, "Okay, no one likes the shit we're peddling, but we'll do it anyway." Then with this episode it was, like, "You want us to do *Star Trek*? This is *Star Trek*. Old school, big as you like, tribbles all over the place." I actually felt like I was doing the *Star Trek* I grew up with, and then we were back to doing *DS9*.

RONALD D. MOORE

My notion for an anniversary show was to go back to Iotia, which was from the original series episode "A Piece of the Action." I had literally pitched this before I was on staff at *DS9*—to go back and find a planet of Kirk and Spock impersonators. For the thirtieth anniversary you go back and you're basically going back to the planet of *Star Trek* fans. They have conventions, they know all the adventures. It's a phenomena and you could comment on *Star Trek* as a whole. I thought it would be interesting. René Echevarria thought it was a dangerous show to do; that we would be talking down to the fans on some level and perhaps it wasn't the best way to go. He wanted to do a *Forrest Gump* episode, combining our characters with the original film footage.

In the room I brought up "Tribbles," and there were two scenes I knew right away from the concept that would be great. One was the big storage compartment opening and throwing tribbles on Kirk's head. And the second is, we're in that lineup after the fight where Kirk confronts a number of officers. Everybody kind of went "Yeah!" and we all started seeing the possibilities. "Tribbles" obsessed us for months; it was a long, long process. So many things had to be answered—the budget, the technical feasibility of doing it with the existing footage. Could we get the rights from all the actors to use their likenesses? Could we bring it in on budget, do we have the right amount of time? All these things, but we kept having faith that, eventually, it was going to happen. And it did.

It's a great piece of television. It's one of the shows for the ages, in my opinion. And it's a salute to the entire production staff from the writers to the director to the lighting, costumes, the set, sound effects, visual effects—*everybody* really put in so much extra time on that episode to really re-create the original *Enterprise* in any way they possibly could. Everybody was staring at film clips, doing research into materials. It was a mania and everybody just threw themselves into it. The entire production staff just went for it. They wanted to make it great. And it shows.

IRA STEVEN BEHR

Just a fun episode, and another show that led to one of the most vociferous arguments we've had: whether or not Sisko should ever meet Kirk before the end of the show. There were people who felt that he should never see Kirk, that they should keep missing each other. I felt that you needed to set it up to see each other and not be able to speak. It became this huge motherfucker argument that in the end we were so deadlocked and there was so much emotion in the air, we actually turned to the writer intern and said, "You, what do you think?" End of stalemate. Of course being an intern and being a smart guy, he sided with his executive producer. And life went on.

Ron and René did a great job with the script. We all had fun working on the story and coming up with things. I was out of town right before that and they faxed me some stuff while I was at the hotel. We were short and I said, "We need to connect these shows in a way that they're not connected yet." That's where the idea of Dax having slept with Bones, which I thought was the biggest hoot, came from. It was a classic moment.

RONALD D. MOORE

Connecting this show to the original was easy to do with these characters, because they could enjoy it on a different level. Dax was the perfect venue for the audience to really get into it, because she had been there before. That gave us a whole element of nostalgia that wouldn't have been present with any of the other series, because Dax is the one character who could look around the old *Enterprise* and say, "I remember this," and she's talking for the audience. "Oh, the tricorder," and she's just grooving on it like the audience is. And O'Brien and Bashir making fun of the whole thing and their look at the *Enterprise*, and Worf trying to explain the difference between the old Klingons and the new Klingons. It gave us so much material to play with and somehow, the way that the original "Tribbles" episode was written and filmed provided all the pieces that we needed. There was never something where we said, "God, I really wish we could do this," and not be able to find a way to do it. It was just one of those things. That show just lent itself very easily to the process of integrating our story into theirs.

ROBERT HEWITT WOLFE

The way we were able to place our characters in that episode had not been done on television before. One of the things I haven't been able to talk about is how amazing our crew was. They could do anything. At some point as CGI became more and more prevalent, the guys stopped saying "We can't do that" and started saying "We can do that, but here's the price tag." It became so much more about how much something would cost. And that's good just in terms of opening things up. We had so much trust in the crew and the actors to deliver whatever we wrote. Every once in a while you adjust something for them, but 99 percent of the time they were just, like, "Yep, we'll do this." Or, you know, "We can only afford three Odo transformations or maybe we can't afford it because we're over budget." But they were *amazing* at pulling off shit like that. They built a third of the original bridge set. Completely re-created it. Re-created corridors, re-created turbo lifts, rebuilt costumes. It was amazing what everyone did. The whole crew—from the art department, the costumers, the visual-effects guys, the extras all looked like they came right off that show and went onto ours. It was amazing and a triumph of television production.

IRA STEVEN BEHR

It was tremendous fun, but it didn't have much to do with *DS9*. It still bugs me when people say it's their favorite *DS9*. It's, like, "Really, is that your favorite?"

ROBERT HEWITT WOLFE

I'd beg to differ. It's *totally* a *DS9* episode. We made that our own and I hope now that when *Star Trek* fans watch the original one, they'll picture Sisko in that bin above Kirk's head, throwing tribbles down.

IRA STEVEN BEHR

I do think that's changed now with the new breed of fans who are coming to it without as much history; the fans who *didn't* grow up with the first series. Yes, you can see the original series anytime you want, but it's not playing on Channel 11 every day. So those fans probably just see it more as a cool episode rather than "Oh, okay, you're finally admitting that you're part of the franchise."

ROBERT HEWITT WOLFE

I left the show after the fifth season. I was burned out. In retrospect there are times I regret it, for sure, but I had sold a pilot, I had sold a feature, and I had done five years in a row of that show pretty much straight through with almost no breaks, so I was a little drained. That was the reason for it. I mean, only Ira did seven years of that show. Everybody else either came later or left sooner. And like I said, sometimes I regret it, but I really was trying to find my own way as a writer and my voice and do my own show. It was really important to me.

There was this sort of unique situation in that I came up on that show, I grew on that show tremendously, but it wasn't a lot of actual producing once I got to the producer level. Just not the way the show was wired. We weren't on set. We weren't really involved with post. And coming from a film school background and knowing the things that I would need to do to be Ira, to be able to run my own show or to be a big contributor on the producer level, there were things that I needed to learn on my own. It felt like the right thing for me to do, but, boy, did I miss those guys. It was fun to go back and do a freelance episode in season seven. It was a lot of fun to do.

IRA STEVEN BEHR

The season ended with the Dominion taking over the station, though it wasn't really a cliffhanger. A cliffhanger is when you leave a situation at a heightened state in terms of the plot, and then you come back and resolve it. Then you find out what happens. That's not what was really going to happen. I didn't view it as a cliff-hanger in the usual sense—it's natural for this show; that's the way we like to put it.

By the end of the fifth season, the staff knew these characters, including ten or more supporting people, to the point where we could take virtually any character—regular or recurring—and in a scene or two scenes could reveal things about that character that kept the audience interested. We had a handle, ultimately, no matter what the first draft might read like, by the time it got to that stage we'd gotten the characters pretty well, for the most part, nailed and the situations nailed, so it just became more and more complex, and motivations became more interesting, as did the way the characters behaved.

It was like a soup that had simmered and sat and been stirred for a long time. Like when my wife makes soup. It's good the first day, it's better the second day, and it's even better the third day, because all of the ingredients have had time to . . . I'd say "gel," but that's a bad word for soup. To mix together, and it just becomes a really complex taste. That's what the show was. *TNG*, the original series, they just didn't hold a candle to what we did. They did other things better, different, maybe more popular. For what we did, we were really good at it and made it a really unique *Star Trek* show for the nine people who got it.

> The season ended with "Call to Arms," which marked the true beginning of the Dominion War as the Dominion, aligned with the Cardassians, take back Deep Space Nine, forcing Starfleet to evacuate the station.

RONALD D. MOORE

A lot was happening in the episode and it moves like a house on fire. You just get pulled into it, and there are so many characters making an appearance and all of these character threads are being manipulated through the episode, but you never lose track of it.

RENÉ ECHEVARRIA

A lot of short scenes, a lot of intercutting between different places. One minute you're on a starbase, one minute you're on the *Defiant,* one minute you're on Worf's ship and one minute you're on Deep Space Nine. You're seeing all these people working toward a common goal. It gives a nice sense of momentum.

In the aftermath of the Dominion/Cardassian alliance taking DS9 at the end of season five, the sixth year began with an unprecedented six-episode arc in which the Federation and Klingons attempt to stop their enemies from destroying the mines in the wormhole. It seems that hope is lost, until an encounter between Sisko and the Bajoran prophets (the so-called "wormhole aliens") turns the tide.

At the end of the six episodes, Starfleet has regained control of DS9, and Dukat, whose daughter (Tora Ziyal) is killed by Damar, suffers a nervous breakdown. The impact of war continues to take its toll on the core group of characters and the season ends with Dukat, no longer seeking power and driven only by a need for vengeance on Sisko for various defeats, embracing the dark side of Bajoran spirituality, the Pah-wraiths, whose power he uses to kill Jadzia Dax and collapse the wormhole, thus cutting Bajor off from their prophets.

IRA STEVEN BEHR

In season six we had to get the station back from the Cardassians, Kira had to give birth to the O'Briens' baby. Also in season six I remember thinking, "Holy shit, have we made Dukat almost *too* sympathetic a character?" The audience just went too far with it, as they are prone to do with certain villainous characters who suddenly become an almost, in some weird way, romantic figure for some people. Just because Marc Alaimo had a very firm sense of who that character was, didn't necessarily mean that it was the same character that *we* saw. He says, "Dukat is not a Nazi," and I would say, "Yeah, he is." "But that's so one-dimensional." "No, it's not." Dukat is a man to whom the ends justify the means. That's the bottom line.

I really thought season six was a season firing on all cylinders with really great episodes. I know that René Aubjeronois wasn't thrilled at first with the Odo-Kira relationship that developed, but what the hell? We thought it was a good way to go. There were a couple of episodes here and there that didn't go where I would have liked them to go, or maybe weren't as strong as they could have been. But that's to be expected, I guess. Like I said, though, there were a lot of stand-out episodes. The overall story was strong enough that I felt we could step away from the main story a little bit.

In season six, the recurring characters grew even more prominent, becoming as integral a part of the show as any of the series regulars. There was Marc Alaimo's Gul Dukat, Barry Jenner's Admiral Ross (Sisko's superior officer), J.G. Hertzler as General Martok, and the Abbott & Costello of space (albeit dryer than the real

McCoys), Jeffrey Combs' Vorta, Weyoun; and Casey Biggs' Cardassian, Damar, who shared many wonderful moments together.

MARC ALAIMO (actor, "Gul Dukat")

I believe the objective in the beginning was to have Dukat be a fairly one-dimensional, aggressive Cardassian. But then I began to add to what they gave me in the scripts and slowly made the character my own. I began to endow him with a number of characteristics, which they then picked up on, and perhaps they realized I was more versatile than they originally thought. So they started writing these wonderful situations for Dukat where he could be seen as being sensitive or irrational or intellectual.

What I like about Dukat is that he can be charming, evil, lovable, mean, funny, vulnerable, and sexy. The heroes on the show never *really* got to be bad. We have a dark side to our nature, but in civilized culture you restrain or control that part of your personality. But Dukat is an opportunist, so he plays both his good and bad sides to get *exactly* what he wants.

BARRY JENNER (actor, "Admiral Ross")

I'm a reserve police officer, and when you go through the police academy in L.A., they talk to you about command presence. Not unpleasantness, but be sure to let them know in situations like that that you're in charge. As friendly as you can be, but here's what's going on, here's what we're going to do, I'm sorry but we have to do it this way. That's the attitude I adopted in my audition for Ross and I got the job.

As an actor, I always try to create a backstory: something that isn't in the show, but that gives me some human history. The history that I created involved having a daughter who was a Starfleet officer who had been killed in this war, so I would do *anything* to bring about the peace. I wouldn't want anyone else to lose their loved ones. Somehow Ira and the writers picked up on what I was doing, because in subtle ways you felt it being incorporated into the character.

J.G. HERTZLER

When my agent originally told me I was up for a Klingon, my response was, "I want to be Hamlet. I spent my life in theater doing Shakespeare." So I went in with the attitude that I wouldn't make it like any other Klingon. I was going to be quite cerebral, conniving, the best I can. Not over the top with anything. Not aggressive openly. So I read for the part and they said, "Thank you. Now, do you know what a Klingon is?" I said, "Oh, okay, you want me to be loud, offensive, abusive, aggressive, angry, over the top." And he said, "Yes." Since I was already pissed off, I picked up a chair and threw it against the wall. It was one of those old folding chairs, and where the little rubber thing comes off it's a really sharp point on the bottom, and it stuck into the wall about twenty feet away. And then I started, although I didn't realize when I threw the chair I ripped half my thumbnail off. I didn't even feel it, because I was so pumped with adrenaline, and I was literally throwing drops of blood on the ceiling.

I got the part.

One of the great things about being able to do a part over a three- or four-year period is the writers start writing *for* you. They have plot and they have to find the objective in the plot, but how he pursues it grows as much from the actor as it does from the writer. And as they began to trust me more, they wrote more *for* me.

IRA STEVEN BEHR

Without any attempt to diss Worf, I always felt that Martok was the truest Klingon that the series had. Martok was a great character and he was full-blown Klingon. I watch that final episode of the series and Martok is just having so much fun. Just his joy at the absolute defeat of the Cardassians was great. "Lots of dead people. Goddamn, let's drink and enjoy it!"

CASEY BIGGS (actor, "Damar")

How brilliant Ira Behr was: he got a stable of writers who were all anarchists and he loved the concept of repertoire-ing. Jeff and I were never regulars, but we were as intrinsically important to that storyline as the regulars were.

JEFFREY COMBS (actor, "Weyoun")

There were swaths of episodes where the series regulars were home by the pool.

CASEY BIGGS

It was, like, *our* show.

JEFFREY COMBS

And that's unheard of. If they hadn't been busy with *Voyager* and launching another *Next Generation* movie, if their energies hadn't been out there, they probably would have said, "No, no, no, you can't do that. We have series regulars, you have to use *them*." But Ira was a magician.

CASEY BIGGS

The writers really liked Jeffrey, and when they killed him off, they said, "Well, shit, let's replicate him. Clone him!"

JEFFREY COMBS

That idea started as a problem solve. "Well, shit, we killed that character. Why did we do that?" That's what they saw in dailies, and then someone said, "We can clone him," and then it became a recurring joke.

CASEY BIGGS

They finally gave Damar a sense of humor, which was great. They knew they needed a foil for Dukat and they saw how Jeffrey and I worked together and built on that.

JEFFREY COMBS

They really were shooting from the hip a lot of the time. They had a sort of plan of storylines, but then a lot of the time they would watch dailies and get ideas from what we were bringing to it. And the next episode we could have those two guys do something else.

CASEY BIGGS

The tension between our characters was great. They'd stick us in the room, and he and I are like in a fucking candy store together when we're playing, and it just works. They liked the way I looked sitting in Quark's bar, and I became a drunk for two years after that. But that's why those writers were so good. Speaking of that, because as a recurring role you don't know how many episodes they have in mind for you, I got a show on Broadway. Ira said, "What are you doing? We've got you scheduled for twelve more episodes." I said, "You didn't tell me that!" You know what they did? They flew me back on my day off and kept our storyline going.

IRA STEVEN BEHR

Then, at the end of the year, we had to suddenly kill Jadzia, which had been kind of a thing all season where we were hearing she was coming back for season seven and then she wasn't. We always assumed it would get resolved.

RONALD D. MOORE

I fought pretty hard to not have Dax die the way she did. I wanted to lose the character in a way that was a gut punch. I wanted Dukat to execute her, but instead he beams into that place to get the Ark of the Orb, and she surprises him or something and gets the drop on him. But the idea in the original was she somehow stumbled across it, or was in the wrong place at the wrong time, and Dukat got her. He just fucking *executes* her. And it was brutal, and it was supposed to be shocking. It was supposed to really hit you, and Rick Berman adamantly refused. He just would not let us do it. "She's got to fire a shot, and she has to die shooting at him. She has to die in a heroic way." And I was just, like, "Come on." I don't think it works the way it is. It's flat

TERRY FARRELL

The problems with my leaving were with Rick Berman. In my opinion, he's just very misogynistic. He'd comment on your bra size not being voluptuous. His secretary had a 36C or something like that, and he would say something about "Well, you're just, like, flat. Look at Christine over there. She has the perfect breasts right there." *That's* the kind of conversation he would have in front of you. I had to have fittings for Dax to have larger breasts. I think it was double-D or something. I went to see a woman who fits bras for women who need mastectomies; I had to have that fitting. And then I had to go into his office. Michael Piller didn't care about those things, so he wasn't there when you were having all of these crazy fittings with Rick Berman criticizing your hair or how big your breasts were or weren't. That stuff was *so* intense, especially the first couple of years.

I started modeling when I was seventeen, so I was used to comments like that, but it was a different experience for me to be around normal, respectful people. And then he's my boss.

According to Farrell, when her *Deep Space Nine* contract was expiring following the end of season six, she requested that she appear in fewer episodes, noting the sheer number of regular and recurring characters featured on the show, which would allow her to work fewer hours.

TERRY FARRELL

Basically he was trying to bully me into saying yes. He was convinced that my cards were going to fold and I was going to sign up. He had [another] producer come up to me and say, "If you weren't here, you know you'd be working at Kmart." I was, like, "What the hell are you talking about? I had a career before this. Why the hell would I be working at Kmart? Who *are* you?" Just to be jerky, he'd call me in my trailer: "Have you been thinking about it yet? Are you going to sign?" Like, right before I had a scene. It was that kind of thing. Rick Berman said I was hardballing him, and I was, like, "I'm not. I just want to have a conversation. You're giving me a take-it-or-leave-it offer and I'm not okay with that." So I finally did have a conversation with him and asked to cut down my number of episodes or just let me out.

RICK BERMAN

To say that this woman was let go is absolutely ridiculous. She was not fired. She requested to not be in all the episodes. She wanted to be a recurring character. You can't be in a situation on our shows where somebody is just going to do seven out of thirteen. I love that people, including some of these actors, love to think that I had all this power. The studio basically said "no way." She's a regular character and she does all twenty-six episodes or nothing. And I think there was a big battle with her attorneys or agents with the studio. I don't remember whether this had to do with money or had to do with her refusal to be in every episode, but she ended up departing. It certainly was not my choice. It was the loss of a character and it was difficult for us.

I've heard stories of her at conventions blaming me and saying that I had something to do with her leaving, which could not be farther from the truth. Brannon and I talk about this all the time, you tend to focus on the nasty things people say about you, and I know that there's been a lot of animosity on the Internet or at conventions that are 100 percent untrue. It's so painful to read stuff like that.

IRA STEVEN BEHR

Let's put it this way: if I had known what was going on, I would have stopped it. There is no doubt in my mind, because that opened a whole can of worms, and I learned more than I wanted to know what was happening under my nose and behind my back of things that were going on. I would have walked over to the Cooper Building and in one conversation I would have stopped that from happening, but everyone chose not to tell me for various reasons. Including, as I found out, to protect me from having to get in someone's face and what that would mean for my position and stuff like that. And I said that was all ridiculous.

HANS BEIMLER

Ira was *really* upset about it when he found out, because it happened on his watch and he wouldn't tolerate that kind of shit.

TERRY FARRELL

When I told Ira what happened years later, I think he almost projectile vomited. Ira was, like, "We were writing *for* you. How could you think we didn't like you?" But I thought he was thinking whatever Rick Berman was thinking. I thought they were *all* thinking the same thing. Rick Berman's representing them, right? But Rick Berman, you don't feel like anyone else could tell him anything. That's the number-one guy. It begins and ends with him so I didn't reach out to talk to Ira, because it didn't even occur to me that he'd have a different opinion than Rick.

Ira, when he found out, was, like, "You would have been recurring?" and I said, "Yes. It would still be thirteen shows." I wasn't starring, Avery starred in it and so did Nana. I was number five. There really was no harm in having me be recurring. But Ira had no idea about the situation. I didn't know I could have talked to him about it at the time.

RICK BERMAN

Terry and I got along perfectly and, for some reason, she departed. Years after she departed, she started saying that I had something to do with her departure, which I can tell you is absolutely untrue. I may have been on the side of refusing to give her seven out of thirteen, but you can't be at a far-off part of the galaxy and just suddenly not show up for half the episodes because you want to go do a movie. Or you want to be with your family. It just doesn't work.

IRA STEVEN BEHR

It *could* have been handled. But you know what? I did not know and no one told me until many years later and that is unfortunate. Other people kept things to themselves, and it went beyond just the actresses. It happened to support staff, too. That's how evil flourishes, when people don't stand up to it. That's the deal. If you don't, they just get away with it.

TERRY FARRELL

I didn't know that I would get the sitcom *Becker* right away. Nobody knew about that. That was just freaking lucky that it was the same lot. I mean, it was easy for me but it could have been on the CBS lot and it wouldn't have seemed so fortunate. It really gave people this false idea that Paramount was saving me or Paramount moved me to *Becker* on purpose. None of that happened.

This wasn't the only behind-the-scenes drama on *Deep Space Nine*. Similar to most television series, over the course of its run there were tensions between some cast members that simmered beneath the surface but never went on to dramatically impact production itself, including interoffice romances between cast members that created friction between some of the actors involved.

ROBERT HEWITT WOLFE

There *was* some drama, but it didn't affect the work. At least from my perception, it didn't affect the way we wrote it. It didn't affect the way the actors worked together. They had whatever stuff was going on down there, but from our perspective it didn't affect things. I've been on shows with casts that have misbehaved in ways that were detrimental to the show, but that was not the case here. There was never a moment when we thought, "Oh, we can't write this scene." They were all super professional.

Every once in a while someone would have a bad day. You do seven years of twenty-six episodes of television, and *someone* is going to have a bad day inevitably. But we never felt like any of that affected the way we wrote the show. Look, we had to deal with Nana's pregnancy, but that *also* happens on a lot of shows. You either shoot around it or you embrace it, and we decided to embrace it and it worked out and it was fun. We turned it into a comedic runner, basically. These were really well-trained actors who knew their shit and were there to do their job, and the job came first. If there was any little bit of drama here and there, it never affected the work.

IRA STEVEN BEHR

There were definitely things going on behind the scenes as in every show. I can't say it had absolutely no effect. It might have had a small effect here and there on a scene or something, but nothing in terms of anything major or anything that was a macro part of the show. No, everyone is a professional, and if we'd taken someone out of a scene at some point, I don't even recall it.

RICK BERMAN

Avery was a very talented and very odd human being. And to this day, I'm sure he hasn't changed. I have not seen him in quite a while. I think you could categorize him as being an angry person. He got along extremely well with half the cast and poorly with half the cast. I know that he was very close to Colm. It had nothing to do with black and white, because Nana and Colm were two of his closest cast members who were both not African Americans. He was very close with Cirroc. And the others all had very odd relationships with him. They were all standoffish and almost frightened of Avery's demeanor. It didn't provide that much of a problem during the course of the show, but it was sad because I had just experienced all these years of a cast that got together so beautifully [on *The Next Generation*]. Every single one of them is still close. And I am still close with every single one of them. I have not gone two months without seeing pretty much every member of the *Next Generation* cast.

With the exception of Kate Mulgrew and a couple of other people from *Deep Space Nine* and *Voyager* and *Enterprise,* I haven't had much contact with them over the last couple of years. But the *Next Generation* cast was a real family. We all sort of began together and started together and they were very close. So when we put together a second cast and you're dealing with people like René [Auberjonois] and people like Siddig, Colm Meaney, Armin Shimerman, and Nana Visitor, you're talking about some heavy-duty actors. Remarkable actors. But still the cast did not have the solidity to it and the warmth that the *Next Generation* had. I think that the tensions that existed did not necessarily get in the way of the show being produced as we all wanted it to be.

ALEXANDER SIDDIG

There was a bit of a falling-out between Avery and I. I don't know if that was growing up and moving on. I'm not sure, really, without being indiscreet, because I could probably go into it, but I think that would be for other people to say. There was tension, but there's always tension with people who live close together as we did. But professionalism won out massively. I didn't even see him as my colleague. He was my boss. He had a temper and I was not going to mess with that. When he got angry, he got *angry*. Everyone knew about it. He's a passionate man.

I had sort of a relationship with Avery for a while, because I was born in Africa and he's African American and there was an affinity there. He would introduce me to Cornel West and militant writers. He loved to talk about African American studies; that was his thing. He was very sensitive to be the color he was in the country he was in, and the history of his people. He took it as a great responsibility, and partly because I am African we talked sometimes. There was an element of fatherliness about him, which I was very grateful for.

> One cannot discuss the sixth season of *Deep Space Nine* without acknowledging a seminal moment from "In the Pale Moonlight," a highlight of the entire series, and discussing "Far Beyond the Stars." In the former, as Federation casualities mount in the Dominion War, Sisko betrays all the ideals he believes in by working with Garak, manipulating the Romulans into thinking they've been betrayed and joining the Federation/Klingon alliance. In the latter, Sisko experiences a vision from the Prophets and finds himself living as fifties science fiction writer Benny Russell, who struggles with inequality and civil rights when he writes the story of a futuristic space station commanded by the African American Benjamin Sisko.

AVERY BROOKS

The fact is that in "In the Pale Moonlight," Sisko ostensibly "confessed" to a computer, looked straight into a camera and talked about it. When we talk about this darker thing, or people have referred to *Deep Space Nine* as this darker thing, in my mind it resembles us. The writers were making a left turn for me [in this episode]. How do you make this palatable? How do you make this comfortable, especially for a man who doesn't want to be here in this situation? *Deep Space Nine* was talking about homelessness and terrorism and all of these things. Gender identity. *That's* us.

IRA STEVEN BEHR

"Far Beyond the Stars" was one of my car moments. Driving from the studio and getting an idea that suddenly seems so good that when I came in the next morning I was ready to jump on it. We'd gotten a story document about Jake being involved with a bunch of writers from the golden age of pulp magazines, and it turned out to be an alien—one of those typical aliens trying to figure out how humanity works or some such nonsense. I liked the idea of the writers, but the rest of it left me cold and we weren't going to do it.

Then, as I was driving home, the whole racism thing kind of got to me. It was really one of those moments that didn't happen a lot, but every now and then going home or in a moment when my head was clear, something would just sync up and I'd get all excited. Suddenly it all became Sisko, and he'd be the guy who couldn't get published, because he was an African American. And the notion that you are both the dream and the dreamer—it just seemed very cool. Plus the idea of all the actors not being in makeup to play different characters.

To an extent it's like shooting ducks in a barrel, because who the hell is going to say that racism is good at this stage of the game? So you're kind of preaching—you would imagine—to the converted already, but I thought it was an interesting way to do it.

AVERY BROOKS

Ira Behr came to me or called me—that's how it is, producers on one side of the lot and soundstage on the other. I went over there and he said, "I have this idea and I want to know whether you are interested, because you will be in front of the camera, but I also want to know if you'd like to direct it." I said, "Well, okay." I thought so many things about it, because the writing talked about 1953, it talked about who we are or who we were, at least. This idea of this brown man writing, or projecting, this vision of science fiction. I thought that was *incredibly* clever. In addition, people didn't have to get up at four o'clock in the morning to put their prosthetic stuff on. I know they were grateful for that.

IRA STEVEN BEHR

That was an episode where Avery and I worked very well together, and that's one of those times he was calling me up at night a lot and we were talking over the show. It was a good experience.

AVERY BROOKS

That statement made to Sisko: "You are the dreamer and the dream." What an *incredible* notion that is. That's at any time, isn't it? Any epoch, any era. Now, later, yesterday.

IRA STEVEN BEHR

At one point I pitched the idea that at the end of the series everything would have been from the imagination of Benny Russell. Of course they wouldn't let me do that—it would have taken away the entire franchise. But what's so crazy about the idea that *DS9* was part of Benny's mind? It's part of Rick Berman's mind and Michael Piller's mind and my mind, Robert's mind, Hans' mind, René's mind, and Ron's mind. So of course it's part of someone's mind.

> The death of Jadzia leads into season seven with the introduction of actress Nicole de Boer as Ezri Dax. Prior to joining the show, the actress had guest-starred on a number of series and costarred in *Beyond Reality, Mission: Genesis,* and *Dooley Gardens.*
> The character of Ezri Dax, as Behr describes it, happened to be the right person in the wrong place, being the only Trill on board a shuttle bringing Jadzia's symbiont back to the homeworld when its life is threatened. With no other choice, an unprepared Ezri becomes the newest Dax host.

IRA STEVEN BEHR

It was awful to lose Terry, but we had to bring in a new character and we knew it was the last season and we had to justify who she was. Ezri's had no training, and she gets all the personalities that are talking to her in her head at the same time not integrated properly. So suddenly she's all these different people, yet not these people. She has all these memories and people's habits and things like that.

It was an interesting and different take on the idea of a Trill. On top of everything else, she was an assistant ship's counselor. As a result, she was the therapist more screwed up than the patients. This allowed us to play a counselor in a much more creative way.

BRADLEY THOMPSON

We wanted to find somebody that was completely opposite of what Terry Farrell was, and we got Nikki, who did a great job. It was Ira's or Hans' idea to dump the symbiont into somebody that wasn't ready, which opened up all kinds of story opportunities that we didn't have.

DAVID WEDDLE

That actually enlivened us, because then we had new stories to tell. It was a good thing. Terry was a loss for sure, but it was fun to bring a new character in and enliven the show and give us more stories to tell.

HANS BEIMLER

I got to bring Nicole de Boer in. I told Rick about her and we had her do a tape. She couldn't get anybody to read the part with her, so she read both parts. She sent us her own tape for her audition. She was marvelous and Rick hired her. I liked her very much and I used her whenever I could. That was my biggest contribution to the casting; I did well on that one. Overall, it was a tough situation, but it was a good tough. You had to redefine the relationship with everybody. It was a good way to sum up why we were here. That's Ira's method of operation: He takes weaknesses, shines a lantern on them, and makes them a strength. Nikki de Boer was just that. Having to redefine her relationship with every character is a great way to bring everybody up to speed so you knew where the characters were.

NICOLE de BOER (actress, "Ezri Dax")

When I joined the show I got some episodes and watched them, but I didn't want to be affected by what Terry had done with Dax. Jadzia was going to be one of many people inside of me, so I played with that. For instance, I did the clasping the hands behind the back thing she did. It was my way of giving a little bit of a nod to her, but she was going to be only one of eight people inside me. Ezri brought with her a different vibe. The energy of the character was lighter.

BRADLEY THOMPSON

Ezri was not planning for this and then, of course, there was the relationship between Worf and her, and you can play with that, saying, "Okay, well, you used to be married." So, how does he feel about being with his wife who really isn't anymore? What are the rules of that? It turned out to be a huge story-generating engine.

NICOLE de BOER

If I'm being honest, the only reason I wanted Worf and Dax to stay together was so that I could jump into the movies with him. But they handled the relationship really well. It was about as good as you could get in a situation like that.

> Additionally in season seven, Sisko and numerous other characters are dealing with the toll of the Dominion War while moral questions are raised as that struggle continues. Most notably, a secret Starfleet organization, Section 31, has developed and introduced a virus that proves deadly to the Founders and will essentially serve as a means of genocide. Shockingly, it's revealed that Section 31 purposely infected Odo in the hopes that he would spread it to his people.
>
> The Dominion forms an alliance with the Breen, which proves devastating to the Alpha Quadrant, and the war intensifies. At the same time, an iron dome is being placed around Cardassia, resulting in Damar leading a rebellion against the Dominion.
>
> In the end, Bashir develops a cure to the Founders' disease, which, despite Starfleet's objections, is administered to Odo, which he uses to cure the Founder by linking with her—the same link that conveys to her that the "solids" are *not* a threat to the Gamma Quadrant (despite the efforts of a group like Section 31). Finally convinced, she ends all hostilities.
>
> The danger is not over, however, as Dukat, working with Kai Winn, attempts to unleash the Pah-wraiths, which leads to a final confrontation between him and Sisko that costs both of them their lives. Sisko, however, in fulfillment of his destiny as the Bajoran Emissary, joins the Prophets. He appears to a very pregnant Kassidy Yates (whom he'd married), telling her that someday he will be back.
>
> As *Star Trek: Deep Space Nine* comes to a close, Odo rejoins his people to cure them and provide assurance that solids aren't a threat; Garak returns to Cardassia to help with the rebuilding after what turns out to be the deaths of

eight hundred million Cardassians; O'Brien is going to teach at Starfleet Academy; Worf joins Martok and becomes the Federation ambassador to Qu'noS; Bashir and Ezri seem on solid footing in terms of a growing romantic relationship; Kira is put in command of *DS9,* Nog is made a lieutenant; and it's unclear whether or not Jake is remaining on the station.

CASEY BIGGS

I died in the last five minutes of the last episode of the last season, which is great. We got the script and it says, "Damar is killed by a nondescript Jem'Hadar." I said, "Oh, c'mon, I can't die like that." The director, Allan Kroeker, said, "Well, how do you want to go?" I said, "I want to go like I'm in a frickin' John Woo movie. I want two big guns. I want to take out fifty Jem'Hadar and I want to die in somebody's arms." He said, "Okay," and I just happened to die in Garak's arms.

IRA STEVEN BEHR

We knew it was the last season and everyone was assuming we were going to start off with a bang, and I made the choice to start with "Image in the Sand" and "Shadows and Symbols," and to do a much more interior, thoughtful show. Like Mike Piller did with the pilot, to get a little more philosophical and spiritual. We had B-stories that had action, but basically it was a man—Sisko—on a spiritual quest. And there was the Prophets. At the time people were kind of pissed off because there weren't enough things blowing up, but I knew by the end of the season there was going to be enough shit blowing up for everyone's taste, so I just wanted to start it differently.

There were people who had problems with Ezri and with us making sure they knew that Dukat was the villain. The guy who became the hero was Casey Biggs as Damar. I'm sorry, but Dukat was *not* a nice man. You might understand him, but that doesn't justify him or validate him. And he was meant to be doomed.

RONALD D. MOORE

I remember when we got into the Dominion War, Rick was adamant at first that the war would only take three or four episodes at the most. And we just said, "Sure," but we lied. We said, "Oh yeah. Okay. No problem." And we just knew that once we got the ball rolling, that we'd never wrap it up in three or four episodes, so that was just trickery. And then as the war went on, Rick would weigh in periodically about how heroic the characters are and "Why does this one have to be so depressing?" and "This one's too violent." And we were, like, "It's a fucking war! What do you mean it's too violent?"

I remember one particularly insane argument that Ira and Rick had when Nog was injured and ended up losing a leg, there was this ridiculous extended argument where I was in a room while Ira was on the phone. We had written the draft where he had lost both his legs, and Rick was just appalled. "We can't lose the character's legs!" And we were, like, "No, we've got to. We've got to have somebody who's injured in this war who's not just a guest star in the background." It was a very important point, but the argument got to the point where they were arguing about, "Well, does it have to be one leg or two? And is it above the knee or below the knee?"

· They were negotiating over where Nog was to lose his leg. It was just absurd. The whole thing is that it's not like he was going to be wheeling around in a wheelchair with stumps. The guy was going to have his leg back the next week, but Rick was flipping out about it.

THOMAS ZELLER (*Star Trek* fan & veteran)

I rarely speak of this, but when *DS9* first came out, I enjoyed it because it was *Star Trek,* and I recalled that *TNG,* too, had taken awhile to gets its legs, so I was patient getting into it, and as time went on I really enjoyed it. It was among the best of *Trek* shows but not my favorite. Now flash forward a dozen years and I had been deployed to Afghanistan and seen my share of war. I am now a 100-percent disabled veteran and am finally moving forward again in my life after three years of Army rehab and now a part of the VA's care.

During this time I've obviously had many disturbing thoughts and feelings. Hard memories and loss. I started watching *DS9* again and amazingly found an outlet that was truly helpful. Long before America or I became well associated with religious extremism and suicide bombers we saw that on *DS9*. We saw the toll of battle and the casualty figures coming in on the faces and the feelings of the characters. And we saw them in the midst of deep desperate battle and the loss of limbs and the struggle to recover. Episodes like "The Sacrifice of Angels" and "The Siege of AR-558" resonate in my consciousness. They are familiar, certainly, but because they take place in an imaginary future far, far from here they are not too close, but just close enough to be cathartic and helpful without tearing me apart.

IRA STEVEN BEHR

I was really getting bummed out how everyone kept asking for these space battles, and I realized that violence and war on *Star Trek* meant nothing, because it was just ships blowing up and we're killing people, but it has no impact and we're just as bad as everyone else in terms of making violence just seem like a plot device. Since ships blowing up were cool, we decided to do a war show, and we tried our best to show what war is.

THOMAS ZELLER

Little did I imagine that anything like a TV show would help me, but it did—and it still does. When I find myself feeling down and missing my soldiers and those days when I was such a vital part of that action I play some *DS9* on the TV and feel at home and not so detached and broken. Today when I go to the VA and meet in groups with other veterans of the desert wars I tell them this, and more than one has told me later that they, too, found help from watching this show. I don't think you have to guess which series is my favorite now and ever shall be.

If I can also reach other veterans and say, "Hey, watch this. You'll be surprised how much better it will help you to feel," then I would give anything I have to accomplish that. The physical wounds we suffer in battle are to varying extents visible, but the wounds we suffer to our hearts, minds, and souls are invisible to all but those who know us. I am willing to lay my heart bare if it will help another veteran, and I am so grateful for the healing I found through *DS9*.

IRA STEVEN BEHR

I knew we were going into a war serialization storyline, and Rick and I argued about how many episodes—eight, ten, twelve. I think we decided on eight and ended up doing ten. He was, like, "Okay, you can only do this many." "But Rick, we have to tell this story." "But this is not the show." It was the last season, so who cares? But that's what this fucking franchise was at that point: rules, rules, rules.

RICK BERMAN

I did feel a responsibility to keep the show in a fashion that would have made Gene pleased. *Star Trek*, I believe, attracted people because of its positive vision of the future. And I've heard that time and time again from everybody from Whoopi Goldberg to twelve-year-old kids. It gives people hope for the future. It's a positive, uplifting vision of where mankind is going to be in the centuries to come. I did not want any of these shows to lose that. Could they bend the rules? Yes. Could the show evolve series after series? Yes. But I wanted to keep that positive essence.

There were times when the writers got quite pissed off about it. But, I felt that if Gene were alive and next to me he would be on my side, and I felt whether I was getting people angry or not there were times that I had to be a little insistent in keeping that vision of Gene's alive. And there were times where I really didn't let things happen that I didn't particularly think should happen.

ROBERT HEWITT WOLFE

Serialization just wasn't how they did things. It wasn't their initial instinct on what kind of show that they thought we were going to do, and they had a successful model and thought we were just going to replicate that model. It was always Michael's and Ira's intent to make a great television show. It *wasn't* their intention to make a Xerox copy of *Next Generation*.

RONALD D. MOORE

Ultimately, I think the studio just had unrealistic expectations about our ability to keep the serialization factor to a minimum. Frankly, we didn't really care. The first half of season seven, after we came back and resolved the two-parter, we then had to do a spate of stand-alones. That was to mollify the great god of the studio so that they didn't freak out. But that gave us more leverage to argue toward the end, "Look, it's the end, you've got to give us this." But we had to give them some stand-alones first.

BRYAN FULLER (coproducer, *Star Trek: Voyager*)

It's fascinating to be in the lower levels watching the frustration that Rick Berman would have with *Deep Space Nine,* because he hated the serialization and he hated that everything didn't tie up in a nice bow at the end. His philosophy was the syndication model, which is you can jump in at any time and you don't need to know characters' backstories. The syndication model is almost anti-character in a way, because it suggests that you cannot grow from your experience. Regardless of how traumatic they are and how life changing they are within the course of any given episode, it has to go back to a blank slate essentially for the next episode so your audience does not have to be burdened with carrying the water from episode to episode.

We have now as television viewers grown so far away from it that it's fascinating to look back and see the different philosophies of the time of what people perceived audiences would or would not reject in terms of what they were willing to sit down and watch. That's something that *Deep Space Nine* and Ira Behr, in particular, would just say, "No, that's not what we're doing. If you don't like it then you can get rid of me, but this is what we're doing." He really stood up for the show and he fought for the show. I learned a lot of lessons from Ira in terms of how I approach a show and in terms of what I am willing to fight for—and I'm willing to fight for a lot.

TOM MAZZA

At the time, the serialized drama was really not the way people saw television. *Deep Space Nine* could get away with it because of the fan base. I think it's easy to say in hindsight, but actually serialization of the show probably helped *build* that core audience and serve that core audience who responded to it. And it's also what made it somewhat distinctive from *Next Gen*. It was about the third season when we realized that it is what it is. It's not going to necessarily get stronger or weaker. We had our audience and rather than try to think it's going to be bigger, we settled into a groove of doing really well with a very different audience.

We just kind of set into what we'll call an attitude of, let's just deliver what the audience is expecting of us. It was that kind of understanding of who the *Deep Space* audience is and knowing it's just not as big. You put *Deep Space Nine* on today on AMC or on a Syfy network—even on a pay tier—the audience will love it.

JEFFREY COMBS

I recently saw Ira and said, "You're a visionary, because now people binge watch television." *DS9* is on Netflix and you can watch the whole thing all the way through. There was a tapestry with *DS9* that lends itself to what's going on right now, because you can sit there and it's a saga. It's a huge interwoven mosaic of characters that the other *Star Trek* shows don't, I feel, possess. It's like *Breaking Bad*. You can't really jump in and watch one episode, you have to start at the beginning. That's the same with *DS9*.

CHASE MASTERSON (actress, "Leeta")

We knew what we had when we had it. That's one of the best things you can ever say about anything, and it's true of *DS9*. Ira Behr said during the fifth season that he thought the show would hit its popularity after production wrapped, when the show was in syndication and people could basically binge watch. As a cast, we knew that the stories that Ira and his team were telling were transcendent. And that's why Michael Piller and Ira took the risk to make it one of the first serialized shows on TV. That was a lot of confidence to have in the audience, because it hadn't really been done before. And look what it's given way to: Ron Moore, David Weddle, Bradley Thompson, René Echevarria, Rob Wolfe—so many top writers came out of *DS9*.

DAVID LIVINGSTON

Ira always felt it was going to be like *The Prisoner*. People are going to feel they're missing something. It's good television and it's got a lot of meat to it.

MICHAEL PILLER

To me, being popular is not necessarily and never has been the signature of success. The original *Star Trek* was supported by a small, dedicated group of fans that kept it on the air, kept it in syndication until it turned into this phenomenon. I believe that *Deep Space Nine* had the difficulty of being on at the same time as all the other *Star Trek* series and during this huge, new rebirth of the science-fiction genre. But, in time, the quality of the writing, the ambitiousness of what we tried to do will become clear, and it will be seen as one of the great *Star Trek* series because it really will stand out from anything else that has ever been done on *Star Trek*.

IRA STEVEN BEHR

This is the thing that I don't think can ever be understood by anyone who wasn't involved in it. Literally everything we did since the middle of the second season was, if not guerilla television, at least had to be generated without the immediate support or understanding of the powers that be. This show had no firm direction. It did not have to develop into anything other than what it was. We all wanted to keep developing it. We had no mandate, no permission, no guidance or direction except for what we came up with on our own. That's a very difficult way to stumble along at times. It's exciting, too, but everything from the backstory to what the Federation is, to latinum, money, and what's Earth, and what's the Gamma Quadrant . . . *everything*. It all had to be kind of created as we were going along.

To suddenly make the show, as we did a couple of times, a slightly serialized show was very difficult. You have shows like *Wiseguy* that did shows in six or seven episode arcs, and that's how that show was geared. That's not like shows like *Bonanza* or *TNG*, where each episode basically, unless it's a two-parter, really had nothing to do with the show that came before and the show that came after. We kept changing as we went on. Certainly the show had a flow in terms of what happened before always had some impact on what happened after, but it's very difficult to do a show like that.

There was no formula on this show, which is also part of my theory that it's not a viewer-friendly show. We did not do what TV is supposed to do. It was not a comforting television series. I'm not talking quality now. Shows can have tremendous quality and be brilliant shows, but each week you basically know what you're going to get. That's why people tune in every week, they like what they get. With us, there was no real formula. We changed it every week. We went down pathways that kept the actors confused, let alone the audience. And that's no way to run an airline.

RONALD D. MOORE

Knowing we could give *Deep Space Nine* an ending allowed us to tilt the show toward a goal for the latter part of the season. Actually, for the last few seasons. To say, "It's going to end there, where do we want the characters to be at the end of the saga?" Having an end point made you look at the series and the characters as a whole. On *TNG*, we didn't really do that. I'm embarrassed to say we didn't even talk about the finale until well into the seventh season. We were deep into it before serious discussion began on what the finale would be. But *Deep Space Nine* had a very different feel to it. We knew this was the last season. We had been talking about it for a couple of years; about various things we could do and ways we could go.

As the Dominion War arc kind of developed, we realized that would be a big part of the finale; we knew that the Prophets had to be involved, that we wanted to bring it back in some ways to things that had been set up in the pilot. I was saying, some of these plot elements, Sisko and Odo, the actual way that they end, I felt might be telling the audience, "Very soon we might be doing a sequel," because Sisko says, "I'll be back," and there are nuggets like that throughout. I didn't really want to jerk off the audience, because there were no plans to do anything.

HANS BEIMLER

When the show was winding down it was very sad, because I was really fond of everybody and we'd done some really good work. It was my first taste of how a team works when it works well over the long haul. That was a really good room. Ron Moore, Ira Behr, Robert Wolfe, René Echevarria . . . Jesus Christ, that was a good staff. I got to make some contributions. We wore our rings—Ira insisted we get rings. He made rings for us all. Really cool rings that had the station coming out of a cloud. It was really sculpted and they were great. Every member of the crew, the cast, every member of the writing team got one. I still have mine; I wear it on special occasions.

But knowing we broke a ten-episode story to wrap it all up . . . I think that's some of the best work I've ever done. And with Ira, we had so much fun doing that. We laughed every day so hard. His wife still tells me it's her favorite time of his career because he laughed every day. He came home every day happy. Why not? We were able to do what we wanted to do.

RENÉ ECHEVARRIA

We never explicitly said we were doing a ten-episode arc. The studio didn't want any "to be continueds" and they didn't want any recaps, strictly because syndication didn't like that. But we proceeded to let the stories guide themselves. A few times we *were* forced to do recaps. And I think there are places you'll find where we were forced to do internal recaps where people talk about what happened. You do your best to not make it sound expositional. For us, it was different to do that. We had some ideas about how things were going to be. We decided that Section 31 was going to be behind the Founders' disease; that Damar was going to rebel against the Dominion; that Ezri and Bashir were going to end up together; that Sisko was in some way going to become a Prophet. But we didn't know exactly how things were going to come down.

RONALD D. MOORE

I will say when we got down to the arc it was more difficult than we had antici- pated. We had done little mini-arcs—the six-episode war arc at the top of season six; we'd tied some episodes together before—but running this many plotlines to- gether over that many episodes was very difficult. It's a different kind of writing. I like the ability to sit down with a story outline and beat sheet and as I'm writing kind of feel my way through it. If I decide something's not working, I change it. Or if I get an inspiration in act three and there's a new way to do a scene, and it will change the whole nature of the show, you do it. Likewise you get to second draft, sometimes the second draft becomes a completely different episode than the first draft. Well, your ability to do that is severely limited when you're at episode three in a nine-episode arc. Suddenly there are domino effects up the line and down the line—it goes both ways.

RENÉ ECHEVARRIA

When we started with the first episode of the arc, "Penumbra," we started throwing the balls in the air, and it was a leap of faith, really, because we didn't know how it was going to turn out. We threw the balls in the air, started catching them and moving things forward. It was a very challenging thing for all of us, because you would be writing an episode and would realize that something wasn't working or something needed to be changed, and the person following you would already be halfway through theirs. You could be rewriting your first draft and suddenly you're making changes that massively affect somebody who's about to turn in their script in three days. To give you an example, I was working on the show where we learn that Section 31 is behind the Founders' disease.

In "When It Rains" we were originally going to find out they were behind it. When I was working on it, I realized that we had a two- or three-episode arc to get there that it was Section 31. First it would be, "My God, this was genetically engineered; my God, it's Section 31; my God, what do we do?" I realized it was basically a "so what?" They had done something in the past to hurt the bad guys. Yes, it's morally corrupt, perhaps, but we're not going to turn and offer the bad guys the cure, even if we could find one. I realized that Odo had to be sick in the middle of the writing, and Ron was in the middle of his script and he said, "Are you crazy? No way, that's going to ruin everything in my script." But we talked about it, he realized I was right, and he had to make that adjustment. So Odo's in danger and you have no choice but to do something about it. That's a good example of how things would change and mutate.

RONALD D. MOORE

The situation caused you to have a lot more communication among the staff, which was a good thing. But it became very dicey because there were times when you need to change plotlines and there were problems that didn't work out. René would find something that he just didn't like or nobody liked and it just wasn't working in his script, and we would just have to change it. That would just force ripple effects everywhere. We were constantly regathering and reworking things. It wasn't something we were used to, because that was a different style of show. If we were to do a show that had more of a serialized format, you're a little more used to working that way. So it was tough. There were some very tense times working through those episodes. But overall it was a very different experience and I'm glad we did it.

DAVID WEDDLE

I haven't seen those episodes in a while, but part of the deal was they had to be stand-alone but the war story could progress within them. When we did "Inquisition," which was really Kafka's *The Trial*, we drew on all these past episodes of Bashir's and brought up all this stuff so it was still a stand-alone show but there were some continuing elements. The war arc, that was revelatory for me. *The Sopranos* had just started and they were having a screening at the WGA of the last episode of the first season. All the writers were going, but I didn't even know what *Sopranos* was. I remember driving over with René and asking, "So what is this show exactly?" He was telling me and then I saw that final episode of the first season and I could tell by the reaction of the crowd that they were reacting to all kinds of continuing storyline things, and I didn't know what they were.

So, then we started to do it in *Deep Space Nine* on Ira's instigation and, to me, that was like a whole door kicked open. Because, honestly, I went into TV to make money. I had been a journalist for years, it was getting harder and harder to make money in journalism. I didn't have tremendous esteem for television as a medium. I always thought of it as what most everybody else did: secondary to film. When we started to do that war arc, which is very much under Ira's leadership, all of a sudden I started to realize, holy shit—there's something you can do with a TV show that no film can do! They can tell a story on a level that Dickens or Tolstoy told a story. That was a real revelation for me. I began to think of TV in totally different terms.

BRADLEY THOMPSON

This is all Ira doing something new and different. He knew how to play that game and get pretty much what he wanted done. And so there were certain things that are part of the arc that were not part of the arc. "Oh, we're going to call it this, but it fit into the arc beautifully even though it was a stand-alone show."

DAVID WEDDLE

Ira deserves tremendous credit. He was always pushing the envelope. Always bending or breaking the rules to see what we could get away with. Tell more complex, darker, richer storylines. And there was considerable tension over that.

BRADLEY THOMPSON

There's a beautiful story that illustrates that. Ron was rewriting a scene for "One Little Ship." We had written this scene, which is pretty much stock television. The Jem'Hadar take over the *Defiant* and they say, "Okay, you're going to do X, Y, and Z. You're gonna get these engines up, or we're going to go do something really, really bad. And if you don't do it we're going to shoot this young ensign." And then the stock version that we gave to Ron was, the captain says, "Don't worry, Ensign. Everything's going to be fine." And Ron took a pass and kept the same line, "Don't worry. Everything will be all right." And the Jem'Hadar blows her head off. And he says, "No, it won't." The studio just totally freaked when they saw that.

Ron came back after the negotiations happened about whether we can blow her brains out or not and says, "Okay, I've good news and bad news. Good news for her is that she doesn't get her brains blown out. The bad news is that she never gets to exist at all."

DAVID WEDDLE

And that's the beginning of the birth of *Battlestar Galactica* right at that very moment.

One of the last tumultuous debates was prompted by the fact that the original ending of the series finale, "What You Leave Behind," had Sisko, following his final battle with Dukat, becoming a Prophet, essentially leaving his worldly concerns—including his family—behind.

IRA STEVEN BEHR

We didn't always intend to have Sisko fulfilling the prophecy, but certainly that season as we started talking about the wrap-up, we talked about it. The one thing

I really wanted to do was *not* have Bajor join the Federation, which was the mission statement in season one. I thought it would be cooler if they didn't. It was too soon, and the idea of Sisko becoming a god, I just thought that the fans consider *Star Trek* captains to be gods to begin with, so we might as well make one an actual god. But Avery saw it as the death of the black captain leaving his son. And I got it, so it was a line change basically. It was, like, "I'll be back," or something like that. It was *not* good-bye. Of course *when* he'll be back is open to interpretation.

RONALD D. MOORE

Avery had some concerns, and there was some validity to what he was saying. Ira, Hans, Rick, and Avery went over it and eventually worked it so that everybody got what they wanted. When push came to shove, they really weren't that far apart. It was more about language than it was about intent or about the concept of the scene or the story or anything like that. It was one of those little mini-crises that, because it happens in the middle of shooting, everybody kind of panics. But if you look back on it, you say, "It was just some dialogue and not that big a deal." Avery did have a point, we had a point, and it was ultimately an easy fix.

BRADLEY THOMPSON

We realized with the Pah-wraiths, all of a sudden we had essentially a battle between good and evil. Between Lucifer and God. It had all of these things that you could put into play. So the conflict was already set. It's, like, how do we make all our players play in very interesting ways and take them to their logical conclusions?

DAVID WEDDLE

I had just seen *El Cid* and I remember saying, "You know, in *El Cid*, he doesn't want to be El Cid. He has plans! He has other plans! I think we should do something like that with Sisko." And then we all together came up with the idea of him building the model farmhouse that he wants to actually build on Bajor, but he'll never live there because he has to sacrifice himself for the greater good, which is what people do in wars all the time. Whatever your plans in life that you had set up, you have to lay that all on the table for the greater good of your society. Being able to tell stories like that coming out of a continuing storyline made that character so much deeper.

In the writers room, people would talk about their most intimate personal experiences. They would talk about novels they read; military history, tactics, World War II. And movies all the time. It was all floating in the air as you're talking. It seems like you're not talking about a story anymore, you're talking about a movie or something, but then that stuff would find its way into the storytelling.

IRA STEVEN BEHR

Deep Space Nine could have kept going, but I kept saying, "Look, we're greedy Americans and we're never satisfied. We always want more. And I get that. But seven is enough." I really convinced myself of that. You know, how dare we be so greedy that we want more? But in actuality, we *could* have kept going. There were lots of places to go that would have been interesting. If we had done a season eight, most likely it would have been the season that, given the time we would have been doing it, where a lot of fans probably would have thrown up their hands because we probably *really* would have gone for it in terms of continuing to question things.

MICHAEL TAYLOR

At the wrap party for *Deep Space Nine*, Ira said, "Not everyone will realize, maybe till later, what a unique experience this was. And you hope to have one of these in your career, never mind two." Certainly for the folks at *Deep Space Nine* I can feel that's what the experience was. For *Voyager*, it was all about learning the ropes for me, with a lot of people who had a lot to teach me and a lot to teach myself. *Battlestar Galactica* was eventually that show for me.

IRA STEVEN BEHR

There is a part of me that is so tired of hearing people accusing me of hating *Star Trek* or of not being a fan. That I only wanted to tear it down. I don't see it that way at all. It's, like, this is the world, let's explore the world. What does it mean? It's just taking nothing for granted. Let's look at it. Let's see what it is. I think we would have continued in that direction, but that's all talk. We left on a very upbeat note among ourselves in terms of feeling like this was a good ending. We knew there wasn't going to be a movie, let's not kid ourselves, and so let's end it. Let's try to actually end it. And that's what we did.

RONALD D. MOORE

I always looked forward to the work on *DS9*. There was just something about being in the room and breaking the stories with that group of guys. It became amazing. You really challenged yourself and each other and the work just kept getting better. It seems like we got out just when we needed to. We got offstage before the applause died down. I'm very happy about that. *TNG*, I think, overstayed its welcome. The last season of that show is kind of rough. With *DS9*, nothing would have pleased me more than to come back for an eighth season, but, creatively, once we started the Dominion War arc, that felt like it should wrap up at the end of season seven. I don't know what the hell we could have done to top that.

IRA STEVEN BEHR

Deep Space Nine was an opportunity and we took it. I don't think that's true of everything that was attached to the franchise. I'm proud for all of us that we did that, and *that's* the legacy of the show. Now, of course, with the all new fans and people binging and without all of that *Star Trek* history meaning so much to people, I think they're able to see the series in a clearer light. Given the fact that it's old, not in terms of dinosaur years but in terms of television years, from what I could see, the last episode still kind of holds up. And that's a good feeling.

ROBERT HEWITT WOLFE

Once we really hit our stride with the show, it was more about the momentum of what was already established and building on the good. I think that there were some growing pains season one and we were figuring things out, but from that point on it felt like a continuous evolution. There were never any radical transformations, even when we did something like bringing Worf on. Whatever it was, it was always a growth from season to season and episode to episode. When you're in the trenches, a lot of the time you're only really looking at an episode or two and you're thinking, "Well, all right. That one didn't work or this one did." As an arc, I think all of the seasons were pretty strong—especially from season two on. We were just trying to tell the best stories we could.

HANS BEIMLER

Ira had said that it was very much a straight line from "Emissary" to "What You Leave Behind," but it's a straight line we discovered looking back. We didn't know where we were going until we got there. We really were keeping options open, discovering the series as we went along. There was a vague notion of what we wanted to do. The one thing nobody may have brought up is that the original mission of DS9 was to bring Bajor into the Federation. That wasn't even mentioned. Nobody cares. In the final arc, all the dangling storylines that were important had to be put together and given a context and meaning and unity at the end. That's what the arc was about. Tie them all up together. Not tie every loose string, but at least address every loose string and give them some sense of unity and purpose. Those were the marching orders at the beginning, what we had to accomplish.

J.G. HERTZLER

The strength of *Deep Space Nine* was the genius of Ira Behr building a family that people could see themselves in. The dynamics of a village. Why did we like *Picket Fences*? You could see yourself there. Why did Andy in Mayberry work? It's about a small town, the characters you become familiar with and you watch them interact and deal with the problems that come into a community when they occur. Here you just add the pressure of invasion or annihilation.

ANDREW ROBINSON

What separated *Deep Space Nine* from the other iterations of *Star Trek* was a darkness, an ambiguity, an ambivalence of morality. For instance, my character, Garak, he lived in the shadows. He had a mystery to him. There's a real appeal and attraction to that. It wasn't so black and white and good and bad and going from planet to planet doing one-night heroic stands. There was a lot of thematic value to *Deep Space Nine*.

ROBERT HEWITT WOLFE

It's a really great show that is about something. It's about family and consequences and how the decisions we make echo. And the weight of them. And the joy of growing with people. It's a very rich show and I'm glad that it seems to hold up really well. A lot of television shows from twenty years ago don't hold up that well, but I hear all the time people saying that they started watching *DS9* for the first time on Netflix and that it holds up and is fun and engaging. *That* I'm really happy about. To me, it's one of the best things I've ever worked on and I'm incredibly proud of all that work. It seems to sustain, and that's really nice.

IRA STEVEN BEHR

If you want to talk about overarching successes, we were a strongly individual series within the franchise. We went places with the show that were unique. Our mode of storytelling was unique. Our character-driven show was unique. The number of ancillary characters who were as interesting as other shows' lead characters was unique. I think we honor the franchise by attempting to move it forward. And at the end of seven years, we basically had a novel for television. Some of the chapters you might want to skip over, but on the whole it hangs together, and as a creative endeavor it honored the actors, it honored the writers and it honored the crew.

We did the best that we could and we owned the failures as well as the successes. Even if our reach exceeded our grasp, we tried our best to make a show that helped rather than hurt the franchise. It's something you could pick up today, look at and go, "Oh, yes, some interesting stuff was done on *Star Trek*." Some other interesting stuff was done on other series, too, and movies, but our little piece of the pie is kind of yummy.

HANS BEIMLER

This show, to me, follows the traditions of the original series more than *The Next Generation*. On the surface, *Next Generation* looks much more in the tradition of the original series, but I think in actuality we were. *Next Generation* to me wasn't about the characters, ultimately. It was about Picard, Data, and not really about the rest of them. After all those years, how much can you tell me about Geordi? Even Riker. There's a few things you can tell me about Riker and Troi, but not that many. I think that *Deep Space Nine,* each one of these characters is well defined and complicated. We could talk pretty substantially about each of them. The same is true of the semi-regulars, like Weyoun, Damar, Kai Winn, and so forth. It's closer in tone to the original series, and not because it's an optimistic view of the world. Kirk and that stuff—regardless of what Gene used to say—wasn't an optimistic view of the world. Every once in a while there was a humanist speech, but their actions were quite different.

What *Deep Space Nine* taught me is that the world is really not that complicated; it's *people* that are complicated. The world itself is pretty damn simple. The people complicate life. That's where the drama is. A man and a woman have a sexual encounter, and then you bring in the fact that it has long-lasting effects. You don't know what the circumstances were, but they were obviously strangers of some kind, and before they even know each other's last name, they're screwing. Then what happens is that you find out she's married to somebody else, so you bring in *that* person. And then the guy feels guilty and that leads you to meet his wife or girlfriend and things track from *there*. People do things because of what happens to them. That's really the motivating factor. The "science fiction" is all about human behavior.

ALEXANDER SIDDIG

This was sci-fi in the true sense, exploring an idea transposed to a different place. Difficult things that normally people don't want to talk about, because they find it uncomfortable. Politics, religion . . . things you're not supposed to talk about, and which is very hard for TV to pull off without being patronizing. *DS9* is the true sci-fi baby of the *Star Trek* world, which is ironic to say because you immediately associate *Star Trek* with sci-fi, but you don't think of *DS9* as *Star Trek*. When you say *Star Trek*, you think Jean-Luc Picard or James T. Kirk, you don't think Sisko. Which is ironic, because the most real sci-fi there is of the whole genre is *DS9* as far as I'm concerned.

NANA VISITOR

We were definitely the black sheep of the family. I remember sitting with Armin Shimerman on set and saying, "They don't really get us, the *Star Trek* fans." And they didn't at the time, but we said, "Ten, twenty years from now they'll get it." That's proven to be true; people are discovering it now thanks to streaming. They're rediscovering the show and it's nice to see. *And* the show holds up.

SALOME JENS (actress, "Founder")

They're all very human stories. What they do is put them in a very dramatic environment, and who you see is yourself and the world you live in. It's certainly reflecting our humanity and the mistakes we make and the mistakes we don't make.

ROBERT HEWITT WOLFE

We were always kind of the ugly stepchild of the franchise, and we never really had our moment in the sun. Except for when we premiered. That *one* episode. We were never the primary focus of the promotional budgets and the attention of the powers that be—which helped us tremendously in some ways, because we were able to get away with a lot. Middle children *always* get away with a lot. But sometimes it's, like, "Oh, c'mon. How about a little bit of love every once in a while?"

TERRY FARRELL

People are always going on and on about what a family the *Next Gen* cast is and how we weren't. Here's my side: I think *Next Generation* are the popular kids in high school. They're totally a clique. They're all dancing to the same song; we're each dancing to our own different songs, but we still come together. I'm not trying to say it's deeper than what *Next Gen* has. It's just different. We're all from broken homes and we come together and make ourselves a group. They all come from the same home. We all came to the space station and we're all coming from a different place, and they all came from Starfleet.

We're the kids from the dysfunctional family, but we survived. We're not the fuckups that come together, we're the survivors that come together.

DAVID WEDDLE

It's hard to imagine *Battlestar Galactica* existing without *Deep Space Nine*. You can see when you watch those last three seasons or so Ron Moore growing as a talent. Because of the space Ira carved out for him. The things that Ira encouraged us to do. Ron just took that ball and ran with it. And then not only his frustrations that we couldn't do everything we wanted to do but also the possibilities that he saw. All of that had a huge impact on *Battlestar*. I'm not sure we could imagine one without the other. It's like Sam Peckinpah and John Ford. It's hard to imagine Sam Peckinpah westerns without John Ford westerns that came first. Two great western filmmakers and there's an interplay and Peckinpah's building on what was done before. And commenting and reacting off of that.

CHASE MASTERSON

Every single day, I hear people say how the show holds up, over fifteen years after we wrapped. Deeply flawed characters, with complicated, messy relationships, hashing out their lives. Boldly going, but not across universes. Boldly going across the boundaries of war—sometimes between species and sometimes within ourselves. *We're* the final frontier.

IRA STEVEN BEHR

We tried to ignore the franchise as much as possible. That's why I'm as proud of the failures as I am the successes in terms of the individual episodes, because we never failed out of conservatism; we never failed by playing it safe. We failed because we dared to go where angels and smarter people would fear to tread. We always went in charging to the sound of the guns. "Let's try and take that story, guys, and wrassle it to the ground!" Sometimes *we* got wrassled. So, fuck it.

DAVID WEDDLE

They had the *Star Trek* exhibit right at the Las Vegas Hilton, and we went the last year and they had a whole museum of *Trek* memorabilia leading up to the ride. For Ron, it was a really pivotal series and mythology in his life, and I remember going up and looking through all these and we'd start looking through the earliest props and then props from shows that Ron wrote and René wrote and Ira. And I remember Ron grabbing hold of René and crying. Crying really uncontrollably. I think it was a mixture of sadness that the *Star Trek* experience was ending for us and also of tremendous fulfillment of everything that had been achieved and how much he got to contribute to it. So, it meant a great deal to him and to René and Ira.

IRA STEVEN BEHR

Seven years is a commitment. As I've said many times, my agents from season three on every year wanted me to leave. But I stayed and I don't regret it. They kept saying, "You're climbing the same fucking mountain. You've climbed it. You've proved it. You did it. Why go back? It's doing absolutely nothing for you career-wise." I was, like, "I get that, but I have to know how it ends."

VOYAGER

(1995–2001)

WOMAN OF THE YEAR

"WE'LL HAVE TO FIND ANOTHER WAY HOME."

In the mid-1970s, Paramount had hoped to launch a fourth television network using *Star Trek: Phase II* as its cornerstone. That series never materialized thanks to its metamorphosis into *Star Trek: The Motion Picture*—and neither did the network. Twenty years later the studio finally achieved that particular corporate goal with the January 1995 launch of both the United Paramount Network (UPN) and *Star Trek: Voyager*, the third live-action spin-off of the original series, created by Rick Berman, Jeri Taylor, and Michael Piller. In the series, the starship *Voyager* has mysteriously found itself transported to the distant fringes of the galaxy and has begun the seventy-year trek back home.

Complicating matters is that *Voyager* had been pursuing a vessel commanded by a crew of Maquis rebels (Federation-born colonists and disaffected Starfleet officers organized against the Cardassian occupation of their homes in a Demilitarized Zone), and has been stranded with them, resulting in the crews having to be integrated, offering the potential of inherent conflict between these characters.

IRA STEVEN BEHR (executive producer, *Star Trek: Deep Space Nine*)

We had done the Maquis on *Deep Space Nine* because they wanted to set them up for *Voyager*. We were doing a two-part episode; Michael Piller wrote part one and I wrote part two. Mike, or maybe it was Mike and Rick [Berman], come in and they go, "Look, *Voyager* is going to be about the Federation and these guys banding together to get home on this ship"—at the time there were all these lawsuits going on with *TNG*—"we don't want there to be any problems, so we're going to put Jeri Taylor's name, Rick's name, and Mike's name onto the story with you." And it's, like, "What? You think I'm going to fucking sue you? You think I'm going to try and get money from *Voyager* because I'm writing this episode?" "No, we don't think that, but . . ." Blah, blah, blah. That was fucking lame. I was pissed off about that. To me that was, like, "Okay, you're basically saying you don't trust me, or not that you don't trust me, but that you're putting your names on it for ownership of something that no one is going to question." It was not a friendly franchise thing to do.

MICHAEL PILLER (cocreator/executive producer, *Star Trek: Voyager*)

Rick really felt that *Deep Space Nine* deserved an opportunity to be on the air by itself and that the franchise could use a little breathing room. He wanted the studio to hold off on *Voyager* for a year at least. The studio came back and more or less said, "Well, Rick, we're going to do this with or without you. We'd rather do it with you, but we're not going to give up the station groups" and things like that. With that edict, Rick came to me and said, "Okay, they want to do another one."

RICK BERMAN (cocreator/executive producer, *Star Trek: Voyager*)

When they knew *Star Trek: The Next Generation* was going to be going off the air and they were going to be left with one show, *Deep Space Nine*, that still had three or four seasons to go, I think the attitude at Paramount was two shows worked successfully, so let's get another one on the air right away so we'll keep the two shows. And both Michael Piller and I were excited about creating another show, but at the same time we felt they were pushing it a little bit. That there's just so much you can do, and it just seemed a little quick because at that point *Next Generation* was ending, *Deep Space Nine* was in the middle of its run, and the movie *Star Trek: Generations* was about to be released. But the studio was very emphatic about it.

And also, unbeknownst to us at first was that the studio had planned to open a new network, which ended up becoming UPN. They felt that the great tentpole of this new network would be the *Star Trek* show. So one piece of good news was that we were in a position to go back onto a spaceship, because *Next Generation* was going off the air. And Jeri Taylor, who had been one of our co-executive producers and eventually an executive producer on *Next Generation,* I adored; she's a wonderful writer and she ended up being the showrunner on *Next Generation* near the end. I invited her to join Michael and myself in creating this show. Again, we knew we were going back on a spaceship, but we had to do something different.

MICHAEL PILLER

We both agreed that a female captain was the next logical step following *Deep Space Nine,* so I said to Rick, "It really makes sense for us to ask Jeri Taylor to join us in creating the show, because then we'll have a female point of view in the room and it won't be the two guys being the creative forces behind the first female captain." In addition, I was very upfront about it when I said, "Look, I will probably only stay on this a year or two, and I want to put somebody into the creative development of this series who is going to stay with it longer than I'm prepared to." That's another reason we recruited Jeri.

TOM MAZZA (executive vice president of creative affairs, Paramount Television)

To be honest with you, I don't believe necessarily that *Voyager* tonally was the right show for UPN, but it was a platform from which the network could jump off. When you look at what UPN was putting on the air and the kinds of shows it was airing, they were going for a different audience than the *Star Trek* audience. So it may not have been the right network and as a result, we got a lot of notes. The hardest thing for the network executives is there would be a development person at the network wanting to call and give notes every week, and so they would call me. I would try and listen as best I could and balance the interest of the *Star Trek* audience with the interest of the network audience. And they're not necessarily the same, so that was a challenge. That was probably my *greatest* challenge over the twelve years or so I worked on *Star Trek*.

KENNETH BILLER (executive producer, *Star Trek: Voyager*)

They were going to call it the Paramount United Network until they discovered PUN would be the acronym.

RICK BERMAN

We wanted *Voyager* to be different, so we made it different in a couple of ways. To start with, we placed a woman in command of a starship. It's something we felt it was time to do and it gave us a new direction. Gene Roddenberry was never averse to the idea of having female captains in guest roles, but this was something that we never did get a chance to discuss with him. Jeri Taylor, Michael Piller, and I all agreed that when we took this on, that it was the next logical step for us. I'm sure Gene would agree.

KATE MULGREW (actress, "Kathryn Janeway")

The character filled a place, a void, in women's lives that only Paramount had the balls to step up to the plate and recognize.

BRYAN FULLER
(coproducer, *Star Trek: Voyager*)

Gay people believed Janeway was the best captain, because she was a strong woman who had a sense of vulnerability that did not detract from her strength as a leader. And as a gay man I can tell you when I first watched *Star Wars*, I couldn't give two shits about Luke or Han, but with Princess Leia I was, like, "This woman is in charge. She's a rebel, she's doing the right thing, she's the one who is not ego-driven in the story. She is driven by what is right for the world and humanity." So with Janeway, young gay men who are growing up without strong, male, gay role models, we often lean toward women because we identify with certain attributes of femininity and also respect the strength and courage and leadership and leadership style from a woman that is often less aggressive and more nurturing than stereotypical male leadership.

JERI TAYLOR

We did an early episode, "The Cloud," which ends with Janeway joining her crew in a game of pool in the holodeck. In that episode, we saw Janeway concerned about the morale of the crew and questioning her role as captain and how she would be able to hold things together in this environment. Then when she comes in to play pool, we show that she's not necessarily going to be the captain of captains past. She is willing to have a different kind of relationship with the crew than Kirk or Picard.

RICK BERMAN

Gene Roddenberry didn't want conflict amongst his characters. That's great, but it doesn't help when you're writing drama, because conflict is what drives drama. Without breaking Gene's rules, we were always trying to find ways of creating conflict. This show featured the inherent conflict between Captain Janeway's crew and that of the Maquis vessel. The Maquis become provisional Starfleet officers, but there will always be conflict between them, and that gave us something new and unique.

Second, we had our people seventy years away from home. They're not necessarily spending the rest of their lives getting home, but they are looking, while at the same time exploring space. The most unique thing about that is that it enabled us to no longer be in contact with Starfleet. It's not like we can call home all the time for instructions. We're on our own.

WINRICH KOLBE (director, *Star Trek: Voyager* pilot episode, "Caretaker")

The conflict between the Federation officers and the Maquis is an old one, but it worked in *The Defiant Ones* and it worked for *Voyager*. We have two groups that at any moment could have serious personality conflicts. The Maquis could suddenly say, "Wait a minute, that's not the way we're going to do it," and *there's* the conflict. I like that the show had inherent possibilities for conflict on the ship itself, which is something that was missing in *TNG*. It just wasn't there, which could be a problem dramatically. There will always be conflict between human beings; we need those conflicts to grow and survive.

JERI TAYLOR

The challenge of staying fresh and original is the main reason that we took the very risky move of throwing our people to the opposite end of the galaxy and cutting ties with everything that's familiar. No Starfleet, no Klingons, no Ferengi—all of those things that have been very comfortable for the audience. It was a universe that they knew well and that they loved exploring, and we turned our backs on that. It was very scary, but we felt that we would force ourselves into having a fresh slant on things and fresh storytelling. It was tough to make that decision.

MICHAEL PILLER

The last thing we wanted to do was to exploit Gene Roddenberry's vision without bringing something new to it. We needed to do something that was unique and hadn't been done before, but at the same time create the kind of environment that a spaceship provides. It was the same process of decision-making that we did on *Deep Space Nine*: "What can you do in a spaceship that is not the same as *The Next Generation*?" One of us said, "You know those shows where Q sends the *Enterprise* off to some strange quadrant and we meet the Borg, but we solve everything in an hour and get back home? Well, what if we *don't*? What if we get stuck there in space and it is completely unknown to us and this is the story of that journey back and of our trying to find our way back?"

JERI TAYLOR

We knew that one of the risks that we took when we developed this show was in cutting off the audience from everything that was familiar. But we felt that that was a good thing to do. It challenged us creatively. The Alpha Quadrant was getting to be a little bit like *Mister Rogers' Neighborhood*. It was very cozy, very comfortable. That sense of the unknown, of the wonder, the excitement, was not necessarily there. So we felt it was our responsibility to populate the Delta Quadrant with fascinating new aliens that would be as interesting to the audience eventually as the Klingons were to them when we started.

MICHAEL PILLER

When we hooked on this idea, we realized in a sense that we were talking about a journey that is very much like the journey that all of us in this country are on. It seems clear that the kind of problems that this country is facing are not problems that are going to be easily solved in our lifetime. We have to begin working on solutions that may take more than one generation to see the final result of. In fact, our children might be the ones who get to see the results of our hard work if we start now.

In a sense, the ship franchise of *Voyager* is that kind of journey, because we are on a ship of men and women who are beginning a journey that conceivably we may not see the end of—and we are working in the best interests of everybody on board to try to solve our problem and to make the best life we can for ourselves on this ship, to find the way back home.

WINRICH KOLBE

They want to go home. Isn't that basically what all of us are trying to do in some sense or another? That gives us a different point of view and a different objective when you have to make a decision. Do you want to get involved in an altercation that happens on planet "X," or do you want to go home? If you want to go home, sometimes you have to go two steps back to go one step forward. That's *very* interesting, particularly if you're forced to ask if the Prime Directive applies or if your primary directive is to go home. But what happens if on the way home there are obstacles that will have to be negotiated in those terms?

JERI TAYLOR

What we concocted was a wonderful action/adventure romp different from *Star Trek: Generations* and very different from the premiere episode of *Deep Space Nine,* which was sort of heavily metaphysical and philosophical and intensely devoted to one character in the form of Sisko. It is a romp and a true action/adventure. We didn't want it to be *Deep Space Nine*. That's a separate show. We didn't want people to be unpleasant and not liking to be with each other. People watch *Star Trek* because it's uplifting and it's positive and hopeful.

MICHAEL PILLER

We thought the best thing we could do was to have a show that really concentrated on adventure. *Deep Space Nine* was a show that went straight to character. It's a much more internal, psychological show—and for some viewers it was too taxing. What the audience was asking for was a slam-bang adventure show, and that's what *Voyager* is. Having said that, you know from my contributions to *Star Trek* that character was the main concern.

WINRICH KOLBE

Rick Berman and Michael Piller may create new series, but they never forget who started this whole thing. Ultimately, as long as it's *Star Trek* it will be Gene Roddenberry's. It's a matter of where you start from. I started in Germany, I still have a German accent, I can't deny it. I'm now living longer here than I did in Germany, but the origins are still there and they will always be there.

JERI TAYLOR

We built in the possibilities for some conflict, but we were just being careful about it. The first season episode "Learning Curve," in which the character of Tuvok runs a boot camp for Maquis, is a warm, positive story which starts out with a lot of conflict. So, being careful, we could have our cake and eat it, too.

MICHAEL PILLER

We learned a great deal from *Deep Space Nine* so that we did not make the same mistakes again this time. When we started *Deep Space Nine,* I said, "We're going to start this series with confidence. We're going to start this like it was the third season of *The Next Generation* and we're going to focus in on the characters. We're going to tell intimate stories that really focus on the characters."

We came in out of the pilot with a belief system that the show could be sort of

Hill Street Blues on a space station. If you took a lot of little stories and brought them together to see life on a daily basis in a sort of crowded, difficult, challenging environment and really focus on the characters, it could be fascinating and, at the same time, save money, because the overages on the pilot were astonishing. A result of that was a lack of scope in the early shows.

I thought that the breadth of the station itself was going to be interesting enough to carry a lot of the stories and, frankly, I am very happy with those, but the audience seemed to be telling me very early on that they felt claustrophobic on this space station. It was very hard to shake that perception, even though the show went all over the place.

DAVID LIVINGSTON (supervising producer, *Star Trek: Voyager*)

Early on, I was hoping that *Voyager* would have the combination of *TNG*, going off to explore new worlds and galaxies, but also have more of an edge. In some ways it paid off with the Maquis being aboard, but I think there should have been more kick-ass going on.

MICHAEL PILLER

So rather than getting intimate with these characters so quickly, perhaps the audience would have more of a stake in who they are after they have gone through a number of adventures together as a family.

ANDRÉ BORMANIS (science consultant, *Star Trek: Voyager*)

The premise of the show was pretty interesting. A strange alien force hurls the starship to the other side of the galaxy 70,000 light years away from Earth. And we have to try to find our way back and we have this block of rebels on the ship, the Maquis, who are opposed to Starfleet. These two factions have to figure out how to work together on a ship that was not designed for the mission that it now needs to undertake. That's a pretty cool premise. We also promised the audience that the Delta Quadrant would be the great unknown. A territory like the Australian outback in the 1870s or whatever. Who knows what you're going to find out there, but it's *really* fucking dangerous. Probably gonna die, assholes.

But that's *not* what the show became, and fairly quickly it's, like, "Okay, well, Chakotay is the first officer, he and Janeway have this cordial relationship, and we meet the Kazon, guys with a different kind of rubber mask than the other aliens we've met in the four hundred or some-odd episodes of *Star Trek* that had been produced to date." It was really the same old thing in a somewhat different package. So there was nothing really different about it, and that ultimately disappointed people.

GLEN C. OLIVER (film & TV critic, *Ain't It Cool News*)

Voyager offered a cast I very much enjoyed, but it hamstrung itself in two ways almost immediately: the notion of colliding two crews of disparate backgrounds on the bridge of a Federation starship was more or less abandoned by the end of "Caretaker," *Voyager*'s opening episode. Any tension and quest for enlightenment which could've been hugely beneficial to the series' dramatic structure was more or less jettisoned from the get-go. And with it went any substantive exploration of the human condition, without which the creation of drama is difficult at best.

KENNETH BILLER (executive producer, *Star Trek: Voyager*)

They were starting casting on the show and decided they would commission a few backup scripts for the prospective series in anticipation of the show going to series after the pilot. René Echevarria was a buddy of mine and he gave some of my material to Jeri Taylor. Based on that and a meeting I had with her, she hired me to write a freelance episode. This is before the show went into production. The episode ended up being called "Elogium," and I shared script credit with Jeri. Based on that script, they offered me a staff position.

> The producing troika of Berman, Taylor, and Piller, along with director Winrich Kolbe, who would helm the pilot episode, "Caretaker," began to assemble the show's cast, always one of a new *Trek* series' biggest challenges. First up was Robert Duncan McNeill as Lieutenant Tom Paris, a former member of the Maquis who serves as *Voyager*'s helmsman.

WINRICH KOLBE

My problem with the character originally was that he was too much an on-the-nose rebel. A little too clichéd, but that changed. We established that he came out of a Federation penal system and that he was not a hardened criminal who is out to slice your throat unless you work for him. He was probably the easiest character to cast. All we needed was someone who had a sense of being a little bit overbearing, a little snotty at times. A character with something in the closet, somebody who's willing to take unusual steps in order to advance themselves. What was important to me was that his father had such high expectations of him, thinking he would be the thirty-sixth and ongoing in a military family, and then he decided, "The hell with that, I'm not going to play that game. I want to do something else."

RICK BERMAN

It had been a while since we had a young, attractive white guy on the show. It just turned out that most of the characters were either alien or black in the previous show, and here we had a woman in a major role. With Robbie, there was something very charming and delightful about him. He was a very good choice.

ROBERT DUNCAN MCNEILL (actor, "Tom Paris")

One thing that I think was interesting about *Voyager* is that every character had a great backstory. That's what made it interesting. Everybody's got sort of a dark side—an edge—which is different than the other *Star Trek* shows.

> Chakotay is the Native American captain of the Maquis vessel, who ends up serving as first officer aboard the *Voyager* under Janeway's command. The actor cast in the role was Robert Beltran, best known at the time for *Models Inc.*, who had also starred in Paul Bartel's cult classic *Eating Raoul* as well as the post-apocalyptic sci-fi dramedy *Night of the Comet*. Chakotay was a difficult role to cast due to the relatively small number of Native American actors available in the Screen Actors' Guild.

WINRICH KOLBE

You're probably talking about a handful of actors who are well-known enough to ask to be considered. We had another actor in mind, but there were pros and cons. Opinions were flying, because that particular actor was older. The question was, without talking about age discrimination, which this wasn't, would he provide a balance? We had nine actors and we had to mix them. The question now is, who do we want as a possible executive officer on the ship? Going with the assumption that usually it was Jonathan Frakes as Riker who led the Away Team, we needed somebody who was physically believable and fit enough to do that.

RICK BERMAN

Beltran, who is basically of Mexican heritage, had, as many people from Central and South America do, a somewhat Native American look to him. He was kind of a hunk and he was a terrific actor. He had his own big role in a movie called *Eating Raoul*. I think he grew a little bit frustrated that his part never got quite as big as he had hoped it would. But he did a good job.

ROBERT BELTRAN (actor, "Chakotay")

At that point in my career, I was thinking it would be good to do a television series, and so I began to concentrate on finding one. Then when my agent called me to tell me about the "Caretaker" pilot, I thought, "Great, I'll be happy to audition for it." It could be an important gig in that it could be a substantial amount of years with steady employment that would make my old age much more comfortable.

I wouldn't have auditioned if I didn't find something valuable in the character. I liked the script very much, and I auditioned wholeheartedly to get the role. It was one of the easiest processes I've ever gone through in getting a job, ironically. I liked the role of Chakotay. I thought that he was open-ended and could really go somewhere with the right kind of writing. I was very much interested in playing the role and seeing what I could do with it.

WINRICH KOLBE

Robert Beltran was extremely soft-spoken in the beginning, and I think that was in part due to the script, where he was described as a calm, stoic Indian. I don't know where we got that from. It's some kind of myth that's still hanging around today, that you can throw a spear through an Indian and he won't even flinch. I'm not an expert on Indians, but I'm a human being and I know Indians are human beings and they will probably react as violently as anybody else. They might deal with it differently, but pain is pain and concentration is concentration.

Living in a Maquis ship and fighting a life-and-death battle with the Cardassians, no one is going to sit around there and calmly say, "Okay, there, give me full forward power and let's get the hell out of here." It's not going to happen. There's got to be that tension there. Robert, I think, developed better and better as he went on.

Serving as security chief of *Voyager* is Tuvok, a full-blooded Vulcan portrayed by Tim Russ *(Mr. Saturday Night)*.

WINRICH KOLBE

Originally Tuvok was supposed to be 160 years old. Again, we had a problem. When we were looking for an established, older actor to play the part of Tuvok, we had some damn good actors come in and read for us, but physically they weren't right. So we kept scaling down. We went from the sixties to the fifties to the forties to the thirties, and it just went down. A little longer and I'm sure we would have to have a tutor on the set. Also playing into this was who was going to be the captain? There was also some concern that Tuvok should be older, or the show might be too yuppie, too young.

RICK BERMAN

I had used Tim in our first movie, *Generations*. He was an unnamed officer on the bridge. I just loved his look. In fact, he was the second choice for the role of Geordi on *Next Generation*.

TIM RUSS (actor, "Tuvok")

There was a very big victory for me in getting this. I had been interested in working on *Star Trek* ever since the original *Next Generation* was created, and I read for Mr. Berman back then. I did not know at the time that LeVar Burton was also going to be considered for the role of Geordi La Forge. So it was in retrospect that I realized that, and Mr. Berman has been in my corner ever since. Tuvok was similar to his predecessor, Mr. Spock, in that he has to maintain a certain consistency with the Vulcan principles and philosophy that we upheld. But there was also an exploration of my character as an individual in terms of the intricacies of his personality and what his intentions may be.

WINRICH KOLBE

The nice thing about Tim is that he came in and gave us a wonderful reading. You have to understand another thing: these stoic parts like Chakotay and Tuvok are very difficult to act. What you're telling those guys is, "I want you to withdraw. I want you to be distant, but I want you to have character. I want you to be a Vulcan, logical, but I don't want you to be boring. I don't want you to be a nerd who pontificates." That is very difficult to do, and Tim is one of the very few actors we saw who could nail it. Leonard Nimoy, obviously, set the tone for this whole thing. There was nothing boring or nerdy or bland about Spock.

TIM RUSS

I had the edge over most people reading for the part, because I *know* that character. Tuvok is definitely based on Spock. Why does everybody like Spock? Why was he genuinely—over Captain Kirk, even—the most popular character on that show? It's because he was what we all want to be. We want to be perfect, we want to be able to overcome all the trials we have to deal with.

The character is so interesting to watch, because every situation that came up you'd want to see what Spock would do, you wanted to see how he reacted—and you enjoyed watching him just completely confused and baffled by human beings. You could forget that he was part human. So, coming into the reading I was armed to the teeth with this character. And casting is generally 80 percent personality and 20 percent talent. I'm not saying I'm able to do the things the way Tuvok does, it's just that I do like to approach things from an analytical or logical standpoint.

If you are 100 percent Vulcan, obviously there's no choice between being human or Vulcan. Spock had to make a choice. Tuvok never had to make that choice. It's like an athlete who trains to do the decathlon and an athlete who's born to do the decathlon. The person who comes into this world destined by nature to do it, has the edge.

Harry Kim (played by *Angry Cafe*'s Garrett Wang) is fresh out of Starfleet Academy in the premiere, and serves as the starship's ops and communications officer.

WINRICH KOLBE

Probably the most inexperienced and naïve character of them all, and he was the character that had to fight hardest to stay in the forefront. When we were casting, we said we wanted a young Asian male, and that's another SAG minority. There are not that many Japanese or Asian actors. It was a very hard role to cast, but we finally wound up with two actors who we liked and we chose Garrett.

GARRETT WANG (actor, "Harry Kim")

I remember thinking at the time that this must have been a dream that I was going to wake up from soon. It is kind of amazing when you think about the legacy we were following, because there really isn't any other TV series I can think of that originally aired in the sixties and kept on going and going and going. It's kind of like an intergalactic Energizer Bunny.

RICK BERMAN

As you might guess, we were looking for a Korean/Asian actor. It was very important for us to have racial diversity in *Star Trek*. It was something that Gene believed in very strongly. And Garrett was, again, a very handsome kid and a very natural actor.

Voyager's seemingly requisite alien-human hybrid was B'Elanna Torres (Roxann Dawson), the half-Klingon chief engineer who, like Spock on the original series, wages an inner war with the intertwining blood of two species.

RICK BERMAN

We always have a hard time when we're casting aliens. B'Elanna is half Klingon and half human. Again, a very hard combination to have a Klingon woman who is even vaguely attractive, because Klingons by definition are kind of monstrous. Because of her name we had obviously decided to have her human side be Hispanic. We read a lot of people and she was just a terrific actress. She turned out to be quite a wonderful director, too.

ROXANN DAWSON (actress, "B'Elanna Torres")

I'm of Latino descent, but that's something that wasn't brought up in any way because it really doesn't make a difference. I love that the attention was brought to the fact that she's half human and half Klingon. I love that the conversation regarding Tuvok centered around the fact that he is Vulcan and that we don't discuss that he's a black Vulcan. And I love the fact that nobody on the crew, except for one little moment, discusses that it's a big deal that we have a female captain. What matters is character, how we're coming across and who we are as people.

WINRICH KOLBE

Roxann might have been the actress that came in on day one and we cast her. Not that we didn't keep looking, but she was pretty well set from the first day. I thought she along with Kim were going to be the two characters most fighting for airtime. One thing she has going for her is a volatile temper, which could go off at any time when things don't work. B'Elanna Torres was a land mine—a hand grenade with the pin pulled out.

ROXANN DAWSON

It's the turmoil and her constantly wanting to reconcile the two sides of her that forms a conflict that I wanted to explore. One of the reasons fans identified with B'Elanna is that we all, to a certain degree, have two or more sides to us that are at work. It's a universal idea and I loved that the character could explore that so tangibly.

She's so afraid of being abandoned that she will leave every situation first. That's why she left Starfleet Academy before she could be expelled, even though she was never going to be expelled. She operates very much on fear. This is not uncommon; we all do that to some degree. A lot of people will often want to have the control in their hands and move away from any situation that would put them at risk or make them vulnerable.

One of the show's most offbeat characters is the Doctor (Robert Picardo, then known for *The Wonder Years* as well as his work with Joe Dante on such movies as *The Howling* and *Gremlins II: The New Batch*), an Experimental Medical Program (EMP). The holographic Doctor is a virtual medical officer taking care of the crew's needs and serving as ship doctor when the vessel is stranded in the Delta Quadrant.

RICK BERMAN

He was just wonderful in the same way that we always have characters that served as a mirror to human culture. Spock did that in the original series, Data did it in *The Next Generation*. Here our decision was to create a doctor who was, in fact, a hologram. Like Data, someone who was not human but wanted to be human. We also wanted this character to be poignant at times, but to be quite funny because he was nothing but a program—but one who would have a sense of ascension to him. That's a very important word in *Star Trek*: ascension. It ends up not meaning what anybody thinks it means, but Picardo was one of the truly natural and talented actors that we have worked with and he provided us with some of the funniest stuff we've ever done.

WINRICH KOLBE

We had a lot of different actors come in once we decided we were going to go with a comedian. Nobody else seemed to get it. They all played it too holographic and computer-like. We wanted somebody who really came out charging and gave us the comic relief we needed. In some ways, the Doctor is similar to Data, maybe not quite as complex, but that would develop. Data at the beginning was not really what he was at the end of *The Next Generation*.

In the beginning Data was just a preposterous windup toy. Then things began to develop. There was, "I want to be human. What about my emotions? What is death?" and so on. He's a guy who, due to his capacity to memorize things—particularly the whole human conundrum—was able to develop. The same was true of the Doctor, although the one disadvantage he had is that he was, in the beginning, restricted to sickbay. However, that changed. He's a very capable doctor with the lousiest bedside manner in the universe.

BRANNON BRAGA (executive producer, *Star Trek: Voyager*)

Early on, we didn't know what the hell we were going to do with the doctor character and were terrified. This guy wasn't going to have anything to do, because he's stuck in sickbay. He's going to be neglected. What a drag. But things turned out *very* differently.

A pair of alien characters amongst the crew were Neelix, described as part scavenger, trader, con man, procurer, and sage; and Kes, Neelix's Ocampa lover, who has a very limited life span.

WINRICH KOLBE

Neelix is a very funny character and also a hustler. In a way he's also, if you go to Joseph Campbell's mythology, the guide. He's the only one who knows that particular area of space. Nobody else knows where we are, really. Nobody knows who the Ocampa are and what's going on there. He does. He's a very important part of things, because he is the sage; he's the guide. And Kes is his alter ego in a way. Plus it gives us a certain romance to explore, because you don't want to have it be strictly business. Neelix and Kes provided romance and a certain amount of comedy on the show.

Neelix was rather easy to cast. We narrowed it down to three actors, and Ethan Phillips was the one who pulled out. He was an inspired choice, and he was the life of the party on the set. Kes was the usual problem you have when you try to cast twenty-something actresses or younger. There are a lot of beautiful women around, especially in Hollywood, but not a lot of them can act. We went through quite a procession of beautiful girls, not bad as actresses but not good enough. You didn't want a ball-buster, you didn't want to have tank-like women saying, "Follow me!" We wanted somebody who could be fragile, but with a steely will underneath. Jennifer Lien gave us that.

ETHAN PHILLIPS (actor, "Neelix")

I think Neelix is a pretty lovable guy. It may be one of the best roles I've ever had an opportunity to play. There's something deep and heightened about him, and playing him was an incredible challenge.

RICK BERMAN

Ethan was kind of our Quark. He was a short, strange alien who could serve as a reflection and to sort of bounce things back on humanity a little bit. This was a great cast. Jennifer Lien was another story. For her character we were looking for sort of an elfin female who played a very important role in the pilot and who was going to come on the ship and become this kind of funny-looking gremlin's girlfriend. It just didn't work. The relationship didn't work, and her character became somewhat superfluous. It was just really hard for the writers to work on it, so eventually we wrote the character out of the show.

The casting of Captain Janeway was an arduous process, with a wide variety of possible names being bandied about, including Lindsay Wagner (*The Bionic*

Woman), Linda Hamilton (*Beauty and the Beast, The Terminator*), Erin Gray (*Buck Rogers in the 25th Century*), Susan Gibney (who had appeared on a pair of *Next Generation* episodes), Joanna Cassidy (*Who Framed Roger Rabbit?*) and Kate Mulgrew.

KATE MULGREW

I was in Ireland with my kids and my manager called me about the audition. I said I wouldn't come home for it; that I didn't know anything about it and I wouldn't leave in the middle of a vacation. When I *did* get home, I asked if they were still auditioning people, and they were. So I went on camera in Times Square and shot an audition, which was *appalling.* It was pouring down rain, I had fallen in love with this guy in Ireland who I was about to meet with, and I said at the end of the audition, directly into the camera, "Forgive me, that was the most abysmal audition of my life, but I've fallen in love, my head's not here, so sorry!" And sure enough, it *was* bad.

JERI TAYLOR

The search for the captain was a long and difficult one. This is the person that gets the white-hot glare of publicity as the first female ever to head one of the *Star Trek* series and she has to be just right. We considered, auditioned, looked at tapes of what seemed like every actress between the ages of probably thirty and fifty-five in Los Angeles, New York, Chicago, Canada, and Europe. We had several people we were happy with. Some of the studio executives didn't necessarily share our feelings. Finally, with days to go, we were made aware that Geneviève Bujold was interested, and we were ecstatic.

Geneviève Bujold is a French-Canadian actress best known for her portrayal of Anne Boleyn in the 1969 film *Anne of the Thousand Days*, for which she won a Golden Globe Award for best actress and was nominated for an Academy Award. Other notable credits include Brian de Palma's *Obsession* (1976), *Coma* (1978), *Tightrope* (1984) and David Cronenberg's *Dead Ringers* (1988).

KENNETH BILLER

Jeri, Rick, and Michael were really excited about it. I think they thought it was kind of cool that she was not American per se in the way that Jean-Luc Picard had not been American, and that that kind of spoke to the international quality of it all. It wasn't just interplanetary, but that the human characters were of the international variety. That it wasn't just about Americans. She was considered a very serious, really interesting actress.

RICK BERMAN

She had been an Academy Award [nominated] movie star. Michael and Jeri adored her. I felt there was something funny there; there was something that didn't seem right.

BRANNON BRAGA

I really pushed for Geneviève Bujold to play Janeway. I was, like, "I *love* Geneviève Bujold from her work in the seventies and early eighties." That turned out to be a bust. I don't think she realized she had to be there every day. If you watch her dailies, you can see she's not very good.

WINRICH KOLBE

On the day we met her, I told Rick, "This will either be a total disaster or a real triumph." At that point I didn't know which it was going to be. I thought there was something in her that could have blown everybody away, but that never came through. I guess it might never have been there. It's a real fine line. At that particular moment, I guess there was a little panic to get somebody so we could get going. Some of us were very high on Geneviève, so we hired her.

JERI TAYLOR

The character's original name was Elizabeth Janeway, but that was changed for legal reasons. There is a prominent Elizabeth Janeway and we were not allowed to use names of prominent people, because it can be sticky, although we heard sort of secondhand that Elizabeth Janeway was flattered about it. It then changed to Nicole at Geneviève Bujold's request, because that is in fact her given name and she wanted that. For two days it was Nicole Janeway.

TOM MAZZA

Things began with, obviously, a long casting process to find the captain. One of the aspects we were looking for in the captain, the attributes of the actor, is that they had to have strength. Every single captain had an internal strength that came through. When Geneviève Bujold's name came up, it was a very interesting choice, but her strength tends to come from within a deeper place. That works sometimes. It doesn't necessarily work for all characters, but historically that role has always had a very strong personality outside, not just inside. Clearly you knew from the ground up that they had it from belly on out. But from the outside her appearance was just a little softer and I think that was generally everybody's question at the time. We debated and the agent and representative said she does not read [for a role in terms of auditoning]. We really went back and forth.

RICK BERMAN

This was a woman who in no way was going to be able to deal with the rigors of episodic television. And I made the point very clear. They all said, "That's nonsense, it's going to be fine." So I said, "Well, at least let's read her the riot act; let's tell her how awful it can be to be a regular on a television series. That she's going to be working with directors she doesn't know; she's going to be working fifteen hours a day," etc., etc.

WINRICH KOLBE

Her concept of the show was completely her own. I do not understand why she took the show in the first place. It seemed to me she was not prepared for what happened. Yet the day before she said yes, Rick Berman told her, step-by-step, what was expected of her and what it would be like.

RICK BERMAN

So we had her in. Of course the studio was in love with the idea of an Academy Award [nominated] movie star. Jeri Taylor and Michael Piller went apeshit. They thought, holy mackerel, we have ourselves an Academy Award–winning [sic] movie star to play Janeway. I spent a lot of time with this woman and I could just see that there was a fragility to her and the way that she talked about making movies, the way that she talked about the kind of relationship that she had with her directors and with her writers.

It was a whole sensibility that told me there was no way this woman was going to be able to do an episodic television show; working ten months a year, fifteen hours a day. So, I took her to lunch and I sat her down and I kind of painted the darkest picture I could of what it would be like. That she would be getting pages five hours before she would go on set. Which, in fact, does happen sometimes. That she would be working with directors that she never met before. That she would be doing seven pages a day as opposed to one and a half, which is what her life had been. I remember she said, "I will go talk to my children and I will let you know on Monday."

And she called me the next day and said, "I've spoken with my children and the answer is *oui, oui,* I will do it." I just went, "Oy, I *know* I'm right about this. I know this isn't going to work." Anyway, to make a long story a little shorter, she quit on the second day. And as chaotic as it was, it was a wonderful sense of vindication for me that I had been right on this.

TOM MAZZA

Casting her was *not* a unanimous decision. We ended up giving her a shot, and she got the role. She was guaranteed her twenty-six episodes. And *then* the dailies started coming in and questions immediately started to come up.

RICK BERMAN

All I said to Jeri and Michael was this is the biggest mistake that we're making. There is no fucking way this woman is going to be able to pull this off. She's lovely, she's beautiful, but it's not going to happen. And everybody disagreed with me, and I was not going to pull rank, and I said, "Great." It wasn't even the first day when she said, "They want to dye my hair." I said, "Yeah, you got gray hair, we want to dye your hair." "But, I like my hair." And then the next day it was "I have costumers who are coming and touching me and adjusting my costume. Who's directing this thing?" It was Rick Kolbe. And she said, "I do not know this man. I need to spend some time with him discussing my character, discussing my story, discussing what this episode is about." And then she started saying things like "Where's rehearsal time?" One thing after another and I just said, "Here we go . . ."

WINRICH KOLBE

We started shooting her on Monday, working hard to get going, and on Thursday afternoon we were just about ready to break for lunch when she said, in front of everyone, "It's just not working out too well. I don't think I'm right for the part." To which I said, "Don't ever say that!" Not because I wanted to lecture her or because she was wrong, but because she shouldn't have said this in front of the crew. It creates a psychological problem. The captain of the ship is supposed to be the captain of the crew, of us. He or she defines how a unit works. Patrick Stewart did it his way, Avery Brooks did it his way. When the star of the show says, "I don't think I'm right for the part," you can feel the reaction from the entire crew. At that moment I got together with her, we had a chat about the situation. I called the producers and about half an hour later it was decided to cancel her relationship with the show. It wasn't Paramount or anyone that fired her, she just decided to pull out.

MICHAEL PILLER

What happened very simply was that Geneviève Bujold was used to working on features and used to working in a very specific manner, with great preparation and great rehearsal, and when she realized that she was going to be working twelve-hour days and that there were none of the luxuries that come with acting for features—I don't mean luxuries in terms of perks, I'm talking about the luxury of time and preparation—she just said, "I'm not going to be able to do this." That was obviously a problem.

TOM MAZZA

Where's the internal strength? We have to have that. But at the same time, what was happening there was the sense that she was not feeling comfortable in the role, which is probably more important than anything, because her being uncomfortable reflects in the performance, right? One thing you can't have as a starship captain is someone who appears uncomfortable and not confident in that role. That was permeating her performance. It was raising huge questions, and you can imagine the cost involved that's mounting on an hourly basis. And the fact that she was guaranteed the entire season.

GARRETT WANG

Before we even shot the first scene, we had a walkthrough on the set with Rick Kolbe, where he took us around and showed us how to operate certain things. We were all there, including Geneviève. Her aura was "approach with caution." She didn't talk to anybody, she just sort of walked around and watched and listened to what was being said. Every now and then one of the cast members would walk up and say, "Congratulations," and she would smile or nod or say thank you and that was it. She just did not further the conversation.

WINRICH KOLBE

She wasn't really a captain. She wanted to be Geneviève Bujold, not Captain Janeway. She didn't want to run the ship. We shot for a day and a half, we did a lot of things and she was pretty much involved in everything. I tried to get her to give us the authority that I wanted from the character, and that never came through.

MICHAEL PILLER

There's no question Geneviève had a problem understanding what the twenty-fourth-century human being was like, and what Roddenberry's vision of humanity was, because an actor would often bring approaches to their character that would not feel comfortable with the context of *Star Trek*. It took us time, saying, "No, that's just not the way Roddenberry sees the future." I think she bristled under that as well.

GARRETT WANG

I asked her how she felt and she said, "I feel like I can't trust anybody." And she left it at that. The interpretation for me was that she was getting in on this show and was being dragged right and left with people saying, "Okay, your hair has to be like this. Okay, your suit has to be like this; you have to wear this kind of shoe. You can't do this, you can't do that." It's kind of like they said, "Geneviève, you're the captain and you can do what you want," and she says, "Great. I want to do this and this," and they say, "Oh, but you can't do that." That's where I think her comment about trust came in.

WINRICH KOLBE

We had a chat about it and I said, "Why can't you give me what I'm looking for in Janeway?" She said to me, "I don't want to be Janeway. I want to be me." Geneviève Bujold is a very fragile human being on the outside, and I felt she had to project a very strong inside for it to work.

GARRETT WANG

She would walk on the bridge and speak in a low, whispery voice, and she's supposed to be the captain. For this role, you've got to raise your volume, not only for the mike, but for the other actors to get psyched. Like where Patrick Stewart is walking across the bridge, the camera zooms in and he says, "Warp one. Engage!" and he's *intense*. Geneviève came out there and the intensity wasn't there. I'm not by any means saying she was a bad actress, but her take was different. She was commanding within, but there are some things you have to do to play the game. You just have to do it a certain way.

There's a scene in the pilot when the *Voyager* is about to pull away from the *Deep Space Nine* station and the things begin to happen when she says, "Engage." We're filming and she walks around and says something to her first officer. He says, "Ready thrusters"; I say, "Thrusters ready." She sits down in her chair and says, "Engage." The way she did it, though, was unusual. She sat down in the chair, closed her eyes for about a minute and softly said, "Engage." It just wasn't working.

RENÉ ECHEVARRIA (supervising producer, *Star Trek: Deep Space Nine*)

The only other actor that I remember having such an extraordinary commitment to the part like the original actors, and this is kind of funny, was Geneviève Bujold. In her first few days in her aborted *Star Trek* career, I remember watching dailies, which I think we had to sneak in and steal a videotape from Jeri Taylor's office to watch them. They would say, "Action!" and she would sit there with her eyes closed for, like, ten seconds. Then when she opened her eyes and started the scene, she was there; she was in space. She was the captain of a spaceship somewhere in another world. For whatever reason, it didn't work out, but it was that same level of commitment that Shatner and those guys brought to it.

ROBERT BELTRAN

I was the last to be cast, so they had actually begun filming before the Chakotay character was involved. I came on doing makeup tests while they were filming. I think it was mostly Geneviève and Tim Russ that had scenes together. I honestly don't really know what happened with that. I do know that when I would see her, she seemed kind of lost and out of it. It didn't seem like she was happy to be there. That's the general sense that I had. I also think that maybe it wasn't totally her fault in the sense that as a captain she would have been the direct opposite of Kate. One of the reasons I wanted to do the show was I wanted to work with Geneviève. I had always loved her work, and I thought it would be great to work with her day in and day out for seven years. So I was really disappointed when she left. She had a different sensibility.

I know they always comment on the one scene where she orders some aliens to be annihilated and she doesn't do it happily. I think the line was "Fire!" and she did it in such a way that the producers thought was not strong enough; not enough of a strong captain. You've got to say, "Fire!" or it doesn't work. Maybe she was starting to realize the limitations of the possibilities of what she could do with so many hands on her character. That's my theory, that they weren't going to let her play the character the way she wanted to play it. It wasn't what they felt was in the best *Star Trek* tradition. But that's where we get into that whole "*Star Trek* tradition" bullshit. She thought it was best for her to bow out. Maybe she was overwhelmed by the television machine, going to the factory every day.

RICK BERMAN

On the first day I got calls from Rick Kolbe, who was directing the pilot, saying that she was having trouble with her lines. She felt that she couldn't memorize seven pages a day. Earlier she refused to dye her hair. Then she finally agreed to dye it. Then one of the hair people came to comb her hair and she said, "Get away, get away; nobody touches my hair." And the makeup person came to touch her up, and then she started saying, "I don't know this Rick Kolbe. How am I supposed to work with a director I don't know?"

TOM MAZZA

Day two comes and we figured we'd see if day two is better. Day two *wasn't* any better. Day three comes and we said, "We can't do this. We're going to have to bite the bullet."

RICK BERMAN

And she finally went to her trailer in tears and I got a call from the director. I went down to her trailer with the director and I was very calm. I looked at her and said, "Look, just pack up your stuff and go home. Everything is going to be fine." And at that point I called the studio people, the chairman of the television division, and told him the story. He agreed and we said, "Let's just shut down."

As sad as I was, I had this gleeful sense of I told you so. The studio was so angry because we had to shut down and it cost a lot of money. They threatened to sue her, which was terrible—and, of course, they never did. All I know is that we then started the casting procedure again and Kate Mulgrew, who had been one of my top choices, we ended up hiring. She came in and read for us and for the studio, and as soon as we had hair situations worked out and uniform situations worked out, within a week we were shooting again.

TOM MAZZA

What happened was ultimately we got a phone call from her agent who said she wasn't happy and did not want to continue. It was like divine intervention, because it really didn't work for both parties. It actually paid for the loss of the first three days, because the first three days were lost in terms of those scenes with her. So, yes, it was a godsend in that regard.

WINRICH KOLBE

It's probably good that the "situation" happened when it did, even though it threw a monkey wrench into our operation. It would have been a disaster if we had shot the whole pilot and *then* found out it didn't work.

KATE MULGREW

We know how great an actress she is. But she was not what they were looking for, and even if she had been, they were not what she was looking for. She had a fourteen-year-old son; she had a different idea of how she wanted to spend the next seven years of her life, and my hat has always been off to her because had she delayed, whether out of fear, greed, or whatever, it would have been a real problem for Paramount. Had she delayed even a few months and continued that long, it would have screwed everything up terribly. The fact that she did it so soon is, I think, a testament to her greatness, and I have always said that.

KENNETH BILLER

I think Geneviève Bujold regretted signing up for it. Of course it's interesting now all the giant stars who all want to do television, because the landscape is changing. Now you have Academy Award winners doing shows on television, because the material is not considered beneath them anymore.

TOM MAZZA

We were really determined to make it a female captain. There was never a time that we opened it up to men. It was really important for the series to have a female captain. We had a few people in again and we went back to the well and Kate emerged. As soon as Kate walked in, and she *did* read, it was immediate.

Susan Gibney [Leah Brahms from *The Next Generation*] was probably the number two frontrunner. In fact, part of the challenge with Geneviève was that Susan Gibney was really good, but she also had that question about that internal strength. She was smart, she was good, but there was still a bit of a younger quality. It almost felt like when you looked at the other captains, there was a history in their life that you thought warranted that position.

And with Susan there was that challenge just by the virtue of the fact that she doesn't appear to have had that kind of experience. Having nothing to do with anything, just by having the performance and the way it was coming across. But there were many who really liked her. *I* really liked her. But as the captain, that was a tall order. Whereas when Kate walked in, you realized right away there was somebody who has that presence. Someone who said, "Okay, I get that they would have achieved the various milestones to get her to being captain."

KENNETH BILLER

They decided they made a mistake and went back to Kate and got her in *very* quickly. Looking back, it's very hard to imagine anybody *but* Kate playing that role. She just owned it completely.

KATE MULGREW

After that terrible audition, the man whom I fell in love with, and who became my second husband, took the script out of my bag and he said, "What is this?" I said, "Don't worry about it, because it's something I'm not going to get." He said, "I think it *is* something you're going to get." "Ridiculous!" But then she quit and they called me back in . . . obviously they saw something.

I came in and they gave me two very big scenes. One was the monologue, "We're lost in an uncharted part of the galaxy . . . ," and the other was with Tuvok, establishing the depth and breadth of our friendship. I loved them both. And I made two very bold decisions in the room . . . not bold, but I played the scene with Tuvok with high humor, as Janeway did throughout her entire relationship with him, because he's *so* Vulcan. I was always trying to ruffle his feathers. So that was full of laughs, and a certain underlying vulnerability, which I thought was very important to show; that her capacity for friendship was great indeed. And necessary to her, as a person. And with the monologue, I did it *to* them. I gave it to the producers. I turned to them as if they were my crew, looked right at them, and I said that I would get us through this. And I remember thinking, "Well, now it's up to you."

I was in and out. There were three or four other women there that day, and I was certain that we would all be put into our little rooms and then you go in for the second round. That's what going to network is, a really appalling process. Torturous . . . unless you're on top of your game, which I was that day. We were told we were dismissed and we went down to the parking lot together with an attitude of "Let the best man win."

Understand, at the time, I knew nothing about *Star Trek*. If anything, I dismissed it. Which stood me in good stead, as it turns out, because ignorance in this case was bliss. And *very* liberating. I went into the audition, then I went to the network, which was harrowing for those who really knew what was at stake. I didn't. I just knew that it was a very good part. I was told it was an important franchise, and that I probably had a guaranteed five to seven years, which is balm to an actress. I just went in and did it, because I liked her. I went in with a sense of humor; I went in with a little bit of cheek. I'm always quite confident in those situations, because they're either going to like me or they're not going to like me. It's very freeing. There must have been fifty people in that room, and I caught Berman's eye right away. I stopped myself just short of winking at him as I left, but we had a nice little frisson.

Anyway, I went home and didn't hear anything for three days. It was the high Jewish holiday, Yom Kippur, which I was unaware of because I am, of course, Irish-Catholic, and I just assumed after the second day that I hadn't gotten it. After my requisite two hours of despondency, I said to my kids, "I didn't get it . . . I'm

going to the market and we'll grill some steaks tonight, have a couple of laughs."
So I went to the market and when I came back, my nanny and my two children
were standing on the front porch, telling me to listen to my messages, which I
never did. So I went in and there it was: "Ms. Mulgrew, this is Rick Berman, executive producer of *Star Trek: Voyager*. I just wanted to say, 'Welcome aboard,
Captain.'"

WINRICH KOLBE

I was shooting when Kate Mulgrew was mentioned. Then suddenly Kate Mulgrew
was hired and I had a meeting with her in the makeup trailer. When she came on
the set, I was very impressed with her. She had a definite presence, and she was
informed about what she had to do. She watched a lot of episodes and I felt so good
about her that I brought her to the set on Stage Nine and said, "Ladies and gentlemen, the captain!" And everyone applauded.

KATE MULGREW

I'm the oldest girl in a very large family of eight. I'm used to walking into situations where everyone else is there first, but I seldom get to save the day. And that
was the feeling. We're going to have fun; I'm here, we're going to help each other.
I had them joking right away. McNeill was the first one . . . in fact, we were laughing so hard that tears were coming down my face.

WINRICH KOLBE

That was all very nice and I suddenly felt that we were taking off. We were just taxi-
ing up the runway until that point. Right from the start, it seemed to me she was
going to do a hell of a lot for women on television. She is definitely a woman, but
she can handle any situation in her own particular way. I would follow her. The
way she moves, the way she thinks, the way she looks is wonderful.

KATE MULGREW

Rick [Kolbe] and I had "a thing" for about three years. I don't normally get involved with people that I work with, but that's how intense the work was. He
understood what I was going through in a way no one else could. Not to mention

his erudition, and he was very sophisticated, very smart and an unusual man. And a war hero. He kept that one way under wraps. A Silver Star. He knew more about that franchise than just about anybody else. He was very well respected, so of course that brought us together. I have no regrets.

Put yourself in my shoes. My four-and-a-half-inch heels that they had to have made for me in Italy, because I was so much shorter than everyone else. Take me away from my nine- and ten-year-old sons. I'm leaving the house at 3:45 in the morning and I'm returning around 11:00 at night. It's an eighteen-hour day. On Friday nights, I go into Saturday mornings. The exhaustion . . . I lost twenty pounds in a month. Rick would call me and say, "You might want to eat something." The challenges, the dialogue, the heart . . . and I was in every scene. For a long time I was in *every* scene. I was trying to make my children understand that this was a good thing; trying to break the mold for women, trying to establish she was a very good commander, whose humanity was still very much intact. Trying to transcend my own gender. I didn't want young men to confuse me for one minute with their mothers; I wanted them to know that I could command a complement of 165 and that I'd get them home.

WINRICH KOLBE

For Kate's character, I knew that we had to find a way of not writing her as a man, but writing her as a woman, which might have been a difficult thing to do because there are not that many female writers on *Star Trek*.

JERI TAYLOR

Would the audience accept that a whole crew would follow her, report to her, trust her in battle? That was the most important selling point in a woman. Kate Mulgrew has that without even working at it. As a person, as a human being, she is everything that we envisioned Janeway being. She has power coming out of her genetic code and the moment she walked out on that bridge the first day, she owned it.

KATE MULGREW

After Geneviève Bujold's defection, which was very, very abrupt, they were scared. How were they going to find the kind of woman they were looking for who could endow this role with the attributes that they needed, who didn't have children? Who didn't have other accomplishments, who didn't have other loves and needs and complexities? I think they were nervous for a good long time with me, and then, after things settled down and in, they realized that I was absolutely committed and highly disciplined.

JERI TAYLOR

Geneviève had a certain approach to the role that was very low key and—who knows?—it might have been effective. Kate came in with a very solid sense of command and authority, and it really seemed like the way to go. Considering that Kate came in after it had already started shooting, she was astonishingly good and professional. She was the captain not just of the crew, but of the cast as well. She was so professional and so prepared that everyone was afraid not to be as prepared as she was. Nobody was late, because she was never late. Everyone knew their lines, because she always knew her lines. She's got such a high standard that she set the caliber of everyone else's work, and that was obvious from the first day.

ROXANN DAWSON

Kate knew how to take control and get into the scenes. There wasn't a question among any of us that in all the scenes she's in control.

ROBERT PICARDO (actor, "The Doctor")

Kate has a natural strength. She has another great asset that all captains on *Star Trek* have had—she has a terrific voice. That's very important. You do all this narration, "Stardate blah, blah, blah." Imagine Edith Bunker as a starship captain.

GARRETT WANG

Kate is the captain. She's leading. Geneviève was not being a captain we would want to follow. She was being a captain, yes, but she wasn't the kind of captain who could lead a ship. Kate has the captain's intensity that she can command *Voyager*. She's very professional, loves what she's doing, and is an attractive woman as well. I had no complaints at all.

The thought was, she's a commanding, tough woman, she's got to be kind of butch, but I think you can have an attractive woman who can be on the money and in command. As an actress, she's a woman of amazing fortitude. Any time I didn't want to wake up in the morning, any time I wanted to feel like complaining about the hours, I would just stop myself and say, "Think of Kate." Kate was there as long as I was. She was there days that I wasn't. That really inspired me.

MAJEL BARRETT RODDENBERRY (wife of Gene Roddenberry)

I was delighted with the Janeway character, and I'm particularly delighted with Kate. She's the greatest gal in this whole wide world. She's a real, honest, and down-to-earth being, and she just owns the screen when she's on it. She's magnificent. She has eyes that sparkle and her whole presence just kind of says "I'm here; this is my ship."

RICK BERMAN

The challenge with Janeway was we wanted her to be a Starfleet captain, which is a very high-ranking military position of authority, but we also wanted her to be feminine. Sometimes those two things don't go hand in hand. If you look at female officers in the military who make it to the rank of admiral or general, they tend to *not* be babes. Now we cast a woman in her forties and we weren't going for a babe look, but we wanted a feminine woman, and that was the great thing about having Jeri Taylor along.

As an executive producer and a writer we had a woman's perspective, which we felt was very important. We wanted basically to balance those two things, and I think with the exception of some hair problems, it worked out very well. [Studio executive] Kerry McCluggage, who I adore and who was running the television division for ten years at Paramount, was a man who was obsessed with hair. If you look at his family, you can see it; they all have perfect hair. And we got a call from Kerry after, like, the first day of dailies saying he hated Kate's hair, and we ended up having to reshoot half of her stuff. Then there was another hairdo. The hair issue continued into *Enterprise*.

There were a lot of hair issues, though probably most of them were with Kate Mulgrew. It used to make poor Kate crazy, because all she wanted to do was act. She had nothing to do with what was done with her hair. She would do a really important day's work—hard stuff—and the next day she'd be told to do it again, because somebody didn't like her hairdo. But we finally ended up getting it worked out.

KATE MULGREW

For months they came to the set. The brass, not just my producers. The Paramount guys came and stood at the lip of the bridge and scrutinized me, my hair, my bosom, my heels . . . all of which was meant to inform me of the importance of this part, and that I was being watched. It was very simple. Nothing was stated. I'm sure they did it with Patrick Stewart . . . for two seconds. And Shatner for even less. But millions, if not billions, of dollars were at stake with this franchise, so they had to make sure. I think in the end they were pleased. It did work, but I would really say that it wasn't easy.

Comparisons, as Oscar Wilde would say, are odious, but the men never had to deal with the physical component, the sexual component, the way that I did. I was scrutinized because of my gender, by all of these guys. "She's got a big bosom, she's got beautiful hair, she's still of childbearing years, how are we going to make this thing work?"

I was in makeup and hair all the time. All of the arguments, all of the conversations and all of the controversy were about my physicality, not about my characterization of Janeway. I really grew to envy, especially, Patrick Stewart, who probably had nothing to do except walk from his trailer to the set. He had a great ease. I had to add an additional three hours to my day, with two young sons at home, and all this technobabble, and wanting to be able to ace that, wanting to be able to understand it, and get underneath it, was quite challenging for the first year.

I'm sure there was some resentment there on my part. I'm sure there was some frustration and anger. Of course, I'm human and, my God, I was tired. But I'm Irish, so the "I'll show them!" part of me surpasses every other thing. Which is why she not only succeeded, she thrived, Janeway, because I was determined.

RICK BERMAN

Kate's a very interesting actor. She's got a deep kind of sexy but odd voice. She's very passionate. She took the work very seriously and she managed to be a feminine woman at the same time she was a leader. She was perfect for the part, and without it looking like boasting, she was my first choice from the beginning.

JERI TAYLOR

I became enormously protective of Janeway and was careful that the character was not put in a light where she might come under siege from anybody. We have a strong male demographic and Janeway managed to be somebody who is the ideal blend of authority, command, and believability as a captain, and yet was not threatening to the male audience. They accept her and they like her. Kate also managed to endow the role with a lovely femininity. She's attractive, she's nurturing, she's sensitive, she's caring. She really owns the whole package, and I am enormously respectful of what she brought to the character.

KATE MULGREW

Janeway was full of conflicts, which I imbue her with. And her conflicts are as timely now as they were then. She was an ardent scientist, but she was first and foremost an explorer. She's got this guy at home, she's engaged, so she has that and she has sensuality. She wants to love and be loved, but first she wants to go to the uncharted parts of the galaxy. I begged Berman to explore her loneliness through-out the course of the series, and he touched on it but not to the level I wanted him to. His argument, which is very solid, was, "Well, we can't expose that too much to the audience. She must lead." I'd suggest, "Let's just see that every now and then, because there's limits." I mean, I had to show that stoicism, but I had to put a brave face on it for my crew, many of whom suffered, some of whom we lost, so it was only in the privacy of my quarters and occasionally in public that I could reveal that stuff.

I'm the one who said, "No sex, no sex." The young male demographic was our biggest, strongest demographic—eighteen- to thirty-year-old men were not going to like it. There would be unending criticism of that person. Want to take me to the holodeck? I can make somebody up there once or twice. Give me Leonardo da Vinci, which was my idea. Let's have a laugh, but I have to run the ship. I felt that way for all seven years. I was of childbearing years the entire time. I didn't want some twenty-two-year-old guy watching it to say, "Ooh, gross!" Let's face it, men are often led by their . . . hmm-hmm. So I decided *not* to give them that. I put *that* much thought into it. Shatner didn't have to; he was expected to engage sexually every week. I always say to him, "Weren't you tired? I'll bet you were tired."

WINRICH KOLBE

There are moments right from the pilot where you get a sense of the difference between the previous captains and Kate as Janeway. There is more concern for and attention to feelings. Yet it's not something that would ever affect her con-duct as captain. If she has to send someone into a life-threatening situation on an unknown planet, for example, she will do that. But if something terrible happens to that crew member, she can agonize openly about it. That's something a woman might talk about, but a male captain probably never would bring it up. He would be staring into space and it would be implied, but he never would talk about it. I think the story approach from a character point of view had a much broader band to work on than if it was a male captain. We've had a lot of women leaders in *Star Trek,* but they've all suffered from the hidden-penis syndrome.

BRANNON BRAGA

Overall, the cast on *Voyager* entered *Star Trek* with an advantage in that with *Next Generation,* most of the actors had never seen *Star Trek* before being cast. Now we had a group of people who knew what *Star Trek* meant. They were good actors and we had a writing staff and production team that had been producing these shows for years. *Voyager* definitely felt fully formed almost from the start, born as an adult instead of as a child. Basically, we thought we had a feel for what worked and what didn't.

MICHAEL PILLER

This was a wonderful cast. We learned from our mistakes on *Deep Space Nine* and to a lesser extent from *Next Generation,* that we needed to immediately find these people as individuals and as a crew. It paid off handsomely.

JERI TAYLOR

The cast stepped into these characters like comfortable slippers. They just seemed to know who they were and they bonded with each other and played in an ensemble way as if it were a seventh season. They felt like a family, and I think that in the pilot it looked like a show that had been on air a lot longer.

ROBERT BELTRAN

It was a short, grueling pilot schedule, but it was fun. The cast came together like magic. I don't know if they could have chosen a better ensemble as far as camaraderie and support goes.

ETHAN PHILLIPS

The cast got along fantastically. It felt like we had been working together for years. They really took their time with the pilot and treated it like a feature. There was never a sense that you were rushing. The show had a reputation for long hours. They would keep you there forever until they got it right.

GARRETT WANG

I remember back in the early days people on the crew told me, "You're going to make a lot of money, but you're going to have no time to spend it." They were right. I would get home at two in the morning and I was out like a rock for the whole weekend to rev up for Monday. In the early days I did wonder why Tom Paris was in these holodeck programs where he got the girls. I went up to director David Livingston during a scene we were filming and asked him about it. He said, "You don't get the girls because you're the nice guy." Then Robert turned to me and said, "You know, I use to play innocent and naïve in my early twenties, and you're going to have to go through that for a while before you can be this stud guy like me." He had a point. Whenever they needed a reaction shot of somebody being amazed by something, they went to Harry Kim.

ROBERT DUNCAN MCNEILL

A great thing about the show is that, as an actor, sometimes you do work and then it's forgotten or you do a play and fifty people see it. One thing that's great about this is that for the rest of our lives, people will know this part of our work, and it's great to have that sort of longevity.

BRANNON BRAGA

Certain challenges of changing shows were the same. What we tried to do was find new voices, and that's a very fascinating process. The challenge that remained the same was coming up with good sci-fi ideas. The first few weeks were me, Jeri, and Michael getting together each day and brainstorming. Who were these people? Where were we going to take them? What are the little arcs we could take them through during the first season? All very basic things. You never know how things are going to turn out. I was writing scripts for this show before it was even cast. I didn't know what these people looked like, which was a challenge, but you just have to go with it. When the actors come in, you get a better feel for speech patterns. Once Kate Mulgrew was cast, for example, I had someone I could imitate, just like I did with Picard. You take the voice and it helps you with the writing.

KENNETH BILLER

One of the biggest challenges that faced the show was that expectations were inevitably high when it comes to *Star Trek*. What gets forgotten is that the franchise may be around for so long, but this was a whole new show with a whole new set of characters and a premise that had its own set of complications and difficulties. In the first year we did some really great episodes and others that weren't quite as great, and I think that's true of any show. When you look back at *Next Generation,* which when taken in its totality is a wonderful show with some of the best stuff done on television in a long time, it's because we only remember the best episodes. When people look back at the first two seasons of *Voyager,* there are a few episodes that you can look back upon as being really good *Star Trek* and really good television.

JESÚS TREVIÑO (director, *Star Trek: Voyager*)

When I got my first opportunity to direct a *Star Trek* episode, which was the *Voyager* episode "Fair Trade," I thought I had died and gone to heaven. It was what I was waiting for my whole life. It was an honor to be able to do this and put my creativity to work on a series franchise that was legendary and that I respect so much. But more than that, helping convey what I think good science-fiction fantasy conveys, which is a sense of wonder. When I was growing up, that was an important element that kept me out of gang life. I couldn't resist the sense of wonder that you felt when you got on to ideas like telekinesis and parallel universes and all these different concepts that expand your sense of wonder.

"Fair Trade" was a great episode, a lot of fun to do, and I had a lot of fun working with the *Voyager* family. The actors really were a family. Everyone respected each other, they were very collaborative, and everybody was seeing the bigger picture. In between shots you talk with the actors and you got to know them. After doing two or three episodes, you become family and you look forward to seeing them and exploring how we're going to work together on a particular episode, and that makes that show come alive.

BRANNON BRAGA

We had a lot of shows about planets with people that look just like humans, whereas I felt that one of the promises of this premise was to be *The X-Files* of *Star Trek*: expect the weirdest, blackest, most dangerous shit you can imagine.

> An aspect of the premise that in many ways failed to deliver was the inherent conflict between crew members in the sense of Starfleet versus the Maquis. Although still touched upon occasionally, most of that conflict was defused early on in the first season.

BRANNON BRAGA

I liked the setup of them being lost in a new part of space, away from *Star Trek*'s usual suspects. I *wasn't* a fan of the Maquis thing—that kind of political stuff just bored me. My feeling was, imagine you're deserted on a desert island with an Al-Qaeda terrorist. How long are you going to bicker about your point of view before you both realize you have to eat and no one else is there to bicker over? You have to survive and you need each other, and I turned out to be right. The Maquis thing just wasn't really going anywhere. The situation defused almost immediately, but it had to. What else would you do? I suppose you could have had a mutiny or something along those lines. I can only speak for my involvement in the show and I was more into doing weird sci-fi; I was in weird sci-fi shit mode.

MICHAEL PILLER

The studio felt the cause of dwindling ratings on *Deep Space Nine* was dark and gritty conflicts, so they said, "This needs to be a bright, wonderful, happy show." Well, what that did to us—and, by the way, I'm not sure Rick disagreed—is that when we created the circumstance that inherently had conflict in it, whereby you basically have the Maquis, the terrorists forced to become one crew with the people who are chasing them, which I think is a terrific premise, it was fundamentally decided that all that conflict was going to disappear almost immediately; everybody was going to wear uniforms, everybody is going to be Starfleet, everybody is going to obey orders, everybody is going to join hands and have the common goal to get home.

And we would *not* play the inherent conflict between the terrorists and

Starfleet. It was very difficult for us to tell stories that made the characters come alive when you can't have them disagreeing about anything. Essentially what you had is a launch to it that lacked the ability to tell character stories as a result of the studio's feeling, and perhaps Rick's, that we needed to get by the premise as quickly as possible and on our journey home, where it's one for all and all for one.

MIKE SUSSMAN (story editor, *Star Trek: Voyager*)

It was just weird, because why even have that element if you're not going to use it? I mean, the only thing that made the Maquis different were the pips on their collar. And every now and then we'd do a Maquis story about some of the Maquis that got killed in the Alpha Quadrant. Ultimately, I don't know what bold plans they had originally, but it was a wasted opportunity. But doing a show like that is constant pressure, even if you're not getting network notes. The pressure is to keep it as much like the other ones, because that's what the fans want, and we as creative people want to do something new.

RONALD D. MOORE
(coexecutive producer, *Star Trek: Voyager*)

When the Maquis put on those Starfleet uniforms at the end of the pilot, the show was dead. That was the biggest mistake, because they went through this whole thing to bring on their enemies. We made up the Maquis on *DS9* just so that they could appear on *Voyager*. Here are Starfleet officers who had become terrorist resistance fighters, guerrilla warriors. The Federation has got them on the run and both of these groups are thrown in a ship on another side of the galaxy and forced to live together.

You'd think that's the setup for a major show about conflict, but at the end of the pilot they all put on the Starfleet uniforms and that's it. It was a huge mistake. It should have been these two sides that were forced to work together that still don't like each other and still are gunning for each other, wondering who's going to come out on top. Who's going to betray who? It should have been gold, but they got scared. Unfortunately, the fact that *DS9* didn't do as well as *Next Gen* scared them and they didn't want another dark show that wasn't as successful. They wanted a show that was more like *Next Generation* and easier to swallow and where people didn't have to think as much. So they drew all the wrong lessons and said, "Let's play it safe."

ROBERT BELTRAN

I don't think it served them well to not exploit that aspect. In the early episodes they created some conflicts hanging over the Maquis-Federation setup, and I thought, "You can't have a much better, built-in crisis for a show like that." I was hoping they would take it further into the series. Maybe the first year or two, but unfortunately, one of the things that I didn't like about the series was that it sort of paid too much homage to *Star Trek* traditions and Starfleet protocol and all that stuff. Most of it was definitely drama-killing traditions that really made no sense as far as creating conflict between characters, which is what you want in a television series. The Maquis quickly became the good Boy Scouts of Starfleet and that treasure trove of possibilities was ended, unfortunately.

ANDRÉ BORMANIS

I know *I* felt disappointed that here we have this great premise of a crew at war with itself in unknown territory. And what do we get? Well, a crew that behaves very politely like the *Next Gen* crew did to one another. Very little conflict and aliens and alien politics that felt completely familiar.

GLEN C. OLIVER

The show did not take chances. It did not commit to its own innate potential. For the first time in *Star Trek* history, *Voyager*'s format . . . a Starfleet craft displaced into unknown space very far from home . . . allowed for the notion in which all *Trek* rules could be legitimately rewritten. *Any* kind of show exploring any type of subject would've been possible—a notion which would've brought the franchise much freshness, and is rampant with eye-opening potential. Alas, Romulans soon showed up, then came the Borg, then came other characters from *TNG* and suddenly . . . *Voyager* felt and looked tiredly familiar. It was a show with a premise more open and far fresher than arguably *any Star Trek* show which had come before it, and it immediately settled into a nest of time-tested and already mundane conceits.

MIKE SUSSMAN

In 1986, Roddenberry was doing a speaking tour around the country and a friend and I went to see him. He announced that he was going to Paramount the following week to talk to them about bringing *Star Trek* back to TV. The whole audience went crazy, and from that moment I was, like, "I don't know what this show is going to be, but I've got to figure out a way to write for it." I'd write spec scripts for *Next Gen* and send them in and wait for a year for a printed rejection letter in the mail.

I lived in Florida at the time, which was heartbreaking. I did some work in TV news as a writer and producer and came out to California and was lucky enough to get a job on the Paramount lot where KCAL Channel 9 used to be, and they were, like, thirty yards away from the *Star Trek* offices. Ultimately I found out about an internship program and applied for it. I got a call from Ken Biller, who was a story editor and brand-new on *Voyager* at the time, saying, "Do you want to come over and do an internship?" I was, like, "Of course!" And it was great. It was the coolest six-week TV film school you could ever imagine.

I came in during the first season of *Voyager* and there were some *great* Brannon Braga episodes of that first season, but there were a lot of stinkers, too. It was nine years since I heard Roddenberry speak, and I finally weaseled my way into there and felt so lucky, but in the back of my mind I'm wondering, "What *are* these writers thinking? Some of these stories are *awful,* and *this* has been done before, and *that* has been done before." I really did feel like the guy who was too late for the party. I mean, the party went on for another ten years because people just didn't want to leave.

It's so funny to even look back on it, because I feel like I was never in it. I was never part of the original series and I was never part of *Next Gen.* For me, those were *the two.* Everything else was just running on fumes. I hate to say it, but it all came down to the writing, and the casting, and the time limits. You need all these magical elements to sort of fall into place. I loved the later shows, but *Deep Space Nine, Voyager,* and *Enterprise* just never had that breakthrough with the general public that *Next Gen* did and that the original had. There were some terrific episodes of all those shows, but . . . well, I just don't know. Maybe it's because the grass is always greener.

JERI TAYLOR

We did hear complaints that some stories bore a similarity to earlier episodes of *Star Trek,* especially the original series. Most of us are not that familiar with the original series. There are only so many stories in the universe, and what's important is the way they're told. And we did want to return to the original series in the sense of being out in the unknown—that sense of adventure that you're going out there where no one has gone before—that's the reason we put them in the Delta Quadrant, to get away from the familiar. That was a conscious attempt to rekindle that sense of adventure. But in terms of storylines, we tried to tell fresh stories as uniquely as we could.

RICK BERMAN

At that point there had been over 350 hours of *Star Trek* produced. I would challenge anybody to come up with a story that would not relate in some way to one of those 350 stories. There are always going to be comparisons and similarities between stories about a group of people on a spaceship that last approximately forty-five minutes. We've had stories that have been pitched and discussed that we all like—and some of them come from our own heads—and then we realize, "My God, that's episode twenty-four of the original series," or something like that, and none of us ever saw it. The potential for similarity is always there when you have so many episodes.

MICHAEL PILLER

The bottom line is that for writers and producers it is very hard to find new science fiction that hasn't been touched before. We sat in rooms every day of the week with ideas and storylines, and as soon as they started to veer into something we'd done before, we'd pull them out of it and go in another direction. I think we did a very good job of coming up with twists on old themes so that they aren't carbon copies. *Next Generation,* for all the remarkable imagination that went into making that series, started off by stealing directly from the original series.

JERI TAYLOR

In the beginning, I'm not sure we consistently delivered on the show's premise, which is that we're in a brand-new, unexplored region of space, we don't know what's going to happen around the next bend or the next star, and there may be monsters out there. We tended to do too many internal, contained, on-the-ship shows and didn't deliver the kind of action, excitement, and new alien quotients that we would have liked to. The reason for that, frankly, is that we did a lot of high-production shows early on and overextended our budget and had to make good on it. We had to come out even at the end of the year, so we had to do some bottle shows that would bring the budget back down again. Our goal for the second year was to provide the action, the adventure, and production values, but to scatter it throughout the season rather than front-loading it.

In the first season of *Star Trek: Voyager,* the series introduced two new species as villains. In the case of the Kazon, the oft-lobbed criticism of familiarity breeding contempt was reflected in this aggressive race—which proved to be a kind of "Klingons Lite." They became a recurring adversary through the first two seasons that, for most people, simply didn't work. Far more successful and imaginative was the Vidiians, introduced in "Phage," a civilization threatened with extinction by an organ-destroying disease known as "the phage," which led them to use highly advanced technology to steal vitally needed organs from others to help their people to survive.

JERI TAYLOR

The Kazon were just sort of big, loutish characters that cause our people to over-act. For some reason, they all turn into moustache-twirling villains as soon as they get that makeup on. They had a cartoon-like quality that I think was not our finest hour.

MICHAEL PILLER

Our intention was to create a sort of disorganized anarchy, them-against-them as much as them-against-us. The wish that I had, which was not fulfilled, was that we would only cast people between eighteen and twenty-five-ish, so that these would be young, angry people who never lived to be old enough to have the kind of experience and perspective on the world that, say, the Klingons and the Romulans might have. The thing is, older actors have more polished performances, and as the things progressed I think they got older and older still, and as a result we didn't fulfill the full potential of the Kazon, even though I think they were written pretty well. They ultimately came out being sort of Klingon-ish and I regret that we didn't stick to our original vision of keeping them young.

JERI TAYLOR

I thought we had an interesting idea. We were likening them to gangs, but I don't know that that ever emerged in a clear enough way to prove interesting. It's one of those things, that we are not as in control as we like to think we are. Through a combination of the stories that we chose to tell with them, the casting, the makeup, and the hair, somehow they became collectively less interesting and more like sort of flat, one-dimensional cartoon characters. Certainly it wasn't our intention, but sometimes we look up on-screen and say, "Wow, how did that happen?"

KENNETH BILLER

The Vidiians, on the other hand, which Brannon created, were so interesting and so different from anything we had seen.

BRANNON BRAGA

The original pitch of "Phage" was that Paris had had his heart blown out by something, and the ship's doctor equipped him with a holographic replacement. It's a great idea. Around that time, Jeri Taylor, Michel Piller, and I had been batting around the idea of an alien race that gathers organs. We said, "Well, what's better than this?" and we put those ideas together to see what we'd come up with. Ultimately I ended up changing the heart to lungs and Paris to Neelix. It was the first time when everything came together just right: the directing, the music, the actors, and you saw *Voyager* hitting its mark.

JERI TAYLOR

The idea of a race that does really unspeakably horrible things, but does them simply because they're trying to survive, we thought was a very complex agenda. We love it when our adversaries are not one-dimensional villains, but have attitudes and textures and layers to explore. I think the Phage people really gave us that. Michael Westmore did an outstanding makeup job on them. They are truly grisly-looking people without looking like horror-monster movie stuff. We were really pleased with that.

WINRICH KOLBE

The Vidiians takes aliens off that pedestal of being weird and gives them some humanity. We were dealing with a very grotesque exterior but a very human emotion. These are a people who are basically dying and are trying desperately to save their species. It's something we're very aware of given organ transplants these days.

JERI TAYLOR

We sat around a number of days talking about new adversaries. Who's interesting? What's interesting? What's an agenda we find interesting? En route we came to these people who harvested organs. We'd gone through cannibalism and a lot more bizarre things, and then we finally hit on the idea of a culture that was dying of an incurable virus, who would go to any lengths to make themselves and their species stay alive. They were creepy and scary and they would do anything to pursue their end, but if you start with a premise like that, it's impossible to make them completely evil because their motivation is completely understandable. If anything, it's more scary if you realize that underneath that grotesque, deformed body there's someone who was once young, strong, and beautiful.

MICHAEL PILLER

Someone compared it to "Spock's Brain" or something like that. I don't know about that, but I can tell you that I liked the idea of an alien culture who are a civilized people forced to do uncivilized things in order to survive. It's a very interesting look at how the human race could devolve if things don't go right. Adversaries shouldn't be pure evil. The Vidiians are a race of people with their own set of values, which are different from ours and driven by different agendas. Even though they're ultimately doing something hideous and terribly wrong as far as our conduct is concerned, from their point of view they're doing it to survive and that makes it okay.

JERI TAYLOR

We thought Janeway was put in a true dilemma when she realized what she was dealing with. In fact, Kate Mulgrew was, herself, fighting tears when she heard the story of those people. She, as a person, was so genuinely affected that she was really fighting not to break down. I think that comes across in the performance of a woman who is torn and struggling and has great sympathy for these aliens, yet she must say, "If you ever come near my people again, I'm going to wipe you all out." That delivered on all counts.

In some ways, the Kazon became an even bigger problem in season two. Piller had left the show in the middle of the first season to produce the western adventure *Legend* for UPN, which was short-lived. The experience, however, did

color what he felt the approach to *Star Trek* should be, and the Kazon would figure heavily into it.

MICHAEL PILLER

When I went out into the cold, real world with *Legend* and saw what was going on,
I found the network was constantly on my case. I wasn't doing anything differently than I had been doing on *Star Trek*, but they were on my case to write shorter
scenes and pick up the pace of the scripts. I used to write three- and four-page
comedy scenes on *Legend* that I thought were great, and they'd say, "We don't want
three- and four-page comedy scenes. Get to the murder!" They'd say, "Make it
more like *ER*, Mike."

I took a look in a cold, analytical way at the television scene, and frankly, it had
changed remarkably in the seven years I was with *Star Trek*. *ER, Law & Order,
NYPD Blue*, and other hour shows told stories in very different ways than we
did. I realized that some of these television shows were writing twenty-second
scenes, and it was less a combination of traditional three- or four-page character
scenes and more like a scrapbook, telling stories with a mosaic of images.

So I came back and I looked at those four shows of ours, and I read the three
other scripts that were completed, and I said, "This is just nineties television." I
came in and sat down with the group and I said, "Guys, I don't think we can get
away with this anymore. The pace of these shows is languid. Yes, we have a loyal
audience, but I think we have to look at ways of telling stories in a much more
vigorous, energetic fashion." Well, people started looking at each other, like,
"Wow, he's just going to change *Star Trek*. He's going to come in here and he's
going to change it completely."

> With the blessing of Taylor and Berman, Piller implemented the changes he had
> in mind, including the idea of a season-long arc involving the Kazon's attempts
> to seize *Voyager* for their own purposes, and the fact that there was a spy se-
> creted aboard the ship in the form of Seska, a surgically altered Cardassian
> working in collusion with the Kazon.

MICHAEL PILLER

I didn't want to rely on the accepted methods of storytelling that we'd become
comfortable with on *Star Trek*, and I think it was successful.

JERI TAYLOR

The Kazon was Michael's push: It was not anything that I thought worked very well. I didn't find them particularly interesting adversaries.

MICHAEL PILLER

I had a number of "orphans" on the show that I adopted. Certain shows, certain characters that I said, "Let's keep with this." Seska was one of those characters. I thought we had an interesting sort of villain with Seska, and she allowed us to go behind the scenes with the Kazon. Creating villains for *Star Trek* is a very difficult matter—giving them a perspective, making them unique. Seska helped define the Kazon for us, and I was very satisfied with the character arc that Seska took us on. As a viewer, I just really enjoyed the whole thing.

KENNETH BILLER

The idea of a season arc was done wrong. The mistake that was made was a clear one. Michael Piller had this notion that we should tell a continuing story, sort of à la *Hill Street Blues, L.A. Law,* or *NYPD Blue.* But if you watched those shows, the continuing story elements are the character threads, the relationships. Somebody's having an extramarital affair and that keeps playing out through the whole season. The A-story, whatever the big case was, gets solved. They arrest the bad guy, and these personal stories continue along. We did it backward. I wrote this episode called "Lifesigns," but that episode will never be a little gem, because right smack in the middle of it are these two bizarre scenes with this guy sending messages off to Seska.

JERI TAYLOR

Given our franchise, which is "We're way over here and we're trying to get way over there," to have the same people cropping up episode after episode gave the curious impression that we were standing still in space, instead of going somewhere else. People began to ask, "Why don't you get out of Kazon space? Surely they don't occupy the whole quadrant." I also thought that we played the same story over and over again. Seska sets a trap and we walk into it—and we get out. I just felt that it got repetitive and, ultimately, not very interesting.

Many of the scripts in those early years failed to engage viewers, often due to repetition of what had come before; characters were underserved, there were conflicting creative visions for the series between Michael Piller and Jeri Taylor (all of which would culminate with Piller departing the series at the end of year two), and most problematic, the show suffered a *massive* ratings drop that saw its audience shrink from season one's average of 11.1 million viewers an episode to season two's 4.5 million.

TOM MAZZA

I think because *Next Generation* was the first reincarnation, it was unique. I don't think it's fair to think that you could produce a show that's necessarily going to perform better than *Next Generation* when *Next Generation* went out into the marketplace and hit it out of the park. If you look at *Deep Space Nine* and *Voyager*, they are different series. Yes, *Voyager* is probably closer conceptually to what *Next Gen* was, but it was different in its own right; having a female captain gave us a whole lot more to play with and very different. But no one over at the studio thought those two shows would actually do better necessarily.

The idea was to perform well and get a slightly different audience. Honestly, a Trekkie was going to come to the shows, most likely, unless we turned them off. But the key was whether or not we were going to be able to get other people who may look at that show versus another. *Deep Space* is a great example. *Deep Space* was a much darker show. It has a smaller fan base, but very loyal and very different. The *Next Generation* audience is very different from the *Deep Space Nine* audience. And in many ways the *Voyager* audience was closer to the *Next Generation* audience than it was to *Deep Space* overall.

MICHAEL PILLER

Just like Gene Roddenberry had an effect on writers like Ron Moore and on others in our audience, Rod Serling had an extraordinary effect on me as a kid with *The Twilight Zone*. Here was a guy who basically did *The Twilight Zone* and burned himself out on it, and then accepted that for all intents and purposes. He was one of the great television writers, an angry young man of the fifties, writer of some of the great hour- and ninety-minute anthology shows, and with *Twilight Zone* he became a celebrity of sorts, but after that, he never entered the tournament again. He wrote a few screenplays, *Planet of the Apes* and *Seven Days in May*, but he didn't have a really distinguished career as a screenwriter because he was more interested in words than in images. I said to myself, "I cannot stay on *Star Trek* for the rest of my life."

KENNETH BILLER

When Michael went off to do *Legend,* Jeri was firmly in charge and we felt a little bit freer in that second season. Michael ran the show, at least from the writing standpoint, with a pretty firm hand. He was tough, he was tough to please. But phenomenal. I mean, I learned how to break stories from Michael Piller and there's a whole generation of very successful showrunners that worked with him—Ron Moore probably being the most successful of us. But Ron, Brannon Braga, René Echevarria, and me—all of whom learned at Michael's knee how to break a show. He was a tough boss and tough to please. I'm now a tough boss and tough to please, but when we look back, we appreciate so much how rigorous he was and how uncompromising he was in making sure we were breaking stories in ways that were honest and the characters were behaving in ways that were honest and felt organic.

I remember later having communication with Michael by e-mail, because, tragically, he'd lost his ability to speak by then. I was able to send him an e-mail and say, "I can't tell you how often I find myself in a writers room with writers who are working for me and I find myself quoting you." He was very touched by that—and it was completely sincere.

At the time we were smart-ass young guys in our mid twenties and we thought we knew better than everybody else. We didn't need Dad telling us how to do stuff. And so he left and we just felt a little bit freer. Then he came back and we bristled a little bit. If I were Jeri, it would have been worse, because she finally had been handed the keys and then he suddenly said, "Oh, sorry, I'm coming back." I'd say that Jeri was gentler. She had a very maternal kind of personality and loved hanging out with all her boys.

She relied on us and depended on us, and made us feel very valued. She could be argued with and persuaded into something by passion. Michael was just tougher. He was just more critical. He didn't mean to be, but he wasn't the most socially graceful. He would sometimes say things without meaning to be that would be very cutting and would make you feel bad. But, like I said, when I look back on it, I'm very grateful for how hard he was on us. He was never mean. He never raised his voice. He never yelled. He never said anything that was intentionally insulting. It was just hard to read him sometimes.

MICHAEL PILLER

At the end of season two, the writers went to Rick and said, "Look, if Mike stays, we're going. He won't let us do the kind of things we want to do and he has very strong opinions about what *Star Trek* is. We think *Star Trek* can be more than what Mike thinks it is, so if he stays, we're leaving. You just need to know that." So Rick came to me and told me this. Of course I felt very bad about it all, but it was done with honor and friendship and no personal feeling. It was basically that you had a bunch of writers who were very frustrated.

Back on *Next Generation,* when I arrived essentially all the writers left at the end of that year because they were frustrated with what the "box" was. I used to call it "Roddenberry's Box," and I loved being in it, because the restrictions forced us to be more creative than going into the routine melodramas that we often see in SF television. So all the writers on *The Next Generation* had had it with Roddenberry's Box and quit. Now here I was, almost ten years later, and suddenly in Roddenberry's absence it had become "Piller's Box" and all the writers were ready to leave again. I guess I read the writing on the wall or listened for whom the bell tolled. I wished everybody well and I went on my way.

JERI TAYLOR

Michael leaving was scary at first. I didn't know what was going to happen. I had never done this without Michael and we had worked very closely together. So I felt really gripped with anxiety, but it gave me and the rest of the staff the opportunity to explore stories which we would not, probably, have developed under Michael's aegis. He had a particular style of storytelling. It is a very good one, but it was not the only one, so we had the freedom to develop things we simply would not have.

MICHAEL PILLER

Star Trek would give me a good living, even in reruns. I know it's a gift that I'd been lucky to get that gave me the freedom to do what I wanted to do, other ways of exploring the human condition. But I realized, I can't settle. I can't sit still. Seven years is long enough. My attitude was, even if I fail, I'm entering the tournament. Even if there were failures, at least they were going to be ambitious failures.

JERI TAYLOR

By the time we got to the third season, we were really talking about embracing the adventure, of bringing more buoyancy and more action, more adventure. I wanted to try to recapture some of the spirit of the original *Star Trek,* which I think everyone would agree was the most fun. We wanted to inject more humor into the show. We did *not* want to do stories in which the crew complains about not being at home, or stories about almost getting home and not making it so that everyone is depressed. Exploration and adventure is the reason why all these people joined Starfleet. And so it seemed to me that they have the joyous kind of time in their exploration that Starfleet people always have.

Doing stories week after week about getting home and the attempt to get home, when it's never going to reach fruition, would ultimately get very, very stale. I also think it had the curious effect of making *Voyager* sort of a dreary place to be. People don't want to be there, they'd rather be home, they'd rather not be in the Delta Quadrant. They're complaining, they're moaning. I don't think that that's what these people would be doing. I think that they would say, "Okay, we're stuck here, we're going to make the most of it, we're going to get home with a database that has the most incredible adventures anyone has ever had," and they would greet it positively.

ROBERT BELTRAN

My greatest criticism of the show was these inviolable traditions. For instance, scenes on the bridge were always the same: "Captain, the shields are down." "Well, reroute this and we'll be good." "Captain, we did that. Thank you, we're saved." And then manufacturing some kind of crisis on the bridge where we're getting rocked by energy bombs and we're doing all this ship shaking, getting flung around the bridge, but the audience knows we're coming back next week, so why spend an ungodly amount of time on the bridge with this manufactured crisis when we know we're going to make it? And maybe one of us will get knocked out and will have to be taken to sickbay. "Is he going to make it? We don't know. We'll see after the commercial." Well, of course we're going to make it, because we are going to be back next week.

They refused to allow anything to be serialized. I guess it was their way of separating us from *DS9*. But you better have something as good. I think that they did have some good episodes here and there, but in general I thought that it was a missed opportunity. The show could have been better and I feel, as just about everybody feels who watched the show, that it missed the possibility of something much bigger and much better.

KATE MULGREW

Year number one, we have to ask ourselves "Are we still breathing?" Year number two, not only are we still breathing, but it seems to me we're all on our feet, which is a good thing. Year number three became "Who are we?" The answer to that comes from relaxation. I thought by the time we got to season three, there was a whole feeling of relaxation, which could not have been achieved without the second season. You can't get from A to D without B and C. I think it had its ups and downs, but season two was quite necessary.

By that time, Janeway and I had become intertwined in many ways. It was very difficult to separate myself from her when I was working and even when I wasn't. I had some odd leakage, and it altered my life dramatically. I really had to be in charge of my life. I had to be more authoritative. I had to be more careful and I had to be more demanding, because I had so much less time than I used to.

The third season furthered Janeway's character growth, had an episode that introduced a futuristic emitter that allowed the holographic Doctor to finally leave sickbay, and saw a deepening (albeit challenging) romance between Paris and Torres. But there were other cast members who did not feel as well served by the writing.

GARRETT WANG

We needed to find out *something* about Harry Kim. For three seasons we had seen a very duty-minded young Starfleet member who everyone thought would be a good guy forever. At least the captain was the captain with a backstory of when she was a commander, when she was a lieutenant. They have that stuff written out. There was a much larger bio that was written on her. Chakotay has the whole thing with the Maquis. Paris had the whole thing with his father and being in jail. Harry's bio said little more than "his parents love him . . . he loves his parents . . . he's an only son, he plays the violin, he graduated from Starfleet, this is his first assignment."

ROBERT BELTRAN

The staff were good writers, but the show manacled the writers in the sense that there were some things they weren't just ready to violate. Some things were sacrosanct and they wouldn't violate, but yet they would. It made no sense to me.

KENNETH BILLER

Rick Berman would say no a lot and was very careful. Maybe he needed to be; I don't know. He was very careful about preserving the rules of *Star Trek* and making sure that we didn't do things in ways that were too different. But it ended up making the show the same a lot. It was hard to deviate from what he was comfortable with. He would tend to make relatively safe choices, and if something seemed too extreme to him, he would shut it down for sure.

ROBERT BELTRAN

I can't remember who brought this up, but some of the fans were saying, "Why isn't Chakotay doing this more? Why isn't he doing *this* more?" and so on. I read in an interview and one of the producers said, "Well, unfortunately, Robert Beltran is playing the second in command, so he suffers from that." And I'm thinking, "Wait a minute, what the hell? There's a human being that's playing the commander, right? It's not the rank that you're writing about, it should be the human being. That kind of thinking to me doesn't make any sense at all.

BRANNON BRAGA

I may be wrong, but my perception is that Beltran looked down at this whole thing. He thought it was stupid or something—whatever the case may be—and he wasn't professional in my opinion. I certainly didn't bend over backward to write for him. I had an issue with him as an actor. I had an issue with him phoning in a performance and, in my opinion, not being prepared. When that happens, you don't write for him, and when you don't write for him, he gets mad. It's like a vicious loop.

ROBERT BELTRAN

It's my duty as an actor to do the best that I can with the material, and I always did. But if you want me to be enthusiastic about it, that's a little bit above and beyond my duties as an actor—*unless* there's something to be enthusiastic about. Otherwise I go in, I clock in, I do my scenes, and I clock out.

I think they were under the impression that all of the actors were totally enthusiastic week in and week out and episode after episode. I think they were fooling themselves. A lot of us got very tired of the way the show was shaping up. More than anything, what kept the enthusiasm level up was just the relationship that all of us had with each other. We were a group that enjoyed working with each other and we had a lot of fun. So going to work was fun in spite of what you were going to work to do. You're getting paid well and it's a steady gig, but it's like being an athlete getting to the NFL. You're on the last-place team, you have a great bunch of guys you're playing with, but you're losing all the time.

BRYAN FULLER

Beltran was hilarious, because he would openly mock the dialogue in dailies. He would turn to the camera and mock the writers to make sure that they saw what he thought of the scenes. That was pretty bratty, but I've certainly been guilty of brattier things.

RICK BERMAN

Star Trek by definition, the original series and *The Next Generation* as well, are series dealing with people who are traveling or going off on adventures, as opposed to people who are trying to come back from adventures. That's a spirit that we realized had been somewhat lacking in the show, because there had been so much focus and concentration on getting home. What we wanted to do was shift the focus of the characters in the sense that they had confidence that they would be finding a way home, whether it's going to be in four months or four years, we didn't know. But there was going to be less brooding and a sense of the excitement of exploration, which is the reason they all joined Starfleet in the first place. We wanted to be meeting new species with a sense of making some headway.

> Not all species were new. Indeed, as established in the second-season episode of *Next Generation*, "Q Who," the Delta Quadrant served as the realm of the popular *Star Trek* villain, the Borg, and as the third season established, *Voyager* had entered their territory. The race of cybernetic super-baddies first showed up in the episode "Unity," which dealt with a colony of former Borg discovered by the crew.

KENNETH BILLER

The problem with the Borg is that they're cool adversaries, but they're pretty boring. They just come at you relentlessly, and so it's not particularly dramatic to see Borg come at you relentlessly. Brannon and Ron Moore had to come up with this really cool notion of the Borg Queen in the movie *First Contact,* because suddenly there's a personality and someone to interact with. But you can't really interact with the Borg. While I was reading an early draft of the screenplay for *First Contact*, I thought of a former Borg. I wondered what that would be like, to have been part of a collective where you could think with one mind and everything was sort of provided to you, and it's suddenly taken away from you.

I think when *Star Trek* is really good, you should think both ideas are right. Someone says, "When we were Borg, we didn't have any disease, we didn't have any ethnic conflict, we didn't have any food shortages." And of course, Soviet Russia had all sorts of social problems, but there are people who are nostalgic for those times. Suddenly they have crime in the former Soviet Union. The Mafia is rampant in the Soviet Union. It didn't exist under communism or it would have been crushed by the government. So, again, that was just an interesting way in which *Star Trek* could take on contemporary issues.

> With the character of Kes was being written out of the show, the writers threw out a season-three finale already in development in favor of a Brannon Braga–Joe Menosky–written two-parter (the first airing as the season-three finale, the second as the season-four premiere), "Scorpion," which would depict the Borg homeworld, a new computer-generated adversary, and pave the way for what would be a seismic shift in *Voyager* on a number of levels, not the least of which was the introduction of actress Jeri Ryan as Borg character Seven of Nine. Prior to *Voyager*, the actress' credits included a number of guest-starring roles and an eight-episode stint on the sci-fi conspiracy series *Dark Skies*.

BRYAN FULLER

I sold two stories to *DS9* and then got to participate in the writers room on breaking those stories, which was a huge deal. There were actually two positions when they were hiring. There was a position on both shows available. Because I had sold my first two stories to *DS9* and I had actually been in that writers room, I was desperate to get the *DS9* job. But I didn't and I *did* get the *Voyager* job, which I was thrilled about. Both shows represented different kinds of learning experiences.

There was a higher degree of camaraderie and brotherhood on *DS9*, whereas *Voyager* was a slightly different dynamic—but no less educational. The things I learned from Joe Menosky and Brannon and Ron Moore in that time were incredibly insightful. I learned so much about character from Joe Menosky, I learned so much about storytelling and structure from Brannon Braga and illustrating the high-concept notions and putting them into a script. And from Ron Moore, the honor of the role we take as storytellers. So those three gentlemen were instrumental in crafting me as a future writer and storyteller.

In any case, I came into *Voyager* for the fourth season at the same time Seven of Nine came into *Voyager,* and that was a creative breath of fresh air.

BRANNON BRAGA

One night I was home, yakking with Joe Menosky—we would have these late-night creative sessions. We'd just done "Scorpion, Part One," the first of our epic two-parters, which is a really cool episode where the Borg meets a species it can't defeat and Janeway decides to forge an alliance with the Borg. It was a really good episode, and it was between seasons, and I said, "What if we have a Borg character on the show?" I mean, *there's* some conflict for you. Then I called Rick—it was the middle of the night—and it was his idea to make it a Borg babe. We formulated the character, who had a proper name at the time—I think it was Perrin, short for Perineum, an in-joke between Rick and me, don't ask me why. But we eventually gave her a Borg designation. I really believe it was an inspired idea.

BRYAN FULLER

The character was so meticulously crafted by Joe Menosky and Brannon Braga. Seven of Nine was their child, this woman who was raised in the wild by wolves and now has to be trained to be human again. It was such a beautiful story and I love the dynamic of Seven of Nine, Janeway, and the Doctor. That's the triumvirate from *Voyager* that I thought was so effective emotionally, which kind of harkened back in a different way to the triumvirate of Kirk, Spock, and McCoy.

Brannon and Menosky introduced the wild child into the crew where she did not respect the chain of command and did not respect the authority of Starfleet, and that was interesting for Janeway to struggle with. I would argue that the dynamic of Janeway and the Doctor and Seven of Nine is as exciting as any of the triangles on the different series. The original series had Kirk, Spock, and McCoy, which has always been the pinnacle of *Star Trek* storytelling and their dynamic between emotion and logic and humanity.

With Seven, Janeway, and the Doctor you had a similar shift from a strong captain who was dealing with new life forms. The Doctor is very much a new life form who was sentient by his programming, but then moved beyond simple sentience into an awareness that brought the humanity. We've seen the Pinocchio story with Data so beautifully told on *Next Gen* and there was a similar sense of discovery for the Doctor. And with Seven of Nine being reformed from a horrible violation of your humanity and not trying to make your way back, being forced by Janeway to re-embrace her humanity against her better judgment and her own wishes, but coming out the other side grateful for what Janeway had taught her, seemed like it was the human core that every *Star Trek* story needs to be effective.

JOE MENOSKY (co-executive producer, *Star Trek: Voyager*)

Seven of Nine was an outgrowth of the more action-oriented *Voyager* that kicked in somewhere mid-third season. Brannon and I knew we were going to do a big season ender involving the Borg. At the same time, we knew we would be losing Kes, a female character, and that people seemed to enjoy the Borg Queen of the movie *First Contact*. All of those things conspired creatively and went into the writing of "Scorpion," so when we came to the point that we had to have a spokesperson, à la Locutus, we just decided to make it a female, someone cool, and a new regular character. All of those things went into the decision.

BRANNON BRAGA

Seven of Nine was something of a fulcrum character for me. Each character on the show was affected by this new infusion of energy and it reinvigorated the show. Some people think she sucked. I remember there was a feeling in the building—I can't remember who, but some of the guys on *Deep Space Nine* thought we were sellouts, just putting tits and ass on the show. I'm, like, "Yeah, we're putting tits and ass on the show. Gene would have approved, by the way. Have you watched the original series? *Star Trek* has a lot of sex in it, man. And the fucking actress is good, give her a chance." What was genius about the character is that she was utterly oblivious to her own sexuality and finds it irrelevant.

JERI RYAN (actress, "Seven of Nine")

I had no problem with an overtly sexual physical appearance, because it was the complete opposite—such a polar opposite—to the character herself. I'm not saying that's why the character works, but it's a huge part of why she worked as well. Look, I'm a mom, so my number one priority when I pick a role is to pick something I'd be proud for my daughter to watch, or my son at the time, because I didn't have a daughter then. I'm proud of this character for any young girl growing up to look at as a kind of role model. It's part of life. You have incredibly intelligent people in all types of appearances.

You can be a bombshell and be really intelligent—you're not a ditz because you're blond and have a figure. And people stereotype someone dressed in tight or sexy clothing and assume you're stupid. That's one of my biggest pet peeves with Hollywood and that's why the role of Seven of Nine was so refreshing. When I read the scene they'd written for her and talked to the producers and listened to where they were going to go with her, it was just the opposite of that. I'm a National Merit Scholar. I was not a dumb kid growing up, but to be assumed to be stupid is something that drives me crazier than anything.

RICK BERMAN

Bringing in Jeri Ryan as Seven of Nine was a similar situation to bringing Worf into *Deep Space Nine*: the ratings were slipping and the studio came to us and said, "What can you do to spice things up a little bit?" And the idea was, what if we brought a babe into the show, but have her be a Borg? The Borg from the movie *First Contact*, which was our second movie, and also from both of the previous series, were incredibly successful and liked. The idea was that a little girl was taken by the Borg and assimilated—basically had her consciousness sucked out. She became part of this hive. We rescue her in a sense, she is separated from the hive and we have to program her back into becoming human. It was just an ideal character.

JOE MENOSKY

One of the things we were very conscious of was the way that Gene Roddenberry created characters that were very simple, but somehow rich with potential. Data— what could be simpler than Pinocchio, a little wooden puppet that wants to be a boy? That was Data, and that was a very rich source of story material. In this case, we wondered what the proper metaphor for this character should be. We had someone who had left the Borg, this powerful, very dangerous alien who had resumed or taken up where her humanity had left off.

We were looking for something that would inspire the writing. Whether we ever came up with it explicitly in dialogue or description or not, one of the things we kicked around was whether or not she was an ex-junkie. Is she someone who has been taken away from her fix and this is essentially a withdrawal? The other metaphor we played with was, is this an ex–cult member? Is this someone taken away from a huge religious cult who has to be given back her individuality; reprogrammed in that sense? But both of those metaphors, for us, were negative.

We played with them and wondered if kids would want to watch someone you think of as being an ex-junkie. That was certainly *not* Pinocchio. Instead, we came up with the inspiring image of a wolf child.

Despite the fact that wolves are considered very dangerous and evil creatures in fairy tales and are merciless, there is still something very elevated about the notion that you once lived among the wolves and survived. That allowed us to write her with a kind of arrogance.

Despite the fact that she's a human, she's always felt at some level that she used to be a part of something very great, and that gives a kind of haughtiness to her. You could argue that it's a defensive posture, but it doesn't matter because it gives you a certain voice and dynamic to that character. Whereas if we had gone with our thinking of the ex-junkie route, what's to be arrogant about?

RICK BERMAN

We read a lot of women, and when Jeri Ryan walked in, everybody's eyes kind of popped out—especially the studio people. We narrowed it down to three people and Jeri Ryan was not my first choice. Jeri Ryan was the first choice of both Jeri Taylor and Michael Piller. My first choice was this wonderful actor who had played Leah Brahms, Susan Gibney. I thought she would be a great Seven of Nine and I was overruled—and probably correctly so.

JERI RYAN

I had seen a couple of episodes of the original series as a kid when I was growing up. I saw the "Tribbles" episode and there was an episode with a planet of kids who kept saying, "grups, grups, grups." That was sort of my whole experience with *Star Trek* up to that point. I had lots of apprehension when they first approached me with it. In fact, when the audition first came along the pipeline I passed on it, like, three times and didn't even want to go in. All I knew about *Star Trek* at that point was that it was sort of notorious for pigeonholing its actors, who were having a difficult time breaking into other things after it. So I was very wary about that.

The second or third time the casting person called my agent and said, "Jeri really needs to look at this," and so they sent over two scenes for me to look at. One I was not terribly thrilled with, which is, of course, the one we used and it ended up on film, which is the now infamous "take off your clothes" scene, which I thought was pretty trite and on the nose and easy. The other scene, which of course never ended up being filmed, showed me the potential of what this character could be, and it was probably the most beautifully written scene that I've ever had for an audition, before or since. It was a scene with, I believe, Chakotay. Seven is having her first memories of laughter, and my son, who was two or two and a half at the time—who is now in college—I could draw on him. It reminded me of all the things I'd seen when he was a baby and he sort of surprised himself and laughed, so I could draw on him, his experiences, and I saw how rich this character could be and what the potential was for her. So I went in and I read for the producers and they wanted to do a screen test.

The way it works is you have to sign a contract, which is usually for seven years, so you basically sign away seven years of your life before you technically even have the job. I'm supposed to test the next day and the show was on that night. My mom happened to be in town because she was taking care of my son for me; she was a nanny for Alex when he was little. I said, "Well, we should probably watch it," because I'd never seen *Voyager*. Well, it was the *worst* hour of TV I'd ever seen. I was literally watching with both hands over my eyes, between my fingers, and I was in tears when it was over. My mom and I kind of looked at each other and I said, "I can't do this." So I called my agent and canceled the test.

The next morning Rick Berman called me at my apartment, personally. He was very sweet. He said, "I understand you have some reservations. I can answer your questions on the phone, but I think it would be better if you came in and sat down with us and we can allay your fears and answer any questions you might have," which was very generous of them. At that point I had nothing to lose, so I said, "Cool. I'll be there." I expressed my feeling that the episode I watched was horrible, and the three of them—Rick, Jeri Taylor, and Brannon Braga—in unison said, "Oh, God, not *that* episode! Don't judge us by that." To their credit, they talked me off the ledge and explained what their vision was for this character, what they wanted her to be and the potential for her. All you can do is kind of trust them or not. I took them at their word, and they were great. They 100 percent lived up to what they told me they were going to do with the character.

They will promise you the moon with a character and then very seldom does it live up to what they're promising you. They're promising to get you to sign on to something. This was one of the rare cases where they absolutely told me 100 percent the truth, and I mean it was even better than they said it would be. As an actor, it was such a gift to play her.

RICK BERMAN

The character had very little recollection of her earlier human existence. She was a character who, during the course of the series, would rediscover—and, in a way, redefine—the humanity that was ripped away from her so many years ago. It was the job of our cast, and Janeway in particular, to try to help bring back the qualities that she once had.

JERI RYAN

I watched the "Best of Both Worlds" episodes of *The Next Generation* and the movie *First Contact*, which was the main one they wanted me to watch. But they were very clear that Seven of Nine was unlike anything the audience had seen before. She wasn't the Borg Queen, she's not Locutus, and she's not a typical drone. So I was trying to figure out who she is when she's the full Borg. I sort of had a grip on what she becomes when she becomes the Seven of Nine she's going to be when she's part of the series, but as part of the collective I wasn't sure.

Director Rick Kolbe was the one who gave me the key to latch on to how to play Seven when she was a Borg. I had to find her physicality, because a lot of the Borg characters are how they hold themselves. He said I should think of a Prussian general—shoulders back, big, straight posture; you don't move your arms a lot when you're walking. It was really very military, and that was the perfect image for me to grasp on to and use. Having said that, it did become slightly problematic with the silver suit—because then I'm stuck in that carriage with the shoulders drawn back and the chest is out, and in highly reflective silver. That was a little troubling, but you can't change the entire posture of the character instantaneously just because she's wearing something different. So that was an issue.

KATE MULGREW

I thought the idea of a female Borg would be cool. She is a human raised by Borg. I wanted to take her inner Borg out. I was on a special mission to humanize her and had a relationship with her. I wanted to strip down her defenses to see if she can assimilate with humans. Kirk wouldn't bother, but Janeway thought of it as a challenge. Janeway brought her over. It's her fault, and therefore her responsibility.

JERI RYAN

Seven was at odds with everyone when she was first brought over to *Voyager*. She didn't want to be separated from the collective; Janeway was forcing individuality and humanity on her. She was making the choice *for* her and there was dialogue where Seven said, "You're no better than the Borg. You're doing the same thing they did. You're forcing me, I'm not choosing!" That was cool, pointing that sort of dichotomy out. Over time, the relationship with Janeway became sort of mother-daughter. There was that intimacy and closeness and tension, especially when Seven got into what I call her unruly teenage phase where they would butt heads a lot.

MICHAEL PILLER

What I think became extremely clear is that once you brought Seven of Nine on board the show, you got cultural conflict from her that nobody else was able to bring. Perhaps partly as a result of that, and I think the quality of the actress had a lot to do with it, she became the most interesting character on the ship, because she was the one person who disagreed with everybody else. What conflict does is bring character out.

BRYAN FULLER

Whenever there is a new character, that means some of the other characters will get less. But I feel like actually what Seven of Nine did do in a fantastic way is bring out a whole other side of Janeway. So I thought Janeway got better with Seven of Nine. And the Doctor got better. And I think there were some characters in the show that were more kind of traditional Starfleet characters than you've seen in previous shows. Bringing in a new character is always a challenge: Now that we've brought in this new interesting character, how can the character's presence make everybody more interesting across the board?

JERI RYAN

I loved the relationship that Seven developed with the Doctor, and I'm still sad Seven didn't fall for him. He was so sweet. I loved the dynamic between them. They shared the same sort of being outside humanity and looking-in aspect. He was a hologram and wanted things he couldn't have, and lived vicariously through Seven a lot. I liked Harry for being like a little puppy dog with his tail between his legs, and they became friends. In fact, I think the first time you'd ever seen Seven crack a smile was because of Harry.

RICK BERMAN

Among the best elements of *Star Trek* since the original series have been characters that Gene Roddenberry believed held a mirror up to humanity. The character of Spock was like that in his half-human qualities. Data was designed specifically for that purpose. The shape-shifter Odo to some degree, and I think the Doctor on *Voyager* to a great degree. Any time we can create a character that lets us reflect or comment on humanity, it does nothing but help the show.

BRANNON BRAGA

Seven of Nine was a galvanizing and polarizing character. I still get criticism from people, including Robert Beltran, who says she was a piece of shit character who ruined the show. I can't imagine how anyone could say Seven of Nine made *Voyager* a worse show.

ROBERT BELTRAN

I know that other people were not happy, but I'll let them speak for themselves. To me it was this endless scene that was written episode after episode of these all-knowing, all-seeing, omnipotent characters that were battling each other, going through the same argument over and over between Janeway and Seven of Nine. I have to say that that made Janeway weaker by making her this all-seeing, all-knowing, never-made-a-mistake-in-my-life kind of character. There's no conflict in that. You really have to search hard to find conflict with those kinds of characters. The Doctor became sort of the same thing. I think they wrote very well for non-humans.

People have misconstrued my criticism as that I felt like I should get more airtime. No, no, believe me. By the time that seven years was over, I was counting the days that I *didn't* have to work. It was not that at all. In fact, I had conversations with writers telling them, "Look, if you just give me one scene in every episode that's a good scene, I will be very happy."

So I thought that this thing between Janeway and Seven of Nine just got taken way too far, for way too long. "Let's make Seven of Nine more human again," and she would make progress and then the next week she'd be back to the same old half Borg/half human. I know that it's hard for any television series to maintain a quality over seven years. I know that the writers have a huge challenge in trying to do that and I sympathize with them. But that's what they're paid for. I think that they took the easy way out in many instances.

RICK BERMAN

Hiring Jeri Ryan caused some problems with Kate Mulgrew. Kate was sort of the Queen of *Star Trek* at that point. She was the star of the show and the first female captain. She hung out with astronauts, she hung out with Hillary Clinton, and she was the spokesman for women in leadership roles and for a lot of things. All of a sudden, this busty, gorgeous, blond babe appears who took away everybody's breath. I literally once remember some press being on the stage and just sort of pushing by Kate to get to Jeri. So there was a little antagonism that existed right through to the end of the show with those two ladies. Which was a shame, because I really liked them both.

ALEXANDER SIDDIG (actor, "Julian Bashir")

Is it really surprising Kate Mulgrew had the reaction she did? She's there thinking she's a feminist trailblazer, first female captain ever, and then a pair of tits walks in the room and you go, "What the fuck is happening here? This is not the show." Jeri Ryan is lovely, obviously, but the costume . . . you don't see her face when she enters a room. It's pretty hard.

BRANNON BRAGA

Kate Mulgrew didn't like the addition of the character at all. To say it was tense is understating the case. We let Kes go, we felt the character wasn't quite working, and we made way for Seven of Nine and it was not pleasant. And suffice it to say when I started to have an affair with Jeri Ryan a year or so later, it was one of the most uncomfortable moments in my career having to go to Kate's trailer to tell her what was going on, because Kate was *not* a fan. I don't think she had anything against Jeri personally, but it was the character. But Jeri was not having it, either. She was, like, "Why is this fucking woman shitting on me? I just want an acting job, for fuck's sake." I think everything cooled off eventually, but it didn't slow things down in terms of production. No one refused to come out of their trailer. But Jeri felt the tension. You know, "There's an intruder in our midst." She was on a bunch of posters, she got all the attention.

GARRETT WANG

Seasons one through three, Kate did every bit of amazing PR that was out there. She was on the cover of *Entertainment Weekly,* she was interviewed by Bill Maher, Jon Stewart had a talk show on MTV and interviewed her, and so on. But the minute Jeri Ryan came in, all the thunder went to her. She did *The Tonight Show with Conan O'Brien,* and Kate was getting much less.

In the beginning, Kate's anger was *not* directed toward Jeri Ryan, it was directed toward the character of Seven of Nine. She complained to the writers and producers and asked that the character be removed. She was the first female captain and now you bring in this borderline T-and-A character. When the writers/

producers said no, she kept complaining and they continued to refuse. Finally her anger was turned toward the actress playing the character, Jeri Ryan. That's when it became horrible.

RICK BERMAN

I think it's something that couldn't have been helped. After three years of being the queen bee, Kate had somebody come in who was younger and sexier and who all of sudden got the attention of the press. It caused some hurt and some alienation and there were problems. Jeri was dating Brannon, which I think added to that problem. It was difficult.

KENNETH BILLER

By the time I became the showrunner in season seven, Kate had a very strong attitude, and I understand it. She was number one on the call sheet and she was the lead of the show, and suddenly some twenty-something bombshell was brought in and there were tons and tons of stories being written for that character and we all knew Kate didn't like it. Now, I will say that the relationship between Captain Janeway and Seven of Nine was a great relationship and it ended up, at the end of the day, there was a lot of really great material for Kate that was written that wouldn't have been written if we hadn't brought that character in. I think she felt like, "I'm the female lead of the show and I'm the star of the show, and now there's this other woman coming in and everybody is acting like *she's* the star of the show." Kate bristled at that.

ROBERT BELTRAN

For some reason, Kate felt there wasn't any room for any other star beside herself. When so much emphasis was given to Jeri, I think she felt slighted in some way or challenged in some way. Which, of course, I could never understand, because you're the captain of the damn show. You're the captain of the ship, so what are you complaining about? What's the problem? You still get to shine in every other scene.

There's an old school in this business where some people believe that you don't give any quarter to anybody that's a challenge to you. Maybe there's a bit of that with Kate. She's kind of old school in that way. But it made the last few years really challenging, because I didn't think it was fair to Jeri and she was my friend. I was a friend of Kate's, too, but I felt that there was a line that Kate crossed and I wasn't going to stand for it. And I voiced my opinion. But to be honest, it wasn't just Kate in the beginning. Several of the actors felt that with all the attention given to Jeri that their characters were going to suffer or whatever.

JERI RYAN

The situation with Kate was very . . . difficult. It was not a fun work experience, particularly that first season. It was very difficult. I completely understand why. I get it, believe me, but it was very difficult. I had mornings, that first season especially, where I'd be nauseous before I went to work that morning, because I was so stressed. The second season wasn't a whole lot easier. . . . Overall, this was not my favorite work experience for that reason.

GARRETT WANG

I used to watch *Voyager* every week and I'd say to Jeri, "Did you see the episode last night?" and she'd say, "Garrett, Kate has made me *hate Star Trek*. I hate coming to work every day."

ROBERT BELTRAN

I remember the actors trying to get together a meeting with Rick to complain about Jeri. I wasn't going to have anything to do with that, because they didn't want Jeri to be at the meeting. So I called Rick and said, "I know you guys are going to have that meeting, but I'm not going to be there." He asked me why not, and I said, "Because Jeri is not going to be there and I don't think it's fair. I think it's all bullshit, because if anybody wants more publicity, all they have to do is hire a publicist and they can get all the publicity they want. If they're not paying for the publicity, then they've got no room to complain."

That was my feeling about it. I told Kate that I wasn't going to be there and she said, "You think it's every man for himself?" And I said, "That's the way it's always been, Kate. That's the way it is in this business. It's every man for himself. I'm not going to be part of any kind of a 'Let's get Jeri' meeting. It's not her fault that they're spending all this time on her and her character and the way she looks. They brought her on for that specific reason, so let's get on with it." Basically the meeting was canceled and it was never brought up again.

GARRETT WANG

I remember a situation where they were interviewing everybody about the Seven of Nine character, and Kate called me in my trailer and asked me to boycott that interview. I said, "Kate, I'm going to go to that interview, because I don't have anything against Jeri." She was *so* mad.

ROBERT BELTRAN

In our own way, Kate and I have reconciled. We're friends and we shared the stage for the first time in San Francisco and had a really good time. But I am *not* going to soft-pedal and say that things weren't as bad as they were, when they were pretty bad. The crew was uncomfortable, the actors were uncomfortable, and there was no reason for it. During filming it could go very beyond what I would have tolerated. If it had been the other way where it was me being insulted and Kate was a man, I probably would have taken a swipe at the guy. But that's me.

GARRETT WANG

At one point Kate pulled the line producer aside and said, "Jeri Ryan is not allowed to use the bathroom unless she uses the bathroom before work or after work, but not during work. It takes too much time to get her in and out of that suit. It's wasting time." Okay, so you're trying to tell another human being that they're not allowed to urinate? She's just got to hold it? Are you kidding me? Obviously it didn't happen; they didn't honor that request.

ROBERT BELTRAN

I know that Jeri had personal costumers assigned to her. It was not easy to wear what she had to wear. It was very difficult for her to spend twelve or fourteen hours in that catsuit that she was wearing and you *do* have to go to the bathroom once in a while. And you want to get comfortable when you're not on the set. It took time to make her look the way that she looked, and that's just par for the course on any film. Some characters need more time and you just deal with it. So there were a lot of things that I saw and a lot of things that I heard about from people that would know. It was maddening that nothing was being done to stop it. I think it goes back to the top. You have to put a stop to that kind of crap. Let's have another three years of fun and enjoyment, which is what the first four years were. It was a lot of fun to go to work then. The last three years *were not*.

GARRETT WANG

Between takes Jeri would take off these three- or four-inch heels and put on slippers, so wardrobe would come over and do that. Kate didn't like that. She was actually standing behind Jeri Ryan, glaring at the wardrobe guy that was putting on her slippers and doing the "kill" signal with her hand. She pulled him aside and basically said, "You leave her in those heels all day long. Don't change them. It's wasting time." Kate had suddenly become like the Caretaker character in the pilot episode who kept saying over and over again, "I don't have time; you're wasting time."

I don't remember the comment, but Kate said something very snarky to Jeri and walked away. Jeri looked at me with a look of disbelief that said, "Can you believe that she said that?" I mouthed to her, "I know. I'm sorry." She was so frustrated, she grabbed a phaser out of the holster of an extra standing near her and aimed it at Kate's back as she walked away, pretending to fire. She was *so* mad. The whole situation was so high school.

BRANNON BRAGA

To me, Seven of Nine was actually contributing to Janeway. The paradigm of the wild child raised by wolves, or in this case the Borg, and having Janeway make this her project, her doomed project to make her human again. I think it made Janeway's character a little more interesting.

KENNETH BILLER

At the end of the day, Seven of Nine was a classic *Star Trek* character. She was really a character who had to struggle to claim her humanity, and the relationships the character developed were wonderful. You talk about serialization, just look at her relationship with the Doctor. She certainly reinvigorated the show from a writing standpoint and it gave us a whole new set of stories to tell. There's no question that at the studio and marketing and producer level they were trying to add T and A to the show. Of course they were. It doesn't change the fact that she wasn't written like Jane Fonda's sex kitten Barbarella. It was written in a very smart way, I thought. And definitely reinvigorated the show for the writers and the fans as well. Whether they were tuning in because they were fascinated by the character or because they liked to look at her. Or both.

TOM MAZZA

No question it benefited the show. She was a huge addition to the show. She represented a real opportunity to reach out and get a little bit more youthful, get a little bit more contemporary, and make it a little bit more relevant to the day at that point. It was a sexy actress playing a sexy character. It brought an element that we quite frankly didn't have on the show. She got that show back onto the front covers of magazines and she became a huge symbol. And she was booking talk shows and she was booking a lot of things, so it was a great character. It really added a tremendous amount.

The dynamic on the set is a little harder; it's harder to add a brilliant, attractive woman like that onto a set and then all of a sudden give her a lot of screen time. One of the things that was always a challenge for the show, and not just for *Voyager*—*Deep Space* as well, and to a degree, *Next Gen*—was constantly handling the actors. And they understand, but they didn't like it. They didn't get much screen time, so for them they are sitting at work fifteen hours a day and they were only truly working three hours, four hours, depending on who it is. That's hard.

So they're sitting in their trailer a lot. And what you tend to do is look at it and go, "How come I'm always in my trailer when Jeri Ryan is not in her trailer?" and all of a sudden, in order to make room for somebody like Jeri, many of the characters have to then start having less page count. At the end of the day, you want it. You're an actor, you want to be performing, you want to be on-screen. And that's hard to accept. A lot of hand-holding had to be done as a result. That's what we had to do and you try your best. It's understandable, but it was a fact of a life and it's not the only show that's ever had that experience.

JERI RYAN

When my character was added, it was a difficult situation. It's always hard when you're writing out one character who's been there from the beginning and you're adding a new person. *And* this was season four, which is never an easy or comfortable situation. There is no best-case scenario. One of the problems with Seven in terms of the other cast members and their characters is that you had a character that was so rich to begin with that the writers wanted to write for her. The writers would be salivating to write for anybody new after three years, so a disproportionate number of episodes had Seven as the A-storyline or a very strong B-storyline, which can be frustrating for actors who have been there for years.

And then you add on the fact that Paramount was very clear—they made no bones about it—that they saw this as their chance to break *Star Trek* into the mainstream media. They said that verbatim in publicity meetings before the character launch, that the sexy part of her was a way of catching attention outside of scifi. And they actually did it, which is why you saw a huge jump in the ratings. People who weren't traditionally sci-fi fans who hadn't watched before, began to watch, because you had to attract their attention. So the marketing was successful, but that was not going to be easy for the actors who have been plugging away for the three previous years. And understandably so.

JESÚS TREVIÑO

I did one of Jeri's first episodes when they were still fine-tuning the costume on her, because she's a gorgeous woman and they wanted to sell her sexuality, obviously. We had other difficulties. There was one scene where she comes into the room and there's a bunch of objects on the table. She picks one of them up as she's talking and the skintight outfit was really showing her breasts. She picked up this thing that happened to be longer than it was wide, and as she held it up she was inadvertently holding it right between her breasts. I turned to the DP and he turned to me and we said, "Let me change that." So I repositioned the camera so that we would get on with the storyline instead of the inadvertent sexual allusion there. Jeri's sex appeal and beauty as a woman was enough, but this was just hilarious. I don't think anyone even got wind of it, except I had to stop and redo the whole thing. People probably said, "He's just a crazy director; he doesn't know what he needs." Well, I knew what I *didn't* need.

BRYAN FULLER

There was a shift in dynamic that is hard not to take personally when you're on a show and they bring in a new element, because they want the show to be different. It basically says what was happening before without that character was not as interesting, so it's hard not to take it personally. I never saw any of the tension, but I was definitely aware of tensions because people had told me about them. But I always saw Kate Mulgrew as the Grand Matriarch of the set. Every St. Patrick's Day she cleared out a stage and filled it with tables and had crew and their loved ones come in for a corned beef hash dinner and got a bottle of whiskey. She would sit there on the stage and talk to you about everything. She was very real and accessible. I loved working with Kate. I loved being able to spend time with her. I love Jeri, too, because we were coming in at the same time and we were about the same age, so it was interesting, too, to see that dynamic and see that there was a shift in the paradigm. But it made the show better.

ANDRÉ BORMANIS

Janeway developed a really interesting relationship with her, Janeway kind of mentoring Seven in her path back to humanity. And of course Seven had a great relationship with the Doctor, Picardo's character. That was a very positive contribution to the show and it was a missing element and Jeri Ryan played her brilliantly. A really significant addition to the show.

BRYAN FULLER

I remember it was, like, the second episode after "Scorpion, Part Two." She was already out of her Borg suit and I was, like, "Ehhhh . . . I wanted to see the transition go much more smoothly and less abruptly." I think that was something that a lot of people wanted internally in terms of the writing staff, but there was that feeling, "Nope, now we've got to settle into the syndication pattern." The solutions for things weren't always creatively based. They were sort of spreadsheet based.

JERI RYAN

As my son grew up, he really became a *Star Trek* fan, and so he would rewatch some of the old episodes and I would catch little things here and there with him. It was funny, because we had sort of progressed the character and then all of us together—the writers and the producers and myself—decided to pull it back, we made it more gradual. If you look at the first couple of episodes, she was much more loose and free than she ended up being later, so we did sort of pull it back.

JOE MENOSKY

We realized we were going too far and too fast and pulled back. It's a real strange feedback phenomenon. You'll do an episode, see what works, and adjust with a new character accordingly if you feel as though you've gone off track. It's also true of characters that we felt weren't working entirely successfully; you find new directions for them based on feedback. Jeri Taylor would say, "If Captain Janeway was only half as cool as Kate Mulgrew, we'd be better off." So in the third season I specifically remember doing some dialogue for Janeway with Brannon, and Kate just played the hell out of it. We realized we should do it more, because we had done something that allowed Kate to inject her personality even more into it. So we gave her more of those kinds of moments, like in "Scorpion" where she's making her deal with the devil, actually the Borg.

BRANNON BRAGA

Kate, her bitching aside, was a consummate professional, and was always. The tension was real and it helped the screen chemistry because Jeri wasn't having it, either.

GARRETT WANG

The writers were *very* passive-aggressive. When they're upset with you, they write it into the script. When Robbie, Robert, and I got heavy one season—we were eating all the junk food on set and gained like twenty or thirty pounds—they gave us girdles to flatten our stomachs. In this one scene in one episode, McNeill and I are in our spacesuits trying to make it across this rocky terrain. Paris is helping me and we're both gasping for air, and he says, "Promise me one thing, Harry. If we make it back alive . . . you'll work out." Later I called Brannon Braga and I said, "What's this crap in the script about working out, man? Is that a dig?" And Brannon said, "Well, Garrett, if you and your fellow actors go down the same path of eating the way you have the past two years, we're going to have to change the name of the show to *Star Trek: Voyager—Pigs in Space*."

So if you watch the episodes of Janeway and Seven, all of the writing where Janeway is trying to teach a lesson to Seven, it's the writers telling Kate Mulgrew you need to learn this when you're dealing with Jeri Ryan. They knew the tension was there, too. If you watch *Voyager* again and watch those scenes, you'll now know exactly what the writers were telling Kate; that you need to do this, do that, you need to be a better person about this.

JERI RYAN

I'm sure the tension did add to some of the scenes between the characters. It can't not. A lot of that was written in the scenes anyway, but real-life tension can help because you can play off of that and feed off another actor. So for some scenes it made it more difficult and in some it helped enrich the scene.

KATE MULGREW

Let's be very straight about something: This is on *me,* not Jeri. She came in and did what she was asked to do. No question about that, and she did it very well. It's on me, because I'd hoped against hope that Janeway would be sufficient. That we didn't have to bring a beautiful, sexy girl in. That somehow the power of my command, the vicissitudes of my talent, would be sufficient unto the day, because this would really change television, right? That's what dug me the hardest, that to pick up the numbers they did that. . . . That was my interpretation of it. And that *hurt* me. I found it sort of insulting. And, of course, she embodied the part, this beautiful girl. But we certainly were utterly professional. I had been nothing short of completely professional, and she did her job. Very well! It was a very good idea that she was half Borg, but it's on me. I'm sorry it has to be part of this legacy, and I should have probably comported myself better. I should have been more philosophical about it, but in the moment it was difficult.

Behind the scenes on season four, things continued to evolve. Jeri Taylor, after a long and successful career in television, announced her plans to retire at the end of the year, and Brannon Braga, who had started as an intern on *The Next Generation,* was now being groomed to take her place as showrunner (the first time he would hold that position). Braga, for his part, wanted to put his own stamp on the series, though it wasn't always an easy thing to do as Rick Berman remained firmly in charge of the franchise.

BRYAN FULLER

I was coming into *Voyager* in Jeri Taylor's last year, and so she was handing the baton over to Brannon, and Brannon was very much a new showrunner. There were things that he really wanted to do and should have been able to do, and which would have made the show even better and bolder and bright, but he was not allowed to. Rick Berman more or less told him, "No, you can't do that, because I can't control Ira Behr on *Deep Space Nine* and I have to control you."

The influences of Rick on Brannon's instincts sort of dampened what the show could have been. Brannon was a great showrunner and had great, bold ideas, but he was working for Rick Berman, who was a daughter of the syndication era. And the show had to be very specifically traditional in a certain sense, and he really squashed some of Brannon's better ideas. I would love to go back in time and see Brannon do the *Voyager* that was his instinct to do.

MICHAEL TAYLOR

They gave me Jeri Taylor's office. It was great. It had a wet bar. Jeri, I still have a model of *Voyager* that was left in your office. It used to light up, no longer does. I hope you won't take it back because I am really fond of it.

BRYAN FULLER

You know, my experience with *Star Trek* consisted primarily of highlights. It was so fantastic to be able to walk onto a Starfleet ship and walk through the corridors. Being in those corridors was surreal and transportive. It was also an interesting time, because I was terrified of screwing it up and yet I was also fascinated with the politics of Rick Berman and Brannon on one show, and Ira on another show. Looking at somebody who had been a showrunner before and had the confidence and the ability to say no with someone who was still reporting to someone and still fulfilling a portion of someone else's vision.

BRANNON BRAGA

I thought *Voyager* could be a big, expansive, cinematic show. I wanted to up the ante from the production point of view. I would eventually get that chance. I remember Joe Menosky and I went to Jeri Taylor and said we wanted to start doing a series of two-part episodes that would let *Voyager* make its own stamp. Every single two-parter we did was fucking great and a barn burner. Real scope, and from a really high concept. I always thought *Voyager* could be high concept.

BRYAN FULLER

Despite Rick's determination to have a stronger hold on *Voyager* than he could on *Deep Space Nine*, I'd not deny how much Brannon actually *did* achieve with the series. He very much was eager to get into more high-concept science-fiction storytelling, like harder science-fiction storytelling. The great stuff with Species 8472, the Borg arc, the "Year of Hell," the Hirogen and "The Killing Game." There was a lot of iconography brought back into the world of the storytelling, and less sort of diplomacy and navigating new species and more "Holy shit, we've got to fight these guys!" And that was really Brannon coming into his own. Actually Brannon and Joe Menosky were really the creative voices of those last few seasons.

BRANNON BRAGA

One of the criticisms the show got was the fact that there was little carryover from episode to episode. There was a two-part episode called "Year of Hell," which was arguably the best two-parter we did. My original pitch for that was "Let's do a season called 'The Year From Hell' where *Voyager* gets its ass kicked and the entire season is *Voyager* barely surviving," and we would play a real continuity between episodes. I don't remember the specifics, but I know it was rejected and it did *not* become a serialized show. So I said, "Okay, I'll do a two-parter that takes place over the course of a year," and that's the closest I ever got.

BRYAN FULLER

In season four, the entire season was going to be *Voyager* getting its ass kicked and the show was really going to go to a gritty and rich place of "We are out of our element and we are in danger and all we have is ourselves," Janeway being this situational, ethical leader who was willing to do whatever it took for her people to survive in these circumstances. And it was so much bolder than what you saw. That's not to say that there weren't some great episodes in that season. You *had* the "Year of Hell," but Brannon had so many bold visions that were brushed aside by Rick just not seeing it and not wanting *Voyager* to be as gritty and bold as *DS9*.

And this was Brannon's first time as showrunner. It's a terrifying thing to be a showrunner, because you're responsible for a huge production. There are huge demands—ridiculous demands—on your brain and your abilities, and it is one of the stupidest jobs in the world. I think it was challenging for Brannon to stand up for his better ideas when Rick Berman was saying no.

One of the things that Brannon really wanted to do is to say we don't have a Federation starbase nearby that we're going to get backup supplies from, so he wanted to start cobbling together an aesthetic for this ship that was a mixture of new technologies that we found in the Delta Quadrant. It was that desire to really change the aesthetic of the show and do something different with *Star Trek*. And what he was told was that the *Voyager* had to look like a starship.

KENNETH BILLER

Back in season three, we had a two-part episode called "Future's End," which guest-starred Sarah Silverman and had the ship ending up in Los Angeles in 1998 or whenever it was. That was early in the season and my recollection is that Rick and Jeri were saying to us that the studio wanted to try and reinvigorate the series and boost ratings. They wanted us to figure out a way that the show could feel different, and my recollection is that I pitched the idea that we could do a whole season where the ship got stuck in present-day Earth. The characters had to assimilate and live lives, and then eventually would be faced with the choice of staying in these lives that they actually had grown accustomed to and maybe forged relationships, and then would have to decide whether or not to continue the journey.

What happened was it went from a discussion of "Gee, could we do it for a whole season?" to "We can't do it for a whole season, can we do a four-episode arc?" And then the four episodes got reduced to two episodes. In the last season we did a two-parter called "Workforce," which was kind of that idea. They got stranded on an alien planet and they were basically immigrant laborers on that planet. We gave Janeway a relationship with a man that she felt attached to and suggested they had been there for a while. We were always trying to find ways to do that, where they could get really emotionally invested with other characters they were meeting, but it was hard to do because of the central premise of the show, which is they are trying to get home.

BRANNON BRAGA

Non-serialization was more or less a mandate. It wasn't the way we did things. Honestly, that's why I did these two-parters. I wanted to do three-parters and that was rejected. I was yearning to tell stories on a larger canvas and stories that required more than forty-five minutes. I have vivid memories of writing those two-parters with Joe Menosky, and it became part of what I was hoping *Voyager* could be. My influence on the show began in season four with the high-concept stories. Like I said, to me the Delta Quadrant should be the weirdest fucking place in the world and weird shit should happen. It's where the Borg live.

BRYAN FULLER

The strength of *DS9* was its serialization. Its ability to say this is an ongoing story and we have to see our characters evolve and change and grow. On *Voyager*, I remember we had an episode where B'Elanna Torres had kind of a religious reawakening and it was going to be a huge deal that this person, who was essentially a recovering Catholic, had turned her back on the Church and had no interest in being a part of it anymore, then has this fantastic experience where she sees the afterlife. She has a religious epiphany.

To me, that was something so fascinating for this character to go through, because she is essentially having a confirmation of things that she had previously denied to herself and to everyone who would listen. Now she has to deal with religion becoming fact in her heart. But the storyline was just *dropped*. It was, like, here we have a character who can rediscover things and yet it was "No, you're holding on to storylines from previous episodes and we have to move forward." The weakness of *Voyager* in its anti-serialization was the strength of *DS9*. And when *Voyager did* embrace its serialized nature or *a* serialized nature it was more rich in its storytelling for it. It really was seeing a very early transition from a syndicated model into what is now more representative of a modern cable model.

BRANNON BRAGA

In season five one of the things I said was: *First Contact* has come and gone. I want to make the Borg *Voyager*'s Klingons. I just full-on embraced the idea that we were in Borg space and we would be doing Borg stories. That's why Seven of Nine was a character, that's why "Scorpion" was our first two-parter about making a deal with the devil to beat a larger foe and trying to get home in the process. There were other two-parters along the way—my favorite was "Dark Frontier," in which Seven of Nine seems to betray Janeway, but in fact she only betrayed her to save the life of the crew. The Borg Queen also made an appearance, so I really wanted to give the thing a cinematic feeling.

> As *Voyager* entered its sixth season it coincided with the end of *Deep Space Nine*. As a result, Ron Moore, who had been such an integral part of that show as well as *Next Generation,* and had proven to be the perfect writing partner to Brannon Braga on a number of occasions, was kept in the *Star Trek* fold by joining the *Voyager* writing staff. What *should* have been an opportunity to elevate the show, instead turned out to be just another divisive conflict behind the scenes.

BRANNON BRAGA

Ron came aboard as a writer and—God, I have a lot of regrets—he came aboard wanting the show to do all sorts of things. He wanted the show to have continuity.

When the ship got fucked up, he wanted it to stay fucked up. For characters to have lasting consequences. He was *really* into that. He wanted to eradicate the so-called reset button, and that's not something the studio was interested in, because this thing was a big seller in syndication. It wasn't until season three of *Enterprise* that we were allowed to do serialization, and that was only because the show needed some kind of boost to it, because it was flat. I made a big mistake by not supporting Ron in that decision or in supporting Ron in general when he came aboard the show. That was a dark chapter for me and Ron and Rick. It was a bad scene.

RONALD D. MOORE

One of my few regrets with my association with the franchise is that brief, but very unhappy period at *Voyager*. It was just a very unhappy experience and a mistake I shouldn't have made. I should not have taken that gig. I think I took it for the wrong reasons and went into it with the wrong expectations. When it went south, I clearly wanted to get the hell out of there. I remember when Brannon said he really wanted me to do it and we had talked about it through that season of *DS9*. I did it because I just didn't want to leave *Trek*. I had been there for ten years. I was comfortable there. I was making a lot of money. I loved *Star Trek*. It was just what I did. It's weird to think of now, but it was ten years of my life and it was my first ten years of being a professional writer. Every year I just kept coming back to the Hart Building. I took my two weeks vacation and showed up and started the next season. That was my life. That was part of my routine and it was hard to imagine *not* doing it. I didn't really want to go out and I didn't have a pilot I was desperate to go pitch and I didn't really want to learn another show. And not one of those reasons was "Oh my God, I'm so intrigued by *Voyager*."

If anything, I stepped into it feeling like I was going to fix *Voyager*. I felt it was flawed and problematic and wasn't working very well. And in my hubris at the time, I thought, well, I'm going to go and I'll show them how to do a *Star Trek* show. I'll fix that show. Brannon and I, we've worked together for years. It'll be fun. He and I together—we'll turn this into a really great show. So I came in and tried to change things, tried to play with the concept, but it was all different. Brannon was in a different space. He was in charge.

KENNETH BILLER

Until you're actually in charge of getting all those scripts out and breaking all of those stories, you really can't understand how much pressure there is. It's like that train starts and it never stops. Brannon—and I think he'd tell you this—was a little overwhelmed at first and he got behind. Brannon's a much more skilled and experienced showrunner now than he was then, but we were always behind. Every weekend it seemed like we were at Brannon's house racing to catch up and trying to break more stories, and it became a very seven-days-a-week job. He had a little bit of a bunker mentality, which is he would go into his office with one writer, which was sometimes me and sometimes not, and just try to figure stuff out as opposed to being in the room with the group. And so it was stressful.

Also, when Brannon took over the show, that was a little tricky for me, because he and I had been very much colleagues and friends and suddenly he was my boss and he had a very different style. He hadn't really done it before, and that was a little tough. Then at the end of season five, I actually left the show, because they brought Ron in, basically above me. They didn't fire me, but they didn't come at me and offer me a big new contract. And, to be perfectly honest with you, I think I felt at the time like I was ready to do something else.

A lot of the time that I was on *Star Trek,* I felt like, "Okay, I've done this. I want to do something new and different." Looking back on it now, now that I've seen how hard it is to be on a show that actually lasts for more than a season or even a whole season, you don't realize how lucky you are. In retrospect, I probably wouldn't have been so quick to leave. But I did leave after season five, and it was a little tough. Back then when you were coming off of *Star Trek,* it *wasn't* considered a sexy credit. It was before the geekosphere had blown up and become the cultural touchstone that it is now. Anyway, I didn't get a job right away coming off of the show, and then a few episodes into season six Brannon and Rick and Ron had some difficulties. They had some friction.

BRYAN FULLER

I'll give you a personal angle into the story. I'm the youngest of five and I watched my parents play my sisters off of each other to the point that they haven't spoken to each other in forty years. I saw that happening with Rick playing Brannon and Ron off of each other in a way that caused them both to behave outside of their natural states, because insecurities were played on, exposed, manipulated. What happened between Brannon and Ron boils down to bad parenting on Rick's behalf.

Rick would taunt Brannon, saying things like "I should have hired Ron to run *Voyager* instead of you." So of course Brannon is going to be insecure and vulnerable. Brannon is a very complicated guy, but an amazing storyteller and a good guy ultimately. Both Ron and Brannon are good guys. But when you're in a situation where you are feeling vulnerable and insecure and you're having somebody essentially say I wish you were more like that guy, you're going to resent that guy.

And when *that* guy is told "I wish Brannon was more like you," then you're going to feel like you should come in and you should be in a position where you're exerting a certain sense of control over the story. So I feel like both of them were victims of bad parenting in that scenario.

BRANNON BRAGA

Ron came in with a very strong point of view and I was irrationally resistant, because I felt that I had just earned my keep as a showrunner. I felt a little threatened by my old colleague, which was silly of me. Ron is always one to push the boundaries, and I wish I'd listened to him.

RONALD D. MOORE

I think at the heart of it is that when we were partners, I was something of the senior partner, because I started a year before him. And in our relationship as people, I took somewhat of a more dominant role. It was a marriage and a partnership. I'm not saying I was number one and he was number two, but there was a certain dynamic between the two of us that I was used to, saying what I wanted to do and not the other way around. And then I was going to work for him and he was a different person running that show. This is from my perspective, but he seemed less willing to take chances. He seemed more afraid of changing the show, and his arguments were feeling a lot like Rick's arguments about what *Star Trek* was and what it wasn't. He still had his Brannon ideas about weird science-fiction things and strange concepts and bizarro time travel. Things that were kind of his signature at the time. But the character work, he was not as receptive to really challenging the characters. A lot of things I eventually put into *Battlestar Galactica,* I started pitching to him originally.

There was a story in development when I was there about them coming across an alien fleet and they were going to shepherd them for a time. I remembering talking about *Battlestar Galactica,* the original show, and saying, "Hey, it could be something like that except we could do it where there's votes by these civilians and they don't want Janeway to always be in charge. And there should be culture there." I kept saying that I want the internal culture on *Voyager* to change over time. Why don't they put the leadership of the starship to a vote at some point? Is Janeway literally going to captain this ship until she's eighty? Is Chakotay always going to be the number two? If these guys really don't think they're getting back to the Alpha Quadrant for seventy or eighty years, shouldn't they start thinking long-term? Shouldn't they sort of let their hair down a little bit? What if they don't want to wear their uniforms on a Friday? What if they want to decorate the halls? What if they start customizing this ship because it's probably a generational ship? And they were not open to those concepts. Brannon was not open to those concepts. It was like changing the show too much: "That's not *Star Trek*. That's not what the audience wants to see. I don't want to see Janeway get votes." He was very contemptuous about some of it, and I bristled at that. I just felt like they weren't willing to try to change the show, because in their minds they thought the show was working fine and it didn't need to be challenged. I was the one saying no, this does not work. This can be better. This is not good.

I kept pushing, and out of that dynamic Brannon stopped wanting to have me in meetings and stopped wanting me to be around, and then the whole thing blew up once I found out that they literally *were* having meetings where I wasn't around and they were developing stories that I wasn't a part of, and the staff had been told not to tell me these things. I walked into Rick's office and said, "I want out." He was shocked and Brannon was shocked, and Brannon and I had it out. It was a hard, very emotional and painful scene. Brannon said, "You're right. I'm sorry. I don't know why it's been like that, but I'd really like you to stay." But I was just done. I just wanted out. It broke my heart and I was angry and hurt. At that point I didn't think I'd see my participation in it. It was his show and I acted like it was my show, which was not the smartest move. I really underestimated what it would be like to go work with him again. In my heart, I was ready to move on. I should have left *Trek* at the end of *Deep Space Nine* and taken on other challenges. Instead I went for comfort and ease and it blew up on me.

BRANNON BRAGA

Now I think it was best he left, because he was frustrated with me. On the one hand I wish I had responded differently, because I think the show would have been better for it. But then again, if he had remained, Ron might not have gone on to do *Battlestar Galactica*—which, in my view, is what he wanted to do with *Star Trek*. Every show creator has their moment, their show, and I really think *Battlestar* was Ron's best work. It was what he was yearning to do with *Star Trek*, but was constrained by the premise.

BRYAN FULLER

I don't think Rick was doing it to be a bad man. I think Rick was doing it because he thought that was the best way to get what he wanted out of the situation. But the way he went about doing it devastated Brannon and Ron's incredible friendship, and that was unfortunate.

MICHAEL TAYLOR

Brannon is an idiosyncratic guy. To a degree, I think he cultivates that sort of thing, but he's really an artist. And that season was his first time running a show. And he just ran it. He had a real instinct for stories. I would take pitches and I wasn't always sure if I had something good. I had something I thought might be okay and ran it by him at a group dinner or something one night, and he said instantly, "That's great. That's *The Diary of Anne Frank*. Aliens hiding in the subspace basement or attic or whatever." He'd really get a feel for what's a story and he could just riff. He would just practically dictate it. I feel I share with him a similar sensibility. Learning from him also about accessing your imagination in a really unfettered way is something that I've kept with me and still serves me. So, he was a really good showrunner. It was a tough show to get done, but we got it done and we did a lot of great stuff.

KENNETH BILLER

This has nothing to do with Ron, but I took a certain amount of pleasure in the fact that Rick called me and asked me to come back and offered to make me an executive producer. They promised me that if I did this together with Brannon for season six, that I would get to be the guy in charge in season seven. And that turned out to be true. They honored that.

By the time I got there, they were way, way behind. After the whole Ron debacle, they basically wanted me to come in and try to very quickly get more stories broken. So I had to put my head down and create a writers' schedule and get everybody going.

> With Kenneth Biller taking over the writing staff for the seventh season, as Brannon Braga felt that he had hit the proverbial creative wall, there was finally an opportunity to do the one thing he and others had been pushing for: more serialization.

KENNETH BILLER

Rick Berman and the studio basically said to me, "Okay, this is the last season and whoever's watching the show in the seventh season are people who are already invested in the show and characters." They allowed me to take a more serialized approach in the final season. So we did storylines that had to do with whether or not Tom Paris and B'Elanna were going to get married, and we got to play that out over a number of episodes. And the quest to get home got played out in a more serialized way than it had been in previous seasons. The lack of serialization before wasn't really driven by the creative desires of the writers or the cast, but driven by the economic realities or at least the *perceived* economic realities of the long-term health of the show and the ability to show it in repeats and to foreign viewers.

BRANNON BRAGA

I had to leave. I'd just done five brutal seasons. The episode I was writing at the time was called "Dragon's Egg," and I just remember I was standing by my pool. It was four o'clock in the afternoon and I was trying to figure out what the hell was wrong with the story, and it almost felt like I had physically hit a wall. I was just, like, "Oh my God, I'm burned out." I soldiered on through season six, which ended up having some good episodes in it, but I knew I wouldn't be back. I couldn't do it anymore. *Enterprise* came along then, too, but I have to tell you: if it hadn't, I probably would have just stepped away from the whole franchise.

Enterprise was positioned to be something new, but it ended up being very familiar—which is a different part of the story.

KENNETH BILLER

I remember going into the writers room dozens of times to see Brannon or Jeri and say, "Oh my God, I've got the greatest idea for a *Star Trek* episode!" And I would pitch them this idea and they'd go, "Yeah, we did that in season two of *Next Gen*" or "We did that in season three of *DS9*" or "That was an original series episode." And it was terrible for me. I thought, "God, how are you ever going to come up with something new?" And it got even worse toward the end of season six and, then, seven, when I was brought on really to run the writers room and be the guy, because Brannon was going off to create the next series. I was just in a panic about how we were going to do it. How were we ever going to come up with twenty-six more episodes? Somehow we did. I'm not sure how, but we did.

Like his predecessors, Biller still needed to answer to Rick Berman, which didn't always prove easy for the fledgling showrunner. At the same time, he expected the other writers to fall in line and follow his lead.

KENNETH BILLER

Rick could be enormously charming and enormously encouraging. And he was really great to me in a lot of ways. He also could be very tough and very cutting when he wanted to be. When I first got the job as showrunner, I don't think he entirely trusted that I was up to the job. By that time I was in my early thirties, and I do remember feeling like he would treat me a little bit as a child. I remember having to stand up to him about that. But I do think that by the end of it, he would tell you he was very pleased with the way the show was run once I took it over. I think he was ultimately pretty respectful and pleased with what I did. But he could be tough.

BRYAN FULLER

I butted heads with Ken quite a bit, to the point where I wasn't asked to join *Enterprise* because I was such a brat. Ken was not Brannon and he was not Ron and he was not Joe. He had a different type of showrunning style, which was "the trains run on time." *That's* where Ken excelled. He knew how to make the trains run on time. He knew how to keep production going, but I didn't think the trains were necessarily going someplace interesting . . . and I behaved so badly. I would just sit there in story breaks and I would huff and puff, sigh, roll my eyes, and complain we had done this before and why are we doing it again? I was a huge thorn in Ken's side because I felt like we needed to do better. We needed to be breaking molds and doing things differently, and Ken's approach was to be responsible to the studio. And responsible to Rick Berman.

He would come in and say Rick Berman's dictation or edict is to go back over previous episodes of *Star Trek: The Next Generation* and see if there is anything that we can mine for new stories as opposed to telling new stories. So there was a familiarity at some times, and then there were times that Ken would totally surprise me and do something unexpected and brilliant and tell a story in a different way where I was, like, "Okay, he is definitely earning his keep." There were moments where I had to respect him.

KENNETH BILLER

Rick, like most powerful people, was complicated. He could be really great and really encouraging and really complimentary. I'm grateful to him. He let me direct, which no writer had done before. He did a lot of good things for my career and I'm very grateful to him. But he could be hard to work for, probably like I'm hard to work for now for some people. And he was like the king of a big kingdom.

That show was hugely popular and he had his way of doing things. It was his prerogative to do things that way. He was the boss and sometimes he would remind you of that. So when I say I was running the show, I was running the show *to a point*. I was breaking all the stories and Rick was dealing with the day-to-day of casting and the production meetings and all of that sort of stuff. But when it really came down to a big decision, I for sure needed Rick's approval.

BRYAN FULLER

Season seven was sort of a safer version of the show, and I had been really excited about the big bold moves of the Brannon and Joe Menosky regime. Ken's regime was a safer *Star Trek* than I wanted as an audience member. But I could have been more mature in how I handled that situation as opposed to spending story breaks doodling on a pad because I thought the story was lame.

It all came to a close as the starship *Voyager* finally made its way home to earth. The final two-hour episode is "Endgame," which deals with the tenth anniversary of *Voyager*'s return to the Alpha Quadrant after spending more than twenty-three years in the Delta Quadrant. A now elderly Admiral Janeway, who lost crew members in the journey home, attempts to travel back to the past and warn her younger self about the dangers of an encounter they're going to have with the Borg and that race's "transwarp corridor." By utilizing advanced Federation technology, the two Janeways are able to defeat the Borg Queen (*First Contact*'s Alice Krige reprising her role), with the admiral sacrificing herself but allowing the ship to return home seven years after it departed. Audiences also see that Seven of Nine and Chakotay became a couple and that Paris and Torres have a baby girl, born just as *Voyager* enters the Alpha Quadrant.

KENNETH BILLER

I wanted to get them home in a satisfying way. I wanted to get them home in a way that wasn't expected. Out of that came the idea that in the final episode they were *already* home, but in a way that wasn't complete. This way Janeway could do this incredibly risky thing to try and put the family back together. I wanted to do something unexpected, so, for example, when somebody pitched to me the idea of Neelix falling in love with this Talaxian woman that he runs into, I said, "The only way I will do that episode is if he stays with her." Because we had to do some things the audience wouldn't expect, and the audience would expect him to say good-bye to her and get on the ship. Or for her to come with him.

I wanted to put some of the characters through the ringer emotionally and, as I said, I wanted to make that last season as serialized as I possibly could, even within the framework of the stand-alone episodes. It was important to me to inject some of that into the show. We certainly did it with the B'Elanna and Tom Paris relationship, and some stuff with the Doctor and Seven.

RICK BERMAN

When ending the show, we considered everything. We considered having Janeway die, we considered having Seven of Nine give up her life, we considered so many things. We knew that the Borg Queen was going to be involved in the final episode. And that there was going to be a great showdown between her and Captain Janeway.

It was a great idea to go in the direction we did with the show, but at the same time there's something about venturing outward and trying to get back home that are diametrically different from one another. *Star Trek* by and large is a show about exploration, and exploration is going forth, it's not trying to find your way home. So it did hold us back in certain ways, but I think that's because we needed to go in a different direction, and *Next Generation* had just ended and *Deep Space Nine* was still on the air, it was the best of both worlds, so to speak.

BRYAN FULLER

We had talked about so many different things to end the series. One of them we sort of used earlier in the season, the idea being Janeway, to get everyone home, allows the crew to be assimilated knowing that the Doctor can activate and disassimilate the way he did Seven of Nine and that *Voyager* was going to cross the finish line in the belly of a Borg cube and then, as it explodes, come bursting out of the debris with everyone safe in this bold gambit that only Janeway could have pulled off. But what we got was sort of a *Voyager* version of "All Good Things." It was a good episode and a satisfying one and there was certainly some nice emotion to it, but it just felt like we had told that story before.

KENNETH BILLER

I thought it was a really cool finale. My recollection is that I was very proud of it. Allan Kroeker did a great job of directing it and it was cool to see the old Janeway, and the fact that she was *so* driven and obsessed with getting her crew home. It was a classic kind of *Star Trek* tale. A *what if . . . ?* story. What if you screwed up and what if you regretted your decision and could put things right? Yes, she had successfully gotten her crew home, but she hadn't gotten them *all* home.

BRANNON BRAGA

My only regret about the Seven of Nine character is that I would have killed the character in the *Voyager* finale. I remember sitting in a room with Rick and Ken Biller. Ken was running the show in the final season, so I had stepped away and couldn't really impose my will. I had written one episode in season seven called "Human Error," where Seven of Nine realizes she can never develop feelings for anyone, because there's this Borg chip in her that will kill her, so she's a woman between worlds. She can't be human and she doesn't want to be Borg again. She's a tragic character, and I really felt she should sacrifice her life at the moment of truth to get her crew home. It would have added a real pathos and would have been a fitting end to a very tragic character. I just can't believe they didn't want to do it.

JERI RYAN

It would have been cool to do that and it would have made perfect sense. It would have been a fitting good-bye to the character. I've heard at conventions over the years that people had a hard time with the storyline of Seven and Chakotay getting together at the end. I had no problem with that, because they had established the continuity. The thing I *did* have a problem with is that there was an episode, might have been in the last season, where Seven was on the holodeck exploring her humanity and she was basically practice-dating Chakotay and fell in love with him. Then she finds out she can't have a relationship because it short-circuits her Borg side. So we'd already established that Seven is in love with him or had fallen in love with him, and the very next episode we shot after that had Seven and Chakotay getting stranded on some planet.

We went to the producers and said, "Okay, is something going to happen? Are we playing this through?" And they all said, "No, don't play any of that; that was just one episode." That was a little weird, but we never played it. *Then,* all of a sudden, we're back together at the end for the finale. That was the one frustration with the character, because as beautifully written as she was, there was a lot of rich stuff that could have been played out in just a glance or a look or a beat or a pause that was missed.

ROBERT BELTRAN

If you look at the Chakotay/Seven of Nine thing that came up, there was no indication that that was even a possibility. I don't even know that we had that many scenes up to that point in the show before they started putting us together. You had Paris and B'Elanna, so any Chakotay/B'Elanna possibility was gone. They had flirted with a Chakotay/Janeway possibility for way too long at the beginning, and so who was left but me and some ensign or me and maybe Seven of Nine? So they just kind of threw us together and it seemed to me that if they had been thinking instead of one episode after the other, but thinking in the long run, what great stuff they could have written preparing for that.

Honestly, I think they were glad to get rid of us. They wanted us out so that they could do their new show, which was *Enterprise*. And I don't blame them. They have their professional careers to think of and all of that stuff. I don't have any bitterness at all; I appreciate the seven years that I was on the show.

KATE MULGREW

Berman had a very strong, principled vision. Without his discipline, I don't think it would have been as good as it was. At least that's how I always felt. When I say it was a privilege and an honor to play Janeway, it sounds terribly clichéd, but you can rest assured that it was. And it continues to be. To have played the first and only female captain of a starship in arguably the world's most successful franchise was no small thing. And to have acquitted myself with some grace and some success makes me feel good all the time.

JERI RYAN

I was ready for the end, because it hadn't been an easy work experience. It had been a long four years, and as much as I loved my boys—the cast members—it was tough. And as great as the crew—this amazing, wonderful, fantastic crew that we got to work with every day—was, I was ready. It was long hours aside from tension and stress and everything else. My average day, because of makeup and costume and all that kind of stuff, was a sixteen-hour day, and the normal now for TV is an eight-day schedule, but we had a seven-day schedule. Added to that was all the special effects and everything else. I had a handful of nineteen-twenty-hour days, so it was a lot of work. But there were a lot of bright spots, and a lot of laughter, and amazing things to play as an actor, which, again, was a gift. But after four years, yes, I was ready to get out of the corset and wear something else.

ROBERT BELTRAN

It was around the fifth year that I just thought, "God, I can't wait till this show is over." I was just living for the end of the show. I wanted out. The scripts are the main reason. The tension was another. Seven years is a long time on any show, and when the writing isn't what you want it to be and there are character conflicts and actor conflicts, it makes it that much more unpleasant. I was ready to get out.

KENNETH BILLER

When I look back at *Voyager*, I think that Captain Janeway, Seven of Nine, and the Doctor are really important parts of the *Star Trek* universe. The first female captain, this really interesting half Borg/half human, and the brilliant performance by Robert Picardo in a character that was fun and funny and different and acerbic. Nothing against the other characters, but those three characters are really an important part of the *Star Trek* landscape and every bit as interesting as some of the other characters that we think about. I'm sure people would argue with me and say they're not as important as Spock and Captain Kirk and Captain Picard, but I would put them up there with those characters.

There's a generation of people for whom *Voyager* was their *Star Trek*. We did really cool character stuff, but it was also an adventure show and a slice of adventure in that universe that in some ways was closer to the original series than *DS9* and maybe even *Next Gen*. I think we created some cool stuff on that show. It may not be everyone's favorite *Star Trek*, but I've been surprised to find out that it's a lot of people's favorite version of *Star Trek*.

BRYAN FULLER

DS9 was for geeks by geeks. Everybody in that room was a *Star Trek* fan. Everybody loved the genre. Everybody enjoyed playing with the tools of the genre. And with *Voyager* there was a small element that was saying, "We've got to be better than *Star Trek*." And it's, like, "No, *Star Trek* is pretty great. Don't worry about being better. Just worry about delivering."

Personally speaking, when I was a kid growing up, I'd watch these things and

I had no idea how they were put together. It seemed all so far away and beyond my reach, yet somehow I found a way to grab hold.

KATE MULGREW

In thinking about the last day . . . Bob Picardo is still one of my closest friends. That was a friendship that just took flight. I'll tell you a wonderful story about him. It's funny what shapes love, isn't it? You work in the trenches for years and years. You meet great people and you're laughing, holding one another's hands and saying, "We're going to get through this together." But then the final day comes and one by one everyone is dismissed. Ethan was the first to go, and it went on from there. I was the last. I'm there to shoot my close-ups and pick-ups as, around me, they were dismantling all of the consoles, all of the other chairs. Then it was "Cut! Print! That's a wrap! Thank you very much, Kathryn." So it was just me and four of the crew, and they had just started to unscrew my chair; I was standing up on another part of the bridge.

Nobody was there; Berman didn't even come down. But who do I see standing in the shadow of the bridge? "Well, Captain, I say it's time for a bottle of champagne." Bob just came in and put his arm around me, and I had one hell of a cry! But *that's* friendship. He's been in my life ever since in that deep way.

Voyager is a chapter of my life that probably has defined a great deal of the rest of my life. It is, suffice to say, a complete, unexpected mystery that I stumbled into. That was not in my idea of my future. In no way did it figure into my imagination as an actress. But it captured me, it took me, it spun me into a different galaxy altogether, didn't it? As an artist, it challenged me on every conceivable level. Patrick Stewart was right the day he came up to me, shook my hand, and we got a cup of coffee or something. I said to him, "How am I going to survive this?" He said, "Take a watch. You see that bridge? Just *own* that bridge. Come for seven years. Do your work. Do it to the best of your ability. Make them follow you. Make them bloody proud."

ENTERPRISE

(2001–2005)

IT'S BEEN A LONG ROAD

"I'M NOT INTERESTED IN WHAT YOU THINK ABOUT THIS MISSION, SO TAKE YOUR VULCAN CYNICISM AND BURY IT ALONG WITH YOUR REPRESSED EMOTIONS."

Star Trek: Enterprise, or *Enterprise* as it was initially (and perplexingly) launched, wasn't the first time the franchise brain trust contemplated a prequel to the original series. Its origins date back to the late 1960s when Gene Roddenberry was already discussing doing a movie in which Kirk, Spock, and McCoy were first united on board the starship *Enterprise*. Although the concept never saw the light of a projector bulb until J.J. Abrams' reinvention in 2009, executive producer Rick Berman, who had overseen the creation of every *Trek* spin-off since *The Next Generation*, had decided the new series would chronicle the first mission of the *Enterprise*.

But it would not be Captain Kirk's first mission, nor even Christopher Pike's. Ignoring canon, which had previously established Robert April as the starship's first captain in the animated episode, "The Counter-Clock Incident," it was decided that the heretofore unknown Jonathan Archer would, instead, sit in the center seat aboard Starfleet's first flagship. This was only the first of many confounding decisions to be made in birthing the series. In the initial concept of *Enterprise*, Archer would be joined by T'Pau, a younger version of the role played by Celia Lovsky as "all of Vulcan in one package" in "Amok Time," a beloved episode of the original series. Outraged fans put an end to that notion, having expressed the feeling that replacing the distinguished and regal Vulcan matriarch with the show's resident sexpot was a bridge too far.

For this new *Enterprise* mission, Berman turned to a familiar face, Brannon Braga, to cocreate the show. Braga, for his part, was leaving *Star Trek: Voyager* following its sixth season and was seeking a change in his career. He had *not* expected to remain in the world of *Star Trek*.

Although the head of the United Paramount Network (UPN), Dean Valentine, opposed launching a new *Star Trek* series so soon after *Voyager*, which had continued to experience ratings erosion throughout its seven-year run, he was overruled by Kerry McCluggage, the president of Paramount Television, who had been there throughout *Star Trek: The Next Generation*'s lucrative run. Although licensing the series to another network and potentially revisiting first-run syndication were both briefly considered by the studio, Paramount wanted to have the control that came with having the series run on their own network and the guarantee of it not being precipitously canceled. With all this in mind, *Enterprise* left dry dock on a four-year voyage timidly going where many had gone before. . . .

KENNETH BILLER (executive producer, *Star Trek: Voyager*)

When Rick told me about *Enterprise,* he told me it wasn't going to be my father's *Star Trek.* They're going to wear sneakers and they're going to do this and that. I do remember looking at *Enterprise* and thinking it just seems like more *Star Trek.* Maybe that was the right way to go. I don't know. He was protecting a brand. A very valuable brand. You can make the argument either way: Should you reinvent the brand or is reinventing the brand too radically going to drive away the people who are loyal to it? Hard to know. When you look at Paul Feig announcing that he's going to do an all-female cast of *Ghostbusters,* everyone freaks out on him. "You're violating the sanctity of *Ghostbusters!*" Really? The guy wants to make something new and he's probably smart to do it that way. But, you know, fans can be really tough. You're damned if you do, damned if you don't. If you keep giving them more of the same, they'll criticize you for not mixing it up, but if you mix it up too much, they'll tell you that's not *Star Trek.*

BRANNON BRAGA (executive producer/cocreator, *Enterprise*)

Star Trek always needs fresh blood. I left before *Enterprise*; I just said, "I can't do this anymore." I remember where I was and what I was working on and where I was standing and at what point in time when I officially burnt out on *Star Trek.* I decided not to do the seventh season of *Voyager* and then I was asked to create *Enterprise.* Rick had a really cool idea for it and I said, "You know what? I'm going to do this one more time." One could argue maybe I shouldn't have. Rick was a really good overlord, but even he needed fresh writers. One could argue maybe we both should have left earlier.

RICK BERMAN (executive producer/cocreator, *Enterprise*)

As *Voyager* was ending, the studio came and said, "Let's get another one up and going." Again, I begged them to let the franchise have a few years' rest. In fact, they wanted it to start before *Voyager* ended and I managed to get them to at least wait until *Voyager* went off the air. The question was, what could we do that was different? I'd been working a great deal with Brannon, and so I asked him to work with me on creating a new series. Our decision, and I still think it was a good one, was to change the time period. We had done three shows that took place in the twenty-fourth century, and I thought it was time to go to another century. To go forward meant spacesuits that were a little sleeker and ships that were a little shinier, but it wasn't that much to invent what had come before.

BRANNON BRAGA

Rick called me and said, "What do you think about setting it between *First Contact* and Kirk's time?" And I said I thought that was a great idea. We started talking about it and considered what it would give us, and it evolved from there. We never considered another concept. We thought that *First Contact* seemed to be more of a relatable film somehow, because it had characters from the near future versus the distant future, and it allowed a more non–*Star Trek* audience to embrace *Star Trek*. You didn't really have to know much to enjoy that movie.

RICK BERMAN

We had no idea what happened between *First Contact* and Kirk–Spock. There was no *Star Trek* canon to respond to how Earth got from being in this post-apocalyptic nightmare to being in the world of Kirk and Spock with Starfleet Academy. So our feeling was to pick a time somewhere within that, when space travel is just beginning. When the first humans are going into space on warp-capable vessels, and they're not as sure of themselves as Kirk or Picard were. They're taking baby steps.

BRANNON BRAGA

As a writer, I don't think I could have written one more line of dialogue for *Voyager*. I really had just about had it with the twenty-fourth century.

RICK BERMAN

There were those who felt that wasn't a great idea; that we should go to a future century. I mean, everybody agreed that it was very good to get out of the twenty-fourth century, but Brannon and I both felt that the past was the wisest choice and that's the show we wrote.

We knew with *Enterprise* that we wanted to turn the ship around. We were dealing with the time when the first warp-drive ship was being developed for a crew of humans. There were no holodecks and people didn't beam themselves anywhere, they just beamed cargo. Nobody would get onto the transporter pad. It just seemed to be the right idea, so it's the one we pursued.

BRANNON BRAGA

Rick does not get nearly enough credit as a writer. Some of my happiest times on *Star Trek* were in those *Enterprise* years. I was so fortunate that I had writing partners like Ron Moore or Joe Menosky or, after *Star Trek*, David Goyer. I've just been blessed in that regard. Suddenly, I was writing with Rick and I didn't know what it would be like to write the pilot with him, but as it turned out some of my happiest days were sitting in his office writing the script together. It was a delightful experience. I usually had a lot of fun creating the show. The biggest challenge was that the studio wanted something, but they were dubious about the prequel idea when we went in to pitch it. I don't think they liked it very much. And they thought *Star Trek* should be about moving forward and not moving backward.

CONNOR TRINNEER (actor, "Charles 'Trip' Tucker III")

We're Lewis and Clark with a warp coil.

FRED BRONSON (writer, *Star Trek: The Animated Series*)

I thought at first, how great, they were going to do Robert April, when I first heard about the concept, but of course it didn't happen.

CHRIS BLACK (co-executive producer, *Star Trek: Enterprise*)

I was not the uber-fan that would have said, "Wait, it should have been Robert April." I probably would have gone with Captain Pike. It should be Captain Pike. He's the first captain! But they went too far back.

BRANNON BRAGA

We wanted to show what happened in the period in *Star Trek* history between *First Contact* and Kirk. How did we end up building the first warp ship? What was it like to meet a Klingon for the first time? People had ball caps and walked dogs and wore tennis shoes and are more identifiable as people than, say, a Captain Picard, who is more of an idyllic man of the future that you probably wouldn't recognize as a person that you could ever meet today.

RICK BERMAN

There's a great irony about developing things that you don't want to be more advanced than things that you know are going to come in ninety years, say at the time of Kirk. The computer that sat on Captain Janeway's desk was bulkier than the one that sits on my desk now. There are cellular phones that are far more compact than the communicators that Captain Kirk used. So we're always walking a very thin line in terms of developing things that are less advanced than from the time of Captain Kirk. But the most fun elements of this series, especially for our fans, were all of the things that they know are coming to *Star Trek* in their infant stages. To be able to see the development of things like transporters and phasers and tractor beams.

From the point of view of some fans, there's the great sense of continuity that the shows have had. And they're very, very particular about that. A lot of them are not happy about things that they felt were outside the canon of *Star Trek*. A lot of them felt that Brannon and I ignored that, which we absolutely didn't. We tried to pay great attention to it and we had people who knew *Star Trek* backward and forward that helped us, but obviously there were things that had to be dealt with.

We couldn't deal with Romulans because it wasn't until the original series that a human ever sees a Romulan. There were things like that, but we also had to have first contact with a lot of different species. We also knew that we were going to be dealing with aliens that no one ever heard of before. If you're dealing with a group called the Suliban, and if they become your bad guys in a series of episodes, how come they were never mentioned with Kirk and Spock? We constantly ran into problems like that. How long can we not have people go on transporters until we wish they had?

MIKE SUSSMAN (producer, *Star Trek: Enterprise*)

You can't go further in the future with communicators getting smaller and our force fields are even more magical. Yeah, go back and let's do *The Right Stuff*. It just sounded so amazing.

SCOTT BAKULA (actor, "Jonathan Archer")

It *is The Right Stuff*. That kind of energy of being the first ones out there and being a little scared sometimes and being a little overwhelmed by the experience, which I think is a great emotion to have to play with. Americans have explored our planet in a variety of different ways. Some successfully, some not. We have a wide history of exploration in this country. Certainly different experiences in Vietnam and places like that where we tried to impose our ideas or philosophies on different cultures, and still are in many places around this planet. Making it more about the experience and less about planting the flag.

In other words, enjoying the experience and learning from it, rather than saying, "Now we're here and we're going to tell you how to do it. We've got good ideas and can do things better than you." So if you're someone out there looking to do good, and looking to explore in a healthy way, there's a great responsibility to that. As well as a great temptation to change and alter and fix. Which became this very wonderful kind of play within the show, which is, how are we all going to deal with not only being out there, but the choices we make?

MIKE SUSSMAN

You go back and look at the original *Star Trek* and this is a criticism you hear now about the J.J. Abrams films, that they weren't really about exploration. The *Enterprise* didn't really leave Earth. But, if you go back and look at the original series, how often Kirk and his crew would show up and they weren't the first on the scene. There's another ship that had gotten blown up. Somebody else was in trouble. Or it was another Constitution-class ship so they could recycle all the sets and they were always like the cleanup crew. Somebody else was always doing the exploration, something got fucked up, and they had to come in and unravel that mystery and solve the problem. But with *Enterprise, we* were now that ship. We were the first ones going out, and there was something in the writing of those stories where it was more fun to be that *second* ship coming along and finding the derelict and what happened to those people rather than to be the derelict.

DAVID A. GOODMAN
(consulting producer, *Star Trek: Enterprise*)

The format hadn't really changed in a sense since *Next Generation,* because the way we told stories on *Enterprise* was very much the same.

ANDRÉ BORMANIS (executive story editor, *Star Trek: Enterprise*)

I saw that there was a certain kind of cautiousness about Rick that was understandable after fifteen years, but I think some of the writing staff was frustrated that he wasn't willing to take as many risks as we might have wanted to take. Maybe some part of that is Rick, but a big part of that is also the studio. Brannon originally wanted to spend the entire first season on Earth building the *Enterprise* and getting a crew together.

BRANNON BRAGA

We wanted to do a show that took place in the first season on Earth, we wanted season one to culminate with the launching of the *Enterprise,* and really tell *Star Trek* a little differently. The closest I've seen it done was in J.J. Abrams' first movie; I was really grooving on the Earth part of the movie with the ship being built, because those were images I was hoping to do myself and wasn't permitted to. I thought it was really cool.

ROD RODDENBERRY (son of Gene Roddenberry)

I loved the first season of *Enterprise*. My one criticism was it would be better if they met the aliens later and it was sort of a slower rollout.

MIKE SUSSMAN

Brannon and Rick really did want to do something pretty different. Would their reinvention have worked and appealed to the fans? I don't know. The show would have been different from what it was, but at the same time it's hard to imagine a show, even if it's not called *Star Trek* in the title, basically being an earthbound show for a year. Maybe that would have been terrific, but maybe the audience would have been, like, "Get on the spaceship already!" I salute them for at least making that attempt. I think they were hamstrung.

ANDRÉ BORMANIS

The way the show was designed, a lot of people on Earth were opposed to the idea of doing this at all. There was a certain kind of xenophobia. We were going to meet all sorts of people who are probably not real happy about us being out here and that could come back and bite us in the ass. Which I thought was great, because I think that that felt real to me. That felt like something that would happen.

FRED DEKKER (consulting producer, *Star Trek: Enterprise*)

I've always been more of a movie guy, so *Star Wars* kind of rocked my world, because of the pure cinema of it. And *Star Trek*, even when I loved it, seemed slightly formal. So I was excited predominantly because I had been told it was going to be a reinventing, a reimagining essentially. We're going back before Picard and before Kirk and back to the beginning of warp travel and that, to me, was very exciting.

ANDRÉ BORMANIS

And the Earth was just getting out of this global multigenerational depression, right? I thought that sounded really, really cool. But the studio would not go for that. The studio was, like, "Nope. *Star Trek* is about a starship going places. You launch the ship in the pilot." Brannon didn't want to have a transporter. Let's save the transporter for maybe second season or third season. Nah, it's *Star Trek*, you've got to have a starship, you've got to have phasers, you've got to have a transporter. So, there were a lot of constraints placed on the show from the beginning.

FRED DEKKER

One thing I can say about that show was that there was never a doubt in my mind that any crazy thing that the writers could come up with, they could pull it off. That production team was not only a well-oiled machine, but they could certainly do a new job every week. I was always amazed at what they accomplished and in awe of those people.

BRANNON BRAGA

We wanted a fresh way to go about things, and the show wasn't really everything we intended. I'm not putting the blame on the studio, because I don't know if they were right or wrong, but I do know that we didn't really go as prequel as we wanted. The whole Temporal Cold War [about manipulations in the timeline from the far future] was put in because they demanded that there be some futuristic thing in it.

I just don't think the Cold War element ever really gelled. There was a spooky guy and there were temporal agents and it all fell into some of the convoluted things that time travel tends to fall into, and it didn't really work. It played something of a role in the third season, but Manny Coto, who took over season four of the show, dropped it completely.

I had in my head been developing an idea for a different show about a Temporal Cold War where you learn in 1981 time travel was discovered by some physicists and they started fucking with it and then China got it and then Iran got it and suddenly people are going back in time and someone did something that fucked the time line. All the countries realized that they had to strike a temporal accord so no one would use it again.

It's kind of like a nuclear weapon metaphor. But of course everyone is so paranoid that the other is going to try and go back and change history, that they have agents in different decades, and it's a cold war throughout many different decades. And I thought well, this could fit perfectly into *Enterprise*. In a way, it was a prequel *and* a sequel.

CHRIS BLACK

Brannon was the only person there in that position to challenge the way things were run. And he might have lost. He might have not gotten what he wanted, but he was the executive producer. The de facto day to day runner of the show. He was approving and disapproving stories. He was putting stuff before Rick and before the network and was in a position to defend it. In my experience, he didn't.

For him now to say, I didn't get to do the show I wanted to do, I say he didn't fight for the show he wanted to do. That might not be fair, because at the end of the day there was a new head of the network at the time at UPN who didn't understand *Star Trek*, who didn't like science fiction, and was not a supporter of the show, but I think they still were the only people in a position to fight for the power they wanted. For them to say now we didn't get to do the show they wanted to, you were the only ones who could.

DOMINIC KEATING (actor, "Malcolm Reed")

The first season under Rick's auspices, they played it way safe and it was cut from the same cloth as the other shows that they had so much success with. Particularly in the first season it became a little derivative, and slightly boring at times. We arrive at the planet, we sort you out, and we're on our merry way. I kind of thought we were going to be like *ER* but in space, and there would be a lot more interaction and drama and storylines about these seven people in space together. Instead, we arrive at a planet, figure it out, sort them out, make them all Republicans and are on our way.

MIKE SUSSMAN

It's funny, on the one hand, it's like the band that goes on tour and the fans only want to hear the classics and not the new music. That's kind of what I think happened with *Enterprise*. We brought back the Andorians, and reinvigorated them. But there weren't a whole lot of nods to the original series, certainly in that first season or two. That's what the fans were kind of crying for and that's something I really wanted to do.

As always when developing a *Star Trek* series, so much would depend on the casting of the show's characters. In command was Captain Jonathan Archer, portrayed by Scott Bakula. Prior to *Enterprise,* the actor was best known for the sci-fi favorite *Quantum Leap,* portraying time-traveling scientist Dr. Sam Beckett. In each episode, Beckett would "leap" into the body of someone in the time stream, quite literally living in their skin. As such, it quickly proved how versatile Bakula was. Between that, other recurring TV roles and a few notable feature films like *Clive Barker's Lord of Illusions*, there was little doubt he would be perfect for Archer.

BRANNON BRAGA

Archer is something between Chuck Yeager and Kirk. He's anything but the fully enlightened man that Picard was.

RICK BERMAN

It was very important for us to have a captain who was not necessarily that sure of himself, because we wanted him to be different than all the other captains. The other captains got on a spaceship and at warp five or warp seven, they never thought twice about it. They ran into aliens every week and they never thought twice about it. We wanted a captain who was taking those first steps out into the galaxy; we wanted him to be a little green. We wanted him to slowly build up a sense of confidence in what he was doing. We wanted him to be a man of great curiosity, an historian of sorts, and a leader of men. But at the same time somebody who was in awe of everything he saw. We ended up making his father somebody who had worked alongside Zefram Cochrane, who was the guy who made the first warp flight. And Kerry McCluggage was a friend of Scott Bakula's and brought him in and we were blown away to have somebody of such popularity. Here was a guy who had a huge TV audience with *Quantum Leap* and it just seemed like a perfect fit.

JAMES L. CONWAY (director, *Star Trek: Enterprise*)

Scott Bakula was the only actor ever discussed for Archer. Problem was, his deal wasn't closed until the table read of the script three days before production began. In fact, there were rumors he was going to a CBS comedy pilot and we got very worried. We had never met him, talked to him, or heard him do the material. All during the casting process the casting director was the only one to read Archer's dialogue. So it was a relief and pleasure to hear Scott brilliantly bring Archer to life at the table read.

SCOTT BAKULA

I responded to the idea of it and this character, and then I got the script for the pilot and everything just fell into place. I liked the character and it was really a return, in many ways, to what the original *Star Trek* was all about. There's a lot of emotion in the show.

CHRIS BLACK

With *Enterprise,* I loved writing for Scott, because he's Scott. He's just the best. And there were a lot of people who criticized him as a choice for captain. Too soft. Too Boy Scout-y. In my opinion, what made William Shatner such a great Kirk was he's kind of an arrogant asshole. And that's who that character is. He's got that swagger and that arrogance. To some extent, Scott is almost too nice a guy. In real life, he's such a delight and such a pro and so respectful and easy to work with that he doesn't have that innate asshole-ness that makes a great starship commander.

RICK BERMAN

Scott was just a *mensch*. He's just one of the most down-to-Earth people I've ever met. There's not a temperamental bone in his body. He's the kind of guy who at the end of a long day will pick up cases and will help the crew carry stuff back to the truck. Always prepared and a peacemaker; a gentle soul and very charismatic. Just a terrific guy.

JAMES L. CONWAY

Scott brought a humanity to Archer that's hard to put on the printed page. Also, as an actor and star of the show, Scott brought a top-notch work ethic and professionalism to the production. As star of the show, he set a great example for everyone.

BRANNON BRAGA

He was great. I can't imagine anyone else being Archer. He was the guy who was a character who was a little in over his head, but that was the point. The funny thing about Scott's take on the character was he spoke in kind of an unusual cadence when he was Archer and I could never figure it out. Someone told me he was a huge John Wayne fan. I've never talked to Scott about it, but I think he may have been doing a little bit of a John Wayne thing. He was our only choice.

DOMINIC KEATING

He's really a trooper. He's not a starry star. He's there for all your off-camera work. He's a real actor's actor. And his experience is good to have around, because he's directed, too. He's got a grasp of just what's going on at a given moment around the set. I have to be honest, when I heard his name was being bandied around to play the part—I had been the first one cast, he hadn't come on board yet—and I was very keen that he was the guy. The minute I heard his name I went, "Oh, yeah, he's perfect for this." I just felt confident that with him in the captain's seat we had a really good shot of being a hit. He's got that handsome man, everyman quality to him. He's perfect for the part. The first day we met him, I shook his hand and I said, "Oh, Captain, we were so worried that the agents had you."

SCOTT BAKULA

We had a different dynamic on our show, and I've thought about it since then, because basically I was the older captain compared to the younger guys on the crew. John Billingsley's in the middle there somewhere. That's why I think the stuff between him and me was always special, even though he was nonhuman. There was a different kind of distance between characters created by the casting. We were building those relationships, but it was still from a different place.

Perhaps in an effort to recapture a bit of the Kirk-Spock relationship (and, physically, a bit of *Voyager*'s Seven of Nine), a female Vulcan was made science officer in the form of T'Pol. Playing her was Jolene Blalock, best known at the time as a model but also a frequent guest star on episodic television.

JAMES L. CONWAY

We were having trouble finding an actress for T'Pol. We read a lot of actresses, looked at a lot of names on a wish list, but couldn't find anyone we liked. The role was critical, because she was a Vulcan and had to be able to "be" a Vulcan, yet still have sex appeal. Thankfully we saw a demo of Jolene's work, loved it, and then met and read and loved her.

RICK BERMAN

That was another case of needing a beautiful woman who could act. This was a big role. We wanted a Vulcan woman, so it had to be someone who you can tell is going to do seven years of a television show and *not* be able to express emotion. It's sort of a death knell of a character. And we wanted her to be beautiful and sexy and be able to act well. Those things, again, you've got your hands tied behind your back. We read hundreds of people, literally. When Jolene came in, I remember she came in with no makeup on and she didn't look all that great. But we saw that there was a remarkable potential and I remember when we called her back, Merri Howard, who was our supervising producer, asked her to put on some makeup, because we had seen film clips of her in a number of things and she was stunning. And she nailed it.

JOLENE BLALOCK (actress, "T'Pol")

I grew up on *Star Trek*. My favorite was Spock. I would sit there with my dad and my brother just watching the show, watching the relationship between Captain Kirk, Bones, and Spock. My favorite relationship was between Bones and Spock, because it was just this animosity and this love-hate relationship. But overall there was such utter loyalty between all three of them. I love the way they worked together, just the way Bones would be, like, "You green-blooded fool." Somewhere in *The Next Generation* I got lost.

BRANNON BRAGA

We wanted a Vulcan babe like Saavik, and wanted a Vulcan on board because the Vulcans were very antagonistic toward humans and she was essentially a chaperone, which really rankled Archer. Their relationship worked kind of nicely, and we saw T'Pol, Archer, and Trip as our triumvirate of characters, Trip being a good old southern boy. He's a guy not fit for encountering space aliens. A couple of our best episodes had him making mistakes with aliens and getting involved when he shouldn't. He just doesn't have the finesse and he's a complete rube. T'Pol is a sophisticate. They had a good chemistry.

CHRIS BLACK

I really felt if anyone got an award for most improved, Jolene deserved it for growing into that role, which was a tough one. Vulcans are hard. Leonard Nimoy was the master, and we would cast Vulcans, and you would have guest actors, and they would come in and play them as robots. And the key to playing Vulcans is not that they don't have emotions, they suppress their emotions. The ones who got it, got it. And Jolene grew into it. She figured it out and she just got better and better. There were times where we went from trying to shoot around her, since she gave the same blank expression, to when we started to love writing *for* her. Obviously, you want to write for your Kirk-Spock-McCoy. So we loved writing for Connor, Jolene, and Scott, because that was your power trio.

BRANNON BRAGA

It was hard to cast T'Pol. It's very hard to cast a role of someone who is stunningly beautiful and can act. Being an actor on *Star Trek* is a whole other thing. Playing a Vulcan is so hard and Jolene did a really good job, but she was not happy playing T'Pol. She and I just never saw eye to eye with the character, and she just didn't like the way the character was going, particularly in the third season when T'Pol became addicted to drugs. She didn't like the romance with Trip. There was a lot of pressure to be basically the ingénue of the show, and the rest of the cast came together pretty easily. You can find interviews where she was dissing the show and me and I never, to be honest, fully understood it. We had to shut down for a month. I think she was going through some shit.

JOLENE BLALOCK

The concept with the shows aren't the problem. The concepts are amazing. The issue is the dialogue. I personally believed that T'Pol should have more of her Vulcan culture. I don't believe she should be so desperate like everyone else, because the original *Star Trek*, which I grew up with, had a very simple message that I took from it, and that is that not everyone is like me, and I'm not perfect, and nobody's perfect, and that's okay. That really helped me. I think T'Pol could be okay with being Vulcan, she shouldn't have to want to be Vulcan. In the dialogue . . . why is that when we're trying to teach each other something, all our analogies involve Earth lore? Don't our cultures have their own lore that might make for good messages?

FRED DEKKER

I remember seeing dailies on the pilot before it was finished. We all were concerned. The shift that Jolene made in that first season was remarkable. I don't know if she was just nervous on the first couple or having a hard time wrapping around it, but once she clicked into it, it was really cool.

JAMES L. CONWAY

Jolene's smart, sexy vibe gave the writers a lot to work with. For a Vulcan, you sensed T'Pol had a lot of emotion deep down, and that really added sizzle to her character. As to her costume, I was shown her wardrobe when the design was fairly down the road, so I don't know if they ever discussed Seven of Nine as a prototype. I do know it was never mentioned when I spoke to Rick, Brannon, or [costume designer] Bob Blackman.

DAVID A. GOODMAN

Jolene is a great portrayal of a Vulcan. Obviously, there were things they wanted me to do which I didn't necessarily approve of, like the drug addiction and the acupressure just to get them naked, but she was stunning, and by season two, it was the second-best portrayal of a Vulcan. You believe her as a Vulcan, and that's not always true with a lot of people who play Vulcans. I think she was amazing, and she could be very funny, too.

JOLENE BLALOCK

In the first season's "Shadows of P'Jem," they made this huge story about how Vulcans were undermining Starfleet and had some kind of agenda, but then they never went on to address it. Then there's an episode in which T'Pol got sick, terminally ill, and they never readdress it. There's the characteristic where Vulcans don't eat food with their hands and yet they wrote scenes where T'Pol is eating popcorn at a movie or Trip will bring T'Pol a peach. It's just so strange to me.

SCOTT BAKULA

There were some little suggestions early on that maybe there could be some possible romance there between Archer and T'Pol, but it wasn't necessary. In what military environment would this be right? There's decorum and rules and we've got Archer in season one flirting with his first officer? It undermines the reality, from my standpoint. I know there was clamoring from fans for it to happen, but I'm glad we never went that way.

CONNOR TRINNEER

It seemed to be, for the first couple of years, that that's what was going to happen, and there were a couple of episodes that bounced into the future that had her taking care of him in old age, and so I didn't know, and nobody seemed to know, and maybe that was good for the relationship in general.

DOMINIC KEATING

There was a sort of human, fun conflict between Bones and Spock. A lot of tongue-in-cheek, wry humor. Scott Bakula is as near as you're going to get to Kirk. There was one moment when the camera came zooming in on a huge crane shot all the way to Scott's face so he could lean forward in his chair and say, "We're going in." It was priceless. We were looking at some massive alien helix and he said, "We're going in." I just love a show where the captain says, "We're going in."

FRED DEKKER

I would take any opportunity for conflict between characters. It worked so well. Not having conflict was like having sex with a steel condom. Drama is conflict. That's what drama is. Once you extract that, you find scenes of people talking and they're relating information. And the other problem is, we talked about "teching the tech." We'll have a scene where we tech the tech. What that meant was the scene was not about anything.

> Chief Engineer of the *Enterprise* and Archer's best friend was Charles "Trip" Tucker, played by Connor Trinneer, a veteran of a number of guest-starring appearances who, following the run of the *Trek* series, would appear in several episodes of *Stargate: Atlantis*.

RICK BERMAN

Connor was the only actor in four television series that I had to fight for. I just love this guy. I think he's a remarkable actor, and I saw four pieces of tape on various things that he had done, and there was just something about him; that this character, or Trip, that we had written, he was just made for. And when we went to Garry Hart, who was the president of the studio at that point, and Kerry was still there as chairman, they didn't particularly like him. And they had us read somebody who had been in something—I forget what he had been in—but he was one of your typical Hollywood pretty-boy types. This was not something I was going to give up, and I constantly bugged Garry until he finally relented and let us hire Connor. To this day he is one of my favorite actors in all of the *Star Trek* series.

CONNOR TRINNEER

I wanted this job *a lot*. It was a good, time-tested franchise with a good audience. It had so many different things happening in it and it gave me the opportunity to play kind of a space cowboy—it was a dream job. Plus you got to use your imagination as you're meeting new species and races. Since this was our first time out, everything was new and we weren't used to anything. You, as the actor, got to take in something as the audience did for the very first time, which was my experience as both an actor and a character. I hadn't had a lot of experience with anything but the first *Star Trek,* and it was fascinating.

CHRIS BLACK

Of the cast, we loved writing for Connor. I think he would respectfully rebel against the folksy southern stuff we tried to give him. He had one too many plates of fried catfish.

CONNOR TRINNEER

This version of *Star Trek* was a bit more irreverent. I looked at it as the less mature *Star Trek*; it was still growing up. We had to meet all the different species like the crews of the other shows have, but everything for us was "Whoa, what was that? Let's check that out." We were exploring in the truest sense of the word. Let's face it, a hundred and fifty years from now isn't too far away. It's something you can grasp your mind around.

> Anthony Montgomery was cast as navigator Ensign Travis Mayweather. Prior to *Trek,* he was a regular on the TV series *Popular.* As the series went on, he would eventually be promoted to MACO Sergeant.

ANTHONY MONTGOMERY (actor, "Travis Mayweather")

It was incredible. There was an electricity that just ran to my core, and it was because I was sitting at the helm of a show, being a part of a franchise that I grew up with and knew about. I'm not a Trekkie by any of stretch of the imagination, but I still understand enough about the franchise that it made me say, wow, this is real! That was even more exciting and intense than when I got the call saying I got the part.

RICK BERMAN

We were looking for an African American actor. We wanted someone young—we wanted this whole cast to be a lot more approachable in ways; we wanted the audience to be able to relate to them more than they could other shows. After all, these people wore sneakers and they were closer to our time than any *Star Trek* group that had ever existed. So we wanted someone who was quite young and Anthony was gorgeous, a terrific actor, and pretty much talked himself into the role the first day we saw him.

ANTHONY MONTGOMERY

It was amazing learning the magic that goes into making a show like *Enterprise*. It was exciting and scary to know it was a prequel, because there was so much history to live up to. Even though we didn't have to match up to everything exactly since we were the "first series," because of the steep tradition of Gene Roddenberry's legacy, in the beginning I was very worried about "getting it right," not just for all the fans out there, but because I wanted to make sure I was honoring the integrity of what it means to be part of the *Star Trek* family.

> The ship's communication officer was Ensign Hoshi Sato, a character who was most afraid to be on a long space voyage. Cast in the part was actress Linda Park, who would later go on to star in the TV version of the film *Crash*.

RICK BERMAN

We wanted an Asian actor to play the role of communications officer and go back to a little listening device like Uhura had had in the original series. We also wanted her to be a translator of almost magical abilities. And Linda nailed it. We wanted somebody very vulnerable and someone who was not into flying on spaceships. In the first audition she completely got it and did very well.

JAMES L. CONWAY

We met Linda early in the casting process and knew she was our Hoshi. Some of the Paramount executives weren't as sure, but after a number of auditions, everyone was convinced.

LINDA PARK (actor, "Hoshi Sato")

There's a lot of growth that happened for me, not only as an actor in front of the camera, but as a businesswoman. Sometimes it's easy to forget that part of being an actor is that you are your own business, especially when you become successful at any level; you see how you work as a business and you can't just say, I'm just an artist, and I don't need to concern myself with the practical, because it's just as important to keep your artistic tools as sharp as your business tool. That's the biggest thing I learned.

At first, I was hesitant about a lot of things; I was twenty-three, all these people know better than I do, so I took an inferior stance on a lot of business decisions, but then had more confidence in what it is that I want and in having an informed opinion and not being afraid to state it, because in the end, it is my career and my life that these decisions are being made about.

FRED DEKKER

I've always loved Hoshi. Partially because I had a bit of a crush on Linda. To me, she was the audience's way in, because she was not comfortable being on the ship, and that was a great way of bringing a character onto a show. In the previous iterations of *Trek,* everyone was comfortable on that ship. But now you have this person who says, "We're going faster than the speed of light, to some place where we don't know what will be there, it's terrifying! And the only thing preventing us from exploding is this big hunk of metal that we're sitting in." I thought that was very compelling.

> Weapons and tactical expert Lieutenant Malcolm Reed was played by British actor Dominic Keating, who had previously starred in the TV series *The Immortal* and *ChromiumBlue.com.*

DOMINIC KEATING

I remember when I first read the breakdown for the part, I wasn't that excited because I just thought I wasn't really what they were looking for. But Rick Berman thought differently. The story goes that I had read for them a couple of years ago for a guest-starring role on *Voyager* and I didn't get it. I don't even remember going back for a callback. I thought to myself, "Well, those people at *Star Trek* think I'm something," but apparently he had my photo in his desk for eighteen months prior to casting *Enterprise* and he remembered me. At the time I'd met him, they must have been in the very early stages of formulating *Enterprise*. You never know, do you?

RICK BERMAN

I had met Dominic on the first day of the last season of *Voyager*. He had a role of an English character. He came in, and we were still a year away from going into production on the new series, but we were already starting to write it. He came in and read for us and I said to Junie Lowry, who was our casting director, "We've got this role for the new series," and I said to him, "We've got a role for you in a series that we're creating that's not going to be going on the air for eight or nine months, whatever it is, but I don't want to use you up here." This guy looked at me and said, "You're right." Coincidentally, he was the first person who came in and read again. We have a lot of British actors in the history of our show and he was, again, a classically trained British actor.

DOMINIC KEATING

I had a chat with Brannon and Rick where I said, "I'm quite excited, and honestly, I'll say whatever you put in front of me, but I would like it that he isn't just the talking head Brit on an American spaceship." Brannon said, "You won't say lines like 'my dear old mum'?'" When I read the breakdown, he's described as "buttoned-down, by the book, wry, dry, shy around women." I'm, like, "Oh, fuck, I've got to *act* this."

ANTOINETTE STELLA (producer, *Star Trek: Enterprise*)

Dominic was one of the fun characters to write for. Malcolm had the reserve that you always wondered what was beneath that surface. Having a character like that was fun.

JAMES L. CONWAY

Anthony, Connor, and Dominic were cast very quickly. We met them early in the process, everyone loved them, and they were set.

Aside from the human characters, there was the need for the requisite alien crew member who in this case would be the ship's doctor, Phlox, a Denobulan who is part of an interspecies medical exchange program on Earth. He was played by veteran character actor John Billingsley.

RICK BERMAN

John is a character actor and somebody else who's in tremendous demand. He's just a wonderful guy. We wanted a sort of a wise, quirky alien to play that role again. Somebody who would be our doctor, and he did a marvelous job. He's another actor I would do anything to work with again.

Like most of the *Star Trek* series—with the exception of *Deep Space Nine*—there generally was not a lot of emphasis put on the idea of recurring characters. An exception for the prequel series was *Re-Animator*'s Jeffrey Combs (Weyoun on *DS9*) as the Andorian, Shran. From as early as season one's "The Andorian Incident" through season four, the versatile Combs (who had already played numerous alien species on the previous series) was even being considered for a series regular in the event that the show was renewed for a fifth year.

JEFFREY COMBS (actor, "Shran")

Actually, at first my nose was a little out of joint, because when I heard they were doing a new series I was hoping to get in as a regular. I thought that on *Deep Space Nine* I'd shown that I should get a promotion or something, but it didn't happen. I was offered a guest-starring role and at first I didn't want to take it. That was my feeling, because after having a run at *Star Trek* and loving and cherishing *DS9* as much as I did, a oner didn't interest me. Then they told me it would probably be recurring and that it was an Andorian. *That* intrigued me, because I knew the original series and this particular Andorian was kind of altruistic. He was a commander of a ship, not a weaselly diplomat, which to me would have been far too similar to what Weyoun was.

When I read the script, whether or not I came back, I really liked the tone and the quality and saw immediately that there was something to play there: weary, suspicious, chip on the shoulder, but also been hurt and burned a lot. I kind of likened it to the Irish and the British. And I love the turn that the Vulcans used logic as a veil to really hide their intentions. That they really did have strategy and cunning, but they hid behind this cool rational veneer, much like the British did. Whereas the Irish are hot. And I like that, too, that the Andorians are hot, yet they were cool.

SCOTT BAKULA

We had a ball. Actors are people and you don't click with everybody, but from the first episode we were right on the same page. And we shared a certain kind of rhythm that worked. I so looked forward to when he was there, and it was obvious to the writers and everybody else that we had something great going on there. He's a great actor and he just ate the scenery with that character and it was all appropriate and right on.

JEFFREY COMBS

Scott's a wonderful actor. He knows the value of what to play in a scene. I also think that he's a very funny man; he's got a great sense of humor, which as Archer he wasn't able to utilize very often. It was there, but he had to be more reserved about all of that. We were always able to find the kind of wry slant on things together in terms of breaking the tension with a little bit of humor here and there. And we could push each other's buttons in this weary game the characters had of you owe me and I owe you, and who owes you and I don't owe you anymore. Those are *really* Andorian: "And now I don't owe you. I did, but now I don't." It was a growing trust.

CHRIS BLACK

I wrote a couple of the Andorian shows, and Jeff Combs is the best. Jeff is versatile. He's almost Shakespearean. He's so theatrical and so perfect for Shran. He would just inhabit that blue skin and those antennae. Those antennae that were flexible and radio controlled. And he and Scott had so much fun together. They were just a delight to watch.

JEFFREY COMBS

And the nice thing is that Shran changed as the show went on, because he realized as he got to know the humans that they *could* be trusted. That he could challenge them and that they could be strong, but they had honor.

RICK BERMAN

We like to think that the Picards and even the Kirks of the world tended to take meeting alien races for granted. This was their daily work. For these seven, it's a pretty spooky occasion. It's always something that's filled with awe and excitement and a little bit of trepidation and fear. It's really almost more like any one of us finding ourselves in the situation where we're about to run into an alien species. It would be a pretty scary thing and certainly not just a day-by-day occurrence the way it would be for a Picard or for a Janeway.

The design of this series' starship *Enterprise* also represented an opportunity to go back to basics, though the basic bridge design remained very much in the vein of its predecessors rather than a homage to Matt Jeffries' brilliant original.

BRANNON BRAGA

In developing *Enterprise,* we kept in mind a tour of a nuclear submarine we had done. We really took our cues from that. This ship is somewhere between a nuclear sub and a starship. We don't have shields. We have something called hull plating. Photon torpedoes don't exist. There's some sort of torpedo that is very much like a high-tech missile. And the list goes on. Some parts of the *Enterprise* look like the space shuttle, some parts look like Kirk's ship, and some parts look like nothing you've seen. But it's definitely more rudimentary and more cramped, and I think much cooler than any of the ships we'd designed so far. It's not Picard's bridge, which looked like the waiting lounge at an airport. It definitely had a more realistic look to it, yet it was no less cool.

RICK BERMAN

Brannon and I had the idea to give it more of a look of a submarine; something that was all business. We and Herman Zimmerman went down to the naval base in San Diego and managed to get on a couple of submarines, to just get the feel of what it is to be confined in a relatively small space. We wanted it to be the antithesis of the luxury of the other starships. And the design that Herman came up with does have a lot of a submarine look. I know the network tried on a number of occasions to get us to spruce it up a little, but we didn't think that was really appropriate. They constantly wanted more color.

MARIE JACQUEMETTON (story editor and writer, *Enterprise*)

The *Enterprise* was just beautiful. It was three hundred and sixty degrees, you walked in and there was a tunnel over your head and an engine room. It was really beautiful. We were literally shooting *Baywatch Hawaii* at a beach with a lifeguard center that was built on the North Shore for our show, because the North Shore lifeguards were going to take it over afterward. It wasn't even really a set.

DOMINIC KEATING

The sets, the effects, the camera stuff is so much more difficult, which for the actor translates to a lot more hours, many more takes, and so on. The spacesuits look great, but, my god, they are heavy. I'm strong. I pitied the female cast members. *You* carry around a five-pound bucket of water for a couple of hours. The helmets alone are sixteen pounds and they're not connected to the bodysuit, so it's your neck that's carrying that thing. I do yoga, so in the claustrophobia of the suit, I would sit down and just close my eyes and go into an almost transcendental state until I heard the bell when you have to stand up again.

> Among the concepts at the outset that were designed to distinguish this series from the other entries in the franchise was to actually omit the name *Star Trek* from the title, and instead call the series simply *Enterprise* (this would eventually change). The other was to do away with the notion of a symphonic title sequence and, instead, feature the song "Faith of the Heart," which had first appeared as the closing titles for the underwhelming Robin Williams vehicle, *Patch Adams*. It proved to be one of the most divisive elements of the series for the fans *and* the staff.

RICK BERMAN

One thing decided in the development of this series was that the show's title should drop the words "Star Trek." Since *The Next Generation*, we've had so many *Star Trek* entities that were called *Star Trek* colon something: *Star Trek: Generations, Star Trek: Deep Space Nine, Star Trek: Voyager, Star Trek: First Contact, Star Trek: Insurrection*. It's just been one after another. Our feeling was, in trying to make the show dramatically different, that it might be fun not to have a divided main title like that. And I thought that if there's any one word that says *Star Trek* without actually saying *Star Trek*, it's the word "enterprise."

MICHAEL SUSSMAN

People were pissed off that it didn't have *Star Trek* in the title and I actually thought that was kind of a cool idea. But they took it as an insult.

RICK BERMAN

When the ratings started to fail in the second season, the first thing that people who had taken over all of this said was "Let's put *Star Trek* back on," as if that was going to suddenly make the ratings jump up. As if anybody out there was going to say, "Damn, I didn't know that was a *Star Trek* show." So it became *Star Trek: Enterprise* the last two years.

BRANNON BRAGA

Rick and I felt that a song would set the slightly more contemporary feeling we were going after with *Enterprise*. For the longest time, we had a temporary song we cut the main titles to, U2's "Beautiful Day." If we had used that—or could have afforded it—that would have been a great song. Those main titles with U2 are amazing. It's hip and cool, whereas the song we ended up with is awful. I'm a big fan of Diane Warren, she's a great songwriter, but this particular song and the way it was sung was tacky. I still cringe when I hear it and, by the way, I think the song had a lot to do with people's adverse reaction to the show. If you look at the main titles themselves, it's a really cool sequence. But the song is awful, just awful.

RICK BERMAN

This is another example of my being stubborn, right or wrong. I thought it would be nice to have a theme song. Nobody had ever done it before. I knew that I wanted the animation at the opening instead of just being the flying through space stuff that had existed on all the other *Star Trek* shows. But I wanted it to be sort of a compilation of the science and the people that led up to the space flight. Our visual effects people put together an amazing visual montage. Then we went to a very famous, contemporary composer named Diane Warren, who's written huge hits. She went through a whole bunch of songs and we came up with this tune that she had written. The lyrics seemed perfect. Then she got all excited, there was a

British singer named Russell Watson and he was a very hot performer. Kind of semioperatic and pop performer, and he agreed to sing it. It basically spoke to exactly what we were looking for—a dream of going out into the unknown and the whole idea of bringing one's heart to what matters. We recorded the song and put it to the animation and everybody thought it was terrific. And the audience *hated* it.

In the second or third year, the network said to us, "Can you rewrite the song and could you make the song hipper?" We left the vocal on, but we did a completely different instrumental with a lot more electric guitars and things to make it a little more rock and roll. I don't know if anybody was truly satisfied with that. I, for one, can tell you that I thought it was a great opening and I'm not alone in that. I don't think I'm in the majority, but I'm not alone.

MIKE SUSSMAN

It gets back to the people running the franchise saying, "We've got to do something different. We've got to shake it up." And kind of shaking it up in many of the wrong ways. Let's say all the wrong ways. I don't think it's a bad idea to have a non–Jerry Goldsmith opening. When they showed us the opening graphics, it was set to U2's "Beautiful Day," which is an amazing song. Obviously we couldn't afford that, it was all temp, but we ended up getting a Diane Warren song and she was a *Star Trek* fan. She gave it to them for next to nothing.

ANTOINETTE STELLA (producer, *Star Trek: Enterprise*)

I was floored, because it didn't sound like a *Star Trek* song. We were in shock. Everybody talked about it after we saw the pilot. Sometimes you try to be different and they work . . . and sometimes they don't.

MANNY COTO (executive producer, *Star Trek: Enterprise*)

I wasn't crazy about it, but I also thought it wasn't as bad as everyone else thought it was. I was neutral. I didn't like the song that much, but it's hard to say. After a while you get used to it, you know what I mean? When you work on a show, they become your opening titles and then you're, like, "Don't criticize my opening titles!" You kind of embrace them in a strange way. But the first time I heard it, I was, like, "Huh?"

MIKE SUSSMAN

I was briefly dating a girl who was in the music industry, and she had never seen *Star Trek*. I turned on *Enterprise,* and when it got to the opening titles, she literally fell out of her chair laughing at how bad and hokey the song was. So, in our attempts to modernize the show and make it cool, not only did we lose the fans, but we gained the disdain of the people we were hoping to convert.

CHRIS BLACK

Is it a great song? No. It's not a great song. I respected what they were trying to do. The visuals of that sequence are spectacular. It tells a story of everything you wanted that show to be. A decision was made by the people who created and ran that show that they were going to do something different. Everything about the conception and design of *Enterprise* was to step away from *Voyager*, which continued to have failing numbers and failing ratings. Did everyone like it? Obviously not. But I respected it for what it was. If you listen to the lyrics of that song, they're appropriate. Are the lyrics cheesy? Absolutely. But is it saying something about the characters of the *Star Trek* universe that I think is appropriate? Absolutely. I don't hate it or love it. Everybody hates it. I don't hate it. I hate Nazis. I don't hate the theme song from *Enterprise*.

BRANNON BRAGA

If you heard the theme to *Next Generation,* it's instantly identifiable, even *Voyager*'s theme to a lesser degree. You know what it is, and you have a certain fondness for it. I don't know a whole lot of people who have anything but a kind of ironic fondness for *Enterprise*'s theme song. It was a little bit out of my hands in terms of selection of the song and the singer. There wasn't a lot I could do about it. I'm not really all that musically knowledgeable. I felt like Rick and Peter Lauritson, who was our post supervisor, were the music men, but there wasn't a lot I could say that would have changed Rick's mind. At the end of the day, Rick was my boss.

LUKAS KENDALL (editor, *Film Score Monthly*)

Is there anybody who likes that song? The choice was ridiculed at the time and comes across no better today. I would not be opposed to the use of a song in principle, but it was the wrong one—a Diane Warren power ballad from *Patch Adams*?

Really? Even the producers seemed to hedge when they had the backing track re-done for season three, but they had too much invested to dump it entirely. The producers broke one of their own rules: *Star Trek* has become pop culture, but there is never pop culture *within Star Trek,* because it punctures the reality. They tried rebranding with a mainstream radio song instead of another "space theme for nerds," so to speak—the desperate attempt to reach a bigger audience—but it was cheesy and lame.

> Unlike the title theme, the series' two-hour premiere "Broken Bow" was greeted enthusiastically by fans and critics who had high hopes for a long and successful run based on the success of the pilot. Their hopes would quickly be dashed as the first season began to air.

DOMINIC KEATING

Its greatest success was we had a bloody good cast. I don't want to be too dispar-aging of past incumbents, but we really did have a very good cast who had some fucking talent. Linda was fresh out of the gate, and she wasn't always my favor-ite person, but she was a good actress. The look of the show was pretty hot and unique insomuch as it was a prequel, so it had to have a sense of going back in time, and yet because of the modern eye in 2001, it couldn't look hokey. They did a really good job in giving you a sense of a pioneering ship. And, God knows, we weren't cheap. That pilot cost about thirteen million.

JAMES L. CONWAY

The *Enterprise* pilot, "Broken Bow," was the best experience of my life, because it was a two-hour, thirty-six-day schedule, twelve-million-dollar budget. I had all the time and money to do it really well and had a great script, so for me of all the things in my career, that was the highlight. Even to the point that we had the cast and crew screening in the big theater at Paramount. On the big screen, and the theater was filled with everybody who had been involved in it. And I'm sitting there with my wife and daughter and it was fantastic.

LINDA PARK

It was definitely nerve-wracking. I had all this nervous energy, which I used toward the character. It was my first year in Los Angeles and literally my third job, so it was maybe my fourth day on a real set. That in itself is really scary when you're embarking on this process of shooting a pilot and you're surrounded by producers and it's their baby. Whether you want it to affect you or not, there's a lot of pressure.

DOMINIC KEATING

We were grooving, we had a fabulous time. It was the finest four years of my whole career. I knew from the read-through that we'd have a good chemistry, and there wasn't any idiot in the cast who was going to fuck this up. It only takes one apple in the barrel, and if that apple happens to be the one at the top of the call sheet, who's a bit of a twit, then it's really difficult. And, God bless Scott Bakula, he is such a gent and so fun and so giving and so generous. His work ethic is extraordinary and his heart is big. And he's a nice bloke, and happy to have a fun time on set and get the work done, but he doesn't take himself seriously. He's very grateful. He's just an actor's actor.

LINDA PARK

By the middle of the pilot, I was feeling more comfortable because we were working a lot of hours, and after the first week, the producers came up to me and they were complimentary. It allowed me to breathe a little easier, because at that point I had very little experience and I needed that assurance, because I was a lot more self-conscious at the beginning of the year.

DOMINIC KEATING

To be perfectly honest, you get offered a gig on a show like *Star Trek* and you know that it's got a very good chance of running seven years. Who am I to turn that kind of opportunity and that kind of financial freedom down? I was very happy to carve out something for myself. I didn't expect to become the action man on the show, but they threw me a nice bone every now and again. The workload wasn't as grueling it was for as Jolene and Connor and Scott.

FRED DEKKER

I would go to the set when I could. I felt comfortable there, that's where the magic was happening. It was always, "How are ya, how do you feel?" Not a lot of artistic or creative discussion, because I didn't feel like it was my place. I felt like if I chose to make it my place, it would have been frowned upon. Scott was a really solid anchor for that group. I'm surprised Connor hasn't taken off as a big star, I always thought he was a generous actor and they all worked very well together.

DOMINIC KEATING

I saw some episodes of *Voyager* and thought that they were a little dry. I did check out some episodes of *Next Generation* out of professional interest, just to see a British actor, who was a stage actor more than anything else, employed in an American TV science-fiction show. He did really well, too. He was perfect for it. I think I'm right in thinking that Shatner had done a lot of theater as well. I could see that this science-fiction stuff has to be said with a very credible, slightly commanding voice that gives it credence. If you don't sell it, it doesn't sell itself. It's too wacky.

ANDRÉ BORMANIS

The premise was not only a prequel to the original series, but the idea that these are people more like us than like the heroic figures of the original series and *Next Gen* and *Voyager* and *DS9*. What if you got a spaceship? What if you and me and our buddies were given a starship and we would go out and cruise the galaxy? How would we react? We'd freak out at a lot of the stuff that would be just another day at the office for Kirk and Picard and the gang. We wanted them to be not sure. Unfortunately, you know that tended to make Archer look kind of weak. So that hurt us a little bit. It was a fine line to try and make it more relatable.

The goal was seeing the experiences of this first crew and how that shaped Starfleet's attitude toward first contact, toward the issue of the militarization of Starfleet and all of these other things. That would be how we laid the groundwork for what became the familiar tropes of the Federation and the Prime Directive. Uneven as it was, I think that worked pretty well.

ANTOINETTE STELLA

In the original, Captain Kirk slept with every single alien female he met and then, by contrast, Scott Bakula became something of a monk, because he always held back. Forty years later, we didn't want trained women out in space just being any port in a storm, so it was respectful to women . . . but it was also less exciting storytelling.

CHRIS BLACK

I think André embraced his role as the science consultant in exactly the right way. You would go to him and say, "Is something like this possible?" To which he would almost invariably answer, "Possible? Sure! It's a big universe. Anything's possible. Is it likely? No." But you would cling to that possibility. As long as it wasn't something so outrageous that people would roll their eyes and tune out. It was not about the science. It wasn't *Cosmos*. We were not teaching people about astrophysics or exobiology. We were trying to write a character-driven show.

FRED DEKKER

André, to his credit, could always come up with great-sounding bullshit. The problem was that we always relied on it. Someone like André was almost a security blanket for Brannon. He knew that if he had to crack a scene, to have the science guy there to write the dialogue and tech the tech, it would make things easier.

SCOTT BAKULA

What I try to do is bring reality to a situation. As much reality as I can, because I see that as my job as an actor. Believability, reality, whatever you want to call it. As I said to Rick and Brannon early on, I don't know why I've done as much sci fi as I have. Part of it, I think, is that I want to believe. If the job calls for me to stand in front of a sixty-foot dragon and battle it to the death, then I want to believe that that dragon is out there. If I believe, maybe I can help the audience believe it. If I believe I can travel in time, then the audience believes it also.

[Creator] Don Bellisario and I got into a thing very early on with *Quantum Leap*, because the network wanted to jazz it up a little bit. They wanted us to be a little more Bill Murray-ish, which is the best way I can put it. I said, "You know what? If you want that, you've got the wrong guy. I don't believe that the heart of the show is going to live on me being a snappy, wisecracking, wiseass time traveler." I said the same thing about *Star Trek*: "I believe that we can be doing this someday. Boy, would I love to be the captain of a starship if people were going out there."

DAVID A. GOODMAN

I thought *Enterprise* was a great show as a *Star Trek* fan. Best pilot of any of the sequel series and just great episodes throughout. But the way we were telling stories *wasn't* so great.

JAMES L. CONWAY

There's a lot of hair issues on *Star Trek*. I had to reshoot the first five days of the pilot because of Scott's hair. When we started shooting, [Paramount Television President] Kerry McCluggage, who was a good friend of Scott's and really had a lot to do with Scott getting the show in the first place, was in New York and didn't see dailies until he came back from New York, and he *hated* Scott's hair. He wanted it one way, Scott wanted it another and somehow the message didn't get to us. So we had to go back and reshoot all of Scott's close-ups for the first five days and change his hair. And then what was interesting was when I did that second-to-last episode in the mirror universe in season four, Scott's hair went back to the way he wanted to wear it for that episode.

STEPHEN BECK
(executive story editor, *Star Trek: Enterprise*)

I always, as a writer, liked beginnings. How people get to where they get to. I thought the pilot was brilliant, the way they introduced everything, and the potential. You could create everything new, but you could also see the beginnings of things.

BRANNON BRAGA

I liked the pilot. It was really high-end, and it cost a lot of money and had a young and exuberant cast. It was exciting to launch a new *Star Trek* show and the pilot was really well done.

MIKE SUSSMAN

I got pulled into Brannon's office and he's, like, "Here's your copy of the script. And then you guys are on vacation. Go away and come back in X number of weeks." I read the script and I was blown away. I was, like, "Oh my God, this is the best *Star Trek* pilot." It was terrific. And so I was super excited about where it was all going.

CHRIS BLACK

I remember what Rick [Berman] said when he was pitching me the show and saying it was going to be *The Right Stuff* in outer space. Dangerous. Risky. The first guys out there, the test pilots of the program, no one's been out here before. A throwback to good old-fashioned, two-fisted *Star Trek*. An acknowledgment that *Voyager* became too intellectual, sterile, and off-putting. The mandate, as I understood it from the network and from themselves, was to make it fun again.

MANNY COTO

I actually thought it would be more fun to go rougher with it, more *Crimson Tide*, meaning there was no captain sitting in a big chair staring at a big screen. And have the ship a bit more claustrophobic, less comfortable. There wouldn't be big viewscreens, you'd have to look into little monitors. Kind of what *Battlestar Galactica* ultimately did.

CHRIS BLACK

This was one of the reasons they cast Scott, to romance alien women and get in fistfights with the bad guys. I was, like, "Sign me up!" I had been waiting for this show for twenty years. I was sold and I thought the pilot, "Broken Bow," kind of promised that. And then it was disappointing when we started getting in and breaking the episodes and that kind of went away.

JAMES L. CONWAY

The pilot of *Enterprise* was terrific. But then the first season was very repetitive and it felt like it was written by people who were burned out. And Brannon copped to this, saying that he had made some bad choices in hiring staff and he was burned out from finishing up on *Voyager*. So I think that first season suffered and it took him awhile to re-steer that ship.

BRANNON BRAGA

When we were shooting the pilot and it was time for me to start writing episodes, I had a lot of things that I wanted to do. But once the ship officially set sail, I felt constrained. I felt, "Here we go again," and I felt very challenged. Also, it was the first time I wasn't working with people I'd worked with before. It was a large staff of ten people, and *Star Trek* was notoriously difficult to find writers for, because it was a hard show to write. I don't even want to say hard; it's unique, and it just had a specific voice, and I had this writing staff that was new to the genre. Out of ten people, I think just a couple survived that first year.

STEPHEN BECK

I was on a show called *Seven Days* before *Enterprise,* and it was a great learning experience. We had three producers who were generous and kind, and each one taught you something different. The show was about a machine that goes back in time seven days. Which was a really neat concept, because you didn't have to worry about killing Hitler and, instead, it was about saving people's lives. So I was on the show and they didn't pick it up, which I was surprised about, but they wanted to interview me for *Enterprise*.

FRED DEKKER

I had lunch with Brannon at Paramount and we hit it off. I said, "I'm in, this is exciting." And sometime after my deal had closed, they had a screening on the lot of the pilot. It was big. It was exciting. It played well. I was thrilled to be a part of this new iteration of *Star Trek*. Brannon said something that stuck with me. He said he wanted the show to be "weird and spooky, but also fun and charming." And that sold me 100 percent. I said, "*That's* a show I would watch."

STEPHEN BECK

My first interview was with Brannon and Rick. I didn't get the job, but three episodes later, they called and said they're adding people on the staff. The interesting thing about the first year was that they wanted to try to do something different than previous *Star Trek*s. But it was difficult for them to find their footing. Too often, I think, they'd gone back to storytelling the way they had done it before. Not that they didn't try, but it really was tough.

ANTOINETTE STELLA

They were looking for people who could write sex and comedy. And I thought, "I was on *Melrose Place,* where there was just sex. I was on *Providence,* which did light comedy . . .", and I thought, "I could do the sex and comedy." I didn't realize they were talking about very twisted alien sex. So it wasn't the sex between the human members of the crew, it was strange alien sex. It was really odd.

MIKE SUSSMAN

Even though they were going to hire a whole bunch of people who were not *Star Trek* veterans, they wanted one or two people who kind of knew it, aside from them, just in case. Rick liked that final script we [Sussman, with writing partner Phyllis Strong] wrote for *Voyager,* which was the last one hour before the finale.

STEPHEN BECK

Brannon called me in and said I had the job. When I was in college, I was a philosophy major with a minor in biology, and I always wrote. When I was a kid I always wrote. But I wanted to be a doctor, because of the good you could do in the world. A friend of mine worked for Universal and he would always bring home scripts. I would read them and say, "I could do that!"

I wrote a spec script for *Chicago Hope* and they hired me. I was, at that point, not only medical director of a clinic, but I was medical director for Sentinel Hospital. And yet it was no decision at all. It was my dream, so I went to *Chicago Hope.* And then my next job was *Seven Days.* Followed by *Enterprise.* I said something that hit Brannon, and he said, "*That's* the philosophy of the show." I said it appealed to me that you get to start over and that you have an infinite amount of stories that you can tell. I remember him saying, "Yes, that's it."

Ten minutes later my name was on the Internet. I hadn't even told anybody. They wanted to shake it up with people that didn't know the system. Now that's where I think part of the problem came from, because there were people that didn't understand the system and were trying to do something different, but their system had been running for twenty-five years.

FRED DEKKER

I always hoped and assumed the actors were happy. They came to work very early and stayed very late. The crew earlier and later. The machine seemed to work very well.

ANDRÉ JACQUEMETTON (story editor and writer, *Enterprise*)

We were on *Baywatch Hawaii*. It was the last gasps of *Baywatch* and we'd written a horror script that our agent sent to Brannon and he really liked it and called us in. By this time, *Baywatch* was finished. We had a good interview and he hired us. So, that's how we started. They were looking for people who didn't know *Star Trek*, because they wanted to reach out to a whole new audience.

MARIE JACQUEMETTON

It wasn't like we didn't know anything about *Star Trek*. We watched *Next Gen*. We had actually worked at Paramount when *Next Gen* was a huge phenomenon, so it was in our awareness. We watched it but we weren't Trekkies. I mean, we couldn't speak Klingon.

BRANNON BRAGA

It was rough. I was pretty depressed, because I felt like the first episode after the pilot was good, and then the third was good, and then there was some episode called "Terra Nova" and it was dreadful. It was a stinker, and I thought, "We're in trouble." It happened that quickly. I was hoping to do something more serialized and felt like I was in a situation where I'm starting to fall into some familiar rhythms.

When the show worked, I thought it worked beautifully. In the first season, there was one of the best episodes of *Star Trek* I ever produced, called "Dear Doctor." It was about Dr. Phlox on an interspecies medical exchange, and he has a human counterpart on another ship. It's about his letters to this doctor and his observations on humanity, and it ends up being about a very serious issue of inadvertent genocide. To me, it had all the humanity and humor that I hoped the show would engender, and it was a show you only could have told on *Enterprise*.

STEPHEN BECK

The difficulty with *Enterprise* was that the culture of *Star Trek* had been around for decades and it was its own inbred culture. Any business, any show, if it's been around long enough, is going to have its own psychological behavior. I think it was dysfunctional behavior, because it had been its own system for so long.

ANTOINETTE STELLA

It was tough to come up with fresh ideas for the show, and the writers wanted to come up with fresh takes on the Andorians and Vulcans, which I thought was a really great idea. Fred's Andorians were interesting . . . much more complex aliens than what the Andorians were before. That was the interesting part: How can we make these *Star Trek* tropes a little fresher?

FRED DEKKER

The positive was that it was an opportunity to reinvent something from the back shelf and start again. That was exciting. The negative is that I got concerned early on that the powers that be were going to fall back on all the things they had done before. What I was excited about was the blank slate. To see aliens we hadn't seen before. We weren't always going to have actors with foam rubber prosthetics. They could be foam clouds. They could be driftwood/intelligent plants. There was an opportunity to blow open this whole concept. What happened was, and the Andorians were the tip of the iceberg, was the inclination to cater to the history of the franchise, to the fans. "Remember the Andorians? They're back!" I thought that was cheap.

Brannon called them the crusty nuggets. To me it's the equivalent of doing kung fu in a James Bond movie. To me, it demonstrates a lack of confidence. I always said to everybody that if we put an hour of a goat eating a tin can and call it *Star Trek,* the fans are going to watch it. So what if we took that concept and pitched it to fans that *didn't* watch *Star Trek*? That was a little bit of a downfall of my time working on that show.

ANTOINETTE STELLA

We were trying to find out what the flaw would be for Scott's captain. How did these astronauts behave when André [Bormanis] was in NASA? In these critical moments, he said, "They had behaved like pros. Astronauts are trained within an inch of their lives and they're also the cream of the crop in every possible category. These guys were, like, genuine superheroes. They behave completely divorced from any emotional response to the emergency." So then we'd say, "What about *Apollo 13*?" And he said, "They had to invent a lot of the conflict, because those guys behaved the way they were meant to behave. In an emergency, they set aside any of their anxiety, fear . . . whatever it is." So that was tough to try to figure out. How do we show they're human when we know how the captain had been trained on handling any emergency?

FRED DEKKER

Brannon and Rick were writing the first batch, and I think the best show of that season was "Fight or Flight." The truth was, we were just sitting in our offices waiting to be called, because Rick and Brannon were writing the show. At some point or another, when the last one they wrote together to inaugurate the series was in the can, that's when we sat down and started talking about what we were going to do.

BRANNON BRAGA

I always said we need to tell stories that we could only tell on *Enterprise,* but once you have a show that's a ship with a captain and his or her crew flying around exploring, you pretty much start to find yourself in a situation that you've been in before. And that was my challenge. But there were some gems in the first couple of seasons.

MIKE SUSSMAN

When we ultimately convened the writers room, we had all of these writers. Maybe ten or eleven writers that first season, and they were all brand-new to the show, basically. With the exception of André [Bormanis], Brannon, Phyllis [Strong], and me. People are pitching like the most clichéd *Star Trek,* but they didn't know any better. I felt bad for them. But it took a long time to rewrite a lot of those scripts and there was just this meandering quality. They wanted the show to be different. I don't know what they were trying to do with it, quite frankly. Rick and Brannon weren't really being allowed to do what they specifically wanted to do, so what they landed on was neither one or the other. It wasn't enough like the previous shows to appease the fans and it wasn't new or ground-breaking.

When the show premiered, the numbers were really good. And I remember *Entertainment Weekly* saying, "They've done it again! Another seven years." Blah-blah-blah. "And everyone was just settling back and ready to coast." And that really wasn't the experience.

MANNY COTO

If you're going to do a prequel, I would have been more interested in seeing something really rough with a sense that this was our first ship. *Enterprise* was going to deep space, but there were characters like Travis Mayweather who had already been to other planets and had been at warp speed. I was, like, "Where's the sense that we're going where no man has gone before? It's the first warp ship to leave our system, scary, there's no one out there." Stick to a submarine, which is dark and scary, like what "Balance of Terror" was. It's still tremendous and those space battles were much more realistic.

In "Balance of Terror," they would fire at each other, but they weren't actually visible on their screens, they were so far away, which is what these kind of super weapons would allow you to do. Nowadays these ships are literally on top of each other and they're firing. I'm, like, "F-16s don't even see the targets they're shooting at in *this* century." I hate it when these ships have to be right on top of each other. I'm, like, "Really, you waited until *now* to fire?"

ANDRÉ JACQUEMETTON

We were really excited. The way Brannon pitched it was we were going to write our own rules and that space was dangerous and scary. It was really exciting to just be there in the beginning, and it doesn't necessarily have to be the best of the best going out there; we're going to make mistakes. For some reason, we kept on thinking at the end of the season *Enterprise* is going to come back to Earth and dock and, basically, it will be maybe half of the ship.

MARIE JACQUEMETTON

I remember Brannon said that in his perfect vision of how the season would end, the *Enterprise* would come limping back to port, falling apart and battered by horrors that they had encountered out there. Clearly, that didn't happen.

ANDRÉ JACQUEMETTON

We didn't stick to that, unfortunately. We didn't stick to a lot of things that first season.

FRED DEKKER

The Borg are brilliant. They're iconographic TV history. We weren't encouraged to do something new like that. We were told to keep the boat in the center of the canal. I wasn't sure if that was a studio edict. I think any writer has the crusty nuggets they like most, so Michael Bay is always going to have a bunch of shaky cam with girls in tight shorts. I was always interested in time travel, but was told that *Voyager* had plundered that to the degree that we would want to hold off on it for a while.

BRANNON BRAGA

I thought one of the strokes of genius about the show was that the Vulcans were antagonists, though they didn't know it at the time. It's a prequel for them, too, and a lot of fans hated that. Some fans said, "How dare you do this to the Vulcans?" And I was, like, first of all, cultures change, even Vulcan culture might have been different and they have their own prejudices. And that's what the show's about.

If you're just putting regular old Vulcans in, why bother? If they're just the Vulcans you're familiar with, why bother? By the way, they were kind of assholes in Picard's day, too. Vulcans are always assholes! In this case the prequel got us an episode called "Stigma," which was a metaphor for the AIDS epidemic, where mind melds were forbidden because they carried a terrible, communicable brain disease. I thought it was a great episode of *Star Trek*.

ANTOINETTE STELLA

I had an assistant, Juan Hernandez, who was a smart, young guy, and we had this episode early on where a Vulcan lies. We knew we were taking a chance, so some guy called the switchboard at Paramount. And he had been up all night, couldn't sleep, calls at six A.M. trying to get to the writers office. Finally at eight A.M., Juan answers the phone. The man, totally irate, said, "You don't know what you just did.

You just violated a basic rule. Vulcans don't lie! Vulcans don't lie! And Mr. Spock said that." And he quotes the show. And Juan took a beat and said, "When Mr. Spock said that, he was lying." This guy was having like a Darth Vader, "Luke, I am your father" moment.

CHRIS BLACK

I remember we would come into work on Monday and the voicemail box for the production office would be full. Overloaded. Completely full of people calling and complaining and bitching. One guy shrieked into the voicemail, "Vulcans don't lie! Vulcans don't lie! Vulcans don't lie!" Just saying it over and over again. Which, to some extent, was something that had been established prior to that as a characteristic of Vulcans.

But we were trying to do something different. That was the whole point of setting it years before and rebooting the whole franchise. We would get letters and vitriolic hate mail. Someone sent us a cardboard box where they had taken their kitchen wastepaper basket and dumped it into a box. Eggshells, coffee grounds. You know, they sent us a box full of garbage. With a note that said, "This is what you've done to *Star Trek*."

I get it to some extent. If you don't like it, you don't like it. Then don't watch it. But there's a sense of ownership. And I've been lucky enough to work on these shows like *Xena: Warrior Princess, Desperate Housewives, Mad Men*...shows with these rabid, vocal, foul people, but there's nothing like the *Star Trek* people. They feel like they own the show. And own those characters. And know what's right. And if you make a choice that they don't agree with or don't approve of, they get *very* upset.

That's why I love *Game of Thrones* so much. I haven't read the books and I watch the show and I say, "Holy shit, I didn't see that coming." And, to me, that's what makes it great. If you're watching *Star Trek* and all of the characters are doing exactly what you want them to do...what's the fun in that?

MARIE JACQUEMETTON

We had this one situation where a student from Temple University called to give us a pitch and we took his phone pitch. It was a story about Vulcans, and we made the mistake of saying, "We can't do this pitch because we have a similar story where T'Pol's fiancé comes onto the ship." So five minutes after our pitch, we get a beep from Terry Matalas, Brannon's assistant. "Brannon wants to see you." We go, "God, what did we do now?" So we go upstairs and Brannon sits us down and says, "Did you just tell a writer about the story that we're doing in your episode?" We had no idea what we had done. "Well, it's on the Internet." It said, "Breaking News from *Enterprise*, they're doing a story with T'Pol with a fiancé." He was fine with it, but he said, "Just be careful what you say at these pitch meetings." That was a big eye-opener about the rabidness of the fan base.

STEPHEN BECK

The third day I was there, still learning my phone, there was a message for me. And I got the message. It was a female voice, speaking Klingon very seductively. I had no idea what she was saying. Unfortunately, I erased it.

MARIE JACQUEMETTON

Brannon had a vision for the show and to some level he succeeded, but then all of a sudden that was being squelched and it was becoming more like traditional *Star Trek*. Whether that was coming from his partner, from the Internet, from the fans, or from fear and us just all sort of falling back on our old Trekkie conventions, we don't know.

Initially, the idea was we were not going to be hemmed in by this sort of utopian view of astronauts being perfect people who have no problems and they're the crème de la crème and that's why they're being sent into space. They're in a tin can floating around the universe and they're going to screw up and they're going to have sex with each other and they're going to insult each other and make mistakes. I don't think we were actually able to have that kind of freedom.

BRANNON BRAGA

You don't set out to make bad stuff, but I'd been doing *Star Trek* long enough that I knew what worked and what didn't. It's not like I knew when a bad one was going out the door. Fortunately, we had a very talented cast and the show looked great. There were still a couple that are really bad and doing twenty-six episodes a year is really rough. I don't even know how we did it.

GLEN C. OLIVER (film & TV critic, *Ain't It Cool News*)

Mankind's first substantive push into space didn't feel magical, or frightening, or unpredictable, or particularly troubled. The sense of this era's early space travel being a dangerous and unpredictable place . . . and the pioneering spirit suggested by *TOS* . . . was nowhere to be found here. The journeys of Jonathan Archer and his crew felt too easy. Too safe. Too clean. And their reactions to what they found "out there" were too tepid, probably because what they found wasn't all that interesting to begin with.

MARIE JACQUEMETTON

A lot of the time we'd start with the characters and what were they experiencing out in deep space for the first time as opposed to "Oh, what cool alien of the week can we bring in?" It's worth saying that one of the things Brannon talked about in our initial interview was he was really looking for writers that could write great characters and create worlds. It was really important to find that. We came from a place where we were writing drama; we would just start with that and it was not so much about that window dressing.

ANDRÉ JACQUEMETTON

The strange thing is we approached each story one at a time. We never really arced anything. We never said this is what we want to accomplish this first season. We didn't do any of that stuff, which was shocking. It was just week-to-week and we had to do twenty-four, so we had to move very quickly and, at one point, we split the room into two. It was different.

STEPHEN BECK

What I loved about *Seven Days*, which was the show I really grew up as a writer on, was we had a big room where everybody gathered. We had our own offices, but everyone spent most of their time there so it was very communal. *Enterprise* felt a little fragmented. We would be called into Brannon's office. Sometimes we would meet without Brannon because of the stresses on him, and come up with stories. We would be spinning our wheels, because we would present it to Brannon, and he would send it up to Rick, and they didn't like it, and we didn't know what they wanted.

FRED DEKKER

We had a lot of fun together. Because we had a lot of time on our hands, Brannon and Rick were writing the show and we would spend some time coming up with the show, but, again, because we didn't have a clear edict all the time, we would just make ourselves laugh. Funny drawings on the dry-erase board . . . it was lovely.

STEPHEN BECK

I happen to think Brannon's brilliant, but this was his first showrunning job and he was still learning how to do it. I have nothing against him. He would often ask us all, separately, to write up a story idea and send it to him written instead of pitching. Which was fine. I never had that done anywhere else, but it's a frustrating way to present. And there were stories I presented to him when I was on staff that ended up being done after I was gone, so I know they were good stories. And this happened with everybody.

MIKE SUSSMAN

Brannon didn't like anything crunchy. If you were eating something and it crunched, it drove him crazy. He's got his quirks. It's fine. Brannon preferred a smaller room. He prefers working with writers one-on-one. And I am kind of like that, too. You get in a room with a million voices and there are people who thrive on that. Ken [Biller], who I worked with on a couple different things, loves that. They're all just like another part of his brain and the more the merrier. I find it overwhelming and I think Brannon finds it overwhelming. So he hired all these people and they would turn into these kind of unruly pitch sessions. Ultimately, the only way to get anything done was to kick everybody out and have just one or two people in his office and figure it out with them. So, the room didn't really exist as a traditional room after that.

CHRIS BLACK

It's funny because when I showed up, everyone seemed demoralized. André and Marie Jacquemetton, who have a growing wall of Emmys from *Mad Men* and are two of the nicest people you'd meet in this business; Stephen Beck, Michael [Sussman], André [Bormanis], Fred Dekker—these people were writers! At the end of the day it *wasn't* about writing. I remember showing up there and you'd sit around all day with nothing to do. Finally, it would get to be six or seven P.M., and I'm, like, "Let's go." *That's* when Brannon would emerge from his office and say, "What do you guys got?" Why don't we start this at ten in the morning so people with kids and family and lives could go off and do that? People *weren't* happy. It was a poor way to run a show.

ANTOINETTE STELLA

What was interesting in the beginning was learning how to be in the writers room. That there are safe snacks and snacks that were not safe. Anything that made a loud crunching sound you weren't allowed to have. You couldn't have potato chips, because Brannon needed to concentrate and he wanted a quiet room. No potato chips, pretzels, crispy cookies, so that's what we all did. And if you did take a bite of a cookie that turned out to be a crisper, you let it sit in your mouth to let it soften because, you know, we didn't want to disturb the flow and the concentration.

We had a guy who came in to do a freelance and he grabbed a bag of potato chips and we were, like, "Oh my God, what are you doing? What are you doing?" And he said, "What are you talking about?" We said, "You can't do that in here!" And he said, "Are you guys kidding?" We said, "No! No! No!" So we actually told him, "You have to put that away now." It was contraband. If he had lit up a joint, it wouldn't have been as alarming to us as eating a pretzel.

CHRIS BLACK

I came in and chewed something crunchy and people just looked at me in horror. I was eating a cracker. And they did the thing like their eyes were big as saucers, and I remember laughing out loud. I think from there on—since the ridiculousness was out—there was never a problem with crunchy food after that. The best shows are the ones that are sort of safe, where no idea or no pitch is off-limits. There was this sort of bunker mentality there that everybody was living in fear of their lives and jobs, and it proved to be true.

ANTOINETTE STELLA

Also, no red marker on the dry-erase board. No red marker because it looked like somebody was correcting things. So black and blue. It looked like, you know when a teacher corrects a paper? So no red marker. The process was to start one and go to the end. I had not been on a show that wrote stories that way before. I've been on shows which broke stories, beginning, middle, end points so you knew how it was going to end and you had your basic structure before you went into scene by scene. But that's not the way we did it. It would be scene one, scene two, scene three, scene four. Also, we broke stories without commercial breaks and without act breaks. He didn't want the story to be compressed any way, unnaturally.

MIKE SUSSMAN

When Manny Coto came, it became a little more of a group room again. But for a long time it was really just people off on their own. You'd go off on your own and meet with other writers and take things around and develop them, but there wasn't that "Okay, let's get the whole staff here" after season one.

MARIE JACQUEMETTON

Every episode we wrote there was really, really difficult. The story breaks took forever, the process of the drafts took forever. It was painful.

CHRIS BLACK

I remember going away for Thanksgiving vacation and standing outside a hotel room in Northern California talking to Brannon on the phone. And my wife is glaring at me, like, "Are you *fucking* kidding me?" But you wanted the episodes to be good and you wanted to tell great stories and you felt a responsibility to the shows and creators that came before. You didn't want to give Scott something disappointing to do. And he was such a trooper, he never complained. But if he called and thought something was "ehh . . ." you felt like crap because you didn't want to disappoint Scott. But the reality was it was kind of like triage. Sometimes if it's not working and it's fighting you, you just have to move on. You could spend another week making this better, but then everything else down the road suffers. And sometimes you don't have a choice. You don't have the resources.

STEPHEN BECK

Rick had veto power and Brannon had to interact with him and that was the biggest problem. We just didn't know what Rick would like. And it was hard, because Brannon could like it but Rick wouldn't like it. Brannon loved the Jacquemettons as writers and they were great. But at the end of their year, he said, "I want to keep you, but Rick doesn't." So that was the biggest dysfunction. The other was we had a lot of new ideas. As a group, I think we were pretty good, but because of Rick I think they tended to go back to things the way they did before.

ANDRÉ JACQUEMETTON

There was a weird political dynamic we were all sort of kind of cautious about from "Breaking the Ice." We wrote the first draft and we were excited and Brannon was excited, and then we had a meeting and it was like everything was tempered.

MARIE JACQUEMETTON

It was basically torn to pieces and reconstructed. There was a weird political dynamic between the two heads of the show. As lower-level writers, that was a huge learning experience, because we'd come from a show where there were basically four writers on *Baywatch* at the end there and our showrunner was very much, like, "Oh, you know, break the story, go write it, I'll polish it, and let's go."

FRED DEKKER

I don't know how to put it besides that the show was in Brannon's head and, to a degree, Rick's. And one of my frustrations of the show was that we as a staff weren't really privy to that. We didn't find the show. It was already in their heads and they didn't always articulate what that was, so we were always running around in the dark. It was partially miscommunication, but they really felt a little under the gun to deliver. And to me, it's a little bit like a sausage factory—you can't contemplate a name for a week like you can if you're writing a screenplay or a novel.

BRANNON BRAGA

The failure is ultimately on me. I struggled, particularly in that first year. It was hard, it was not a great time. What the show needed was probably a better showrunner, quite frankly. Maybe it needed Ron Moore. I wanted to do what Ron Moore had done with *Battlestar Galactica*.

STEPHEN BECK

My second episode was called "Oasis" and you'd go down onto a haunted planet with survivors there. Very similar to a show they did on *Next Generation,* that they had done before. And often they did that. Now, Brannon took the staff to his house and treated us to a nice wonderful evening. He took us to restaurants. He was very generous in those ways. And he could afford to be . . . he was hugely successful. At the end of the year, my contract ran out with three episodes left and I was let go.

DOMINIC KEATING

Brannon keeps his cards very close to his chest, but I always enjoyed his company, and whenever we see each other, he's very generous. He's fucking loaded, bless him; you never put your hands in your pocket when you're with him. It's always a very fun night when we see each other and we all hang out.

STEPHEN BECK

The people that they ended up keeping were people who really knew the *Star Trek* universe and knew how to write for *Star Trek.* The theory behind *Enterprise* was that you could loosen up the storyline, the character dynamic, and it could be a little more like the first one. Yet it ended up being mostly stylistically like *Next Generation* and *Voyager,* and a little less dynamic.

CHRIS BLACK

There was a consistency in the show that was carried through by the creative people who designed the show. Brilliant people. Nice people. Bob Blackman, Michael Westmore, all of these show effects guys. There was a consistency that carried over to the storytelling, too. There was a template, a *Star Trek* way. We were all huge *X-Files* fans, so we were excited when John Shiban came in during the second season. He came in with enthusiasm about wanting to shake things up. We would come into the room and start breaking stories, and John would come in and say that this was the new way of doing things. But it didn't really stick. That's not to say it would not have worked, but there was this inertia that this was a huge space-going *Titanic* that had been moving in the same direction for thirty years and it just wasn't going to turn. Not for the lack of deckhands trying to turn it.

STEPHEN BECK

When being a doctor, you do what you do and you do it well. You're rewarded by the patients getting better. *Enterprise* was the first job where I knew I was doing a good job and didn't get a proper reward. And you've got to learn that in Hollywood. Believe me, I look back and I was cleaning my garage and I found some typewritten ideas that I submitted and they were good. I was feeling a disconnect with what I thought were good ideas and not getting a response at all. Let alone a response I liked. But it taught me. For a long time it was painful, because I thought I was a failure. But you know, you do learn things, to be a part of that marvelous cultural experience. To this day, I am proud that I was a part of that and that I had the opportunity.

ANTOINETTE STELLA

The first season was eleven people . . . and one by one people left rather quickly.

MARIE JACQUEMETTON

We were close to everyone. There were no dividers, there was no room politics like you get on some shows. We were all trying to survive. Trying to get a story upstairs that got green-lit. That was it.

ANDRÉ JACQUEMETTON

And there was a lot of blood in the water. There was a revolving door . . . and a lot of people came through. Which is not good for morale. So, it made it difficult, but we all sort of banded together and did the best we could under the circumstances.

MARIE JACQUEMETTON

We were warned before we took the job, too. It was sort of known around town that *Star Trek*, in general, was a revolving door–type show where a lot of writers came in and out. But on the good side of that, it was an open policy, you know? Like you could pitch there even if you had no credits, and that was another thing that we got involved with that was a learning experience for us.

FRED DEKKER

It was a great living, I revere these people, I love them all to this day, but I was just feeling like I wasn't being valued. Nothing against Rick and Brannon, but if I wasn't invited back it wouldn't crush me. Brannon came into my office, the only time he did. He closed the door and I said, "I know why you're here." I was writing and directing my first feature within the first few years of joining the Writers Guild and so I was, for lack of a better term, spoiled as an auteur. There was a little bit of a disconnect coming into someone else's sandbox, because it wasn't my sandbox and I wasn't sure what was allowed.

> With the departure of virtually all the new writers who had been hired on staff first season, second season began with a new face in the writers room in the form of John Shiban, a producer on *The X-Files*, whose tenure would be short-lived. Also joining the staff was longtime *Star Trek* fan David A. Goodman, a veteran of numerous animated series, including *Futurama,* where he wrote the justly lauded *Star Trek* homage, "Where No Fan Has Gone Before."

DAVID A. GOODMAN

I was looking for work and I got an interview with *Firefly,* which was coming on its first season. The interview with Joss Whedon went very well. Joss is a very off-beat guy, very sweet, and I was a huge fan of that script, but I did not get a job offer. But Joss liked me and he basically told my agent that he would keep me in mind. I'd been a half-hour writer for so many years, I didn't think about trying to get a job on the staff of *Enterprise* because I really didn't have writing samples that were appropriate, but I had my *Futurama* scripts. So my agent calls Brannon and said, "Hey, you should look at this guy." And Brannon hadn't seen my *Futurama* episode, but the other people in the office had.

What my agent didn't know at the time is that Brannon had just lost a writer he wanted to hire, Jose Molina, to *Firefly.* They had been negotiating with Jose and he'd gotten a better offer at *Firefly* and he took that offer and didn't go on to *Enterprise.*

JOSE MOLINA
(co-executive producer, *Agent Carter*)

Brannon was one of the first people I ever met in Hollywood and is one of the reasons I got into TV writing in the first place. When he offered me a job on *Enterprise,* I felt like he was doing me a favor. My first show, *Dark Angel*—which was run by his friend René Echevarria—had just been canceled, I'd just gotten married, and I desperately needed a job or I'd have to go back to answering phones. I was . . . and am . . . enormously grateful to Brannon, but I felt lousy about getting a job offer out of what I assumed was pity. It didn't make me feel any better when Business Affairs contacted my agents with what was essentially a demotion: less money, lower title, etc. But I needed a job, so I accepted the job and asked my agents to negotiate a few details. It took about a week for the deal to close, and I took that time to e-mail everyone who had interviewed me that season to thank them for their time.

On the day before my *Enterprise* deal closed, I got a message on my answering machine from Tim Minear telling me not to take the *Star Trek* job just yet and to call him. So I did. He offered me a job on *Firefly* on the phone. I knew Tim and Joss Whedon from my assistant days, so I didn't even have to interview. The offer included a promotion and a raise. My *Firefly* deal closed that afternoon.

DAVID A. GOODMAN

My agent, not knowing any of this, said to Brannon, "I think you should meet with David because I think Joss is going to make him an offer." Now, Joss Whedon was *not* going to make me an offer; he was nice, he liked me, but Brannon was wanting to get back at Joss Whedon for stealing the writer he wanted, so he took a meeting with me thinking he was going to be stealing a writer from Joss, so I owe Jose Molina my career on *Star Trek.*

JOSE MOLINA

Years later I found out that Brannon didn't have a clue about the lowball Business Affairs offer. He'd offered me the *Enterprise* job fully on my merits, and not remotely because we had a personal relationship or because he felt bad for me. If the "business" side of "show business" hadn't interfered, my career would be very, very different . . . and that comedy hack David A. Goodman would've never soiled the good name of *Star Trek* with his so-called writing.

DAVID A. GOODMAN

I have the meeting with Brannon and in the meeting are John Shiban and Chris Black, who is a huge *Star Trek* fan and loved my *Futurama*. I go into this meeting having read every interview Brannon Braga has ever given at this point. I know the man very well and, not only that, I am basically parroting things he's said about *Star Trek* in the interview back to him: "The great thing about *Star Trek* is one week we can write a western and one week we can write a mystery." I was quoting him, but he didn't know that. He just thought I thought that, too, and that's how I always felt, so I was never better prepared for an interview. I was light in the interview and joking around and Brannon and Rick wanted *Enterprise* to be lighter, so they thought bringing a comedy writer on board was a good idea. I found out later from John Shiban that he didn't think I was a good fit and didn't think they should hire me, but Chris Black lobbied heavily for me and I became good friends with John as well.

John was trying to convince Brannon that this wasn't a good idea, but Brannon liked me enough to say I should get a meeting with Rick. The only thing I remember about the meeting with Rick was he had just gotten off the phone with Wil Wheaton and told him he'd been cut out of the movie *Nemesis,* which I thought was interesting. Then, I literally went home, and turned on the TV and saw Wil Wheaton talking about it and I was hearing the same conversation from a different side.

They hired me as a consulting producer on *Enterprise,* and I got there, and it was not what I expected. I got a very nice office that had its own bathroom and it was the office I had pitched to Brannon in years before when he was running *Voyager.* I had gone to the Hart Building so many times to pitch and never sold a freelance script, but now I was on the staff at *Star Trek*. It was sort of this dream come true.

CHRIS BLACK

Star Trek is this unique and special thing. But people look at the people who work on this show and it was like going to church every day. The fact is that it was a job. And at times, a very hard job. You're doing twenty-six episodes. The schedule was crazy! And you're trying to do stuff and get stuff done, and it's not that you're punting stories or that you don't care. You care deeply. But the reality of doing an hour-long episode is that you're not sitting around every day thinking how you're going to preserve Gene Roddenberry's legacy. You're thinking, What are they going to shoot tomorrow when the crew shows up at seven A.M.? And we have a production meeting later that day for an episode that's half a million dollars over budget. And Rick just gave us a bunch of notes. And we haven't even started break-ing this episode. And I'm calling my wife telling her I'm not going to make it home for dinner.

DAVID A. GOODMAN

Literally, my first day there, Chris Black, who by the time I had gotten there was clearly depressed, goes through everybody who got fired after the first season. There's a writer, Dave Wilcox, who was very friendly to me, and the week I start, he gets fired. I've never been on a show with that much turnover. I've been on shows where people got fired, but they wouldn't dump the whole staff in the first year. Chris really kind of scared me.

CHRIS BLACK

People look at my credits and say, "How could you do *Star Trek* and *Desperate Housewives*? How are you able to do both types of writing?" Writing is writing. It shouldn't be about the spaceship. If you're telling a good story, it can take place on Wisteria Lane or *Enterprise*. It doesn't matter. And that was the watchword, that if you're pitching a story that starts with *Enterprise* running into a weird spatial anomaly, that's not a story. If you're pitching a story that starts with Trip and Ar-cher discovering that T'Pol has a secret past? Oh! What's *that* story? It starts from character. The tech just comes after.

DAVID A. GOODMAN

I didn't have a lot of one-hour writing experience, so I got off to a rocky start. There was an idea floating around that would become "Precious Cargo," and it was Rick and Brannon's story. Brannon brought all the writers into his office and said, "Okay, Rick has this idea, this is the idea, who wants to write it?" And no one is raising their hand. So I said I'll take a shot, I'll write it, which was a mistake. I write dozens of outlines that John and Chris are trying to help me with and then, finally, I go off to draft and I turn it in.

Up to this point Brannon has been very friendly and he liked me, and then the door closes. He's not interested in seeing me anymore. This is sort of the pattern at *Enterprise*: You get one shot. It's not like there's something unfair about it, it's not a school, they're looking for people who know how to write, and he didn't think I did a good job and he didn't even think there was anything worthwhile for me to even keep rewriting. He took it away from me and Chris rewrote it.

MIKE SUSSMAN

There was nothing cutting-edge about *Star Trek* anymore in seasons one and two. We were, like, "Let's do more character-oriented shows." So we ended up doing some super low-concept shows and the character work we were doing wasn't fun. We were still doing very traditional *Star Trek* character stuff, but getting rid of the cool science-y, high-concept premise, the time travel and such. And we hadn't really replaced it with anything that was bringing us new viewers. We were just alienating the old viewers.

DAVID A. GOODMAN

It looked like I was going to get fired and I was desperately trying to figure out how to keep my job and get my option picked up. We're heading into December and I keep sending story documents to Brannon to no effect. There was a story going around that Brannon liked involving a Klingon trial, so I kind of worked it into this idea of this Klingon trial/flashback, weirdly similar in structure to my *Futurama* episode. I write this document up and I send it to Brannon. I don't hear anything and then I spent a lot of time trying to hang out at Brannon's assistant's [Terry Matalas] desk, trying to get to see Brannon and get a laugh out of him to see if I could ease the tension. I looked at Terry's desk and I see my idea that I wrote up for Brannon in this memo of story ideas he's sending to Rick. So he must have liked the idea but, in my opinion, he didn't want to give me credit for it because that would mean I would have to write it and then if I was writing a script they would have to pick up my option.

GENNIFER HUTCHISON (assistant to John Shiban)

I feel like there was more of an atmosphere at *Enterprise* of fear. If you don't do good, you're fired. That might not have been the intent, but I think that certainly was what was coming through. I feel like when people are in that situation, they're doing just enough work to not get fired. Just enough to not get yelled at or to not get in trouble. And that goes for any business. I just feel you could get so much more if you let people feel more safe and comfortable enough to really pick those ideas that might seem weird at first but turn out to be something great.

DAVID A. GOODMAN

I think Brannon didn't want to pick up my option, but he liked the idea. So he sends that memo over to Rick, and I'm in a writers' meeting with Brannon. I had heard that Rick had approved the Klingon story, but there was no way for me to confront Brannon about this, because he's my boss and I knew it would just upset him that I was looking at Terry's desk and it would get Terry in trouble. So we're in the writers' meeting and Brannon says we're thinking about the scripts we're going to write. He wasn't going to assign me one, and I said "Well, you know that Klingon story that you wrote up for Rick, I would love to do that."

In a certain way, in that moment I felt like Brannon knew I knew what he'd done; there was nothing he could do, no one else was chiming in. In that moment I sort of let him know, "Look, I know you sent that over there and I know I didn't get any credit for it, and that's okay, just give me the fucking script." And he did. I wrote the outline and he really loved my outline and he really liked my script. "Judgment" is an episode that fans hate for some reason, but I love it. It harkens back to sort of tying the Klingons from the original series to the Klingons in the *Next Gen* series.

I got my option picked up for the rest of the season, but at the end of the season they were not picking up John's option. In his last meeting with Brannon and Rick, on the way out the door, he said, "Keep David, he's really good." I thought that was an interesting arc in that I sort of succeeded with John, who is very talented. I learned a lot from him about one-hours. It was a great accomplishment, because Brannon still wasn't sure. Chris also lobbied heavily for me to come back, because he liked working with me, and then I came back for season three.

Season three would mark a dramatic departure for *Enterprise,* the show embracing a more serialized form of storytelling that had always been anathema to the series. Although Ira Behr had been able to serialize *Deep Space Nine* in its later seasons, he didn't have a network to answer to and Rick Berman had largely lost interest in the series as he focused his efforts on saving *Voyager.* In the season-long arc, the Earth is devastated by an attack by the Xindi, an attack that kills Trip's sister along with millions of other civilians. Starfleet learns an even more powerful attack is coming and dispatches the *Enterprise* to enter the Expanse, a mysterious region of space in which the Xindi, an alliance of several species, reside to prevent an even more devastating attack on the planet from being launched.

SCOTT BAKULA

I felt the second year had been successful in many ways in terms of introducing some stories and concepts, and continuing some from the first year. But I was feeling like we needed to get a little more serious and address some of these issues—I felt like we could not ignore the Temporal Cold War, ignore the Suliban, ignore the fact that I'm now a wanted escaped prisoner from the Klingon Empire—there were issues I felt needed to be addressed by this captain and this crew. It just felt like the show needed to take a heavier, more serious turn for a while.

BRANNON BRAGA

It wasn't until the end of season two when Jonathan Dolgen, king of all of Paramount, called us in and said, "You have to do something; the show is being renewed but you have to do something to shake things up." So we finally got to do what we wanted to do all along, which was a seasonal arc, which at that time was like a big deal. *24* was doing really well, and everyone was saying maybe we can do something serialized, too. I became creatively energized, and season three was actually really fun to do.

RICK BERMAN

When a show is having problems in the ratings, which *Enterprise* definitely was, the powers that be come and say, "What can you do to fix it?" Brannon and I spent a great deal of time thinking about that. We finally decided on doing something that *Star Trek* had never done before, which was to create a seasonal arc. On *Next Generation,* an arc never lasted more than two episodes. But you look at all of the shows that were having continuing storylines and we decided to try it. And we created a seasonal arc and I think it helped the ratings. Not a lot, but it definitely helped. It also allowed Archer to become a stronger character and a tougher character. The same thing is true with most of the cast.

SCOTT BAKULA

I say this, and I've never heard from Rick Berman or Brannon Braga if they hate that I say this, but there's a big part of me that feels that 9/11 influenced our show, influenced the writers and their state of mind. When they said, "We want to go in this darker direction," I said, "That feels appropriate to the times." You look at shows like *JAG*, which was still on then, and *NCIS* and shows that came out of the war . . . it's funny how all the war movies pretty much died, but the TV stuff that touched on it lived on. I felt like it was appropriate. I wish it had been that way from the top.

Joining the show was writer Manny Coto, who had recently wrapped showrunning his own sci-fi series, *Odyssey 5*, for Showtime. Coto, much like Fred Dekker before him, had started his career directing several popular cult horror films, including *Dr. Giggles*. He would subsequently go on to work on such acclaimed series as *24* and *Dexter*, after assuming command of *Enterprise* in season four.

MANNY COTO

I had no idea there was a mandate to hire people who didn't know *Trek*. I had created and produced a series called *Odyssey 5* for Showtime, which ran only one season, but Brannon had read the script and liked it very much. He thought it was really kind of *Star Trek* in tone, and so I just came in for a meeting. I remember they were in the middle of the Borg episode for *Enterprise* and Brannon was inspecting a prop. We sat down and I told him that I was very much a huge original series fan and that I was a pretty big *TNG* fan. I was kind of spotty at the time, quite frankly, with *Voyager* and *Deep Space Nine*.

I don't remember him being put off by it at all, I think we just hit it off on what kind of science fiction we liked and he brought me on. I was replacing somebody who had just been let go, so he was in pretty desperate straits. He had just lost a big writer that he'd let go [John Shiban] and the other writers weren't delivering scripts that made him happy, so he was pretty frazzled when I came on.

GENNIFER HUTCHISON

It was interesting because I was also a huge *Quantum Leap* fan, so I was so excited to be on a show with Scott Bakula. John was very enthusiastic to be there, but was working in a very entrenched system. *Enterprise* was the last of so many shows and I think there was a sort of a system that was going on and as a new writer coming on, it was hard to adapt to that. And to know these are the ideas that they're going to respond to. This is how it's going to work. There were a lot of personalities that had been there for so long. And it's hard to bring in your own voice without getting in trouble for it in some ways.

Also, it's *Star Trek*. So every idea has been done and as a result there's this huge barrier for entry there. Because as you come and prove yourself valuable, the first thirty things you pitch they're, like, "We almost did that one, but it doesn't work for this." As big as that world is, there's not a lot of room to sort of let your voice be known when there is such a history.

I remember one of the rules was they didn't want anybody to die in an episode. It was still really early on in the show. Ultimately they ended up killing so many people on that show with the war storylines. But John had an episode where Archer does the space walk on the hull of the ship, and originally there were going to be some redshirts in the episode. And they were, like, "No, you can't. You can't have anybody die."

So I think there was this frustration at not being able to tell a story that felt like it had higher stakes because of these rules that had been set out. It's just generally hard when there isn't that flexibility. This is what the show is and we don't deviate from it.

MANNY COTO

When I met with Brannon, he pitched me the whole Xindi arc. I remember being a little disappointed. I thought the idea was cool, but one of the things I was looking forward to doing on *Star Trek* was coming up with stand-alone episodes; sci-fi concepts that I could explore. When it became a season-long arc, I said, "Okay, I guess I won't be doing that." It was kind of a 9/11 allegory in a sense, so I signed on to the idea. Brannon wanted to make the show darker and a little more gritty, because it was perceived as kind of staid, so I was all for that.

BRANNON BRAGA

We *weren't* trying to do 9/11. The show premiered a week or two after 9/11. We didn't do the Xindi arc as a 9/11 metaphor. We did it because an attack on Earth hadn't been done in a while. Let's put Earth at stake so there's a larger purpose. And Manny Coto came on board and he was a fan of *Star Trek*. He got the show instantly and he could write the hell out of it, so I felt between him and Chris Black I finally had my core. By then I had the season figured out. I knew where it was all going to go, I knew how it would end, so it was a pleasure to do.

CHRIS BLACK

It's so funny, I don't remember any of that. I know now Brannon talks a lot about how it was supposed to reflect the darker worldview and faceless terrorist threats we can't deal with. I was at Paramount when 9/11 happened. I was standing in Brannon's office with [writer] Phyllis Strong, who worked in the financial district in New York. She was terrified that she had lost friends there, and Brannon said, "Go home if you want, stay here if you want." I remember the studio being shut down and our first day back at work. I think David Livingston was directing. We were all standing on set, everyone holding hands and having a moment of silence before they went on with the day's work.

MIKE SUSSMAN

We were shooting an episode that I had cowritten when 9/11 happened. It was a light-hearted romp on an alien planet and I can barely stand to watch the episode now, because it's like the light goes out of everybody's eyes.

CHRIS BLACK

I remember the line at the Paramount gate with the mirrors on sticks looking at cars for bombs. But I don't remember it affecting the storytelling. It was still to me, after I passed through the gauntlet of security, going into the writers room and doing the same job we were always doing. But I think it might have been the fact that Rick and Brannon excluded us from that process.

CONNOR TRINNEER

The show, after a couple of years, had to deal with the politics of survival, so then that became something that we all thought about, like how far could we go? And then at the end of the day you have to remember that 9/11 happened to us and that changed our show, I think it changed everybody and everybody's perspective, and our show got darker with the times. People either love that season or hate that season.

DAVID A. GOODMAN

In general, we didn't really work it out in a way that you needed to. It wasn't that detailed thing that you do on *24*, probably the most extreme version of it, where every script has to be so tightly connected to the next one. We needed to get a little closer to that than we got. We had ideas, Brannon had ideas that had to come out during the season, and he would sort of put them in episodes or build episodes around that stuff, but we weren't tightly engineering the season, really, until the tail end as you're leading up to the ending.

SCOTT BAKULA

The whole Xindi thing really captured my imagination. Part of it was really fanciful and appropriate for the world we were in, and I felt that had a lot of magic. I thought the pilot was really great. I got to do a lot of wonderful stuff that for me was challenging. It's why you do sci fi: to run across a bridge while the whole thing is blowing up behind you. You only get one shot at it. That's the kind of stuff that I love to do. All the stuff in the spacesuit, as painful as it was to do, was kind of great. The time travel stuff—I got a kick out of it. It was so wacky, but what are the odds that a guy who's done a series as a time traveler would roll into another series so many years later and a time element is introduced again, only completely different? For sci-fi fans like myself, that was just ironic and wonderful.

CHRIS BLACK

The Xindi was not something we cooked up in the writers room. It was not the network demanding something to shake things up. We're now confronting this radically different world. Let's brainstorm something different to do. It was just Brannon and Rick going off and saying, "Let's do this." And then coming back to the writers and saying, "Here's how it's going to be . . ." And us going, "Okay. Then we'll do that."

Which may be part of why I disinvested. I didn't feel like we were telling these darker stories about a post-9/11 world because we didn't participate in coming up with that. And there's nothing wrong with that. It's their show.

MIKE SUSSMAN

I remember very long meetings at Brannon's house over the summer before we started. I was equating it to *Star Blazers,* where we're off on a mission to save the Earth, and can we steal from that? I loved that we were allowed to get really dark. It was kind of this delayed response to 9/11, because *Star Trek* has always really so closely mirrored what's going on in politics in the real world in a peripheral situation, in the dynamics.

The third season when we did our sort of 9/11 allegory, that was almost two years later. And, strangely enough, the show was already struggling for relevancy *before* 9/11. After 9/11 it was *completely* irrelevant to a lot of people. Even certain fans of the show. What were we doing? I think like the rest of the world we were kind of in shock. And maybe in a little denial. Ultimately, we did a lot of 9/11 parallels in season four, which I think in many ways were done better with the whole Vulcan and Romulan situation, and stuff going on behind the scenes with people launching wars under false pretenses.

One of the more controversial choices during the third season was having Archer torture an Oosarian pirate, Orgoth, in the episode "Anomaly." But Jonathan Archer was no Jack Bauer, and while many viewers applauded his actions, even more were appalled.

MANNY COTO

I immediately found myself comfortable. When I came on during the Xindi arc, there was conflict and Bakula was torturing people in airlocks, so it was not the same *Star Trek* that others had come onto. I didn't really find myself butting heads. I thought it was a fairly mild torture scene; you got the impression that he wasn't actually going to kill the guy—at least I never thought he would. It was a question of stakes. He's protecting the lives of four billion people and, by the way, this wasn't even a nice guy, this was a thug, who he's just depriving of oxygen enough to knock him out. At the same time, it was totally against the *Star Trek* ethos; this was a prequel, people aren't the same as they were in the original series.

SCOTT BAKULA

My argument was always "Look, we don't really know how far Archer was going to take it and only Archer knows that." It's great food for thought. At the same time, if you contemplate the reality of the situation, what would you do to continue your mission if your mission were to save a planet full of people? What would Archer do? Different guys would do different things. Dick Cheney would do one thing and I would do a different thing, so it's just interesting to see a guy that you think you know and you've grown accustomed to and how he deals with situations for two years of shows. Whether you agree or disagree with the choice that we wrote, the fact that it got people talking showed that it's television that's working.

MIKE SUSSMAN

I just didn't understand it from the beginning. It's like, okay, there's a Pearl Harbor attack on the Earth, but the bad guy aliens are testing their weapon. And they're testing it on the planet they're going to attack—thereby giving a year's notice to these people. It's like the Japanese sending one plane over to Pearl Harbor and dropping a bomb. It just made no sense to me from the get-go. Why are these things happening aside from the fact that it'd be cool?

MANNY COTO

There was a lot of talk about making Bakula a stronger captain, that in the first two seasons he was indecisive, but a lot of that I felt was in the situations. For example, there was one episode where he was obsessed with finding out what was creaking underneath his floor. It's not Bakula's performance, he was told to get on his hands and knees and look for a sound. He's never going to come off as a heroic captain like that. In season three, we were going to toughen him up, but in my opinion, you don't toughen him up by making him hysterical and running around screaming at people, you make him weaker. The quiet strength is the guy who is able to govern his passions.

DOMINIC KEATING

I didn't have much to do other than come rescue the captain the whole time. In all honesty, there were several of those scripts I never read all the way through. I flicked around the scenes I was in, I don't have to know anything else. The Xindi stuff came out heartfelt and well-meant. It was a reaction to 9/11, but I thought some of the handling of the subject matter was a little jingoistic, so to speak. It was certainly in step with a lot of the feeling in America. With hindsight it comes off a little heavy-handed.

MANNY COTO

In making Bakula so angry, Trip became someone whose point of view got lost throughout the season, his feeling for losing his loved one was kind of muted because Archer was so nuts, and I don't even know what Dominic's point of view was. If we were doing the airlock scene now, I would probably make Trip be the one who took the bull by the horns against Archer's orders and put the guy in the chamber and have Bakula come in and stop him at the last minute. The season was set up with Trip being the one saying I want to kill these motherfuckers, so that was the perfect setup to have Trip be the one to lose his shit and Bakula being the one who has to rein him in.

If I was pitching for that season now, I would argue for an interesting arc where Trip leads a mutiny against Archer for being too weak, and do a kind of *Crimson Tide* where Trip ultimately comes back to his senses. *That* would have been interesting and have made both characters stronger.

DAVID A. GOODMAN

I always feel looking back that we didn't do a good enough job working out the details. It was cool stuff, but we didn't fully flesh it out. Years later, I got to write this book, *Star Trek: Federation,* which was this sort of faux history of the Federation, and I had to figure out some way to make the Xindi stuff make sense, and it doesn't make sense because, as writers, we didn't do enough figuring out, the way the writers did on *Deep Space Nine*'s Founder's Saga.

CONNOR TRINNEER

For the first couple of years, no one seemed to know if it was going to be Trip and T'Pol or the captain and T'Pol. During the Xindi arc when she was doing all that neuro-pressure or whatever it was called to help him get through the death of his sister, she and Trip began to develop a deepened relationship. I don't think it was ever on the page initially. What I liked about it was that it was a complicated relationship and it was one where he was trying to find common ground where they could relate to one another. That's definitely kind of real life-ish. The fact she was a Vulcan and he was a human was a nice facet of the relationship. It was an odd couple.

CHRIS BLACK

There was an effort to make the show sexier. Obviously every show has that character. *Voyager* had Seven of Nine and Jolene was Jolene. This striking actress in a tight outfit. There was a component of that show that was supposed to be sexy. And that goes back to the original series. Look at the costumes originally designed for those women. It's like the joke, something you threw on and almost missed. The decontamination stuff got a little out of hand. I admired what they were trying to do with the T'Pol/Trip relationship. I thought that was interesting.

If you look at the original series, Spock had a Vulcan father and a human mother, and I always wondered how that worked. And they don't talk about it much. A couple of scenes in the original series, but not much. What kind of marriage is that? A marriage with one person who can't be demonstratively passionate or emotional. What is that like? So the idea of a relationship like that playing out between two of your leads was really appealing. Let's try to make this a real romance. But it became what it was. A little lurid. I can't honestly recall where that came from. I know the actors weren't hugely enthusiastic. I cannot argue with the assessment that it felt gratuitous.

MANNY COTO

I thought they were silly; it was less about the obvious attempt to get hot bodies on there, but are you really going to be decontaminating by spreading this gel all over your body? It doesn't seem like a very efficient way to decontaminate. I would rather have them strip and get hit by a beam. Not "We're going to spread gel all over each other." What if you missed a spot?

DAVID A. GOODMAN

I didn't like the decontamination chamber scenes mostly because what those scenes show you is what you *can't* do. If everybody is good with the stuff and Trip isn't going to get an erection being with T'Pol, then they take their clothes off and they rub it all over themselves, but instead, because it's network TV, they have to stay half dressed. What about the parts of their bodies that are covered by their clothes? All of the things you can't do because it's TV and we're suggesting something really sexy, but if we want to show the future, we're going to take their clothes off. If Roddenberry's idea of the future is accurate or possible, that's what would happen.

CHRIS BLACK

After three seasons I was done. They offered me a lot to come back. To be executive producer. They offered me more money than I had ever made on a show before. But after three years, I couldn't work creatively this way.

DAVID A. GOODMAN

In the two years I was there, *Family Guy*, which I'd worked on, had gone off the air but had come into its own on DVD and reruns. Rick Berman had become a fan through his son, so I get these calls during the day from Rick wanting to talk about *Family Guy*, like, "How did you get away with saying that Ted Turner fucked the dog?" And so it helped in my work situation, because I arranged for Seth MacFarlane, who was my friend, to come in and meet Rick and Rick's son, who was a huge fan. After Seth leaves, I said to Rick that Seth's an actor and he'd love to be on *Star Trek*. So then Seth's first cameo is as an engineer in "The Forgotten." Then he came back in season four, and that's how he and Brannon became friends and ended up doing *Cosmos* together.

At the end of season three, *Family Guy* was coming back, and Seth asked me to go run it with him, so I left, but it was this sort of fulfillment of a lifetime dream where I got to write *Star Trek*.

BRANNON BRAGA

When season three was over, I was done. Manny had great ideas for season four and I was turning it over to him.

SCOTT BAKULA

I didn't want to stop, because we were really starting to go into new places. Which is hard to do when you're the fifth series in a franchise. It was a great time. In four years, there was some pretty intelligent, rich work there.

ANDRÉ BORMANIS

Where we disappointed the fans was in not really embracing the prequel element. For instance, Fred Dekker very much had to push and fight for the Andorians. "Bring in the Andorians. Let's see how humanity first met these guys with the antennas." And again, Rick and Brannon, not big fans of the original. They're just not that familiar with it. And they were harder to convince to do those explicitly prequel kind of shows. You're never going to please everybody.

DAVID A. GOODMAN

The problem with *Enterprise* to me, having been there, was that Rick and Brannon, in some ways, didn't like their own ship. You can sort of see it in the design, the *Enterprise* bridge is gray and dark, and it's attempting to be cool, but it feels like a place you don't really want to be.

LINDA PARK

I think we hedged between going where no other show has gone before and not wanting to upset the fan base, and that's somewhere in the middle. You can't run a show based on those thoughts, you have to run a show on telling the best story.

DOMINIC KEATING

Rick [Berman], God bless him, gave me the job, but Brannon Braga was the creative mind behind that show for at least fifteen years. With Rick, he was an accountant, really. He was a bean counter that was put in charge of Roddenberry to make sure the crazy, wacky dude didn't spend too much money.

DAVID A. GOODMAN

I think that, honestly, they were done with *Star Trek* and, artistically, they didn't create a place that anyone wanted to be, because *they* didn't want to be there. It was always an uphill battle on *Enterprise* to write real *Star Trek* stories and they didn't want to. As a result, we went back to a lot of retreads that had been done on previous series. I remember getting a call from J. Michael Straczynksi about *Star Trek,* and he said it's like they have this pristine Cadillac and they're keeping it in the garage.

J. MICHAEL STRACZYNSKI
(creator/executive producer, *Babylon 5*)

In the *Star Trek* universe we've overcome everything. The policy among the writers of that series is that the characters can have no inner doubts or flaws or fears, and I think the process of overcoming is more interesting than having overcome.

It's more dramatically interesting. You never see a shot of Picard using the men's room on the *Enterprise*.

BRANNON BRAGA

The people who took over the network I don't think liked the show. It wasn't part of their game plan when CBS took over UPN. They didn't understand it and it wasn't part of how they wanted to brand things, and they wanted it to be younger. They made a deal with a music company of some sort, and they had access to some hot acts, like boy bands, that were popular at the time. They wanted us to try and work in these musical acts on the show. I remember I was pitching some season-two ideas and they were, like, "Can you get a song on the show every week?" I asked, "Where would they be playing?"

MIKE SUSSMAN

There was a changeover in administration at the end of season two with the whole CBS/Viacom split. I can't remember the details. Basically all the UPN guys who had been our best buddies since the mid-90s were gone. We had this new group of people sort of running things. And they were looking at the numbers going south and they weren't particularly fans of the franchise. They didn't know what it meant institutionally, because they were a brand-new institution. It wasn't Paramount anymore. It was this split-company and CBS. And it's funny, because CBS has now sort of rediscovered the value of the franchise. The consumer products are all over exploiting *Next Gen* and the original show now. There's more stuff than there was ten years ago. And of course the Blu-rays came out of that. But at the time I think they were looking at the raw Nielsen numbers of the show and saying "Why is this still on the air?"

RICK BERMAN

When CBS took over, we had developed a degree of trust with the people at Paramount who basically ran UPN or the syndication. So, it was just one set of executives. They trusted us, they believed us, and they didn't give us any notes. When people like Dean Valentine got involved with UPN, he pretty much had been told, don't bother giving notes, and he didn't, and we had a great relationship. Most television producers and writers get notes from both the studio and the network. We were getting notes from neither. And then CBS took over halfway through *Enterprise* and we started getting notes.

You had these young executives who feel they are not doing their job unless they are giving you notes. And it was frustrating, but it was more frustrating for Brannon than me. The rule of thumb became that there were three categories of notes. You're far too busy to spend a lot of time on these notes. Give them a quick look. If a note is a good note, don't be stupid, take advantage of it. If a note is a note that doesn't hurt one way or another, for example they want to change an adjective, give them the benefit of the doubt and do the change. If the note is harmful or stupid, ignore it. That's the rule that we all came up with and that's the rule that we followed. The network rarely came back and said, "You didn't do note seventeen."

But, it was a pain in the ass to get faxes of sheet after sheet of notes every day coming from people who didn't know really what we were doing. But we managed to get ourselves around it.

BRANNON BRAGA

I was pitching a story where our captain and another crew member spend the entire episode stuck on the hull of the ship, which was a daring production challenge, and I was asked "What's a hull?" by the network. And so we were the only people who understood the show. To be blunt, I don't think they appreciated the show, and at a time when *Star Trek* was at its most vulnerable, it was at a place that was not protecting it or nourishing it, so that didn't help.

MIKE SUSSMAN

I certainly think that the people I was working for could have done a better job of welcoming their new overlords and bringing them in and saying "This is what we're trying to do." Instead there was a lot of "these are the new guys and we don't like them and they don't like us." Inevitably, you're going to get canceled in that situation when you're at war with the people who run the network.

DOMINIC KEATING

Les [Moonves] was the golden boy of Viacom, and CBS was the most watched network in the universe. Les was charged with bringing UPN similar success. He put

Dawn Ostroff in the big chair at UPN, and Rick started getting notes. After four hit shows and being the Prince of Paramount, he's getting notes about his show. Some of them are legendary: "Can we put a boy band in the mess hall scenes? Does Jolene have to wear the pointy ears? She'd be so much cuter without them." Rick just ignored it.

I was in the *Star Trek* directing school and I was very close to getting my first episode to direct, I put hours and hours into shadowing directors and sitting in the edit suites and many, many meetings with Rick. Then he had to call me in and let me know that it was looking very unlikely that I would ever get to do this, because he just basically ignored these stupid notes and the suggestions of how he would run his show. In response to that, the edict came down from UPN that they had last call on all directors and writers and that no new directors and writers could be brought on the show without their say-so. So he wasn't going to go to bat for me and lose his bargaining chip and it never happened. Whatever way they could yank his chain . . .

MANNY COTO

When the ratings sagged, they tried to insert themselves and come up with these notes and Rick was "Nope, I'm going to do what I want." Ultimately, no one interfered with him. For season four, some executives took me to lunch and they were trying to reinsert themselves a little more, and Rick found out about it and they were quickly shut down. They weren't going to give notes. So there might have been feeble attempts, but no real interference.

SCOTT BAKULA

I don't read that stuff, because I'm a baby and don't want to read negative comments, because when you're in the midst of it and having to do the work every day, how does that help you? I'm not writing the show, I'm not creating the show, and for me to hear that people don't like my dog or don't like the theme song . . . it doesn't help me. So I don't search that stuff out. But I thought that if you really break it down, in the middle of the second season we were kind of flowing into that Xindi arc and I thought the show from then on never really slowed down. I *love* that whole arc and that's where I thought the show just got better and better.

MIKE SUSSMAN

We didn't know if we were coming back for a fourth season, and I think whether Rick and Brannon had planned it or not, they'd done something absolutely brilliant in that they ended season three with a cliffhanger. The network was unaware of this. When we sent them all the scripts, nobody read them apparently, and we realized after we had sent the crew home and the actors were on vacation and the sets had been struck, that we'd written and filmed a cliffhanger. They were seriously considering canceling the show, but they knew the blowback they would get from canceling *Star Trek,* of all things, on a cliffhanger. They basically demanded that we undo the cliffhanger in editing or a reshoot, which was impossible. So did that help us get a season four? Maybe it did. Maybe it didn't. I know they lowered the license fee for the following year.

RICK BERMAN

For the fourth season it wasn't so much what we did, it was really what the studio did. The studio went to the people and UPN and talked them into giving us one more season. We were all the same company and, basically, if you can get up to a hundred episodes, it makes a television show much more valuable. At that point we were around the seventy five episode mark. They offered to lower the license fee a little bit, which made it more attractive to the network, and they finally agreed to give us a fourth season.

MANNY COTO

My idea was, let's find cool ideas that have some tie, some relevance with the original series; let's use this as a prequel, let's make a prequel. And let's have fun. We were all huge *Star Trek* fans, André and Sussman and I were all original series fans, so let's have fun and do stories that we'll all really enjoy.

DAVID A. GOODMAN

Manny came in and said, I'm here to help you, what do you need me to do? So he earned Rick and Brannon's trust in some way, and they gave him the freedom to run the show in season four and do what he wanted. The rest of us would butt heads a little too much, and as a result, you're not going to succeed that way. There's only going to be so much original series references in this, we're not going to really be drawing a connection to the original series even though we take place before most of the things we've done before. There were things we could have done, but Rick and Brannon were locked into their kind of show for a long time and they were going to keep doing it and you couldn't really break the way they did it.

BRANNON BRAGA

I didn't know how long the show would run; I thought maybe it would run four years or it could run seven, but I was just done. I thought season three was a blast and I was done. Manny was poised to take the show to a whole other level, which he did. I think I rewrote an episode for him in season four, but I really had nothing to do with it. It was all Manny.

MIKE SUSSMAN

Brannon never left. There was this weird narrative like he wasn't there. He was still writing. He was still giving notes. The day-to-day running of the staff Manny had sort of taken over. I remember even a couple of times being told he was taking a step back, but Brannon was still my boss and he was still Manny's boss.

MANNY COTO

Brannon's a little more anal-retentive and a little bit more exacting. He's got his own way of doing things; we would talk through the stories and then Brannon would get into the room with the writer of the episode, a story assistant, and he would dictate the outline as the story assistant would write it out, beat by beat, so the writer wouldn't write the outline, Brannon wrote the outline, which was an astounding feat. I couldn't do that. He would dictate the whole outline and the writer went off and wrote. My feeling was that once you beat out an episode, the writer should go off and write the outline, it's their episode, they're the ones who should see the outline through and flesh it out. They're the ones who are going to have to write the script. So I don't know if that helped or not, but I wasn't about to stand in front of a script assistant and dictate a whole outline that a writer is supposed to be writing. Everyone was going to write their own episodes, we'll beat it out together line by line and whiteboard card by card, but you go off and flesh it out.

ANDRÉ JACQUEMETTON

The way Brannon worked is, his juices didn't start kicking in until late in the day, and Marie and I had a young child at the time. When you do your eleven, twelve hours, you're ready to go home, and then you get summoned at seven o'clock at night, and Brannon's, like, "Hey, we're ready to go! Have a drink!"

MANNY COTO

As far as the room goes, when I was there, Brannon didn't have much of a room. The writers would meet on their own and come up with ideas and stories and they would be pitched to Brannon and Brannon would say yes or no. So there wasn't a working room that I was part of. Brannon and I worked together a lot, he liked my work, so I guess he thought this is great.

My room was different in the sense that there was a room. We all got together and would come up with stories and beat them out. In season three, there was Sussman and Chris Black, who was great, and that was kind of it as far as the writers went. David A. Goodman was great, but he was leaving to go do animation, so there weren't many people writing. For season four, I brought in the Reeves-Stevenses and Alan Brennert and a couple of other writers and André [Bormanis] was there, so we had a room. Different showrunners run things differently and Brannon did a lot on his own. I don't know if one way is better or not.

GARFIELD REEVES-STEVENS (coproducer, *Star Trek: Enterprise*)

We got a phone call one day from our agent, who said Manny Coto had called him. This was toward the end of season three and Manny knew we wrote *Star Trek* novels and had asked if we'd ever written scripts. For all the years we had hung out at Paramount to do the behind-the-scenes books, we had early on decided that we would always present ourselves as book writers and *not* as scriptwriters, because it seemed everybody in the world was trying to pitch those guys and they were under siege, so to put them at their ease, we never said anything about our script writing.

JUDITH REEVES-STEVENS (coproducer, *Star Trek: Enterprise*)

I also think that Mike Sussman had mentioned the fact that we'd written *Federation* and that spoke to the themes of what Manny was interested in developing in season four.

GARFIELD REEVES-STEVENS

Before season four was officially picked up, Manny and Mike and André all got together at Paramount, sort of off the record, to start talking about what they wanted to see in season four.

JUDITH REEVES-STEVENS

And when they called us in, they did so before they got going on season four. Then we didn't hear from them again until, I believe, August of that year. They were already shooting Mike's episode, "Home," and they were up to about episode six, and we joined them, with that one in progress, and within two weeks we were writing the outline for the next episode. We were just thrown into it. But it was fun, because they still had things to niche up, and that's something that we love doing and that we've done in books before with *Trek*.

GARFIELD REEVES-STEVENS

We particularly liked the idea in the pilot and all through the first three seasons that the Vulcans weren't really good guys. They were sort of holding us back, because that, to us, really fit in with *Star Trek*'s themes: that our enemies can become our friends. The Klingons were the bad guys in *The Original Series*, but you could see in *The Next Generation* they were coming around to someday they were going to be firmly the Federation's allies.

JUDITH REEVES-STEVENS

Those stories hadn't been told, so we were able to contribute and add to *Star Trek* lore with that. That was a real privilege.

With Brannon Braga sidelining himself from the action, Manny Coto was in a position to deliver the *Enterprise* season most fans had always wanted, a show that paid homage to the original series and revisited fan favorite elements. In a strange way, *Enterprise* season four was redolent of the final year of the original *Star Trek* in which the network had been alienated by the series overlord, a new showrunner was in place, and budgets were cut in anticipation of imminent cancelation. Unlike season three of the original series, *Enterprise*'s final year is considered its best by most viewers.

RICK BERMAN

Manny is a huge *Star Trek* fan. When I say *Star Trek,* I'm talking mainly the original series. So what he brought to the table was a great love for what was going to be coming in ninety years. He was able to bring to the canon things that the fans loved; things that set up storylines that the fans of the original series knew would be paid off in various episodes of the Kirk and Spock era. He created storylines from many episodes that did tie into the original series, and the fans of the original series enjoyed that.

ANDRÉ BORMANIS

Manny Coto initially had to convince Rick to go in that direction. And Brannon gave him the reins. It was his show to do what he wanted to do. He made the case that people want to see these kinds of stories. We were going to get a fourth season, which was in doubt at the end of the third season, and Manny very much argued that if we want to have a shot at a fifth, this is what we need to do. And he was absolutely right.

GARFIELD REEVES-STEVENS

When Manny took over, we saw a similarity to *Next Generation* in that at the beginning Gene wanted to draw that line between the original series and *Next Generation*. He didn't want to sort of explicitly make that connection. He wanted the series to stand on its own, and it finally reached a point where he said, "Okay, let's test the waters. Let's bring in Sarek as a character, and really unite the two series." Once *Next Generation* had established itself firmly, then of course it could draw on *The Original Series* and make all those connections. And that led to *Generations,* where the two captains met. So for *Enterprise* it seemed to us that Rick and Brannon drew that line. They said, "Let's make sure the show stands on its own."

JUDITH REEVES-STEVENS

When they opened the barn door, we were fortunate enough to be there and go through it.

RICK BERMAN

You have to understand, because I didn't really watch the original *Star Trek* until twenty years after it was made, it was very hokey for me. The way it was lit, the performances, the set decorations. It was a hokey show from the sixties. It had some great stories and some great philosophy and some great concepts, but I just really couldn't get into it that much twenty years later having not been a fan earlier.

Manny, who is a remarkable writer and incredibly enthusiastic, was passionate about wanting to do certain things . . . and it was my nineteenth year of doing *Star Trek*. The ratings were not great and both Brannon and I felt why not let Manny do what he wants, God bless him. He did it—and it didn't change the ratings—but it did make a lot of fans happy, which I was pleased with.

DOMINIC KEATING

I remember when Manny came on board as a staff writer and he wrote a Xindi episode. I read that one all the way through and immediately rang him up to say, "Welcome aboard, mate, that was really a very special reading," and he said, "Oh, thanks, man." He did a great job. From what I hear from the fans, we were really hitting our stride and there was some interesting stuff for Malcolm with Section 31 and his torn allegiances. We easily had another three years in us, that's for sure.

MANNY COTO

I just went in and said, "This is what I think we should do for the last season." Season three had ended, and the ratings were really low, and they didn't know if they were coming back or not, and they ended up getting a slightly reduced order. Brannon said, "You're running the show, and basically it's going to be what you want to do." I had already pitched to him what I thought it should be, and so I went in to see Rick and told him what we wanted to do. He was very excited about it. I was a little bummed, because I got left with the old Scott Bakula in World War II cliffhanger from season three, and for a while Rick was pitching doing the whole season in World War II. At that point, I was, like, "I'm not doing this, I might have to leave. I am not doing an entire season in World War II."

MIKE SUSSMAN

Between season three and season four, we hadn't gotten the official pickup, and Manny is in the office and he told me, "I don't know that we're actually coming back, but if you want to come in and brainstorm some ideas just in case, because we are going to be fucked if they give us a late pickup." Which they ended up doing. And we didn't have anything done. I went in and on his whiteboard he had basically all the big two- or three-episode arcs: "Vulcan Reformation," "Romulan," "Mirror Universe," etc. He just had this laundry list of things he wanted to do, and we just started talking more and more about these stories, and I'm thinking, it's never going to happen. The show's going to get canceled. We're not going to get to do the show that we always wanted to do. And what a tragedy that's going to be. And then, bizarrely enough, we got renewed for another year, and "it was glorious," to quote Commander Kor. It was a ton of fun.

MANNY COTO

Even those first two episodes that were going to take place back in time in World War II, I pitched the alternate universe where you have the Nazis occupying the United States. At least to me, I can find that interesting. I love all that stuff. So from that point, I said we'll do two and then I want to do other cool stuff and Rick was, like, "Okay, do it."

MIKE SUSSMAN

Now, *Enterprise* ultimately got pulled into a very fan service-y kind of direction, but that was the kind of the thing I wanted to do at the beginning. When Manny came on board we were able to do it, because people honestly just stopped caring. They were just rounding out the syndication order. We got to have fun with it. And that last year of *Enterprise* is the most fun I've ever had working in TV, because they did just leave us alone. We rebuilt the sixties sets and brought Brent Spiner back on our show. It was probably a little too much. And that was after years and years of incredible restraint.

JAMES L. CONWAY

The last season of *Enterprise* was very fresh. I thought they rejuvenated that series.

MIKE SUSSMAN

I was an intern on *Voyager* in the mid-90s, and one of the things that Michael Piller's assistant told me was, don't show them that you're a fan. They'll think you're nuts.

CHRIS BLACK

I must confess I did not watch a single episode of season four. And it was not bitterness or sour grapes, it was just that you're just kind of done. You just walk away. I did that job and that job's behind me. I still had friends on the show, and I heard Manny really stepped up in a way that, quite frankly, I did not. He seized the reins and said these were the stories we should tell. It was an opportunity for him to take control of the show. And from what I understand, for the better. A lot of people were very happy. But to me, as fun as it is to see Scott wearing a velour tunic or Jolene in a short minidress, that's not what *Enterprise* was supposed to be.

In a way, we gave up trying to do something different. The premise and promise of that show was to take *Star Trek* to the next level. Let's do something people haven't seen before and get them excited about that. We did three seasons of that and it didn't work so, fuck it, we'll give them the old *Star Trek*. Give them what they want. Give them the Mirror Universe. Whatever. To me, it felt like giving up.

MIKE SUSSMAN

Ultimately, having a familiarity with a franchise as a writer only helps you. With *Enterprise* they brought in all these new writers after they pretty much got rid of the entire *Voyager* writing staff. But some of these writers just weren't aware of the six hundred episodes that had been done before. And people were constantly pitching stories that had been done or were clichés or we were never going to do. On the one hand, you need people who maybe had not seen every hour of the six hundred or seven hundred hours of whatever it is, but if you haven't, stories are going to get repetitive pretty quickly. That's going to be a challenge for the franchise moving forward at some point.

SCOTT BAKULA

We got into kind of the wrap-up mode on the fourth season. I felt like the pilot had that flavor, that dark side to it, and then we lost that and got kind of into more traditional, conventional *Star Trek* kinds of episodes, some of which were fantastic, some of which felt a little bit like we'd seen it before, and then we got away from that and it thrilled me. I encouraged them every step of the way to go there. Again, it wasn't my show to run, but I did throw in my two cents every once in a while.

MIKE SUSSMAN

I adore Scott and I think he is really wonderful. The role as originally intended was much more Scott's forte. He did his best and rose to the occasion, but for me, aside from Shatner and Patrick Stewart, none of the captains have quite had that whatever "it" is. That Shakespearean heft that those two guys had. That role really changed through a number of years. But I never heard any whispers of Scott being fired. I don't think that would have helped the show. I think that would have just pissed off the fifty fans we had left at that point.

MANNY COTO

We were always going to stick with Scott. I remember at one point we debated actually killing Scott as a way to inject a dramatic situation into the fourth season, where the characters now have to get used to someone brand-new coming on board. This person would have a totally different way of doing things and have a totally different outlook, and so you would have Trip and the rest of the characters kind of butting heads against this individual, whoever he or she might be, but we decided not to. It's a little like the shift in *M*A*S*H*.

I figured you could do the same thing with this; start off with a character nobody liked, butting heads, and they end up respecting him. That was one where Rick said no. It was a radical change, but I probably would have done it if we had known we were going for seven seasons. We didn't have to kill Bakula, he would have just been gone part of the season.

> One of the most inventive concepts Coto implemented in season four was the idea of mini-arcs, multiple-part episodes that would allow the producers to amortize their costs over several episodes and provide an even more epic scale to the series despite the show's reduced budget.

MANNY COTO

I said you've done the season-long arc and we're not going to do that again, but let's do mini-arcs. I knew there was an interesting opportunity with the Vulcans. The Vulcans that Rick and Brannon had set up were very different from the Vulcans we remember from the original series, and I thought there was a great opportunity to do an episode which bridged those two cultures and to develop a story about how they'd floundered from the original teachings of Surak, but that felt to me like a sweeping *Dune*-like epic. I didn't want to do it as the whole sea-son, so I said let's do these three-episode arcs. My fantasy was that someday some-one would cut them together and do *Enterprise* mini-features.

MIKE SUSSMAN

It was a blessing in disguise ultimately, because we couldn't build as much since the budget had been cut, so we had to do two- or three-parters. If you're going to build a giant Vulcan set or re-create the original series bridge, you're going to have to use it in more than one episode. Which meant we could then delve deeper into the characters and spend more time in these environments.

JUDITH REEVES-STEVENS

Those two- and three-parters are interesting in that they're like shared universe writing, because you can start it off and even if you're involved on the arc, you don't know exactly where it's going once it goes into someone else's hands.

GARFIELD REEVES-STEVENS

I remember Brannon commenting on the Vulcan arc, saying, "Whoever got the last one, it was a thankless job, because they had to pull everything together."

MIKE SUSSMAN

It's funny how everyone talks about serialization in terms of TV and serializing something over twenty-four episodes or thirteen or ten episodes. But we were doing two- or three-part stories that were great for *Star Trek*. They were movies basically spread over two or three episodes that worked perfectly. Twenty-two episodes felt really unwieldy for a single story. And the one-hour stand-alone feels like old-timey sixties television. We sort of stumbled upon this happy medium simply as a matter of this was all we could afford to do.

MANNY COTO

From that point on, we just jumped onto that. It wasn't something that came out of cost. That wasn't the original plan, although it helped. The original plan was just to tell larger arcs, larger stories that we couldn't tell in forty-two minutes and that we didn't want to spend the whole season on. We settled on this and we started plotting out the season that way—let's do the Vulcans, let's do the Augment story—and so it became a great way to do it.

The storyline of "The Augments" dealt with genetically enhanced beings designed by Dr. Arik Soong (ancestor to Data's creator, Dr. Noonian Soong), and saw *Next Generation*'s Brent Spiner cast in the role as a eugenics pioneer.

MANNY COTO

That was actually Rick and Brannon. Originally, the character was going to be Colonel Green, because I've always been obsessed by Colonel Green [from *TOS* "The Savage Curtain"], don't ask me why. And then Rick said Brent Spiner wants to do one, so we retooled the part for him and he was great.

JUDITH REEVES-STEVENS

That was in place before we got there. They were bringing together all sorts of elements, and favorite people and characters, and pulling threads together. Very much an integrated season.

GARFIELD REEVES-STEVENS

Along those lines, one of the last ones we pitched to Manny was that we bring back the woman who played the Borg Queen [Alice Krige] and have her as a Starfleet medical technician who was investigating the Borg technology from that earlier episode, and she ends up being kidnapped by the Borg. We all know what happens to her. Manny liked it, but he said he didn't want to get into *Next Generation* in that season. He wanted to concentrate on the original series.

MIKE SUSSMAN

We'd been trying to do the Mirror Universe all season. In fact, we were trying to find a way to take that Nazi cliffhanger and say, "Hey, we're actually in the Mirror Universe," but we couldn't make that work. And then there was a long period of time when they were negotiating with Shatner about him being on the show, but he just wanted too much money to come back.

MANNY COTO

The Reeves-Stevenses had a story idea, which was a really cool idea, based on the original "Mirror, Mirror" episode where the Tantalus Field would make people vanish. The idea was people wouldn't actually die, that they were transported to a pocket universe and, in theory, the James T. Kirk character/Tiberius Kirk from the alternative universe would end up there as a result of his own Tantalus Field at the end of the episode, since Good Kirk had given Spock advice about the Tantalus Field in his cabin. So Tiberius and a number of other unsavory individuals from the Mirror Universe are there in this pocket universe and our ship accidentally penetrates it. Tiberius Kirk finds a way to get the fuck out of there and he's going to take over our ship. It would be our ship against evil Tiberius Kirk. Fantastic! We pitched this to Rick and he thought it was great.

JUDITH REEVES-STEVENS

What we said to Bill was that instead of being Captain Kirk, you're Tiberius.

GARFIELD REEVES-STEVENS

And the idea was that Tiberius is the guy who causes the split in the timeline that creates the Mirror Universe.

MANNY COTO

So we had lunch with Shatner—Rick, Brannon, and myself—and pitched it to him. He thought it was great, too. During that lunch, Brannon and I had to show him how to use his new cell phone. I remember he was having trouble; it was like Kirk trying to figure out how to use a cell phone. He was, like, "I have to get it to work . . . this is important . . . what am I going to do?" So we finally got it to work and after lunch Bill made one comment, as we were leaving and said, "You know this is going to cost you?"

And Rick was laughing, but ultimately what happened was that Paramount did a study or survey and didn't feel bringing back Shatner would raise ratings enough to warrant the amount of money he wanted, which was considerable. Paramount felt they had already decided this was the last season. "We're going to move on, so why bother trying to do anything truly exciting?" And that's what happened. The episode would have made a lot of money, but at the time they really didn't give a shit.

MIKE SUSSMAN

I remember I was in Rick's office and UPN was trying to figure out if it was worth spending the money to get him. It was like $100,000 an episode. They put together a little commercial that just had file footage of Kirk. And they're, like, "The Legend Returns." And they were showing it to the people in Vegas to see what they would say, and there wasn't really that much of a bump. It would have been great to have him on the show, but you're also getting Bill Shatner in his mid-seventies, not even *Wrath of Khan* Shatner. He had a story that he cooked up with Judy and Gar that I'm sure would have been a lot of fun, but when that fell through, I said, "Great, I'm doing my Mirror story."

MANNY COTO

I remember Rick looking at the dailies and he was commenting on how great the actors were and how much they had come to life and how much fun they were having. He said we should transfer that to the regular universe. Those were expensive episodes, but we amortized them. That's where the two-parter helped. We were able to do those big things. We wanted the original series look with the high-key lighting and the colors and gels and all that. We could do as much fun stuff as we wanted. My argument to Rick about changing the opening title sequence for those episodes was to use footage from *First Contact,* which was an idea that I had fallen in love with. Rick was okay with that. I said we want these episodes to look as if they came from the Mirror Universe, so finally he just signed on and we had great fun with it.

CONNOR TRINNEER

The "Mirror, Mirror" episodes I didn't like because I didn't like what I was doing in them.

ANTHONY MONTGOMERY

Having never seen the Xindi arc nor the Mirror Universe episodes, I can say I've heard from many fans on both sides of the spectrum: some fans *love* the season-long Xindi arc, while others have shared that is was "good, but too long." *All* of the fans *love* the Mirror Universe episodes.

From an acting perspective, Travis was not utilized very much during the Xindi arc, but I had a fantastic time playing my villainous doppelganger in the Mirror Universe episodes. I never get cast as "evil" in most projects, so it was a lot of fun to play a bad guy.

JAMES L. CONWAY

It's great because a lot of times actors, when you're rehearsing the scenes and they're bored, will exaggerate the scenes in their rehearsal just to get through it without being too bored, and then when you have an episode where they actually play it that way, they just relished it. That was a fun episode, because everybody played these big exaggerated versions of themselves. For actors it was a lot of fun.

> It was during filming of "In a Mirror, Darkly," the Mirror Universe episode, that the cast and crew learned that season four would be the show's last. While this was not surprising, it did come as a tremendous disappointment to everyone involved who could feel the show belatedly gaining its space legs throughout the season.

SCOTT BAKULA

Everybody is saying, "seven years, seven years, seven years," and I'm saying, "Not so fast everybody, because the world has changed and the situation we're in with UPN is different than if we were syndicated." And then everything else blew up around us and a lot of changes happened at the network. I said, "You can't plan on seven years," and that meant with the storylines also. There needed to be a sense of urgency and let's not just meander and do as many episodes as we can in seven years and everybody goes away. That was kind of my drumbeat underneath it all, let's really try and focus on the right now with every episode and every day on the set.

JUDITH REEVES-STEVENS

When they took away the daily fruit basket, we knew we were in trouble.

GARFIELD REEVES-STEVENS

It was a fruit basket that was delivered to the writers every day and it cost twenty-five dollars.

JUDITH REEVES-STEVENS

When that disappeared, we knew . . .

GARFIELD REEVES-STEVENS

The writing was on the wall.

BRANNON BRAGA

Season four of *Enterprise* is probably what it should have been in the beginning, but, you know, where the fuck was Manny when I needed him? By the way, I'm being really hard on the show; people like the show and have revisited it on Blu-ray and are much kinder to the show now. Some will say, I wish I'd watched it when it was on and supported the show more because it's actually really good.

I feel like *Star Trek* was in its waning days; I mean, even *Gunsmoke* got canceled. Every show goes away. After a while, people are looking for what else is new. And Rick and I happened to be in the thick of *Star Trek* when it was at its apex in the 90s with *Generations* going, *First Contact*, *Voyager*, and *Deep Space Nine* being on the air and successful. And then after that it slowly started to degrade until Rick and I happened to be at the helm when the show went away.

RICK BERMAN

I'm not a great believer in blaming things. Jonathan Dolgen was chairman of all of Paramount at the time, and he used the phrase "franchise fatigue" with me, which I think was one of the best explanations of what was going wrong. At the same time, we made a movie with one of the top screenwriters in Hollywood, John Logan, called *Star Trek: Nemesis,* and it just died. Simultaneously, there were problems going on with *Enterprise.* So I think it really had to do with a sense of "franchise fatigue" and the fact that there had been so much *Star Trek.*

GLEN C. OLIVER

Even with so many misgivings regarding the direction these shows often took, it is my strong contention that *TNG, DS9, Voyager,* and *Enterprise* did not bring about "franchise fatigue," as some have asserted. My contention is that their style, tone, frequently unimaginative storytelling, and the soft-shoe payoffs their stories often advanced were what promoted franchise *disinterest.* "Fatigue" suggests too much. In this case, I think many fans simply stopped caring, because *Star Trek* maneuvered them into that position. By decisions which were actively and repeatedly being made, and also by the decisions which *weren't* being made.

Over the course of the years, *Star Trek* ceased to be *about* anything tangible. And, at the end of the day, who wants to watch shows which don't seem entirely sure of their own identity? Shows which almost seemed to shun their own potential?

BRANNON BRAGA

Were we partly to blame? Yeah, of course. *Enterprise* took a lot of the heat because that's the show that took *Star Trek* down, but I don't think it helped that a couple of the movies didn't do as well and weren't as well received. It's just people were really brutal on *Enterprise.*

> As the series began to wind down, the show's two most controversial choices were still to come. First, the killing of Trip in the penultimate episode, and the series finale which, instead of providing a swan song for the crew of the NX-01, revisited "The Pegasus" episode of *Next Generation* with guest-stars Jonathan Frakes and Marina Sirtis reprising their roles as Riker and Troi, respectively.

CONNOR TRINNEER

I was super satisfied with how they handled the end of Trip and that's because I'm the only one on the show who had a completed arc. My story was told in its entirety and I really liked that. I liked the idea that you don't have to ask whatever happened to him. They sent me the script a few days before shooting and Brannon said, "I want to know what you think," and I said, "Are we canceled?" "We're done." So I said, "I think it's great then." For an actor, it's a real satisfying thing to have the completion of a story.

BRANNON BRAGA

The series finale was an hour that's very controversial and I'll take the blame for this with Rick since we wrote it together, but we wanted to end an eighteen-year run that was a huge part of our lives and the audience's with a valentine to this era of *Trek*. Manny had just done a stellar three-part episode, which I considered to be *Enterprise*'s finale in its own right. We wanted the final episode to be a very high-concept idea where we're on Picard's *Enterprise* and Riker's in the holodeck to look at one of his heroes, Captain Archer. What an interesting way to look back at *Enterprise,* through the eyes of a different *Star Trek* character. I thought it was great, but the episode was flat and I don't think it really worked. And killing Trip felt flat and just pissed people off. It certainly pissed the cast off. They hated the script.

RICK BERMAN

We have Riker come on board, go into the holodeck to study the famous day ninety years earlier when something happened to Jonathan Archer which eventually led to the formation of the Federation. He's watching Archer at a very critical moment with a group of aliens and a friend who's in danger, and it was a very moving story. We thought that, in a sense, we would be honoring our characters by seeing them through the eyes of future generations. But a lot of people took it as being disrespectful to the cast and felt that we had turned the final episode into an episode of *The Next Generation,* which was very far from the truth. But you can't control how people feel about it. Both Brannon and I have wondered in the years since that perhaps it was a mistake. There were those who thought the episode was terrific and there's a lot more who thought that it was sort of a disrespectful way to end the series.

JUDITH REEVES-STEVENS

There was *such* controversy over that. I don't even mean among the fans; even on staff there were a lot of people who reacted positively and a lot of people who reacted negatively toward it. We felt it was saying good-bye to all the years of them working in this franchise.

GARFIELD REEVES-STEVENS

To us, that was the last episode of the Rick and Brannon era.

JUDITH REEVES-STEVENS

We were in the episode. I was in one of the outfits from Gates McFadden and Gar was dressed up as an admiral [Admiral Brad Yacobian, an homage to the series unit production manager]. We were sitting up in the bleachers while they were filming. Manny was beside us, and it was so strange to see it all coming to an end.

GARFIELD REEVES-STEVENS

For us, it was the end of a chapter in *Star Trek*.

JEFFREY COMBS

That episode was a bit of a mess. I think the message that was being sent there by Rick Berman, frankly, was: "OK, we may have been canceled, but I want to put in front of you that I also had a successful *Next Generation*." I thought then and I still do that it was insulting to the series regulars of *Enterprise* that they weren't even given the dignity and the time therefore to wrap up their own damn show. And you know, even Jonathan Frakes felt the same way. "Why am I here? What is this? It's a job, I'll take the paycheck and I'll do this, because if I don't, somebody else will."

JONATHAN FRAKES (actor, "William T. Riker")

Rick called me and said, "We'd like you to do the last episode of the show as a valentine for the fans." I thought, "Okay, it's Rick and it's *Star Trek* and I always say yes," but it was at least my feeling that it was an uncomfortable situation to be brought into a show that, first of all, has been prematurely canceled. And to essentially be part of their finale when it was really Scott's show. And he was *such* a gentleman. He was notably generous and civil and thoughtful, and I thought in-side he's got to be thinking, "What the fuck are you guys doing? My show's already been canceled and you guys are coming here to try to close it out?" I would have been *so* insulted. I didn't think that was our finest hour.

JEFFREY COMBS

No one bore any resentment there. The actors are not to blame. Not at all. Scott couldn't have been more welcoming. But, being the leader that Scott is, he was a *true* leader, like a quarterback on the field. He's a consummate professional. He'd never let anybody know, but I bet you that there were quite a few conversations.

BRANNON BRAGA

Scott Bakula was the nicest guy, and we had a great relationship, and it was the only time where he called me about the script and said he had big problems with it. He was pissed that we were doing an episode that really wasn't an *Enterprise* episode, but was a *Next Gen* episode. Everyone, including the fans of the show, felt the same way.

MANNY COTO

My feeling was that "Demons" and "Terra Prime" were the final *Enterprise,* that's how I always pictured it. It was evident that this was the end of the long run, the eighteen-year run, so Rick and Brannon wanted to do an episode that would pay homage not just to *Enterprise* but to all the years, and I had no problem with it whatsoever. I liked the idea at first, but it wasn't as great as it could have been.

BRANNON BRAGA

Unfortunately the script was written and we were going to shoot it. There wasn't a whole lot I could do. It just is what it is. I'm still asked about it to this day, and I think I made a mistake doing it. At the time it seemed like a cool thing, but it turned out to not really work. It was sweet and it had a nice little ending with the ships from *Star Trek,* and our heart was in the right place, but we should have just done a great *Enterprise* finale and called it a day. It was a little bit of an over-reach.

DOMINIC KEATING

I know Scott talked quite openly about finding it a little irksome, but by the time we came to shoot the last episode, we'd known for about two or three months that we were done, so I kind of moved on in my head. If anything, I think the device to get Marina and Jonathan was a bit clunky and not altogether plausible, but given that Rick and Brannon were tying up sixteen-seventeen years of their watch, I thought it was rather fitting that they would bring in *Next Generation*. And it was such a treat working with Marina, who I knew very well from doing conventions. And Jonathan, I tell you that scene I shot with him in the galley was one of the funnest days I ever had on set. Hysterical, he's a really fun guy and a real actor's actor.

MANNY COTO

Everything is either great or horrible, and it's kind of amazing. When I was doing *Enterprise* and I just started, I would look at some of these fan sites and there was one guy whose whole purpose was to kind of shit on every episode. When I was a fan it would never occur to me to sit and write shitty letters putting down all the work that everyone had done. We were in love with the show and every now and then we would comment about how this didn't work or that didn't work, but this vitriol that people have, I'm like, "Do you *really* enjoy this?"

BRANNON BRAGA

By the time we got pretty deep into season four, we knew that they weren't going to renew it, and when the somewhat unceremonious phone call came in, I happened to be in Rick's office, and the person in charge of the network at that time said, "It's time to put this one to rest." And we were, like, "Okay." It was a ten-second conversation.

MANNY COTO

The e-mail was: "I'm hearing rumors that *Enterprise* is being canceled and the rumors are really strong today, what do you know?" And I said, "I don't know anything." But sure enough, when I got to work Brannon came in and said we're canceled. But everybody knew—the odds were that it was the last year—it was kind of understood that season four was it, so it wasn't a big shock. I don't remember a lot of tears. I know people were disappointed, but everyone kind of knew.

BRANNON BRAGA

It was truly a mix of feelings, because on the one hand I was greatly relieved, I was moving on to other things, and it was such a scalding experience toward the end with an estranged network and an apathetic fan base. At the same time, it was a show that we thought was finally really good, so it was upsetting that it was over.

I really think we could have continued for another two or three years with Manny at the helm. We were already cutting corners, the shows had shifted to high-definition video the fourth season and I thought it looked like shit, but even with cutting corners, the show could have continued creatively.

Star Trek is a long-term investment, but at the end of the day, I think I was very ready to do other things. In fact, I'd already had another project sitting in front of me that I had to tackle, which was another science-fiction show for CBS, *Threshold*. It was doomed to failure, but I'd been doing *Star Trek* for fifteen years. I was ready to do something else, but looking back it was bittersweet—more bitter than sweet, because it should not have been canceled.

MANNY COTO

I would have loved to have built more toward the Romulan War and explored that and continued to set up the Federation. I loved Jeffrey Combs and I wanted to find a way to bring Combs onto the bridge as a character on our show. I wanted to make him a regular. He was tremendous and he had such a great energy. To have him as an interspecies exchange would have supercharged the season.

MARIE JACQUEMETTON

It was great experience. It's funny, because I know there's a lot of negativity surrounding the hours and the rewriting and all the stuff that goes on, but we learned so much there. Brannon is an amazing writer. Just to watch him work and pitch out a story and analyze how he built suspense and expand on the kernel of an episode was so instructive to us. That's a lot of the way we worked at *Mad Men*, because Matt [Weiner] works a little bit in that same way. He'll start a story from a conversation that he had in his head with the characters.

ANDRÉ JACQUEMETTON

To work with so many creative people and to write a paragraph about an alien world and actually see it come to light was just extraordinary for us. It really was. Especially coming from *Baywatch*. To see people create these incredible worlds was really inspirational. We learned a lot and it helped us a great deal with *Mad Men,* working in a difficult situation. It always is a difficult situation; you're working with volatile individuals and these are skills that you need to develop as a writer.

DAVID A. GOODMAN

From 1987 to 2005, there was always a new *Star Trek* on. It was great. But there was something to be said about being hungry for it again. I took it for granted that it was always going to be there. And when it wasn't, I was, like, "Oh wait, there's no *Star Trek*."

ALEXANDER SIDDIG (actor, "Dr. Julian Bashir," *Deep Space Nine*)

I would have hated to be on either *Enterprise* or *Voyager*. It would have been a living hell, because there was no food for the actor. If Ira had been in charge, things may have been different. On *Enterprise,* those guys didn't know what they were doing. Brannon was a mini-Rick. Brannon came up with innovative ideas on *Next Generation* and I've got to give him credit for that. But something happened. I think Hollywood may have gone a bit to his head. The thing that I desperately tried to avoid. That and Bush getting elected.

BRANNON BRAGA

It was hard doing *Star Trek*. I just did two TV shows, *Cosmos* and *Salem,* both of which had thirteen episodes apiece. We used to do twenty-six episodes a year with *Star Trek*. I can't even imagine how we did it. I was younger, but that's a lot of episodes on a show that was really challenging. *Star Trek* was held to a very high standard and to do that over and over every week was really challenging.

SCOTT MANTZ (film critic, *Access Hollywood*)

There were, like, 790-something episodes.

BRANNON BRAGA

It is staggering. By the way, nothing was recycled. There was always an effort to keep everything new. They're all pretty original. You couldn't really repeat story-lines, because *Star Trek* viewers know all the episodes. So it's not like if you watched the ten seasons of *Bewitched*, you're going to say they redid that. We couldn't do that. You have almost a thousand episodes of *Star Trek* and they're all pretty different, which is amazing.

DOMINIC KEATING

I blame *Voyager*. We'd have done our seven years, that's for sure. The fact of the matter is they'd gone to the well many, many times, and thank God we got the four, but it was just time for a rest. Year after year, series after series, you're writing a variation of a theme. It was incredible and it will never be done again in the history of television. There's not a chance. Seventeen years and four hit shows. It's unprecedented what Brannon and Rick did.

BRANNON BRAGA

If *Star Trek* was created today, you might very well see more of a *Game of Thrones* approach with a highly serialized, intricate storyline going on.

MIKE SUSSMAN

And ten-episode seasons instead of twenty-six.

DOMINIC KEATING

When we did the final farewell photograph at the gates of Paramount, it was a huge production and they had a massive load of makeup people putting various extras in the guises of all the various creatures. So Brannon, Connor, and I were standing in the sunshine at Paramount waiting for the full setup of all the production crew along with cast members and the various incarnations of aliens that we'd met along the way. There was a lull in the conversation between the three of us, and there was this guy dressed up as a Tellarite who was just a couple of feet away. He was sweating his tits off in the sun and Brannon turned back to me and said, "It's time."

I was really just crestfallen that we were being cut short and weren't doing the full seven, but I have to say that caught me unaware and tickled me pink for days. It still does. He was very dry, Brannon. Bless him.

CONNOR TRINNEER

We really got along well; there was rarely any significant drama. It helps to get along and we did. We see each other now at conventions or around town. I'm still pretty close to a few of the cast members, and I personally feel like it was a special time and I don't think I'm alone in that.

DAVID LIVINGSTON

To me, *Enterprise* was the best experience of all. I got to do great stuff. . . . I even did a zombie episode. . . . I loved the cast, I loved shooting with two cameras in HD. You knew what you were getting. I thought it was a travesty they pulled the plug while it was getting better. Scott was great, too. What a privilege and a gift it was to work on the show. I didn't know anybody appreciated what we were involved with. We both got it. We knew it was special. Unfortunately, to me, it ended too soon.

MIKE SUSSMAN

The writing was on the wall. But, in this business you live so much in denial, I think, because we were having so much fun. Creatively, the show was better than ever. I felt like at least we kind of got to go out doing what we wanted to do. It was sad to be there at the end of this whole franchise and to get into that final episode. But, overall, I think we went out on a high note in terms of the season.

JAMES L. CONWAY

Many of these people had been there for ten to eighteen years, and it was almost an entire career. They knew they were on borrowed time to be in one place for so long. So, though it was sad to see it go, I think a lot of them understood that it was time.

MIKE SUSSMAN

I would just love to be involved with something like that and have that much passion. I don't know if I'll have that in my career again. I chased that *Star Trek* dream for so long and then finally caught it and was incredibly lucky to do so. I've created shows [TNT's *Perception*] since then, but it's not the same thing.

CHRIS BLACK

To go work on that show was a dream come true for me. I had been a *Star Trek* fan since I was young. I went to my first *Star Trek* convention in Columbus, Ohio. I must have been fifteen, because my dad had to drive me from Toledo to Columbus, which was a pretty long drive. God bless my father, who was willing to drive me and my geeky friends to a *Star Trek* convention. And then the chance to go to Paramount and play in that universe and go to the sets was spectacular. There were people running around with pointed ears and phasers and standing on transporter pads and talking in communicators. It was like I had died and gone to heaven.

It's fair to look back at all the mistakes we made collectively and the frustrations we had with the showrunners, but the fact is, I wasn't in charge of the show and you have to respect the person in that position. You have a couple of choices. You can quit in a huff and say, "I refuse to be a party to this," or you can fight to the point you get fired. *Or* you can do your best to do good work within the limitations of that parameter. I was there for three seasons and, in many ways, Rick and Brannon were so generous to me in allowing me to be a part of that and to tell some of the stories I really wanted to tell. I don't want to seem ungrateful or ungracious about it even though looking back I would have done it differently. The fact is, it wasn't my show to run.

MIKE SUSSMAN

It's funny, because Brannon has this record for being the anti–*Star Trek* guy, but he feels the thing about *Star Trek* is you can take almost any idea that you had for a story and turn it into a *Star Trek* episode. You can't do that on any other show. I created a police procedural and there are very limited types of stories after a while. You don't get that with *Star Trek*. You could do a legal show one week, you could do action-adventure the week after that, and a comedy the week after that. You're stretching all these different muscles and it's terrific. There are other shows like that, but most shows aren't. Most shows are a formula.

SCOTT BAKULA

I had *such* a good time. The creative process there was so interesting and the people involved were so gifted and so talented. At the end of the year wrap party they'd put together a reel, or at the beginning of the next season you'll see a promo that says "Last season on *Enterprise*," and you sit there and go, "Wow, we did an *unbelievable* amount of creative, inventive, stunning work." And we only had eight days to do it and only so much money to do it, and we pulled it off week after week. That part of it was great. But I think it would have been nice if we had had a longer go at it, because I feel like we had really discovered something and, in my opinion, we were starting to push the envelope of what the show could be—but it took a while to get there.

FRED DEKKER

The last time I saw Rick was at my doctor's office. We share a doctor, so I was sitting there, waiting for my appointment, and he was there and I said, "How are you?" He said, "Great." I asked what he was working on, and he said, "I'm done."

RICK BERMAN

I've been working on a book, which is not really a book about *Star Trek*, it's a book about *Star Trek* and a lot of the other things that I have done in my life. I've been doing a lot scuba diving and enjoying my family. I don't think I will be getting involved in doing any television. I'm not quite sure how serious he is, but [*Nemesis* screenwriter] John Logan is always saying come to Dublin and help me on *Penny Dreadful*.

I've had a couple of instances where people have asked me to get involved in things that didn't interest me. I put twenty years of my life into making documentary films—and I put another twenty years of my life into doing *Star Trek*—and I think that that was plenty.

JAMES L. CONWAY

At the time that *Enterprise* ended, I was on the Paramount lot directing *Charmed*. For me, the reality of the show finally being canceled was the alley between Stages 1 and 2 and Stages 8 and 9 that was always mobbed with trailers—all the makeup trailers and the actors' trailers for *Star Trek—that's* when I knew that the show was over forever, when, after eighteen years, that alley was empty.

J.J. ABRAMS &
BEYOND

(2009-2016)

STAR-TING OVER

"YOU KNOW, COMING BACK IN TIME,
CHANGING HISTORY . . . THAT'S CHEATING."

Not since 1969 when NBC first canceled *Star Trek* had the franchise ever seemed so definitively dead. Few anticipated its rebirth and growing popularity at the time. The threat of network cancelations during seasons one and two should have been the end, but letter-writing campaigns changed NBC's mind. Even when the show was canceled at the end of year three, instead of slipping into oblivion, it shattered syndication records. Over thirty years ago it was resurrected as *Star Trek: The Motion Picture,* which, given its cost overruns and critical lambasting, *should* have been the end.

Instead, Paramount Pictures handed *Trek* over to their television division and producer Harve Bennett, resulting in *The Wrath of Khan,* eight additional big-screen features and four spin-off TV series. But by 2005, it appeared *Star Trek* had finally reached its end. *Nemesis* had proven a box-office bust three years earlier, *Enterprise* had been ignominiously canceled by UPN after four years, the official *Star Trek* Web site was shutting down, and the licensed magazine was ceasing publication. For all intents and purposes, *Star Trek* was truly dead this time.

However, with many fervent fans having subsequently become successful industry professionals themselves, it's not surprising that subsequently there were a few notable attempts at interesting the studio in a reboot and other proposals that were developed to present to Paramount, with some heavyweight (and lightweight) industry names behind them.

In the case of a proposed *Star Trek* IMAX film, the project was announced as early as 1997, prior the franchise's precipitous decline. The idea was for a forty-minute, ten- to twelve-million-dollar film to be shown exclusively in big-screen IMAX-equipped theaters. Written by Rick Berman and Hans Tobeason, the idea was that it would feature characters from the various television series united in one film.

RICK BERMAN (executive producer, *Star Trek: The Next Generation*)

I've always felt that the script we developed for *Star Trek: IMAX* was wonderful. The IMAX people loved what we came up with and Paramount loved it. The film would have featured a bunch of new characters, but with Colm Meaney as Miles

O'Brien at the center of it. But for business reasons between Paramount and IMAX, it was back-burnered.

In 2005, *Star Trek: The Beginning* was developed as a feature film to be produced by Rick Berman and written by Erik Jendresen (HBO's *Band of Brothers*) that would have served as a bridge between the television series *Enterprise* and the original show. It would have chronicled the pre-Kirk war between the Romulans and the Federation. A regime change at the studio, however, spelled the end for *The Beginning*.

ERIK JENDRESEN (writer, *Star Trek: The Beginning*)

Shortly after *Band of Brothers*, I got a call from my agent, who said, "Would you be interested in getting into *Star Trek*?" And I said, "No." First of all, because I don't really like science fiction. I'm kind of an odd purist that way. If it's not Jules Verne or H.G. Wells or Edgar Allen Poe or Arthur Conan Doyle, I'm not that interested. The space opera genre of science fiction is just something that has never held any interest for me. But they didn't take no for an answer. [Producer] Jordan Kerner really wanted to have a conversation, so they called me back and said, "Would you come consult with us?" And I said, "Sure." And I was very honest with them. I loved two things about *Star Trek*. The first was this sort of Horatio Hornblower aspect to Kirk. All of that boldness. It's sort of a throwback to a great kind of literary figure and hero. Second, I realized I loved the fact that the stories were always, at the time, of political or social relevance. There was a message behind them all. And it was kind of lovely. I really respected that.

So they wanted to talk more about it. I said, "Look, guys, I've got to take a pass on this." They called me again. And they said, "Could we just talk?" They wanted me to give them any thoughts that I might have. And so I finally said okay. I decided to tell them something that I thought they'd never go for. I said, "Imagine this baby as a trilogy. It should be something that fills that missing place in the canon. It was sort of like having an encyclopedia. This encyclopedia is missing the letter T. There's a gap. And interestingly enough, at least for the original series, an inciting incident that's referred to but we've never seen is the Earth-Romulan War that started the whole thing."

I said, "I'd ever so loosely fashion the first one on *The Iliad*. And the sequel would be ever so loosely based on *The Odyssey*. I would love to leave the hero and his crew stranded and having to make their way slowly back to Earth having no idea whether Earth exists or not. It's going to take them years to get back on this crippled ship. And that journey in the sequel to the prequel would also involve some of the interesting moments that harken back to the original series. But it happened decades before. It would be a tremendous trek on the way back." Then I added, "And then the third one, I have no idea what it will be." And they loved it!

GLEN C. OLIVER (film & TV critic, *Ain't It Cool News*)

Jendersen's *Star Trek: The Beginning* was massive in scale and rich in emotion. The script felt complex thematically, and suggested settings which were more vibrant and sprawling than anything the *Trek* movies had shown us to date. *The Beginning* was, fundamentally, a classic World War II-esque tale focusing on a young and somewhat rudderless Tiberius Chase, who we infer was a forefather of James T. Kirk, although this is never clearly stated. Chase is forced to quickly define his purpose in life when Romulans show up to smite Earth as part of an ethnic cleansing campaign against the Vulcans.

ERIK JENDRESEN

This is all happening during the Serbian-Croatian conflict. So the whole notion was of this interstellar ethnic cleansing going on. It was really about something. And the fact that the Earth stands up against the Romulans [in defense of the Vulcans, whom they've had a strained relationship with since *Enterprise*] and says, "No." The needs of the few outweighs the needs of the many. That is the moment when the Earth stands up and says no.

RICK BERMAN

Jordan Kerner came on as a movie producer under contract at Paramount. Part of his deal was to develop a *Star Trek* movie. He came to me and they said that they wanted me to work with him and I said great. We came up with a project and a writer was found. It just petered out.

ERIK JENDRESEN

It was Jordan Kerner and Kerry McCluggage. Rick Berman didn't have anything to do with the film. He showed up at my office at Paramount. But that was it. I was also well aware of a lot of the animosity among Trekkies or Trekkers toward the

Berman regime. And I never got to know the guy. He was perfectly pleasant, but he seemed vaguely disinterested. Which was perfectly fine for me. So, it was a whole gaggle of producers and Mark Evans, who was the exec on the project. We went in to pitch it to the head of the studio, Donald De Line. We sat down and started telling the story. I've been in a lot of rooms in Hollywood. I've pitched a lot of projects. I've never been in a more preternaturally dead room than this one. It was like being in a sensory deprivation tank. There was not a sound, and in the middle of the pitch I thought, "This is really odd."

In the middle of it, I look over to the sofas and one of the producers is sitting there and he started doing that "Kennedy just got shot" with his fist under his chin. So, I think, to hell with it, I'm going to go take a really big swing here and I told the whole story. I took forty-five minutes to do the entire thing. And I was just riffing and also sort of discovering and creating things as I sort of started embellishing on my story. I get to the end. Dead silence. And then De Line clears his throat and he says, "Umm, how long would it take you to write this?" I said, "Eight to ten weeks." And then he sticks his hand out and just shakes my hand and says, "Write it fast." He bought it in the room. And so we walk out and all the producers are just falling all over themselves. They're so thrilled. "We're doing the next *Star Trek*! This is unbelievable!" And I'm thinking to myself. I've got to go home and write this *now*, goddamn!"

GLEN C. OLIVER

Set between *Enterprise* and *TOS*, *The Beginning* addresses the origins of many issues which would become instrumental in the *Trek* mythos. For example: Starfleet's peculiar, and previously underexplored, balance between militarism and exploration is touched on here to considerable extent. As is *Trek*'s critical, time-tested conflict arriving from the conundrum of knowing when to follow orders, and when to buck the system.

"*. . . I will still, and forever, wonder how one can go boldly and follow at the same time?*" ponders Chase in one the script's many voiceover letters to the girl he loves, all patterned in tone and style after many of those wonderful Civil War–era messages soldiers sent to family and friends back home.

ERIK JENDRESEN

By the time I was finished writing it, I was quite shocked about the whole thing. I really enjoyed the process. I was also very well aware of the fact that because of the agnostic feeling I had toward the genre, and I wasn't a die-hard fan, I was able to serve it better, because I wasn't precious. My own feelings about a story or a canon of material are as strong as most Trekkies are for the Arthur Conan Doyle books. That was something I was crazed about as a kid. To this day, I still am. So, I thought, well, I have to think of this legion of folks who hold this so dearly and try to serve that. It really served canon. And I went deep in my research and tried to make sure that this entry didn't in any way defy the canon. Having to come up with some kind of clever way to be able to have a human encounter a Romulan and deal with the notion that no one lives to tell of it. And it was really fun to try to tackle the idea of Kirk's progenitor. Who is this guy that he was named after? Where did his spirit originate from? I really embraced it.

GLEN C. OLIVER

As written, *The Beginning* suggests a very, very different brand of *Star Trek* which smartly, even brazenly, upholds the mythology's core values, while concurrently wrapping them in a very different package for delivery. There are a few connections to Berman-era lore; species introduced in that time frame are present, and there's a reference to *Enterprise* NX-01's sister ship, but they are tenuous and even dispensable. Characters and situations featured in *The Beginning* are predominantly new and placed within an extremely militarized ethos.

ERIK JENDRESEN

I was well aware of the fact that this story was a departure from that intention Roddenberry had always held close [for *Star Trek*]. I was trying to be respectful of it. And those issues are sort of addressed in the story. But, I had them also face the simple fact that Starfleet came out of a conflict, that sort of wonderful swords-to-plowshares thing that ultimately happened can't happen without the swords part.

GLEN C. OLIVER

Perhaps what's most compelling about *The Beginning* is that its setting is, in a way, as much a character as the people populating its story. The way things are, a hyper-militarized, early space-exploration Earth, and the way things need to be to survive—is every bit as critical as the people we're getting to know throughout

Jendresen's story. As much as *The Beginning* is about characters, it's about how the *Trek* universe so many of us love came to exist. That's quite a narrative manifesto, and the script handles such matters admirably, even effortlessly.

As a screenplay in itself, the script works very well—as long as one is not put off by the reality that *Trek*-ish value systems can be successfully deployed within a harder, more *Starship Troopers*–esque package than we're accustomed to. It's difficult to completely assess the full success of Jendresen's overall intent here, though. My understanding is that *The Beginning* was the first of three intended movies, and as such it ends somewhat ambiguously. Thus, the payoff of several important plot threads is currently, and will likely forever be, unclear. If whatever he planned next was as forward-thinking and out of the box as his first installment. We'd have seen a very unusual, very grown-up *Trek* for the ages.

ERIK JENDRESEN

I was so looking forward to the second one, because it was going to be a chase from Romulan space. And also, the great notion being that most of the Romulan fleet would be heading back to Romulus from Earth so they are sort of on a collision course with the whole Romulan fleet. During the course of this, there would be conflict, tension, and suspense. But, I was looking forward to inventing the adventures of Odysseus on his way home—back to Penelope.

I did have one person in mind when I wrote it. But it's a tertiary character. Tiberius is Kirk's great-grandfather. So his great-great-grandfather is Tiberius' father, Otto Chase, who leads this group of xenophobes, and I was just absolutely convinced there was only one guy to play him. And that was Christopher Walken. I would have brought him back in the sequel. He was such a colorful character. The idea of Walken in this subterranean cavern with all of these ancient rotting Nazi UFOs would've been great.

GLEN C. OLIVER

Would this have worked? *The Beginning* feels like exactly what the franchise needed, exactly when it needed it. If produced as clearly intended on paper, it would've become *Trek*'s equivalent of Nolan's *Dark Knight* films, for better or worse. It would've taken time-tested themes and familiar conceits, and folded them into a world which is bigger, bolder, darker, and more naturalistic than anything anyone familiar with the franchise had come to expect. *The Beginning* would've asserted, very loudly, that *Trek* could be so much more than what it often is. And *Trek* can take so many more forms than it often does. By my measure, this kind of thinking is critical to *Trek*'s long-term survival, no matter who is in the driver's seat.

ERIK JENDRESEN

To this day I don't know and will never know if it would've worked. But, of course, I went ahead and wrote it and turned the script in and on Wednesday of that week, the head of the studio [Donald De Line] was fired. It's a tried and true, honored tradition of Hollywood that regime change is a slate-wiper. Any new regime coming in, even if a film is going to be a success, it's bad news for them because they had nothing to do with it. So they can't really risk it. It was just so unlucky.

In 2004, *Babylon 5* creator J. Michael Straczynski and *Dark Skies* creator Bryce Zabel developed a fourteen-page treatment titled *Star Trek: Reboot the Universe*. It was a concept the duo never had the opportunity to pitch to Paramount because it was announced that J. J. Abrams and Bad Robot Productions already had plans for rebooting the universe and would be developing a new feature film for the studio.

BRYCE ZABEL (cocreator/executive producer, *Dark Skies*)

Joe [Straczynski] and I were working on a network pitch for a limited series called *Cult,* and we started talking about the state of the *Trek* universe. Before we could stop ourselves, we banged out a fourteen-page treatment. At that moment, we had a lot in common, both producing sci-fi series and, in particular, a devotion to five-year plans. Joe had crafted one for *Babylon 5* and Brent Friedman and I had done the same for our NBC alien invasion series *Dark Skies.*

I seem to recall having lunch at Art's Deli and our conversation veering off into the *Trek* situation. The take we came up with included using the original characters, but not as young officers at Starfleet Academy. We wanted to do what they would do in the world of comics: create a separate universe for all the past TV and film *Trek* continuity in order to free ourselves creatively so we could embrace the good stuff, banish the bad, and try some new things. In our reboot we wanted to start over, use Kirk, Spock, and McCoy and others in a powerful new origin story about what it was that bonded them in such strong friendship and show them off as you'd never seen them before. It was, admittedly, pretty audacious.

Another unrealized pitch for *Star Trek* developed in 2005 was *Star Trek: Federation*, a concept from directors Bryan Singer (*X-Men, The Usual Suspects*), Christopher McQuarrie (*Jack Reacher, Mission: Impossible–Rogue Nation*), and Robert Meyer Burnett (*Agent Cody Banks, Free Enterprise*), which was written as a treatment by Geoffrey Thorne.

In the pitch many Federation members have abandoned the alliance and Starfleet is stretched thin when a new enemy, the Scourge, attacks and destroys a starship and several Federation colonies. The only survivor is Lieutenant Commander Alexander Kirk. Dubious of his account of what happened, Vulcan, Bajor, and Betazed leave the Federation, leaving the Ferengi as the dominant power in the galaxy. With the Vulcans reunifying with the Romulans, a new U.S.S. *Enterprise* is tasked to return the Federation to its goal of going boldly, but with the ulterior objective of finding the Scourge. After its captain and first officer are killed, Commander Kirk (third-in-command) is promoted to captain.

GEOFFREY THORNE (writer, *Star Trek: Federation* pitch document)

What I tried to do was go back to brass tacks and asked myself, "What was *Star Trek* actually about? What were Gene and Dorothy Fontana trying to do when they first started the show? What was going on in the world at the time and what is the job of a good TV show?" The job of a good TV show is to speak to its *mass* audience, not what we would call the core audience. The core audience is people like me who are going to show up because it's called *Star Trek*. We already have them; they'll tune in just to see if we screw it up. That's a given. What you want is a show that is competitive with the other networks that are not *Star Trek*. I considered *that* to be my job.

If you take the history of *Star Trek* as we've been presented with it, the Federation ultimately wins every fight. We either destroy the thing, convince the thing not to destroy us, or absorb the thing into us. So what happens when utopia actually happens? That was actually part of the problem of *Star Trek* as a social phenomena—it started to get church-like for too many people. Even people backstage, which was humans don't have any issues with one another and there wasn't a need for commerce. The only problems came from outside. But that's not how *Star Trek* was when it started; it was very rough and tumble and I wanted to get back to *that*.

My idea was, every episode would start with a video letter home from one of the crew, and that crewman might not necessarily be in the episode, it would just inform what we were about to see. So I said, "Utopia has occurred and everything has stagnated." Innovation is driven by necessity, so if you've got everything you need, you've explored everything, you've embraced your enemies, and everything is cool, then you're not making any new stuff. You're not pushing. That's not how evolution works. I pictured a Federation that had hit its plateau and stayed there for three hundred years. Basically using a lot of the same tech from the time of *Next Generation*, and these are old ships. People are pulling out of the Federation because there's no need for a Federation in such a time of peace—but of course it turns out that that's completely wrong. *That* was the starting point.

Everyone seemed very happy with the pitch and were about to present it when J.J. Abrams came in and said, "I want to make these movies." The new *Star Trek* films destroyed the possibility for *Federation* to get off the ground, and that was the end of it.

> Before the bottom fell out of the final frontier, there was also an animated *Star Trek: Final Frontier* pitch, developed as a Web series for Startrek.com. As it was moving through the preproduction process, Paramount Pictures and CBS Television Studios were split into two separate companies in January 2006, and the future of the Web site came into question. While Viacom/Paramount held on to the motion picture rights for *Star Trek,* CBS Television retained the lucrative consumer products licensing and TV rights, past and future. Impressed with the potential for the animated webisodes, studio executives at Paramount Home Entertainment briefly considered the property as a made-for-video project. But with CBS taking control of all *Star Trek* licensing, and Paramount Pictures only controlling the films, the project languished until a management change in December 2007 put an end to it once and for all.

DAVE ROSSI (producer, *Star Trek: Final Frontier*)

We initially envisioned six-minute webisodes in serial format, each installment ending with a "Same Bat time, same Bat channel" feel. The premise was that a hundred and fifty years or so from the end of *TNG*, in the wake of a vicious attack, warp travel has been rendered useless throughout much of Federation space. There's a hint of Romulan involvement and, thirsty for justice, the Federation goes to war with the Romulans. The war drags on with no victory in sight and the two sides sign a treaty. It's fifty years later and the Federation has become isolationist, staying within its own borders. One man, Captain Alexander Chase, aboard a small ship called the *Enterprise,* seeks to reclaim what was best about Starfleet, the Federation, and the tenets that make *Star Trek* what it is: exploration, betterment of mankind, scientific advancement, hope.

Our target audience was not only existing *Star Trek* fans, but also kids, introducing them to a *Star Trek* that, due to the freedom of animation, had an epic scope to the galaxy and, while peppered with lots of great action, also told a story.

> But there was a seismic shift in the *Star Trek* galaxy when producer/director J. J. Abrams and his Bad Robot shingle signed a deal with Paramount to produce a new *Star Trek* movie. Ultimately, the decision was made to resurrect *Star Trek* on the big screen under the aegis of Bad Robot, but in a film that would reboot the franchise in the way that *Casino Royale* had for James Bond and *Batman Begins* for the Dark Knight.
>
> Abrams and his creative team quickly decided that the film would be a reinvention featuring the iconic original series crew of Captain Kirk, Mr. Spock, Bones, and the rest, and it would show how that group first came together, particularly the duo of Kirk and Spock. But this wasn't the first time a reboot had been considered. It was *Trek* movie producer Harve Bennett's original attempt at depicting the early days of Kirk, Spock, and McCoy being rebuffed by the studio in the late eighties that ultimately led to his acrimonious parting from the *Star Trek* franchise and Paramount.

GLEN C. OLIVER

Star Trek: The Academy Years, often erroneously referred to as *Starfleet Academy,* was scripted by *Star Trek V*'s David Loughery for Harve Bennett; it chronicled how young Kirk and Spock, and other *TOS* mainstays meet, and become friends, at Starfleet Academy. Colored by more than a few shades of *Top Gun*, the screenplay was filled with tremendous moments of warmth and heart—and focused heavily on its characters' journeys toward understanding themselves individually, and recognizing their potential as a group.

It was as character-centric as *The Wrath of Khan* and *Search for Spock,* and featured the same unapologetic devotion to exploring the human condition demonstrated by those titles. Despite a few misplaced, miscalculated attempts at humor, there's a lot of "truth" in Loughery's work in *The Academy Years*—touchingly, surprisingly, admirably so at times. This would've been a very nice and affecting origin story when factored into the broader framework of the franchise, and that it didn't make it to screens remains highly regrettable.

Regarding this project and its obvious correlation to J.J. Abrams' 2009 film, it should be noted that "recasting" *TOS* roles . . . and exploring the relationship of these characters in different ways . . . was actually a notion Gene Roddenberry himself acknowledged early on in *Trek*'s history. Not only did he feel this was possible, he even expressed some level of enthusiasm for the conceit. Meaning: those dismissing such projects on the basis that "this wasn't the creator's intent" don't actually have much of an argument in this regard.

Much like director Philip Kaufman, who considered Spock the key to *Star Trek*'s enduring success when he was developing *Planet of the Titans* in the mid-70s, writer/producer/director J.J. Abrams seemed equally enamored of the Spock character, which led to him approaching actor Leonard Nimoy to reprise his role of Spock before even moving forward with his plans for a reinvention of the franchise.

LEONARD NIMOY (actor, "Spock")

I was surprised when I got the call, but then I thought in a way it made sense. *Star Trek* was out of gas and needed something fresh. It needed a departure, and I felt this came at the right time with the right people. If I was surprised, I was very pleasantly surprised. After *Star Trek: The Motion Picture*, the franchise was like a beached whale, and Harve Bennett got it back in the water. I think that was the situation with this film.

BRYAN BURK (producer, *Star Trek* [2009])

I had been scarred seeing *Star Trek: The Motion Picture* in theaters when I was a kid. That was my introduction to *Trek*. I'd only gone to see it because *Star Wars* had come out two years earlier, and I was so hooked, I felt I had to. But when I was watching the film, I felt left out, because everybody was cheering every time a new character came on and I didn't know who they were. But when I saw *Wrath of Khan*, I remember being really moved, because it was accessible and fun. But all of the other films that followed it became more and more of a niche franchise as they went along. So the filmmakers had less and less resources to make the films. You would see with the visual effects that the technology was getting better, but the effects got smaller and smaller because they didn't have the ability to do the same thing financially on these films. So the idea for us was how to bring *Star Trek* up to date with the rest of the film world. That's what we hopefully did.

GERALD ISENBERG (producer, *Star Trek: Planet of the Titans*)

My partner at the time when I did *Star Trek: Planet of the Titans* was J.J. Abrams' father, Jerry. I've known J.J. since he was five. My first memory of J.J. was when my boy, Josh, had his fifth birthday and J.J. was the entertainer. He dressed as Superman and did a forty-minute routine that was fabulous. He was an immensely talented and inventive kid from the time he came out of the womb. The fact that he's directing both *Star Trek* and the new *Star Wars* is a mind-bender.

J. J. ABRAMS (director/producer, *Star Trek* [2009])

I think he is conflating two things here [*laughs*]. Yes, I did a magic show for his son's party. But I didn't dress up like Superman for *that*! But when I was six, I *would* dress up like Superman, because . . . I was six.

MANNY COTO (executive producer, *Star Trek: Enterprise*)

The end of *Enterprise* was all ratings and the fact that the last movie had underperformed, so there was a sense that the franchise was waning and needed a creative boost—and, by, the way, I predicted what was going to happen. When they were talking about whether to bring *Star Trek* back, I said they were going to find a hotshot filmmaker to revamp the series. And that's exactly what happened. By the way, that's what I would do if I were Paramount. I would look for someone who was big, powerful, and had made successful properties and is a *Star Trek* fan. Not that hard—there's a lot of Trekkies.

ROD RODDENBERRY (son of Gene Roddenberry)

He didn't need to, but J.J. came to see us when he decided to make the film. It was very nice and very different from how Paramount had treated us in the past. Even though he probably would have proceeded if he hadn't, he came to us for our blessing and that was just a very nice gesture that made us feel included once again.

RONALD D. MOORE (executive producer, *Battlestar Galactica*)

I liked the idea of this "reboot" as soon as I heard it, and it was something I was vocal about. I said that the idea of going back to the original and recasting and starting over was brilliant. When I left the show, I felt like there had been so much *Star Trek* and it was so much continuity and so many things to keep track of, that it was hard to come up with new stories. You'd be in the writers room pitching stories and you'd have to stop and go, "But does that contradict episode twenty-five?" It was a burden. All the backstories of Romulans and the Klingons and Starfleet and the history and all the franchises . . . It was just an enormous burden and I really felt like it was becoming impenetrable to the audience. Especially if you weren't a completely dyed-in-the-wool fan who watched every episode and knew the stuff backward and forward.

J. J. ABRAMS

I didn't make this movie in comparison with others. I'm not saying it isn't compared, and it's obviously part of a bigger series, but we just felt honored to be able to present our take on *Trek*. But the truth is, *Star Trek* at a certain point very early on decided that it was not going to reach out to other viewers. That it was not going to try and reach out beyond what it was. It almost became more and more myopic as it went on in terms of its appeal.

RONALD D. MOORE

I don't want to take a college course to understand the show, so I was a big advocate of going back to the beginning and starting over. And when they announced J.J., I thought that was a great move. He's done some great television and this seemed like the perfect thing. J.J. sent me a very nice note after that saying he appreciated what I said, because he was taking a lot of flack.

J. J. ABRAMS

I was not a huge *Trek* fan in the beginning. I came late to this particular party, but—with all due respect to the films and the TV spin-offs—the original series, to my mind, is what *Star Trek* was. All of the subsequent series and films felt to me, as they went on, that they were less and less relatable. It felt to me that if you were going to do a version of *Star Trek,* you would have to do it in such a way that it would bring it to life in a way that never had been done before. What I realized was that in my mind Kirk and Spock were the key, the heart, of *Trek*. Approaching this movie, [screenwriters] Alex Kurtzman and Roberto Orci, [producers] Damon Lindeloff and Bryan Burk, and I discovered that's what we wanted to examine and explore: what Kirk and Spock were all about.

ROBERTO ORCI (writer/producer, *Star Trek* [*2009*])

Part of it was looking at what's been done, and it just seemed interesting to us that there has never been a movie that's been simply called *Star Trek*. That in itself seemed to suggest a gap or an area or a hole in what has been done in canon. The idea for this film kind of came from that. It was definitely a challenge, but once we figured out what we wanted to do, we had such a clear impression of what it would be and wouldn't be. Language matters here on whether or not we call it a reboot or something else.

What it really is, and one of the things we were most excited about, is how you keep surprises operating in a world where everybody thinks they know what continuity means and they think they know every element of canon, because they think it's been recorded. That was one of the surprises or challenges of the story, but we did know that we wanted it to be a reintroduction to people who may have never heard of *Star Trek* or have a negative association with it.

ALEX KURTZMAN
(writer/producer, *Star Trek* [2009])

Star Trek had, at that point, over forty years of history and a fan base that's incredibly intelligent and passionate about what they feel is true or not true to *Star Trek*. Figuring out how to bring new life to it, while staying true to everything everyone knows about *Trek,* was obviously very challenging. *And* wonderful, because we were in this kind of crazy, miraculous position of getting to make these movies which inspired us as kids for a whole new generation of kids.

J. J. ABRAMS

My whole take on it was that I needed a way in. I was challenged by and excited about giving people who had no idea of what *Star Trek* was or had seen it and felt a little bit like I did, that it was for them and not for me. To give *them* a way in. To make Kirk and Spock and the other characters as relatable and as unformed or in process as possible. For example, and I've said this a lot, *Star Wars* was, for me, a ride that was undeniable.

When I saw the first *Star Wars,* and even now when I watch those original movies, they were wonderful adventures that were completely relatable, because Luke Skywalker was you. Luke was this kid who didn't know where he was going to go, didn't know what his life was going to be. He was an average farm boy who gets this insane call to adventure.

Kirk was always a cocky, brilliant, shoot-from-the-hip guy who I never felt connected to. I enjoyed it. I appreciated it, but his character was objectified to me, because I just didn't connect with who that guy was. The other main guy was Spock, and he was obviously wildly logical and incredibly deliberate in his consideration, yet I never was really him. So I was disconnected from these characters, even though I could appreciate them.

ALEX KURTZMAN

Bob and I wrote the script, but there were five brains in the room conceiving what we wanted the movie to be, between us, J.J., Damon Lindeloff, and Bryan Burk. In those five brains were various degrees of fandom. Some of the more rabid fans, like Bob and Damon, were saying, "You know, love this idea, but it feels like a violation of what we know *Trek* to be." And people who are absolutely fans, but a little more neutral, like J.J., Bryan, and myself, were constantly walking the line of figuring it out. In a way, we were the eyes of a new audience that hadn't seen *Trek* at all. We were saying to ourselves, "Okay, we want to make a movie that's for fans, but we also want to make a movie that's for a whole new generation of people. What do I need to see if I don't know anything about *Trek*?" Between everybody there was a really good checks and balances system.

ROBERTO ORCI

It was a great situation, because it automatically went through multiple points of view. It wasn't a bad thing as long as we had our wits about us.

ALEX KURTZMAN

I actually think that variance of perspectives is critical to *Trek,* because the spirit of the show was very much Roddenberry's and it's always maintained an optimistic, hopeful universe about exploration. Ultimately about family and friendship, but I think the character points of view reflected different writers who came along over the course of time. I do think it was important to have those voices.

ROBERTO ORCI

We only jumped into a project when we already felt we had a reason. We didn't just sign and say, "We're going to reinvent this today. We don't have an idea, but we're going to take the job." We went into it having an idea of where we were going to go. Doing so obviously takes into account how much we were going to have to change in terms of what the fans expect. It's definitely challenging, and it's definitely something you want to keep in touch with the fan perspective on. But we knew what we were going to do.

About a year earlier, we were talking to Paramount about *Star Trek,* even before we were doing *Mission: Impossible III,* and we didn't quite have the angle on it yet, so we didn't jump on it. Luckily nobody did in that time, and when it came back around and we'd done *Mission: Impossible III* with J.J., and they approached us all as a team, we'd spent a year thinking about it enough where finally something bubbled up and we said, "Now we have a reason to do this."

ALEX KURTZMAN

We are in an entirely different millennium than when *Star Trek* originated; it was the twentieth century when the show began. Cell phones didn't exist. The future we presented in this movie is much closer to the reality that currently exists than has ever been the case. As a result, it isn't so much a fantasy; it could be humans traveling in space and accomplishing things. That's a given now, even on a street level, and because that's a given now, you have to ask, "What is the story?"

ROBERTO ORCI

We were watching the twenty-third century from the twentieth century. We're now a century closer.

ALEX KURTZMAN

The reason we built the sequence with young Kirk in the Corvette in the trailer is because we wanted the audience to immediately understand that the touch points feel a lot more present than they did when *Trek* first came out.

ROBERTO ORCI

It's not some fantasy universe. It's an extension of where we are.

ALEX KURTZMAN

It's not an accident that that was the first thing you saw in the trailer, because there's no way your mind says, "It's going to be *Star Trek.*" When he says his name is James Tiberius Kirk, you go, "What?" That was all part of bringing people into it from a new place.

ROBERTO ORCI

Science fiction can be very cold and very abstract, so the idea was to make it still be science fiction, but have it be visceral. Our code word for that was "rock 'n' roll."

J. J. ABRAMS

There were people who knew and loved *Star Trek* and would be thrilled to see these characters living again. To see scenes and sequences that you've heard referenced and never seen before, and answering certain questions and seeing how this group is reborn. So for me, it was a way to take three groups of people who represent the whole audience, and say, "Let's bring everyone together and tell a story that starts at the beginning, when Kirk is unformed. When you meet him and he's an aimless punk who goes to bars, drinks, picks up women, starts fights." Yet you know, and even the neophytes to *Star Trek* will watch and say, "Kirk? Isn't he Captain Kirk? How does he go from here to there?"

So for me, it was giving people a way into this world in a way it's never been done. By doing this film with the kind of resources that certainly a *Trek* film has never been allowed to have before. By delivering on a level of visceral fast-paced action that *Trek* has never really had as its signature. What we came up with was a story of incredible characters, of incredible potential, of real optimism and wonder, and treated it in a way that provides a kind of emotional connection, visceral excitement, visual spectacle that *Trek* had never seen before.

ROBERTO ORCI

One of the ways "in" for the audience, and for us, was the idea of creating an alternate timeline that would not negate the original continuity. We were using the rules of quantum mechanics. This time travel is different from classical time travel in that the time travel posited by quantum mechanics avoids paradoxes like the grandfather paradox. You can't erase your existence if you run into your grandfather, you merely create a new timeline in which you run into your grandfather.

ALEX KURTZMAN

At the same time, so much of this movie still conforms to what canon might have been if it had been rendered before; if the story of their origins had been told.

SCOTT MANTZ (film critic, *Access Hollywood*)

I love the timeline. They can go off and do whatever they want. The original timeline is intact. So for those of us who are purists, it's still there.

In the film, a Romulan vessel commanded by Nero (Eric Bana) pursues Leonard Nimoy's Spock into the past seeking vengeance for what he believes is Vulcan's responsibility for the destruction of the Romulan homeworld. Nero's arrival in the past—actually twenty-five years before Spock arrives—results in him attacking the starship *Kelvin*, nearly killing the young James Kirk as he's being born, and through his actions generates a completely new timeline that is similar but different to the *Star Trek* we've known from the previous decades.

BRYAN BURK

The thought process was, if we're going to do this, let's make it a place where, if you're a fan, you can go back and see these origins you never saw, and if you are new to the universe, it's a new entryway. That was kind of the logic, which was, let's make a thing that everyone can get on board with, whether or not you've seen it before; this is a new experience for you. Really the justification was, when you see this movie, anyone familiar or not with the world will come out and say, "I'm now a part of the *Star Trek* universe." And if you've never seen it before, hopefully you'll be excited and inspired to go back and watch all the previous episodes. And if you have, hopefully you'll start filling in holes that at least in the film world had not been filled in before.

ROBERTO ORCI

The feeling was that if you become addicted to Kirk and Spock from this movie, you have a ton of adventures you don't have to wait for. This film is a continuation of the previous *Star Trek* and, as we've said, your DVDs will not cease to exist because of this movie. They're still a part of continuity.

ALEX KURTZMAN

Because our story meets Kirk before the events of *The Original Series,* the fun for us was the idea that he was not ready to assume his position of captain. So watching the evolution of that character was reason enough to do this story.

ROBERTO ORCI

And the idea of being this kid who grew up in Iowa, which has been referred to in the movies but never seen, as opposed to meeting him in space, you get to see him very much grounded in a world you can imagine in the cornfields of Iowa. And when we originally met Spock on the series, he was very much a controlled Vulcan. His history has been referred to many times in that he had a real struggle with his Vulcan and human halves, and that he was something of an outcast on Vulcan. He finally defied his father by not pursuing the life his father was hoping for him at the Vulcan Science Academy. Those have all been referred to and never seen.

ALEX KURTZMAN

Along those lines, from the minute you've ever known Kirk and Spock, they've been friends. What this movie posits is that perhaps they *didn't* start out as friends; that it was a friendship that had to be earned. In a way they're opposites, and when opposites first meet, they don't always attract. It's kind of like two brothers learning to respect each other.

ROBERTO ORCI

We looked at John Lennon and Paul McCartney's friendship as part of our model for Kirk and Spock when we were writing. They were opposites and they bonded very young because they both lost their mothers when they were teens. They might not have actually gotten along at the time had it not been for that kind of a bond. They were the only ones who understood each other's pain, so they were definitely an influence on our view of Kirk and Spock. You know, *Star Trek* and the Beatles were products of the sixties, so sometimes you have to tie it all together. By the way, Spock is Lennon, because Paul is the optimist who can see through the pain and still keep his chin up. That's Kirk. Spock is a little more fatalistic with his logic, as John Lennon was.

It's been suggested elsewhere that part of the newfound appeal of *Star Trek* has to do with the current world climate. The 60's show connected with audiences when America seemed to be teetering on the knife's edge; the threat of the Cold War, the ongoing conflict in Vietnam, the battle for civil rights in America, and assassinations of our most respected and beloved leaders. In essence, *Star Trek* served as a prism through which to explore the current state of humanity. In the aftermath of September 11 and the global threat of extremism, which has created an ongoing environment of fear and paranoia, perhaps the appeal of an optimistic depiction of the future once again seems a welcome relief.

ROBERTO ORCI

As we all say, the fact that *Star Trek* represents a future to begin with is one of its most optimistic qualities. I think we take for granted the last few years before September 11. *Star Trek* came at a time when just saying there was a future was an extremely optimistic thing to say. That time is back. *The Original Series* stands out in terms of being societally relevant. It had a Russian, it had a black woman—it was really trying to address the situation in the world while also trying to be escapist. We couldn't agree more that this was a perfect time for *Star Trek*.

ALEX KURTZMAN

It's funny, because if you watch those episodes now, the thing that strikes you is how unbelievably sophisticated those shows were for the time. They didn't pander to anybody; in a way you had to catch up with a lot of the technology and what was happening, and yet it also managed to entertain and have this very relevant social parable behind the whole thing. Shows that can do that are absolute miracles.

ROBERTO ORCI

When we were writing *Star Trek*, it was our goal in developing the story to embrace all the goals that *Star Trek* has, which is not to shy away from what the situation in the world is while simultaneously not failing to be fun or escapist.

ALEX KURTZMAN

That's part of what makes *Star Trek* what it is. It's entertaining and all the things we love about it, but if you stop and look at the deeper meaning, there's real substance there. It's making a comment about basic human relations and politics and everything that you can ever want to think or feel. That's what makes *Trek* and what makes it unique. You certainly couldn't imagine doing *Trek* without taking that into account.

> Several Bad Robot stalwarts were assembled to help maintain the elements that had made *Star Trek* popular in the past while continuing to push it inexorably into the future.

DANIEL MINDEL (director of photography, *Star Trek* [2009])

The goal of J.J. and I was to provide a "movie" feel for the franchise. In many ways the previous movies felt the same as the shows. We gave the *Enterprise* and the other ships scale and weight and depth, and you feel that; you see that. As a result, it gives the movie so much more gravity when you watch it.

Guys of my generation, or some of them at least, love to shoot widescreen, which is what I love to do. What that means is that apart from having a huge picture area the detail and the rendition of the negative is enormous. That means the makeup and the sets and everything else have to be able to stand up to that scrutiny when it's projected on a screen fifty feet wide and twenty feet high, which is the way I see it. I don't look at it as something that's going to be watched on a laptop or home theater. As far as I'm concerned, if it looks good on the screen, it's just going to be huge at home.

Many people in the industry said we needed to shoot this film in HD because it's cheaper, it's better for the effects and all of that. But I was determined that we weren't going to do that. We were going to do it the other way. We were going to do it on film using old technology, which, as far as I'm concerned, is far superior even now than digital technology in terms of image gathering and the quality of the image, which is really what I care about.

SCOTT CHAMBLISS (production designer, *Star Trek* [2009])

From a creative standpoint, there's a real difference between approaching a piece of new material that doesn't have any history and expectation based on what's come before, and this *only* having history and expectations.

In designing the *Enterprise* we started with the original from the TV show and saw what they did to it in the various movies, but we stayed pretty close to the original. And applying the notion of what the great designers of that era were doing on top of what that thing looks like, which is very rigid. I remember taking a red Magic Marker to one of the sketches one of my illustrators had done, which looked like the original. I started to make it a little more supple, a little more curvy and sexy in certain ways, and gave it back to another illustrator to detail that out a little more fully. Ultimately what we came up with was a result of that. It's the same ship, pretty much. The properties are not that different. Certainly the dish and the nacelles are there, but there's a suppleness to them. Not that air plays a part in space, but there's this kind of aerodynamic sexiness about it that we went for.

MICHAEL KAPLAN (costume designer, *Star Trek* [2009])

When I first met with J.J. Abrams, I wasn't sure how the meeting was going to go, but he liked the fact that I *wasn't* a Trekkie. He felt that was a plus, because he wanted something really fresh. He wanted new eyes.

I told him it would be really fun to create a whole new world, yet do an homage to the TV show, because that's where our world in *Star Trek* would end. There were certain things we wanted to be recognizable. Updated, but not done away with, like the *Enterprise* costumes. There's a sixties sensibility I thought was important to keep intact. It was really about finding a balance. I would do some sketching and say, "I love this costume idea, but it doesn't feel like *Star Trek*," and we would abandon it. A design could have been more *Star Wars*, for example. There's a vocabulary that was needed and, of course, I studied the *Star Trek Encyclopedia*.

With the colors of the uniforms, I didn't just say, "Go out and get red, yellow, and blue fabric." We dyed all the fabrics over and over again and did screen tests until we found harmonious colors. The command shirt, for instance, is not really yellow. It's kind of a golden mustard. They're not the same colors that were originally used, but I thought it was necessary to use those *types* of colors. Why complicate something that could be very simple? We want to know who these people are, who they end up being at the end of the movie, and it's kind of how we get there, so why complicate things for the sake of change? It was just coming up with colors that I felt were appealing and would photograph well.

I also wanted to do something more sophisticated than they had done on the TV series, so I created a new fabric where a pattern of the boomerang logo was utilized. You can also see a new black shirt that's a part of the uniform. Back on the TV show, it was all one piece. This is like the undershirt and the uniform is on top of that. It made sense to me that the uniform would have an undershirt, and that it would still be consistent. The shirt is a dark charcoal gray, as are the pants, and the color of the jumpers describe what the person's job is.

I wanted to have a different flavor and a different look on the *Kelvin*. I looked back into 1950's sci-fi films like *Day the Earth Stood Still* and *Forbidden Planet* and kind of wanted to take that retro futuristic feeling and infuse it. J.J. was very happy with that look. That's the kind of research I did, certainly not copying any of those but trying to get that kind of retro flavor so that when you saw it, subconsciously you'd know you were in an earlier world.

MICHAEL GIACCHINO (composer, *Star Trek [2009]*)

There was a lot of discussion early on about what we would use or not use, if anything. The decision was made that it had to be pretty much all fresh. If we were approaching characters from a fresh point of view, and we were approaching everything from this new place, even the music would have to be. The second you play Jerry Goldsmith's theme, it put you in a different place. We found that it kept placing you in this whole different universe that has its own connotations, baggage, and the whole thing. As much as we loved it, it wasn't what we were doing.

Our question was what were we going to do that fits what we were building as opposed to taking something that was made to fit a different thing that was built? That was a tough decision, because obviously we love all of that stuff, but I have always felt that, for me, the cornerstone for *Star Trek* as far as music is concerned is the Alexander Courage theme. That's the one thing that remains. But, again, what we had to ask ourselves was, when do you use it? It's finding the right place, because you can't throw it in all the time. You need to build to it and it has to be something that is born out of the story. That was kind of a tricky problem to work out, but I think we had a lot of fun with it in the end. It's all about when and how and why. Why is always the question, because its so easy to throw in a theme because it's cool, but you need to think, *why* do you need it? *Why* do you throw it in?

Kirk and Spock certainly have their own ideas and motifs and themes. And then there are ideas tied into different things within the film. With Kirk you've got kind of an unfinished guy who's kind of rough around the edges, very instinctive and gutsy and all of those things. He kind of reacts as things are thrown at him, and that idea needs to kind of be reflected in what his music is. Spock is all about thought, all about working things out, all about logic, but then deep down underneath it there is, admittedly or not, an emotion going on there. So those are the kind of things you're trying to figure out and work on while you're writing a specific theme for somebody. An approach from inside them.

What I like about film music is that a character's theme changes with the story, so that Spock's theme, for instance, can be played in a different way in one situation than the way it was played when he was just sitting there alone with his own thoughts. I really think that it's similar to the way an actor emotes differently for different situations. The theme, too, is played differently.

We had an emotional story and it had to be treated that way. It's loud and big when it needs to be, so no worries there, but it's also subdued and gentle when it needs to be. It's one of those things that anytime you approach something like this—especially something that's as huge and epic as this and, on top of that, something you actually like from when you were a kid—that's always scary, but in the end you just say, I'm going to go with what I think fits and so be it.

LUKAS KENDALL (editor, *Film Score Monthly*)

Michael Giacchino's theme for the new films is memorable, but eight bars long. It's like *half* a theme. But he said he tried playing the existing *Star Trek* themes against the picture and they didn't work. It showed you the nature of franchise movies today, how they need constant music, yet move so quickly they never have time to finish a thought.

> One of the greatest challenges facing the film was finding its cast, which would be inhabiting the iconic shoes of its predecessors. While the look and approach to the material was important, as were the action sequences and visual effects, much of it would rise and fall on who was cast for the ensemble.
>
> Those people, of course, were Chris Pine (*Just My Luck, Smokin' Aces*) as James T. Kirk, Zachary Quinto (*Heroes*) as Spock, Karl Urban (*Lord of the Rings, The Chronicles of Riddick, Dredd*) as McCoy, Zoe Saldana (*Vantage Point, Avatar*) as Uhura, Simon Pegg (*Mission: Impossible III, Hot Fuzz*) as Scotty, John Cho (*American Beauty, Harold & Kumar*) as Sulu, and Anton Yelchin (*Huff, Terminator Salvation*) as Chekov.

J. J. ABRAMS

It was critical that we find actors who were not just wonderful to watch and talented and great, but actors who really spoke to the spirit of the characters that Roddenberry originally created. And *not* trying to do impersonations of the actors who originally brought them to life, but rather had elements of those people. This was the approach we took conceptually in terms of the story, visually in terms of the design of the film, the sets, the wardrobe, the props, and certainly with the performances. It needed to feel, and at a glance look, like *Star Trek*. It needed to be cut from the same cloth, because otherwise why the hell would we be doing this film? And yet everything needed to be filtered through the context of today. What is relevant now?

APRIL WEBSTER (casting director, *Star Trek* [2009])

We weren't afraid of recasting these iconic roles, but we knew it was going to be a challenge. We also knew we weren't going to be able to match people exactly, but we did want to give at least a close indication to people; to give a sense of the characters they've known and loved for so long.

For Kirk we weren't looking for someone doing a Shatner impersonation. We wanted somebody who would embody that spirit. Chris Pine did. He was a lifesaver, because we really wanted someone who could give us the cockiness, but still be likable. If you look at the old episodes of Shatner and that character, he was always cocky, but there was also something enormously appealing about him. We auditioned a lot of people all over the place, but there was something that he was able to bring in, that sort of swagger. Not that other people couldn't get that, but Chris just fit the bill. We had narrowed it down to a couple of people and he became the guy.

BRYAN BURK

J.J. and I were in a casting session and there were three potential Kirks outside. Chris came in and couldn't look less like William Shatner. He was *amazing*. It was also the weirdest thing in the world. He came in as himself, but then he started reading and he *became* that character. It was such an out-of-body experience. Co-incidentally, Zachary Quinto, who had already been cast as Spock, was around. We asked them to read a scene together and they did. Instantly it was, like, "Yeah, there they are. Kirk and Spock."

ZACHARY QUINTO (actor, "Spock")

There's a real sense of trepidation at first between Spock and Kirk; and a sort of skepticism and a little bit of uncertainty about where each of the characters is coming from, because it's from such opposite ends of the spectrum. And then there's an appreciation, I think, that is discovered between them. And respect, also, and trust that eventually they both come to regard and understand in each other.

The other thing is that Chris and I knew each other before we did this film. We came to the table with the rapport already forged. We have a lot of mutual friends and we both worked out with the same trainer before either of us got the movie.

He's a friend of ours and I'd be working out and he'd say, "My buddy Chris is on his way over." "Oh yeah, I've heard about that guy. Never met him." So we passed each other, then we met and we both ended up working on the film. So we had a history a little bit and built on it.

CHRIS PINE (actor, "James T. Kirk")

When I heard I'd gotten the part, there's a period of fifteen to twenty minutes or so where you couldn't be any more excited and you're jumping up and down and you're calling everybody you know, and your parents are planning celebratory dinners and all that. And then there's months of anxiety about the fact that you actually have to do it! And that there's going to be a lot of scrutiny. So my response was a mixture of absolute excitement and absolute panic, but the great thing about working with the people involved with this project—J. J. Abrams especially—is that you never felt like there was this heavy responsibility on your shoulders. He always made sure that we were having fun and enjoying the experience, because it is a really unique experience that very few people get to have.

Making the character my own, it's not like I had a checklist of things, like, I should do this, I shouldn't try to do that. These would be good things to emulate, and these would be good things to make my own. I watched much of the original series to get a sense of the aesthetic and the relationship between the characters and what the series had already established, and then I just very simply read my script and tried to do the best job possible to bring to life the character that I read on the page.

RONALD D. MOORE

What I really liked about Chris Pine and that take on the character is that it harkened back to the first-season Kirk, who was a little bit more kickass; a little bit more of a temper, a little bit more of a wildcard, and was a little bit closer to Robert Conrad. I liked that Kirk. The Kirk who is parodied is the third-season Kirk. He's more histrionic and broader. But the early and younger Kirk was a little edgier, a little more dangerous. A little bit more willing to throw a punch and kiss a girl. *That* was the take in the movie, and I liked that.

APRIL WEBSTER

Zachary Quinto was cast as Spock almost right away. At first we weren't even sure what we were really looking for. Did they want a more human Spock? The completely Vulcan Spock? The combination? We did it, like, twenty different ways, but this is something that Zachary has always wanted to play. I guess when you have intention that strong, it sort of became inevitable in this case.

Susan [Bay], who is Leonard's wife, said backstage at Comic-Con how scary it was that he looked like Leonard when he was younger. That's a very tough part for anyone to play. Even if you look like them, it's a hard part for someone to play. How do you play someone caught between these two personalities? Or caught between these two realities of having been shamed his whole life for being half human and having to keep that aspect of himself in control all of the time? I think that Zachary really found a fine line there for us. In the end, his casting was a no-brainer.

ZACHARY QUINTO

I believe that part of the reason I got the role was that it was a place that I understood. There's a duality about Spock and a need to understand that duality and wrestle with it to a certain extent that I can relate to in my life. I think a lot of people can. That sort of disparity sometimes between your heart and your head, and I think that there are many experiences that I've had that informed this iteration of the character and where he is in his journey.

APRIL WEBSTER

Who would have ever thought that a guy from New Zealand would be Bones? We had a general meeting with Karl Urban about the project, and when he left both J.J. and I said, "Bones!" He's got those blue-blue eyes and the dark hair and a DeForest Kelley element. We just had to see if he could do the accent. Karl was just amazing in the role. He did a great, great job. He has a wonderful sense of humor, he's a man of heart and that so totally came through with the scenes with Kirk he had to do. Besides being the grumpy curmudgeon, which is also part of the role, he got to bring the heart to it, which was a friend of Jim's who really cared about him.

KARL URBAN (actor, "Leonard 'Bones' McCoy")

The way it worked was that I took a meeting with April Webster and J.J. and really felt it was up to them to determine how they could see me fitting into their vision. At that point, like everybody, I knew nothing about the story. So I went along, and after that meeting we got word that J.J. would really love to see me try out for

Bones, and I was thrilled to bits, because I've always had a very strong affinity for Bones and for what DeForest Kelley did as being such an integral part of the original triumvirate.

McCoy is a character full of compassion and pain. He has an amazing personal prime directive to help and heal others, whether friend or foe. That's his calling in life. I see him as a staunch and avid supporter of Jim Kirk. Through the course of the film, we get to see their friendship develop from their initial meeting to their days in Starfleet, and we come to understand the bond of their friendship. To me, that was often the most interesting dynamic in material I got to play, because there is a distinct difference between how McCoy *feels* about Kirk or, say, any given situation and how he reacts.

At the beginning of this film, when we find McCoy, he is literally running away to join Starfleet. At the same time, he has this incomprehensible fear of space flight and space itself. You know, Alex and Robert wrote the most amazing dialogue for me. Lines like "Space is full of disease and danger wrapped in darkness and silence"—that, to an actor, is just gold.

APRIL WEBSTER

We *love* Simon Pegg. He did *Mission: Impossible III* for us, so any time we do a film we have to try and have Simon in it. He's so delightful, so inventive. He always brings something special to the part. We saw lots of Scottys, but we kept coming back to Simon. We didn't know what his availability was and ultimately we went to him, because he and J.J. have a great relationship. Simon is a character actor, so he becomes whoever you want him to be. You look at *Mission: Impossible* and he was that tech guy. You look at him in this and he *is* Scotty. I think people like seeing him, as opposed to feeling, like, "Oh, what's Simon Pegg doing in that movie?"

SIMON PEGG (actor, "Montgomery 'Scotty' Scott")

Because I'd worked with J.J. on *Mission Impossible,* I didn't think there was a chance for *Star Trek.* But then I received an e-mail asking if I would be interested in playing Scotty. I couldn't believe it. I told my wife and she laughed, because she's Scottish and also because it's a major iconic sci-fi character. I thought about it for a few days and I just wasn't sure. But then J.J. came back to me and said, "The worst thing that can happen is that every couple of years we get together and have some fun." That seemed like a very good argument for me, and I said yes. Next thing I knew, I was on the bridge of the *Enterprise.*

APRIL WEBSTER

Simon brings wit and speed and cleverness and a very dry humor to him that I just adore. I know I use the word "unexpected" a lot, but you never know what's really going to come out of Scotty's mouth. That's the way you feel when you're watching Simon, because he just embodies the character so well that the character has his own language and rhythm. It's not just him reading lines. He adds a little bit here and there. It's like when Will Smith did *Independence Day*. There were a lot of things that they let him improvise, because he brings so much of his Will Smith-ness to it. It's the same thing with Simon.

SIMON PEGG

I wanted to reach out to someone in Doohan's family, but his son, Chris, beat me to the punch. I said to him, "Look, I'm not going to do anything that disrespects your dad. This is something I want to do in honor of him and in tribute to him and carry on in the spirit of a character that he created." And, really, one that he made one of the most iconic sci-fi characters ever. For a supporting player, if you say *Star Trek* to people, chances are they'll bring up "Beam me up, Scotty."

APRIL WEBSTER

We saw a lot of really good ladies for Uhura. It was a very tough audition, because we weren't using scenes from the script to find someone who could give us that "I'm smarter than you" quality without being obnoxious. But Zoe Saldana was able to do it with some humor, so that she wasn't only defensive, because she has to have an attitude of "I've got to set these guys straight."

There's this whole interaction she has with Chris and what their relationship is. He tried picking her up and she's, like, "Yeah, I don't think so," whereas another woman might have said, "He's cute." But she has a great insight. You get a sense that that character is enormously perceptive, and that's Zoe. She has a deepness to her, a depth that she wears on her, yet she's fun and being beautiful doesn't hurt. You wanted someone you would believe had the authority.

ZOE SALDANA (actress, "Nyota Uhura")

There's an androgynous essence to Uhura. Even though she's very beautiful and her feminine presence is obvious, there's this energy and leadership to her that sort of gives you that feeling that her sex appeal is probably observed and admired by the audience, but her coworkers just acknowledge her energy and authority. And I love that. She's in charge of so many things and she has so much control of herself, her emotions, and she is considered capable enough to run the linguistics department on her own, and I just find that amazing.

In the first movie, there's definitely the curiosity that all the characters have for each other, because they are meeting for the first time. That's one thing I absolutely loved. Here you've got Kirk, who is a very cocky young man who was born to do this. It's a gift. Whether he wants it or not, he possesses it. Things are very easy for him, whereas a character like Uhura is someone who has had to work really hard for everything that she's earned. There's just an awareness of each other, and she's, like, "Why is he so the boss of it all and so disrespectful and so funny?" And I'm pretty sure Kirk goes, "She's sexy, she wears that little dress, she knows what she's doing." Maybe he's not used to dating smart girls or something. So there's definitely a very awesome sense of intrigue that all of the characters are possessing that I absolutely love.

APRIL WEBSTER

We were really concerned about finding someone Japanese for Sulu because of George Takei. We saw so many people for this role, but John Cho just brought the best to it. We actually asked George about *not* casting a Japanese guy, because we were very concerned about that. George said it wasn't Gene Roddenberry's intention that only a Japanese be considered for that part. He explained to us about how the character was to be a representative and that made us feel a lot better.

We were all very familiar with John Cho. I needed someone who was manly and could be a swashbuckler, because the thing about Sulu is that he was someone who had enormous authority himself, would take a lot of risks, and when you think of that fencing scene where he went nuts, he was obviously daring. What's important whenever we cast these parts is that people have humor and are able to see the lighter side. He was also someone in the scenes we were reading who stood up for what he believed in. He had great conviction and integrity. In the read that we did, John was the guy for that. Not that other people couldn't get there, but he just had all of the elements combined. That really makes a big difference when you're representing the character.

ANTON YELCHIN (actor, "Pavel Chekov")

I wasn't just going to make Chekov some Russian character, because that defeats the purpose of playing him. The accent has to be Chekov's accent in terms of past episodes and films.

APRIL WEBSTER

When we said that Chekov was going to be a nineteen-year-old whiz kid, I did bring in a couple of other guys, but I immediately sent Anton's press kit and tape to J.J. because there was no question in my mind that he was the guy. Not a single question in my mind. The nice thing is that Anton is really Russian, can speak Russian, and was raised by Russian parents, so it wasn't going to be Boris and Natasha Russian. The idea for the character in the film is that he was recently recruited and hadn't had an opportunity to perfect his English. Anton is such a smart young man and that comes across instantaneously as far as I'm concerned. I think he brought his innocence to Chekov.

ANTON YELCHIN

I thought a lot about the spirit of Chekov and his genial nature. I think that partially came from the fact that they kind of brought him on as a [The Monkees] Davy Jones-esque comic relief in the second season. And also from the way Walter Koenig played this character and the way that they had Chekov exist. Something I use as an example for how I felt about Chekov is an episode where they land on this planet and are researching it. Instead of doing his work, Chekov spends most of his time with his girlfriend. He's dedicated and hardworking and he's a brilliant navigator, but he has no qualms hanging out with his girl. Just funny things that I wanted to bring to the character to make him both funny and perceptive and intelligent, and yet somewhat awkward the way he is in the series.

J. J. ABRAMS

These actors truly blow my mind with how great they are. It really was because they embodied these characters. They just brought their own wonderful personalities, their great energy and knowledge of what had come before. There were moments when Zoe as Uhura would touch her ear, listening to an incoming message; or when Chris Pine as Kirk is sitting in the captain's chair and would hit the communication button; and certainly Zachary as Spock, who looks so much like Nimoy that it's eerie—watching him raising an eyebrow or walking down the corridor of the *Enterprise*. There were moments when we were shooting where I would get chills, because it was this weird thing where it was so alive. It felt so right, and yet I felt like I was watching this weird resurrection of these characters. As someone who had become a fan by the time we were shooting, it was like watching these old favorites being reborn. Especially having Nimoy around, which was a spectacular thing. He was just the most wonderful and thoughtful and gracious guy.

LEONARD NIMOY

My approach to the character has changed, because Spock has evolved in the sense that a lot of personal experiences have affected him. On the other hand, you've got Zachary Quinto coming into this movie, who is even slightly before the Spock I played in the original series. So you see him even before the place I was playing the character on the original series, and you're seeing me giving a performance that's totally after all of that. This movie contains a very broad spectrum of Spock's character.

I had a wonderful time making the movie. It was very close to myself. I felt totally comfortable, very much like I feel personally. Having arrived where I am as a person, and the place that Spock has arrived, I felt very, very comfortable with it. It was totally like slipping into a warm bath or an old, comfortable sweatsuit.

> Supporting players in *Star Trek* include Bruce Greenwood (*National Treasure: Book of Secrets*) assuming the role of Jeffrey Hunter's Captain Christopher Pike; Chris Hemsworth (soon to be known the world over as Marvel's Thor) as George Kirk, who sacrifices himself so the crew of the starship *Kelvin* (including his just-born son, James) survives Nero's attack; Sonita Henry as an alien doctor aboard the *Kelvin*; and Faran Tahir as the *Kelvin*'s captain, Robau.

BRUCE GREENWOOD (actor, "Captain Christopher Pike")

To find the character of Christopher Pike, I really had nothing to go on but Jeffrey Hunter's portrayal of the character in the first *Star Trek* pilot, "The Cage." The fundamental difference between the Hunter Pike and the Greenwood Pike is that our dilemmas are different, Hunter's being that he was terribly ambivalent about his place in the Federation; he was torn by whether or not he wanted to go back and have a smaller life or that of a commander. My Pike doesn't have an internal wrestling match the way the earlier one did, but he does have second thoughts and mis-givings about the way Starfleet is training officers as by-the-book products that may not, at the end of the day, be what's required for a great leader. So he keeps his eye out for that kind of special young man, and as it happens, Kirk seems to fill that bill.

CHRIS HEMSWORTH (actor, "Captain George Kirk")

I'd never seen a production of that size and that kind of equipment on a set. It was really kind of daunting and I was well aware that I was not in Kansas anymore. The difference being that I'm still as wowed by it now, but it's a little more familiar to me.

To be honest, I knew *Star Trek,* but not in any great detail. It wasn't until after I shot it and the film came out that I started to understand the following and the hysteria and the dedicated fans that surrounded it. Then it was, like, I hope I did an all-right job. I think if I had known all of that beforehand, it would have been a little more uncomfortable and nerve-wracking. Thankfully, my naïveté kept me safe. Getting to the premiere and all around that period, I started thinking, this is *huge.*

SONITA HENRY (actress, "Alien Doctor Aboard the *Kelvin*")

I was just happy to be working, but I was also happy to be part of *Star Trek* in any way, shape, or form. We shot that sequence on the *Kelvin* in Long Beach, and I just remember it being very frantic and hectic and lots of explosions going off. They had basically put an entire can of hairspray in my hair, and I had explosions and sparks about two feet from my head. As I'm running down corridors, I'm think-ing to myself, I am going to have a Michael Jackson Pepsi commercial moment!

FARAN TAHIR (actor, "Captain Robau")

Let me tell you, you walk on the set the first day—the doors open just like they used to do for Shatner with that little "pffffttt." You walk in and you're on the bridge and for five minutes I couldn't believe it. It's the stuff that dreams are made of. All your life it's Shatner's *Star Trek,* I've seen *Next Generation* and all of that, and in that moment you forget that you're an actor. All of a sudden you're that ten-year-old boy, and *then* a crew member comes over and says, "That's your captain's chair." Inside you're doing *cartwheels.* "Oh my gosh, *I'm* the captain. That's *my* chair."

ERIK JENDRESEN

Just prior to J.J.'s film coming out I suddenly got this document in the mail from the WGA [Writers Guild of America]. The WGA was filling a protest on my behalf, because I had not been included in the chain of title of the writers when J.J.'s film and Kurtzman and Orci's script was submitted to the WGA. So they'd already gone ahead and essentially they were going to stop the release of the film. I had no idea of this. I got this notification from the WGA and I immediately called them. I said, "What the hell are you guys doing?" "Well, we're trying to protect you." I said, "Wait a minute. Hang on. What I did had *nothing* to do with the Abrams approach. It's a hundred and thirty years later, it's literally a completely different approach." I said, "Let's do this, let me talk to Kurtzman or Orci or whoever. Get them on the phone and let me have a chat."

And so it was [Roberto] Orci who called me. He knew about the script, but he'd never read it, and he proceeded on the phone to tell me the entire story of their film. Obviously there was no crossover to say the least. I was able to call the WGA and say, "Forget it. Cancel all this stuff. Call off your dogs. This is an incredible waste of time and energy."

Orci called me again shortly thereafter, because he had gone and read my script [*Star Trek: The Beginning*]. It was very gracious of him actually because of what had happened with the whole WGA mess. I reached out and solved it quickly, and I think he appreciated it, and so he read the script and called me and he simply said, "Holy smokes, this should be the basis of a new television series. This is perfect." Because he knew they were sitting on a new franchise. He thought the storyline was such that it could be done as a TV series. It does seem to be a no-brainer. And it would be an appropriate thing actually to go ahead and finally fill in the canon.

While that appears unlikely, the effort to make *Star Trek* more mainstream was deemed a major success, as became instantly apparent upon its May 8, 2009, release. In addition to receiving largely critical plaudits, the film, made at a cost of $150 million (by far the highest budget of any previous *Trek*), earned an impressive worldwide gross of $385 million (the highest ever for the franchise). Most important, it marked the triumphant return of *Star Trek* to the zeitgeist and raised interest (primarily) in the original series again.

ROD RODDENBERRY

My mom [Majel Barrett Roddenberry] loved the film so much. When they were making the movie they reached out to her and said they wanted to use her voice on the *Enterprise*. At the time her health was really failing, but the minute she heard that, she perked up. I mean, she had changed her personality. She couldn't really get out too much at the time, but the day they came over to the house to record her, she got dressed, she walked, she was vibrant. It made her *so* happy. That's what she lived for. Like my father, she was *Star Trek*.

DAVID A. GOODMAN
(consulting producer, *Star Trek: Enterprise*)

I really enjoyed J.J. Abrams' movie, because I liked seeing a reinvention of Kirk and Spock in a modern way. I bumped on things in the movie like beaming across the galaxy, which is something they should have thought twice about, but I liked that idea of taking these actors and saying, "Okay, let's explore these characters." There's so much fun to have with Kirk and Spock interpreted in a new modern way.

BRANNON BRAGA (executive producer/cocreator, *Star Trek: Enterprise*)

Two things struck me about the movie. These characters are so iconic, and there's such a hunger to go back to them, that other actors playing them is acceptable. There was great skepticism, myself included, that they could pull it off, and they did. Also, it's the first *Star Trek* movie since *The Motion Picture* that actually had a real budget, certainly compared to the movies I worked on. So you were able to get some spectacular sequences. The caution was that I thought a couple of the sequences were things you could see in any movie. There was one thing the *Star Trek* movies did well, and that's the action sequences always had something going on and were character motivated. The best example being the Nebula cat-and-mouse game from *Wrath of Khan*.

RONALD D. MOORE

J.J. Abrams extended me a lovely courtesy: he was shooting the first movie and invited me to go down to the set. I went back to Paramount for the first time in years and they were shooting on one of our old soundstages right on *Star Trek* alley. I got to walk in and I was on the *Enterprise* again. This time more as a fan. As somebody who didn't know, who wasn't on the inside, I was seeing people running around in *Star Trek* uniforms armed with phasers. And here's the transporter room, and that's the shuttlecraft, and I was, like, "Wow! This is kind of neat." It was kind of nice to be on that side of the curtain and again and *not* know what this all means. I told them I didn't want to know what the story was. Whatever they were shooting that day was fine and I wouldn't be asking any questions.

DAVID A. GOODMAN

I went to the premiere and I'm sitting in the row with George Takei and Walter Koenig and I'm watching the Chekov scene and him doing the Russian accent joke. I look over and Koenig is laughing his ass off. He's just enjoying the moment. I thought there was an audacity to it and I enjoyed the hell out of it.

BRANNON BRAGA

I was at the premiere with my best friend, who's a rabid *Star Trek* fan, and he did not like Vulcan being destroyed. I worked on the franchise for a long time and I thought it was a breath of fresh air.

RENÉ ECHEVARRIA (supervising producer, *Star Trek: Deep Space Nine*)

It surprised me. I always thought you could recast Sulu, McCoy, even Spock, but never thought they could ever recast Shatner as Kirk. But they did. And it worked!

BRYAN FULLER (executive producer, *Pushing Daisies*)

The cast was amazing. It was thrillingly directed, though the villain wasn't necessarily the smartest problem-solver in the universe—which is always kind of frustrating. But beyond the villain and his two-dimensional reasoning—and the fact that there were so many better ways to solve that problem that he had and the path that he took, and also certain parts of the storyline were removed, so there was confusion as to what they were doing for the last twenty years, I really enjoyed the first movie. *That* was a summer movie I wanted to show up for.

SCOTT MANTZ

What I liked about J.J.'s first movie was that all the years of *Star Trek* films opening huge, playing for a couple of weekends to just the fans, and dropping off had ended. With the exception of *The Motion Picture* and *The Voyage Home*. They needed a *Star Trek* film that was going to appeal to everyone, and that's what the 2009 movie was. It wasn't just great *Star Trek,* it was a great movie, too, because you didn't need to know anything about *Star Trek* the way it reset everything by being in an alternate timeline. So your origin story of bringing the crew together worked and there was magic in it, because there were some cool action scenes, but there were a lot of moments between the characters. Especially between Kirk and Spock.

NAREN SHANKAR (executive producer, *CSI: Crime Scene Investigation*)

J.J. is an amazing director and he's really able to bring a sense of exhilaration to movies. However, I didn't buy the story that much. It kind of felt like the Muppet Babies in space. The kind of analogy I would use is this: The U.S.S. *Nimitz,* the aircraft carrier, is grievously damaged in battle and a precocious midshipman goes, "Hey, my last name is Halsey, put me in charge of the ship" and everybody goes, "That's a great idea! Let's go do that!" That's essentially the movie and I didn't buy it.

Now, does that mean I didn't enjoy sitting down and watching it? The way it's pulled off is pretty thrilling and enjoyable. It's a different thing than the original series. Maybe it's just a function of the times. J.J. is one of those guys who's so good at engaging the pulse of things. He doesn't love *Star Trek* the way he loves *Star Wars* so I got the impression that he was trying to fix what he felt was wrong with it so that it wasn't boring and stodgy and too intellectualized.

KARL URBAN

J.J. made a film for not just the fans of *Star Trek,* but fans of movies. He made an exciting, engaging, action-packed, character-driven film. The characters at the core of this film are the core strengths of it. But beyond that, you just haven't seen a *Star Trek* like this movie.

ZOE SALDANA

What I love about this movie is the way that the characters all grow up so much. They all start as young kids that are studying, working hard; for some it's easy and for some it isn't. And they're going to be faced with all of these challenges that they've only tested for, things that they've never experienced for real. This is the beginning and viewers got to see where this alliance became pure rock, when they all sort of unite and become the team that they are on the *Enterprise.* That sort of gave us chills at times, because J.J. was so nice about giving everybody that journey where you start off in one place and end up someplace else.

LEONARD NIMOY

It's fascinating to watch the roots of the characters that Bill Shatner and DeForest Kelley and myself and the rest of us played. To watch the seeds of those characters being planted is amazing. When we started doing the show, we were a crew on the *Enterprise* going out and doing our missions. In this movie we see the seeds of those characters being planted; where they came from before the *Enterprise*, where they came from before they met each other, how they met each other and what the circumstances were, and how they became the crew that we eventually played. It was great fun to watch.

ZACHARY QUINTO

The strength of this film is about J.J. and his point of view. It's his manner of storytelling and his undeniable gift for expressing universal ideas, but filtered through these kind of established or relatively established worlds and group of characters. He just looks at things differently, switches things back on themselves. Aesthetically this movie is really magnetizing and beautiful and it's about character and connection and about things that everybody can relate to.

LEONARD NIMOY

I believe the audience for this film was looking for two very specific things. One, they wanted big entertainment and, two, I think they found great heart in the relationships of the characters. That's one of the things that this movie accomplishes brilliantly. The heart at the core of this movie is excellent and it's very exciting to see. It's a very big and grand adventure, but the people at the heart of it are all solidly in place. You know who they are, how they're dealing with each other, how they're coming together as a crew, and it's really exciting to watch.

BRYAN BURK

The press was always saying that we were making a movie for a lot of different people. You feel, like, obviously there were forty years of fans. You're taking on a great franchise or property that has been around for a long time. It's funny, when J.J. first started burying himself into the world of *Star Trek,* he began by coming to understand what Gene Roddenberry wanted with the property, why he created it, what he was thinking about, what his view of *Star Trek* in the world was. He wanted to go back and be as truthful to that vision as he could. But if you do your job right, you're really making a movie for yourself and your hope is that it's a movie you'll love and the people out there will love. But you never want to make a movie for others.

J. J. ABRAMS

This movie was not trying to appeal to *Star Trek* fans only. It's trying to appeal to people. If they happen to be *Star Trek* fans, great. Of movies in general, better. This is a movie that is hopefully something that, in a Roddenberry-ian way, redefined what it is to be a Trekkie.

ROBERTO ORCI

When we were first doing *Star Trek*, it was definitely a turning point, and I'd like to think the turning points in the history of *Trek* have always in a way made *Trek* better as it's gone on. I feel that we have been so incredibly influenced by so many of the wonderful decisions that the different teams that have worked on *Star Trek* over the years have made. It's simply an honor to be a part of it and to have inherited the mantle. We couldn't have been doing that without the instruction that everyone else had given us and the road map that was set out for us. We owed it to everyone who came before us to kind of do this right.

RICHARD ARNOLD (*Star Trek* archivist)

J.J. has done a brilliant job of bringing *Star Trek* back to life. It was about as dead as it could have been, to the extent that the studio had gotten rid of everything— they felt it was a waste of money to keep any of it in storage. As for Gene, in his last interview he had been asked what he thought *Star Trek*'s future would be. He felt that the current people in charge would drive it into the ground and kill it. When asked if there was anything he could do to stop that, he said no, it had become too valuable. But he hoped that some day, years from then, some bright young thing would come along and reinvent it, and possibly do a better job of it than he did. And he wished them luck.

HEART OF DARKNESS

"YOU SHOULD HAVE LET ME SLEEP!"

J.J. Abrams' 2009 reboot of *Star Trek* did *precisely* what was expected of it, giving the franchise a shot in the arm, providing a gateway for new fans and, to a large degree, thrilling old fans who were happy to see their favorite crew of the *Enterprise* brought back to life, albeit with new actors portraying the iconic roles. The question was, of course, whether its success could be repeated. The *other* question was why it would take four years for the sequel to reach theaters after so much momentum had been built up with the critically acclaimed first film. In modern Hollywood, four years could seem like an eternity in terms of audience attention spans that communicate in 140 characters or less.

Star Trek had always underperformed overseas, which had been acceptable in the past with the domestic box office and home video easily covering the smaller budgets. With the new films, the much larger budgets (exceeding $200 million for the second film reportedly), it was essential that the films work both in the United States and internationally.

ROBERTO ORCI (writer/producer, *Star Trek Into Darkness*)

We can't deny that the second film might have been hurt at the box office by the delay. Normally, though, screenwriters and directors and such are accused of being crassly after the dollar, and suddenly with this movie, it was, like, "They waited too long to cash in!"

ALEX KURTZMAN (writer/producer, *Star Trek Into Darkness*)

I would argue the opposite . . .

ROBERTO ORCI

How dare you?

ALEX KURTZMAN

Internationally, *Star Trek* has always been a real challenge. It just hasn't been embraced in the way that *Star Wars* was, but in fact Paramount did a very good job
in the four years between movies of getting the world to know that this *Star Trek*
was something different from what the international market had not fully embraced before.

ROBERTO ORCI

And that includes giving out DVDs of the movie in international markets, and just
really being generous with the material and letting it go out there.

ALEX KURTZMAN

So when you look at our international numbers and see that they're 80 percent
higher than they were last time for the most challenging part of the marketplace,
that's actually an enormity. I don't know if it could have been accomplished *without* the four years' lead time to educate the audience on how our last movie was
different from what everybody knew before. So I would call that a huge win for
Star Trek.

ANTON YELCHIN (actor, "Pavel Chekov")

Even though it was four years between films, you can quickly see *why*. You see all
of the work that's been put into it, you see the complexity of the relationships, the
complexity that builds on what was discovered in the first one, which makes it that
much more interesting. You get that much more insight into these people. And
then the world that you're in, the scope and the scale of the film, is that much bigger. But the kind of human being that J.J. is, the kind of filmmaker that J.J. is, and the
intellect that he brings, views one thing as the most important: quality. Which is
what you want. He takes his time; he doesn't really give a damn whether it's two
years, three years, or four years between films. He wants people to pay their ten or
eleven dollars and have that money worth it to them. You want people to like the
film, to get drawn in, and you don't want to jeopardize that by just churning one out.

During the four-year hiatus there were attempts to keep the "Abramsverse" alive
via fiction for fans. Some novels reached the public and some did not. In terms of

the latter, there were four sequel novels that were written, edited, and ultimately canceled out of concern that they might conflict with future films. Those novels were Alan Dean Foster's *Refugees*, Christopher L. Bennett's *Seek a Newer World*, David Mack's *More Beautiful Than Death* and Greg Cox's *The Hazard of Concealing*.

All four authors were excited about the possibility and ultimately disappointed when publication plans were canceled. It wouldn't be the first time Bad Robot would bump heads with Paramount over conflicting thoughts about the licensing of the property, with the studio looking to milk as much money as possible out of the ancillaries and Bad Robot wanting to be more conservative in exploiting *Star Trek* outside of the movies, which included their unrealized hope of limiting the release of merchandise based on non-Abramsverse *Trek*, controlled by CBS Consumer Products division and not Paramount.

ALAN DEAN FOSTER (author, *Star Trek: Refugees*)

The altered timeline opened up a raft of possibilities in the sense that anything is fair game now, because nothing is canon. You can start all over again with the same characters and same general background and do anything you want. By the same token, just as the people who did the film realized, you don't want to alienate the legion of fans who have grown up with *Star Trek*, so while you've got unlimited range to your storytelling, you have to keep in mind that you don't want to do something so outrageous that it turns everybody off.

CHRISTOPHER L. BENNETT (author, *Star Trek: Seek a Newer World*)

The new timeline is an intriguing mix of the familiar and the new. On the one hand, it's a chance to explore the formative years of the characters we know so well; to write about a younger Kirk, Spock, McCoy, etc. as they're still getting to know each other and feeling out their relationships. But at the same time, there are fresh angles and twists that add spice to the experience and give you new things to discover. And while it can be limiting to be deprived of the ability to build on past *Trek* continuity, it's also somewhat liberating not to be bound by such an enormous canon, to build a story purely on one movie and the fundamentals of the *TOS* characters and universe.

DAVID ALAN MACK (author, *Star Trek: More Beautiful Than Death*)

All bets were off. The past of the *Star Trek* universe changed, and so might its future. As an author of original *Star Trek* tie-in novels, I was able to write a book based on the new film without having to worry about forty years of trivia and continuity. I had to respect only the details established in the new movie and I was encouraged not to muddy the waters with references to other books. The result, I hoped, was that *More Beautiful Than Death* would feel familiar and accessible to fans from whom the new movie was their entry point into the franchise.

GREG COX (author, *Star Trek: The Hazard of Concealing*)

I'd written over a dozen previous *Trek* novels and short stories, but I really tried to shake off any mental cobwebs and approach this book as a brand-new thing. The most important effect of the new timeline, of course, is that the destinies of Kirk and Spock and the rest are no longer set in stone. We don't know what the future holds for them anymore.

ALAN DEAN FOSTER

I was led to believe that the books were canceled because Paramount didn't want to chance having anything come out that might contradict or otherwise adversely affect anything that future writers or directors might wish to do. In other words, there should be nothing a third or fourth or more films should have to worry about in regards to non-cinematic canon. . . . But my book, *Refugees,* is a good one, and I'm sad that fans can't get to read it.

> What they *could* read was the series of IDW comic books that took place between the two films, and have continued since *Star Trek Into Darkness*, all of which have been written by Mike Johnson, a veteran of Roberto Orci and Alex Kurtzman's former production company, K/O Paper Products.

MIKE JOHNSON (writer, IDW *Star Trek* comics)

Having close access to the movies meant that I could shape the comics to complement the films and avoid any conflicts. For the comics that appeared between the first two films, I tried to emphasize that the crew was still very new, both to serving in Starfleet and to each other. We wanted to show them gaining experience, but not so much that they would be perfectly at ease in their jobs by the beginning of *Into Darkness*.

By the time *Star Trek Into Darkness*, which saw J.J. Abrams returning as director, finally reached theaters on May 16, 2013, expectations were at a fever pitch among fans anxious for the latest *Star Trek* adventure.

CHRIS PINE (actor, "James T. Kirk")

The first one was a great position to be in, because no one was expecting much of anything, so you could either live up to people's low expectations or beat them by a mile. I hope we did the latter and, so yes, for the second one there was the sophomore effort. We were not making an album, but we were making a film and you want to be sure it's as good as the first one and that it lives up to people's expectations.

JOHN CHO (actor, "Hikaru Sulu")

I wasn't overwhelmed by expectations, mostly because of J.J. I think he does what a leader does, which is to shoulder the responsibility. I never sweated it. I realized that there were expectations. I realized intellectually that we would have to meet certain expectations or exceed them, but I didn't emotionally sweat it, so to speak, because I felt very confident in our captain.

ZACHARY QUINTO (actor, "Spock")

What sets J.J. apart is the emphasis he puts on humanity and character. He doesn't do things by the book and he certainly hasn't with *Star Trek*.

J. J. ABRAMS (director/producer, *Star Trek Into Darkness*)

This movie goes further than the first movie in every way. There are volcanic planets, wild spaceship chases, and massive effects, but there is also a more nuanced story. The goal we had was to keep all the comedy, humanity, and buoyancy while going into more complex and darker territory. For the story to move forward, this had to be a more ambitious movie than the first. The action and the scale were light-years ahead. Bringing in IMAX and 3D technology gave audiences yet another kind of excitement and fun to be had. But at the same time, no matter the scale or the format, the thing that still mattered most to everyone was to tell the most exciting and emotional story yet.

MICHAEL GIACCHINO
(composer, *Star Trek Into Darkness*)

Set pieces are always great, but without a character reason to have them, they get kind of boring. That's one of the things I really love about what J.J. does—he does his best to make sure that the characters are always at the forefront of everything. Whatever is happening, it's because the characters either did something or need something and not just because of some random reason to have a chase scene or some sort of action moment. It always revolves around the characters, and the thing that I really enjoyed about this movie is the evolution of the characters from where they were in the first film. The first film was basically like your first day at school for all of these guys storywise, and *Into Darkness* was more about how they're fitting into this world that they've opted to be a part of.

J. J. ABRAMS

I can't tell you how many story meetings we had. We were constantly collaborating, making adjustments, figuring out what needed to be set up. I felt really lucky to be working with Bob Orci, Alex Kurtzman, and Damon Lindelof again. They were tireless, and they created a story in which, at one point or another, each of the main characters has their life and their ideals on the line.

Early on, the film was officially described by Paramount in a press release as follows: "When the crew of the *Enterprise* is called back home, they find an unstoppable force of terror from within their own organization [in the form of 'John Harrison'] has detonated the fleet and everything it stands for, leaving our world in a state of crisis. With a personal score to settle, Captain Kirk leads a manhunt to a war zone world to capture a one-man weapon of mass destruction. As our heroes are propelled into an epic chess game of life and death, love will be challenged, friendships will be torn apart, and sacrifices must be made for the only family Kirk has left: his crew."

ROBERTO ORCI

We were thinking about this story from the moment the first movie ended and it never really left our minds. We were doing other things, but *Star Trek* was always in the back of our minds.

ALEX KURTZMAN

We felt very protective of the first movie and we knew what a weird needle it was going to be to thread, because we wanted to appeal to die-hard fans as much as people who didn't like *Star Trek*. We all felt very gratified at the reaction we got to the first movie, which meant an even stronger sense of protecting it the second time around. And that responsibility never stopped being daunting. The minute it does, we have no right to be doing it anymore.

> In a piece of thinly veiled secrecy that didn't prove all that shocking to fans, the so-called John Harrison turned out to be Khan Noonien Singh, the twentieth-century genetic superman originally played by Ricardo Montalban in *The Original Series* episode "Space Seed" and the feature film *Star Trek II: The Wrath of Khan*. Rather than being discovered by Captain Kirk and the *Enterprise*, this time, he is, instead, discovered by a Starfleet's Admiral Marcus (Peter Weller), who is aggressively searching for solutions to problems such as the one presented by Nero in the first film and the means of transforming Starfleet into a more militarized organization.

ALEX KURTZMAN

We knew going in that we were biting off an enormous amount by taking on Khan, and it took us literally a year of debate about how to proceed, whether or not it was the right thing to do, and what it would mean to do that. *And* what the expectation would be by taking that on. You certainly can't fault us for not taking the time to consider our choice—some people may disagree with the choices that we made, but we did not go into it blindly. I think that we feel, for the most part, that we accomplished everything we wanted to.

ROBERTO ORCI

It's easy to fall in a trap when you're using a known character or a known situation to think that the audience is somehow going to be aware of it, and therefore bring love, or meet you halfway, and the expectations are on the story, so it had to stand on its own. It had to be a story where you didn't need to know who the hell Khan was. Our movie had to stand on its own, just like the first movie did. If you knew Kirk and Spock, great. Now you get to see their childhood and you get to go, "Oh, that's why they're that way." If you hadn't seen Kirk and Spock ever before, you're, like, "Oh, look, human kid, alien kid get together and they become best pals. Amazing. Great story." Same thing with Khan—the story is about Starfleet waking up a cryogenically frozen, genetically engineered super human and using him for nefarious purposes.

ALEX KURTZMAN

There's a point where Kirk and Khan have to work together. What fascinated us was what happens when you have to partner with Hannibal Lecter if that's your only option. For us, you take all of the things that you think about Khan—Can he be trusted? Who is he *really*?—and you say, "Let's devise a plot whereby Kirk has no choice but to partner with the one man who can either destroy him or help him." And the fun of that is playing the game with the narrative of having Spock contact Spock Prime in the middle of that sequence in order to remind everybody, "This guy is going to fuck you over; nothing that you do is going to change that." So the bomb is symbolically put under the table and now you're waiting to see if he's going to be the Khan from *Wrath of Khan* or somehow our version is going to deviate enough from canon that it pays homage to everything we know about Khan, but brings a new context to the character. And *that* was the fun of it for us, just moving right in to what the audience's expectations were with Khan, because those expectations were *our* expectations, and if we can get ourselves to feel, to be asking those questions and to be unsure of the outcome, which was the whole point of creating an alternative timeline, then I felt we were making the right choices.

ROBERTO ORCI

Alex makes an incredible point, and two things about that: one is that's why it's *not* a remake of what's come before. There's no precedence for that with Khan. Alex just articulated what works best for fans who actually have expectations. For fans who said we threw it all away, you only get the juiciness of contrasting the fact that, is time going to repeat . . . oh, wait, they're working together now. *That's* for fans. If you're not a fan, it doesn't matter; you're just watching a story of "Can I trust this man or can't I?" and that works on its own. But for fans, using

Khan gives it a whole other layer, and we thought it was *not* just homage to *Wrath of Khan*, but also something for fans to play with, as evidenced by the fact that we are fans and this just tickled us.

ALEX KURTZMAN

In *Wrath of Khan*, despite the fact that Khan was such a bad guy, when he monologues about having been marooned on the planet and having lost his family, it's a very relatable and understandable motivation, and that's what made him such a great villain. And that was something we felt we could not change about Khan on any level. He had to be someone who was ultimately dedicated to family, and the protection of his family. That was going to perfectly mirror in our minds Kirk's arc, and the idea that he doesn't quite understand what it means to be a captain yet.

Some of the fans said in their criticisms of the first movie, "Well, gosh, it certainly seemed easy for Kirk to be made captain," and "The Kirk we knew got there in a very different way." You could certainly say that, but on the other hand, Kirk *did* save the world in the first movie, and that does feel like it should qualify him to be captain.

That being said, whereas Kirk and Spock worked together to accomplish the goal in the first movie, Kirk certainly does not have the maturity or the experience. Only experience can give you what the Shatner Kirk had, and our Kirk didn't have that yet. But that's the fun of the game that we're playing and the story we're telling, because we're watching our Kirk become a man, and he's not there yet. That's why our villain was so exciting to us, and that's why we ultimately chose Khan, because Khan is the perfect foil for that arc.

In the film's climax, the writers cagily played with a reversal on *Wrath of Khan*, where instead of Spock sacrificing his life to save the ship, it's Kirk who pays the ultimate price (though the use of Khan's blood reverses that in the film's coda).

ROBERTO ORCI

They see the final death scene that is reversed as some kind of retread that doesn't resonate because in *The Wrath of Khan* Kirk and Spock were already friends. Well, in this movie we reversed their meaning—in *The Wrath of Khan* that was two friends who were old friends saying good-bye to each other. In our movie, it's two friends realizing that they *are* friends, and the situation works just as well to solidify that point. For some fans, their preconceived notions prevented them from evaluating the fact that the movie is actually worthy on its own, and that's why they were having a slight dissonance with people who didn't know *Star Trek* very well and obviously had a great reaction to it.

ALEX KURTZMAN

It's only exact dialogue for the first few lines, and then it branches off into separate dialogue. So we obviously were paying homage to it, and while some of the circumstances were similar, which is reflected by the line "Ship, out of danger?" everything after that is different.

ROBERTO ORCI

Think about it: You've decided to reverse that scene. Kirk is trying to save the ship just like Spock was. What are you going to do, rewrite those lines? "Hey, are we okay?" "Hey, did I save the ship?" It feels dumb *not* to use the lines that apply specifically to that scenario, so instead of saying "I'm trying to save the ship, did it work or not?" we said "Hey, man, let's just pay homage to it and use *Star Trek*." And after that it goes into an entirely different thing of Kirk being afraid to die and the situation being totally reversed. So, sure we debated it, and sure it was something to think about, but put yourself in that situation and try and rewrite good stuff—we'd be equally harassed for "Oh, they tried to rewrite that scene and failed." It's the Kobayashi Maru *every* time.

ALEX KURTZMAN

I've always said *Wrath of Khan* and the death scene was about the ending of a friendship, and our death scene was actually about the beginning of a friendship, because it's not until the death scene in our movie that Spock finally understands what Kirk is trying to tell him about the meaning of friendship.

ROBERTO ORCI

Khan survives at the end of the film and is put back on ice. We're of two minds. On the one hand, we never want to count sequels before they hatch. We want every movie to be internally consistent and stand on its own and not require a previous knowledge. But if you *have* knowledge of previous incarnations, then you're rewarded through sort of inside information.

But we like to make sure we leave things that are consistent with the movie. So Khan being alive . . . well, that's the theme of the movie: We're not going to execute someone without him going through a trial, so him being alive at the end could be perceived as some Easter egg to save ourselves in the future, but it's also the logical and moral conclusion of the movie. What happens next is anyone's guess. But *this* movie closes by being consistent with its own theme and morals, and we don't know how to do anything other than that.

You may say we're saving Khan for later, but we're thinking we're saving Khan for his trial where you actually get to see whether he's guilty or innocent, and what it all means in the future. But are we also saving ourselves this easy bad guy for later? We could be. That could be a nice bonus to our incredible integrity-filled decision to keep him alive at the end.

Returning from 2009's *Star Trek* were a number of the key behind-the-scenes personnel, who are mainstays of "Team Abrams," and who, like everyone else, felt the challenges of production. Among those crew people were composer Michael Giacchino, director of photography Dan Mindel, visual effects supervisor Roger Guyett, costume designer Michael Kaplan, and production designer Scott Chambliss.

MICHAEL GIACCHINO

For me, it was always about really focusing on each character's storyline and making sure that when I'm writing for them, it's appropriate for that moment and it's not just me saying I want to write a big piece of music. I'm always having to remember what came before and what is coming after. Hopefully the steady ramp-up for the audience is exactly that, a steady ramping up to an emotional climax in the film. It's always a challenge, especially on this film it just seemed more intricate. More mature in a way in a lot of facets.

DANIEL MINDEL (director of photography, *Star Trek Into Darkness*)

We tried to preserve the fact that the *Enterprise* was a brand-new ship and really shiny and new. The bridge looked and felt like an Apple Store. It was all clean and sparkly. We tried to preserve all of that, but what we brought to this one was the fact that we were outside more. We opened up the world a bit more in the sense that we had another interior location to set the guts of the *Enterprise* against as opposed to just having the Budweiser brewery in L.A. We went up to Northern California to a real high-tech laboratory that we were allowed to use as a backdrop and we shot on the streets of L.A. and a couple of other locations around. Which gave a huge scope. Plus we also created a planet, which we got to go outside on and that's really cool.

MICHAEL GIACCHINO

The theme is very different than what you have been used to from any of the *Star Trek* movies and that was by design. When I first started writing that theme, I must have written thirty versions of it, and most of them were much more akin to what you would expect from a *Star Trek* theme. Very big, grandiose spacefaring music, but none of them felt right against our movie. There was something just not right about it. The truth was we weren't making the old *Trek*. We were doing something slightly different, taking the characters in a slightly different direction and doing some different things with them. I was at a point where I just didn't know what to do, and Damon Lindelof said to me, "Listen, why don't we just forget that this is a *Star Trek* movie. Forget that it even takes place in space. Go home and write a theme that is about two people who meet and become the best of friends."

I got that, because that's essentially what we were doing, making a movie about these two people who cross paths and ended up being the best of friends. Once I let all of that emotional baggage go, and the fact that I was a *Star Trek* fan and even a huge fan of all the scores of those movies, I was able to focus on what this movie really was and what it needed. Once I wrote the theme, I showed that to J.J., and he said, "That's *our* movie." It was a really interesting process to go through and one I had never gone through on a film. I'm usually pretty focused and know exactly what to do when it comes to writing for a movie. At the beginning of that first movie it was a very difficult process for me.

DANIEL MINDEL

The thing that we like to do with CG work is, first of all, have some realism to it so that when we do shoot it, we shoot it outside when it's possible. We shoot in the elements so we get a wind and atmosphere. To go downtown we shoot outside and then ILM takes out the things that are anachronistic that people might recognize and turn them into twenty-third-century buildings and architecture and what have you. We have the sunlight and the road and the pavement that are real. At least it retains a bit of something.

One particular challenge was shooting the *Enterprise* in the water. I don't know how another person would do it, but for me I'm an avid scuba diver so I know what it's like to be underwater and the difference between light and color under the water as opposed to above the water. Not that I've been in space, but I've seen a lot of photography of space. I just try to follow the laws of physics, basically. The reality of the *Enterprise* is that it's a CG ship and so it lives in a world where the effects guys can put in space or underwater. The rendition they give is based upon photographs and sketches and what have you. My job is to then—where we interact with those backgrounds through a window or something like that—where I come in is I soften the lights to be underwater; I make it more subdued, cooler, or bluer in color. It's very simple, really.

ROGER GUYETT
(visual effects supervisor, *Star Trek Into Darkness*)

At one point the ship tilts radically as it begins a crash landing. We called that the "roly-poly sequence." The ship is turning and the artificial gravity is failing, and when that happens, people are going to start sliding around. J.J. got very interested in the idea that if you move the camera in certain ways and if people behaved in certain ways, it would really feel like everything on the ship had wrapped around upside down. And he was right.

MICHAEL KAPLAN
(costume designer, *Star Trek Into Darkness*)

The second movie was a lot bigger, but there were other challenges. I'd gotten over the basic reinventing of the Starfleet uniforms, but there were other uniforms, a lot more complicated costumes to do. Also I felt that I needed to surpass what had been done the first time, because people are always looking as time goes on for a franchise to keep getting bigger and better. One particular challenge was the wet suits used. They were really difficult to make. If you're doing a contemporary movie, just buy a wet suit, or you can have them made. I wanted the fabric printed, we needed different colors for the different actors who are wearing them that corresponded with their placement and their uniform colors. We had to try experimental dying and getting them to fit just right. We did them all in-house. I'm really happy with the way they turned out.

SCOTT CHAMBLISS
(production designer, *Star Trek Into Darkness*)

Stepping back into a project four years later was totally surreal; I'd never done that with any project before. On the one hand it felt really familiar, like we never left, and on the other hand it just felt like it was so long ago because we all looked so much older.

The ship gets bigger in this one. It was really satisfying to do that. We also got to take over the stage in L.A. at Sony—the old MGM stages—and we filled the entire Stage 15 with all of our different *Enterprise* sets and literally connected them so that on-screen the camera could go from one end of the stage to the other and remain on the *Enterprise*. That was *really* satisfying. The connectivity is a great pleasure.

J. J. ABRAMS

The set being contiguous, we were able to go from the bridge, down a hallway, into the turbo plaza area, and go around a corner into the med bay. It gives the ship a sense not only of scale, which is a fun by-product, but a real sense of being interconnected. It elevates everything—the performances, the lighting, the camera work.

SCOTT CHAMBLISS

Into Darkness let us get to know the *Enterprise* a little bit better, and it becomes a very active, action-packed place for our crowd as opposed to walking and talking in the hallways.

J. J. ABRAMS

A number of our sets were more vertical than horizontal, and the use of IMAX makes the scale feel even bigger. We used it for the volcanic jungle planet Nibiru in the beginning of the film, the Klingon planet Kronos, and especially the end chase through San Francisco. It became a rule that when the action was outdoors, we shot using IMAX, and when we were indoors, we used anamorphic 35. Obviously, you can't do a movie called *Star Trek* and not have green screen elements, but one of the things we continued from the first movie in *Into Darkness* is the idea of finding locations or building sets whenever we could to create a world that isn't synthetic or sterile, but feels very real.

The guest actors of *Star Trek Into Darkness* include Peter Weller (*RoboCop, Buckaroo Banzai*) as Admiral Marcus, one of the actual antagonists of the film, who is pushing against the very tenets of *Star Trek*; Alice Eve (*Entourage*) as the admiral's daughter, Carol, who, in the Prime Universe (specifically, *The Wrath of Khan*) was played by the late Bibi Besch and revealed to be a former lover of Kirk's who gave birth to their son, David; and in a role originally offered to Benicio Del Toro (*The Usual Suspects, Sicario*), Benedict Cumberbatch (*Sherlock, The Imitation Game*) as John Harrison, revealed to be the eugenically bred superman Khan Noonien Singh.

ALICE EVE (actress, "Carol Marcus")

I knew very little about *Star Trek*, but did research before I started shooting. It was great for me to step on the bridge, though I fell on my bum the very first time. Which is a testament to how clean and shiny they kept the floors.

MICHAEL GIACCHINO

For Khan, it wasn't about writing so much as what he wanted or the things that he's doing in the film. It's more about his past and the way his brain works. For me it was one of those things where I found him to be a very interesting character, especially because it's Benedict, who's such a great actor. Sometimes all he needs to do is look at you and that's all you need. So for me the music was all about what was going on inside that guy's head. I kept looking at him and saying, "What is he thinking right now?"

BENEDICT CUMBERBATCH (actor, "John Harrison"/"Khan")

I'd seen the first film and I thought it was just terrific. It was an amazingly witty, intelligent romp at the same time as being faithful to the original. J.J. creates an atmosphere on the set that is absurdly good fun.

J. J. ABRAMS

In the first film, we had extraordinary actors who took these iconic characters and made them their own, with a spirit that completely validated what they were doing.

Benedict did exactly the same thing with his character. He came to the table with a whole new attitude, personality, background, and strength, but he's such a compelling and powerful actor that it works. He has a wry sophistication to his approach that is so right. To me it nullified any concerns of how he might look. We are not in any way undoing what's come before, but he is our version of this character. It was the right way to go, because he was so damn good.

BENEDICT CUMBERBATCH

J.J. and I talked a lot about my character, about who this man is and what role he played in Starfleet. I also enjoyed the physical aspect of the film, which Zachary Quinto and Chris Pine helped me on. Zach and Chris are just brilliant at this stuff, very strong and fast, but they were also really kind and considerate with me. They were always concerned about safety—but then they just let the emotions rip.

KARL URBAN (actor, "Leonard 'Bones' McCoy")

I loved watching Chris and Benedict when they were doing scenes together, because the sparks would literally fly.

CHRIS PINE

Benedict went at this character like a scalpel. His performance is so precise, I watched in awe as a fan and a fellow actor. It was chilling and creepy, and hands down, I think he has created some moments that will stand in the pantheon of great *Star Trek* moments.

> Beyond Khan and his impact on Starfleet, a primary goal of the screenplay for *Star Trek Into Darkness* was to explore the continuing evolution of the *Enterprise* family.

ROBERTO ORCI

It was important to see where they are in the evolution of their friendship, but not to the point they were in the five-year mission in the original series, because they're not quite there yet. You're between the 2009 movie when it started and the solidified friendships or relationships you saw in the original series.

MIKE JOHNSON

The guiding theme throughout the movies and the comics is that the new cast is at a younger point in their lives. The crew is learning how to do the job, learning how to work together, learning how wondrous and dangerous uncharted space can be. Our Kirk needs to prove himself more than the original Kirk did in any given episode. Spock deals with the ongoing ramifications of Vulcan's destruction, and Spock and Uhura are obviously in a romantic relationship. Scotty has a more skeptical view of Starfleet than he did in the original series. Sulu demonstrates his leadership abilities earlier than his original counterpart. Chekov is more demonstrably a prodigy and arguably the smartest person on the ship. I'd say Bones is the one who differs the least from the original, as befits Karl Urban's brilliant performance.

ALEX KURTZMAN

The mistake we did *not* want to make was assuming that the result of them coming together is that they're the bridge crew we knew before. It was particularly critical in relation to Kirk and Spock, because at the end of the first movie, they've come together as a means of necessity. It isn't like they joined forces because they're the best of friends. They're not the Kirk and Spock you remember from *The Wrath of Khan*. They still have to earn their friendship; they have trials to go through together before they can get to that place.

CHRIS PINE

Kirk in the second film has to deal with humility, and if the first film was Kirk getting the chair rather quickly due to an unforeseen series of events, the second is about him really earning the chair and understanding what it means to be the captain of a starship—the captain many, many people depend on for survival . . . or not. So it's a growing process.

ROBERTO ORCI

Like we said, that's actually a good example of where criticism from fans of the first film played a role in the story of the second. People were saying, "Gosh, Kirk became the captain so fast," so when you meet him in this movie, part of the struggle he's going through is that very perspective in this universe. People think maybe he made captain *too* fast and he needs to be slowed down a bit and maybe he's not ready. And in a way the movie becomes about Kirk proving that he *is* ready and very much incorporating some of the criticisms of the first movie and making it a dramatic obstacle in the second, which is great.

BRUCE GREENWOOD (actor, "Christopher Pike")

Because of Kirk's actions, he ends up serving under Pike again. I think they were wise to examine this mentor relationship and what it means. In spite of someone being your mentor and handing over the reins because, at least for the moment, he's unable to continue, doesn't absolve the recipient of responsibility. If the responsibility is deemed to be unmet or called into question, then there's issues. I was always hoping from the end of the first one that this mentor relationship between Pike and Kirk would continue and evolve, and it did.

MICHAEL GIACCHINO

It's that feeling of "You betrayed me. I stuck my neck out for you, I did this for you, I supported you and I believed in you and this is what you do?" It's really a father-son sort of situation, which everyone has been through at one point in their life. It makes it very real and everyone can identify. Bruce plays it so well. He's sitting there yelling at Chris, and you feel completely like you let your best friend down.

BRUCE GREENWOOD

In this situation, it's not about Kirk making amends. It's making a personal journey to a place where responsibility comes naturally. When I say responsibility for your actions, it's about making considered choices. Choices that aren't made out of bravery. Choices that aren't made out of ego. It's getting the big picture. The Kirk of old just imagines that if you win every freakin' battle, you've got the war down. And if you lose a battle on the way, it's fine, but it's gonna bug him. Here he's got to make decisions that are more complicated.

CHRIS PINE

Kirk's getting older and he comes face to face with his insecurities about his capabilities as a leader and himself as a person. Why is he doing what he's doing? Why is he captain of the starship? Why is he leading people? What does it all mean?

SIMON PEGG (actor, "Montgomery 'Scotty' Scott")

Scotty was less bitter in the second film, because he's found a place in the world. In the first film he's disillusioned because he's been disciplined in a rather unceremonious way, and now he's got a position and it's a ship he really likes. But he's still as cantankerous as he was. The thing about Scotty is that he thinks he owns the ship he's working on. It's *his* ship and everyone else is staff, so he has that slightly protective attitude.

JOHN CHO

You can almost feel sorry for Sulu and all of the characters, because they have to mature so quickly. They feel like children who had to take care of the house in Mom and Dad's absence or something. It's the crises that are so enormous, and they're so young and have had to shoulder so much. To me it feels like all the characters in the film were prematurely mature.

KARL URBAN

To me, the core of *Star Trek* has always been that it's about a group of people who aren't necessarily geared to get along perfectly with each other, but who always overcome their differences to defeat a common adversary. I see Bones as being at the opposite extreme of Spock. If Spock is logic, then Bones is humanism, and Kirk has to find the middle ground between the two to be a great captain.

SCOTT CHAMBLISS

If you look at the first movie, it's some kids in college graduating who get their first jobs. That's basically the *Star Trek* version of that. In the second movie, the kids have had their jobs for a while and they're starting to deal with real-life problems that go deeper. They have issues that reach to the very core of who they each are as individuals—what the sense of their own character is—and that is something they each have to face in their own way. They also have to deal with the notion that the idealism that the Starfleet unit embodies may not be as perfect as all of them would like to believe it is. That leads to a whole world of trouble.

BRYAN BURK (producer, *Star Trek Into Darkness*)

The script for *Into Darkness* started with one question: How can we put the *Enterprise* team into the greatest jeopardy and conflict? We felt that if the first film was about how this team came together, then this story had to be about them really growing up and how they are becoming adults.

SIMON PEGG

The point is, we've all just become a family, the whole crew, in the absence of a blood family. We're a proxy family, and Kirk is the patriarch. It's joyously exhausting to watch, but at the heart of it, it's a very human story about looking after the people you love.

ZACHARY QUINTO

For Spock, the movie was about understanding what it is to be emotionally available. In the beginning of the film, Kirk makes some cavalier decisions that come back to bite him in the ass, but the basic setup is that Spock is willing to die in order to obey the law, and Kirk is not willing to let his friend die just because of some rules. There comes a moment when Spock really gets what best friends are for. He admits to himself how deeply he can feel for people.

CHRIS PINE

This film deals with really archetypical, huge things about growing up and life and death. So from the beginning of the film to the last moment, the characters go on an extraordinary journey. Now, there's been a lot of talk about the darkness of it, which is there, but the levity from the first one is certainly there, too.

ROBERTO ORCI

When people heard the title, the first thing they thought was, "Oh, they're trying to be *The Dark Knight*." Our point of view is that the optimism that Gene

Roddenberry created is still there, and *Into Darkness* is indicative of the obstacle that comes in to threaten this optimistic utopia. Not that the world is dark, but lightness sometimes faces the dark, and how you overcome that determines what your nature is. In our version, the values of *Star Trek* overcome the darkness.

CHRIS PINE

No matter how dark things may get, at the end of the day the bridge itself is the beacon of hope. It's the family coming together, facing almost insurmountable odds and being able to overcome. People from these disparate backgrounds and a woman of color all made the original *Star Trek* very new and novel in the sixties, but in many ways it remains true now. Maybe it's not as novel or new, but it's a family, a unit made up of many different parts, people, background, age, sex, color, gender. It's all of that coming together to beat the odds. It's not Batman, it's not the lone wolf, it's not the antihero. These are good people with good intentions who are struggling to be better.

ROBERTO ORCI

We wanted to explore the notion of the utopia of the Federation. A utopia is supposed to be a society without conflict, but how do you aspire to a utopia while also acknowledging the barriers *to* utopia? No matter how advanced the Federation is and no matter how advanced the twenty-third century is, there are still going to be things that intrude, that make it difficult. We're the most advanced nation, we are prosperous and we are powerful and plentiful, and yet there's a lot of darkness and a lot of things we have to overcome. Although our ideals are right and although our lip service to what we want is worthy, there are real barriers, both from within and externally.

ALEX KURTZMAN

Starfleet in its conception represented American government and our ability to work or not work with different governments and cultures. And *Star Trek* at its best—which is something we've talked about a lot—always reflects the time from where it comes, and the politics of the world. Obviously right now that's a huge question for us and it will continue to be a huge question for us for a long time, so it felt like the right idea to infuse into our version of *Trek*. Without wanting to make it a polemic or too overt an analogy or to hammer politics, because obviously the goal first and foremost is that it's entertaining, but *Star Trek* uniquely allows us to ask questions about our world. And I think that people expect that of *Star Trek*.

ROBERTO ORCI

Some fans would say, "Your *Star Trek* does not reflect the utopia that Gene Roddenberry envisioned." Well, Gene Roddenberry was also a fan of drama, so I think he would have agreed with that up-front. But on the other hand, there's precedence in *Star Trek*. *Star Trek VI* deals with a cancer on the presidency—let's call it—and the intention of this movie is to very much raise the issue that utopia is being subverted by darkness, and that's why you have Scotty saying things like "We're supposed to be explorers, man. This isn't *Star Trek*. We're not supposed to be out there killing people."

So the movie is conscious of where it wants to be, but, as Alex says, we cannot fail to reflect where we're at. By the way, in the end utopia wins. If Kirk and the gang resign from Starfleet to become a rebel group, then utopia is over. But if they win in the end and restore Starfleet to what it's meant to be, *that's* utopian.

ALEX KURTZMAN

That's the point we're making at the end of the movie in Kirk's speech, because in Kirk's speech he says we've gotten off course from the original vision of what *Star Trek* is supposed to be as evidenced by these words, "Space . . . the final frontier." Roddenberry, I think, would be proud that the legacy has been preserved in the way that we feel it deserves to be preserved.

Star Trek Into Darkness, like the 2009 film, was a financial hit, grossing $467 million globally. The distinction between the two, however, was that many critics (and fans) seemed less enamored with the follow-up, particularly its decision to ape *The Wrath of Khan* storyline from three decades earlier.

SCOTT MANTZ (film critic, *Access Hollywood*)

Everything that *Star Trek* (2009) did was undone by *Into Darkness*, because they had no canon to adhere to; they could do whatever they wanted, and what do they do? They remake *Khan*. Not only did they remake *Khan* in a way that was cringe-inducing when Spock yelled "Khan!!!!" but they tried to amp up the action and they did. *Into Darkness* was definitely more action-packed than the first film, but what happened was by amping up the action, they—Bad Robot, Orci, Kurtzman, J.J.—robbed the film of the magic that defined *Star Trek* (2009). It wasn't about the characters, it was just another action movie.

CHRIS GORE (founder, *Film Threat*)

My feeling about the two J. J. Abrams *Star Trek* films are mixed. As a ride, I really enjoy the first film, as it seemed to respect the original series and characters while rebooting the universe. The essence of the characters seemed to be preserved as they are presented with new and unfamiliar circumstances. Unfortunately, the second film just seemed to be a rehash of lines, moments, and awful winks to the audience, which only served to remind us what a much better movie *The Wrath of Khan* is. It actually made me like the first film *less*.

DAVID A. GOODMAN (consulting producer, *Star Trek: Enterprise*)

I was disappointed in the second film, because I wasn't seeing any writers taking a real chance. I wanted to see writers using *Star Trek* in a way that was more exciting, and they sort of fell back on the Khan story, which I just didn't enjoy seeing again. I've seen *Wrath of Khan* too many times to enjoy seeing that character played by someone else.

BRYAN FULLER (executive producer, *American Gods*)

I thought the second movie was more of a deconstruction/reconstruction as opposed to an organic narrative. And so many acrobatics were bent around "He's *not* Khan, he *is* Khan." So much of the lip service of "No, we're not doing Khan," and then when he actually ends up being Khan, it had the opposite effect than the filmmakers intended, which was to build anticipation and be a pleasant surprise. It was more about the fact that they were lying the entire time during their press for the film, and the story is sort of confusing and muddy, and I have a lot of questions.

When I saw it in theaters and Spock yelled "Khan!!" the audience erupted into laughter. It made me want to cry. That was very sad. It became a laughable experience. It was silly. And Uhura stopping an important mission to bitch at her boyfriend I thought was insulting to everyone and not just the women. There were things that I thought were giant missteps.

ADAM MALIN (cofounder, Creation Entertainment)

The J.J. films have been a gateway opportunity for new fans and they have indeed brought in a new generation of fans that had not sampled *Star Trek*. From the J.J. films they've gone in and explored *Star Trek* and found things about it that they love, and that they don't like. Every fan is different and likes different things about the legacy of all the different *Star Trek* series.

NICHOLAS MEYER (director, *Star Trek II: The Wrath of Khan*)

I love Benedict Cumberbatch. I love *Sherlock*. And I loved him in *Parade's End*. I just thought he was great, but I have to confess that I don't understand these new *Star Trek* movies. Maybe I just sound like an old fogey or something, but it doesn't seem to have anything do with what made *Star Trek* compelling. I don't think seeing Spock endlessly slugging somebody captures the idea of Spock as a character; it just seems kind of dopey. And, you know, Khan is Khan. I don't get how anybody else can be him and not be Ricardo Montalban.

So a lot of it just didn't track for me. I didn't understand it, and I also sort of don't understand what those movies are about. I understand what *Star Trek II* is about; it's about friendship, old age; it's about death. I understand what *IV* is about; it's an ecological, cautionary tale. And I understand what *VI* is about. But other than doing all the things that people expect in a *Star Trek* movie, I didn't understand what those movies are about. I think the difference between an homage and a rip-off is that in an homage you're supposed to add something. They should try to do something else besides trying to do *Star Trek II*.

ED NAHA (producer, *Inside Star Trek* LP)

The last *Star Trek* film came close to parody. Today filmmakers often confuse on-screen bombast with brilliance. And a lot of fans are too caught up in deifying personal pronouns. When everything is big, nothing is. I hope all involved will very soon get back to basics and engage in storytelling that reaches the head and the heart as well as the ancillary markets. I hope that idealism and forward thinking make a comeback.

J. J. ABRAMS

Our first *Star Trek* movie was, if anything, an exercise in perfection of casting. April Webster and Alyssa Weisberg helped us find the absolutely perfect actors. I'm proud of its telling and humor, but of course only see what's wrong with it. Among other things, I wish we had given Eric Bana a bit more to do other than be full of rage, given that he is such a fine actor.

Into Darkness was in some ways a harder film to make. I'm not sure we ever fully realized the story, and I take full responsibility for that. I think we leaned too much on the series' past in telling that story. One thing I'm enormously happy with was how powerfully Benedict Cumberbatch brought Khan back to life. And I really enjoyed some of the action sequences, mostly the ship-to-ship scene and end chase through a futuristic San Francisco.

CHRIS BLACK (coexecutive producer, *Star Trek: Enterprise*)

I don't love J.J.'s movies, but I respect he's reinvigorated interest in the franchise and to some extent with the first movie, did what we were supposed to do with *Enterprise*. He did what we were tasked to do, but failed, which was to make it fun again. If the mission was to make *Star Trek* fun again: mission accomplished.

Celebrating the franchise's fiftieth anniversary, the third film in the series was *Star Trek Beyond*, the fourteenth big-screen *Enterprise* outing, released on July 22, 2016. The entire cast reprised their roles and were joined by the likes of Idris Elba (*Luther, Pacific Rim, Beasts of No Nation*) and Sofia Boutella (*Kingsman: The Secret Service*).

Though originally intended to be cowritten and directed by Roberto Orci, creative differences led to a parting of the ways, with the studio reportedly deeming the script "too soft." Although initial discussions about the project had centered on the return of Khan and a potential cliffhanger that would lead into the next film with a Klingon occupation of Earth, Orci's film was to deal with a super-powerful being à la "Who Mourns For Adonais" and was abandoned in mid-prep while many of the sets were already being designed, including a Vulcan embassy and a Federation starbase. With Orci now out as director, Paramount needed to scramble to make their intended fiftieth-anniversary release date and retool the film in the vein of *Guardians of the Galaxy*, their reported preferred template for the new movie.

After several productive conversations on the set of *Mission: Impossible–Rogue Nation*, J. J. Abrams and Bryan Burk set about replacing the writing team of J. D. Payne and Patrick McKay, who had been working under Orci, with Simon Pegg and Doug Jung. Deep into producing, directing, and cowriting *Star Wars:*

The Force Awakens, Abrams (who remained aboard as a producer) gave up the center seat to director Justin Lin, whose greatest commercial success had been with multiple installments of the blockbuster *Fast and Furious* films as well as the *Scorpion* TV pilot.

Beyond was tasked with picking up where *Into Darkness* left off, with the crew of the starship *Enterprise* finally having embarked on its five-year mission and boldly going where no one had gone before.

MIKE JOHNSON

In the aftermath of *Into Darkness,* the characters definitely found themselves dealing with a new status quo, given that they uncovered a massive conspiracy at the heart of Starfleet. I think it had negative and positive effects. Negative given that their faith in the institution they serve was shaken, and the damage to both Starfleet and San Francisco was considerable. But positive in that Starfleet now has a clean slate, and the crew has a new mandate to embark on their five-year mission.

SIMON PEGG

When Doug Jung and I began writing, it was apparent to us that the crew would be out on the mission that made the show popular in the first place—a deep space mission for five years. The first two films were spent with us really getting to know each other, and in the case of the last film, having an adventure which stayed within our own solar system. Doug and I felt, let's get them out there now and get onto that wagon train in space and start boldly going where no one has gone before.

CHRIS PINE

I think what you see in this film, which I love, is a close-up look at this crew. I've always thought about a crew in a submarine or something. It's like you go out for six months at a time and it's not like every day is dealing with potential nuclear disasters. It's like you're out there swimming a bit, and sailing and nothing's happening.

SIMON PEGG

They're about two years into the mission and experiencing what anyone would if they'd been on a spaceship for two years. It's been fun to play with that as well. That was never really questioned in the movies, about the fact that they were on this five-year mission, away from all their loved ones and just basically all cooped up together in one spaceship. What that would be like? Not just for Kirk, but for all of them. That's a nice thing to look at.

CHRIS PINE

So it looks at what it's like to be with the same crew of people for five years. What is the boredom of that kind of monotony; of having to find meaning and vision when you have to grab a fourteenth cup of coffee to stay awake to get through the night?

KARL URBAN

It's really interesting in that we come face-to-face with the reality of actually being in a confined environment for two years with each other. There's a lot of fun, fertile, funny material to explore in that. This movie really explores what is beyond what we've set up. It questions why we are doing what we're doing. What is the validity of it? What is the meaning of it? Through this movie we disperse and go on these amazing individual journeys of growth, and then come together. It's a lot of fun to watch.

SIMON PEGG

There is a moment in this group where they separate and we felt like the Kirk/ Spock dynamic was explored quite a lot in the first two movies. And myself and Doug always loved the dynamic between Bones and Spock, because they are opposites. They're like the devil and the angel on Kirk's shoulders.

CHRIS PINE

I agree that the first films were very much Spock and Kirk–centric, which, of course, I love because I got to work with my good friend Zach, but in *Star Trek Beyond* it seems like there's a dispersal of the prime elements of *Star Trek*, so everybody has space and time to explore their characters and the relationships between the characters.

KARL URBAN

Zach and I had a lot of fun together. You get the polarity of those two characters that are quite often talking cheese against each other, and you throw them into the deep end, because it's just so much fun to watch these characters get together to try to figure it out. And there is such a deep respect between them. They may philosophically and ideologically and emotionally be polar opposites, but when the chips are down, they come together to overcome a common adversity. That's one of the strengths of *Star Trek* and always has been.

CHRIS PINE

There are a lot of big questions for Kirk in the film. He's not a young man, at least as defined by the first film, dealing with rage issues, or having to prove himself. He's been there, he's done that. Now he *is* the captain, and he's looking around thinking, what next? What now? It's like you got the award and people have told you you're good enough, and you're thinking, well, I thought that it was going to be *this* thing, and it's actually not. So it's redefining boundaries and parameters, and desires and interest and focus, really, for Kirk in terms of what is meaningful to him.

SIMON PEGG

To put them in perilous situations felt like a gift. Like I've said, there's a little bit of separation in the movie for a while, but the characters are all closer than they ever were. They've known each other longer, they've been through a lot together, so the stakes are higher, because their feelings are deeper. So it's great to take a group of fifty-year-old characters like that and to give them a new context and new sort of adventure.

CHRIS PINE

What was a little daunting about the film is that there was a new creative crew behind it. New writers and producers and Justin Lin and Justin's creative team.

We started early in 2016 and didn't have much time. And Justin's done an incredible job of pulling this together. Obviously from *Fast and Furious* he brings a sense of action and that kind of kinetic shape of a film.

KARL URBAN

It was wonderful to have a fresh injection of energy, and of course the way that Justin approaches this material is obviously different from the way that J.J. does. Justin being a long-term fan of *Trek*, he is very vigilant that he imbues his movie with, I guess, a real sense and spirit that is akin to what Roddenberry created in the sixties.

SIMON PEGG

People forget this, but Justin Lin's debut [*Better Luck Tomorrow*] was a fantastic little Sundance movie. Studios will often find a gifted director who's done something kind of cool and small and throw them into the fiery franchise arena. That's what happened with Justin with *Fast and Furious*, and what Justin did with those movies is clearly something that worked, because that franchise has become a behemoth.

DAVID ELLISON (executive producer, *Star Trek Beyond*)

Justin's vision for the third movie was unbelievable. One of the things that was very important to everybody, including J.J., and actually most important for J.J., was for somebody to come in and very much put their own stamp on the movie. Obviously, in this film, to truly do what *Star Trek* promises, which is to go where no one has gone before. *That* was a challenge, and Justin had a vision for exactly how he wanted to do that. The result is a film that I believe is worthy of the fiftieth anniversary of *Star Trek*.

SIMON PEGG

With *Star Trek*, Justin is able to exercise all of his talents. Not just in terms of having a stage and executing action, but also how he can sort of bring characters to life.

CHRIS PINE

Justin is super direct and explicit about what he wants. The man works nonstop; he was sleeping, like, three hours a night. We'll shoot, he'll go home, edit, and come back with exactly what he needs to be done. I'd say this one more than anything else is probably three-quarters action—it's nonstop—while maintaining a really good kind of character core. And that's what Simon brings to it. He knows us and what we do well. He knows how to write to our strengths. The thing I've always wanted and my favorite thing to do, is the comedy. I was probably most nervous about retaining that kind of core, which is what J.J. brought to the first one. It was fun and a tone that was not Marvel superhero aware and not Batman super dark. It's very eighties' pop with a commercial sensibility. That is serious and can deal with great themes, but is also really fun and a great way to spend two hours in a movie theater.

SIMON PEGG

Let's face it, the *Star Trek* of 2016 has to be different. We can't make those kinds of small, thoughtful little plays like the episodes used to be now. In terms of a cinematic sense, the studios just wouldn't bankroll it, and it's not what the larger audiences who have now gone to see *Star Trek*—and who have as much right to it as the fans—want. We have to make something that people are going to come in and see so we can keep making it. It doesn't mean we can't keep what made the show special and try and invigorate what *Star Trek* 2016 means with what *Star Trek* 1966 meant as well.

KARL URBAN

This film feels a little bit retro and a little bit contemporary.

J. J. ABRAMS

The fiftieth anniversary is such an important milestone for the series. I hope that Justin's picture celebrates the spirit, tone, and characters so beautifully brought to life by Roddenberry. I think *Star Trek Beyond* is addressing some elements that our first two films did not, including, of course, going on the five-year mission.

SIMON PEGG

It was so important to us that *Star Trek Beyond* be out in time for the fiftieth anniversary. Even more since Leonard Nimoy passed away. We wanted to sort of tie all of that in together. I don't mean having Leonard in the movie, but just acknowledging *Star Trek*'s legacy and Leonard's legacy and everyone that's been involved with it from the beginning. It feels right that it be the fiftieth-anniversary year. We wouldn't have wanted to miss that.

It felt so appropriate to bring this movie out this past summer. It celebrates everything that made this story great. We've really put our heart and soul into it. The actors as well have brought so much to it. We always talk through the scenes, they know their characters better than anyone. So many times we've discussed things, minutiae, at the beginning of the day to fill it with kind of faithful and exciting *Star Trek* stuff. At the end of every day, Doug and I would sit and watch two episodes of the original series as a treat—*if* we felt like we'd done good work that day. There are a couple of moments of dialogue, a couple of McCoy expressions, that we just took as his parlance. Like "in a pig's eye" from the end of "Amok Time," and we thought, if that's in his parlance, he can say it in this movie. So there were little things that I think fans will go, "I know that!"

DAVID ELLISON

It was obviously wildly important to deliver something that lives up to the amazing universe that Gene Roddenberry created. We're very excited about what we worked on, and very much hope that people feel the same.

CHRIS PINE

What Justin Lin wanted to do was explore *why* this franchise needs to be around. Why it's so important. So it's revisiting a big essential theme of what this is all about, and it's exactly what made *Star Trek* so special in the sixties. It's really the relationship between selflessness and selfishness. It's, Are you going to serve yourself or are you going to serve the greater good? It seems like the story that we keep on retelling each other, the thing that resonates the most, is what Spock always says: The needs of the many outweigh the needs of the few. Or the one.

SIMON PEGG

I'd love it if kids discovered *The Original Series* and watched it after seeing this film. You know, it'll be strange to them, because it won't have the state-of-the-art look we have today, but I hope the story gets them because that's what always got me. It's like when you discover a band and you go into their back catalog.

J. J. ABRAMS

I'm honored to have been the temporary captain of the ships that Lucas and Roddenberry built. I only hope that my involvement helped bring more people into these universes, so lovingly and wonderfully drawn by their creators. It was an honor to have lived in these worlds, for a time, and to have been even a small part of their enduring legacies.

STILL BOLDLY GOING

GOING

(1966–24th Century)

TO INFINITY AND BEYOND

"THE ONLY REASON I KNOW THAT IS BECAUSE THAT'S WHAT ALMOST HAPPENED IN 'THE PARADISE SYNDROME' WHEN KIRK LOST HIS MEMORY AND BECAME AN INDIAN GOD."

Even with a succession of new series and movies in the 1990s, the importance of the so-called mothership, the original *Star Trek,* remained clear, even if many years of repeats had taken their toll on viewership as well as the quality of the deteriorating broadcast prints themselves.

For the then-fledgling Sci-Fi Channel (now called Syfy), *Star Trek* remained the most highly coveted off-network series they could acquire—conveying to television viewers and the advertising community that the channel had arrived—even if the ratings themselves eventually proved a disappointment.

BARRY SCHULMAN (founder, Sci-Fi Channel)

It was a really big win. I went out on a number of advertising calls with Pepsi and some other big companies and there was no question in the advertising world that *Star Trek* was something they expected to see on the Sci-Fi Channel. It *was* the holy grail, at least to the affiliates, and even more so to potential viewers than *The Twilight Zone* since it was in color and of a newer vintage.

Plus the fact that the night we launched the channel, we ran three *Star Trek* movies back to back. The first three *Star Trek* films had never been owned by one entity at the same time ever. The cable systems, the advertising community, and the viewers expected to be given the best, most important science-fiction projects that had ever been made. *Star Trek* and *Star Wars* were both that. There was no question that it added to our distribution on cable systems and we got a lot of attention. Viewers who hadn't discovered the channel discovered it as a result of all the press coverage and the marketing about *Star Trek,* so I don't think anybody looked at it as a failure.

In all honesty, it was not acquired when we were launching the channel. We did not have it in our bag of goodies, so to speak, until a couple of years later. Even though we were owned by Paramount and they owned the rights to the series, the deal hadn't been locked. The deal hadn't been signed, sealed, and delivered for a while. Securing it at the price that Paramount thought it was worth and we could afford was a challenge; getting it in the condition we wanted to, getting the permission to enhance it. The remastering was essential, because this series launched in 1966 and it ran three years on NBC. Now, flash forward to the year 1992 when we launched and the series is old. It needs to look brand-spanking-new. It has to look exceptionally clean and state of the art. You know, *Star Wars* had come along and a lot of science-fiction movies had come along that were far more vivid, so it was critical that Paramount upgrade the prints and invest the kind of money they needed to, which they did. That may have been a contributing factor to not locking a license fee and a deal until they saw what was involved in terms of their costs, in all fairness. Ultimately this became a very big deal. It was very expensive.

For new episode wraparounds, both William Shatner and Leonard Nimoy would film segments (for which they'd be paid handsomely) introducing the episodes and sharing stories about the making of the show. This allowed the fledgling network to program the show in a ninety-minute time slot and avoid having to edit the episodes, given the additional commercial time since the 1960s that would be needed in a sixty-minute slot. Unfortunately, due to low ratings, the Nimoy wraps, for which the actor did extensive preparation and research, were never broadcast.

BARRY SCHULMAN

It was very important for us to get press. We had a limited advertising budget, so if we could get written up, the press would pick up on it. That, in effect, *was* our marketing. People would come to see Nimoy and Shatner reflecting on this iconic series. We spent about a quarter of a million dollars building the set at Raleigh Studios. The set looked like the *Enterprise*. It was beautiful.

Over a decade later, as the fortieth anniversary approached, *Star Trek* was now part of CBS after the split with Paramount, and the series was even *more* shopworn. The evolution of programming to high-definition was ubiquitous, and while remastering the series' picture and sound for hi-def broadcast would be a relatively routine task, the problem remained that the original special visual effects had all been composited on film. Since those elements had long since been destroyed, all that remained were the final composites of multiple passes of original miniature photography that were soft and grainy. It's not that the effects were bad—they had been groundbreaking in the sixties—but upgraded to hi-def they would show their age. *And* they would not match the pristine live-action photography, which looked superb as it was retransferred from the original episode negatives. As a result, CBS made the unprecedented (and expensive) decision to re-create the original visual effects in CGI and integrate them into the existing episodes, which are the versions currently in syndication and on streaming platforms (though the Blu-rays thankfully provide an option to watch the remastered episodes with the groundbreaking original visual effects upgraded to HD—albeit still soft and grainy from too many passes through the optical printer).

One of the producers on the project was David Rossi, a production associate on *Star Trek: The Next Generation* and longtime *Star Trek* fan who continued to work at the studio after the end of *Enterprise*. The biggest challenge for the producers and the visual effects team at CBS Digital would be to seamlessly replace the existing visual effects without changing the running time or sound mix of the original elements.

DAVID ROSSI (producer, *Star Trek Remastered*)

I was approached by David LaFountaine, the executive VP of CBS Television Syndication. He told me they were trying to reintroduce *The Original Series* into syndication, but that stations weren't biting, because it was, at that time, a forty-plus-year-old television series, and the appeal had tarnished somewhat. David was tasked to figure out how to entice them. We met for lunch, and while they had a few ideas, the biggest was to introduce all-new visual effects and matte paintings as well as remastering the series. I told him it was the worst idea I'd ever heard. Coming off the backlash the remastered *Star Wars* movies had received from fans, I felt he was heading for the same cliff. He asked me to think about it, and two weeks later we met again for lunch. I told him the idea was still bad, because he'd never find someone who wouldn't do what Lucas did, which is to get carried away and have the *Enterprise* doing barrel rolls and launching fighter ships. He then surprised me and asked if I wanted to do it, and I said yes without hesitating.

We were enormously successful, given the budget and schedule limitations and that we were asked to work with a visual effects company [CBS Digital] that had relatively no experience doing science-fiction episodics. We almost bankrupted that poor company, but to their credit, they stepped up in a huge way and did some really amazing work in the time they were given and for next to no money. But it took its toll.

I think we accomplished our goal of updating the effects. Captain Kirk and the crew's adventures were what the show was about episode to episode, and we never wanted to take people out of that with too much flash. What would I have done differently? I would have had a year of prep time beforehand instead of two weeks until the first airing, and a budget and schedule that would have let us breathe between shows. It was a crushing, unforgiving schedule.

The fact is that since its debut fifty years ago, *Star Trek* has been a touchstone of American popular culture. In the early days of the series, Leonard Nimoy guest-starred—*as* Spock—on *The Carol Burnett Show,* and as the cult around the show grew, references could be found virtually everywhere. "Beam me up, Scotty" became as ubiquitous a phrase as "Play it again, Sam," while "warp speed" and "phasers" entered the vernacular. But it was undoubtedly guest host William Shatner, playing himself as an exasperated guest at a 1986 *Star Trek* convention, who exhorts the assembled uber-fans to "get a life," that may rank as the most memorable homage of them all.

It was actually the second time the venerable *Saturday Night Live* series dissected *Trek,* the first being during its inaugural year when John Belushi as Kirk fell prey to Elliott Gould as an NBC executive who canceled the series in mid-trek and proceeded to tear down the set around him and the rest of the cast.

Years later, Patrick Stewart would make a less memorable appearance on the series, this time playing Picard as captain of *The Love Boat Enterprise* in which the cruise ship played host to a lovestruck Ferengi (played by now Senator Al Franken), Charo, and David Brenner. Actor Bernie Kopell even put in a cameo appearance in the skit, which featured Chris Farley as Riker and Rob Schneider as Data.

PATRICK STEWART (actor, "Jean-Luc Picard")

I had a wonderful time doing it. It was exhausting, exhilarating, and absolutely terrifying, and I would have not missed a moment of it for all the world.

BRENT SPINER (actor, "Data")

That's what happens when you have a giant [Stewart] standing among pygmies. If everyone had been as good as Patrick, it would have been a good show.

Saturday Night Live was not the only variety show to parody *Trek,* as witnessed by *In Living Color*'s "The Wrath of Farrakhan."

KEENAN IVORY WAYANS (actor/writer, *In Living Color*)

That was one of the smartest sketches we ever did. Basically it was a parody of *Star Trek: The Wrath of Khan*. But in ours, Minister Farrakhan beams aboard the

Enterprise and creates racial dissension among all ethnic groups and points out how Captain Kirk has been exploiting everybody on the starship. It was just the right mix of everything.

Other now-classic *Star Trek* references could be found frequently in music and literature, including *Bloom County*; Nena's "99 Luftballoons," in which the German singer crooned "everyone's a superhero, everyone's a Captain Kirk"; and "Spock's Brain" was parodied in a famous episode of *The Wonder Years,* which had Fred Savage as Kevin Arnold impersonating Shatner's most pained moments from that episode after being zapped by a wristlet-wearing Winnie Cooper, a dead ringer for one of the episode's "givers of pain and delight."

Actor/director Ben Stiller, is such an uber-fan of *The Original Series* that he named his production company Red Hour, taken from the episode "Return of the Archons" ("Festival! Festival!") He also named the villain played by Will Ferrell in *Zoolander* after the Mugatu, the horned beast first seen in "A Private Little War." Stiller also used the classic fight music from "Amok Time" during another fight to the death, this one in *The Cable Guy,* while references to "Arena" popped up in both *Bill & Ted's Bogus Journey* and Eddie Murphy's *Boomerang*. And, of course, few who saw it could forget ABC team captain William Shatner on *Battle of the Network Stars* confiding in host Howard Cosell, "I know a little something about being a captain. . . ."

The ongoing battle between the original *Trek* and *Next Generation* was gently made fun of in an episode of *Night Court*, which pitted classic Trekkers against *TNG* fans in Harry Anderson's courtroom, as well as in a famous MCI phone commercial in which the original stars of *Star Trek* communicate in a "Friends and Family" calling circle, only to be joined by a bemused Jonathan Frakes.

And while Quentin Tarantino worshiped at the altar of Shatner in his screenplay for *True Romance,* it's probably Tarantino's uncredited rewrite of *Crimson Tide* that has his most unforgettable *Trek* movie reference. In Tony Scott's classic film, Denzel Washington exhorts a crew member to repair their damaged submarine: "Now I'm Captain Kirk, you're Scotty, I need more power. I'm telling you if you do not get this radio up, a billion people are gonna die; now it's all up to you." Likewise, *Star Trek* comedy is often mined on the CBS hit series *The Big Bang Theory*, in which its band of geniuses frequently obsess over the series, none more than Sheldon, who, to steal a seventies phrase, truly "groks" Spock.

But perhaps the greatest *Star Trek* tribute of all was on the TV series *Futurama* in its now-classic episode, "Where No Fan Has Gone Before," written by David A. Goodman, who previously wrote and produced the TV movie *The Adventures of Captain Zoom in Outer Space,* a precursor to *Galaxy Quest*, costarring Nichelle Nichols. Following *Captain Zoom,* Goodman was the showrunner on the syndicated sequel to *Knight Rider, Team Knight Rider,* in which he also paid tribute to his science-fiction favorite.

DAVID A. GOODMAN (writer, *Futurama*)

We had a character on the show named Trek Sanders, and we said his parents were huge *Star Trek* fans. In one episode we find out Trek Sanders' mentor is a scientist named Jackson Roykirk, who was a scientist mentioned in the original *Star Trek* series ["The Changeling"]. He created an earthquake machine. It was a weird *Trek* crossover.

Years later, I got a job on a show called *Family Guy,* which was created by Seth MacFarlane, who is a huge *Star Trek* fan. Part of why I got hired was Seth and I could trade quotes from *Star Trek* and *The Next Generation*. When *Family Guy* got canceled after the third season, Seth helped me get on *Futurama*. He made a call to David X. Cohen, who was running it. I got an interview there and I brought with me a communicator keychain, which I got at *Star Trek:* The Experience in Las Vegas with Seth and two of these *Family Guy* writers. David was a big *Star Trek* fan and he hired me.

When I got there, they were talking about doing a *Star Trek* episode, and the idea they were talking about at that moment was this weird notion of a giant William Shatner and a giant Leonard Nimoy fighting over Manhattan. David said, "Should we do that or should we do a *Star Trek* homage?" I thought the homage would be better and would be fun. Within two weeks of being there, we were breaking the episode.

The original idea *Deep Space Nine* had been considering for "Trials and Tribble-ations" was going back to the "Piece of the Action" [from original *Star Trek*] planet, and it's a planet of fans. I was kind of inspired by that idea. I thought, why don't we have this fan on this planet who is taking the crew hostage and the *Futurama* crew would have to rescue them? But we couldn't figure out who this fan is, and I said, "What if it's an energy being?" *That* was the tipping point. We broke the story together, and then I went off to write my first draft based on all the notes we had compiled. I had two weeks to write the script, but I had jury duty the first week, sprained my ankle the second week, and still I'm writing this script. And it's *still* the most joyous writing I've done. They were very pleased, the script was well received, it got nominated for a Nebula Award against *Minority Report, Lord of the Rings: The Two Towers,* and *Finding Nemo.* I, of course, did not win.

The episode reunited the entire living cast of *Star Trek* (and a mute Dr. McCoy) with the exception of James Doohan, who told the producers "no way" would he participate if Shatner was involved. As a result, Scotty was replaced by a new character, Welshy.

DAVID A. GOODMAN

My original title was "We Got Everyone But Scotty," because James Doohan passed on doing it. There was a sense that if we could get Nimoy, we would get Shatner, but when Shatner read the script he said no. [*Simpsons* and *Futurama* creator] Matt Groening agreed to get on a conference call with me and [showrunner] David Cohen. Shatner gets on the phone with us, and Matt, who created *The Simpsons* and is the sweetest guy, says, "We want to figure out some way to do this. You're so special to us." He was very complimentary and, truth be told, Matt wasn't a giant *Star Trek* fan, but he wanted to do this. Shatner says, "Well, I might be interested if it was good or funny or original, but I just don't see anything about in here that I haven't done before." At that point Matt, who's richer than God and really doesn't need to be taking insults from Shatner, got very quiet, and it was sort of up to me and David Cohen to try and save it.

David asked if there was anything we could change about the script, and Shatner explains that the thing about *Star Trek* that appealed to him was his friendship with Leonard. David says we can certainly write something like that, and we could also record you guys together. Shatner said that would be marvelous. So there's a scene in the episode that was written for Shatner where he's saying good-bye to the cast, and then to Nimoy he says, "Good-bye, my friend." It's really not anything about their friendship at all, but it seemed to be enough to please Shatner.

We screened that episode at the Pasadena *Star Trek* convention and there were two jokes that nobody laughed at: Fry talking about *Star Trek* and how "there are seventy-nine episodes, thirty good ones," which was always my view of the original series. The other joke is when the energy being's mother tells him to come in for dinner and Fry says, "All the time we thought he was this great being and he was just a child," and the mother being says, "He's not a child, he's thirty-four." I've had a lot of pleasure from that one episode.

Dreamworks SKG's *Galaxy Quest* poked gentle fun at *Star Trek* and does such a good job of re-creating the feel of classic *Trek* and its stars that it's been called the "best *Star Trek* film ever made" by some. In the film, aliens abduct the stars of a *Star Trek*–like show, believing they're real space explorers who can fend off an alien invasion. Tim Allen plays the Shatner-like captain with the late Alan Rickman as a Spock-like first officer.

GLEN C. OLIVER (film & TV critic, *Ain't It Cool News*)

Galaxy Quest explored and embodied the conceits and core values on which *Star Trek* was built far more interestingly, and far more fully, than *Trek* of that era usually did. It clearly loved and understood the tenets driving *Star Trek,* while simultaneously celebrating the very lifeblood of the franchise, its fans. And, in both cases, it pointedly, even brilliantly, asserted that it was okay to embrace that which we love. That we should not reject that which defines who we are. In saying this, it was referring to its own thematic heartbeat as well as the fandom the film was exploring. *Galaxy Quest* asserted that in diversity there is strength. That adversity brings courage and growth and unity. That the needs of the many outweigh the needs of the few, or the one. These were brilliantly acknowledged, utterly pure and unapologetic *Star Trek* ideals . . . ideals the franchise is struggling to remain in touch with even now. Yet *Galaxy Quest,* not officially a *Trek* movie, knew how to nail the conceits so very well.

RONALD D. MOORE (executive producer, *Outlander*)

The year I left the franchise was the same year that *Galaxy Quest* came out. Everyone was telling me I should see it and I just couldn't. I didn't want anything to do with it. But, years later, I don't even know how many years later, I think I was on *Battlestar* by then, I watched *Galaxy Quest* on TV and *loved* it. It literally brought me back to the franchise. It was made with such affection by people who know and love *Star Trek.* It was such a *Trek* salute. It warmed my heart and it made me feel good about the show again and it touched me emotionally a couple of times. It kind of opened up the franchise for me again and rekindled my love of *Star Trek.*

GLEN C. OLIVER

If *Galaxy Quest* isn't the best *Star Trek* film, it's damn close. Another contender would be *Master and Commander: The Far Side of the World.* If *Trek* of that era had used this picture as a tonal and stylistic template, the franchise might've headed in some wondrous directions.

RONALD D. MOORE

There was a short story called "Visit to a Weird Planet Revisited" in a *Star Trek* book [of fan short stories], *New Voyages,* that came out in the 1970s, that had Shatner, Nimoy, and DeForest Kelley stepping onto the transporter on the stage of the original *Star Trek* series. The lights blink and then they find themselves transported and, literally, beamed aboard the real *Enterprise.* It was really funny. And it *was* that movie. There's a great moment in the story where Nimoy goes up to the bridge and tries to figure out how to look into his viewer. He didn't know how to turn it on. I loved it.

Another classic and critically acclaimed look at *Star Trek* and its fans was the award-winning 1999 motion picture *Free Enterprise*, in which William Shatner played himself and encounters two die-hard *Star Trek* fans (played by Eric Mc-Cormack and Rafer Weigel) who discover their idol, William Shatner, is more screwed up than they are. It's a romantic comedy that can best be described as Woody Allen's *Play It Again, Sam* meets *My Favorite Year*.

WILLIAM SHATNER (actor, "Bill," *Free Enterprise*)

The writers had an idea for a script which involved me. Apparently, as kids, they would conjure me up and seek my advice. And I, as a figment of their imagination, guru-like, would offer wise pearls. So they wrote the script and raised the money to make a movie and they contacted me. They said, "Here's a script we'd like you to be in." So, I read it and this guru talks and offers pearls. And the fictional writers fawn all over Shatner and discourse on the aspects of his career. It was very bizarre and I said, "Thank you very much, I don't want to be in it." And they said, "You got to be in it." And I said, "I can't be in it. It's just too embarrassing."

SCOTT MANTZ (film critic, *Access Hollywood*)

When you're ten, you're looking for a role model. My role models growing up were not sports heroes. All my friends' role models were sports heroes. My role model was Captain Kirk. I wanted to be that guy. I still want to be that guy. When I was dating a lot and I wanted to get pumped up for my date, I would watch "The Conscience of the King" because in that scene in the observation deck he goes, "Worlds may change, galaxies disintegrate, but a woman always remains a woman." I saw that line in *Free Enterprise* and I just was freaking beaming from ear to ear. It was great! It was perfect! It didn't work for Shatner, but it did work for me.

GLEN C. OLIVER

Free Enterprise may well be the most insightful and truthful examination ever of why fans love what they love, and what it means to so fully embrace what they love. In my dating years, I regularly showed the movie to potential girlfriends, contextualizing it by saying, "If you can understand and accept what this is about, you can understand me." This was very true then, and it remains as true today.

WILLIAM SHATNER

They proceeded to pursue me for a long time. Finally, because I'd heard they got the money and they were upset, I called them. I said, "Look, I'm calling you because I empathize with you that you've sold a script and you want an actor. I've been in your position, but you don't understand. It's embarrassing to me to do what you wrote.

"If you made me a screw-up I suppose that might work," I said. "But I'm not going to be in your film. Even if you rewrite it, I'm not going to be in your film. And if you should rewrite it where I screw up and everything, I'm still not going to be in your film. But, I'll read the rewrite." When the rewrite was finished I read what I had to do and I thought, I'm really putting myself out on a line here. I get drunk, I smoke, I fall down, I chase girls. We went through every scene that I was in and I proceeded to suggest things that were Shatner, the character.

In a way I tried to have an improvisational feeling. Attempting to take my performance to another, if not level, another way of going. You have to have your performance in your mind. At the same time, there is an element of spontaneity that film acting should have.

ERIC MCCORMACK (actor, *Free Enterprise*)

I had to come clean with these guys and tell them that I don't know anything about *Star Trek* and that most of the references were lost on me. I had to find something that I could connect with. For me, it was the *Planet of the Apes* references. I think I was in there from the beginning, but what clinched it was when I mentioned *Planet of the Apes* and I did my Charlton Heston impression—because I believe that Charlton Heston in *Planet of the Apes* is one of the great awful acting performances of all time. Truly over the top.

WILLIAM SHATNER

This whole part of William Shatner was total experimentation. I took advantage of the fact that they wanted me, and were willing to change the script. I thought the only way to do this is to make, me, Shatner, a screw-up who is trying to learn as well. So, I learned from them as they learned from me. And that kind of happened in real life as well. The film was a very interesting opportunity for me.

The movie itself culminates with the Shatner character finally realizing his dream of producing a one-man musical version of *Julius Caesar,* which he performs as a rap with hip-hop artist The Rated R.

WILLIAM SHATNER

I was listening to a station playing rap music when I was driving someplace and I thought, that's the way to do "Friends, Romans, Countrymen," and *Julius Caesar.* And so I suggested a rap version. In the past, I had taken some lyrics and acted some lyrics where I took literature and had new music written to it, with the idea being that literature can be music, and music can be literature. The lyrics could be poetry. I've been kidded about it over the years, and so it sounds kind of idiotic where I'm acting a song.

In a way this was something like that. I was never terribly fond of rap music, because I've always thought of it as aggressive and kind of shocking for a non-street person. But the people for whom the music is attractive, who have the anger, and have the rhythm, and have that impulse, the music speaks to them. I was trying to understand that music. I thought that Shakespeare, who was universal and eternal, could fit into that rap paradigm. I met the most charming group of talented rap artists. Rated R had written some poetry and we laid down some tracks. The whole thing is so way-out. It so pushed the envelope, and it was fun, and I had the best time.

ERIC MCCORMACK

I was amazed at some of the stuff he did in the film, particularly the end of the movie. It would be very easy for someone in his position to be a big pain in the ass, but I think he absolutely played ball. It's just great to watch. I came into the film with no major *Star Trek* past. I had to play it in a way that others just naturally fall down and wet their pants when Shatner comes in the room. But, of course, I'm a huge *Rescue 911* guy. So, I have my touchstone.

More recently two of television's most critically acclaimed dramas have both had their share of fun with *Star Trek*. In the case of Matthew Weiner's sixties-era *Mad Men,* a character from the series, Paul Kinsey, attempts to get his spec *Star Trek* script, "The Negron Complex," to Gene Roddenberry.

MARIE JACQUEMETTON (producer, *Mad Men*)

[*Mad Men* creator] Matt [Weiner] loves *Star Trek*. He loves science fiction, too. First season Paul Kinsey was talking about *Outer Limits* and Matt always wanted Paul to go off and write a *Star Trek* episode. I don't think it actually ended up working its way into the series until that fourth season ["The Christmas Waltz"], because we'd always have plans to do things every season on *Mad Men*, but because our storytelling style was so elongated, things got pushed and pushed.

Even more outrageous was the infamous *Star Trek* pie-eating contest episode pitch in which *Breaking Bad*'s Jessie Pinkman's friends, the very stoned Badger and Skinny Pete, are discussing their slam dunk pitch for an original *Star Trek* episode during a drug-fueled rant in the "Blood Money" episode, which led off the series final year.

GENNIFER HUTCHISON
(coexecutive producer, *Better Call Saul*)

The pie-eating contest is something that [creator] Vince [Gilligan] would pitch every now and then in the writers room when there would be a lull and we would start talking *Star Trek* or the transporter. He would always say, "I have this great idea for a *Star Trek* episode," and then he would pitch basically what you saw on-screen, which was the idea of using the transporter to win a pie-eating contest and it going horribly awry. It was something that we'd always laugh at.

PETER GOULD
(coexecutive producer, *Breaking Bad*)

We knew we had a scene where Jesse was more or less shattered and we wanted Badger and Skinny Pete to be talking about their own crazy stoner stuff. Vince actually had pitched a version of this *Star Trek* incident years ago in the writers room. Gennie and I both had a little bit of a, let's call it a philosophical disagreement, about the function and use of the transporter. So I asked Vince's permission to use his *Star Trek* pie-eating story and combine that with the disagreement that Gennie and I had about the transporter. I don't really know what stoners talk about, but I do know a lot about *Star Trek*.

VINCE GILLIGAN (executive producer, *Breaking Bad*)

Sometimes what you do in a writers room when you can't move the story at hand forward, and you can't come up with a good idea, is you find yourself making up other stories. Sometimes in the writers room we'd come up with adventures for a detective we called McTaint. In other words, we find ourselves writing a really terrible cop show centered around a guy who breaks all the rules named McTaint. But this was one of those days where I was pitching what I thought would have been a great *Star Trek* episode of the original series, but Paramount nor Gene Roddenberry probably would have let me write the pie-eating contest scene. I don't think the stakes would have been high enough, unfortunately.

PETER GOULD

I can't believe they never thought of the idea that you could eat anything you wanted and then just have Scotty beam it out of your stomach. I can't picture a much better use of the transporter.

VINCE GILLIGAN

However, I will say this: there were no fatties in the twenty-third century. Except for Harry Mudd. The only guy who *isn't* having stuff beamed out of his stomach.

However, if you think that's the craziest notion involving *Trek* you've ever heard, then you hadn't heard about writer/director Nicholas Meyer and *Undiscovered Country* cowriter Denny Martin Flinn's own short-lived post–*Star Trek VI* plans.

NICHOLAS MEYER (writer/director, *Star Trek VI:
The Undiscovered Country*)

I was once involved in trying to make a *Star Trek* opera with Denny Martin Flinn, who wrote *Star Trek VI* with me. A literal opera. Denny had originally been a dancer on Broadway. He took it very seriously, he wrote several books about the American musical. He also wrote a wonderful book that I use when I teach called *How Not to Write a Screenplay*. He was a terrific, imaginative, and organized person, and he also had some really interesting ideas.

At some point, somebody from New York City Opera contacted me and asked whether we thought it was possible to make a *Star Trek* opera. We went to work on a libretto or, at least, a story outline for a libretto. Then he became ill and he ultimately died. It sort of died aborning. But, at one point Cliff Eidelman, the composer of *Star Trek IV*, that most unusual score, was on board to write the music for it.

And a yet even stranger phenomenon has proliferated among *Trek* die-hards recently, the creation of fan films in which Trekkers create their own original adventures of the starship *Enterprise* (often playing the roles themselves) and her sister ships for exhibition on the Web. The most popular of these include Vic Mignogna's *Star Trek Continues* and James Cawley's *Star Trek: New Voyages*. Some of the series have even included guest stars from various *Trek* series moonlighting in these amateur productions, including George Takei, Walter Koenig, Denise Crosby, Gary Graham, and others. Even *Voyager*'s Tim Russ stepped behind the camera to direct another fan film, *Star Trek: Renegades*.

GLEN C. OLIVER

As a writer and as someone who is interested in filmmaking, I always, *always* tip my hat toward anyone with the tenacity to create and finish a film project of any kind. Filmmaking is rarely an easy task, even when taking on relatively small-scale projects. Conceiving, realizing, and finishing a project and putting it out there for the world to see? Takes a special kind of person, without question. I've seen some wonderfully produced fan films over the years, and I understand why someone might be compelled to mount such an undertaking. I understand loving something so much that the hunger to be a part of it pushes one to suffer great sacrifice to make themselves a part of it.

Conversely, as a creator myself, I have to question: When bringing so many resources to bear on such productions, wouldn't it be even more rewarding to put one's own, self-created material on-screen instead? To make a statement to the world not by interpreting someone else's universe, but by presenting your own ideas and vision?

I'd never discourage anyone from making a fan film, but I would strongly encourage them to consider being bold and generate something original, instead. You never know where it might lead, especially these days when studios are regularly and voraciously putting into motion feature films based on viral video successes and self-generated proof-of-concept reels.

RONALD D. MOORE

I don't know how they can do it, because it takes an enormous amount of time to make a real show—and it must take them quite a while, because I assume they're working on less than a shoestring budget, even with Kickstarter, setting all those lights and getting the gels just right for the shadows, the special effects. People have been doing visual effects on computers for ages, so that's expected, but to build those sets, light them, and shoot them, that's an enormous undertaking.

BRANNON BRAGA (executive producer, *Star Trek: Enterprise*)

They're fun to watch. What's really interesting is seeing the special effects, which are better than anything we did. And then you take a look at the sets, which are okay, passable, but then you get to the scripts and the acting and they're generally awful, but look, the fact that you're writing this book and that I'm talking to you is evidence that *Star Trek* is not going anywhere.

THE NEVER-ENDING TREK

"HIS JOURNEY ENDS NEVER / HIS STAR TREK / WILL GO ON FOREVER / BUT TELL HIM / WHILE HE WANDERS HIS STARRY SEA / REMEMBER, REMEMBER ME."

As *Star Trek* celebrates five decades of cosmic adventures and twenty-first-century technology catches up with the twenty-third-century wizardry first introduced in 1966, one can only wonder how much longer the franchise can continue to enthrall and obsess audiences around the world. What is its enduring legacy, and will we continue to honor and celebrate the hopeful, optimistic vision of *Star Trek* in another fifty years? No matter what other iterations may follow, including the new 2017 TV series from Bryan Fuller and ongoing movie saga, it seems the root of *Star Trek*'s phenomenal success will continue to be mined from the DNA of *The Original Series,* which has spawned everything that's followed.

DOROTHY FONTANA (story editor, *Star Trek*)

I don't know why people keep coming back to it, but I have had so many people, whether they're in my business, or whether they are outside— civilians, if you will—coming in to say, "*Star Trek* still talks to me. But I like the original series." They always come back to the original series. We were talking to an audience that was listening. We were trying to tell intelligent stories with good actors and good messages, and I think we succeeded. The goal on any show is to tell the best stories you can. We succeeded admirably, especially in the first two seasons of *Star Trek.*

LINDA PARK (actress, "Hoshi Sato," *Star Trek: Enterprise*)

William Shatner and Spock, they're American mythical icons, and *Star Trek* has so many cultural connotations. Even if somebody has never watched *Star Trek* in their life, they can still tell you a whole list of things that they know about it, and that's a pretty amazing thing. So in that sense, I knew what I was getting into, but on another level, you can never know until you're into it. There's also a difference in hearing about it and being in it. Before the pilot for *Enterprise* even aired, we had bags of fan mail, and that was strange. But it's part of being on *Star Trek*. People embrace you before they even see you, because you're part of something they love.

BRENT SPINER (actor, "Data")

I kind of sometimes think fame is like paying your rent. If you don't have it, you want it really bad. And once you have it, you never think about it. But once you've lost it, you think about it *a lot*.

DAVID LIVINGSTON (producer/director, *Star Trek: The Next Generation*)

It was about the future of humanity, that we survive and we're a force of good in the universe. It's not a dystopian view of the future, it's a positive view that humanity can survive. I'm a great fan of *Blade Runner*, but that's not *Star Trek*. You don't see people having huge conventions with costumes and makeup to celebrate that movie. You do see it for *Star Trek*, because it's a positive future. It's like the sacred and the profane. *Star Trek* is a religion to some people. It's like a religious experience at some of these conventions; people coming together to celebrate a singular thing. And Rick [Berman], to his great credit, always protected that vision.

BRENT SPINER

Star Trek, as it relates to the history of television, is an animal of its own. I don't think it compares to anything else. I don't think there's anything in the history of television that's been as big a phenomena as *Star Trek* is. Even prior to television you had the Tarzan series, the Andy Hardy series, and James Bond, which was a really big phenomenon that made United Artists a lot of money, but none of them compare to what *Star Trek* did for Paramount Pictures.

Star Trek is the goose that laid the golden egg, but I don't think it compares to any other television or film. It's like when I read reviews of a new *Star Trek* movie, they're not reviewed as a regular film on their merits. Are the performances good? Is the shooting good? Is the story and writing well done? It's never really looked at like that. It's looked at like, is it a good *Star Trek* movie or a bad *Star Trek* movie?

JONATHAN FRAKES
(actor/director, *Star Trek: The Next Generation*)

When it was good, it was one of the best shows on television . . . and when it's bad, it's still good.

ROD RODDENBERRY (son of Gene Roddenberry)

I'll be honest with you, one of the reasons I'm not in entertainment or doing *Star Trek* or trying to do *Star Trek* is a fear that no matter what I do, even if it is pretty spectacular, it'd get criticized and torn apart. So, I'd rather do things for myself. If I'm going to come up with a story I'm going to keep it to myself and enjoy my own goddamn story.

BRANNON BRAGA (executive producer, *Salem*)

One of the reasons I didn't burn out sooner and I was able to do this for fifteen years was truly a credit to the premise. Anything you can think of you can really and truly do on *Star Trek*; any idea you want to explore, you can explore. It's an open book. It's kind of like when I think about it, I'm, like, "God, I miss this show." I could write for the show again, it never really got old. Every episode had its own challenges, but different sensibilities come and go, and I think the J.J. Abrams movies definitely infuse a new energy and budget into the whole thing.

RONALD D. MOORE (executive producer, *Outlander*)

It's a very special and warm feeling. I'm very proud of it and surprised by it. I can't believe that something of my childhood became part of my adult life in such a profound way, and that I got to literally walk the halls of the *Enterprise*. It's kind of weird.

There're parts of it I've never really reconciled. Trying to figure out why, in *Generations,* I wanted to kill Captain Kirk, my childhood hero; why that meant so much to me and why it was important for me to tell that story, even though it didn't work as well as I wanted it to. Who does that? Why would you do that and what does it say about me? Those things are still puzzling parts of my psyche I've never quite understood.

BRYAN FULLER (executive producer, *American Gods*)

It's a beautiful world that has been created to promote inclusivity and a better man than the man that we have today on this planet. Anything that encourages us to grow and strive and be the better versions of ourselves is a wonderful thing to have in our culture.

MICHAEL TAYLOR
(coexecutive producer, *Turn: Washington's Spies*)

Hopefully, we can have a future like that. A future where everyone gets along. That was always bullshit, though. The belief of Gene Roddenberry was that somehow people would evolve past hatred and prejudice. That's fucking childish. But, all the shows, no matter how dark *Deep Space Nine* might have gotten or *Battlestar Galactica* was, for that matter, it was still about people trying to remain hopeful. Trying to struggle and make connections. In *Battlestar,* they're making connections with the robots that were trying to kill them, because in the end, if you're a sentient being, what choice do you have? The one thing none of these shows was is cynical. Any new *Star Trek* should embrace that kind of optimism. That kind of hopefulness.

DAVE ROSSI (production associate, *Star Trek: The Next Generation*)

Hope. Inclusion. Acceptance. *Star Trek* works best when it's espousing these tenets. It's a story that says we're not only going to make it as a species, but we're also going to learn to accept each other, differences and all, and in fact embrace those differences. What a world that would be, huh?

ROD RODDENBERRY

Does the world still want *Star Trek*? I know the answer, yeah, everyone still wants *Star Trek*. I am curious, though, as we all get older, are the people who are brought up with the current movies going to care? *Star Trek* will be more of a historical footnote than something that's really affecting people.

LEONARD NIMOY (actor, "Spock")

It's pretty clear to me that we did such an amazingly incredible wonderful job of building a foundation on which one could build forever, that it's unstoppable. It's taken on a life of its own where it won't go away. It's a wonderful monster we've created.

PATRICK STEWART (actor, "Jean-Luc Picard")

One cannot escape the impact that this series and the whole *Star Trek* mythology continues to have. I have been overwhelmed and made extraordinarily proud to continue to be associated with a program like this, because I have been reminded every day of the continuing impact in all possible areas of what this show does.

RONALD D. MOORE

I'll miss the *Enterprise* no matter what else I do. *Star Trek* was all about "These are the voyages of the starship *Enterprise*." That's always been something special to me. Other series will have other joys. This show was my first sale, my first staff job. It's something from my childhood, and that's why it will always stand alone for me.

LEONARD NIMOY

Star Trek means a lot to me. I do believe it has a great positive effect on a lot of people. I have met some wonderful people who have told me with great passion about the positive effect it had on their lives. I continue to run into people who say, "This thing gave me a sense of what my life could be about."

THOMAS DOHERTY
(professor of American Studies, Brandeis University)

The nice thing about *Star Trek*, in the end it's pretty good-humored. Like Shatner on *Saturday Night Live* and *Free Enterprise*, it's all done with good humor and affection and there's still the love there for the show even as you're appreciating the ludicrousness of the lizard monster.

WIL WHEATON (actor, "Wesley Crusher")

Not everything in the world is super-serious. I think it's really okay to make fun of those things. In *The Walking Dead* nothing in the universe is as clean and flawless and meticulously cared for as a sponsor's vehicle in the Zombie Apocalypse. It's just a fact and it pulls me out of the show every time I see it.

Even those of us who love *Star Wars* before George Lucas went and fisted our childhood, still make fun of Luke Skywalker whining about having to go to Toshi Station to get power converters, because that's who we were when we were kids. We wanted to be Han Solo because he was cool, but we were Luke because he was awkward and whiny and weird.

BRENT SPINER

I know it sounds absurd, and it is absurd, but I think in ways *Star Trek* may be the most important television drama there's ever been, because of its support of ideas that are helpful to mankind. It promotes the ideas of quality and tolerance and things that are truly important, and it says it to people in their homes on a nightly basis. They're getting a dose of some good old liberal ideas, and I think *Star Trek* is instrumental in this country in leading us toward the idea of one world, which is clearly what we have to get to.

ROD RODDENBERRY

One of the main things that's great about *Star Trek* is how it inspired people. Whether it is to believe in themselves, believe in the future, or believe in the people around them. I've met Elon Musk a few times, who I heard is a *Star Trek* fan, and I'm in love with him as a person. He is the epitome of what our future innovators and philanthropists need to be like, because he didn't let anything get in his way. He has passion, he had a belief, and had tons of people saying no, and he saw it through and he blew up rockets and he was a failure, and he was a failure over and over and over again, but he kept going. And now look at him. Fucking amazing.

I'm also a huge fan of Peter Diamandis of the XPrize. He's incredibly inspirational. I think he and my father would have been best buds. Every time I talk to him, every time I hear him talk about the future and what we're capable of, I think of my father.

BRENT SPINER

With *Star Trek*, Gene created a world that says not only that it's a United Federation of Planets, but we've already solved all the problems on Earth and have the ability to interact in an interplanetary way. I think it's a great idea that they actually got it together on Earth and realized that it is one world here and requires everyone understanding they're in the soup together. What's done that better than *Star Trek*?

And there is silliness in *Star Trek*, but that's the beauty of the show. It's always been the perfect blend of silly and serious so that it's not like taking medicine. They make the medicine really palatable by cloaking it in a certain silliness. I can't think of another television show that's been able to impact as many people in a positive way.

ROD RODDENBERRY

My parents gave me an amazing gift with the money they made, and being a genuine believer in that future I was introduced to the idea of philanthropy and what could be done trying to make a positive impact. I talked to my advisors about starting a foundation and kind of built the idea of a foundation with basically four pillars: humanitarian advances, science, technology, and education.

What we do is we look for organizations, institutions, and individuals that are on the cutting edge of technology, that are working toward that *Star Trek* future. No Band-Aid solutions. So, as much as it pains me and sounds horrible when I say we don't give blankets to homeless, we try to solve and go to the root of what is the systemic issue that is causing homelessness.

BOBAK FERDOWSI
("Mohawk Guy," Jet Propulsion Laboratory)

There is a lot in *Star Trek* that I would love to see come true: warp drive, transporters, replicators, especially, but one thing that doesn't get a lot of love in *Trek*, but is very valuable, is faster-than-light communication. When people are talking across great distances, we're limited by the speed of light—for something in our own solar system as close as Mars, the shortest delay is four minutes. But the idea that we could communicate in real time and not have to wait for the signal to travel is incredible, and as we learn more about physics, it seems like a real possibility.

RONALD D. MOORE

I started as a fan of a show that was dead and was never going to come back. And then it came back and then I was on the show, and then when I was on the show I felt like this is going to go forever. They can't do enough series, they can't do enough movies. There's no such thing as too much *Trek*—and then there was too much *Trek*. I stepped away from the franchise and I didn't really do conventions anymore. I did my first real *Star Trek* convention a couple of years ago. It was in London or Vegas. It was the first one I had done in a long time. I didn't know what to expect and I thought I was going to see a withering away, but it was gang-busters and there were kids in *DS9* uniforms and Bajoran earrings and it was still a fandom. There were still people who watched every episode, there was still mer-chandising, and I was surprised and very pleased that it was still going. Now it does feel like it will outlive me.

It is one of those pop sensations, like Sherlock Holmes or *Star Wars*. They are mythic characters. They will just continue because they are part of our cultural heritage at this point.

ADAM MALIN (cofounder, Creation Entertainment)

I think *Star Trek* might hold the claim of having the greatest entertainment legacy of them all, and it's obvious to me that it will be vital for another fifty years, and my hope is that as many of us will be around to celebrate it and be grateful for all the ways that *Star Trek* has enriched our lives.

GLEN C. OLIVER (film & TV critic, *Ain't It Cool News*)

At *Trek*'s seventy-fifth anniversary, we'll continue to look back in awestruck rec-ognition that for one shining moment in history, mass entertainment was vision-ary enough to believe its audience could recognize and comprehend a better imagining of the future. That this better future could only be reached through cre-ating better versions of ourselves. That we deserved some sort of template which encouraged us to question and think and evolve.

We'll still be acknowledging that *Star Trek* dared to present to us a universe filled with wonder and ideals and hope. That it was brazen enough to assert that our shortcomings are forgivable and surmountable as long as we struggle to reach for something better—both individually and as a species. There must be some truth to such precious, wondrous notions, as we're still exploring and discussing these ideals to this day. And, yes, we'll still be doing so twenty-five years from now. Because we're human. And the human adventure is just beginning.

ROD RODDENBERRY

When my son grows up and wants to know more about *Star Trek*, I'll certainly take him to the *Star Trek* movies that come out in the years to come. Assuming it's good enough to watch, we'll watch the TV shows. Will I force him? No. Will I say, "Hey, have a seat with me, check this out." Yes. If he gets up halfway because he's bored, that's fine. You know he'll do it on his own. If my son wants to be a fireman, be a ballet dancer, be a writer, be an airline pilot, I'm fine with any of those things. As long as he does something that he's passionate about. He's got to be passionate. Find an interest. Find a passion, because that's the only way you'll be great at it.

SUSAN SACKETT (assistant to Gene Roddenberry)

I was so happy to be the first person who could hear Gene's thoughts. He only dictated on a Dictaphone, which is in some museum today. He'd put his foot on the pedal, and I'd put a little earpiece on, and I could hear his voice in my ear as he was sharing these thoughts for the first time with me, and I would hear whatever he was writing. That was an amazing experience. He was one of the great minds of the twentieth century, despite everyone's critiquing and giving him a hard time. He wasn't perfect, but he did have a lot of original thoughts that are just now beginning to be appreciated, and I was lucky to be able to participate in that.

NICHOLAS MEYER (director, *Star Trek II: The Wrath of Khan*)

I must say I was terribly surprised by the evolution of my feelings with regard to *Star Trek*, if you go back to the sixties when I just clicked past it because I didn't understand what I was looking at, to the conversations with Harve Bennett and, later, with Leonard Nimoy, making these movies where you're sort of immersed in this world.

People always say: What do you attribute the popularity of this to? And they always ask you about Sherlock Holmes. I really never know the answer to these things. I speak in generalities and so forth. But, one thing is for sure, over these years there are hundreds of people who have either written to me or come up to me and told me how much this stuff has meant to them; half the staff of NASA, and fathers or sons who have told me about going to see *The Wrath of Khan* together every year and how meaningful it is to them. I'm not going to look down my nose at any of that. I'm humbled by it. How many people in this life get to be a part of having moved or made happy so many people? No, I am not going to look down my nose at that ever again.

JOHN LOGAN (writer, *Star Trek: Nemesis*)

What has always attracted me to the world of *Star Trek* is the idea of hope and that there's a better future ahead of us. No matter what happens to the individual players, the journey goes on with hope. I couldn't envision a *Star Trek* world or any *Star Trek* movie that didn't have at least a whisper of hope to it in terms of these people and their continuing mission.

ED NAHA (producer, *Inside Star Trek* LP)

One of the nicest aspects of the *Trek* philosophy itself was that of inclusion. In the *Star Trek* universe, there were equal rights. Your race and your gender didn't hold you back from sitting on the bridge or rising in the ranks of the Federation. In Gene's head, these were not radical ideas. This was just common sense. In order to thrive, a society has to invite *everyone* to participate. If *every*one is working toward the same goals, those goals will be realized. In a way, this shows the practicality of idealism.

In today's real world, of course, this attitude is considered dangerous. Look at the conservative bleating over Obamacare. It's a threat! To what? To everything! Why? Because it *is*! Do you have facts to back that up? We don't need facts! We just know! In the *Star Trek* universe, the Tea Party wouldn't exist.

ROD RODDENBERRY

I bought into it. I started believing in that future, too. I became a real genuine fan of the *Star Trek* philosophy, of that better future. Listening to the fans and learning that people from all walks of life, all around the world, all believed in this one future, that was an incredibly uplifting idea and something I became very proud of. I love the idea of the United Federation of Planets.

RICHARD ARNOLD (*Star Trek* archivist)

It's been said time and again, but it's worth repeating: Gene gave us a future where we survived our current immaturity and did so with dignity. We're not out there empire building, we're out there exploring and learning. His vision has changed so many people's lives and will continue to do so for a long time.

ADAM MALIN

I think Gene's optimism for the future of the human condition is a message that is just as vital today as it was fifty years ago and is part of what inspires new generations of *Star Trek* fans. Whatever Gene may have been as a business associate, a writer, a showrunner, a producer, he was a man with a very noble vision for society, and that has come through in the spirit of *Star Trek* through all these years, and for me remains his greatest achievement, simply saying to the world that in the future our society will be better, and that's a beautiful message and I think it's Gene's greatest legacy.

GREG STRANGIS (executive producer, *War of the Worlds*)

One wonderful story I've always heard about Gene Roddenberry is he resented the fact that Scientology was a religion and not *Star Trek*. Because he considered himself a better writer than L. Ron Hubbard.

KATE MULGREW (actress, "Kathryn Janeway")

We know that it's going to be the headline on my obit, no matter what. Even if I married the Pope. "Captain Janeway Marries the Pope," right? Having played her, I understand in myself that the contribution was so much more than the playing of the character.

WILLIAM SHATNER (actor, "James T. Kirk")

Star Trek has been a wonderful vehicle for me, and I know that I'm identified as the Captain Kirk character to a large extent, although it's amazing how ephemeral that kind of fame is. When I was shooting *T.J. Hooker* on the streets of Los

Angeles, they would say, before the show aired, "That's where Captain Kirk is," and the day after it aired, it was "Oh, T.J. Hooker is in that dressing room."

GENE RODDENBERRY (creator/executive producer, *Star Trek*)

All I've done in *Star Trek* is have fun, daydream—and Paramount has graciously given me an office to do that in, has paid me more money than I really feel I deserve—and they earned more for themselves than I really feel *they* deserve.

HAROLD LIVINGSTON (writer, *Star Trek: The Motion Picture*)

I've never understood the cultishness. Never understood it. I'm astonished. I can't tell you why people love *Star Trek*. I think everybody is nuts.

ACKNOWLEDGMENTS

The authors would like to thank everyone who graciously took the time over the years to be interviewed by us, in some cases multiple times for many, many hours. In addition, we're deeply indebted to David E. Williams, Sheldon Teitelbaum, Steven A. Simak, Joe Nazarro, Jeff Bond, Dr. Mitchell Rubinstein, Karen E. Willson, Scott Mantz, Jeff Goldsmith, and Jennifer Howard/the Archive of American Television (for additional Rick Berman quotes; visit emmytvlegends.org for more information), who were willing to share their own original material to help supplement this volume, where necessary.

In almost all cases, material is taken from original interviews conducted by the authors over the last three decades, with the exception of the aforementioned additional material as well as comments excerpted from public appearances at press conferences and/or conventions, along with original memo excerpts. Certain quotes from Michael Piller are excerpted from his unpublished manuscript, *Fade Out: The Making of Insurrection*, with the gracious permission of his wife, Sandra Piller.

Again, we would be remiss not to mention our patron saint, editor Brendan Deneen, his intrepid assistant Nicole Sohl, and our publisher, the terrific Thomas Dunne. Our gratitude as well to our agent, Laurie Fox at the Linda Chester Agency, for all her enthusiasm throughout the process, as well as our diligent copyeditor, Edwin Chapman.

In addition, special thanks to our research assistants, without whose help we would probably be publishing this book for the sixtieth anniversary. A very special shout-out to our sensational and irreplaceable senior research assistant,

Jordan Rubio, as well as Derek Hedbany, Marie Lombardi, and New York University professor Andrew Goldman for his gracious assistance, as well as the enormously helpful Julie Graham at the UCLA Library Special Collections, and the entire staff of the Academy of Motion Picture Arts & Sciences Margaret Herrick Library—thanks for the use of the room.

The authors would also like to thank Steven Pizzello of *American Cinematographer* magazine for his contributions to this volume, as well as *Cinefantastique* magazine, and acknowledge the inestimable contributions to the genre, and this volume in particular, of the late Frederick S. Clarke, founder of *Cinefantastique*, without whom none of this would have been possible. Fred was a mentor and an inspiration and, along with Kerry O'Quinn, founder of *Starlog*, was a legendary pioneer in the field of erudite sci-fi film and television journalism long before the world had ever heard of the Internet.

And, of course, our most profound thanks to the late, great visionary Gene Roddenberry, without whom we would not still be talking about (and watching) *Star Trek* five decades later.

We would be remiss not to mention the thoughtful, supportive, and immensely talented Michael Piller, who left this world way too soon, as well as the late gentleman writer Robert Lewin, Robert H. Justman, Harve Bennett, Maurice Hurley, Herb Wright, Grace Lee Whitney, Bernie Williams, *TNG* publicist Larry Goldman, and the incomparable Leonard Nimoy, who could've lived and prospered a little longer.

To contact the authors with comments, questions or for requests for author appearances, please e-mail us at 50yearmissionbook@gmail.com.

Follow us on twitter at:
@50yearmission
@markaaltman
@edgross

ABOUT THE AUTHORS

MARK A. ALTMAN has been coexecutive producer on such TV series as TNT's *The Librarians* and *Agent X*, a writer/producer for ABC's *Castle* and USA Network's *Necessary Roughness*, as well as the executive producer and showrunner of HBO's *Femme Fatales*, which *Entertainment Weekly* called "a badass-chick anthology series" and the *Huffington Post* hailed as "pulpy fun."

He has been dubbed "the world's foremost Trekspert" by the *Los Angeles Times* and worked for over a decade as a journalist for such publications as as *The Boston Globe*, *The Manchester Guardian*, *Cinefantastique*, *Sci-Fi Universe*, and *Geek*, for which he was a founding publisher and editorial consultant; Altman also wrote numerous issues of the *Star Trek* comic book for DC and Malibu Comics. Altman, however, is probably best known to rabid *Star Trek* fans as the writer and producer of the beloved love letter to *Star Trek* and award-winning cult classic, *Free Enterprise*, starring William Shatner and Eric McCormack (*Will & Grace*), the feature film about two dysfunctional *Star Trek* fans who meet their idol and find out he's more screwed up than they are. Among the numerous awards for the film, Altman was honored with the Writers Guild of America Award for Best New Writer at the AFI Film Festival along with Best Film.

In addition, Altman produced the thirty-million-dollar film adaptation of the bestselling videogame *DOA: Dead or Alive*, as well as James Gunn's superhero spoof, *The Specials*, and the *House of the Dead* films, based on the videogame series from Sega.

Altman has spoken at numerous industry events and conventions, including the New York University Tisch School of the Arts and ShowBiz Expo, as well as the Variety/Final Draft Screenwriters Panel at the Cannes Film Festival. He was a juror at the prestigious Sitges Film Festival in Barcelona, Spain, and has been a frequent guest and panelist at Comic-Con, held annually in San Diego, California, and a two-time juror for the Comic-Con Film Festival. He is also a graduate of the Writers Guild of America's Showrunners Program and a member of the Television Academy.

Altman lives in Beverly Hills, California, with his wife, Naomi; children Ella and Isaac; three cats named Ripley, Giles, and Willow; and one tribble . . . which is hardly any trouble at all.

EDWARD GROSS is a veteran entertainment journalist who has been on the editorial staff of a wide variety of magazines, among them *Geek, Cinescape, SFX, Starlog, Cinefantastique, Movie Magic, Life Story,* and *SciFiNow.* He is the author of such nonfiction books as *Above & Below: The Unofficial 25th Anniversary Beauty and the Beast Companion, X-Files Confidential, Planet of the Apes Revisited,* and *Rocky: The Ultimate Guide.* He currently serves as an executive editor of *Empire* magazine's Web site: empireonline.com/us.

Gross lives in New York with his wife, Eileen, their sons, Teddy, Dennis, and Kevin, and a lovable mutt named Chloe.